CAMPING AND CARAVANNING GUIDE

GREAT BRITAIN AND IRELAND

1992

Published by RAC Publishing, RAC House,
Bartlett Street, South Croydon CR2 6XW.

© RAC Enterprises Limited 1991

ISBN 0 86211 155 2

Cover illustration Roy Westlake

Advertising Agents
Kingslea Press Limited
137 Newhall Street, Birmingham B3 1SF
Tel: 021 - 236 8112

Designed and typeset in Great Britain by
Product Communication Limited
London W1V 1HH

Printed and bound in Great Britain by
The Guernsey Press Co. Ltd, Guernsey,
Channel Islands.

Contents

Entries in the Guide

RAC recognised sites

The RAC inspects and recognises camping & caravanning sites throughout the country. They are of many types, from large holiday parks with the full range of sporting and entertainment facilities, to smaller quiet sites in rural areas.

RAC recognised sites are divided into 'Listed' sites which have all the necessary facilities and 'Appointed' sites which have a large number of amenities and superior facilities (see under 'Requirements' page vi). These sites are shown in the guide with the RAC logo and the designation letters L or A next to the site name. All are visited regularly to see that standards are being maintained.

Every RAC recognised site is included in this guide. They are distinguished from non-RAC sites by the site name appearing in bold, capital letters and the presence of the RAC logo.

Sample RAC recognised site entry (fictitious)

HAPPY VALLEY CARAVAN PARK   RAC L
Mill Lane. ☎ (0733) 455572
Open: 1 March-31 October
Size: 3 (8) acres, 28 touring pitches, 5 with elec, 10 with hardstanding, 10 level pitches, 40 static caravans, 3 chalets. 6 hot showers, 15 WCs, 2 CWPs

Car & caravan £4.50, Motor caravan £4, Car & tent £3.50, M/cycle* & tent £3; all up to 2 people; elec £1, awn 75p, dogs 50p; WS
cc Access, Amex, Diners, Visa/B'card
Level, grassy site beside river; fishing possible (permit required). Sauna, children's playground and evening entertainment. 10 caravans for hire (own WCs). Calor gas only. Shop and restaurant 2 miles.
3 miles N of Tonbridge on A227 turn E opposite church; site on right.

A site entry explained
Size: the first figure is the area of the site reserved for touring caravans; the figure in brackets is the total area of the site. We give the number of pitches for touring visitors in caravans, motor caravans and tents, and how many of these pitches are level, and how many have electric hook-ups and hardstanding. We also give the number of static caravans and chalets on the site.
Please note that these are not necessarily for hire and are not inspected by the RAC.
Where caravans and chalets are available for hire, it is mentioned in the description.
We next list the number of hot showers, cold showers, WCs and chemical waste disposal points (CWPs) on the site.

Disabled facilities ♿
Sites shown with this symbol have some facilities for the disabled. It is essential to ask the site in advance whether your personal requirements are catered for.

The remaining symbols indicate the main features of the site as follows:

⚋ Caravans accepted

⚌ Motor caravans accepted

▲ Tents accepted

⚎ Laundry room

⚏ Shop

⚐ Snacks/take away food

✖ Restaurant

╲ Swimming pool

⚐ Shelter for campers

⚑ Dogs accepted

Non-RAC recognised sites

Sample non-RAC site entry (fictitious)

Happy Valley Camping Site
Lower Road. ☎ (0123) 4567
Open: April-October
Size: 10 acres, 15 touring pitches, 5 static caravans
6 hot showers, 3 WCs, 1 CWP

Charges on application
On A456 3 miles S of Tonbridge.

Touring pitches - non-RAC site entries

Where the number of pitches is given as, eg. `15+' it represents the number of touring caravan pitches + an unspecified number of tent pitches.

Hardstanding - non-RAC site entries

`Hardstanding' indicates that some pitches have this facility.

Hot showers, WCs - non-RAC site entries

Where the number of these is given as, eg. `4b hot showers, 6b WCs' this indicates `blocks' of facilities.

Swimming symbol - non-RAC site entries

For non-RAC site entries **only** this symbol indicates that there is swimming available on site **or nearby**, ie. there **is not necessarily a swimming pool on site**.

Prices

The prices are those quoted to us by the site management and are per night for the 1992 season, except where indicated otherwise.

In some cases VAT, which is applicable to most camping and caravanning sites, may not have been included.

It is always advisable to confirm charges before your arrival at a site.

An asterisk against Motorcycles indicates that the site only accepts motorcyclists who are RAC members. A valid membership card must be produced. Many sites are reluctant to accept large groups of motorcyclists, though happy to accommodate individual motorcyclists. Groups of motorcyclists should inquire before arriving at a site whether they will be accepted.

`WS' shows a site which has winter storage for caravans. Please contact the site direct (NOT the RAC) if you wish to store a caravan.

Credit cards

If a site accepts credit cards, which cards are accepted are shown after the price information.

Description

The short description of the site gives an idea of what sort of site it is, what amenities it has and what the surroundings are like.

The directions should enable you to locate the site from the nearest main road.

Dogs

Most sites accept dogs, but owners are expected to keep their pets under control (often on a lead while on the site) and to exercise them with consideration for other campers. Some sites will not accommodate certain breeds - it is advisable to check before arriving. Sites which accept dogs are shown by a symbol.

Gas supplies

Most sites have supplies of bottled gas. Where no mention is made in the description, it indicates that both Calor gas and Camping Gaz are available. Otherwise the description states Calor gas only, Camping Gaz only or No gas available. N.B. this information has not been obtained for the non-RAC sites in the guide.

Booking

We are not including any booking information in the site entries in this edition of the Guide. As a general rule, **it is necessary to book at peak periods for all sites**. Out of high season, it is advisable to book if you want to stay at one specific site, or in an area with few sites. Even in low season it is sensible to telephone ahead to check on the space available and to time your arrival so that if a site is full you have time to find space in another site.

The RAC is not responsible for the control or management of any of the sites listed in this guide and booking arrangements must be made with the site owners.

Requirements for RAC Camping & Caravanning Sites

There should be not more than 30 units per acre of campable area, and at least 20 feet spacing between units. Drinking water points should be no more than 100 yards from any unit. Points for disposal of waste water should be no more than 50 yards from any unit, and there should be at least one per acre.

Toilets: Male - 1 WC and 1 urinal
        per 30 units
        Female - 2 WCs per 30 units
(if chemical toilets, double the number)

Wash basins: Male - 2 per 30 units
        Female - 2 per 30 units
        (Hot water if over 60
        units)

Showers: (for sites with over 60 units)
        Male - 1 per 60 units
        Female - 1 per 60 units
        These should have hot water

Adequate arrangements should be made for the collection and disposal of rubbish. There should be a properly designed chemical toilet disposal point with an adequate supply of water adjacent for cleaning containers. Listed sites must have a minimum number of 10 touring pitches.

RAC Appointed sites must have in addition to the above qualifications - Flush WCs, hot water in wash basins, and a minimum number of 20 touring itches.

Other requirements for Appointment:

Electric shaver points

a shop on site (unless a supermarket or similar store is so near that an on-site shop would be uneconomic)

fresh milk supplies

first-aid facilities

at least one recreational activity within the mileages shown: swimming (¼); boating (¼); golf (5); tennis (2); fishing (2); riding (2).

Static Caravans for hire
RAC Appointed and Listed sites are inspected and assessed purely for touring caravans and tents. Information is given where static caravans and chalets are for hire at sites **but no inspection is made of such units and the RAC does not accept any responsibility for the nature or quality of accommodation offered.**

Camping and Caravanning Club sites
The Camping & Caravanning Club sites in this guide have not been inspected by the RAC, but they are all managed to the C&CC's exacting standards and each is supervised by a resident warden. A few of the sites have only minimum facilities; where this is the case it is clearly stated in the site description.

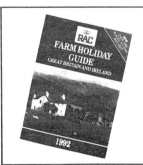

⚜
—— **RAC** ——
FARM HOLIDAY GUIDE GREAT BRITAIN & IRELAND 1992

This exciting new guide features farms who welcome guests throughout England, Scotland, Wales and Ireland. Illustrated entries give full details of accommodation, prices and places of interest nearby, plus a useful map section to help you locate the farms.

Price: £5.99.

Choosing and buying equipment

STARTING OUT CAMPING AND CARAVANNING

More and more people have turned to camping and caravanning in recent years. Not only does it provide a holiday with greater freedom of choice, it also offers opportunities for getting away throughout the year even if only for weekends. Caravanning in particular has grown at an astonishing rate: there are now reportedly half a million or more touring caravans in this country alone.

Our guide will give you a good idea of what to expect when you go camping or caravanning. Interestingly, in this country we tend to differentiate between the activities of camping, caravanning and motor caravanning more than in most other countries in Europe. In Scandinavia, for example, the term 'camping' applies whatever kind of unit you stay in - even applying to the chalets which most sites over there provide.

You will, no doubt, already be 'camping' in one form or another.

You may have just started out. You may have just come back to it after a number of years away - in which case you will find a great many differences. You may be considering changing from one kind of camping to another, joining the great numbers of people who, over the years, experience a number of transitions in the way they camp. Whatever your present activity, our guide to what you need and which factors you need to consider when buying will be of help.

But camping and caravanning isn't just about equipment - it is about getting 'out there' and using it. How to make the most of your opportunities is just as important as choosing wisely. With thousands of camping and caravanning sites to choose from, stretching from one end of the country to the other, there is naturally a great variety. Facilities on sites may be extensive; others prefer sites with few facilities for all sorts of reasons. What will appeal to you as a camper or caravanner more than anything else is that the choice is yours.

More and more people have turned to camping and caravanning in recent years.

INVESTING IN NEW EQUIPMENT

The least expensive way to start is undoubtedly camping. With large frame tents of good quality available for just a few hundred pounds, they will more than repay the outlay in years to come provided they're looked after. Designs for family use extend to tents with separate kitchen areas, inner compartments for sleeping in at night, even hanging wardrobes. However, they are at their best when staying in one place for several days at least. More convenient for touring purposes are the large ridge tents with extended porches, or the new vis-a-vis designs which combine elements of design from several types of tent.

Weight may be a consideration if you are to be using a small car, but packed size is more likely to be your concern. Frame tents particularly are bulky items to pack despite usually having separate pole bags. Ridge tents and large dome tents have far more compact pole systems.

When choosing a tent it is necessary to allow for all the gear which must be stowed in it too, most of it at floor level. All the bedding has to be kept somewhere during the day if a separate bedroom isn't available. The kitchen area, too, usually requires a lot of room.

Trailer-tents get around some of these problems. By being essentially a tent built onto a solid construction in the form of a trailer they can make use of the solid base to include some fixed storage space. But those which open out to provide beds at either end offer another possibility - small 'tents' which can be fixed under the trailer-tent's bed areas, providing lots of extra storage. These can also be used by children at night - though they then lose one of the main advantages of this sort of camping which is off-the-ground sleeping.

There is a gradual transition from the simple canvas trailer-tent to the folding caravan. In between are all manner of different products. Some are lightning quick (ie. two or three minutes) to erect - which usually means that they are simply a shell once erected. Some require pegging out and others don't. One even makes use of PVC coated polyester rather than cotton canvas which

Trailer-tents can make use of the solid base to include some fixed storage space.

There are many factors to consider when choosing a caravan - careful study of all the options is vital before you make a choice.

makes for less worry when packing away wet. The real advantage of the trailer-tent, apart from its comfort relative to tent camping, is its ease of towing because it is low and offers little wind resistance. It can also be much easier to store as some can be turned their side and even fit into a larger garage as well as the car.

Those considering a more sophisticated model would do well to read the following section on choosing a caravan as some of the thinking necessary behind the purchase will be relevant.

Setting out to buy anything new is a serious business. But with caravans costing many thousands of pounds, and with some motor-homes costing tens of thousands of pounds, it requires careful study of the options before making the wisest choice, and a commitment to get the best use from it.

Making an informed decision isn't easy: there are many factors to consider and, of all the different units available, choosing a caravan is perhaps hardest of all.

Making the choice should involve two quite separate exercises. Firstly, it is necessary to sit down at home and work out the basic requirements - factors which won't change, at least for some time. You will want to consider the probable weight of the loaded caravan in relation to your car, number of berths and, ofcourse, the price you are willing to pay - bearing in mind the accessories you may still have to buy. Why should this be done at home? Simply because it is too easy to be swayed by other factors once you are at a dealers. Too many purchasers finish up with a caravan heavier than was their intention because they have been attracted by its interior.

Deciding on the number of berths isn't necessarily as straightforward as counting heads. Children can always sleep in an awning or in a small tent beside the caravan, giving the family the option of large two-berth layouts too. Older couples, on the other hand, often opt for a four- or five-berth layout so they can occasionally take their grandchildren away.

Weight, however, is a much more restricting factor to deal with. Ideally, your loaded caravan should not exceed 85% of your car's kerbweight. You've now calculated the greatest 'maximum laden weight' or 'gross weight' which your car will cope with comfortably, assuming it has sufficient power and torque in the engine. Work out the likely weight of everything you will load in your caravan. Don't forget to allow for the items which are out of sight like gas bottles, and for items you may load afterwards like bicycles. Once you've calculated what your likely loading figure is to be, you now know what 'loading margin' you are looking for.

By deducting the loading margin from the maximum laden weight of any caravan you calculate the third weight you will come across: the 'ex-works weight'. All three figures for any new caravan will be readily available. Most manufacturers quote in both hundredweights and kilograms, though a few have gone entirely metric.

An outfit in which the loaded caravan weighs more than 85% of the kerbweight of the car is more likely to get involved in a situation where 'the tail is wagging the dog'. In other words, the caravan takes control rather than the driver of the towing vehicle being able to determine how the outfit as a whole behaves.

You will see advice that experienced caravanners may exceed the '85% rule' but, in reality, most of us seriously underestimate the weight of all that we pack so it remains a good 'rule' for all.

The factors of brake horse power and torque affect how capably your car will tow in different conditions. Flexibility is helpful and that means having something in reserve. Assess the engine speeds at which peak power and peak torque are attained. Torque is only useful if it can be achieved at the relatively low engine speeds maintained whilst towing.

The weight of the car itself must also be considered in relation to power and torque. Heavier cars are good from the stability point of view but that weight has to be propelled. Comparing power to weight ratios, then, is also important when choosing tow-cars.

Not surprisingly, both the Caravan Club and the Camping and Caravanning Club receive more requests for advice on outfit-matching than any other single topic.

One other factor to think about is whether or not a twin-axled model would be of benefit. Whilst a greater loading margin can be allowed than for the single-axle version of the same model, manoeuvrability by hand is more difficult. A compromise is offered by Lunar who provide the option of lifting one axle to get round this problem.

As for price, only you can decide how much to spend and whether or not you wish to extend your purchasing power by using a finance agreement. If you do choose to borrow as a means of purchasing, you don't have to accept the dealer's finance arrangements. Remember that he makes money out of you this way as well: be prepared to negotiate a lower interest rate. If necessary, make enquiries of finance companies direct or, better still, approach your bank.

Having determined these factors, take the time to look around as many caravans as possible just to get the feel of the different ranges. You will quickly realise that there is a great overlap in terms of basic layout - but some are caravans you could enjoy being in. Others won't suit you at all. Just as at home, decor is a very personal matter.

The serious business of looking at specific ranges and models within those ranges will bring you into contact with salesmen - but you must treat them as demonstrators. Ask them to actually show you - not just to explain - how beds are made up, how the table is stored, how the blinds and flyscreens work. And when they've demonstrated these things, try them yourself. It is essential to see what the caravan is like with all beds made up, to see how easily (or otherwise) the bunks operate, and to see what access is like to the toilet at night. Most caravans are also displayed without their tables in place because this makes them seem more spacious.

By going through this process on every model which is of interest, you will quickly realise that certain layouts will suit you better than

Most caravans are displayed without their tables in place, to make them seem more spacious.

others. The degree of privacy afforded the adult couple in models with a centre dinette converting to beds for the children is far less than on models with beds at both ends. Children also need an area to call their own, with their own storage for toys and books and their own table to play on.

On some models the area afforded to children in a separate dinette may seem generous, but when the dividing curtain is drawn at night those same areas can seem very claustrophobic. And do the children need a light on at night? If so, will that disturb your sleep?

Seating arrangements are fairly standard, though some models offer upholstery with a 'knee-roll' - a rounded edge to add greater support behind the knee and under the thigh. Some also offer shaped end- and scatter-cushions to improve comfort still further. But all these increase the complication of converting seating to beds and back again in the morning.

Larger tables can be free-standing with folding legs which makes them easy to store and equally easy to use outside. So-called 'fixed' tables usually attach at one end and have a folding leg arrangement at the other so that these too can be removed and stored. Table storage has until recently tended to be in the toilet/shower compartment, usually making it necessary to remove it in order to have a shower. This inconvenience has led to ingenious 'hidden' storage methods being developed in the last couple of years.

Although use of tables for making up the front double bed has given way to the use of pull-out slatted bases, the smaller tables from rear- or centre dinettes are still used to bridge the gap between the seats at night. Other options include various designs of a pull-out base which fits over the existing seat base and simply slides out. Bessacarr actually use this system on the front dinette too, also allowing seating to be moved nearer to the table for children during the daytime.

Cooking facilities start with a hob and grill. The simplest hob has just two burners, now giving way to a three-burner hob as standard on most basic models. The option of four burners is often available, and will be a standard fitting onbetter equipped models which may also offer an oven too. Recent advances have meant the increased use of electronic ignition on both cooking appliances and fridges. You can expect the latter to run on gas, mains electricity or 12 volt power - though the last is intended only for whilst you are towing as the drain would otherwise be too great for your battery.

Toilet and washing facilities depend largely on the price of the caravan. The simplest arrangement is no more than an empty toilet compartment in which you can place a portable chemical toilet. If you have been away from camping for some time, you will find that today's portable toilets are much more sophisticated, incorporating their own flush mechanisms. But the single greatest improvement in recent years has been the development of the cassette porta-potti. This is a built-in chemical toilet with either manual or electronic flushing system and which uses a pullout cassette waste container which is both easy and far less unpleasant to empty.

Most toilet compartments offer at least a tip-up washbasin with running cold water provided. But the vast majority of new caravans now offer hot water systems at least as an option and often as standard. Where it is an option there may be a shower

tray fitted as standard. Where hot water is already standard you can usually expect a shower too.

Heating is to be considered a very useful addition. A simple space heater is the budget van's usual fitment, progressing to one which is thermostatically controlled and even further to one which has the addition of blown air central heating which distributes ducted warm air through vents around the caravan.

Using your caravan outside the summer season necessitates thinking about gas too. Propane, rather than butane, will be necessary if temperatures are likely to drop below 4° Celsius.

As far as power for your caravan's electrics is concerned, there are several possibilities. The simplest method is to plug your caravan's grey 12S lead into your car's 12S socket. The I2S and 12N sockets are the two seven-pin sockets you will see by the tow-ball. The 'N' stands for 'normal' and this provides power to the caravan's or trailer's roadlights. The 'S' stands for 'supplementary' and provides power for additional equipment such as interior lighting, fridge and so on. The 12S socket/plug will be grey and the 12N will be black.

Provided you use it only for lighting in the evening and for intermittent use of the water pump and you give your car a run every day to recharge the battery, using the car's 12S socket will be adequate. However, it does cause problems when someone wants to use the car whilst others want to stay in the caravan or trailer-tent.

The way round this is to use a leisure battery solely for the caravan or trailer. These are normally rated at between 60 amp and 90 amp. Many caravans fit a separate battery compartment to avoid the dangerous practice of keeping the battery in the gas locker. If staying put for more than a few days, this battery will need charging too but this service is often offered by site-owners for a small fee. Alternatively, your car can be wired so that you can charge the battery in the car on an occasion when all the family is going out. Serious caravanners often work with two such batteries, swapping them over as necessary.

Those with mains electricity will find that a charger is incorporated to top up the 12 volt battery. However, there are a number of popular continental models like Adria which do not offer such a provision and whose 240 volt and 12 volt electrics are quite separate. In this case no provision at all is made for abattery and use has to be made of the car's 12S socket if 12 volt power is required.

Lastly, as far as caravans are concerned, some mention must be made of the effects on the market of the recent recession combined with the over-production of new models during the preceding year. Over-production had already become evident when the downturn in the economy was seen. Stocks of new caravans at certain manufacturers were an embarrassment. Dealers, having had a couple of good years, were left carrying a lot of stock they had taken in part exchange as well as more new caravans than they could easily sell. From a total production of around 35,000 the estimate for the coming production year is around 25,000. At the end of the 1991 caravanning season, large dealers were discounting heavily the stock they still held to make way for new models. At the extreme, reductions of over £3000 could be found on top of the range models.

Some 1991 caravans will continue to be found new early in 1992 - and secondhand in the years to come - at bargain prices.

Those looking to invest in a new motor caravan or larger motor-home have to consider not only the design factors but also the base vehicle and its engine. All offer a compromise between ease of use as a vehicle and ease of use as a mode of living. The classic example of that compromise is the elevating roof, allowing a more aerodynamic body whilst motoring but greatly improved headroom whilst on site. Larger models opt for that headroom permanently, with some making good use of the over-cab area for sleeping accommodation.

With only 4000 new motor caravans sold last year by an enormous range of convertors and manufacturers, the business of getting to view new models involves a lot of travelling around. Undoubtedly the best method is to visit one of the major exhibitions. Much the same problem applies to viewing tents and trailer-tents as showrooms which display a wide range of these already erected are all too few.

BUYING SECONDHAND

The traditional route for people buying their first trailer-tent, caravan or motor caravan has been to buy an older model - perhaps ten years old or so - to see if they enjoy the activity. Once they've got hooked they gradually move up to a new model in two or three leaps.

And after two to three years, you may well look to trade up to a model with a higher specification so that you can enjoy your new acquisition in all weathers and in greater comfort.

Better condition older caravans - even those around ten years old -

tend to command higher prices than you might expect. Look around the dealers and you'll see many 1981 and 1982 models with asking prices in excess of £2000. And reasonable condition family vans of that age with four or five berths can often reach £2500. Such caravans will sell privately for much less - but represent greater risk unless they are thoroughly inspected. (Refer to the section on Carascan for more information.)

Those caravans from the mid 1980s which offer family accommodation and reasonable specification come with quite high asking prices - expect to pay at least three or four thousand pounds. Look for a caravan which has been looked after both inside and out; look for one with as many 'extras' as possible double-glazing, heater, fridge and mains electrics in particular. If you have a family, then look out for a three- or four-burner hob rather than a two-burner one.

All these, at one time, cost someone extra money. But, just like the money spent on improving your house, it is rarely returned when you sell it.

Caravans in this country are manufactured to a set of specifications not matched by foreign manufacturers, with certain exceptions. But even those made to BS 4626 will still be cheaper by far than British models. Whilst they are cheaper to buy, they are harder to resell too.

The main factor governing the asking price varies. A family selling privately a model they have cherished for years will place a higher value on it than is realistic. A businessman who has used a caravan for working away (and many do) will deem that it has long since paid for itself, being far cheaper than a hotel, and will probably undervalue it. Dealers take condition into account, but take greater account of the year of manufacture.

Motor caravans, like houses, are worth what you can get someone to pay for them. Surprisingly high prices are asked for quite old models because they can still serve their main function just as well. Low mileage examples can be an excellent buy - but they bring their own problems too. Low mileage means they've been standing idle. Tyres can have lots of tread left but side walls can be in poor condition. Other rubber parts can dry and crack. Any engine suffers through not being used at all. A better buy is often a vehicle which has had light but regular use.

On entering a caravan, trailer-tent or motor caravan - or on opening out a tent - if you detect a musty smell, no matter how faint, leave this one alone. Mustiness indicates damp. The smell may be only be faint because the owner or dealer has given it a good airing. In any case, examine material thoroughly. Go over floorboards and panelling. Better still, use a damp meter which will detect damp in places you can't examine.

Looking for wear and tear on tents and awnings means at least spreading the material out but try to see it erected if at all possible. Examine pegging points and, on lightweight tents especially, the condition of the groundsheet. Polework should be examined for sections which may have been bent and re-straightened, and for damaged joints.

Prospective purchasers of trailer-tents should use a combination of these and some of the points specifically on caravans which follow.

In considering a caravan, it is vital to

confirm the year of manufacture and the ex-works and maximum laden weights first of all. Only then should you think of examining the caravan itself. Start outside with an examination of the bodywork, paying particular attention to seams and joints for signs of possible water ingress. Not all water entering a caravan is visibly noticeable from the inside; hidden damp is a serious and expensive business indeed.

Smooth finish aluminium panels are far easier to clean than stipple-effect finishes but show up minor dents and scratches much more. Ribbed-effect aluminium falls between the two. The sandwich construction of the panelling has an insulating filling of polystyrene foam which is bonded to both inner and outer panelling. Examine body panels for signs of delamination.

You may still be looking at a caravan with toughened glass windows but it's increasingly likely to have acrylic ones. Examine these closely if the caravan is generally dirty. If they've been cleaned in the past with anything mildly abrasive, they'll look like they've been cleaned with wire wool and won't clean up as well as you think.

Examine the towing hitch and the A-frame, though the latter may be hidden beneath a fairing. The hitch should work smoothly and lock into place as required. Some rotational movement is necessary - but it should not feel loose or wobbly. Try pushing the hitch back against the gaiter, too. Several inches of movement (provided the handbrake is off) is normal as you simulate the overrun brake mechanism coming on. Also check that the jockey wheel winds up and down smoothly.

Accident damage which might affect the chassis will be evident elsewhere - but a chassis can be twisted in other ways. Look too at the corner steadies for signs of twisting and other misuse. If possible make use of the van's jockey wheel to raise or lower the front end so you can wind each corner steady in turn to its greatest extent and back again.

Having taken with you something to lie on, crawl underneath to check for soft floorboards, signs of damaged gas piping and stray wiring.

All gas appliances should be checked for poor connections and actually operated. They may not work immediately as there will be air in the system. This is not unusual and appliances should light after several attempts. If no cylinder is fitted, get the owner to fit one. Similarly, every electrical appliance should be checked which means fitting a battery and a mains lead if necessary. Caravans sold by dealers should have been checked - but take nothing for granted. Gas and electrical faults are rare but, when they happen, as serious as they come.

The water system should be operated too, including any water heater fitted, and any fittings in the washroom. Whilst there, check that the flush works if a cassette porta-potti is fitted.

Most of these things, if the caravan has been in regular use, should be in working order. The trouble with 'the bargain' is that it probably hasn't. It may not even have been towed for several years, in which case the tyres, the running gear and brakes, and the roadlights and connecting seven-pin plug will certainly need immediate attention.

The handbrake should work smoothly over three or four notches and the breakaway cable should be checked too. Check wheels for sideways movement, indicating worn wheel bearings - and don't forget to ask if the owner has a spare. One of the main advantages of buying privately can be the extras you acquire with the caravan. For example, the owner may no longer need his existing awning if it won't fit his next van.

As for soft furnishings and furniture, look for obvious signs of wear and tear which will reduce resale value later on. Fittings like hinges and catches can always be replaced - but try every locker door, every cupboard. Behind that woodwork could be signs of damp. As most furniture is fitted over the carpet at manufacturing stage, you probably can't lift the carpet - but feel it in several places for any wetness.

If any of the items referred to need attention, they could easily cost you more than an inspection by Carascan.

ACCESSORIES - MAKING LIFE EASIER

The basic requirements of any form of camping are shelter, warmth, food and comfort. The first you already have; the rest depend on accessories.

More adventurous campers will tell you that being wet doesn't matter as long as you're warm - but most will want to stay both warm and dry. For users of tents and cotton canvas trailer-tents, that means two things. Firstly, all new cotton products need to be 'weathered' to go through several cycles of getting wet and drying out - so that the cotton fibres fill out. These have been compressed whilst the material has been stored in huge heavy rolls. Secondly, the seams will benefit from a dose of seam sealant, readily available in tubes from camping shops. Take a tube with you on holiday, too.

Cold certainly is the real enemy, and it is vital to realise that cold comes upwards from the ground. Extra insulation below is far more important at night than an extra quilt or blanket above. There are several types of sleeping mat available: dense foam ones which roll up compactly and are favoured by backpackers; self-inflating ones again good for lightweight camping; good old-fashioned air beds, and two inch thick foam ones - though these are exceptionally bulky especially if there are several of you.

Awning carpet is available for caravanners planning to sleep part of the family in the awning but they provide virtually no insulation at all.

For either the motor caravanner or caravanner, the awning is a very useful addition. For the latter, it can represent a considerable outlay with prices ranging from a hundred pounds for a secondhand cotton full awning to a thousand pounds for a new acrylic one.

The full awning attaches along the entire side of the caravan. Neither cotton nor acrylic versions should be left packed away wet but cotton ones take much more drying. Porch awnings cover a section of the side of the caravan where the door is - as the name suggests. These are useful for short term use when it is wet and provide a place to hang wet clothes and keep muddy boots.

Enthusiastic caravanners often use a full awning whilst staying put in one place at holiday time (taking it down near the end of their holiday if rain threatens) and a nylon or acrylic porch awning for frequent weekend use.

Choice of clothing, too, is determined largely by our unpredictable weather. If it's muddy nothing can beat the traditional wellington boot. But in wet

Full awnings attach along the entire side of the caravan. Porch awnings cover a section of the side, where the door is.

weather experienced campers often opt for shorts and trainers without socks after all, legs dry more quickly than trousers.

Modern advances in fabric technology are well worth making use of. Breathable waterproofs aren't all expensive - cheaper versions are quite adequate if you're not engaged in active pursuits. Polypropylene thermal tee-shirts are warm and dry very quickly when wet. Fleece fabrics have replaced wool entirely on the outdoors scene because they are light, extremely soft and comfortable, windproof in certain forms, and they wick moisture away so quickly they dry in no time - all ideal properties for campers and caravanners. Inside the tent or caravan some extra footwear is needed for comfort: be it a pair of slippers or a pair of walking socks with extra-thick soles.

Anyone planning to go outside the summer season will require some form of heating. In a caravan or motor caravan this will be be in the form of a properly fitted and flued gas heater. In a tent, however, the only option is a free-standing space heater connected by hose to the gas cylinder, or a bowl-type heater which screws directly onto a Camping Gaz cylinder. It is necessary to realise, however, that butane will not vaporise readily below around 4° Celsius. Propane will work well below freezing but it is stored at a higher pressure. Different regulators are needed and you should check that any appliance connected is suitable.

It is worth noting that small resealable-valve butane/propane mix cartridges are available for a range of lightweight camping appliances including a small heater. Alternatively, get the kettle on and climb into your sleeping bag. You will also find that gas lanterns give off a surprising amount of heat and the pressurised Tilley designs even more.

Cooking appliances for family campers are mostly simple two-burner units with a grill beneath. You can always take pans from home but sets of pans which sit neatly inside one another take up far less room; these are available in non-stick versions too. One very useful addition in the kitchen area is a small pressure cooker. And if you are frying, use one of those ingenious mesh 'lids' which stop the fat from spitting everywhere as this will damage furnishings and waterproofed material.

Of course, frying has generally given way to barbecues and many of these are available in different shapes and forms. But what many newcomers to camping don't realise is that there are gas barbecues and griddles too, which are clean and easy to use. There is also a Camping Gaz table-top fondue set making use of a tiny gas cartridge - so all sorts of cooking are at your fingertips.

Keeping your food fresh is easy these days and a good cool box will serve you well for many years. Don't underestimate the size you will need. Some models will run off a 12 volt supply so you can plug them into your car's cigarette lighter, but they can drain the car battery completely in a day so careful use of this facility is necessary.

The most vital item, though, is the kettle. Most campers use a simple and inexpensive one but you can get quickboil versions using a special base. Low wattage electric ones are available through camping and caravanning accessory shops for those with mains electrics. At one time this meant only the more privileged caravanner. Now the majority of new caravans have mains connections and so do some trailer-tents.

But now campers can use mains hook-ups too. Specially designed leads incorporating the necessary safety devices and a number of three-pin sockets are available and can be used on some sites - though it is wise to enquire first.

The essential thing to understand is that you cannot simply plug in all manner of domestic electrical equipment as you will overload the system. A number of specially designed products are on the market, like 500 watt fan heaters and low wattage kettles. A black and white television from home will only use one and a half amps, with a colour version doubling that figure. But ordinary electric kettles and similar appliances may take up most of your available amperage. Most hook-ups offer a six, ten or sixteen amp supply. Exceeding this results in your supply being 'tripped' and, more importantly, in an unhappy site warden.

Other accessories which are essential include a water container - and a waste water container for those in trailer-tents, caravans and motor caravans. The easiest water containers to use are the cylindrical ones which are rolled ratherthan carried. Whilst these were designed for those using electric submersible pumps, there is now a camping version with a tap incorporated in the cap and a stand to sit the container on.

Chemical toilets have improved greatly in recent years and one of these is a useful extra, though bulky, for when you want to use minimum facility sites or to attend rallies. Campers will also require a toilet tent.

Toilet facilities on quality sites are extensive and often include other facilities like washing machines. For this reason it is worth taking a small collapsible clothes drier and some pegs as well. A plastic washing-up

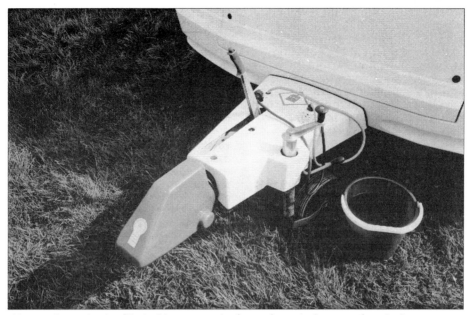

Always place a bucket filled with water at the front of your unit, as a safety device.

bowl is indispensable for carrying either the washing or the washing-up across to the toilet block.

Safety shouldn't be forgotten either. Not only should you make up a comprehensive first aid kit, you should take a fire extinguisher and always place a bucket filled with water at the front of your unit. A number of caravan manufacturers even fit fire blankets as standard now and they have to fit smoke alarms by law.

If you are towing, as well as spare bulbs, don't forget a suitable jack and spare wheel for your trailer or caravan. Most accessory shops only stock the wheel which you've then got to take away to get a suitable tyre fitted.

You will also need towing mirrors as you must be able to see behind or at least along the side of your caravan or trailer. Trailer-tents present no problem because you can see over them through your interior mirror.

Finally, many people use a stabiliser for towing. This accessory is not an essential - in fact, few people in the trade use them at all because they are towing ever-changing combinations of vehicle and caravan. But it is true that the majority of caravanners use one. It is necessary to realise that a stabiliser won't prevent a badly matched or badly loaded outfit from behaving badly. Snaking can still begin, but the first sideways movements are dampened fairly quickly.

Snaking starts with small but increasing sideways swaying movements of the trailer or caravan. This is sometimes caused by instability caused by poor loading. More often it is caused by another factor - a sideways force exerted by wind or a mass of air forced aside by another vehicle, as a boat pushes water aside.

Because your towing coupling allows movement, and because your caravan or trailer has only two wheels rather than four, it will be affected more than your towing vehicle. A stabiliser dampens the initial movement at the coupling, stopping the caravan from increasing the arc of the swing with each sway. Fitting a stabiliser is certainly a good idea, but it will tend to hide the 'feel' of the outfit from the less experienced caravanner.

SECURITY MATTERS

Theft of and from caravans is a fact of life. During 1990 the total value of caravans stolen reached a staggering six and a half million pounds. There is no doubt that many of these were stolen to order, backed by highly organised thieves.

Motor caravans do not suffer the same degree of attention, and one rarely hears of tents being stolen or entered on site. This is a reflection of two things: there is a ready market for stolen caravans, and thefts of already owned models tend to be from storage areas and from the drive at home.

Sites themselves, while not being totally immune, are very rarely the scene of a theft. Campers and caravanners are generally gregarious, quickly getting to know one another with a passing greeting, and an unwelcome visitor is easily spotted.

For the thief to break into a caravan is not difficult. Door frames are aluminium and a jemmy will spring a door open in seconds. The locks which are normally fitted use one of a relatively small number of keys - the bunch you see a salesman with would, between them, open almost every caravan in the country. Windows are only acrylic and can be cut through easily. However, a high security lock with tens of thousands of key combinations can be fitted, and so can an alarm system. Neither

will stop the thief from breaking into a caravan in a quiet storage area.

Theft of the caravans themselves is the major concern - and this can be prevented. Unfortunately, the greater the degree of prevention, the greater the inconvenience when you want to use it yourself.

Hitch locks prevent the trailer or caravan from being attached to the thief's towball. Once thieves started to steal complete hitches from old caravans to replace locked hitches on newer ones, a new design of hitch lock emerged. This types covers the hitch and its mounting bolts entirely.

One company manufactures a steel post, designed to set deep in your drive-way, onto which your hitch attaches and locks in place. Similarly, some people use heavy chains to secure their pride and joy.

It isn't only the police who use wheel clamps - they are available in a variety of forms to caravanners too. Removing the wheels entirely is one option during the winter months. Corner steady locks can be fitted to

Wheel clamps are available in a variety of forms to help make caravans secure.

prevent the steadies being wound up.

But whatever single form of security device you fit, someone will have a tale to tell of how a thief overcame that type of crime prevention. So what's the answer?

Most caravan theft is opportunist - but that doesn't mean it isn't premeditated. Thieves drive around assessing the ease with which they can steal certain caravans, coming back when least likely to be noticed.

The thief needs time to get past your preventative measures. For every extra measure, he needs more time. By fitting a simple hitch lock, four corner steady locks and a wheel lock the caravanner presents the thief with a lengthy and increasingly obvious task - yet all those locks can be removed by the caravanner in minutes.

Much of the above can be applied by the trailer-tent camper too, and motor caravanners can make use of a combination of wheel locks and conventional car security devices. At the end of the day, vigilance and the practise of good habits count for a great deal.

The Caravan Registration and Identification Scheme (CRIS for short) is a new idea set up by the National Caravan Council. Every touring caravan, starting with the 1992 model year, will be registered and security marked with its own unique number. The numbering system used will be the standard VIN (Vehicle Identification Number) system using seventeen characters. The VIN number will be die-stamped onto the chassis and will also be chemically etched on the caravan's windows. The same number is present on a registration document which will also record future changes of ownership. In essence, the system will follow the pattern used for car registration documents. That hasn't stopped car theft either - but it does make it more difficult.

WHAT OF THE OTHER SIX MONTHS?

Having invested in your camping and caravanning equipment, what you do with it during the colder half of the year is important too. If it is to be

A Vehicle Identification Number can be chemically etched on the caravan's windows for added security.

stored, then it should be readied for storage. If it is to be used, a number of additional factors need to be borne in mind.

Any canvas material - be it tent, trailer-tent or caravan awning - must be properly clean and dry. If any stains need washing, use only pure soap and warm water as detergents will remove water-proofing. Allow to dry thoroughly: any hint of damp may result in mildew.

Tyres on caravans and trailers should be up to pressure and during the course of the winter should be rotated so that one spot has not carried all the weight for months on end. Some people actually remove their wheels, temporarily replacing them with lockable stands as additional security.

If it is a trailer-tent or caravan which is being stored, all kitchen surfaces should be given a thorough clean with Milton or a similar cleansing fluid. Any toilet should have been properly cleaned and disinfected. The upholstery should preferably be removed and the interior well aired. Periodic airing during the laying-up period is a good idea too.

Any water system needs thorough draining in order to prevent damage through water freezing in the pipes and appliances. Whilst the Carver Cascade hot water system (as fitted to the majority of caravans) has a drain tap, any additional drain tap which is a few inches lower than the plumbing is more effective. An additional method of helping clear the system of water is to open all taps and to blow down them.

Finally, draw the curtains or blinds to prevent sunlight from affecting the colour of your upholstery, though modern fabrics are more resistant to fading.

Any form of trailer should be serviced before it goes into storage - not after. When it is taken out in the Spring you are anxious to use it and the temptation then is often to ignore getting it serviced. Brakes need checking and adjusting, all moving parts like corner steadies and brake linkages need greasing. Any work on the gas, water or electrical systems should be done now too.

Finally, a thorough washing and a good coat of polish will make it so much easier afterwards to get rid of the dirt the winter rain will bring.

It may well be that you won't store your caravan or trailer at home. In some cases, bye-laws may prevent this; it may block your drive and access to your garage; you may have nowhere at all to keep it. Two popular options are to store it in a proper storage area, or to keep it with a friendly farmer.

The cost of storage varies regionally. With thefts of caravans at alarming levels, you may feel justified if you have a valuable caravan in paying more for storage offering better security. Most storage areas need to be accessible enough to allow caravanners to come and go regularly, which makes security difficult without employing costly electronic systems.

Farms, in this respect, make good locations because those who don't belong stand out immediately. However, they are often less handy for frequent to-ing and fro-ing. Wherever you choose to leave it, make sure you leave it secure. (Refer to the section on security for more detailed advice.)

Finally, park it on the flat and leave it level as six months' constant twisting of its framework and door and window frames won't do it any good.

If, on the other hand, you aren't the sort to let cold and wet weather deter you from winter camping and caravanning, read on.

Whilst the ground is sometimes wetter it can also be a lot harder once temperatures start dropping to freezing at night. Stronger pegs are needed for tents and awnings, as well as something to knock them in and a peg-puller for getting them out.

Snow brings its own problems. Both tents and awnings need more steeply sloping roofs in order to shed snow, the accumulated weight of which can be considerable. Deep snow makes pegging almost worthless, so a valance is necessary around the base of the awning or flysheet. This can then have snow (and preferably boulders or other available materials) heaped on it to weigh it down.

Choice of gas must come down to propane - readily available in either 3.9kg or 13kg bottles. In certain areas an intermediate 7kg size is available from less well-known companies. For the lightweight camper propane is available in small cartridges as well as cylinders using a butane/propane mix. The latter will generally be sufficient for lightweight campers in our climate.

Modern caravans are well insulated and have double-glazing and, though they can be cold until you've had the heater on a while, the problems aren't as great as for the tent or trailer-tent camper.

Insulation and heating have been dealt with in the section on accessories but it is worth re-emphasising here the need for good insulation between you and the ground. Your sleeping bag, too, needs to be up to the job. Down bags are more efficient weight for weight than those with man-made fillings but a good down or quality feather and down bag is expensive. All-year round sleeping bags with man-made fillings are bulkier and considerably cheaper and perform better when wet than down bags. Look for a baffle behind the zip to prevent cold spots, for overlapping sections so that the bag isn't sewn through, and the benefit of a mummy-style bag will be appreciated when it is cold enough to draw the hood around your head.

The real problem you have to face is the long night - so the last accessory on your shopping list is a good book.

by Andrew Stansfield

November 1991

RAC Carascan inspection scheme

More than 90% of first-time caravanners buy a secondhand caravan when starting the pastime. More than 75% of first-time caravanners buy their first caravan from a private individual or from a non-specialist dealer. This means that 79% of all first-time caravanners buy a used caravan without any sort of guarantee to its condition. They are examining a caravan with totally inexperienced eyes.

Needless to say stories of first-timers `buying a pup' are legion. With an ever increasing number of people taking to caravanning as a means of avoiding the holiday rush, or as a way of pursuing another hobby - it was obvious that there was a need for a service providing an expert inspection of secondhand caravans.

Thus was formed a liaison between the world's first motoring organisation and the world's first camping and caravanning organisation, which led to the introduction of `RAC Carascan' endorsed by the Camping & Caravanning Club.

The scheme is simplicity itself. After completion of a single form, an RAC Engineer is sent to inspect the caravan. The engineer will travel to the caravan, whether it is at a dealership or on private property.

The engineer examines every aspect of the caravan's construction, including chassis, tow-hitch, brakes, wheels, tyres, body construction, lights (both internal and external), wiring fuse boxes, power points, water system, toilet, shower, gas and cooking facilities. Everything that relates to the caravan's construction or use is covered by the RAC Carascan inspection report.

The owner, or seller, of the caravan will receive an unbiased and comprehensive report which will highlight essential repairs, and the conditions of all body and mechanical components.

RAC Carascan will give you peace of mind, and improve your negotiating power when purchasing the caravan of your choice. An RAC inspection prior to warranty expiry may identify any faults which can be rectified under warranty at no cost to yourself. You can improve the resale value of your caravan as an RAC Carascan report will prove that your caravan has been well maintained.

Enjoy the same benefits when you make use of the RAC Vehicle Examination Service to inspect your car.

So if you are buying, selling or hitching-up for the start of a new caravanning year, play safe and get the RAC on your side. For full details contact the RAC on 0800 333660.

The Law relating to Caravans and Trailers

This summary refers only to the more important motoring laws relating to trailers and caravans. It is believed to be correct at October, 1991.

AVOIDANCE OF DANGER

A motor vehicle, every trailer drawn thereby and all parts and accessories of such vehicles and trailers shall at all times be in such condition that no danger is caused or likely to be caused to any person in or on the vehicle or trailer or on a road.
This includes passengers and/or load, and is endorsable with 3 Penalty Points.

LIGHTING

Number plate
Must be of similar dimensions to that of the towing vehicle and bearing the same mark and numbers. It must be illuminated at night.

Front lamps
If a trailer exceeds 1600mm in overall width or 2300mm in overall length, and was manufactured after 1/10/85, it must be fitted with two white front lamps.

Rear lamps and reflectors
Two red rear lamps and two red rear reflex reflectors must be fitted to a trailer. The reflectors must be of the triangular type, marked BS.AU 40L111 or L11A, or bear an approval mark incorporating 111 or 111A.

Stop lamps
Two red stop lamps must be fitted to most trailers, but where the stop lamps at the rear of the towing vehicle can be seen by an observer standing centrally 6 metres behind the trailer no stop lamps are required, provided the trailer was manufactured before 1/10/90.

Direction indicators
Direction indicators must be fitted to most trailers, but where the direction indicator on each side of the towing vehicle can be seen by an observer standing centrally 6 metres behind the trailer no direction indicators are required, provided the trailer was manufactured before 1/10/90.

Rear fog lamps
At least one rear fog lamp must be fitted to a trailer manufactured after 1st April 1980 that exceeds 1300mm in overall width. A trailer that is being drawn by a vehicle that is not required to be fitted with a rear fog lamp is not itself required to be fitted with a rear fog lamp.

Side reflex reflectors
A trailer that exceeds 5 metres in overall length, excluding its drawbar, is required to be fitted with amber side reflex reflectors bearing an approval mark including the Roman numeral I.

Parking without lights
The provisions permitting certain types of motor vehicles to park without lights on roads subject to a speed limit of 30mph or less do not apply when a trailer is attached to the vehicle.

BRAKES

Unbraked trailers
Existing and new trailers do not require breaks if:
(a) the sum of their maximum design axle weights does not exceed 750kg, *and*
(b) their laden weight on the road does not exceed half the towing vehicle's kerbside weight.

Trailers that can be towed by motorcycles do not require brakes. Unbraked trailers must have at least one wheel prevented from turning by means of blocks, chain, etc., when disconnected from the towing vehicle.

Braked trailers
All trailers required to have brakes must also be fitted with a parking brake.

Trailers first used before 1st April 1983 must comply with the Road Vehicles (Construction and Use) Regulations. These permit brakes to apply automatically if a trailer overruns, i.e. overrun (inertia) brakes. These brakes must be efficient but no specific performance is set.

Trailers first used after 1st April 1983 must comply with the latest EEC Braking Directives or the Europe Braking Regulations (ECE). These also permit overrun brakes. However, in order to comply with international standards, it is usually necessary for the design to undergo a type approval test. The trailer's braking efficiency must be at least 45% and the parking brake must be capable of holding the laden trailer on an 18% gradient.

A modern braked trailer must be fitted with an emergency device which will automatically apply the trailer's brakes if it becomes uncoupled from the towing vehicle; except that this does not apply to a single axle trailer up to 1500kg maximum gross axle weight, provided that it is fitted with a chain which will prevent the coupling head from touching the road if the trailer becomes detached.

MOTORWAY LANES

No motor vehicle drawing a trailer shall be driven in the right-hand lane of a motorway with three or more lanes which are open for use, except where this lane has to be used to pass a vehicle carrying or drawing a load of exceptional width.

PASSENGERS

No passenger may be carried in a moving caravan with less than four wheels or two close coupled wheels on each side.

CLOSETS

The contents of closets or urinals must not be discharged, or allowed to leak, onto the road. Closets in caravans must be either of the chemical type or must empty into a tank, which must be ventilated from outside and supplied with an efficient deodorant or germicide. The waste from any lavatory basin or sink may not be emptied into this tank.

INSURANCE

A driver intending to use his vehicle for towing must make sure that his insurance policy for the towing vehicle covers such use. If he is taking a trailer abroad he must ensure that his green card mentions the trailer.

SPEED LIMITS

When towing a trailer the towing vehicle is restricted to 60mph on motorways and dual carriageways, and 50mph on all other roads except where a lower speed limit is in force.

TYRES

Tyres fitted for use with the old maximum speed of 50mph may not be suited to the current maximum of 60mph. Trailers first used after 1st April, 1987, must be fitted with tyres suitable for 62mph (100kph) at the maximum design axle weight. From 1st January, 1992, the minimum tyre depth is 1.6mm.

MIRRORS

The driver of a towing vehicle must have an adequate view to the rear. Any rear view mirror must not project more than 200mm outside the width of the caravan when being towed or the width of the towing vehicle when being driven solo.

Very long and very heavy caravans and trailers are governed by further regulations. If you require more detailed information please contact the RAC Legal Department.
☎ Bristol (0272) 232444.

The Caravan Towing Code

Reproduced by kind permission of the National Caravan Council.

SCOPE OF THE CODE

The Code applies to all trailer caravans of maximum laden weight not exceeding 2030kg (4475 lbs), overall width not exceeding 2.3m (approx. 7' 6'') and overall length not exceeding 7m (approx. 23'), excluding the drawbar and coupling. This is legally the maximum size of trailer that can be towed by a motor car.

OBJECTIVES

The Code's objectives are:

To provide simple, easily understood advice on the safe matching of towing vehicles to caravans;

To make recommendations on the

selection of the ratio of caravan weight to towing vehicle weight so that safe towing may be achieved under the varying conditions which may be met on the road;

To give advice on the engine size and power required for satisfactory towing both for the ability to restart on a gradient and to maintain a reasonable speed relative to the traffic flow on various types of road;

To set out the factors the caravan user needs to take into account before towing a caravan.

Definitions of terms used in the Code:

THE CARAVAN

Ex works weight:
The maximum weight of the caravan as stated by the caravan manufacturer, as new with standard fixtures and fittings. (Note: Because of the differences in the weight of materials supplied for the construction of caravans, variations of + or -5% of the manufacturer's stated ex works weight can be expected.)

Actual laden weight:
The total weight of the caravan and its contents when being towed.

Maximum laden weight:
The maximum weight for which the caravan is designed for normal use when being towed on a road, laden.

Noseweight:
That part of the weight of the caravan supported by the rear of the towing vehicle.

THE TOWING VEHICLE

Kerb weight:
The weight of the towing vehicle as defined by the vehicle manufacturer. This is normally:
with a full tank of fuel;
with an adequate supply of other liquids incidental to the vehicle's propulsion;
without driver or passengers;

without any load except loose tools and equipment with which the vehicle is normally provided;
without any towing bracket.

THE CARAVAN/TOWING VEHICLE COMBINATION

Caravan/Towing vehicle weight ratio:
The actual laden weight of the caravan expressed as a percentage of the kerb weight of the towing vehicle, ie:

$$\frac{\text{actual laden weight of caravan} \times 100}{\text{kerb weight of towing vehicle}} = ...\%$$

How to estimate the actual laden weight:
The *basic* items required for two people to go caravanning will weigh a *minimum* of 100kg in total. These will include: food, crockery, cutlery, cooking utensils, clothing, bedding, gas bottles and water carrier.
The weight of any additional items required (eg battery, awning, portable toilet, spare wheel, TV etc) must be added to the *basic* total.
A further 25kg for each additional person should be allowed for *basic* items.

Having established the total weight of items to be carried by the caravan this must be added to the ex works weight to obtain the estimated actual laden weight.

If in doubt this can be done on a public weighbridge.

The address of the nearest public weighbridge in a locality may be obtained from the area Trading Standards Department (Weights and Measures).
The Department's telephone number will be found under:

County Council;
Metropolitan Council;
London Borough Council;
or Regional Council (for Scotland).

Note: Weighbridges have varying weight tolerance levels.

FACTORS WHICH MUST BE CONSIDERED FOR SAFE TOWING

Driver's towing experience

Experience of towing is not essential for taking up caravanning but drivers without experience should take greater care when manoeuvring. Speed should be built up gradually in order to get used to the different handling and braking characteristics.

For those who would like training, there are courses available and details may be obtained from the specialist clubs.

Further experience should be gained before tackling the more difficult elements of towing (higher weight ratios, mountain passes, difficult terrain, etc).

Caravan/towing vehicle weight ratio

This ratio has a major influence on stability. It is recommended that:

(a) the actual laden weight of the caravan should always be kept as low as possible. The lower it is when the caravan is being towed on a road the safer the caravan/towing vehicle combination will be.
(b) as a general rule, **the actual laden weight of a caravan should not exceed the kerb weight of the towing vehicle,** particularly if the latter is a conventional car (saloon, coupe, hatchback, estate, convertible, etc).
(c) the greater the actual laden weight of the caravan is in relation to the kerb weight of the towing vehicle, the more careful and experienced the driver needs to be.
(d) care must always be taken not to exceed the towing vehicle's loading and towing limits.

The law requires that caravans and their towing vehicles and the loads they carry must be is such a condition that no danger or nuisance is caused.

Power to weight ratio of towing vehicle to caravan

The performance of the towing vehicle has an important bearing on its suitability for towing and, therefore, on the selection of the caravan to match the towing vehicle.

There are many factors involved, which are often contradictory, such as brake horsepower, gearing, torque characteristics, turbo-charging and fuel injection.

No hard and fast rules can be stated but, as a general guide, conventional petrol engines with a capacity up to approximately 1500cc should be adequate for towing a caravan weighing around 85% of the kerb weight of the towing vehicle. Above 1500cc such engines should manage a caravan weighing up to 100% of the kerb weight of the towing vehicle and still give adequate performance but it should be noted that the towing vehicle manufacturer's limit is, in some cases, less than the kerb weight. While the towing vehicle may manage 100%, attention is again drawn to the recommendation under the previous heading, 'Caravan/towing vehicle weight ratio', that a weight ratio of 85% is an ideal starting point.

Diesel engines of whatever size have a lower performance for a given cubic capacity compared to petrol engines.

When climbing, a 10% loss of power with a petrol engine and slightly less with a diesel engine should be expected for every 1000 metres gain in height. A good reserve of power is, therefore, very necessary for towing up gradients at altitude.

Vehicles with automatic transmission may need additional cooling for the gearbox when towing. The advice of the vehicle manufacturer should be sought.

WHEELS

Caravan wheelnuts should be tightened to the setting stated by the caravan manufacturer (user instructions) and should be checked with the use of a torque wrench regularly. If a spare wheel and tyre is carried it must be suitable for use on that caravan.

Types of tyre fitted

The tyres specified by the caravan manufacturer should be satisfactory for towing in the United Kingdom of speeds of up to 62mph (100kph) at the maximum laden weight of the caravan. In certain countries overseas it is legal to tow at higher speeds. If it is intended to visit such countries and tow up to the higher speed limits then it is important that the suitability of the tyres is first checked with a caravan dealer.

Tyre pressures

Caravan and towing vehicle tyres must be at the pressures recommended for towing or heavy loading. Towing stability may otherwise be affected. The pressures should be given in the towing vehicle and caravan handbooks.

DISTRIBUTION OF WEIGHT IN THE CARAVAN AND CAR

Equipment and effects should be loaded in the caravan so that any heavy items are low down near the floor and mainly over or in front of the axle(s). The remainder should be distributed to give a suitable noseweight at the towing coupling.

Incorrect caravan loading will result in poor towing stability. Overloading of the towing vehicle's rear suspension will also result in poor towing stability.

The weight should be distributed so that each caravan wheel carries approximately the same load.

Noseweight

It is recommended that the noseweight should be varied to find the optimum for towing, dependent upon the actual laden weight of the caravan. Experience has shown that the noseweight should be approximately 7% of the actual laden weight (i.e. between 50 and 90 kg).

Measurement of noseweight

The noseweight may be measured using a proprietary brand of noseweight indicator. Such equipment is obtainable from caravan dealers.

Another simple method is to use bathroom scales under the coupling head with a piece of wood fitted between the coupling head and the scales, of such length that the caravan floor is horizontal with the jockey wheel raised.

STABILISERS

A stabiliser should **never** be used to try to improve a caravan/towing vehicle combination which has poor stability, because instability will reappear at a higher speed.

However, a good stabiliser can make an acceptable caravan/towing vehicle combination more stable and safer to handle.

TOWING VEHICLE'S REAR SUSPENSION

It is important that the towing vehicle's rear suspension is not deflected excessively by the noseweight on the tow ball. If it is, the steering and stability will be affected.

The greater the towing vehicle's tail overhang (the distance between the rear axle and the towing ball) the greater the effect the noseweight will have on the towing vehicle's rear suspension.

After trying out the caravan it may be found that stiffening of the rear suspension is necessary, but note that this may give the towing vehicle a firmer ride when not towing. There are a number of suspension aids available and advice should be sought on which to use and how to fit them.

It is important to ensure that the caravan is towed either level or slightly nose down.

SERVICING

A caravan is a road vehicle and, therefore, requires regular servicing, with particular attention to the braking system, wheels and tyres, and road lighting. These items are fully covered in the standard servicing schedule of the Caravan Service Centre Scheme run by the NCC. There are over 150 RAC inspected workshops in the Scheme, which is operated in conjunction with both the RAC and the Caravan Club.

MIRRORS

The driver of the towing vehicle must have an adequate view to the rear. If there is no rear view through the caravan windows it is essential that additional exterior towing mirrors are fitted to provide a view along both sides of the caravan.

Any rear view mirror must not project more than 200mm beyond:
(a) the width of the caravan when being towed
(b) the width of the towing vehicle when driven solo

Note: Any rear view mirror fitted shall be 'e' marked and cover the field of view as stipulated by type approval requirements.

ROADLIGHTING

Make sure:
(a) All cable connections are of correct length to avoid disconnection or trailing of the cable on the ground.
(b) All road lights and indicators are working correctly before setting off.

Conventional connection of 12N and 12S seven-pin sockets

Power for the caravan's roadlights and electrical equipment is transferred from the towcar by means of a pair of seven-pin plugs (on the caravan) and sockets (on the car). Though these look similar at first glance they are not interchangeable because they have different arrangements of pins and contact tubes.

The roadlight plug/socket is known as type 12N (normal) and is usually coloured black. The second plug/socket is known as 12S (supplementary) and is conventionally coloured grey.

An arrangement whereby the car's rear foglights are extinguished when the caravan roadlights are connected (to prevent glare from light reflected off the caravan's front wall) is permissible. All other lights on the rear of the car must work when the caravan is being towed.

Connections for the caravan battery charging and refrigerator circuits should be controlled by relays. These will ensure that the caravan battery is never recharged at the expense of the car battery; and that power is transmitted to the fridge only when the car engine is running, to avoid the risk of flattening the car battery.

BRAKES

For caravans exceeding a maximum weight of 1500kg the braking device must be such that the caravan is stopped automatically if the coupling breaks.

For caravans below 1500kg a breakaway cable is required. If there is no automatic stopping device always ensure that the breakaway cable, when fitted, is secured to the towing vehicle.

VEHICLE CARAVAN CONNECTION

Always ensure that the towing hitch is correctly locked to the ball prior to setting off.

SPEED LIMITS
See pxxvi

MOTORWAY DRIVING
See pxxvi

Reduce speed:
(a) In high or cross winds
(b) Downhill
(c) In poor visibility

HIGHWAY CARE

High sided vehicles
Extra care should be taken when passing or being passed by high sided vehicles. As much space as possible should be given between vehicles to avoid air buffeting.

Courtesy and safety
Be considerate to other road users and remember, with the caravan behind, everything takes a little longer than solo motoring. Overtaking and stopping distances increase when you are towing, so always indicate in plenty of time.

Useful Addresses

The Camping and Caravanning Club
Greenfields House,
Westwood Way,
Coventry,
West Midlands CV4 8JH
(0203) 694995

The Caravan Club
East Grinstead House,
East Grinstead,
West Sussex.
RH19 1UA
(0342) 326944

The Motor Caravanners' Club
22 Evelyn Close
Twickenham,
Middlesex TW2 7BN
081-893 3883

Master Dealers' Association
44-45 Leigh House,
Devizes Road,
Swindon,
Wiltshire
(listings of members available)

British Holiday & Home Parks Association
Chichester House,
31 Park Road,
Gloucester GL1 1LH
(0452) 26911/413041

National Caravan Council Limited
Catherine House,
Victoria Road,
Aldershot,
Hampshire GU11 1SS
(0252) 318251
(comprehensive listing of members available includes manufacturers, dealers, parks and traders)

Society of Motor Manufacturers & Traders Ltd, Motor Caravan Section
Forbes House,
Halkin Street,
London SW1X 7DS.
071-235 7000
(listing of members available)

Motor Caravan Information Service Advisory
36 Grosvenor Gardens,London SW1

UK Towing Bracket Suppliers

Towing brackets should be made to British Standard BSAU 114b or the equivalent international standard ISO 3853.

Anchor Towbars Ltd.
Orchard House,
Appleby Hill,
Austrey,
Atherstone,
Warwickshire CV9 3ER
(0827) 830039

Bumper to Bumper Ltd.
38 Melford Court,
Hardwick Grange,
Woolston,
Warrington,
Cheshire WA1 4SD
(0925) 815661

B. Dixon-Bate Ltd.
Unit 45,
First Avenue,
Deeside Industrial Park,
Deeside,
Clwyd CH5 2LG
(0244) 288925

Exhaust Ejector Co.
Wade House Road,
Shelf,
Halifax,
West Yorks HX3 7PE
(0274) 679524/5/6

PCT Leisure Ltd.
Holbrook Industrial Estate,
Halfway,
Sheffield S19 5GH
(0742) 510210

Peter J. Lea Co. Ltd.
Shaw Road South,
Shaw Heath,
Stockport,
Cheshire SK3 8JG
061-480 2377

Speedograph Ltd.
Rolleston Drive,
Arnold,
Nottingham NG5 7JR
(0602) 264235

Tanfield Ltd.
Guildford Road,
Horsham,
West Sussex RH12 1LT
(0403) 61393

Towsure Products Ltd.
151-183 Holme Lane,
Sheffield S6 4JR
(0742) 340542

Watling Engineers Ltd.
88 Parkstreet Village,
St. Albans,
Hertfordshire AL2 2LR
(0727) 873661

Witter Towbars Ltd.
18 Canal Side,
Chester CH1 3LL
(0244) 341166

British Tourist Authority

The British Tourist Authority was set up to encourage people to visit Great Britain, and people living in Great Britain to take their holidays there. It also encourages the provison and improvement of tourist activities and facilities in Great Britain. Likewise, the English, Scottish and Wales Tourist Boards have similar functions in respect of England, Scotland and Wales except that they have no mandate to promote tourism outside the actual areas they cover, leaving all overseas publicity to the British Tourist Authority.

Tourist Boards have set up Regional Tourist Boards to cover more compact areas of their respective countries, and Tourist Information Centres are located in cities and towns throughout Great Britain for the supply of information on places of interest to tourists. These Information Centres are indicated by distinctive 'i' signs placed in their vicinity.

The addresses of the National and Regional Tourist Boards are as follows:

ENGLISH TOURIST BOARD

Head Office: Thames Tower, Black's Road, Hammersmith, London W6 9EL.
(written enquiries only)

West Country Tourist Board
60 St David's Hill, Exeter, Devon, EX4 4SY
(0392) 76351

**Southern Tourist Board
(including the Isle of Wight)**
40 Chamberlayne Road, Eastleigh, Hampshire SO5 5JH.
(0703) 620006

Isle of Man Dept. of Tourism
Sea Terminal Building, Douglas.
(0624) 74323

South-East England Tourist Board
The Old Brew House, Warwick Park, Tunbridge Wells, Kent TN2 5TU.
(0892) 540766

London Tourist Board
26 Grosvenor Gardens, London SW1W 0DU.
071-730 3488

East Anglia Tourist Board
Toppesfield Hall, Hadleigh, Suffolk IP7 5DN.
(0473) 822922

Thames and Chilterns Tourist Board
The Mount House, Church Green, Witney,
Oxon OX8 6DZ.
(0993) 778800

Heart of England Tourist Board
Woodside, Larkhill, Worcester.
(0905) 763436

East Midlands Tourist Board
Exchequergate, Lincoln LN2 1PZ.
(0522) 531521
(written and telephone enquiries only)

North-West Tourist Board
Swan House, Swan Meadow Road,
Wigan Pier, Wigan, Lancs WN3 5BB
(0942) 821222
(written and telephone enquiries only)

Cumbria Tourist Board
Ashleigh, Holly Road, Windermere,
Cumbria LA23 2AQ.
(096 62) 4444
(written enquiries only)

Yorkshire and Humberside Tourist Board
12 Tadcaster Road, York YO2 2HF.
(0904) 707961

Northumbria Tourist Board
Aykley Heads, Durham DH1 5UX.
091-384 6905

SCOTTISH TOURIST BOARD

Head Office: 23 Ravelston Terrace,Edinburgh
EH4 3EU.
031-332 2433
(written and telephone enquiries only)

Aviemore and Spey Valley Tourist Board
Grampian Road, Aviemore PH22 1PP.
(0479) 810363

Ayrshire Tourist Board
Suite 1005, Prestwick Airport,
Prestwick KA9 2PL.
(0292) 79000

Caithness Tourist Board
Tourist Office, Whitechapel Road, Wick,
Caithness, KW1 4EA.
(0955) 2596

Clyde Valley Tourist Board
Horsemarket, Ladyacre Rd, Lanark ML11 7LQ.
(0555) 61661

Dumfries and Galloway Tourist Board
Campbell House, Bankend Road, Dumfries,
DG1 4TH.
(0837) 50434

Dunoon and Cowal Tourist Board
Tourist Information Centre, 7 Alexandra
Parade, Dunoon, Argyll PA23 8AB.
(0369) 3755

East Lothian Tourist Board
Brunton Hall, Musselburgh, EH21 6AE.
031-665 3711

Fort William and Lochaber Tourist Board
Fort William Cameron Centre, Cameron
Square, Fort William.
(0397) 703781

Forth Valley Tourist Board
Annet House, High Street, Linlithgow, West
Lothian, EH49 7EJ.
(0506) 844600

**Inverness, Loch Ness and
Nairn Tourist Board**
23 Church Street, Inverness IV1 1EZ.
(0463) 234353

**Loch Lomond, Stirling and
Trossachs Tourist Board**
41 Dumbarton Road, Stirling, FK8 2LQ.
(0786) 75019

Mid Argyll, Kintyre and Islay Tourist Board
Area Tourist Office, The Pier, Campbeltown,
Argyll PA28 6EF.
(0586) 52056

Perthshire Tourist Board
45 High Street, Perth, PH1 5TJ.
(0738) 27958

Ross and Cromarty Tourist Board
Information Centre, North Kessock,
Inverness, IV1 1XB.
(046 373) 505

St. Andrews and N.E. Fife Tourist Board
2 Queens Gardens, St. Andrews,
Fife KY16 9TE.
(0334) 72021

Scottish Borders Tourist Board
Haliwell's House, Selkirk.
(0750) 20054

Shetland Tourist Board
Market Cross, Lerwick, Shetland ZE1 0LU.
(0595) 3434

**The Isle of Skye and South West Ross
Tourist Board**
Tourist Information Centre, Meall House,
Portree, Isle of Skye IV51 9BZ.
(0478) 2137

Sutherland Tourist Board
Area Tourist Office, The Square, Dornoch
IV25 3SD.
(0862) 810400

Western Isles Tourist Board
4 South Beach Street, Stornoway,
Isle of Lewis PA87 2XY.
(0851) 3088

WALES TOURIST BOARD

Head Office: Brunel House, 2 Fitzalan Road,
Cardiff CF2 1UY.
(0222) 49909

North Wales Tourism Council
Civic Centre, Colwyn Bay, Clwyd.
(0492) 531731

Mid-Wales Tourism Council
Owain Glyndwr Centre, Machynlleth, Powys
SY20 8EE.
(0654) 702653

South Wales Tourism Council
Pembroke House, Charter Court, Phoenix
Way, Enterprise Park, Swansea, SA7 9DB.
(0792) 781212

NORTHERN IRELAND TOURIST BOARD

Head Office: St. Anne's Court, North Street,
Belfast BT1 1ND.
(0232) 731221

London Office: 11 Berkeley Street, W1X 5AD.
071-493 0601

IRISH TOURIST BOARD (BORD FAILTE)

Head Office: Bago St. Bridge, Dublin 2.
(010 3531) 765871

London Office: 150 New Bond Street,
W1Y 0AQ.
071-493 3201

CHANNEL ISLANDS

States of Guernsey Tourist Committee
PO Box 23, White Rock, Guernsey.
(0481) 26611

States of Jersey Tourism Committee
Weighbridge, St Helier, Jersey.
(0534) 78000

National Parks

Countryside Commission,
John Dower House, Crescent Place,
Cheltenham, Gloucestershire
GL50 3RA.
(0242) 521381

Under *The National Parks Access to the
Country Act 1949,* the following areas
have been designated National Parks,
and Areas of Outstanding Natural
Beauty:

National Parks

Brecon Beacon
Dartmoor
Exmoor
Lake District
Northumberland
North York Moors
Peak District
Pembrokeshire
Snowdonia
Yorkshire Dales
The Broads Authority

Areas of Outstanding Natural Beauty

Anglesey
Arnside and Siverdale
Blackdown Hills
Cannock Chase
Chichester Harbour
Chilterns
Clwydian Range
Cornwall
Cotswolds
Cranborne Chase & West Wiltshire
Downs
Dedham Vale
Dorset
East Devon
East Hampshire
Forest of Bowland
Gower Peninsula
High Weald
Howardian Hills
Isles of Scilly
Isle of Wight
Kent Downs
Lincolnshire Wolds
Lleyn

Malvern Hills
Mendip Hills
Norfolk Coast
North Devon
North Pennines
Northumberland Coast
North Wessex Downs
Quantock Hills
Shropshire Hills
South Devon
South Hampshire Coast
Suffolk Coast and Heaths
Surrey Hills
Sussex Downs
Solway Coast
Wye Valley

The purpose of the Act is primarily to ensure the preservation and enhancement of the natural beauty of the areas concerned. It does not confer any right of access to an area designated an Area of Outstanding Natural Beauty. From 1 April 1989 a similar status was conferred on the Norfolk and Suffolk Broads.

Scotland does not have National Parks as such. Instead, many of the most outstanding areas of Scotland have been identified as National Scenic Areas where development is closely watched. They include much of the Western Isles, Wester Ross, Ben Nevis and Glen Coe, the Cairngorms, Loch Tummel, Loch Rannoch, Loch Lomond and the Trossachs.

National Forest Parks

The Forestry Commission,
231 Corstorphine Road, Edinburgh
EH12 7AT.
031-334 0303

The Forestry Commission control these Parks which are areas of Forestry Commission land not immediately required for forestry purposes and which have been made available to the general public. The National Forest Parks (which are not connected with the National Parks) are set amidst some of the finest holiday country in Great Britain.

Caravan and campsites have been established in some of the National Forest Parks. They vary from fully equipped campsites with the all the facilities one would expect - hot showers, toilets, often washing machines and shops - through semi-equipped sites with basic facilities - some just with toilets and a water supply - to informal campsites, where campers must have their own chemical toilet, as the only facility may be a standpipe nearby.

All Forestry Commission campsites are in attractive surroundings offering peace and quiet. They make particularly good sites for those campers who are interested in wildlife and the natural world.

Sites are listed in this guide under the heading shown in brackets.

Forest of Dean and Wye Valley, Gloucestershire. (Forest of Dean).
New Forest, Hampshire. (New Forest).
East Anglian Forest, Norfolk. (Thetford).
East Anglian Forest, Suffolk. (Woodbridge).
Border Forest Park, Northumberland. (Kielder).
North York Moors, N. Yorkshire. (Pickering).
Snowdonia National Forest Park, Gwynedd. (Beddgelert).
Queen Elizabeth Forest Park, Central. (Aberfoyle and Drymen).
Glen Trool Forest Park, Dumfries & Galloway. (Newton Stewart).
Glencoe Forest, Highland. (Glencoe).
Glenmore Forest Park, Highland. (Aviemore).
South Strome Forest, Highland. (Balmacara).
Argyll Forest Park, Strathclyde. (Arrochar).
Rannoch Forest, Tayside. (Kinloch Rannoch).

Sites near Motorways and Ports

To help you plan your journeys, these lists show which places have campsites within about 5 miles of the motorway or port.

Motorways		Sites at
M2	Junction 3	**Rochester**
	Junction 7	**Faversham**
M20	Junction 2	**Brands Hatch**
	Junction 8	**Maidstone**
	Junction 9	**Ashford**
	Junction 13	**Folkestone**
M1	Junction 14	**Newport Pagnell**
	Junction 20	**North Kilworth**
	Junction 34	**Rotherham**
	Junction 36	**Worsborough**
	Junction 39	**Wakefield**
M4	Junction 5	**Slough**
	Junction 6	**Windsor**
	Junction 10	**Wokingham**
	Junction 18	**Badminton**
	Junction 21	**Aust Severn Beach**
	Junction 22	**Chepstow**
	Junction 28	**Newport**
	Junction 36	**Bridgend (no caravans)**
	Junction 37	**Porthcawl**
M5	Junction 3	**Halesowen**
	Junction 7	**Worcester**
	Junction 9	**Tewkesbury**
	Junction 11	**Cheltenham Gloucester**
	Junction 12	**Gloucester**
	Junction 14	**Berkeley Wotton-under-Edge**
	Junction 17	**Severn Beach**
	Junction 20	**Clevedon**
	Junction 21	**Weston-super-Mare**
	Junction 22	**Burnham-on-Sea**
	Junction 24	**Bridgwater**
	Junction 25	**Taunton**
	Junction 26	**Wellington**

M5	Junction 27	**Uffculme**
	Junction 28	**Cullompton**
	Junction 30	**Exeter**
M6	Junction 2	**Nuneaton**
	Junction 17	**Congleton Sandbach**
	Charnock Richard Service Area	**Chorley**
	Junction 33	**Garstang**
	Junction 34	**Lancaster**
	Junction 35	**Carnforth**
	Junction 36	**Kirkby Lonsdale Milnthorpe**
	Junction 37	**Sedburgh**
	Junction 38	**Tebay**
	Junction 40	**Penrith**
	Junction 44	**Carlisle**

From London north to Edinburgh
A1(M)/A1

St Neots
Newark
Tuxford
Worksop
Wetherby
Boroughbridge
Bedale
Scotch Corner
Morpeth
Alnwick
Belford
Berwick-on-Tweed
Cockburnspath
Dunbar
Haddington
Musselburgh

From Glasgow south to Carlisle
M74/A74

	Junction 2	**Motherwell**
	Junction 12	**Douglas Moffat Beattock Lockerbie Ecclefechan Kirkpatrick Fleming**

Ports	Sites At		
Dover	**Dover**	Harwich	**Harwich**
	Barham		
	Folkestone	Holyhead	**Holyhead**
Ramsgate	**Manston**		
	Sandwich	Hull	**Barton-on-Humber**
Portsmouth	**Portsmouth**	Newcastle-upon-Tyne	**Newcastle-upon-Tyne**
Plymouth	**Plymouth**		
		Stranraer	**Stranraer**
Fishguard	**Fishguard**		**Portpatrick**
	Newport		**Sandhead**
Swansea	**Swansea**		

The National Trust

The National Trust is an independent charity and is responsible for the preservation of many historic houses, industrial monuments, formal and romantic gardens, nature reserves, open countryside and hundreds of miles of Britain's coastline. Details of these NT sites and NT activities can be obtained from:

36 Queen Anne's Gate, London
SW1H 9AS.
071-222 9251

North Wales Office, Trinity Square,
Llandudno, Gwynedd LL30 2DE.
(0492) 860123

South Wales Office, The King's Head,
Bridge Street, Llandeilo SA19 6BB.
(0558) 822800

Northern Ireland, Rowallane House,
Saintfield, Ballynahinch, Co. Down,
BT24 6LH.
(0238) 510721

The National Trust for Scotland
5 Charlotte Square, Edinburgh
EH2 4DU.
031-226 5922

English Heritage

Over 350 ancient monuments, buildings and sites are looked after by English Heritage (formerly the Historic Buildings & Monuments Commission). Further details can be obtained from:

English Heritage,
Fortress House,
23 Saville Row,
London W1X 1AB.
071-973 3000

The Country Code

Enjoy the countryside and respect its life and work;
Guard against all risk of fire;
Fasten all gates;
Keep your dogs under close control;
Keep to public paths across farmland;
Use gates and stiles to cross fences, hedges and walls;
Leave livestock, crops and machinery alone;
Take your litter home;
Help to keep all water clean;

Protect wildlife, plants and trees;
Take special care on country roads;
Make no unnecessary noise.

You are asked to respect these maxims of the 'Country Code' published by
The Countryside Commission
John Dower House
Crescent Place
Cheltenham
Gloucestershire
GL50 3RA

General Advice

Roadside camping

Camping or siting a caravan on verges or lay-bys is not allowed. However, permission to camp on land nearby can often be obtained from the farmer or landowner.

If an outbreak of foot and mouth or swine vesicular disease occurs, campers must be very careful to follow all necessary precautions.

London

If you are visiting London with a caravan on tow, try to avoid travelling across the centre of London, particularly during the rush hours Monday to Friday 0800-1000 and 1600-1800 hours, and if you are unfamiliar with the route.

Parking of car/caravan outfits at meter bays is not permitted. It is best to leave a caravan at the site and visit central London solo, or by public transport. If it is essential to park an outfit in London, find a suitable car park. Underground and multi-storey car parks often have a height limit which will not permit access for caravans or motor caravans.

As well as the sites listed under London, the following RAC recognised sites are within reasonable distance:
Brands Hatch, Thriftwood Camping site.
Hoddesden, Dobb's Weir Caravan Park.
Windsor, The Willows Riverside Park.

Motorway Service Areas

Caravans are permitted to park at Motorway service areas for the purpose of utilizing the facilities. Parking for the purpose of cooking meals, etc., is not usually permitted and at some service areas it is forbidden to lower the corner legs of a caravan for any reason. Charges for overnight stops are available on application to the individual service areas.

Travel Information

For information on current UK traffic conditions and roadworks call the RAC 'Motorist's hotline' (0898) 500242. Calls charged at 48p per minute 8am-6pm Monday to Friday, and 36p per minute at all other times.

To contact the RAC Camping and Caravanning Department please telephone 081-686 0088, or write to RAC Enterprises
P.O. Box 100
Bartlett Street
South Croydon
CR2 6XW

ENGLAND

HARWOOD BAR CARAVAN PARK   RAC L
Mill Lane, Harwood Bar, Great Harwood, BB6 7UQ.
☎ (0254) 884853
Open: 1 February-31 December
Size: 1 (9) acres, 25 touring pitches, all level,
25 with elec, 4 with hardstanding, 104 static
caravans. 4 hot showers, 8 WCs, 1 CWP

Car & caravan £6, plus 50p per person above 2,
child 50p; elec £1, awn 50p
*Quiet picturesque park in elevated position
overlooking Pendle Hills and beautiful countryside.
3 caravans for hire. Shop and restaurant ½ mile.
Swimming pool 1 mile. 3 nights minimum stay in
letting holiday homes.*
*On A680 2½ miles N of Accrington, 2½ miles S of
Whalley, signposted to east side of A680.*

CLIPPESBY HOLIDAYS   RAC A
Clippesby, NR29 3BJ. ☎ (0493) 369367
Open: Easter-End October
Size: 10 (34) acres, 80 touring pitches, 30 with elec,
50 level pitches, 25 cottages. 8 hot showers,
21 WCs, 3 CWPs

(1991) Car & caravan, Motor caravan, Car & tent,
M/cycle & tent £5-£9, plus 90p per person above 2;
elec £1.50, awn £1.20, dogs 65p
cc Access, Visa/B'card
*Quiet, family-run country park in centre of Norfolk
Broads. Tennis courts, licensed clubhouse and
children's play area. Permit required for dogs.
From A47 Acle by-pass turn left at roundabout on
to A1064 for just over 2 miles. Fork left on the
B1152 for ¾ mile, turn left to site on right in
¼ mile.*

REEDHAM FERRY CAMPING &
CARAVAN PARK   RAC L
Ferry Road, Reedham, NR13 3HA.
☎ (0493) 700429
Open: Easter-end September
Size: 4 acres, 20 level pitches. 4 hot showers. 4 cold
showers, WCs

Charges on application.
cc Access, Visa/B'card
*Well-kept site, with children's play area, next to the
River Yare and the Ferry Inn. Boating, fishing and
birdwatching. No gas available. Shop 1 mile.
7 miles S of Acle on B1140, on the N bank of the
River Yare.*

Woodthorpe Hall Caravan Park
Woodthorpe Hall. ☎ (0507) 450294
Open: March-January
Size: 5 acres, 70 touring pitches. 6 hot showers,
15 WCs. 150 static caravans

*Situated on the B1373 between Withern and
Alford. From Louth take the A157 E to Withern or
the A1104 from Alford.*

Camping & Caravanning Club Site
Dunstan Hill, Craster, NE66 3TQ.
☎ (066576) 310
Open: 30 March-26 October
Size: 8 acres, 160 touring pitches. 12 hot showers,
18 WCs

Charges on application.
cc Access, Visa/B'card
*This grassy site is 1½ miles from a sandy beach,
accessible by footpath.
Take the B1339 to Embleton, follow the signs for
Craster. The site is ¾ mile on the left.*

Star Caravan & Camping Park
Cotton. ☎ (0538) 702219
Open: February-December
Size: 25 acres, 120 touring pitches. 4 hot showers,
12 WCs

*From Stoke, travel E on A52 following signs to
Alton Towers. Site on left by Star Inn, Cotton.*

Clennell Hall
NE65 7BG. ☎ (0669) 50341
Open: All year
Size: 13½ acres, 50 touring pitches. 6 hot showers,
7 WCs. 18 static caravans

*On B6341 W of Rothbury, follow signs to Alwinton.
Near village, turn right over cattle grid after bridge
and follow road by river to site.*

Low Wray Camp Site
Low Wray, LA22 0JA. ☎ (053 94) 32810

▣ Snacks/take away   ☒ Restaurant   ◺ Swimming pool   ▣ Shelter for campers   ⊞ Dogs accepted   1

Open: April-October
Size: 5 acres, 200 touring pitches. 12 hot showers, 36 WCs. 5 static caravans

From Ambleside, take B5286 to Hawkshead. Signposted off that after 2 miles.

National Trust Camp Site
Great Langdale. ☎ (096 67) 668
Open: All year
Size: 9½ acres, 300 tent sites. 12 hot showers, 26 WCs

8 miles W of Ambleside on B5343.

SKELWITH FOLD CARAVAN PARK   RAC A
LA22 0HX. ☎ (05394) 32277
Open: 1 March-15 November
Size: 12 (125) acres, 150 touring pitches, all level, 130 with elec, all with hardstanding, 300 static caravans. 28 hot showers, 60 WCs, 4 CWPs

Car & caravan £6.65, Motor caravan £6.15; elec £1.30, awn £2.50; WS
Family-run park set in former country estate with an abundance of flora and fauna. Ideal centre for exploring the Lakes. Restaurant 1 mile. Swimming pool 5 miles. No motorcycles.
From Ambleside, travel SW on A593 for almost 1 mile, turn S on to the B5286 for ¾ mile to site entrance on right.

ANDOVER *Hampshire*   Map 2 B3

Wyke Down Caravan & Camping Park
Picket Piece, SP11 6LX. ☎ (0264) 52048

Open: All year
Size: 7 acres, 150 touring pitches. 4 hot showers, 15 WCs.

All signposted from A3093 from Walworth roundabout.

APPLEBY *Cumbria*   Map 4 B1

Low Moor Campsite
Kirkby Thore. ☎ (07683) 61231
Open: April-October
Size: 1½ acres, 12 touring pitches. 2 hot showers, 7 WCs. 25 static caravans

Signposted off A66, between Appleby and Penrith.

Three Greyhounds Inn
Great Asby, CA16 6EX. ☎ (07683) 51428
Open: March-October
Size: 2 acres, 12 touring pitches. 2 hot showers, 3 WCs. 6 static caravans

A66 to Appleby or M6 Junction 38. Signposted off A66 on B6260.

WILD ROSE CARAVAN PARK   RAC A
Ormside, CA16 6EJ. ☎ (07683) 51077
Open: All year
Size: 10 (40) acres, 177 touring pitches, all with elec, 90 level pitches, 90 with hardstanding, 240 static caravans. 20 hot showers, 45 WCs, 3 CWPs

(1991) Car & caravan, Motor caravan, Car & tent

🖢 Facilities for Disabled   🖾 Caravans accepted   🖻 Motor caravans   🅰 Tents   🖾 Laundry room   🖢 Shop

£6.10-£9.20, plus £1.10 per adult above 2; elec £1.40 (£2.00 in winter), awn £1.50; WS
Friendly, welcoming, peaceful family park in unspoilt Eden Valley twixt Lakes and Dales. Spotless facilities including teenage room, toddlers' room, safety-surfaced play park. Free equipment, super flowers. No unaccompanied young people; no dangerous breeds of dog.
From Appleby travel S on the B6260 and at 1½ miles on turn left as signed 'Ormside' and at 1½ miles further again turn left for 500 yards, then turn right to site.

ARNSIDE *Cumbria*   Map 4 B1

Bottoms Farm
Silverdale, LA5 0TU. ☎ (0524) 701243
Open: March-October
Size: 4 acres, 6 touring pitches. 2 hot showers, 3 WCs.

| | 🚐 | 🚙 | ⛺ | | | | | | | 🐕 |

Off A6, 4 miles NW of Carnforth. 2 miles S of Arnside.

Gibraltar Farm
Silverdale, LA5 0TH. ☎ (0524) 701736
Open: March-November
Size: 6 acres, 40 touring pitches. 2 hot showers, 5 WCs

| | 🚐 | 🚙 | ⛺ | | | | | | | 🐕 |

Minor road N of Carnforth, signposted Silverdale. Follow signs to Hospital and Gibraltar to t-junction. Site opposite.

Hollins Arnside Farm
Far Arnside, Silverdale. ☎ (0524) 701767
Open: April-October
Size: 4 acres, touring pitches. 6 WCs

| | 🚐 | 🚙 | ⛺ | | | | | | | 🐕 |

M6 (Junction 35) into Carnforth. Follow signs to Silverdale into Cove Road and farm is on the left.

ARUNDEL *West Sussex*   Map 3 A3

Camping & Caravanning Club Site
Slindon Park, Slindon, BN18 0RG.
☎ (024 365) 387
Open: 30 March-28 September
Size: 2 acres, 46 touring pitches

| | 🚐 | ⛺ | 🏪 | | | | | 🐕 |

Charges on application.
Site in National Trust parkland estate. Minimum facilities - campers must have their own chemical toilets. Shop 1 mile.
From the A27 turn towards Eartham, then towards Slindon and the site is on the right.

Fontwell Racecourse Caravan Club Site
Fontwell, BN18 0SX. ☎ (0243) 543335
Open: May-September
Size: 70 touring pitches. 5 hot shower, 12 WCs

| ♿ | 🚐 | 🚙 | ⛺ | | | | | | | 🐕 |

W from Arundel on A27, site just past junction with A29.

MAYNARD'S CAMPING & CARAVAN PARK   RAC L
Crossbush, BN18 9PQ. ☎ (0903) 882075

Open: 1 March-31 October
Size: 3 acres, 70 touring pitches, all level, 36 with elec. 4 hot showers, 8 WCs, 1 CWP

| ♿ | 🚐 | 🚙 | ⛺ | 🛏 | | ✖ | | | | 🐕 |

(1991) Car & caravan, Motor caravan, Car & tent £6.00; plus £1 per adult above 2, child 50p; extra car £1; elec £1.40; WS
Small, quiet site in village. Hotel and restaurant adjacent. Shop and swimming pool ½ mile.
Site 200 yards S of the junction A27/A284, ½ mile SE of Arundel. Turn into 'Howards Hotel' car park.

ASHBOURNE *Derbyshire*   Map 5 A3

Bank Top Farm
Fenny Bentley. ☎ (0335) 29250
Open: Easter-September
Size: 3 acres, 50 touring pitches. 4 hot showers, 9 WCs.

| | 🚐 | 🚙 | ⛺ | 🛏 | 🏪 | | | | | 🐕 |

2 miles N of Ashbourne on A515, bear right on to B5056. Site in 100 yards.

CLOSES CARAVAN PARK   RAC L
Kniveton, DE6 1JL. ☎ (0335) 43191
Open: Easter-31 October
Size: 2½ acres, 35 touring pitches, all level, all with hard standing, 18 with elec. 4 hot showers, 6 WCs, 1 CWP

| | 🚐 | 🚙 | ⛺ | | | | | | | 🐕 |

(1991) Car & caravan, Motor caravan £4, Car & tent, M/cycle & tent from £3.50, all plus £1 per adult above 2, child 50p; extra car 50p; elec £1, awn £1
A rural site, central for many attractions in Derbyshire, Peak District National Park, Alton Towers. Quiet, secluded, suitable for walkers and lovers of countryside and total relaxation. Shop 500 yards. Restaurant and swimming pool 2½ miles. No large groups. Bank Holidays only - minimum stay 3 days.
From Ashbourne travel NE on the B5035 for 3 miles to Kniveton, turn left to site in ¼ mile.

Gateway Caravan Park
Osmaston. ☎ (0335) 44643/43274
Open: March-October
Size: 15 acres, 150 touring pitches. 20 hot showers, 20 WCs.

| ♿ | 🚐 | 🚙 | ⛺ | 🛏 | 🏪 | | | | 🏕 | 🐕 |

SE from Ashbourne on A52, first turning to Osmaston. Site in 100 yards.

Highfield Caravan Park
Fenny Bentley. ☎ (0335) 29228
Open: March-October
Size: 16 (55) acres, 55+ touring pitches. 10 hot showers, 20 WCs. 1 static caravan

| | 🚐 | 🚙 | ⛺ | 🛏 | 🏪 | | | | 🏕 | 🐕 |

Off A515, 3 miles N of Ashbourne. ½ mile N of village.

SANDYBROOK HALL HOLIDAY CENTRE   RAC A
Buxton Road, DE6 2AQ. ☎ (0335) 42679
Open: April-November
Size: 8 hectares, 70 touring pitches, 28 with elec, 15 level pitches, 5 with hardstanding, 20 static caravans. 9 hot showers, 13 WCs, 1 CWP

⬜ 🏠 🚐 ⛺ 🛏 🛍 ☕ ✕ 🛌 | 🐕

(1991) Car & caravan, Motor caravan, Car & tent, M/cycle & tent £5.50-£6.50, plus 75p per person above 4; elec £1.50, awn 75p

Friendly, family site in picturesque setting close to Derbyshire Dales and Alton Towers. Licensed bar and club rooms.

1 mile N of Ashbourne on A515. Opposite Dovedale turn-off.

ASHBURTON *Devon* — Map 1 B3

ASHBURTON CARAVAN PARK — RAC L
Waterleat, TQ13 7HU. ☎ (0364) 52552
Open: Easter-31 October
Size: 2 (4) acres, 35 touring pitches, all level, 4 with elec, 40 static caravans. 6 hot showers, 7 WCs, 1 CWP

♿ | 🚐 ⛺ 🛏 🛍 | | | | | 🐕

From £2.75 per adult per night, from £1.75 per child; elec £1.25, dogs 50p

Situated in secluded south-facing wooded river valley within Dartmoor National Park. ETB 4 ticks and Rose Award 1992 Caravans. Best S England Campsite 1989-1990 (AA). Restaurant 1¼ miles. Swimming pool 1½ miles. 6 caravans for hire (minimum 3 nights).

From A38 to centre Ashburton, North Street, bear right before bridge, signed "Waterleat" and camping. 1¼ miles north towards moor.

Churchill Farm
Buckfastleigh, TQ11 0EZ. ☎ (0364) 43800
Open: Easter-October
Size: 3½ acres. 1 hot shower, 1 WC

⬜ | 🏠 🚐 ⛺ | | | | | | 🐕

From A38 (Exeter) take slip road to Buckfastleigh. At top of slip road, turn right, take second right at telephone box towards Buckfast Abbey, follow road then turn left at mini-roundabout at top of hill, turn left into No Through Road until the Parish Church. Site opposite.

Cockingford Farm
Widecombe-in-the-Moor, Buckfastleigh
☎ (036 42) 258
Open: Easter-October
Size: 2½ acres, 30 touring pitches. 4 hot showers, 6 WCs

⬜ | 🏠 🚐 ⛺ | | | | | | 🐕

Take A38 to Ashburton towards Buckland-on-the-Moor.

HIGHER MEAD FARM — RAC A
TQ13 7LJ. ☎ (0364) 52598
Open: 4 April-November
Size: 5 (370) acres, 40 touring pitches, all level, all with elec, 5 with hard standing, 20 static caravans. 5 hot showers, 5 cold showers, 6 WCs, 2 CWPs

♿ | 🏠 🚐 ⛺ 🛏 🛍 | | | 🏪 🐕

Car & caravan, Motor caravan, Car & tent, M/cycle & tent £4-£6, plus £1 per adult above 2, child 80p; elec £1.40, awn £1, dogs 50p

A very pretty site on a real 370-acre farm, on the edge of Dartmoor National Park. New shower block. All facilities free. 20 caravans for hire (own WCs). Restaurant 1 mile. Swimming pool 2 miles.

On the A38 Exeter to Plymouth road, when you see the sign "26 miles to Plymouth" take the second left at Alston Cross, marked "Woodland Denbury". We are ¼ mile from A38.

River Dart Country Park
Holne Park. ☎ (0364) 52511
Open: Easter-September
Size: 12 acres, 120 touring pitches. 12 hot showers, 16 WCs

♿ 🏠 🚐 ⛺ 🛏 🛍 ☕ | | 🛌 🏪 🐕

From A38 Exeter-Plymouth road, follow brown signs from Ashburton exit. 1½ miles on the left.

ASHFORD *Kent* — Map 3 B3

BROAD HEMBURY FARM CARAVAN AND CAMPING PARK — RAC L
Steeds Lane, Kingsnorth, TN26 1NQ.
☎ (0233) 620859
Open: All year
Size: 3 (5) acres, 60 touring pitches, all level, 48 with elec, 25 static caravans. 6 hot showers, 16 WCs, 1 CWP

♿ 🏠 🚐 ⛺ 🛏 🛍 | | | 🏪 🐕

(1991) Car & caravan, Motor caravan, Car & tent, M/cycle & tent £3.50; all plus £1.50 per adult, £1.20 per child; elec £1.50

Quiet country park with every facility. Convenient for Channel Ports and many places of interest in South East. Top quality grading: BTA 5 Ticks. 5 caravans for hire (own WCs) including caravan hire for disabled persons. Restaurant 1 mile. Swimming pool 3 miles.

From Ashford take A2070 South for 3 miles. Turn left at second crossroads in Kingsnorth. Park signposted from here.

Dean Court Farm
Westwell. ☎ (0233) 712924
Open: All year
Size: 2 acres, 30 touring pitches. 2 WCs

[icons: caravan, trailer tent, tent, shelter, dog]

M20/A20, turn off towards Westwell, head South.
Site 1 mile on right.

ASHINGTON Northumberland — Map 7 B3

Wansbeck Riverside Park
☎ (0670) 814444
Open: All year
Size: 5 acres, 44 touring pitches. 7 hot showers,
11 WCs

[icons: disabled, caravan, trailer tent, tent, electric hook-up, laundry, cup, dog]

Off A1068, 1 mile SW of Ashington centre.

ASKAM-IN-FURNESS Cumbria — Map 4 B1

Marsh Farm
☎ (0229) 62321
Open: March-October
Size: 4 acres, 25 touring pitches. 4 hot showers,
6 WCs

[icons: caravan, trailer tent, tent, electric hook-up, dog]

A595 to Askam. Over railway crossing to shore.
Site signed to right.

ASTON CANTLOW Warwickshire — Map 2 B2

ISLAND MEADOW CARAVAN PARK   RAC L
The Mill House, B95 6JP. ☎ (0789) 488273
Open: 1 March-31 October
Size: 3 (7) acres, 24 touring pitches, all level,
19 with elec, 56 static caravans. 4 hot showers,
12 WCs, 1 CWP

[icons: caravan, trailer tent, tent, laundry, dog]

(1991) Car & caravan, Motor caravan £6, Car & tent,
M/cycle & tent from £2.50, plus 50p per person
above 2; elec £1.50
*Quiet, secluded park on sheltered island by
picturesque village. Fishing free to guests.
6 caravans for hire (own WCs). Restaurant ½ mile.
Swimming pool 6 miles. 3 nights minimum stay
over Bank Holiday weekends.*
From A46 or A3400 follow signs to Aston Cantlow
village. Park is ¼ mile west of village in Mill Lane.

AXMINSTER Devon — Map 2 A3

ANDREWSHAYES CARAVAN PARK   RAC A
Dalwood, EX13 7DY. ☎ (040 483) 225
Open: 1 April-31 October
Size: 4 (11) acres, 90 touring pitches, all level,
80 with elec, 30 with hardstanding, 80 static
caravans. 18 hot showers, 21 WCs, 2 CWPs

[icons: disabled, caravan, trailer tent, tent, electric hook-up, laundry, swimming pool, dog]

Charges on application. WS
*Peaceful farm site with lovely views of Axe valley.
Games room and play area. Superb new toilet
block built to continental standards. 30 caravans
for hire (own WCs). Restaurant 200 yards. No
teenage or single-sex groups.*
3 miles W of Axminster on A35, turn N at second
turning to Dalwood, follow site signs.

Hunters Moon Touring Park
Hawkchurch, EX13 5UE. ☎ (029 77) 402
Open: March 15-31 October
Size: 11 acres, 179 touring pitches. 12 hot showers,
23 WCs

[icons: caravan, trailer tent, tent, electric hook-up, laundry, cup, restaurant, shelter, dog]

A35 out of Axminster towards Dorchester for
3 miles, left at major intersection on to B3165
(signposted to Crewkerne), follow this for 2 miles,
take left turn to Hawkchurch and site is on left.

AYLSHAM Norfolk — Map 3 B1

Hevingham Lake Caravan & Camping
Hevingham. ☎ (060 548) 368
Open: Easter-October
Size: 14 acres, 25 caravans & tents. 2 hot showers,
5 WCs. 5 static caravans

[icons: caravan, trailer tent, tent, electric hook-up, laundry, dog]

From Norwich take A140, near Airport branch off to
left on to Holt Road (B1149) for 5 to 6 miles, take
second turning to Hevingham. Follow signposts.

Landguard House
Erpingham, NR11 7QB. ☎ (0263) 761219
Open: March-October
Size: 1½ acres, 25 touring pitches. 4 hot showers, 6
WCs

[icons: caravan, trailer tent, tent, dog]

From Aylsham take the A140 north towards
Cromer. Signposted off A140.

AYSGARTH North Yorkshire — Map 5 A1

WESTHOLME CARAVAN & CAMPING SITE   RAC A
Near Leyburn, DL8 3SP. ☎ (0969) 663268
Open: 1 March-31 October
Size: 4 (22) acres, 46 touring pitches, mostly level,
40 with elec, 3 with hardstanding, 44 static
caravans. 6 hot showers, 12 WCs, 2 CWPs

[icons: caravan, trailer tent, tent, electric hook-up, laundry, cup, restaurant, shelter, dog]

(1991) Pitch per night £5.50-£7.25, M/cycles £3.50,
plus £1 per adult above 2, child 50p; elec £1.50,
awn £1
*Quiet park on terraces alongside trout stream in
the heart of Wensleydale in walking country.
Swimming pool 18 miles.*
Turn off A684 1 mile E of Aysgarth.

BACTON Norfolk — Map 3 B1

CABLE GAP CARAVAN PARK   RAC A
Coast Road, NR12 0EW. ☎ (0692) 650667
Open: 21 March-31 October
Size: 2 (6) acres, 27 touring pitches, all level, all
with elec, 47 static caravans. 6 hot showers, 9 WCs,
1 CWP

[icons: caravan, trailer tent, electric hook-up, dog]

Car & caravan, Motor caravan £6.50-£7.50, plus 75p
per person; elec £1.25
*Quiet, family-run, award-winning park with direct
access to sandy beach. Hook-up to satellite TV
available on all pitches. 13 caravans for hire (own
WCs). Calor gas only. Shop and restaurant
30 yards from entrance. Swimming pool 10 miles.
No motorcycles. Maximum stay 28 days on touring
field.*

[icon] Snacks/take away   [X] Restaurant   [icon] Swimming pool   [icon] Shelter for campers   [icon] Dogs accepted   5

Situated at the end of B1150 from Norwich and between Great Yarmouth and Cromer on B1159 coast road. Follow tourism signs from Bacton village.

BADMINTON Avon Map 2 A2

Petty France Farm
☎ (045 423) 665
Open: April-September
Size: 2 acres, 20 touring pitches. 2 hot showers, 2 WCs

From M4 junction 18, A46 N for 5 miles. Site on left.

BAKEWELL Derbyshire Map 5 A2

GREENHILLS CARAVAN AND CAMPING PARK RAC A
Crow Hill Lane, Near Ashford-in-the-Water, DE4 1PX.
☎ (0629) 813467/813052
Open: All year
Size: 4 (8) acres, 100 touring pitches, 35 with elec, 50 level pitches, 65 static caravans. 6 hot showers, 15 WCs, 1 CWP

Car & caravan £7.50, Motor caravan £6.50, Car & tent £6.50; all plus £1.10 per adult, 70p per child; elec £1.75, awn £1.75, dogs 60p
A family-run site in the heart of the Peak District National Park. There's a clubhouse with licensed bar on site. Restricted facilities November-March. Shop on site in season, otherwise ½ mile away. Restaurant ½ mile. Swimming pool 8 miles. Five nights minimum stay over Bank Holidays (except May Day). No motorcycles.
1 mile NW of Bakewell on A6, turn S as signed 'Over Haddon and Monyash' to site on right.

BAMBURGH Northumberland Map 7 B2

GLORORUM CARAVAN PARK RAC A
Glororum, NE69 7AW. ☎ (06684) 457
Open: 1 April-31 October
Size: 6 (20) acres, 100 touring pitches, all level, 68 with elec, 150 static caravans. 16 hot showers, 35 WCs, 4 CWPs

Car & caravan, Motor caravan, Car & tent, M/cycle & tent £5-£7, incl. up to 2 adults & 2 children; extra adult £1, extra child 50p; elec £1, awn £1
Cheques with cheque cards only
A well-kept site in lovely country close to Bamburgh Castle and the sea. Children's play area. Families and couples only. Restaurant 1¼ miles. Swimming pool 14 miles.
Site on N side of the B1341, just over 1 mile SW of Bamburgh.

WAREN CARAVAN PARK RAC L
Waren Mill, NE70 7EE. ☎ (06684) 366
Open: 1 April-1 November
Size: 4 (100) acres, 200 touring pitches, 57 with elec, 140 level pitches, 345 static caravans. 32 hot showers, 16 WCs, 2 CWPs

(1991) Car & caravan, Motor caravan, Car & tent £6.20-£8.20, plus 50p per person above 4 (1 child under 7 free); elec £1.50, awn £1.50, dogs £1
cc Major cards accepted
Well-planned level site with magnificent sea views. Recreation field and children's play area. 15 caravans for hire (own WCs). Restaurant 1½ miles. Swimming pool 15 miles. No motorcycles.
At ¼ mile S of Belford on A1 turn E on B1342. Site in 2½ miles.

BAMPTON Devon Map 1 B2

Lowtrow Cross Inn
Upton, Taunton, TA4 2DB. ☎ (039 87) 220
Open: April-October
Size: 2½ acres, 21 touring pitches. 5 hot showers, 5 WCs. 1 static caravan

7 miles N of Bampton on B3190. 1 mile E of Upton.

BANBURY Oxfordshire Map 2 B2

BARNSTONES CARAVAN & CAMPING SITE RAC L
Great Bourton, OX7 2BB. ☎ (0295) 750289
Open: 1 March-31 October
Size: 3 acres, 50 touring pitches, all level, 44 with elec. 3 hot showers, 5 WCs, 1 CWP

(1991) Car & caravan, Motor caravan £4, Car & tent, M/cycle & tent £3, plus 50p per person above 2, child 50p (under 5s free); elec £1, full awn £1/porch 50p; WS
Barnstones is a very high quality site set in 3 acres of grounds, landscaped with many varieties of trees, shrubs and flowers; with excellent toilet block, free showers, laundry room, children's play area; low level lighting around site roads. Shop ½ mile. Restaurant 150 yards. Swimming pool 2½ miles. No gas available.
If arriving from new M40 motorway, leave motorway at Junction 11 (Banbury turn-off) and follow signs A423 to Coventry and Southam. In 2 miles turn right, signposted Great Bourton and Cropredy, site entrance is 100 yards on right. (Barnstones is 3 miles N of Banbury on A423.)

BANHAM Norfolk Map 3 B1

Banham Zoo
The Grove, NR16 2HB. ☎ (095 387) 476
Open: All year
Size: 8 acres, 100 touring pitches. 4 hot showers, 6 WCs

On B1113, 2 miles N of Kenninghall.

BARHAM Kent Map 3 B3

Ropersole Farm
Dover Road, Near Canterbury, CT4 6SA.
☎ (0227) 831352
Open: All year
Size: 2¾ acres, 85 touring pitches, 24 with elec. 4 hot showers, 12 WCs

7

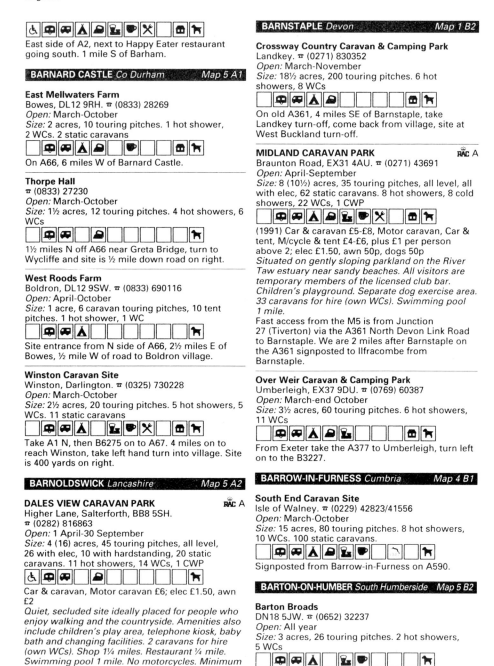

East side of A2, next to Happy Eater restaurant going south. 1 mile S of Barham.

BARNARD CASTLE Co Durham — Map 5 A1

East Mellwaters Farm
Bowes, DL12 9RH. ☎ (0833) 28269
Open: March-October
Size: 2 acres, 10 touring pitches. 1 hot shower, 2 WCs. 2 static caravans

On A66, 6 miles W of Barnard Castle.

Thorpe Hall
☎ (0833) 27230
Open: March-October
Size: 1½ acres, 12 touring pitches. 4 hot showers, 6 WCs

1½ miles N off A66 near Greta Bridge, turn to Wycliffe and site is ½ mile down road on right.

West Roods Farm
Boldron, DL12 9SW. ☎ (0833) 690116
Open: April-October
Size: 1 acre, 6 caravan touring pitches, 10 tent pitches. 1 hot shower, 1 WC

Site entrance from N side of A66, 2½ miles E of Bowes, ½ mile W of road to Boldron village.

Winston Caravan Site
Winston, Darlington. ☎ (0325) 730228
Open: March-October
Size: 2½ acres, 20 touring pitches. 5 hot showers, 5 WCs. 11 static caravans

Take A1 N, then B6275 on to A67. 4 miles on to reach Winston, take left hand turn into village. Site is 400 yards on right.

BARNOLDSWICK Lancashire — Map 5 A2

DALES VIEW CARAVAN PARK   RAC A
Higher Lane, Salterforth, BB8 5SH.
☎ (0282) 816863
Open: 1 April-30 September
Size: 4 (16) acres, 45 touring pitches, all level, 26 with elec, 10 with hardstanding, 20 static caravans. 11 hot showers, 14 WCs, 1 CWP

Car & caravan, Motor caravan £6; elec £1.50, awn £2
Quiet, secluded site ideally placed for people who enjoy walking and the countryside. Amenities also include children's play area, telephone kiosk, baby bath and changing facilities. 2 caravans for hire (own WCs). Shop 1¼ miles. Restaurant ¼ mile. Swimming pool 1 mile. No motorcycles. Minimum 3 nights stay over Bank Holidays.
Site on W side of B6251, 1 mile S of Barnoldswick. Approach the site from the N through Barnoldswick.

BARNSTAPLE Devon — Map 1 B2

Crossway Country Caravan & Camping Park
Landkey. ☎ (0271) 830352
Open: March-November
Size: 18½ acres, 200 touring pitches. 6 hot showers, 8 WCs

On old A361, 4 miles SE of Barnstaple, take Landkey turn-off, come back from village, site at West Buckland turn-off.

MIDLAND CARAVAN PARK   RAC A
Braunton Road, EX31 4AU. ☎ (0271) 43691
Open: April-September
Size: 8 (10½) acres, 35 touring pitches, all level, all with elec, 62 static caravans. 8 hot showers, 8 cold showers, 22 WCs, 1 CWP

(1991) Car & caravan £5-£8, Motor caravan, Car & tent, M/cycle & tent £4-£6, plus £1 per person above 2; elec £1.50, awn 50p, dogs 50p
Situated on gently sloping parkland on the River Taw estuary near sandy beaches. All visitors are temporary members of the licensed club bar. Children's playground. Separate dog exercise area. 33 caravans for hire (own WCs). Swimming pool 1 mile.
Fast access from the M5 is from Junction 27 (Tiverton) via the A361 North Devon Link Road to Barnstaple. We are 2 miles after Barnstaple on the A361 signposted to Ilfracombe from Barnstaple.

Over Weir Caravan & Camping Park
Umberleigh, EX37 9DU. ☎ (0769) 60387
Open: March-end October
Size: 3½ acres, 60 touring pitches. 6 hot showers, 11 WCs

From Exeter take the A377 to Umberleigh, turn left on to the B3227.

BARROW-IN-FURNESS Cumbria — Map 4 B1

South End Caravan Site
Isle of Walney. ☎ (0229) 42823/41556
Open: March-October
Size: 15 acres, 80 touring pitches. 8 hot showers, 10 WCs. 100 static caravans

Signposted from Barrow-in-Furness on A590.

BARTON-ON-HUMBER South Humberside — Map 5 B2

Barton Broads
DN18 5JW. ☎ (0652) 32237
Open: All year
Size: 3 acres, 26 touring pitches. 2 hot showers, 5 WCs

From A1077 follow signs from Barton.

Silver Birches Tourist Park
Waterside Road, DN18 5BA. ☎ (0652) 32509
Open: April-November
Size: 2 acres, 25 touring pitches. 4 hot showers,

ℹ️ Facilities for Disabled   Caravans accepted   Motor caravans   Tents   Laundry room   Shop

6 WCs

From A15 follow signs to Humber Bridge Viewing Area. Site just before Viewing Area and "The Sloop" public house.

BASLOW Derbyshire — Map 5 A2

Leam Farm
Grindleford, S30 1HL. ☎ (0433) 50460
Open: All year
Size: 1½ acres, 20 touring pitches. 1 WC

Site 2½ miles N of Eyam, on E side of Eyam Moor.

Stocking Farm
Calver, S30 1XA. ☎ (0433) 30516
Open: April (Easter)-October
Size: 1 acre, 10 touring pitches. 2 hot showers, 4 WCs. 10 static caravans

A623 first right after Bridge Inn, bear to right few yards later, take FIRST left turn.

BASSENTHWAITE Cumbria — Map 4 B1

Robin Hood Caravan Site
CA12 4RJ. ☎ (076 87) 76334
Open: Easter-November
Size: 2 acres, 16 touring pitches. 4 hot showers, 6 WCs. 19 static caravans

Turn right off A591 at Castle Inn (7 miles N from Keswick). Right after 1 mile to site.

BATH Avon — Map 2 A3

NEWBRIDGE CARAVAN PARK RAC A
Brassmill Lane, BA1 3JT. ☎ (0225) 428778
Open: All year
Size: 4 acres, 88 touring pitches, all level, all with elec, all with hardstanding. 9 hot showers, 1 cold shower, 14 WCs, 3 CWPs

Car & caravan, Motor caravan £7, all plus £1 per adult, 50p per child (over 5 under 16); elec £1.30, awn £1
cc Access, Visa/B'card
88 carefully landscaped, individual, all-weather hardstandings. Overlooking the River Avon, 1½ miles from Bath city centre. Updated to AA 4 Pennant standard. Restaurant 200 yards. Swimming pool 1½ miles. No motorcycles.
At 1½ miles W of Bath on A4 bear left and follow signs.

NEWTON MILL TOURING CENTRE RAC A
Newton St Loe, BA2 9JF. ☎ (0225) 333909
Open: All year
Size: 23 (43) acres, 195 touring pitches, all level, 90 with elec, 90 with hardstanding. 18 hot showers, 32 WCs, 1 CWP

Charges on application.
Country site in a picturesque valley with play area and a pub/restaurant on site. TV satellite hook-up.

Swimming pool 2½ miles.
Travel SE from junction of A4 and A39 on B3110 to site on left.

BATTLE East Sussex — Map 3 A3

Brakes Coppice Farm Park
Crowhurst, TN33 0SJ. ☎ (0424) 83322
Open: March-October
Size: 3½ acres, 30 touring pitches. 2 hot showers, 4 WCs

1½ miles SE of Battle on A2100, take turning to Crowhurst. Left fork in ½ mile. Site 1 mile further.

BEADNELL Northumberland — Map 7 B2

Swinhoe Links
NE67 5BW. ☎ (0665) 720589
Open: April-November
Size: 26 acres, 20 touring pitches. 12 hot showers, 32 WCs. 130 static caravans

B1340 Alnwick to Beadnell. Head toward harbour. Signposted from harbour.

Camping & Caravanning Club Site
Anstead, NE67 5BX. ☎ (0665) 720586
Open: 30 March-28 September
Size: 6½ acres, 150 touring pitches. 6 hot showers, 17 WCs

Charges on application.
cc Access, Visa/B'card
In an Area of Outstanding Natural Beauty. Close to sandy beaches of Beadnell Bay. Camping Gaz only. Shop 1 mile.
From the A1 follow the signs for Seahouses, the site is between Seahouses and Beadnell.

BECCLES Suffolk — Map 3 B1

Waveney Lodge Caravan Site
Elms Road, Aldeby. ☎ (050 277) 445
Open: All year
Size: 1 acre, 15 touring pitches, 10 with elec. 2 hot showers, 3 WCs

Turn right on A146 at Gillingham on to A143, in 1 mile turn right into Holloway Hill. Signposted Aldeby. After 1½ miles turn left into Elms Road. ¼ mile later, site on right.

BEDALE North Yorkshire — Map 5 A1

Pembroke Caravan Park
Leeming Bar, Northallerton, DL7 9BW.
☎ (0677) 22652
Open: April-October
Size: 1 acre, 14 touring pitches. 2 hot showers, 3 WCs

From A1 left and then right on to A684, come into Leeming Bar, bear left for next 2 junctions and site is 800 yards up the road after the second junction.

Snacks/take away · Restaurant · Swimming pool · Shelter for campers · Dogs accepted   9

España

England

BELFORD *Northumberland* — Map 7 B2

Budle Bay Camp Site
Waren Mill, Bamburgh, NE70 7EE.
☎ (06684) 544
Open: Easter-October
Size: 7 acres, 125 touring pitches. 5 hot showers, 7 WCs

[icons: Facilities for Disabled, Caravans, Motor caravans, Tents, Shop, cup, tap, X, dog]

On B1342, 2 miles E of Belford and A1.

BERE REGIS *Dorset* — Map 2 A3

ROWLANDS WAIT TOURING PARK RAC L
Rye Hill, BH20 7HL. ☎ (0929) 471958
Open: Easter-4 October
Size: 8 acres, 71 touring pitches, 45 with elec, 50 level pitches. 10 hot showers, 10 WCs, 1 CWP

[icons: Caravans, Motor caravans, Tents, Laundry room, dog]

(1991) Car & caravan, Motor caravan, Car & tent, M/cycle & tent £2.30, all plus £1.30 per adult, 75p per child; elec £1.35, awn £1
Situated in an Area of Outstanding Natural Beauty with direct access into woods and heathland. Ideal situation for walking or touring Dorset. Family-run site. Shop and restaurant ¾ mile. Swimming pool 5 miles. Maximum stay 21 days.
At Bere Regis take road to Bovington Camp and Wool. About ¾ mile from Bere Regis at top of Rye Hill turn right. Site 300 yards along lane.

BERKELEY *Gloucestershire* — Map 2 A2

Hogsdown Farm
Lower Wick. ☎ (0453) 810224
Open: All year
Size: 4 acres, 25 touring pitches. 2 hot showers, 5 WCs

[icons: Caravans, Motor caravans, Tents, Laundry room, cup, tap, dog]

Between Junctions 13 and 14 on the A38. 1 mile off the A38 opposite the Berkeley turning.

BERWICK UPON TWEED *Northumberland* — Map 7 B2

HAGGERSTON CASTLE HOLIDAY PARK RAC L
Boal, TD15 2RA. ☎ (0289) 81333
Open: 1 March-5 January
Size: 8 (70) acres, 120 touring pitches, all with elec, all level, all with hardstanding, 1012 static caravans. 16 hot showers, 16 WCs, 2 CWPs

[icons: Facilities for Disabled, Caravans, Motor caravans, Laundry room, Shop, tap, X, swimming, dog]

Car & caravan, Motor caravan £7-£9, both plus 85p per person; £2.50 extra per night for private shower and toilet
cc Access, Visa/B'card
Holiday park offering easy access to Northumbrian countryside, castles and beaches. On site facilities include bowling green, tennis, entertainment, boats on the lake. Level site in beautiful rural setting with lakes, swans and various other water fowl. 480 static caravans for hire (own WCs). Calor gas only. No motorcycles.
7½ miles S of Berwick on A1.

Marshall Meadows Caravan Site
TD15 1UT. ☎ (0289) 307375
Open: Easter-October

Size: 5 acres, 40 touring pitches. 6 hot showers, 10 WCs. 55 static caravans

[icons: Caravans, Motor caravans, Tents, dog]

North on A1, Berwick by-pass, right 1½ miles down road. Just before English/Scottish border.

ORD HOUSE CARAVAN PARK RAC A
East Ord, TD15 2NS. ☎ (0289) 305288
Open: 1 March-31 October
Size: 6 (43) acres, 70 touring pitches, 50 with elec, 27 level pitches, 18 with hardstanding, 200 static caravans. 9 hot showers, 25 WCs, 2 CWPs

[icons: Caravans, Motor caravans, Laundry room, X, dog]

Car & caravan, Motor caravan from £5 to £11 maximum; WS
cc Access, Visa/B'card
40 acre wood-lined estate with 18thC manor house. Licensed club has lounge, bar and family room with ball pool, soft play, pool tables, etc. Recreation area has crazy golf, giant draughts, badminton, 9 hole practice golf course. Shop 200 yards. Swimming pool 1½ miles. No tents, no teenage groups.
On Berwick by-pass (A1) turn off for East Ord. Follow caravan symbol signs.

BEWDLEY *Hereford & Worcester* — Map 2 A1

ACRE FARM CARAVAN PARK RAC L
Far Forest. ☎ (0299) 266458
Open: March-October
Size: 7 acres, 10 touring pitches. Hot showers, WCs

[icons: Caravans, Motor caravans, Laundry room, Laundry]

Charges on application.
Wooded site, with children's play area, suitable for overnight stay. Calor gas only.
3½ miles W of Bewdley on A456, turn right on A4117 for 1 mile and observe site sign.

The Blount Arms Caravan Park
Forest Park, Cleobury Mortimer, DY14 9BD.
☎ (0299) 270423
Open: March-October
Size: 1½ acres, 25 touring pitches. 2 hot showers, 3 WCs

[icons: Caravans, Motor caravans, Tents, tap, dog]

Site between Bewdley and Cleobury Mortimer. Take A417. Site 2½ miles E of Cleobury Mortimer.

BIDEFORD *Devon* — Map 1 B2

Knapp House
Churchill Way, Northiam, EX39 1NT.☎ (02374) 74804
Open: Easter-October
Size: 7 (70) acres, 60 touring pitches. Hot showers, 20 WCs. 10 static caravans

[icons: Caravans, Motor caravans, Tents, Laundry room, cup, swimming, dog]

Turn right off A39 Junction 27. Take the link road to Bideford, turn right at roundabout at Bideford Bridge. Site on right in 1 mile.

BILLINGSHURST *West Sussex* — Map 3 A3

LIMEBURNERS CAMPING RAC L
Newbridge, RH14 9JA. ☎ (0403) 782311
Open: 1 April-End October
Size: 2¾ acres, 42 touring pitches, all level, 21 with

⬡ Facilities for Disabled ⬡ Caravans accepted ⬡ Motor caravans ⬡ Tents ⬡ Laundry room ⬡ Shop

elec. 3 hot showers, 3 cold showers, 6 WCs, 1 CWP

🚐 🚑 ⛺ | 🍵 ✖ |

(1991) Car & caravan, Motor caravan, Car & tent,
M/cycle & tent £4.75, plus £1 per person above 4;
elec £1, awn £1; WS
*Quiet, country, family site attached to 16th century
public house. Shop 1½ miles. Swimming pool
9 miles.*
On B2133 between A272 and A29. 1½ miles W of
Billingshurst.

BISHOP'S CASTLE *Shropshire* Map 4 B3

The Green Caravan Park
Longden Road, SY9 5EF. ☎ (058 861) 605
Open: Easter-October
Size: 16 acres, 140 touring pitches. 10 hot showers,
21 WCs. 20 static caravans

🚐 🚑 ⛺ | 🔋 💧 ✖ | | 🐕

Take Longden road off A5 Shrewsbury by-pass.
Site 15 miles on right.

Powis Arms
Lydbury North. ☎ (058 88) 254
Open: All year
Size: 1 acre, 26 touring pitches. 2 hot showers,
4 WCs

🚐 🚑 ⛺ | | 💧 ✖ | 🏠 🐕

From Bishop's Castle 3 miles down B4385 S
towards Craven Arms. Entrance on right next to
pub and opposite entrance to nature reserve.

BLACKPOOL *Lancashire* Map 4 B2

High Moor Farm Caravan Park
Weeton. ☎ (0253) 836273
Open: March-October
Size: 6 acres, 60 touring pitches. 8 hot showers,
14 WCs

🚐 🚑 ⛺ 🔋 🔋 💧 | | 🏠 🐕

Junction 3 off M55, Fleetwood road (A585 N) for
3 miles. Turn left (B5269) and left again (B5260)
opposite barracks.

KNEPS FARM HOLIDAY HOME & PARK RAC A
River Road, Thornton Cleveleys, FY5 5LR.
☎ (0253) 823632
Open: 1 March-31 October
Size: 4 (10) acres, 65 touring pitches, all level,
55 with elec, 55 with hardstanding, 100 static
caravans. 16 hot showers, 16 cold showers,
25 WCs, 2 CWPs

♿ 🚐 🚑 | 🔋 🔋 🍵 ✖ | | 🐕

(1991) Car & caravan, Motor caravan £2; all plus
£1.50 per adult, £1 per child; elec £1
*The site has a games room and children's play
area and is on the banks of the River Wyre.
Swimming pool 2 miles.*
Take A585 N from M55 as far as River Wyre Hotel,
turn N on to B5412 for 1¼ miles, turn right into
Stanah Road at St John's Church and continue
towards River Wyre.

Mariclough and Hampsfield Camp Site
Preston New Road, Peel. ☎ (0253) 61034
Open: March-October
Size: 2 acres, 60 touring pitches. 3 hot showers,
6 WCs

🚐 🚑 ⛺ 🔋 🔋 🍵 | | | 🐕

From M55 Junction 4 turn left on to A583. At set of
traffic lights go straight through for another
250 yards, site on left.

MARTON MERE CARAVAN PARK RAC A
Mythop Road, FY4 4XN. ☎ (0253) 67544
Open: 1 March-31 October
Size: 93 acres, 421 touring pitches, all with elec, all
level, all with hardstanding, 912 static caravans.
36 hot showers, 70 WCs, 8 CWPs

♿ 🚐 🚑 | 🔋 🔋 💧 ✖ 🏊 | 🐕

Car & caravan, Motor caravan from £7.95-£9.95;
Caravan to hire from £30-£40; elec included, dogs
75p
*Marton Mere is set in 93 acres of beautiful scenery.
All facilities are well maintained and we are a
National Caravan Council and Tourist Board
graded park. We are also a Rose Awarded park.
44 static caravans for hire (own WCs). No
motorcycles. 3 nights minimum stay over Bank
Holidays.*
Take junction 4 off the M55, (A583), towards
Blackpool. At the second set of traffic lights turn
right, (Mythop Road), and we are 150 yards on the
right.

Pipers Height Caravan Park
Peel. ☎ (0253) 63767
Open: March-October
Size: 10 acres, 100+ touring pitches. 10 hot
showers, 20 WCs. 16 static caravans

♿ 🚐 🚑 ⛺ 🔋 🔋 | | | | 🐕

Junction 4 off M55. Turn left, down to traffic lights,
turn right and then sharp left within traffic lights.
Site on the right.

Stanah House Caravan Park
River Road, Thornton. ☎ (0253) 824000
Open: March-October
Size: 5 acres, 50 touring pitches. 4 hot showers,
6 WCs

🚐 🚑 ⛺ 🔋 🔋 | | | | 🐕

From M55 take Exit 3 to Fleetwood. A couple of
miles down the road will be a large roundabout.
Follow signposts to Little Thornton (right turn),
second right signposted "Stanah Picnic Area and
Caravan Park", follow to river.

Windy Harbour Holiday Centre
Singleton. ☎ (0253) 883064
Open: March-October

💧 Snacks/take away ✖ Restaurant 🏊 Swimming pool 🏠 Shelter for campers 🐕 Dogs accepted   11

Size: 54 acres, 130 touring pitches

[icons]

¼ mile N off A586, 2½ miles E of Poulton-le-Fylde.

BLANDFORD FORUM *Dorset*　　Map 2 A3

THE INSIDE PARK CARAVAN & CAMPING　RAC A
DT11 0HG. ☎ (0258) 453719
Open: Easter-30 September
Size: 7 (12) acres, 75 touring pitches, 45 level
pitches, 32 with elec. 6 hot showers, 9 WCs, 1 CWP

[icons]

(1991) Car & caravan, Motor caravan, Car & tent,
M/cycle & tent £1.84, all plus £2.04 per adult, 51p
per child; elec £1.28, dogs 51p; WS
A unique blend of convenient and comfortable
family camping in spacious, rural surroundings in
the heart of our family-run farm. Modern facilities
and a friendly, personal welcome. Restaurant and
swimming pool 2 miles.
Travelling S on the A350 Blandford by-pass take
the Blandford St Mary exit to W. Then road to
Winterborne Stickland, follow camping signs to
site in 2 miles.

LADY BAILEY CARAVAN PARK　RAC L
Winterborne, Whitechurch, DT11 0HS.
☎ (0258) 880786
Open: 16 March-31 October
Size: 8 (18) acres, 50 touring pitches, all level. 6 hot
showers, 18 WCs, 2 CWPs

[icons]

Car & caravan, Motor caravan, Car & tent, M/cycle
& tent £4.25 per person; awn 50p; WS
cc Access, Visa/B'card
There's a children's play area at this peaceful,
grassy site in lovely countryside. Restaurant
500 yards and swimming pool 5 miles.
At 5 miles SW of Blandford on A354.

BLUE ANCHOR BAY *Somerset*　　Map 1 B2

BLUE ANCHOR BAY CARAVAN PARK　RAC A
☎ (0643) 821360
Open: March-October
Size: 45 acres, 75 touring pitches. Hot showers,
WCs

[icons]

Charges on application.
Large, well-cared-for site on the seafront. Caravans
and chalets for hire. Shop closed after mid
September and showers closed after end of
September.
From junction A39 and B3191, 4 miles E of
Minehead, travel E on B3191 for 1½ miles.

BODIAM *East Sussex*　　Map 3 A3

BODIAM CARAVAN & CAMP SITE　RAC L
Park Farm, TN32 5XA. ☎ (0580) 830514
Open: 1 April-30 October
Size: 5 acres, 50 touring pitches, all level, 25 with
hardstanding. 5 hot showers, 7 WCs, 1 CWP

[icons]

Car & caravan, Motor caravan, Car & tent, M/cycle*
& tent £5, plus £1 per adult above 2, 50p per child;
WS

Beautiful rural setting. Many walks including one
to Bodiam Castle along River Rother. Free fishing.
Large area for children to play. Restaurant 1 mile.
Shop 3 miles. Swimming pool 10 miles. No gas
available. No camp fires allowed.
Signposted on the A229, 3 miles S of Hawkhurst.

Lordine Cou:t Caravan & Camping Park
Ewhurst Green, Staplecross
☎ (0580) 830209
Open: Easter-October
Size: 4½ (11) acres, 120 touring pitches. 21 hot
showers, 40 WCs. Static caravans

[icons]

At Cripp's Corner (A229), NE on B2165 for 3 miles.
Site on left.

BODMIN *Cornwall*　　Map 1 A3

Camping & Caravanning Club Site
Old Callywith Road, PL31 2DZ. ☎ (0208) 73834
Open: 30 March-28 September
Size: 10½ acres, 175 touring pitches. 6 hot
showers, 18 WCs

[icons]

Charges on application.
Grassy site, with some trees, on the edge of
Bodmin and convenient for main road. Children's
play area. Camping Gaz only.
From the A389 follow the signs for the site.

BOGNOR REGIS *West Sussex*　　Map 3 A3

CHURCH FARM CARAVANS　RAC L
Pagham, PO21 4NR. ☎ (0243) 262835
Open: 1 March-31 October
Size: 2½ (62½) acres, 50 touring pitches, all level,
50 static caravans. Hot showers, WCs

[icons]

Charges on application.
Handy for the sea, this holiday park is situated
around a lagoon and a natural harbour which is
also a bird sanctuary. Children's play area, club
with entertainment. Calor gas only.
3 miles W of Bognor Regis, follow roads signed to
Pagham.

BOROUGHBRIDGE *North Yorkshire*　　Map 5 A1

THE OLD HALL CARAVAN PARK　RAC L
Skelton Road, Langthorpe, YO5 9HS.
☎ (0423) 322130
Open: 1 April-31 October
Size: 10 acres, 12 touring pitches, all level, 8 with
elec, 99 static caravans. 2 hot showers, 2 cold
showers, 5 WCs, 1 CWP

[icons]

(1991) Car & caravan, Motor caravan £6.15, Car &
large tent £6.15, Car & small tent £5.10, M/cycle &
tent £5.10; elec £1; WS
The farmstead on which the park lies existed in
Saxon times. ½ mile from Boroughbridge, the site
is close to river amenities, fishing, boating, sports
centre ½ mile away. Shop 500 yards, restaurant
100 yards, swimming pool 6 miles.
From the junction of the A1 and B6265 (N of
Boroughbridge), travel SE on the B6265 for
1½ miles, turn right for 400 yards to site on left.

PONDEROSA CARAVAN PARK   RAC L
Wetherby Road, YO5 9HS. ☎ (0423) 322709
Open: 1 April-31 October
Size: 6 acres, 50 touring pitches, all level, 20 with elec, 9 static caravans. 4 hot showers, 4 cold showers, 9 WCs, 1 CWP

	⊡	🚐	🛆	🛆					⊞	🐕

(1991) Car & caravan, Motor caravan, Car & large tent £5.65, Car & small tent, M/cycle & tent £3.85; elec £1; WS
Level, well-sheltered site central to major tourist attractions. Hot water to all wash basins. Sports centre and supermarket within easy walking distance. Restaurant 100 yards. Swimming pool 6 miles. 2 tourer caravans for hire.
At the S end of Boroughbridge by-pass (A1) turn E as signed "Boroughbridge" and observe international camping signs.

Riverside Holiday Park
Bar Lane, YO5 9LS. ☎ (0423) 322683
Open: March-October
Size: 6 acres, 30 touring pitches. 6 hot showers, 14 WCs. 75 static caravans

	⊡	🚐	🛆	🛆	🛆					🐕

¾ mile from A1. Turn to go through Boroughbridge. Follow signs to Roecliff. Along road you will find a farm and guest house. Take the turn-off and site is ¾ mile down the road on river bank.

Lower Pennycrocker Farm
St Juliot. ☎ (0840) 250257
Open: Easter-September
Size: 4 acres, 40 touring pitches. 2 hot showers, 2 WCs

	⊡	🚐	🛆							🐕

2½ miles N of Boscastle on (B3262). Follow signs to site.

Trebyla
Minster, PL35 0HL. ☎ (0840) 250308
Open: Easter-September
Size: 2½ acres, 32 touring pitches. 1 hot shower, 2 WCs. 3 static caravans

	⊡	🚐	🛆	🛆						🐕

From A39 at Tresparrett Posts, take B3263 for 1½ miles towards Boscastle. Site on right.

BOURNEMOUTH *Dorset*   *Map 2 B3*

CARA CARAVAN PARK   RAC L
Old Bridge Road, Iford, BH6 5RQ.
☎ (0202) 482121
Open: All year
Size: 7 acres, 36 touring pitches, all with elec, all level, all with hardstanding. 7 hot showers, 9 WCs, 2 CWPs

	⊡	🚐		🛆	🛆					

Car & caravan £5.50-£7.50/£8.85 (2/4 persons), Motor caravan £4.60 (low season); extra person 75p-90p; extra car 75p-90p; elec £1.55-£1.65, awn £1.85-£1.95
A well-run site beside the River Stour. Very quiet and peaceful. Restaurant 100 yards. Swimming pool ¾ mile. Calor gas only. RAC motorcyclists only admitted with caravans. Maximum stay 28 days.
3 miles E of Bournemouth (pier) on A35 just before crossing River Stour.

Chesildene Touring Caravan Site
☎ (0202) 513238
Open: April-October
Size: 3 acres, 70 touring pitches. 6 hot showers, 16 WCs

	⊡	🚐		🛆	🛆				⊞	

From A338 to Bournemouth, turn right on to A3060 and follow camping signs for 1 mile.

BRAMPTON *Cumbria*   *Map 7 A3*

Irthing Vale Caravan Park
Old Church Lane, CA8 2AA.
☎ (069 77) 3600
Open: March-October
Size: 4½ acres, 20 touring pitches. 6 hot showers, 8 WCs. 25 static caravans

	⊡	🚐	🛆	🛆	🛆					🐕

On A6071 at Brampton, ½ mile north of Brampton.

Talkin Tarn Country Park
☎ (069 77) 3129
Open: Easter-October
Size: 1¼ acres, 12 touring pitches. 4 hot showers, 3 WCs

	⊡	🚐	🛆							🐕

Off A69 on to B6413 to Castle Carrock. Site 1 mile south of Brampton.

🔲 Snacks/take away ☒ Restaurant ◩ Swimming pool ⊞ Shelter for campers 🐕 Dogs accepted   13

BRANDS HATCH Kent · Map 3 A3

Thriftwood Camping & Caravanning Park
Plaxdale Green Road, Stansted, TN15 7PB.
☎ (0732) 822261
Open: Closed February
Size: 18 acres, 150 touring pitches. 9 hot showers,
20 WCs

150 yards off A20. Signed off M20, M25 and M26.
Behind Horse and Groom public house at top of
Wrotham Hill.

BRANDSBY North Yorkshire · Map 5 A1

Water End Farm
Stillington Road, YO6 4RT.
☎ (034 75) 236
Open: March-October
Size: 3 acres, 15+ touring pitches. 3 WCs

On B1363 Helmsley-Stillington road, ½ mile S of
Brandsby.

BRAUNTON Devon · Map 1 B2

Chivenor Holiday Centre
Chivenor, Barnstaple. ☎ (0271) 812217
Open: March-November
Size: 1½ acres, 30 touring pitches. 4 hot showers, 6
WCs. 25 static caravans

3½ miles from Barnstaple on A361 to Ilfracombe.
The entrance is off the only roundabout.

LOBB FIELDS CARAVAN & CAMPING PARK RAC A
Saunton Road, EX33 1EB. ☎ (0271) 812090
Open: May-September inclusive
Size: 14 acres, 100 touring pitches, 25 with elec.
20 hot showers, 38 WCs, 2 CWPs

(1991) Car & caravan £4.50-£7, Motor caravan, Car
or M/cycle & tent £3-£5.50; £1 per adult above 3,
child 50p (5-14); extra car 50p; elec £1.50, awn
50p,dogs 50p
*Large, level, meadowland site with panoramic
views facing south across Braunton Burrows to
Saunton and across Taw/Torridge estuary to
Bideford and Appledore. Quiet site 1 mile from
Braunton village centre and 1½ miles to Saunton
Beach. Restaurant 1 mile. Swimming pool 7 miles.
Site is on the N side of the B3231, 1 mile W of
Braunton town centre.*

BRENTWOOD Essex · Map 3 A2

Camping & Caravanning Club Site
Warren Lane, Frog Street, Kelvedon Hatch,
CM15 0JG.
☎ (0277) 72773
Open: 30 March-28 September
Size: 12 acres, 150 touring pitches. 2 hot showers,
11 WCs

Charges on application.
*Meadowland site sheltered by wood and hedges.
Shop 1½ miles. Calor gas only.*

From A128 take the turning next to the Bentley
Golf Club House. After the sharp right hand bend
take the next right, the site is on the left.

BRIDGETOWN Somerset · Map 1 B2

Exe Valley Caravan Club Site
Mill House. ☎ (064 385) 432
Open: March-October
Size: 4 acres, 30 touring pitches. 4 hot showers,
5 WCs

Site in Bridgetown village centre.

BRIDGNORTH Shropshire · Map 2 A1

STANMORE HALL CAMPING PARK RAC L
Midland Motor Museum, Stourbridge Road,
WV15 6DT.
☎ (0746) 761761
Open: All year
Size: 8 acres, 60 touring pitches, all level, 15 with
elec, 6 with hardstanding. 7 WCs, 1 CWP

Charges on application. WS
*Attractive site in parkland around lake. Children's
play area. Restaurant 2 miles. Swimming pool
3 miles.*
From the junction of the A442 and
A458 (Bridgnorth by-pass), travel E on the A458 for
1 mile to site on right.

Camp Easy
Rays Farm, Billingsley, WV16 6PF.
☎ (029 924) 255
Open: 1 April-31 October
Size: 1 (10) acres, 20 tent pitches (tents provided,
no caravans, motor caravans or touring tents
allowed). No showers, 1 WC

8 miles from Bridgnorth off the B4363 Cleobury
Mortimer Road or 7 miles from Bewdley off the
B4363 to Bridgnorth.

BRIDGWATER Somerset · Map 2 A3

Currypool Mills
Cannington, TA5 2NH. ☎ (0278) 671215
Open: Easter-October
Size: 1½ acres, 35 touring pitches. 4 hot showers, 7
WCs. 3 static caravans

A39 through Cannington. Turn left at sign for
Spaxton/Aisholt. Site 500 yards on left.

MILL FARM CARAVAN & CAMPING PARK RAC A
Fiddington, TA5 1JQ.
☎ (0278) 732286
Open: All year
Size: 15 (50) acres, 200 touring pitches, 140 with
elec, all level. 14 hot showers, 60 WCs, 3 CWPs

Car & caravan, Motor caravan, Car & tent, M/cycle*
& tent £6.50, plus £1 per adult above 2, child 50p;
extra car £1; elec £1.50, dogs 50p; WS
*Inland family holiday park situated in a picturesque
valley between the beautiful Quantock Hills and the*

sea. Children's paradise: swimming, boating, riding, large sandpit, games rooms, TV rooms. Canoes and ponies for hire. Tourist Information, laundry, camp shop.
From Bridgwater travel W on A39 for 6½ miles, turn right on unclassified road towards Fiddington, ¼ mile on turn right to site in ¼ mile.

BRIDLINGTON *Humberside* · Map 5 B1

BARMSTON BEACH HOLIDAY PARK   RAC A
Sands Lane, Barmston, Driffield, YO25 8PJ.
☎ (0262) 86202
Open: Easter-End September
Size: 1½ (13) acres, 16 touring pitches, 8 with elec, all level, 350 static caravans. 18 hot showers, 12 WCs, 2 CWPs

(1991) Car & caravan, Motor caravan £6.13-£9.20; elec £3.07, dogs £2; WS
cc Major cards
Small and friendly, direct access to beach. Entertainment throughout the season. Tiger Club activities for children. Heated outdoor swimming pool. 28 static caravans for hire (own WCs). Calor gas only. No motorcycles.
6 miles S of Bridlington on the A165. Turn left at Little Chef, signposted Barmston Beach.

Old Mill Caravan Park
Bempton, YO16 5XD. ☎ (0262) 673565
Open: Easter-October
Size: 2 acres, 25 touring pitches. 4 hot showers, 14 WCs

Come in from Flamborough on B1255. Follow road and signs to Marton, left at mini roundabout to Bempton. Left again 200 yards.

The Poplars
45 Jewison Lane, Sewerby, YO15 1DX.
☎ (0262) 677251
Open: All year
Size: 1¼ acres, 30 touring pitches. 4 hot showers, 8 WCs

2 miles NE of Bridlington.

SHIRLEY CARAVAN PARK   RAC A
Jewison Lane, Marton, YO16 5YG.
☎ (0262) 676442
Open: 1 March-30 November
Size: 2 (25) acres, 46 touring pitches, all level, all with elec, all with hardstanding, 430 static caravans. 12 hot showers, 26 WCs

Car & caravan, Motor caravan £7; elec £1, awn £1
Rural site - level grass with hardstanding for tourers. 12 static caravans for hire (own WCs). Swimming pool 3 miles. No motorcycles.

At roundabout on A165 take B1255 to Flamborough for 2 miles, turn left on to unclassified road signposted Jewison Lane and Bempton, after ¼ mile site on left over level crossing.

SOUTH CLIFF CARAVAN PARK   RAC A
Wilsthorpe, YO15 3QN. ☎ (0262) 671051
Open: 1 March-30 November
Size: 11 (79) acres, 200 touring pitches, all level, all with elec, all with hardstanding, 750 static caravans. 15 hot showers, 18 WCs, 2 CWPs

(1991) Car & caravan, Motor caravan, Car & tent, M/cycle & tent £5.75-£7.15; elec £1.20, awn £1.20
cc Access, Visa/B'card
Flat, level site with easy access to EEC Blue Flag award-winning sandy beaches. Swimming pool 1½ miles. 8 weeks maximum stay.
1½ miles south of the resort of Bridlington, off the A165.

BRIDPORT *Dorset*   Map 2 A3

Eype House Caravan & Camping Park
Eype, DT6 6AL. ☎ (0308) 24903
Open: April-10 October
Size: 4 acres, 20 touring pitches. 4 hot showers, 8 WCs. 35 static caravans

On A35 signposted Eype. Site 200 yards from beach.

FRESHWATER CARAVAN PARK   RAC A
Burton Bradstock, DT6 4PT.
☎ (0308) 897317
Open: 15 March-15 November
Size: 20 (45) acres, 425 touring pitches, all level, 60 with elec, 250 static caravans. 40 hot showers, 60 WCs, 4 CWPs

(1991) Car & caravan, Motor caravan, Car & tent, M/cycle & tent £5.25-£10.75, plus 90p-£1.50 per person above 4; elec £1.25, awn £1.15, dogs £2.30
cc Visa/B'card
Situated at the mouth of River Bride with its own private beach. Nightly entertainment in High Season. Golf course adjoins site. 60 caravans for hire (own WCs).
At Bridport take B3157 Weymouth road. Park entrance 1½ miles on right from Crown Roundabout.

GOLDEN CAP CARAVAN PARK   RAC A
Seatown, Chideock, DT6 6JX. ☎ (0308) 22139
Open: 23 March-3 November
Size: 8 (28) acres, 150 touring pitches, 120 level pitches, 110 with elec, 33 with hardstanding, 195 static caravans. 15 hot showers, WCs, 3 CWPs

◪ Snacks/take away   ☒ Restaurant   ◩ Swimming pool   ▣ Shelter for campers   ☗ Dogs accepted   **15**

(1991) Car & caravan, Motor caravan, Car & tent, M/cycle & tent £5.15-£7.45, plus £1.05 per person above 2; elec £1.30, awn £1.20
cc Major cards
Overlooked by the famous Golden Cap clifftop and surrounded by the heritage coastline, the park is an ideal location from which to explore and enjoy West Dorset. 9 static caravans for hire (own WCs). Swimming pool 2 miles.
From Bridport travel W on the A35 for 2¾ miles to Chideock, turn S on unclassified road to site on left.

HIGHLANDS END FARM HOLIDAY PARK RAC A
Eype, DT6 6AR. ☎ (0308)22139
Open: March-October
Size: 10 (28) acres, 120 touring pitches, 100 level pitches, 90 with elec, 45 with hardstanding, 160 static caravans, 3 chalets. 15 hot showers, 30 WCs, 2 CWPs

(1991) Car & caravan, Motor caravan, Car & tent, M/cycle & tent £5.15-£7.45, plus £1.05 per person above 2; elec £1.30, awn £1.20
cc Major cards
Extremely well-kept clifftop park with views across Lyme Bay. Lounge bar. 16 caravans and 3 chalets for hire (own WCs).
At 1 mile W of Bridport on A35, turn left for ¾ mile to Eype church, where turn left.

Uploaders Farm
Dorchester Road. ☎ (0308) 23380
Open: April-October
Size: 1 acre, 25 touring pitches. 2 WCs, CWP

3¾ miles E of Bridport, S of A35.

WEST BAY HOLIDAY PARK RAC A
West Bay. ☎ (0308) 22424
Open: March-October
Size: 18 (40) acres, 255 touring pitches, 30 with elec, 11 with hardstanding, 11 level pitches, 250 static caravans. 27 hot showers, 75 WCs

Charges on application.
A well-organised family park by West Bay beach and the River Brit, with a children's play area, a club and pub with entertainment in high season. Caravans for hire.
At 1 mile S of Bridport on B3157, keep right to West Bay. By church, turn right, cross harbour bridge to site.

Brightlingsea Caravan Club Site
Lower Park Road, CO7 0JX.
☎ (0206) 303421
Open: Easter-October
Size: 4 acres, 55 touring pitches. 6 hot showers, 10 WCs

B1027 to Brightlingsea, right fork signposted "Waterfront". Turn right before Community Centre.

BROOK LODGE RAC L
Cowslip Green, Redhill, BS18 7RD.
☎ (0934) 862311
Open: 1 March-31 October
Size: 2½ acres, 29 touring pitches, all level, 20 with elec, 3 with hardstanding, 1 static caravan. 4 hot showers, 7 WCs, 1 CWP

Charges on application.
A sheltered, secluded site in the grounds of Georgian House, with woods nearby and a stream. Swimming pool and children's play area. Caravan for hire. Restaurant 1 mile.
Site on E side of the A38, opposite 'Paradise Motel', 9½ miles SW of Bristol, 3 miles NE of Churchill.

Centry Touring Caravans & Tents
Gillard Road, TQ5 9EY. ☎ (0803) 853215
Open: Easter-October
Size: 1½ acres, 32+ touring pitches. 4 hot showers, 12 WCs

Follow signs to Berry Head from A3022. Site on left past Centry Road.

Galmpton Park Camping Site
Greenway Road, Galmpton. ☎ (0803) 842066
Open: Easter-October
Size: 10 acres, 120 touring pitches. 10 hot showers, 16 WCs. 2 cottages

Site signed from A380 (Paignton to Brixham road).

HILLHEAD CAMP RAC L
TQ5 0HH. ☎ (0803) 842336
Open: Easter-October
Size: 20 acres, 330 touring pitches, 200 with elec, 280 level pitches. 30 hot showers, 49 WCs, 1 CWP

Charges on application.
Family-run site with panoramic views of the sea and countryside. Facilities include a large clubroom with licensed bar and live entertainment nightly for adults and children, a large heated swimming pool and a children's pool.
From the junction of A379 and A3022 (2 miles W of Brixham) travel S on A379 for 2 miles and turn left on B3205 towards Dartmouth Lower Ferry for 200 yards.

Upton Manor Farm Camping Site
St Mary's Road, TQ5 9QH. ☎ (0803) 882384
Open: May-September
Size: 10 acres, 250 touring pitches. 18 hot showers, 25 WCs

At traffic lights in the centre of Brixham turn right into Bolton Road, left into Castor Road, leads to St Mary's Road.

SHAKESPEARE COUNTRY

Leedons Park, situated in the charming Cotswold Village of Broadway is within easy reach of Cheltenham, Evesham, Warwick and Stratford Upon Avon.

The forty acre park, open all year, caters for both caravanner and camper alike with it's Pet and Pet free areas, Electric Hook-ups (10 amps) and children's play area, all overlooked by the Cotswold hills.

Our Modern Caravan Holiday Home Hire Fleet is available for your main holiday or just a few days break. Also Luxury Caravan Holiday Homes **For Sale** on the Park.

Whether your stay is a couple of days or longer you will be assured a warm welcome.

For booking and colour brochure write, phone or call.

Open All Year

Discover the Beauty of the Cotswolds at

LEEDONS PARK BROADWAY
CHILDSWICKHAM ROAD
BROADWAY. WORCS WR12 7HB

Tel: 0386 852423

BROADWAY *Hereford & Worcester*   *Map 2 B2*

LEEDONS PARK   RAC A
Childswickham Road, WR12 7HB.
☎ (0386) 852423
Open: All year
Size: 30 (54) acres, 450 touring pitches, all level, 180 with elec, 119 static caravans, 3 chalets. 28 hot showers, 40 WCs, 2 CWPs

(1991) Car & caravan, Motor caravan, Car & tent, M/cycle & tent £6-£9, plus £1 per person above 2, child £1; extra car £1; elec £1.50, dogs £1
cc Access, Visa/B'card
An excellent site with modern, spotlessly clean WC and shower blocks. Situated in the Vale of Evesham and Shakespeare country: Gateway to the Cotswolds. 19 static caravans and 3 chalets for hire (own WCs). Maximum stay 28 days (tourers). At ¼ mile W of Broadway, at the junction of A46 and A44, travel SW on A46 for 200 yards, where turn NW on unclassified road for ¾ mile. Site on left (signposted from A44 Evesham to Broadway road).

BROMYARD *Hereford & Worcester*   *Map 2 A2*

Saltmarshe Castle Caravan Park
☎ (0885) 483207
Open: March-October
Size: 20 (50) acres, 14 touring pitches. 12 hot showers, 25 WCs. 250 static caravans

On A44 Leominster-Worcester road. Bromyard turn-off, follow the Stairport Road (B4203), site is

signposted off that road.

BROUGHTON-IN-FURNESS *Cumbria*   *Map 4 B1*

Birch Bank Farm
Blawith, Ulverston. ☎ (022 985) 277
Open: May-October
Size: ½ acre, 6 touring pitches. 1 WC

From A5092 ½ mile W of Gawthwaite turn right for Woodland. Site is 2 miles down the road.

BRUTON *Somerset*   *Map 2 A3*

BATCOMBE VALE CARAVAN PARK   RAC L
Batcombe, Shepton Mallet, BA4 6BW.
☎ (0749) 830246
Open: 1 May-30 September
Size: 5 acres, 30 touring pitches, all level, 16 with elec. 2 hot showers, 4 WCs, 1 CWP

(1991) Car & caravan, Motor caravan, Car & tent £4.50-£6.50, plus £1.50 per adult above 2, child 50p; elec £1.50, awn £1, dogs 50p; WS
An Area of Outstanding Natural Beauty, with its own secluded valley of lakes. Short distance from Longleat, Stourhead and Glastonbury. Shop and restaurant 1 mile. Swimming pool 5 miles. Calor gas only. No motorcycles. Family groups only. Access to site must be off the B3081 between Bruton and Evercreech, from where it is well signed.

● Snacks/take away   ✗ Restaurant   ◿ Swimming pool   ⬚ Shelter for campers   ⊞ Dogs accepted   **17**

BUDE *Cornwall* — Map 1 A3

HAVEN VIEW TOURING PARK — RAC L
Gillards Moor, St Gennys, EX23 0BG.
☎ (08403) 650
Open: 1 April-31 October
Size: 6 acres, 100 touring pitches, all level, 6 with elec. 5 hot showers, 11 WCs, 1 CWP

Car & caravan, Motor caravan, Car & tent, M/cycle & tent £1.80, plus £1.80 per adult, 80p per child; elec £1.50, awn 80p; WS
Level, open, grassy park with views overlooking the valley down to Crackington Haven and the sea beyond. Licensed bar, lounge/TV room, children's play area, dog walk. Restaurant 3 miles. Swimming pool 8 miles.
8¾ miles S of Bude on the W side of the A39.

Bude Holiday Park
Maer Lane. ☎ (0288) 355955
Open: March-October
Size: 23 acres, 250 touring pitches. 40 hot showers, 44 WCs. 136 static caravans

From A39 follow campsite signposts towards Bude.

BUDEMEADOWS TOURING HOLIDAY PARK — RAC A
Poundstock, EX23 0NA. ☎ (0288) 361646
Open: All year
Size: 9½ acres, 100 touring pitches, 27 with elec, 15 with hardstanding, most level. 7 hot showers, 16 WCs, 1 CWP

Car & caravan, Motor caravan, Car & tent, M/cycle & tent £3.45 per person, £1.50 per child; elec £1.75, dogs 60p; WS
Well-maintained park in a beautiful setting, panoramic views and 1 mile from surfing beaches of Widemouth Bay. No additional charges for our first class facilities. An excellent centre for exploring this magnificent part of North Cornwall. Restaurant 1 mile, swimming pool in Bude - 3 miles.
From Stratton (E of Bude), travel S on the A39 for 3½ miles to site on left.

CORNISH COASTS CARAVAN PARK — RAC L
Middle Penlean, Poundstock, EX23 0DR.
☎ (0288) 361380
Open: Easter-End October
Size: 3½ (4) acres, 78 touring pitches, 6 with elec, 30 level pitches, 5 with hardstanding, 3 static caravans. 4 hot showers, 9 WCs, 1 CWP

(1991) Car & caravan, Motor caravan, Car & tent, M/cycle & tent £4-£5, plus 80p-£1 per adult above 2, child 60p-80p; elec £1.30
Quiet family park with glorious views towards the sea at Widemouth Bay. 3 static caravans for hire (2 with own WC). Restaurant ½ mile. Swimming pool 5 miles.
Site is on the W side of the A39, 5½ miles S of Bude.

EAST THORNE CARAVAN & CAMPING PARK — RAC L
Kilkhampton, EX23 9RY. ☎ (0288) 82618

Open: Easter-31 October
Size: 1½ (2½) acres, 29 touring pitches, 25 level pitches. 2 hot showers, 5 WCs, 1 CWP

(1991) Car & caravan, Motor caravan, Car & tent, M/cycle & tent £3.75-£6; awn 50p
Small, grassy site with a children's play area. Children's bikes for hire. 1 static caravan for hire (own WC). Restaurant ½ mile. Swimming pool 5 miles.
Travel on A39 from Bude to Kilkhampton, turn right on B3254 for ½ mile to site on right.

KEYWOOD CARAVAN PARK — RAC L
Whitstone, Holsworthy, EX22 6TW.
☎ (0288) 84338
Open: Easter-31 October
Size: 2 (8½) acres, 25 touring pitches, 10 level pitches, 8 with elec, 14 static caravans. 6 hot showers, 6 cold showers, 18 WCs, 1 CWP

(1991) Car & caravan, Motor caravan, Car & tent, M/cycle & tent £5; elec £1, dogs 50p; WS
Very quiet secluded site, ideal centre for touring north coast of Devon and Cornwall, yet far enough away from the usual hustle and bustle of tourist centres. 14 static caravans for hire (own WCs). Restaurant and swimming pool 8 miles. Dogs must be kept on a lead.
From the junction A3072/B3254 (4 miles E of Bude), travel S on B3254 for 4¼ miles where turn right as for Whitstone Head, for 1 mile.

RED POST INN & HOLIDAY PARK — RAC L
Launcells, EX23 9NW. ☎ (0288) 81305
Open: 1 March-31 October
Size: 3.9 acres, 64 touring pitches, all level, 10 with elec. 4 hot showers, 8 WCs, 1 CWP

Car & caravan, Motor caravan, Car & tent, M/cycle & tent £1.60-£2.70, plus 80p per person above 2; elec £1.35; WS
cc Access, Visa/B'card
Village pub and restaurant and camping and caravan site. Old 16th century coaching inn. Shop 100 yards. Swimming pool 5 miles.
From the junction of the A39 and A3072 at Stratton, travel E on the A3072 to Red Post (3 miles) to site on right.

Tamar Lake Farm
Thurdon, Kilkhampton. ☎ (0288) 82426
Open: April-October
Size: 0.8 acres, 15 touring pitches. 1 hot shower, 4 WCs. 3 static caravans

A39 - 3 miles south of Kilkhampton towards Tamar Lake on the B3254 OR north on B3254 from A3072. Site signposted off road.

Widemouth Bay Caravan Park
Widemouth Bay. ☎ (0288) 361208
Open: March-October
Size: 20 acres, 100 touring pitches. 12 hot showers, 10 WCs, 131 static caravans

From Bude(A3072), follow Widemouth Bay road for

Facilities for Disabled Caravans accepted Motor caravans Tents Laundry room Shop

4 miles.

Willow Valley Camping Park
Dye House, Bush, EX23 9LB. ☎ (0288) 353104
Open: April/Easter-October
Size: 4 acres, 45 touring pitches. 2 hot showers,
5 WCs. 1 static caravan

On A39, 1 mile N of Stratton.

WOODA FARM CARAVAN & CAMPING PARK RĂC A
Wooda Farm, Poughill, EX23 9HJ.
☎ (0288) 352069
Open: April-October
Size: 6 (12) acres, 160 touring pitches, 80 with elec,
140 level pitches, 53 static caravans. 18 hot
showers, 29 WCs, 2 CWPs

Car & caravan, Motor caravan, Car & tent, M/cycle
& tent £5.10-£9.50, plus 60p per person above 4;
elec £1.55, awn £1, dogs 80p; WS
cc Access, Visa/B'card
*Quiet, family park with scenic views. ETB rating:
Excellent 5 ticks. Own woodland walks, coarse
fishing, 9 hole golf, clay shoots, archery in main
season. Free showers and hot water. 49 static
caravans for hire (own WCs). Swimming pool
1½ miles.*
Through Bude north to Poughill, at top of village
turn left. Park is 200 yards on right.

BUDLEIGH SALTERTON *Devon*　　　*Map 1 B3*

LADRAM BAY HOLIDAY CENTRE RĂC A
Otterton, EX9 7BX. ☎ (0395) 68398
Open: 1 April-30 September
Size: 10 (52) acres, 54 touring pitches, all level,
35 with elec. 475 static caravans. 12 hot showers,
12 cold showers, 52 WCs, 1 CWP

(1991) Car & caravan £7-£10, Motor caravan £6, Car
& tent £4-£9.50, plus £1 per person above 2; elec
£1.50, awn £1.50
*A grassy site with private beach; swimming,
boating and fishing. Licensed bar, family room and
children's play area. 104 static caravans for hire
(own WCs). No motorcycles.*
At 2 miles N of Budleigh Salterton, on A376, turn E,
continue through Otterton for 1½ miles.

BUNGAY *Suffolk*　　　*Map 3 B1*

Outney Meadow Caravan Park
Broad Street, NR35 1HG. ☎ (0986) 892338
Open: All year
Size: 4 acres, 30 touring pitches. 6 hot showers,
10 WCs. 1 static caravans

Site at junction of A144 and A143 north of Bungay,
signposted.

BURNHAM-ON-CROUCH *Essex*　　　*Map 3 B2*

Silver Road Caravan Park
5 Silver Road.
☎ (0621) 782934
Open: Easter-mid October
Size: 1½ (3) acres, 70 touring pitches. 2 hot
showers, 4 WCs. Static caravan

From the West, through town to Victoria Inn, Silver
Road, and bear left.

BURNHAM-ON-SEA *Somerset*　　　*Map 2 A3*

Channel View Caravan & Camping Sites
Brean Farm, Brean Down. ☎ (0278) 751241
Open: Easter-October
Size: 4½ acres, 90 touring pitches. 8 hot showers,
18 WCs

From M5 Junction 22 take B3139 to Brean.
Through village and site is 2 miles down coast
road.

Edithmead Trailer Park
☎ (0278) 783475
Open: March-October
Size: 10 (14) acres, 105 touring pitches. 8 hot
showers, 8 WCs. Static caravans, chalets

Site on the A38 next to junction 22 of the M5.

HOME FARM CARAVAN PARK RĂC A
Edithmead, TA9 4HD. ☎ (0278) 788888
Open: All year
Size: 40 acres, 750 touring pitches, all level,
600 with elec, 50 with hardstanding. 35 hot
showers, 56 WCs, 4 CWPs

Car & caravan, Motor caravan, Car & tent, M/cycle*
& tent from £4.20, plus £1 per adult/child; car £1.50;
elec £1.40, awn £1.20, dogs 75p
cc Access, Visa/B'card
*A family-orientated park with adventure
playground, Go Karts, BMX track, children's club
and sports, extensive leisure facilities. Shop open
Easter-end September. Swimming pool ¾ mile.*
From junction 22 of the M5 (A38) travel W on the
B3140 towards Burnham-on-Sea for almost ½ mile,
turn right to site entrance on left.

New House Farm
Mark Road, Highbridge, TA9 4RA.
☎ (0278) 782218
Open: March-October
Size: 4½ acres, 30 touring pitches. 4 hot showers, 6
WCs

From M5 Junction 22 take A38 toward Highbridge.

💙 Snacks/take away　✕ Restaurant　◺ Swimming pool　⌂ Shelter for campers　🐾 Dogs accepted　　**19**

UNITY FARM HOLIDAY CENTRE
For a fun packed, water splashing, roller-coaster family caravan and camping holiday.
DIAL A COLOUR BROCHURE (0278) 751235
COAST ROAD, BREAN SANDS, BURNHAM-ON-SEA, SOMERSET TA8 2RB

First roundabout take second exit and follow Industrial Estate signs. Next roundabout take first exit on to the B3139, go over motorway bridge and site is a couple of yards.

Northam Farm Caravan & Camping Park
Brean. ☎ (0278) 751244
Open: Easter-October
Size: 40 acres, 300 touring pitches. 30 hot showers, 3b WCs

Junction 22 off M5 (signed Burnham-on-Sea). Follow signs to Brean along coast road. Look out for Brean Leisure Park, 500 yards past it is Pontins. Site is 500 yards past Pontins on right.

Unity Farm Holiday Centre
Coast Road, Brean Sands
☎ (0278) 751235/6
Open: March-October
Size: 60 acres, 700 touring pitches. 40 hot showers, 60 WCs. 550 static caravans (150 for hire)

Leave M5 at Junction 22, follow signs for Berrow and Brean. Site is 4½ miles down this road from motorway.

Warren Farm
Warren Road, Brean. ☎ (0278) 751227
Open: April-October
Size: 40 acres, 400 touring pitches. 40 hot showers, 70 WCs

M5 Junction 22 follow signs for Brean and site is on B3140.

BURNSALL North Yorkshire   Map 5 A1

Howarth Farm
Skyreholme, Appletreewick
☎ (075 672) 226
Open: March-November
Size: 5 acres, 10 touring pitches. 4 hot showers, 6 WCs

From A59, B6160 N for 3½ miles. Right at Barden Tower for 1½ miles to t-junction. Right signposted Skyreholme then right at fork in ½ mile. Site 200 yards.

Howgill Lodge
Barden. ☎ (075 672) 655
Open: April-October
Size: 3 acres, 20 touring pitches. 2 hot showers, 6 WCs. 4 static caravans

From A59 take the B6160 for 3½ miles N. Turn right towards Appletreewick at Barden Towers. 1 mile later there is a signpost to site up gravel road on your right.

Mill Lane Caravan & Car Park
Ainhams House, Appletreewick
☎ (075 672) 236
Open: April-October
Size: 2½ acres, 40 touring pitches. 3 hot showers, 5 WCs

Site 1 mile SE of Burnsall.

BURTON-UPON-TRENT *Staffordshire*   Map 5 A3

Little Park Farm Holiday Homes
Park Lane, Tutbury, DE13 9JH.
☎ (0283) 812654
Open: All year
Size: 1 acre, 20 touring pitches. 2 hot showers, 2 WCs. 4 static caravans

A30 take exit and follow signs towards Tutbury and take fork towards Tutbury Castle - entrance to site is just beyond Tutbury Castle entrance.

BURWARTON *Shropshire*   Map 2 A1

Three Horse Shoes Inn
Wheathill. ☎ (058 475) 206
Open: March-October
Size: 2½ acres, 50 touring pitches. 1 hot shower, 4 WCs. 1 static caravan

On B4364, 7 miles NE of Ludlow.

BUXTON *Derbyshire*   Map 5 A2

Butchers Arms
Reaps Moor, Longnor, SK17 0LL.
☎ (0298) 84477
Open: All year
Size: 2 acres, 60 touring pitches. 1 WC

B5053 S from Longnor for 1½ miles, then right fork for ¾ mile.

COTTAGE FARM CARAVAN PARK   RAC L
Blackwell, Taddington, SK17 9TQ.
☎ (0298) 85330
Open: 1 March-31 October
Size: 3 acres, 30 touring pitches, all with elec, 25 level pitches, 25 with hardstanding, 1 static caravan. 2 hot showers, 5 WCs, 1 CWP

(1991) Car & caravan £4.50, Motor caravan £4, plus 50p per person; elec £1.15, awn 50p
Small, friendly, family-run site (open in winter with tap and hook-ups). Centre of Peak District National Park. Ideal for walking and touring. Hot and cold running water. Site lighting. 1 static caravan for

---

🗓 Facilities for Disabled 🚐 Caravans accepted 🚐 Motor caravans ⛺ Tents 🧺 Laundry room 🛒 Shop

hire. Restaurant 1 mile. No motorcycles.
At 5 miles SE of Buxton on A6, turn N on road to Blackwell, follow caravan park signs.

Limetree Park
Dukes Drive, SK17 9RP. ☎ (0298) 22988
Open: March-October
Size: 12 acres, 35 touring pitches. 6 hot showers, 12 WCs. 32 static caravans

Signposted off A515, 1 mile south of Buxton.

Pomeroy Caravan & Camping Park
Street House Farm, Pomeroy, Flagg, SK17 9QG.
☎ (029 883) 259
Open: Easter-October
Size: 2 acres, 30 touring pitches. 4 hot showers, 6 WCs. 1 static caravan

5 miles SE of Buxton on A515. Site entrance signed over cattle grid.

Thornheyes Farm
Longridge Lane, Peak Dale, SK17 8AD.
☎ (0298) 26421
Open: Easter-October
Size: 2 acres, 15 touring pitches. 1 hot shower, 2 WCs

2 miles N of Buxton, turn right (E) at sign saying Peak Dale, turn right at crossroads.

CAISTER-ON-SEA *Norfolk*　　　**Map 3 B1**

GRASMERE CARAVAN PARK　　RAC L
7 Bultitudes Loke, Yarmouth Road, NR30 5DH.
☎ (0493) 720382
Open: April-October
Size: 5 acres, 46 touring pitches, all level, all with elec, 63 static caravans, 1 chalet. 12 hot showers, 21 WCs, 1 CWP

Car & caravan, Motor caravan from £4.35-£5.95 incl. 2 persons; elec £1
Rural holiday park, all pitches level and well-drained, each pitch has own water tap, drain, electricity and TV hook-up. Restaurant and shop 400 yds. Swimming pool 3 miles. No dogs. No teenage or single sex groups.
Enter Caister from A149 at Stadium roundabout, after ½ mile turn left 50 yards past Esso petrol station.

OLD HALL LEISURE PARK　　RAC A
High Street, NR30 5JL. ☎ (0493) 720400
Open: 30 March-30 September
Size: 2 (4) acres, 35 touring pitches, all level, 30 with elec, 36 static caravans, 4 chalets. 6 hot showers, 12 WCs, 1 CWP

(1991) Car & caravan, Motor caravan £5-£8; awn 50p-£1
cc Access, Visa/B'card
A small, family-owned and managed park offering excellent facilities and personal service. Shop 10 metres. Calor gas only. 32 caravans and 4 chalets for hire (own WCs). No dogs. No all-male

or all-female parties.
Take A149 out of Great Yarmouth, follow tourist road signs from Yarmouth Stadium - park opposite Caister church.

SCRATBY HALL CARAVAN PARK　　RAC A
Scratby, NR29 3PH. ☎ (0493) 730283
Open: Easter-31 October
Size: 4½ acres, 108 touring pitches, all level, 64 with elec. 10 hot showers, 2 cold showers, 18 WCs, 1 CWP

Car & caravan, Motor caravan, Car & tent, M/cycle & tent £4.00-£7.00; elec £1, awn 85p
Well-maintained, quiet, level, grassy site, near the sea and close to Norfolk Broads. Restaurant ½ mile. Swimming pool 2½ miles. No single-sex groups.
At roundabout, junction of A149 and B1159, 1½ miles N of Caister, turn N along B1159 for 1 mile. Site on left.

CAISTOR *Lincolnshire*　　　**Map 5 B2**

Nettleton Park
☎ (0472) 851501
Open: March-October
Size: 140 touring pitches. 6 hot showers, 12 WCs. 213 static caravans

From A46 N, left onto B1434. Right onto B1205. Site in 1½ miles.

CALLINGTON *Cornwall*　　　**Map 1 B3**

Mount Pleasant Caravan Park
St Ann's Chapel, PL17 8JA.
☎ (0822) 832325
Open: April-September
Size: 6 acres, 18 touring pitches. 1 hot shower, 5 WCs. Static caravans

On A390, 4 miles E of Callington.

CALNE *Wiltshire*　　　**Map 2 B2**

BLACKLAND LAKES HOLIDAY AND LEISURE CENTRE　　RAC A
Knights Marsh Farm, Stockley Lane, SN11 0NQ.
☎ (0249) 813672
Open: All year
Size: 8 (17) acres, 180 touring pitches, all level, 96 with elec, 30 with hardstanding. 13 hot showers, 23 WCs, 2 CWPs

Charges on application.
Relaxing, not overcrowded, scenic, rural farm site. 6 sheltered paddocks for campers/caravanners. Conservation area. Very good holiday and touring centre. Quiet but not isolated, interesting site and area. Very good access - improved in 1991. Mother and baby facilities. Restaurant and swimming pool 1 mile. Weekend Breaks 1½/2½ nights minimum stay.
From the junction of the A4 and A3102 in Calne, travel E on the A4 for ¾ mile, turn right to site on left in ¾ mile.

◨ Snacks/take away　⊠ Restaurant　◪ Swimming pool　◙ Shelter for campers　◪ Dogs accepted　　　21

CAMBORNE *Cornwall* — Map 1 A3

MAGOR FARM CARAVAN SITE ♔ A
Tehidy, TR14 0JF. ☎ (0209) 713367
Open: March-October
Size: 7½ acres, 164 touring pitches, all level. 14 hot showers, 14 WCs, 1 CWP

Car & caravan, Motor caravan, Car & tent, M/cycle & tent £3.50, plus 50p per person above 2, child 50p; awn £1, dogs £1; WS
Holiday park with level standings, close to country park and beaches. Free hot water for showers. Spring water. Shop and restaurant 1¼ miles. Calor gas only. Drive in and take your own position.
From the junction of A30 and A3047, W of Camborne, travel N on unclassified road for 1½ miles to site on left (signed from junction of A30 and A3047).

CAMBRIDGE — Map 3 A1

Camping & Caravanning Club Site
Behind 19 Cabbage Moor, Great Shelford, CB2 5JU.
☎ (0223) 841185
Open: 25 March-28 October
Size: 12 acres, 100 touring pitches, all level, 24 with elec. 6 hot showers, 19 WCs, 2 CWPs

Charges on application.
cc Access, Visa/B'card
Level, grassy site with a children's play area.
From the M11 junction 11 turn N on to the A10. At traffic lights turn right on to A1301 for ½ mile to site on left.

CAMBRIDGE *Cambridgeshire* — Map 3 A1

HIGHFIELD FARM CAMPING PARK ♔ A
Long Road, Comberton, CB3 7DG.
☎ (0223) 262308
Open: 1 April-31 October
Size: 8 acres, 120 touring pitches, 100 with elec, 60 level pitches, 40 with hardstanding. 10 hot showers, 10 cold showers, 21 WCs, 3 CWPs

Car & caravan £5.50-£6.50, Motor caravan, Car & tent £5.25-£6.25, M/cycle & tent £4.25-£5.25, plus £1.20 per adult above 2, child 60p; elec £1.30, awn 75p
A grassy, well-maintained, family-run park on a working farm. Children's play area on park. Restaurant 2 miles. Swimming pool 5 miles. Children under 16 must be accompanied by an adult.
From M11 leave at junction 12. Take A603 (Sandy) for ½ mile, then turn right on B1046 to Comberton. From A45 turn south at Hardwick Roundabout and follow international camping and caravanning signs to Comberton.

ROSEBERRY TOURIST PARK ♔ L
Earith Road, Willingham, CB4 5LT.
☎ (0954) 60346
Open: Easter-October
Size: 10 acres, 80 touring pitches, all level, 40 with elec, 1 static caravan, 1 chalet. 6 hot showers, 12 WCs, 1 CWP

Car & caravan, Motor caravan, Car & tent, M/cycle & tent plus £1.50 per adult, 75p per child; car 50p; elec £1.25, awn 50p; WS
A 10-acre holiday park set amid 1000 pear trees, taking only 80 tourers. 1 static caravan and 1 chalet (own WC) for hire. Restaurant 1 mile. Swimming pool 4 miles.
Turn off M11/A604 at Bar Hill on to B1050. Site is on left in 6 miles. (1 mile after Willingham).

CAMELFORD *Cornwall* — Map 3 A1

JULIOT'S WELL HOLIDAY PARK ♔ A
PL32 9RF. ☎ (0840) 213302
Open: 1 March-31 October
Size: 8½ acres, 55 touring pitches, 8 with elec, 38 level pitches, 3 with hardstanding, 48 static caravans, 1 chalet. 10 hot showers, 10 cold showers, 14 WCs, 1 CWP

Car & caravan, Motor caravan, Car & tent, M/cycle & tent £5.50-£8, plus £1 per person above 2, child 50p; elec £1.50, dogs 50p; WS
Woodland and meadow setting with views across countryside. Fully licensed Old Coach House, skittle alley, children's play area, undercover hot and cold washing-up facilities for campers. Tourist Board 5 Ticks rating, plus Rose Award. 40 static caravans for hire (own WCs).
Turn NW off the A39 at Valley Truckle, S of Camelford, on the B3266 for ¼ mile, at crossroads turn left, ¼ mile to site on right.

LAKEFIELD CARAVAN PARK ♔ L
Lower Pendavey Farm, PL32 9TX.
☎ (0840) 213279
Open: Easter-31 October
Size: 5 acres, 30 touring pitches, 18 with elec, 30 level pitches. 4 hot showers, 5 WCs, 1 CWP

Car & caravan, Motor caravan £6, Car & tent, M/cycle & tent £3.50-£6, plus 50p per person above 2 (under 5s free); car 50p; elec £1.30, awn 50p, dogs 50p
A quiet, secluded site with its own lake and valley views, set in 5 acres on a working farm. Farm animal corner with a variety of hand-reared animals. Restaurant 1½ miles. Swimming pool 1 mile. Calor gas only.
In Camelford on the A39, turn NW onto the B3266. Site 1 mile N of Camelford.

CANTERBURY *Kent* — Map 3 B3

The Red Lion Caravan Park
Old London Road, Dunkirk, ME13 9LL.
☎ (0227) 750661
Open: All year
Size: ¾ acre, 17 touring pitches. 2 hot showers, 5 WCs

M2 junction 7, A2 Canterbury-Dover. 3 miles from junction signed Dunkirk and Caravan Park. 3 miles from A2.

Rose & Crown
Stelling Minnis. ☎ (022 787) 265

Open: March-October
Size: 2½ acres, 37 touring pitches. 3 WCs

5 miles S of Canterbury on B2068, E to Stelling Minnis. First left for site.

ST MARTINS TOURING AND CAMPING PARK ☂ L
Bekesbourne Lane, CT3 4AB.
☎ (0227) 463216
Open: 1 April-30 September
Size: 18 acres, 200 touring pitches, mostly level, 12 with elec. 22 hot showers, WCs, 1 CWP

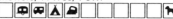

(1991) Car & caravan, Motor caravan, Car & tent £6.20; extra car £1.80; small tent only £3.50; elec £2, awn £1.80; WS
Tree-surrounded, rural meadowland site, all grass, quietly situated. Children's play area. Restaurant 1½ miles. Swimming pool 3 miles. Minimum stay 7 nights.
At 1½ miles E of Canterbury city centre on A257 to Sandwich. Turning opposite Canterbury Golf Club.

SOUTH VIEW CARAVAN PARK ☂ L
Maypole Lane, Hoath, CT3 4LL.
☎ (0227) 86280
Open: All year
Size: 2.3 acres, 45 touring pitches, all level, 14 with elec. 5 hot showers, 5 cold showers, 9 WCs, 1 CWP

Car & caravan, Motor caravan, Car & tent, M/cycle & tent £6.50, plus £2 per person above 2; elec £1.50, awn £1; WS
Quiet, clean, level, grassy site. Ideal touring site for east Kent. Shop ½ mile. Swimming pool 6 miles.
From Canterbury follow the A28 to Sturry, cross level-crossing and turn right, ½ mile further bear left for 2¾ miles, then turn right for site.

Yew Tree Park
Stone Street, Petham, CT4 5PL.
☎ (0227) 70306
Open: Easter-October
Size: 3 (4½) acres, 30 touring pitches. 4 hot showers, 4 WCs. 18 static caravans

4 miles S of Canterbury on B2068, turn W into road by Chequers Inn. Site 100 yards.

CARLISLE Cumbria   Map 7 A3

DALSTON HALL CARAVAN PARK ☂ A
Dalston Road, CA5 7JX. ☎ (0228) 710165
Open: 1 March-31 October
Size: 4 acres, 60 touring pitches, all level, 26 with elec, 30 with hardstanding, 9 static caravans. 4 hot showers, 18 WCs, 1 CWP

Charges on application.
Well-maintained, family-run site by the river with individual pitches. Fishing available. Play area.
4 caravans for hire (own WCs). Restaurant 100 yards. Swimming pool ½ mile.
3 miles SW of Carlisle on B5299.

DANDY DINMONT CARAVAN & CAMPING PARK ☂ L
Blackford, CA6 4EA. ☎ (022 874) 611
Open: 1 March-31 October
Size: 3 (4½) acres, 47 touring pitches (20 for tents), all level, 20 with elec, 14 with hardstanding. 4 hot showers, 14 WCs, 1 CWP

Car & caravan, Motor caravan £5.50, Car & tent, M/cycle & tent from £4.25, Tent only £3.25; extra car £1; elec £1, awn £1
A quiet, rural site just off M6, ideal base for visiting Hadrian's Wall, historic Carlisle, Scottish Border country and Lake District. Also a convenient overnight halt. Shop 2 miles. Restaurant 1½ miles. Swimming pool 4½ miles. Calor gas only. Dogs must be kept on leash at all times.
Just off M6 (Junction 44) on A7 to Galashiels - the tourist route to Scotland. Just over 1 mile, follow site signs, turning at the Blackford Church crossroads. Cross over next crossroads (100 yards) and site entrance is on the right (30 yards).

ORTON GRANGE CARAVAN PARK ☂ A
Wigton Road, CA5 6LA. ☎ (0228) 710252
Open: All year
Size: 4 (6) acres, 50 touring pitches, all level, 25 with elec, 14 with hardstanding, 22 static caravans. 6 hot showers, 11 WCs, 1 CWP

Car & caravan, Motor caravan £3.80-£5, Car & tent, M/cycle & tent £2.20-£5, all plus 80p-£1 per adult, 50p -70p per child; elec £1.20-£1.40, awn 90p-£1
cc Access, Visa/B'card
Small, wooded park, large children's play area. 4 caravans for hire (own WCs). Caravan and camping accessory shop and tent sales. Restaurant 400 yards.
Travel SW on the A595 from Carlisle for 4 miles.

CARNFORTH Lancashire   Map 4 B1

HOLGATE CARAVAN PARK ☂ A
Cove Road, Silverdale, LA5 0SH.
☎ (0524) 701508
Open: 1 March-mid November
Size: 7 (106) acres, 70 touring pitches, all level, all with elec, 30 with hardstanding, 350 static caravans. 10 hot showers, 19 WCs, 2 CWPs

(1991) Car & caravan, Motor caravan, Car & tent, £10.20-£11.75 (1992 prices + approx 10%); elec £1.50, awn £1
Situated in an area of outstanding natural beauty. Holiday park with 10 static caravans for hire (own WCs). No motorcycles. Minimum stays at Bank Holidays and weekends.
At the traffic lights in Carnforth on A6, turn W and follow roads to Silverdale. Site is 5 miles NW of Carnforth.

BOLTON HOLMES FARM ☂ L
off Mill Lane, Bolton-le-Sands, LA5 8ES.
☎ (0524) 732854
Open: April-September
Size: 4 acres, 25 touring pitches, 45 static caravans.
4 hot showers, 4 cold showers, 16 WCs, 1 CWP

Charges on application.
*Simple `working' farm site with views over bay.
Calor gas only. Restaurant ½ mile. Swimming pool
5 miles.*
At 1½ miles S of Carnforth on A6, turn W into Mill
Lane, continue to the sea and fork left to site.

CAPERNWRAY HOUSE CARAVAN PARK   RÁC A
Capernwray, LA6 1AE. ☎ (0524) 732363
Open: March-October
Size: 5½ acres, 60 touring pitches, 47 with elec,
10 level pitches, 1 static caravan. 4 hot showers, 10
WCs, 1 CWP

Car & caravan, Motor caravan, Car & tent, M/cycle*
& tent from £4.50; elec £1.25, awn £1.25; WS
*Quiet rural site set in rolling countryside. Ideal
base for touring Lakes and Dales. Adventure
playground on site. B&B available at Capernwray
House. 1 static caravan for hire (own WC). Shop
and restaurant 2 miles. Swimming pool ½ mile.
Calor gas only.*
M6 (Junction 35), then B6254 to Over Kellet and
Kirkby Lonsdale. At t-junction, left into Over Kellet.
At crossroads, turn left, Capernwray House
Caravan Park 2 miles on right.

DETRON GATE CARAVAN SITE   RÁC A
Bolton-le-Sands, LA5 9IN.
☎ (0524) 732842
Open: 1 April-31 October
Size: 8 (10) acres, 90 touring pitches, 6 with elec,
6 with hardstanding, 35 level pitches, 42 static
caravans. 4 hot showers, 16 WCs, 1 CWP

Charges on application.
*An attractive farmland site with converted
farmhouse and outbuildings containing shops, cafe
and TV/games room. Children's play area.
Restaurant and swimming pool ½ mile.*
1½ miles S of Carnforth on A6. Site visible from
this road.

The Hawthorns
Nether Kellet. ☎ (0524) 732079
Open: March-October
Size: 10½ acres, 31 touring pitches. 4 hot showers,
6 WCs, 39 static caravans

From M6 (Junction 35) turn off on to
B6294 heading right. Cross motorway and take first
left toward Nether Kellet. ½ mile to t-junction, turn
left and site is 200 yards on left.

Marsh House Farm
Crag Bank, LA5 9JA. ☎ (0524) 732897
Open: April-October
Size: 5 acres, 120 touring pitches. 8 hot showers,
7 WCs. 30 static caravans

From M6 junction 35, S through Carnforth, site
signposted. Site 1 mile off A6, by shore.

NETHERBECK CARAVAN PARK   RÁC L
North Road, LA5 9NG. ☎ (0524) 735133
Open: 1 March-31 October
Size: 1½ (4) acres, 20 touring pitches, all with elec,

32 static caravans. 2 hot showers, 2 cold showers,
3 WCs, 1 CWP

Charges on application. WS
*A family-run site, with children's play area and a
caravan for hire. Shop and restaurant 1 mile. Calor
gas only.*
In centre of Carnforth, turn E on to B6254 (Market
Street), take first turning on left (North Road), site
in ¾ mile on right.

Red Bank Farm
Bolton-le-Sands. ☎ (0524) 823196
Open: March-October
Size: 6 acres, 5 touring pitches. 4 hot showers,
15 WCs. 39 static caravans

From A6 turn right on to Morecambe Road
(A5015). Right over railway bridge on to shore and
site.

Sandside Caravan & Camping Site
St Michaels Lane, Bolton-le-Sands
☎ (0524) 822311
Open: March-October
Size: 6 acres, 50 touring pitches. 4 hot showers,
12 WCs. 35 static caravans

Exit M6 at Junction 35. Follow A6 through
Carnforth. Turn right (W) at Little Chef at Bolton-le-
Sands. Site ½ mile down road.

CASTLE HOWARD *North Yorkshire*   Map 5 A1

CASTLE HOWARD CARAVAN SITE   RÁC A
Coneysthorpe, YO6 7DD. ☎ (065384) 366
Open: 1 March-31 October
Size: 6 (12½) acres, 40 touring pitches, all level,
28 with elec, all with hardstanding, 122 static
caravans. 6 hot showers, 6 cold showers, 24 WCs,
2 CWPs

(1991) Car & caravan, Motor caravan from £5, Car
& tent, M/cycle & tent £2.75-£5, plus 50p per
person; elec £1.20, awn £1; WS
*Close to Castle Howard, situated by the Great Lake.
Recreation area and fishing on site. Restaurant
2½ miles.*
At 4½ miles SW of Malton on A64, turn W, at
1½ miles on turn right and 2 miles further, again
turn right. Site in ½ mile.

CERNE ABBAS *Dorset*   Map 2 A3

LYONS GATE CARAVAN & CAMPING PARK   RÁC L
☎ (030 05) 260
Open: Easter-end October
Size: 8 acres, 60 touring pitches, all level, 3 static
caravans. 4 hot showers, 7 WCs

Charges on application.
*Peaceful country site surrounded by woodland.
Indoor swimming pool, coarse fishing lake,
playground. 3 caravans for hire (2 with own WCs).
Bar with terrace. Restaurant ¾ mile.*
3¼ miles N of Cerne Abbas on the W side of the
A352.

Ⓐ Facilities for Disabled   Ⓞ Caravans accepted   Ⓜ Motor caravans   Ⓐ Tents   Ⓛ Laundry room   Ⓢ Shop

CHACEWATER Cornwall — Map 1 A3

CHACEWATER CAMPING & CARAVAN PARK RAC L
Coxhill, TR4 8LY. ☎ (0209) 820762
Open: Easter-October
Size: 3½ (6½) acres, 80 touring pitches, all level,
12 with elec, 20 static caravans. 7 hot showers,
16 WCs, 1 CWP

Charges on application.
*Quiet, level park surrounded by farmland, with TV
and games rooms and children's play area.
Families or couples only. 20 caravans for hire (own
WCs). Restaurant 1 mile.*
3½ miles W of Truro on A390 fork left signed
Chacewater for 2¾ miles. In village turn S signed
St Day and take first turn right.

CHALFONT ST GILES Buckinghamshire Map 3 A2

HIGHCLERE FARM COUNTRY TOURING PARK RAC L
Newbarn Lane, Seer Green, HP9 2QZ.
☎ (024 07) 4505
Open: 1 March-31 January
Size: 1½ acres, 30 touring pitches, all level, 28 with
elec, 20 with hardstanding. 4 hot showers, 4 cold
showers, 8 WCs, 2 CWPs

(1991) Car & caravan, Motor caravan £5.50, Car &
tent, M/cycle & tent £3.50; elec £1.50
*Quiet meadowland site with a farm shop selling
fresh produce. Restaurant ¼ mile. Swimming pool
½ mile.*
From the junction of the A413 and B4442, turn W
along Pheasant Hill and through Chalfont St Giles.
Site on right in 1 mile.

CHARD Somerset — Map 2 A3

Alpine Grove
Forton, TA20 4HD. ☎ (046 06) 3479
Open: Easter-September
Size: 7½ acres, 40 touring pitches. 2 hot showers, 5
WCs

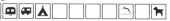

From A30 Chard-Crewkerne road, take B3167. At
first signpost for Forton follow signs to site.

Five Acres House
Beetham, Combe St Nicholas, TA20 3PZ.
☎ (046 034) 364
Open: All year
Size: ½ acre, 6 touring pitches. 1 hot shower,
2 WCs

100 yards away from A303 London-Exeter road.
Signposted 2 miles W of Combe St Nicholas.

Turnpike Woodlands Caravan Park
Exeter Road (A30), Howley, TA20 1QD.
☎ (0460) 66036
Open: April-November
Size: 7 acres, 75 touring pitches. 12 hot showers,
18 WCs

Site on A30. 2½ miles out of Chard heading

towards Honiston.

Camping & Caravanning Club Site
The Turnpike, TA20 1QD.
Open: 30 March-23 November
Size: 20 acres, 75 touring pitches. 12 hot showers,
16 WCs

Charges on application.
This site has direct access from the A30, 4 miles W
of Chard.

South Somerset Holiday Park
The Turnpike, Exeter Road, Howley
☎ (0460) 62221
Open: Easter-November
Size: 7 acres, 140 touring pitches. 12 hot showers
21 WCs

Off A30, Howley.

CHARLBURY Oxfordshire — Map 2 B2

COTSWOLD VIEW CARAVAN & CAMPING SITE RAC A
Enstone Road, OX7 3JH. ☎ (0608) 810314
Open: Easter or 1 April-30 September
Size: 7 acres, 90 touring pitches, 51 with elec,
45 level pitches. 9 hot showers, 10 WCs, 1 CWP

(1991) Car & caravan, Motor caravan, Car & tent,
M/cycle & tent £6.65; child 80p; elec £1.45
*Situated on the hillside close to the picturesque
township of Charlbury. Here you will not only be
able to enjoy the breathtaking and uninterrupted
views over the Cotswolds, but also the up-to-date
conveniences of a modern and sensitively
landscaped site in a peaceful setting. ETB 5 Ticks,
AA 3 Pennents. Swimming pool 7 miles. 3 nights
minimum stay over Bank Holidays.*
Travelling from London and the east via M40 and
A40, ring road until June - Enstone left on
B4022 to Charlbury, approx 2 miles on the left.
Travelling from the west and Cheltenham, take A40
as far as Burford, left on to A361 signed to
Chipping Norton, turn right on to B4437 to
Charlbury, follow signs to Enstone on B4022.
¾ mile on right.

CHARMOUTH Dorset — Map 2 A3

MANOR FARM HOLIDAY CENTRE RAC A
DT6 6QL. ☎ (0297) 60226
Open: All year
Size: 15 (30) acres, 345 touring pitches, 40 with
elec, 5 with hardstanding. 100 level pitches,
15 static caravans, 12 chalets/houses. 24 hot
showers, 57 WCs, 2 CWPs

(1991) Car & caravan, Motor caravan, Car & tent,
M/cycle & tent from £5; extra person £1.50, child
£1; elec £1.50, awn £1.50, dogs £1; WS
*Large, open holiday park in area of outstanding
natural beauty, 10 minutes' level walk from beach.
15 static caravans and 12 chalets/houses for hire
(own WCs).*
At east end of Charmouth by-pass (A35) enter
Charmouth Manor Farm ½ mile on right.

📓 Snacks/take away ☒ Restaurant ◿ Swimming pool ▣ Shelter for campers 🐾 Dogs accepted 25

Newlands Caravan & Camping Park
DT6 6RB. ☎ (0297) 60259
Open: March-October
Size: 23 acres, 196 touring pitches. 20 hot showers, 36 WCs. 81 static caravans

½ mile E of Charmouth on A35.

MONKTON WYLDE FARM CARAVAN PARK   RĀC L
DT6 6DB. ☎ (0297) 34525
Open: Easter-End October
Size: 3 (6) acres, 40 touring pitches, all level. 5 hot showers, 7 WCs, 1 CWP

Car & caravan, Motor caravan, Car & tent, M/cycle & tent £1.10-£2.20, all plus £2 per adult, up to 75p per child; awn £1, dogs 50p-75p
A small and secluded, high quality site with spotless facilities on a 200 acre working sheep and cereal farm in tranquil countryside. Generously sized pitches with plenty of space for children to play. Easy access to many and varied tourist attractions including seaside. Shop and restaurant ¾ mile. Swimming pool 2½ miles.
A35 W from Charmouth. After 3 miles at Greenway Head turn right to B3165 signed Marshwood. Site ¼ mile down lane on left. NB Do NOT take lane to Monkton Wylde village.

CHATTERIS *Cambridgeshire*   Map 3 A1

Sunset Campsite
Huntingdon Road. ☎ (035 43) 3649
Open: May-October
Size: 5 acres, 40 touring pitches. 2 hot showers, 5 WCs

On A141 from SW approaching Chatteris, right at roundabout then sharp right.

CHAWLEIGH *Devon*   Map 1 B2

YEATHERIDGE FARM CARAVAN PARK   RĀC A
East Worlington, Crediton, EX17 4TN.
☎ (0884) 860330
Open: Easter-September
Size: 9 acres, 85 touring pitches, 60 with elec, 35 level pitches, 2 static caravans. 12 hot showers, 17 WCs, 2 CWPs

(1991) Car & caravan, Motor caravan, Car & tent, M/cycle & tent £5.50, plus 65p per person above 2; elec £1.45, awn 65p, dogs 25p; WS
Panoramic views; secluded, spacious farm park. Peace and freedom to roam the farm, see the animals (some to touch). Ideal for touring, coasts and moors. 2 static caravans for hire (own WCs). Restaurant 1¼ miles.
At 4 miles E of Chawleigh on B3042.

CHEADLE *Staffordshire*   Map 5 A3

Hales Hall Caravan & Camping Park
Oakamoor Road, ST10 1BU. ☎ (0538) 753305
Open: Easter-October
Size: 20 acres, 50 touring pitches. 4 hot showers, 20 WCs

From Cheadle, take B5417 E towards Oakamoor. Site in ¾ mile.

CHEDDAR *Somerset*   Map 2 A3

BROADWAY HOUSE CARAVAN & CAMPING PARK   RĀC A
Axbridge Road, BS27 3DB. ☎ (0934) 742610
Open: March-November
Size: 30 acres, 200+ touring pitches, 150 with elec, mostly level, 10 with hardstanding, 34 static caravans. 9 hot showers, 75 WCs, 2 CWPs

(1991) Car & caravan, Car & tent, M/cycle* & tent £3, Motor caravan £2, plus £2.50 per person, £1-£1.50 per child; elec £1.50, awn £1, dogs 50p
cc Major cards
Situated at the foot of the Mendip Hills, wonderful central position for exploring the area. Excellent for family caravan and camping holidays. All facilities. 34 static caravans for hire (own WCs). Restaurant 1 mile. No large motorcycle groups.
M5 Exit 22, 8 miles to park following brown tourist signs to Cheddar Gorge and Caves.

BUCKLEGROVE CARAVAN PARK   RĀC A
Rodney Stoke, BS27 3UZ. ☎ (0749) 870261
Open: 1 March-31 October
Size: 5½ acres, 125 touring pitches, 66 with elec, 50 level pitches, 6 with hardstanding, 35 static caravans. 11 hot showers, 22 WCs, 2 CWPs

Car & caravan, Motor caravan, Car & tent, M/cycle* & tent £4.50-£7.50, plus £1.60 per adult above 2, child 90p; car 60p; elec £1.30, awn £1.05; WS
Quiet, select, family site situated at the foot of the Mendip Hills on the A371, midway between Wells and Cheddar. 12 static caravans for hire (own WCs). Restaurant ½ mile. No dogs. 3 nights minimum stay over Bank Holidays and during High Season.
3½ miles SE of Cheddar on A371.

Church Farm Camping Site
☎ (0934) 743048
Open: Easter-October
Size: 4 acres, 48 touring pitches. 6 hot showers, 6 WCs, 2 static caravans

Site on S side of Cheddar on A371.

Froglands Farm
☎ (0934) 742058/743304
Open: Easter-October
Size: 3 acres, 62 touring pitches. 6 hot showers, 9 WCs

Site on A371 in village of Cheddar.

Glendale Farm
Wedmore. ☎ (0934) 712257
Open: April-October
Size: 1½ acres, 5 touring pitches. 2 WCs

On B3151, 2¼ miles S of Cheddar.

  Ⓖ Facilities for Disabled ⊞ Caravans accepted ⊡ Motor caravans Ⓐ Tents ▣ Laundry room ▣ Shop

Netherdale Caravan & Camping Site
Bridgwater Road, Sidcot, Winscombe, BS25 1NH.
☎ (0934) 843481
Open: March-October
Size: 3½ acres, 25 touring pitches. 4 hot showers,
12 WCs

	🏕	🚐	🅰							🐕

On A38, 1 mile SE of Winscombe.

Rodney Stoke Inn
Rodney Stoke. ☎ (0749) 870209
Open: All year
Size: 3 acres, 41 touring pitches. 3 hot showers,
3 WCs

	🏕	🚐	🅰			☕	✖		🔲	🐕

On A371 midway between Cheddar and Wells.

CHELTENHAM *Gloucestershire*   *Map 2 B2*

Cheltenham Racecourse Caravan Club Site
The Racecourse, Prestbury Park
☎ (0242) 523102
Open: May-October
Size: 7 acres, 84 touring pitches, 22 with elec, part
level, hardstanding. 5 hot showers, 25 WCs, CWP

	🏕	🚐		🅿						🐕

Site well-signposted.

Folly Farm
Notgrove, GL54 3BY. ☎ (0451) 20285
Open: All year
Size: 3 acres, 20 touring pitches. 8 WCs

♿	🏕	🚐	🅰			☕			🔲	🐕

On A436 2½ miles from Bourton-on-the-Water.

Longwillows
Station Road, Woodmancote, GL52 4HN.
☎ (0242) 674113
Open: March-October
Size: 4 acres, 80 touring pitches. 5 hot showers,
11 WCs

♿	🏕	🚐	🅰	🅿		☕	✖			🐕

Site signed from B6432 and signed from A435.

CHESTER *Cheshire*   *Map 4 B2*

Chester Southerly Caravan Park
Balderton Lane, Mariston-cum-Lache, CH4 9LF.
☎ (0244) 671308
Open: March-November
Size: 8 acres, 90 touring pitches. 8 hot showers,
14 WCs

♿	🏕	🚐	🅰	🅿	🔋					🐕

Turn off Chester Southerly by-pass (A55) on to
A483. After 300 yds, turn right into Balderton Lane.

Fairoaks Caravan & Camping Park
Rake Lane, Little Stanney, CH2 4HS.
☎ (051) 355 1600
Open: March-November
Size: 6½ acres, 120 touring pitches. 10 hot
showers, 22 WCs

♿	🏕	🚐	🅰	🅿						🐕

From M53 junction 10, take A5117 W, signposted
Queensferry, signposted to site.

Netherwood House Caravan Site
Whitchurch Road, CH3 6AF.
☎ (0244) 335583
Open: March-October
Size: 1½ acres, 29 touring pitches. 2 hot showers, 3
WCs

	🏕	🚐	🅰							🐕

On A41 (Chester-Whitchurch) about 1 mile from
Chester by-pass. Signposted.

CHESTERFIELD *Derbyshire*   *Map 5 A2*

Mill Field Mobile Home Park
Old Tupton. ☎ (0246) 862296
Open: March-October
Size: 1½ acres, 10 touring pitches. 2 hot showers, 3
WCs

	🏕	🚐	🅰				✖		🔲	🐕

1½ miles N of Clay Cross on A61, at Old Tupton
roundabout, turn W on Ashover road. Turn left
after 1½ miles to site.

CHICHESTER *West Sussex*   *Map 2 B3*

Bell Caravan Park
Bell Lane, Birdham, PO20 7HY.
☎ (0243) 512264
Open: March-October
Size: 7 acres, 13 touring pitches. 4 hot showers,
12 WCs. 50 static caravans

	🏕	🚐								🐕

Due S from Chichester on A286. At Birdham turn
left on to B2198. Site is 350 yards on left hand side.

Goodwood Racecourse Caravan Club Site
☎ (0243) 774486
Open: April-September (restrictions)
Size: 2½ acres, 66 touring pitches, all level, 16 with
elec. 4 hot showers, 26 WCs, CWP

	🏕	🚐	🅰	🅿						🐕

From A286 Midhurst-Chichester, E at Singleton.
Site 1¾ miles.

SOUTHERN LEISURE CENTRE   RAC L
Vinnetrow Road, PO20 6LB.
☎ (0243) 787715
Open: April-October
Size: 5 (200) acres, 300 touring pitches, 20 with
hardstanding. 24 hot showers, 65 WCs, 8 CWPs

	🏕	🚐	🅰	🅿	🔋	☕			🏊	

Charges on application.
*By a lake, this attractive site not only offers boating
and fishing but also water-skiing too. There's a
swimming pool, children's play area and evening
social activities at the site.*
At roundabout junction of A27 (Chichester by-pass)
and A259, 1 mile SE of Chichester, turn into
Vinnetrow Lane for ¼ mile to site. Site signed at
roundabout.

CHIPPING NORTON *Oxfordshire*   *Map 2 B2*

Camping & Caravanning Club Site
Chipping Norton Road, Chadlington, OX7 3PN.
☎ (0608) 41993
Open: 30 March-26 October
Size: 4½ acres, 75 touring pitches. 4 hot showers, 8

🔲 Snacks/take away   ✖ Restaurant   🏊 Swimming pool   🔲 Shelter for campers   🐕 Dogs accepted   27

WCs

☐ 🚐 🚙 🏕 ☐ 💺 ☐ ☐ ☐ ☐ 🐕

Charges on application.
cc Access, Visa/B'card
Level, grassy site sheltered by trees.
Turn off the A361 at the signposts for Chadlington
and the international camping signs.

CHITTERING *Cambridgeshire* Map 3 A1

The Travellers Rest
Ely Road (A10), CB5 9HP. ☎ (0223)860751
Open: March-October
Size: 2 acres, 40 touring pitches. 2 hot showers,
4 WCs showers, 4 WCs

☐ 🚐 🚙 🏕 ☐ ☐ ☕ ✕ ☐ ☐ 🐕

Halfway between Ely and Cambridge on A10.

CHORLEY *Lancashire* Map 4 B2

ROYAL UMPIRE CARAVAN PARK RAC A
Croston, Near Leyland, PR7 5HP.
☎ (0257) 793377
Open: Mid December-Mid November
Size: 11 (60) acres, 125 touring pitches, all level, all
with hardstanding, 99 with elec. 11 hot showers, 24
WCs, 2 CWPs

♿ 🚐 🚙 🏕 ☐ 💺 ☐ ☐ 🎮 🐕

(1991) Car & caravan, Motor caravan, Car & tent,
M/cycle* & tent all £2.60-£3.20 per person, £1.05-
£1.35 per child; elec £1.35-£1.55
cc Access, Visa/B'card
Level, grassed site. Large children's play area.
Indoor games room. Garden area. Information
boards. Eating-out information. 2 restaurants
within 200 yards. Swimming pool 2 miles.

Minimum booking 2 nights, Bank Holidays
3 nights, except Easter which is 4 nights.
From the N, leave M6 at junction 28 and travel S on
the A49 for 2¾ miles, turn right on the A581 to site
in 4 miles.

CHRISTCHURCH *Dorset* Map 2 B3

GROVE FARM MEADOW HOLIDAY PARK RAC L
Stour Way, BH23 2PQ. ☎ (0202) 483597
Open: 1 March-31 October
Size: 2 (10) acres, 48 touring pitches, all level, all
with elec, 1 with hardstanding, 193 static caravans.
7 hot showers, 14 WCs, 1 CWP

☐ 🚐 🚙 ☐ 🗲 💺 💿 ☐ ☐ ☐ ☐

(1991) Car & caravan, Motor caravan £4.50-£10,
plus 50p per person above 2; elec £1.20
cc Access/Mastercard, Visa, Eurocheque
English Tourist Board Rose Award park situated in
lovely rural surroundings on banks of the River
Stour, fishing on the park. British Graded Holiday
Parks graded Excellent. 77 static caravans to hire
(own WCs). Restaurant 1 mile. Swimming pool
2 miles. No single sex parties. No groups.
From Ringwood take A338 S, take Christchurch exit
at about 6 miles. At end of exit road turn left and
then right at first roundabout into St Catherines
Way/River Way, then second right into Stour Way.

Heathfield Caravan & Camp Site
Avon Causeway, Hurn. ☎ (0202) 485208
Open: March-October
Size: 2 acres, 10 touring pitches. 2 WCs

☐ 🚐 🚙 🏕 ☐ ☐ ☐ ☐ ☐ ☐ 🐕

On A338 turn off to Hurn. Follow signs to Avon
Causeway. Site is directly opposite the Causeway
Hotel.

Royal Umpire Caravan Park

This attractive riverside park is full of atmosphere. It is delightfully located near the picturesque and historic village of Croston, and makes an ideal base for a Holiday Break touring the Lake District, Yorkshire Dales, Peak District and the North Wales Coast.

The park comprises of 60 acres of level meadows.

Nearby are Martin Mere Wildfowl Trust, Formby Nature Reserve, and a natural Bird Sanctuary north of Southport – also Camelot at Charnock Richard, Leyland's Commercial Vehicle Museum, Granada's Studio Tour, Science and Technology Museum both in Manchester, Wigan Pier Industrial Heritage Centre and many other places of interest are all close at hand.

We are also situated in between Western Europe's largest tourist attractions; Blackpool's famous Pleasure Beach and Liverpool's famous Royal Albert and Victoria Docks, which house the National Maritime Museum and the Tate of the North Gallery.

A little beyond Southport, yet far beyond comparison.

Situated on the A581 from Chorley to Southport only 4 miles from (M6) Junction 28 and 5 miles from (M6) Junction 27 and (M61) Junction 8, which makes an ideal stopover from the North to the Channel Ports and from the South to Scotland.

The Park facilities include over 100 electric hook-ups, two modern toilet blocks with free hot water for showers, two launderettes, Spar shop, a fun childrens adventure play fort, landscaped gardens, tuition swimming pool adjacent, two superb pubs and restaurants within 100 yards. Minimum facility Rally Area only £2.00 per unit per night for exempt organisations.

Ring or write to: THE PARK MANAGER, THE ROYAL UMPIRE CARAVAN PARK, SOUTHPORT RD (A581), CROSTON, NR. PRESTON, LANCS PR5 7HP.

REDUCTIONS FOR SENIOR CITIZENS STAY & SPECIAL OFFERS FOR OUR LATEST DETAILS RING NOW FOR OUR MID-WEEK STAY

TEL: 0772 600257

Snacks/take away ☒ Restaurant ◺ Swimming pool ▣ Shelter for campers ✦ Dogs accepted

HEATHFIELD CARAVAN PARK
RAC L

Bransgore. ☎ (0425) 72397
Open: March-October
Size: 14 acres, 200 touring pitches, 34 with elec,
200 level pitches. 16 hot showers, 39 WCs, 2 CWPs

☐☐☐☐ ☐☐☐☐☐☐ ☐☐

Charges on application.
Well-appointed site on the edge of the New Forest.
Restaurant 3 miles.
On A35, 8½ miles SW of Lyndhurst and 5¼ miles
NE of Christchurch, turn W as signed
"Godwinscroft, Bransgore, Sopley" and take first
turn right. Site in 500 yards.

Mount Pleasant Touring Park
Matchams Lane, Hurn. ☎ (0202) 475474
Open: March-October
Size: 7 acres, 145 touring pitches. 8 hot showers,
8 WCs

☐☐☐☐☐☐☐☐ ☐☐☐☐

From A338 take Christchurch exit. Turn right at end
of slip road towards Hurn. At roundabout take
second exit then immediately turn left into
Matchams Lane. 1¼ miles on right is site.

CHUDLEIGH *Devon*   Map 1 B3

FINLAKE LEISURE PARK
RAC A

TQ13 0EJ. ☎ (0626) 853833
Open: Easter-end December
Size: 25 (130) acres, 450 touring pitches, 370 with
elec, 390 level pitches, 370 with hardstanding,
40 chalets. 33 hot showers, 80 WCs, 9 CWPs

☐☐☐☐☐☐☐☐☐☐ ☐☐

Charges on application.
cc Access, Visa/B'card
Wooded site with a wide range of facilities
including boating, water slide, golf, tennis, grass-
skiing, fishing and licensed bar. Calor gas only.
From Plymouth, take the A38 towards Exeter, leave
at signpost to Chudleigh Knighton (B3344), site
1½ miles on right.

HOLMANS WOOD TOURIST PARK
RAC A

TQ13 0DZ. ☎ (0626) 853785
Open: March-October
Size: 12 acres, 120 touring pitches, all level, 67 with
elec, 63 with hardstanding. 8 hot showers, 12 WCs,
3 CWPs

☐☐☐☐☐☐☐ ☐☐☐☐

(1991) Car & caravan, Motor caravan £5.25-£8.25,
Car & tent, M/cycle & tent £5.25-£6.25; adult £1.25-
£1.75, child £1; awn £1-£1.50, dogs 75p
cc Major cards
Superb setting on the edge of Dartmoor. Beautiful
countryside, ideal for the touring holidaymaker.
Swift access to Torquay, Plymouth, Exeter and the
South Devon coast. Excellent and modern facilities
on the park. Restaurant ½ mile. Swimming pool
5 miles.
Follow the M5 to Exeter and take the A38 towards
Plymouth. Continue up Haldon Hill past the Exeter
and Devon Racecourse on the left, and down the
other side. About ½ mile on to the left is an exit,
signposted to Chudleigh, next to a garage. The
entrance to Holmans Wood Tourist Park is at the
end of this short slip road on the left.

CHURCH STRETTON *Shropshire*   Map 4 B3

SMALL BATCH SITE
RAC L

Ashes Valley, Little Stretton, SY6 6PW.
☎ (0694) 723358
Open: Easter-30 September
Size: 2 acres, 12 touring pitches, all level. 2 hot
showers, 5 WCs, 1 CWP

☐☐☐☐☐☐☐☐☐☐☐☐

Car & caravan, Motor caravan £5, Car & tent £4.50
Pleasant site in superb walking area. Shop and
restaurant ¼ mile. Swimming pool 2 miles. No gas
available. No motorcycles.
Turn off A49 into Little Stretton, on to B4370. Turn
left at Rogleth Inn - site is ¼ mile to the right.

Spring Bank Farm
62 Shrewsbury Road, SY6 6HB.
☎ (0694) 723570
Open: Easter-September
Size: 12 acres, 3+ touring pitches. 1 WC

☐☐☐☐☐☐☐☐☐☐☐☐

In Church Stretton on A49, site on B4370 bisecting
school playing fields.

Wayside Inn
Marshbrook, SY6 6QE. ☎ (069 46) 208
Open: Easter-October
Size: 3 acres, 5 touring pitches. 3 WCs

☐☐☐☐☐☐☐☐☐☐☐☐

50 yards off A49 in Marshbrook village.

CIRENCESTER *Gloucestershire*   Map 2 B2

COTSWOLD CARAVAN PARK
RAC A

Broadway Lane, South Cerney, GL7 5UQ.
☎ (0285) 860216
Open: Easter-End October
Size: 30 (70) acres, 305 touring pitches, all level, all
with elec, all with hardstanding, 158 static
caravans, 56 chalets. 38 hot showers, 82 WCs,
6 CWPs

☐☐☐☐☐☐☐☐☐☐☐☐

(1991) Car & caravan, Motor caravan £6.50-£13.50,
Car & tent, M/cycle & tent £4.50-£11
cc Only accepted in restaurant
Flat, open site comprising 3 touring fields, static
holiday caravans and timber lodges situated round
3 fishing lakes. 36 caravans and 26 chalets for hire
(own WCs). Prices include electricity and awning.
Minimum stays: May Day Bank Holiday 3 nights
(tourers), other Bank Holidays 4 nights (tourers),
static holiday accommodation 1 week (Saturday to
Saturday).
At 4 miles SE of Cirencester on the A419, turn SW
as signed Cotswold Water Park. Turn right at
second cross-roads after 1½ miles. Site is ¼ mile
on left.

MAYFIELD TOURING PARK
RAC A

Cheltenham Road, Perrotts Brook, GL7 7BH.
☎ (0285) 831301
Open: Easter-31 October
Size: 2 (12) acres, 36 touring pitches, 24 with elec,
22 level pitches, 20 with hardstanding. 4 hot
showers, 4 cold showers, 5 WCs, 1 CWP

☐☐☐☐☐☐☐☐☐☐☐☐

Car & caravan from £5, Motor caravan from £4, Car & tent, M/cycle & tent from £3.50, all low season prices; plus 50p per adult above 2, child 30p; elec £1, awn 75p
The park is situated in an elevated position overlooking the picturesque Churn Valley, an ideal position to tour the Cotswolds. 12 months' licence, 12 acres suitable for rallies and 28 day camping and recreation/sport/games area. Restaurant 5 minutes' walk. Swimming pool 2 miles. No minimum stay. No dogs.
Situated immediately off the main A435 Cirencester to Cheltenham road, 2 miles N of Cirencester, 13 miles S of Cheltenham.

CLACTON-ON-SEA *Essex*   Map 3 B2

SACKETTS GROVE CARAVAN PARK   RAC L
Jaywick Lane. ☎ (0255) 427765
Open: April-October
Size: 10 (26) acres, 220 touring pitches, static caravans. 18 hot showers, 60 WCs

Charges on application.
Level parkland site with swimming pool, clubhouse and children's play area. Caravans for hire.
At 1¼ miles N of Clacton or 1¾ miles S of Little Clacton on A133 turn W at roundabout on to B1027 for 1¼ miles, then turn S into Jaywick Lane for ¾ mile to site.

Tower Caravan Park
Jaywick, CO15 2LF. ☎ (0255) 820372
Open: March-October
Size: 43 acres, 100 touring pitches. 8 hot showers, 10 WCs. 517 static caravans

A133 from Colchester. Take B1027 right at Clacton and turn left into Jaywick Lane for 3 miles.

Weeley Bridge Caravan Park
Weeley. ☎ (0255) 830403
Open: March-October
Size: 10 acres, 250 touring pitches. 4 hot showers, 10 WCs. 25 static caravans

On A133. Site adjoins Weeley Station.

CLAPHAM *North Yorkshire*   Map 4 B1

FLYING HORSESHOE HOTEL CARAVAN SITE   RAC L
LAE 13ES. ☎ (046 85) 229
Open: 1 April-30 November
Size: 2½ acres, 20+ touring pitches, all level, 16 with elec. 4 hot showers, 6 WCs, 1 CWP

Charges on application. WS
This small site has a children's play area and a games room, and is ideally situated for fell-walking and fishing. Shop 1 mile.
At Clapham on the A65, turn S onto an unclassified road, signposted Keasden. Site ¾ mile.

CLEETHORPES *South Humberside*   Map 5 B2

Humberston Fitties
DN36 4HG. ☎ (0472) 813395
Open: April-October

Size: 5 acres, 90 touring pitches. 6 hot showers, 24 WCs. 1250 static caravans, 350 chalets

A1046 takes you north, Sea Lane connects to Anthony's Bank Lane. Site is in front of you.

CLEVEDON *Avon*   Map 2 A2

Warrens Holiday Park
Colehouse Lane. ☎ (0272) 871666
Open: March-January
Size: 14 acres, 75 touring pitches. 6 hot showers, 17 WCs. 54 static caravans

Exit M5 at Junction 20. Follow B3133 towards Congresbury. Right into Colehouse Lane.

CLITHEROE *Lancashire*   Map 4 B2

Camping & Caravanning Club Site
Edisford Bridge, Edisford Road, BB7 3LA. ☎ (0200) 25294
Open: 30 March-26 October
Size: 5.8 acres, 100 touring pitches. 6 hot showers, 14 WCs

Charges on application.
Children's playground. Camping Gaz only. At edge of town.
From Clitheroe take the B6243, the site is on the left just before the River Ribble.

CLOVELLY *Devon*   Map 1 B3

Dyke Green Farm Camping Site
Higher Clovelly. ☎ (0237) 431279
Open: Easter-October
Size: 3½ acres, 25 touring pitches. 2 hot showers, 5 WCs

Site on A39 at B3237 junction to Clovelly. 1½ miles from beach.

CLUN *Shropshire*   Map 4 B3

Bush Farm
Clunton, Craven Arms, SY7 0HU.
☎ (058 87) 330
Open: March-January
Size: 2 acres, 15 touring pitches. 1 hot shower, 3 WCs. 4 static caravans

On B4368 towards Clun, turn left at Crown Inn, Clunton. Cross river, bear left and follow signs to Bush Farm.

COCKERMOUTH *Cumbria*   Map 4 B1

THE BEECHES CARAVAN PARK   RAC L
Gilcrux, Near Aspatria, CA5 2QX.
☎ (069 73) 21555
Open: March-November
Size: ½ (2½) acres, 10 touring pitches, all level, with elec, all with hardstanding, 22 static caravans. 3 hot showers, 6 WCs, 1 CWP

● Snacks/take away   ✕ Restaurant   � Swimming pool   ▥ Shelter for campers   �🐾 Dogs accepted   31

Car & caravan, Motor caravan, Car & tent, M/cycle & tent £6; awn £1, dogs £5 per week
Small, secluded, landscaped, family-owned site with excellent facilities, bistro and bar, regular entertainment in season. 20 static caravans to hire (own WCs). Swimming pool 2 miles. 2 nights minimum stay (for hired caravan).
From Cockermouth, leave as for Maryport on the A594 for 1¾ miles, turn right to Tallantire for 1½ miles. On leaving Tallantire, turn left for 1¼ miles, turn right to Gilcrux, site signposted in village.

VIOLET BANK CARAVAN PARK   RAC L
Simonscales Lane, CA13 9TG.
☎ (0900) 822169
Open: 1 March-15 November
Size: 3 (6) acres, 30 touring pitches, 15 with elec, 6 with hardstanding, 20 level pitches, 79 static caravans. 4 hot showers, 8 WCs, 1 CWP

Charges on application.
Grassy, meadowland site in tranquil rural setting with magnificent views of the Buttermere Fells. Play area. 3 caravans for hire (own WCs). Restaurant and swimming pool 1 mile.
Leave Cockermouth town centre via Lorton Road (B5292), after ½ mile turn W into Vicarage Lane. Site is fifth turning on left - just under ½ mile.

Whinfell Hall Farm
Lorton. ☎ (090 085) 260
Open: Easter-October
Size: 4 acres, 35 touring pitches. 4 hot showers, 10 WCs. 16 static caravans

Take B5292 from Cockermouth for 3 miles. Briefly join B5289, turn right at Lorton Hall, over River Cocker, then left and campsite is about 100 yards.

WYNDHAM HALL CARAVAN PARK   RAC A
Old Keswick Road, CA13 9SF.
☎ (0900) 822571
Open: 1 March-15 November
Size: 4 (12) acres, 40 touring pitches, all level, 17 with elec, 8 with hardstanding, 106 static caravans, 18 chalets. 12 hot showers, 21 WCs, 2 CWPs

(1991) Car & caravan, Motor caravan, Car & tent, M/cycle & tent £4.80, plus 50p per person above 2; elec £1.25, awn 60p, dogs £1; WS
Licensed bar, snooker and pool tables, play area and putting green at this family site. 40 caravans and 18 chalets for hire (own WCs). Restaurant and swimming pool ¼ mile.
Leave A66 at Dubwath, travel W on unclassified road (old A66) for 4½ miles, site on left.

COLCHESTER *Essex*   Map 3 B2

COLCHESTER CAMPING & CARAVAN PARK   RAC A
Cymbeline Way, Lexden, CO3 4AG.
☎ (0206) 45551
Open: All year
Size: 12 acres, 185 touring pitches, 102 with elec, all level pitches, 12 with hardstanding. 8 hot showers, 26 WCs, 3 CWPs

(1991) Car & caravan, Motor caravan, Car & tent £3, all plus £2.30-£2.75 per adult, £1-£2 per child; elec £1.30; WS
cc Major cards
An international site with high standards, well-ordered and tidy. No motorcycles. Maximum stay 14 nights.
Look for tourist signs off A12 for directions via A134 slip road to Colchester.

Mill Farm Camp Site
Harwich Road, Great Bromley, CO7 7JQ.
☎ (0206) 250485
Open: March-October
Size: 3 acres, 20 touring pitches. 2 hot showers, 5 WCs. 23 static caravans

Signed from A120 and from A133 (Colchester), turn left at traffic lights at Elmstead Market. Site on right. Entrance through nursery.

COLEFORD *Gloucestershire*   Map 2 A2

Woodlands View Caravan & Camping Site
Sling. ☎ (0594) 35127
Open: All year
Size: 1½ acres, 20 touring pitches. 4 hot showers, 7 WCs. 5 static caravans

Site is 1½ miles S of Coleford on B4228.

COMBE MARTIN *Devon*   Map 1 B2

SANDAWAY BEACH HOLIDAY PARK   RAC A
Berrynarbor, EX34 9ST. ☎ (0271) 883155/866666
Open: March-October
Size: 1 (2) acres, 23 touring pitches, all level, all with elec, 90 static caravans, 12 chalets. 12 hot showers, 16 WCs, 2 CWPs

Charges on application.
cc Access, Visa/B'card
Beautifully located park with coastal views and private beach. Club and children's play area. 90 caravans and 12 chalets for hire (own WCs).
Site on N side of the A399, 3½ miles W of Ilfracombe, 1¾ miles E of Combe Martin.

CONGLETON *Cheshire*   Map 5 A2

Capesthorne Hall
Macclesfield, SK11 9JY. ☎ (0625) 861221
Open: March-October
Size: 60 acres, 100 touring pitches. 2 hot showers, 8 WCs

Signposted off A34, midway between Congleton and Wilmslow.

CONISTON *Cumbria*   Map 4 B1

Coniston Hall
☎ (05394) 41223
Open: March-October
Size: 20 acres, 150 touring pitches. 12 hot showers, 24 WCs.

⟨15th⟩ Stowford Meadows
Combe Martin, Ilfracombe, Devon

Come and enjoy the spaciousness and freedom Stowford Meadows is renowned for – 450 acres of glorious Devon countryside, all of which is available for you and your family to enjoy. Take the chance to explore the delights of nearby Exmoor National Park or the magnificent North Devon coastline.

We have all the quality facilities you would expect of a first-class family owned park, designed especially for the tourer including: ★ The Old Stable Bars (**FREE**) ★ Barn Dances and Discos in High Season (**FREE**) ★ **HEATED INDOOR POOL** (open Spring Bank Holiday) ★ 4 spacious modern amenity blocks ★ Laundry facilities ★ Games room and pool tables ★ Take-away food and 70 seater cafe ★ 2 full size snooker tables ★ Extensively stocked camp shop ★ Horse Riding ★ 18 Hole Pitch and Putt ★ **Electric Hook-ups: Bookable.** Great for families – Large children's play area, beautiful on-site nature walks and a superb choice of 5 local beaches.

Special New Feature: Discounts at some of North Devon's leading tourist attractions **SAVE £££**

SUPERB VALUE for '92 – e.g. Car, Caravan + 4 people inc. VAT £3.50 to £8.20; electric hook-up £1 to £1.50; Special reductions for over-50s; Awnings **FREE** in low season; pay for a week and **SAVE** £5 in high season.
Summer '92 storage – only £40 incl. VAT.

TEL: (0271) 882476
for free colour brochure

---

1 mile S of Coniston on A593, site signposted.

Croft Caravan & Camping Site
Hawkshead, Ambleside, LA22 0NX.
☎ (09666) 374
Open: March-October
Size: 5 acres, 50 touring pitches. 4 hot showers, 10 WCs. 20 static caravans

In Hawkshead on B5286.

Hawkshead Hall Farm
Hawkshead. ☎ (09666) 221
Open: March-October
Size: 4 acres, 50 touring pitches. 6 hot showers, 5 WCs

5 miles from Ambleside, just before Hawkshead on B5286.

Pier Cottage Caravan Park
LA21 8AJ. ☎ (05394) 41497
Open: March-October
Size: 1 acre, 10 touring pitches. 2 hot showers, 3 WCs

From Coniston take Hawkshead road. ¼ mile turn right over cattle grid. In 350 yards is Pier Cottage. Site signposted from that point.

Waterson Ground Farm
Outgate, Ambleside, LA22 0NJ
☎ (09666) 225

Open: March-Nov (caravans)/Camping all year
Size: 6 acres, 43 touring pitches. 2 hot showers, 5 WCs

4 miles from Ambleside on the right on the road to Hawkshead.

CONSETT *Co Durham* — Map 7 B3

ALLENSFORD CARAVAN PARK ⓡ L
Castleside, DH8 9BA. ☎ (0207) 509522
Open: 1 April-31 October
Size: 14 acres, 20 touring pitches, 38 static caravans. 6 hot showers, 14 WCs, 2 CWPs

Charges on application.
Well-cared-for, grassy site bordered by trees, with children's play area, next to the River Derwent. Restaurant 2 miles.
From Castleside, 2½ miles SW of Consett, travel N on A68 for 1 mile and turn right at Allensford for ¼ mile.

Manor Park Caravan & Camping
Rippon Burn, Castleside, DH8 9HD.
☎ (0207) 501000
Open: Easter/April-October
Size: 7 acres, 35 touring pitches. 4 hot showers, 8 WCs. 10 static caravans

3 miles S of Castleside on A68, turn E for ¾ mile.

Byreside Farm
Hamsterley, NE17 7RT. ☎ (0207) 560280
Open: All year

⬛ Snacks/take away ☒ Restaurant ◻ Swimming pool 🔲 Shelter for campers 🔲 Dogs accepted   33

MANOR PARK

Broadmeadows, Castleside, Consett, Co. Durham   Tel: 0207 501000

A well appointed site in a woodland setting — ideal stop for those visiting beautiful Northumbria. A peaceful, secure and family operated park.

Size: 3 acres, 40 touring pitches. 2 hot showers, 4 WCs

From Consett, head N on A694. Turn off towards Hamsterley. Turn into High Westward.

CORFE CASTLE *Dorset*   Map 2 A3

WOODLAND CAMPING PARK   RAC L
Glebe Farm, Bucknowle, Wareham, BH20 5NS.
☎ (0929) 480280
Open: Easter-31 October
Size: 6½ acres, 65 touring pitches, mostly level.
5 hot showers, 13 WCs, 1 CWP

Car & caravan, Car & tent £7, Motor caravan, M/cycle* & tent, Bicycles & tent £6; plus £1 per child (3-16 yrs), £2.50 per adult above 2; dogs £1
A quiet family site with all essential facilities. Direct access by public footpath to Purbeck Hills. Own riding stables on farm. Bookings not accepted.
Approaching Corfe Castle on A351, turn W for ¾ mile.

COVERACK *Cornwall*   Map 1 A3

LITTLE TREVOTHAN CARAVAN PARK   RAC L
Near Helston, TR12 6SD. ☎ (0326) 280260
Open: March-October
Size: 4½ (10) acres, 25 touring pitches, all level,
4 with elec, 30 static caravans. 6 hot showers,
14 WCs, 1 CWP

Charges on application.
Level, grassy site in rural situation with licensed club, children's playground. 30 caravans for hire. Close to beaches.
Entering Coverack on the B3294, turn right at Zoar Garage, signed Coverack, take third turning on left to site.

Penmarth Campsite
Penmarth Farm, Helston. ☎ (0326) 280389
Open: April-October
Size: 2 acres, 25 touring pitches. 2 hot showers,
4 WCs. 4 static caravans

From Helston past Cold Rose Air Station and Naval Base. Garage on right, take first right and third left.

CRANTOCK *Cornwall*   Map 1 A3

Cottage Farm Tourist Park
Treworgans, Cubert, Newquay
☎ (0637) 830389
Open: Easter-October
Size: 2 acres, 45 touring pitches. 4 hot showers,
6 WCs. 1 static caravan

Follow A3075 S from Newquay. At Rejerrah crossroads turn NW to Cubert. At next t-junction turn N towards Crantock, then site is ¾ mile on your left.

Crantock Plain's Farm
☎ (0637) 830955
Open: May-September
Size: 3 acres, 40 touring pitches. 4 hot showers,
9 WCs

S from Newquay on A3075, take second Crantock right-hand turn. Site in ½ mile.

Quarryfield
☎ (0637) 872792
Open: March-October
Size: 5 acres, 15 touring pitches plus 125 for tents.
12 hot showers, 26 WCs. 6 chalets, 40 static caravans

1½ miles S of Newquay on A3075, turn W to Crantock. Site NW of village.

TREAGO FARM CARAVAN SITE   RAC A
TR8 5QS. ☎ (0637) 830277
Open: April-October
Size: 4 acres, 93 touring pitches, 23 with elec, static caravans, chalets. 10 hot showers, 13 WCs, 1 CWP

Charges on application.
There is a footpath across fields to the beach near this attractive and quiet site. Caravans and chalets for hire (own WCs). Shop open 20 May to 10 Sept.
2 miles S of Newquay on A3075, turn right for 2 miles to Crantock, and continue as signed "West Pentire". Site in ½ mile on left.

Trebellan Tourist Park
Trebellan, Cubert, Newquay
☎ (0637) 830209
Open: Easter-September
Size: 11 acres, 150 touring pitches. 14 hot showers,
14 WCs

4 miles S of Newquay on A3075, turn W for Cubert. In ¾ mile turn left on minor road to Trebellan. Site on left opposite Smuggler's Den Inn.

TREVELLA CARAVAN & CAMPING PARK   RAC A
TR8 5EW. ☎ (0637) 830308
Open: Easter-October
Size: 25 acres, 270 touring pitches, 104 with elec,
36 with hardstanding, 50 static caravans. 18 hot showers, 53 WCs, 2 CWPs

---

🔲 Facilities for Disabled   🔲 Caravans accepted   🔲 Motor caravans   🔲 Tents   🔲 Laundry room   🔲 Shop

TREVELLA NEWPERRAN THE FAMILY RUN HOLIDAY PARKS

TREVELLA PARK
27 CRANTOCK, NEWQUAY, CORNWALL
TR8 5EW.   TEL: 0637 830308

Trevella just outside Newquay and its seven golden beaches. A breathtakingly beautiful secluded family park. As well as touring pitches there are holiday caravans for hire with toilet, shower and colour T.V.

NEWPERRAN TOURIST PARK
27 REJERRAH, NEWQUAY, CORNWALL
TR8 5QJ.   TEL: 0872 572407

Newperran has been developed from a small Cornish farm in a picturesque, beautifully cared for setting. It is a level park with perimeter pitching ideal for caravans, tents, motor homes and the perfect family holiday.

Both parks have spotless facilities inc. modern toilet and shower blocks with individual wash cubicles, razor points, babies room, hairdressing room, hairdriers, launderette, crazy golf, games room, TV room, cafe, shop and off licence, free htd. swimming pools and adventure play areas.
Our reputation for cleanliness friendly and courteous service have earned each park the highest AA rating of 5 pennants and the Top AA Assessment of "Excellent" for Sanitary installations.
*Concessionary green fees at Perranporth's excellent links course.
*The well stocked lake at Trevella offer Free Fishing (no closed season)

TELEPHONE FOR COLOUR BROCHURES **(0637) 830308 24 hr**
OR WRITE FOR BROCHURE TO THE SITE OF YOUR CHOICE

(1991) Car & caravan, Motor caravan, Car & tent, M/cycle* & tent £2.35-£3.95 per person
cc Access, Visa/B'card
Attractive site with own fishing lakes and 5-acre nature reserve, near Crantock beach. Children's play area on site. 50 caravans for hire (own WCs). 2 miles S of Newquay on A3075, turn right signposted Crantock.

CRASTER Northumberland — Map 7 B2

Proctors Stead
NE66 3TF. ☎ (0665) 576613
Open: March-October
Size: 3 acres, 62 touring pitches. 6 hot showers, 9 WCs. 2 static caravans

From A1 take the B1340 for 2 miles and follow signs.

CROMER Norfolk — Map 3 B1

Beeston Regis Caravan & Camping Park
West Runton. ☎ (0263) 823614
Open: March-October
Size: 60 acres, 15 touring pitches. 12 hot showers, 40 WCs

On A149, 1 mile from Sheringham, 3 miles from Cromer.

Camping & Caravanning Club Site
Holgate Lane, West Runton, NR27 9NW.
☎ (0263) 75544
Open: 30 March-26 October

Size: 11.6 acres, 250 touring pitches. 20 hot showers, 30 WCs

Charges on application.
cc Access, Visa/B'card
Secluded site with views of sea. 1 mile from beach. From the A148 take the road opposite the Roman Camp Inn and turn right at the National Trust sign. The site is along this road.

FOREST PARK CARAVAN SITE   RAC A
Northrepps Road, NR27 0JR.
☎ (0263) 513290
Open: Easter/1 April-31 October
Size: 30 (65) acres, 429 touring pitches, 192 with elec, 379 level pitches, all with hardstanding, 272 static caravans. 26 hot showers, 26 cold showers, 60 WCs, 5 CWPs

(1991) Car & caravan, Motor caravan £4.85-£5.63, plus 50p per person above 2, child 50p (over 5 years); elec £1, awn £1
A well-arranged, beautifully-kept site with an indoor swimming pool, licensed clubhouse and children's play area. Dogs must be kept on leads. 28 days maximum stay.
From Cromer on A148, left at traffic lights onto B1159, fork right at Northrepps Road. Site in ½ mile.

Manor Farm Caravan & Camp Site
East Runton, NR27 9PR. ☎ (0263) 512858
Open: Easter-September
Size: 16 acres, 280 touring pitches. 12 hot showers, 48 WCs

A148 SW from Cromer for 1 mile. Right to East

■ Snacks/take away ☒ Restaurant ◠ Swimming pool ▣ Shelter for campers ⊮ Dogs accepted   35

Runton.

Roman Camp Caravan Park
West Runton, NR27 9RD. ☎ (026 375) 256
Open: April-September
Size: ¾ acre, 11 touring pitches. 4 hot showers,
8 WCs. 85 static caravans

[icons]

A149 from Cromer to Sheringham for 2½ miles.
Head S at West Runton on to minor road for 1 mile.

SEACROFT CAMPING & CARAVAN PARK   RAC L
Runton Road, NR11 8TU. ☎ (0263) 511722
Open: March-October
Size: 5 acres, 120 touring pitches, 50 with elec,
10 with hardstanding. 14 hot showers, 30 WCs,
1 CWP

[icons]

Charges on application.
cc Visa/B'card
*A well-managed site with sea views; areas, and
some pitches, divided by shrubs. Field for ball
games, TV lounge, games room, licensed bar and
play area as well as its own swimming pool.
W of Cromer on the A149. Site on left in ½ mile.*

CROWBOROUGH *East Sussex*   Map 3 A3

Camping & Caravanning Club Site
Goldsmith Recreation Ground, TN6 2TN.
☎ (0892) 664827
Open: 30 March-26 October
Size: 13 acres, 60 touring pitches. 4 hot showers,
7 WCs

[icons]

Charges on application.
cc Access, Visa/B'card
*On the edge of Ashdown Forest with an adjoining
leisure centre. Useful overnight stop en route to
Newhaven ferry port. Shop 1 mile.*
Turn off the A26 towards the Leisure Centre, the
site is on the right.

CROYDE BAY *Devon*   Map 1 B2

Bay View Farm
Braunton, EX33 1PN. ☎ (0271) 890501
Open: March-September
Size: 10 acres, 70 touring pitches. 16 hot showers,
13 WCs. 2 static caravans

[icons]

From Braunton take B3231, site on right as you
enter Croyde village.

CROYDE BAY HOLIDAYS   RAC A
Moor Lane, EX33 1NZ. ☎ (0271) 890351
Open: Easter-31 October
Size: 4 (65) acres, 79 touring pitches, all level, all
with elec, 50 static caravans. 18 hot showers,
16 WCs, 3 CWPs

[icons]

(1991) Car & caravan, Motor caravan, Car & tent,
M/cycle & tent from £3.60; plus 60p per adult, 50p
per child (low season prices); elec £1.95; extra car
80p
cc Access, Visa/B'card
The park is situated behind the sandhills in

*65 acres of meadows offering gentle walks, nature
reserve and coarse fishing. Privately owned beach.
WCTB Grade 5 Ticks Excellent and Rose Award for
1992. Swimming pool 300 yards. 50 caravans for
hire (own WCs). Minimum stay 2 nights/tents (high
season only).*
Leave the M5 at Junction 27 and take the new
North Devon link road to Barnstaple. Follow the
A361 Ilfracombe road from Barnstaple and turn left
to Braunton on to the B3231 to Croyde, carry on
through Croyde village, turn left at the bridge then
turn left into Moor Lane, signposted to Croyde Bay,
the site is approximately ¼ mile on the left.

Putsborough Sands Caravan Site
Manor Farm, Putsborough, Georgeham
☎ (0271) 890231
Open: Easter-October
Size: 2 acres, 20 touring pitches. 2 hot showers,
2 WCs

[icons]

On B3231 Braunton to Croyde and Georgeham,
follow signs to Putsborough.

CULLOMPTON *Devon*   Map 1 B2

FOREST GLADE INTERNATIONAL
CARAVAN & CAMPING PARK   RAC A
Kentisbeare, EX15 2DT.
☎ (0404 84) 381
Open: 1 April-End October
Size: 5 (10) acres, 80 touring pitches, all level,
64 with elec, 4 with hardstanding, 37 static
caravans. 10 hot showers, 12 WCs, 1 CWP

[icons]

(1991) Car & caravan, Motor caravan, Car & tent
£7.70, plus £1.35 per person above 2, child 60p;
M/cycle £3; elec £1.50, awn £1, dogs 40p; WS
cc Access, Visa/B'card
*Forest Glade is situated with easy access to most
of the West Country. A quiet park maintained to a
high standard by resident owners. Please book
during school holidays. Indoor heated swimming
pool. 22 caravans for hire (own WCs). Dogs must
be kept on a lead at all times whilst on the park.*
From M5 junction 28, travel E on the A373 for
3 miles, after Keepers Cottage pub take first left
signed Sheldon for 2½ miles to site. (Touring
caravans must book in advance or telephone for
details as to best access route to Forest Glade).

CUMWHITTON *Cumbria*   Map 7 A3

Cairndale Caravan Park
Headsnook. ☎ (076 886) 280
Open: March-October
Size: 2 acres, 5 touring pitches. 2 hot showers,
5 WCs. 4 static caravans

[icons]

On A69 exit at Warwick Bridge, follow signs to
Great Corby and then Cumwhitton. Sign at end of
village to site.

DARSHAM *Suffolk*   Map 3 B1

Haw Wood Caravan Site
Near Saxmundham. ☎ (098 684) 248
Open: Easter-October
Size: 7 acres, 80 touring pitches. 4 hot showers,

9 WCs

☐ 🏕 🚐 ⛺ 🛁 ☐ ☐ ☐ ☐ 🐕

E side of A12, 6 miles N of Saxmundham.

DARTMOUTH *Devon* — Map 1 B3

DEER PARK HOLIDAY ESTATE
RAC A
Stoke Fleming, TQ6 0RF. ☎ (0803) 770253
Open: 1 March-5 November
Size: 14 acres, 160 touring pitches, all level,
100 with elec, 4 static caravans, 4 flats. 16 hot
showers, 20 WCs, 1 CWP

♿ 🚐 🚿 ⛺ 🛁 🛒 ☕ ✕ 🏊 ☐ 🐕

Charges on application. WS
cc Access, Visa/B'card
*We are a family site with an adventure playground,
pub with family room, games room, swimming
pool and sunbathing area. All facilities are free on
site. 4 caravans and 4 flats for hire.
At 2 miles S of Dartmouth on A379, observe bus
stop at site entrance.*

Leonards Cove Holiday Estate
Stoke Fleming, TQ6 0NR. ☎ (0803) 770206
Open: March-October
Size: 1 acres, 10 touring pitches. 8 hot showers,
12 WCs. 80 static caravans

☐ 🏕 🚐 ⛺ 🛁 🛒 ☕ ✕ ☐ ☐ ☐

A379 out of Dartmouth. Site in middle of Stoke
Fleming.

LITTLE COTTON CARAVAN PARK
RAC L
TQ6 0LB. ☎ (080 43) 2558
Open: March-November
Size: 7 acres, 95 touring pitches, 75 with elec. 8 hot
showers, 12 WCs, 2 CWPs

♿ 🏕 🚐 ⛺ 🛁 🛒 ☐ ☐ ☐ 🐕

Charges on application.
*Family-run site near Dartmouth. Restaurant
1½ miles. Swimming pool ½ mile.
On the S side of the B3207, 1¼ miles W of
Dartmouth.*

WOODLAND LEISURE PARK
RAC A
Blackawton, TQ9 7DQ. ☎ (080 421) 598
Open: 15 March-15 November
Size: 8 (60) acres, 80 touring pitches, all level,
60 with elec. 12 hot showers, 12 WCs, 1 CWP

♿ 🚐 🚿 ⛺ 🛁 🛒 ☕ ✕ ☐ 🐕

Charges on application.
*Most attractive modern touring park near to but
separate from extensive leisure park with animals,
wooded nature and action trails, to which resident
campers and caravanners have free entrance.
6 miles S of Totnes on the A361, at Halwell, turn E
on the B3207 for 2½ miles. Site on right.*

DAWLISH *Devon* — Map 1 B3

COFTON FARM CARAVAN & CAMPING PARK RAC A
Starcross, EX6 8RP. ☎ (0626) 890358
Open: Easter-31 October
Size: 16 acres, 450 touring pitches, 300 with elec,
62 static caravans, 5 cottages. 46 hot showers,
97 WCs, 2 CWPs

♿ 🏕 🚿 ⛺ 🛁 🛒 ☕ ✕ 🏊 ☐ 🐕

(1991) Car & caravan £4.60-£7.70, Motor caravan
£4.60- £7.15, Car & tent £4.10-£6.60; 70p-£1.55 per
person above 2, child 70p-£1.35; awn 70p-£1.55,
dogs 70p-£1.35
*Clean and tidy landscaped holiday park in rural
countryside. Short drive to Dawlish Warren beach.
Modern pool complex with "Swan" pub and sun
patio. 62 caravans and 5 cottages for hire (own
WCs). Family groups and mixed couples only. No
all male or female groups. No motorcycles. Dogs
must be kept on a lead.
From Junction 30/M5, follow A379 Dawlish. Park
½ mile on left after Cockwood village and harbour.*

LADY'S MILE TOURING & CAMPING PARK RAC A
EX7 0LX. ☎ (0626) 866986
Open: 16 March-4 November
Size: 7 (16) acres, 400 touring pitches, all level,
300 with elec, 1 static caravan. 35 hot showers,
27 cold showers, 69 WCs, 2 CWPs

♿ 🏕 🚐 ⛺ 🛁 🛒 ☕ ☐ 🏊 ☐ 🐕

(1991) Car & caravan, Car & tent £7.70, Motor
caravan £7.15, plus £1.55 per person above 2, £1.35
child; car £1.55; elec £1.50, awn £1.50, dogs £1.35;
WS
*Clean, well-maintained, friendly holiday park.
Baths with Aquatech whirlpool systems. Water
chute. New adventure fort and children's play area,
completely enclosed, soft white sand for added
safety. Restaurant ¾ mile.
Site on the E side of the A379, 1 mile N of Dawlish.*

DEAL *Kent* — Map 3 B3

Clifford Park Caravans
Thompson Close, Walmer. ☎ (0304) 373373
Open: March-October
Size: 11 acres, 20 touring pitches. 4 hot showers,
5 WCs

☐ 🏕 🚐 ⛺ 🛁 ☐ ☐ ☐ ☐ ☐

From Canterbury, along by-pass to Dover Docks,
up to roundabout on Jubilee Way, turn left on Deal
Road. 4 miles along is site, just past Mill service
station.

Leisurescope Deal Holiday Caravan Park
Golf Road. ☎ (0304) 363332
Open: Easter-October
Size: 2½ acres, 30 touring pitches. 4 hot showers, 4
WCs. 25 static caravans

☐ 🏕 🚐 ☐ ☐ ☐ ☐ ☐ ☐ 🐕

🍴 Snacks/take away ✕ Restaurant 🏊 Swimming pool 🏕 Shelter for campers 🐕 Dogs accepted   37

A258 to Deal, to end of road, turn left at Godwin Road to end of road, turn left into Golf Road, past the golf course.

SUTTON VALE CARAVAN CLUB   RAC L
Sutton-by-Dover. ☎ (0304) 374155
Open: March-October
Size: 2 (6) acres, 20 touring pitches, static caravans, chalets. 8 hot showers, 20 WCs

Charges on application.
A secluded rural site, 3 miles from Deal beach, has a clubhouse and children's play area. Caravans and chalets for hire (own WCs).
From the roundabout, junction of the A2 and A256, proceed N for 30 yards, turn right (Archers Court Road) for 4 miles to site on left.

DELABOLE *Cornwall*   Map 1 A3

PLANET PARK   RAC L
Westdown Road. ☎ (0840) 213361
Open: All year
Size: 3 (3½) acres, 50 touring pitches, 24 with elec, 45 level pitches, 6 static caravans. 4 hot showers, 10 WCs, 1 CWP

(1991) Car & caravan, Motor caravan, Car & tent £4.50- £5.50, M/cycle & small tent £2.50-£3.50, plus £1 per person above 2, child £1 (over 5 years); elec £1.35; WS
Friendly, terraced, well-kept family park on edge of village. 2 miles from the sea. Fantastic views. 6 caravans for hire (own WCs). Shop 200 yards. Restaurant 300 yards.
From the junction of the A395 and A39, travel S for 1½ miles, turn right on unclassified road signed Delabole for 1½ miles to the B3314, travel 2½ miles through village to site on left.

DERBY *Derbyshire*   Map 5 A3

Caravan Club Site
Elvaston Castle Country Park, Borrowash Road, Elvaston, DE7 3EP. ☎ (0332) 573735
Open: April-October
Size: 3 acres, 55 touring pitches. Hot showers, WCs, CWP

From A6, 5 miles SE of Derby, turn N on to B5010 for 1 mile. Turn left for site.

DEVIZES *Wiltshire*   Map 2 B3

Bell Caravan & Camp Site
Andover Road, Lydeway, SN10 3PS.
☎ (0380) 840230
Open: Easter-October
Size: 3 acres, 30 touring pitches. 3 hot showers, 5 WCs

3 miles SE of Devizes on A342 Andover road.

LAKESIDE   RAC A
Rowde, SN10 2LX. ☎ (0380) 722767
Open: 31 March/Easter weekend-31 October
Size: 6 acres, 40 touring pitches, all level, 18 with

elec. 4 hot showers, 8 WCs, 1 CWP

Car & caravan, Motor caravan, Car & tent, M/cycle & tent £6, plus 75p per adult above 2, child 50p; elec £1.50, awn 75p
A rural site surrounding a large, well-stocked spring fed lake set under the Roundway Hills, 1 mile from famous Carnhill Locks. Bike hire available. Restaurant 150 yards. Swimming pool 1 mile.
1 mile NW of Devizes on A342.

Potterne Wick Caravan Park
Potterne. ☎ (0380) 723277
Open: Easter-October
Size: 1¼ acres, 30 touring pitches. 2 hot showers, 5 WCs

On A360, 2½ miles S of Devizes, turn left for Urchfont. Site 250 yards.

DISS *Norfolk*   Map 3 B1

Honeypot Camp & Caravan Park
Wortham. ☎ (037 983) 312
Open: April-October
Size: 3 acres, 32 touring pitches. 2 hot showers, 3 WCs

Entrance to site S side of A143 (Bury St Edmunds to Diss road), 4 miles SW of Diss in Wortham village.

THE WILLOWS CARAVAN & CAMPING PARK   RAC L
Diss Road, IP21 4DH. ☎ (0379) 740271
Open: 1 April-30 September
Size: 4 acres, 30 touring pitches, all level, 14 with elec. 2 hot showers, 7 WCs, 1 CWP

Car & caravan, Motor caravan, Car & tent, M/cycle & tent £4.50, plus 50p per person, 25p child; elec £1, awn 25p
An attractive, quiet and level rural site on bank of River Weaver, part-planted with conifers, part open. Shop and restaurant 400 yards. Swimming pool 1 mile. No groups.
From Scole (junction of A140 and A143), travel W for ¼ mile to site on left, or 1½ miles E of Diss on A143, site on right.

DOLTON *Devon*   Map 1 B2

Dolton Caravan Park
The Square, EX19 8QS. ☎ (080 54) 536
Open: April-September
Size: 2 acres, 25 touring pitches. 2 hot showers, 4 WCs

From B3220, turn opposite Beacon Garage to Dolton. Proceed for 1½ miles and turn right at Union Inn. Follow road and site at rear of Royal Oak public house.

DORCHESTER *Dorset*   Map 2 A3

GIANT'S HEAD CARAVAN & CAMPING PARK   RAC L
Old Sherborne Road, Cerne Abbas, DT2 7TR.

☎ (0300) 341242
Open: Easter-October
Size: 3½ acres, 50 touring pitches, all level, 20 with elec. 2 chalets. 2 hot showers, 2 cold showers, 7 WCs, 1 CWP

Car & caravan, Motor caravan, Car & tent, M/cycle & tent from £3.50, plus £1 per adult above 2, child 50p; elec £1.25, awn 50p, dogs 50p; WS
An ideal position for a motoring holiday - peaceful, rural site with wonderful views. 2 chalets for hire (own WCs). Restaurant 2 miles. Swimming pool 8 miles.
Into Dorchester, avoiding by-pass, at Top o' Town roundabout take Sherborne road. After approx 500 yards fork right at Loders (BP) Garage. Signposted from here. From Cerne Abbas take Buckland Newton road.

Heathfield Park
Crossways, DT2 8BS. ☎ (0305) 852357
Open: March-October
Size: 8½ acres, 160 touring pitches. 10 hot showers, 25 WCs

9 miles E of Dorchester (A35), turn S on B3390 for 5 miles.

Railway Triangle Caravan Site
Poundbury Road, DT1 2PL. ☎ (0305) 268645
Open: All year
Size: ½ acre, 10 touring pitches. 4 hot showers, 6 WCs. 20 static caravans

From town centre head out on Bridport Road, 100 yards on right is Poundbury Road. Site on right after ¼ mile.

Home Farm Camping & Caravan Site
Puncknowle, DT2 9BW. ☎ (0308) 897258
Open: Easter-October
Size: 2 acres, 22 touring pitches. 4 hot showers, 8 WCs. 2 static caravans

Take A35 Dorchester to Bridport, left at beginning of dual carriageway to Little Cheney, then signposted.

DOVER *Kent*   Map 3 B3

HAWTHORN FARM   RAC A
Martin Mill, CT15 5JU. ☎ (0304) 852658

Open: 1 March-31 October
Size: 14 (28) acres, 160 touring pitches, all level, 80 with elec, 156 static caravans. 24 hot showers, 30 WCs, 2 2 CWPs

(1991) Car & caravan, Motor caravan, Car & tent, M/cycle & tent £2.05-£2.55, all plus £2.05-£2.55 per adult, £1-£1.50 per child; elec £1.25; WS
Country site, roomy with lots of trees, mostly flat, overlooking the Kentish Downs. Restaurant 500 yards. Swimming pool 3 miles.
From A2 at top of Dover Hill, turn left towards Deal. Site 1½ miles further on left of road.

DULVERTON *Somerset*   Map 1 B2

Halse Farm
Winsford, Near Minehead. ☎ (064 385) 259
Open: March-October
Size: 3 acres, 24 touring pitches. 1 hot shower, 4 WCs, 1 static caravan

4 miles N of Dulverton on B3223, turn right (NE) to Winsford. Site ¾ mile.

DUNWICH *Suffolk*   Map 3 B1

Cliff House
Minsmere Road, IP17 3DQ. ☎ (072 873) 282
Open: April-October
Size: 30 acres, 120 touring pitches. 11 hot showers, 11 WCs

From A12, 5 miles N of Saxmundham, turn E to Dunwich. Near Dunwich, turn S across Dunwich Heath into Minsmere Road. Site signed.

DURHAM *Co Durham*   Map 7 B3

FINCHALE ABBEY FARM   RAC L
Finchale Abbey, DH1 5SH.
☎ (091) 386 6528
Open: All year
Size: 6 acres, 80 touring pitches, 20 with elec, 20 with hardstanding, 100 static caravans, 3 chalets. 10 hot showers, 4 cold showers, WCs, 2 CWPs

Car & caravan, Motor caravan, Car & tent, M/cycle & tent £6, plus £1 per person above 4; elec £1; WS
Rural site, with a stream, beside Finchale Abbey.

🍴 Snacks/take away   ✖ Restaurant   🏊 Swimming pool   ⛺ Shelter for campers   🐕 Dogs accepted   **39**

Touring pitches in two fields next to the farm. Swimming pools at Durham and Chester-le-Street. From junction of A167 and A691 (NW of Durham), take road to Framwellgate Moor. At 1 mile on, turn right, then ¼ mile further keep right; pass under railway bridge and ¼ mile beyond turn left.

EASINGWOLD North Yorkshire — Map 5 A1

Easingwold Caravan & Camping Park
White House Farm, Thirsk Road, YO6 3NF.
☎ (0347) 21479
Open: March-October
Size: 5 acres, 30 touring pitches. 2 hot showers, 5 WCs

Site on A19, 1¼ miles N of Easingwold.

Hollybrook Caravan Park
Stillington Road, Penny Carr Lane, YO6 3EU.
☎ (0347) 21906
Open: March-December
Size: 2 acres, 30 touring pitches. 4 hot showers, 5 WCs. 1 static caravan

S of Easingwold, turn E off A19 signposted Stillington. Right in ½ mile into farm road.

EASTCHURCH Kent — Map 3 B2

Warden Springs Caravan Park
Warden Point. ☎ (0795) 880216
Open: March-October
Size: 50 acres, 30 touring pitches. 8 hot showers, 1b WCs

M20/M2 exit on to A249. Site on B2231, 2½ miles N of Eastchurch.

ELLESMERE Shropshire — Map 4 B3

FERNWOOD CARAVAN PARK RAC A
Lyneal, SY12 0GF. ☎ (094875) 221
Open: 1 March-30 November
Size: 48 acres, 60 touring pitches, 40 level pitches, 40 with elec, 165 static caravans. 9 hot showers, 20 WCs, 3 CWPs

Car & caravan, Motor caravan £7.30-£8.75; elec £1.75
Country site with a lake, near the Shropshire Union Canal. Children's playground. Calor gas only. Restaurant 1½ miles. Swimming pool 4 miles. From Ellesmere, travel E on the A495 to Welshampton, bear right on the B5063, take first turning right (after crossing the canal) to site on right.

TALBOT CARAVAN PARK RAC L
2 Willow Street
☎ (0691) 622408/622285
Open: Mid March-November
Size: 1 (2) acres, 21 touring pitches, all with elec, 20 level pitches, 20 with hardstanding. 4 hot showers, 6 WCs, 1 CWP

(1991) Car & caravan, Motor caravan, Car & tent,

M/cycle & tent £6.50, extra person per night £1; elec £1.20, awn 50p
cc Access, Amex, Diners, Visa/B'card
Sheltered in a valley with hardstandings on grass, near to town centre, hotels and lake. Calor gas only. Shop 200 yards. Restaurant 400 yards. Swimming pool ½ mile.
N side of the town in Talbot Street.

ESKDALE GREEN Cumbria — Map 4 B1

Fisherground Farm
☎ (09467) 23319
Open: March-November
Size: 3 acres, 30 touring pitches. 6 hot showers, 6 WCs. 5 chalets

From Eskdale Green head towards Hardknott Pass. At King George IV Inn turn left. Site is first on left about 400 yards from the Inn.

Hollins Farm Camp Site
Boot, Holmrook, CA19 1TH. ☎ (09467) 23253
Open: All year
Size: 2½ acres, 35 touring pitches. 2 hot showers, 5 WCs

From A595 head E to Eskdale Green and Beckfoot. Site between Beckfoot and Boot - signposted.

EVERSHOT Dorset — Map 2 A3

Clay Pigeon Caravan Park
Wardon Hill, DT2 9PW. ☎ (0935) 83492
Open: All year
Size: 3¾ acres, 60 touring pitches. 2 hot showers, 6 WCs

On A37 midway between Dorchester and Yeovil.

EVESHAM Hereford & Worcester — Map 2 B2

RANCH CARAVAN PARK RAC A
Honeybourne, WR11 5QG. ☎ (0386) 830744
Open: 1 March-30 November
Size: 8 (48) acres, 120 touring pitches, all level, 96 with elec, 180 static caravans. 10 hot showers, 24 WCs, 2 CWPs

(1991) Car & caravan, Motor caravan £7.20-£9.25, plus 75p-£1 per person; elec £1.75, awn £1.25-£1.50, dogs 75p-£1
This is an established family-run park located in the Vale of Evesham on the edge of the North Cotswolds. The park has the benefits of an outdoor heated swimming pool, a licensed club serving meals and a shop, all exclusive to the park. 4 caravans for hire (own WCs). No motorcycles. No tents. Dogs accepted on a lead. From Evesham travel E on the A44, turn left onto the B4035 to Bretforton. Then turn left to Honeybourne, turn left - site on left in ¼ mile.

WEIR MEADOW HOLIDAY & TOURING PARK RAC L
Lower Leys, WR11 5AB. ☎ (0386) 442417
Open: 1 March-31 October
Size: 5 (10) acres, 100 touring pitches, all level, 45 with elec, 25 static caravans, 3 chalets. 18 hot

🖢 Facilities for Disabled Caravans accepted Motor caravans Tents Laundry room Shop

showers, 18 cold showers, 16 WCs, 1 CWP

Car & caravan, Motor caravan £6.14, plus £1 per person above 2, child £1 (over 5 years); awn £1.20
We are in town centre of Evesham, with own full river frontage of our 10 acres; a level, grassy holiday park. No tents, no motorcycles.
From town centre, leave in easterly direction, on A44, cross old river bridge, then take second left into Burford Road, then left again into Lower Leys, also signposted from the Evesham by-pass.

Yessel Farm
Boston Lane, Charlton. ☎ (0386) 860377
Open: April-October
Size: 20 touring pitches. 6 hot showers, WCs

From A44 take Boston Lane to Charlton. Site along road in corner on double bend.

EXETER *Devon*   Map 1 B3

BARLEY MEADOW CARAVAN & CAMPING PARK   RAC L
Crockernwell, EX6 6NR. ☎ (0647) 21629
Open: 15 March-15 November
Size: 4 acres, 40 touring pitches, all level, 10 with elec, 6 with hardstanding. 4 hot showers, 9 WCs, 1 CWP

Charges on application. WS
Mainly level, grassy site with easy access. Children's play area. Restaurant 75 yards.
From the junction of the M5, A30 and A38 (S of Exeter), proceed on the A30 towards Okehampton. Approximately 10½ miles from the M5, turn left for Cheriton Bishop/Crockernwell, go through Cheriton Bishop to site on left, ½ mile W of Crockernwell.

Haldon Lodge Caravan & Camping Park
Kennford, EX6 7YG. ☎ (0392) 832312
Open: All year
Size: 4½ acres, 75 touring pitches. Hot showers, WCs

From end of M5, take A38 for 1½ miles and turn off at Kennford Services. Pass Anchor Inn and over bridge. Follow Haldon Lodge signs.

KENNFORD INTERNATIONAL CARAVAN PARK   RAC A
Kennford, EX6 7YN. ☎ (0392) 833046
Open: All year
Size: 8 acres, 120 touring pitches, all level, 110 with elec, 22 with hardstanding. 12 hot showers, 47 WCs, 2 CWPs

Car & caravan, Motor caravan, Car & tent, M/cycle & tent from £7, plus £1.30 per person above 2; elec £1.50, awn £1.30, dogs £1
cc Access, Visa/B'card
High quality touring caravan and camping park with all individually-hedged pitches with electric hook-ups and many picnic tables. Excellent touring centre for South Devon, Exeter, Torquay.
1 mile from end of M5 alongside A38 opposite Kennford Service Area.

Rewe Campsite
Heazille Barton. ☎ (0392) 860253
Open: April-October
Size: 4 acres, touring pitches. 2 WCs, CWP

From A396, 6½ miles NE of Exeter, turn E for ¼ mile.

SPRINGFIELD HOLIDAY PARK   RAC A
Tedburn Road, Tedburn St Mary, EX6 6EW.
☎ (0647) 24242
Open: 16 March-31 October
Size: 8 (9) acres, 88 touring pitches, 62 with elec, 78 level pitches, 16 with hardstanding, 12 static caravans. 8 hot showers, 8 cold showers, 20 WCs, 2 CWPs

Car & caravan £5.65, Motor caravan £5.10, Car & tent £3.60, M/cycle & tent £4.65, plus £1.55 per adult above 2, child £1.05; elec £1.55, awn £1.55, dogs £1.05; WS
British Tourist Board Graded park - 5 Ticks and Rose Award 1991. Set in beautiful, peaceful countryside. Centrally located and adjacent to Dartmoor National Park. Beaches 30 minutes. Sparkling toilets/showers, separate cubicles. 6 8-6-4-berth holiday caravans for hire (own WCs). Restaurant 200 yards.
From junction 31 of M5, A30 and A38 (S of Exeter), proceed on the A30 towards Okehampton. At second signpost for Tedburn St Mary, approx 10½ miles from the M5, turn right to roundabout, then left, site signposted on right through village.

CLIFFORD BRIDGE PARK   RAC A
Clifford, Drewsteignton, EX6 6QE. ☎ (0647) 24226
Open: Easter-30 September
Size: 6 acres, 24+ touring pitches, 18 with elec, all level, 3 static caravans, 2 chalets. 6 hot showers, 10 WCs, 1 CWP

Car & caravan from £6.20, Motor caravan from £5.50, Car & tent, M/cycle & tent from £5; £1.35 per adult above 2, child £1.10; elec £1.25, awn £1.20, dogs 50p; WS
Clifford Bridge is a small and level park within the Dartmoor National Park, surrounded by woodland and bordered by the River Teign. The Gorge is noted for its superb viewpoints and magnificent woodland tracks. 3 caravans for hire.
From the junction of the M5, A30 and A38 (S of Exeter), proceed on the A30 towards Okehampton. Approximately 10½ miles from the M5 turn left for Cheriton Bishop/Crockernwell. At the Old Thatch Inn turn left for Clifford Bridge, at cross-roads (1¾ miles) turn right to site in 1 mile.

EXFORD *Somerset*   Map 1 B2

Downscombe Farm
☎ (064 383) 239
Open: All year
Size: 3 acres, 35 touring pitches. 2 hot showers, 6 WCs

From B3223 in Exford, take Porlock road but keep to left, past Post Office then fork left and site is within ½ mile.

◼ Snacks/take away   ☒ Restaurant   ◹ Swimming pool   ▣ Shelter for campers   🐾 Dogs accepted   **41**

WESTERMILL FARM RAC L
TA24 7NJ. ☎ (064 383) 238
Open: 1 May-31 October
Size: 6 acres, 60 touring pitches, all level, 6 chalets.
6 hot showers, 10 WCs, 1 CWP

Charges on application.
In a lovely setting by the River Exe, this sheltered site offers fishing, bathing and paddling. 6 chalets for hire (own WCs). Restaurant 2½ miles.
Leave the B3224 at Exford onto the Porlock road. After ¼ mile fork left. Fork left in 2½ miles at site sign.

EXMOUTH *Devon* Map 1 B3

DEVON CLIFFS HOLIDAY PARK RAC A
Sandy Bay, EX8 5BT. ☎ (0395) 265333
Open: Easter-Mid October
Size: 143 acres, 200 touring pitches, 50 with elec, 1728 static caravans, 143 chalets. 11 hot showers, 11 cold showers, 47 WCs

(1991) Car & caravan, Motor caravan, Car & tent
£12.00- £16.00
cc Access, Visa/B'card
Large park situated on the cliff top, overlooking Sandy Bay. 428 caravans and 143 chalets for hire (own WCs). No motorcycles. No under 21s. No all male or all female groups.
Turn off the M5 at Exit 30 and take the A376 for Exmouth. At Exmouth follow the signs to Sandy Bay.

Webbers Farm Caravan Park
Castle Lane, Woodbury, EX5 1EA.
☎ (0395) 32276
Open: Easter-September
Size: 7½ acres, 85 touring pitches. 12 hot showers, 13 WCs

From M5 junction 30 take A376 towards Exmouth. After 1¼ miles, left on B3179 to Woodbury. Left at village crossroads. Follow signs.

FAKENHAM *Norfolk* Map 3 B1

CROSSWAYS CARAVAN SITE RAC L
Holt Road, Little Snoring, NR21 0AX.
☎ (0328) 878335
Open: All year
Size: 1¾ acres, 25 touring pitches, all level, 12 with elec, 12 with hardstanding. 2 hot showers, 7 WCs, 1 CWP

(1991) Car & caravan, Motor caravan £4.75; elec £1.20, awn 50p
This simple little rural site is of level grass surrounded by trees. Restaurant 1 mile. Swimming pool 3 miles.
3 miles NE of Fakenham on A148.

FAKENHAM RACECOURSE RAC L
NR21 7NY. ☎ (0328) 862388
Open: Good Friday-1st week in October
Size: 11.4 acres, 150 touring pitches, all level, all with hardstanding, 106 with elec. 9 hot showers, 33 WCs, 3 CWPs

(1991) Car & caravan, Motor caravan, Car & tent, M/cycle & tent £1-£2; all plus £1.85-£2.25 per adult, 85p-£1.05 per child; elec £1-£1.20; extra car £1; WS
Grassy, sheltered site with all modern facilities. Excellently maintained, ideally situated for touring north and west Norfolk. Swimming pools 1 and 13 miles. No minimum stay.
Travel S from Fakenham on the A1065 for 1 mile to Hempton. Turn E for ¼ mile, turn S on the B1146 for 400 yards, entrance to racecourse on left.

FALMOUTH *Cornwall* Map 3 B1

MENALLACK FARM RAC L
Treverva, Penryn, TR10 9BP. ☎ (0326) 40333
Open: Easter-31 October
Size: 1½ acres, 30 touring pitches, 15 level pitches, 2 with elec. 2 hot showers, 6 WCs, 1 CWP

(1991) Car & caravan, Motor caravan, Car & tent, M/cycle & tent £2.30, all plus £1 per adult, 70p child (under 15 years); elec £1, awn 50p, dogs 30p
Peaceful, 30-pitch touring site with lovely views over rolling, wooded countryside of the Helford Conservation Area. Restaurant 3 miles. Swimming pool 4 miles.
Leave A39 at double roundabouts, go towards Helston (A394) to next roundabouts, go straight across first one, take second exit from second (to Argal Reservoir). In Mabe Burnthouse, over slightly staggered crossroads, follow road for 2 miles to next crossroads. Turn right towards Gweek, through Lamanva and Treverva, but not Constantine. Site ¾ mile beyond Treverva on left.

Pennance Mill Farm
Maenporth, TR11 5HJ. ☎ (0326) 312616
Open: Easter-October
Size: 4 acres, 50 touring pitches. 4 hot showers, 6 WCs. 4 static caravans

From A39 follow international camping signs into Falmouth, turn right at second mini roundabout. Head to Swanpool Beach. Site on left at bottom of hill.

Tregedna Farm Camp Site
Maenporth, TR11 5HL. ☎ (0326) 250529
Open: April-September
Size: 10 acres, 40 touring pitches. 4 hot showers, 8 WCs

From A39 Truro to Falmouth, right at Kimberley Park traffic lights. Past Hospital to t-junction. Turn left and continue for 2½ miles towards Maenporth. Site on right.

Tremorrah Camping Site
Swanpool, TR11 5BE. ☎ (0326) 312103
Open: May-October
Size: 3 acres, 75 touring pitches. 4 hot showers, 13 WCs

1½ miles SW of Falmouth. Site signed.

FANGFOSS North Yorkshire — Map 5 A1

Fangfoss Old Station Caravan Park
YO4 5QB. ☎ (075 95) 491
Open: March-October
Size: 4 acres, 45 touring pitches. 6 hot showers,
9 WCs

From York, turn left off A1079 at Wilberfoss, then
second left into minor road signposted Fangfoss.
Site 1½ miles.

FARNHAM Surrey — Map 2 B3

Tilford Touring
Tilford. ☎ (025 125) 3296
Open: All year
Size: 4 acres, 80 touring pitches. 2 hot showers,
6 WCs

Leave Farnham by-pass, go S over Farnham level
crossing, fork right immediately, proceed to Tilford
and ask for Duke of Cambridge pub. Site is down
lane beside pub.

FAVERSHAM Kent — Map 3 B3

Painters Farm Caravan & Camping Site
Painters Forstal, Ospringe
☎ (0795) 532995
Open: March-October
Size: 2 acres, 50 touring pitches. 4 hot showers,
8 WCs

On A2 turn S at Faversham/Ospringe. Signposted
from A2 and Painters Forstal.

FELIXSTOWE Suffolk — Map 3 B2

PEEWIT CARAVAN PARK   RAC A
Walton Avenue, IP11 8HB. ☎ (0394) 284511
Open: 1 April-31 October
Size: 3 (13) acres, 65 touring pitches, 22 with elec,
220 static caravans. 24 hot showers, 24 WCs,
1 CWP

Car & caravan, Motor caravan, Car & tent, M/cycle
& tent £3.50-£7.25, plus 50p per person (children
under 10 free); elec £1
*Well-established, tree-lined, level, sheltered, quiet
site under the personal supervision of the owners.
Very convenient for continental ferries.
Motorcycles admitted if quiet. Restaurant ¼ mile.
Swimming pool ½ mile. 10 caravans for hire (own
WCs). 3 weeks minimum stay in most cases.*
Site SW of town centre on NE side of Walton
Avenue (A45).

SUFFOLK SANDS HOLIDAY PARK   RAC A
Carr Road, IP11 8TS. ☎ (0394) 273434
Open: Easter-October
Size: 27 acres, 36 touring pitches, all level, all with
elec, 21 static caravans. 12 hot showers, 15 WCs,
1 CWP

(1991) Car & caravan, Motor caravan, Car & tent,
M/cycle & tent £5;£8; elec £2, dogs £2

cc Visa/B'card
*Large site close to shoreline, with children's play
area, evening entertainment, bar and billiards.
21 caravans for hire (own WCs). Restaurant 1 mile.
Swimming pool ½ mile. Calor gas only.*
From Ipswich take the A45 towards Felixstowe, for
5 miles to roundabout, turn right, on for 2 miles to
second roundabout, turn left, then right at traffic
lights. Site in ¾ mile.

FILEY North Yorkshire — Map 5 B1

BLUE DOLPHIN HOLIDAY PARK   RAC A
Gristhorpe Bay, YO14 9PU.
☎ (0723) 515155
Open: Easter-End September
Size: 12 (87) acres, 400 touring pitches, 60 with
elec, 100 level pitches, 800 static caravans,
99 chalets. 15 hot showers, 39 WCs, 3 CWPs

(1991) Car & caravan, Motor caravan, Car & tent
£7-£8- £11; elec £3, dogs £2
*Family holiday park with entertainment venues,
bars, food court, amusements, facilities for all the
family. 280 caravans and 99 chalets for hire (own
WCs). Restaurant 1 mile. No motorcycles.*
On the A165 between Scarborough and Filey,
signposted from main road.

CROWS NEST CARAVAN PARK   RAC A
Gristhorpe, YO14 9PS. ☎ (0723) 582206
Open: 1 March-31 October
Size: 6 (20) acres, 40 touring pitches, all level,
40 with elec, 230 static
caravans. 12 hot showers, 20 WCs, 1 CWP

Charges on application.
*A well-maintained, modern site close to the coast.
Bar and games room; children's play area.
Caravans for hire (own WCs). Restaurant ½ mile.*
2¼ miles NW of Filey, 5 miles SE of Scarborough
on A165.

FILEY BRIGG TOURING CARAVAN SITE   RAC A
☎ (0723) 366212
Open: April-October
Size: 9 acres, 140 touring pitches, all level, all with
hardstanding, 36 with elec. 10 hot showers,
16 WCs, 2 CWPs

Charges on application.
cc Access, Visa/B'card
*The site is part of Filey Country Park and has
access to Filey Bay. Swimming, boating, fishing,
tennis and miniature golf all on site. Restaurant
½ mile.*
Enter Filey on A1039, turning N into Church Cliff
Drive.

FLOWER OF MAY CARAVAN PARK   RAC A
Lebberston Cliff, YO11 3NU.
☎ (0723) 582324/584311
Open: Easter-September
Size: 13 acres, 300 touring pitches, all level, all with
elec, all with hardstanding, 194 static caravans.
24 hot showers, 63 WCs, 3 CWPs

Car & caravan, Motor caravan, Car & tent £5.30-

▣ Snacks/take away ☒ Restaurant ◹ Swimming pool ▣ Shelter for campers 🐾 Dogs accepted   43

Widely acclaimed as one of the best privately owned holiday parks in the country, the Flower of May is constantly updated to provide the most comprehensive facilities, right on the coast between Scarborough and Filey.
* Indoor Heated Swimming Pool
* Lounge Bar and Family Lounge
* Children's safety play area
* Games Room * Self Service Shop * Fish and Chip Shop
* Cafe * Special terms early and late season – ask for details*

the happy family holiday park

Please send for colour brochure from the resident proprietors:
Mr & Mrs J. G. Atkinson, Dept. E, Flower of May, Lebberston Cliff, Scarborough YO11 3NU.
Telephone (0723) 584311

£8.65; 6-7 berth static caravan £95.70-£310.75 per week; elec £1.50, awn £1.15
Acclaimed as one of th? *best privately-owned holiday parks in the country, The Flower of May provides the most comprehensive facilities, right on the coast between Scarborough and Filey. ETB 5 Ticks and Rose Award park. 194 caravans for hire (own WCs). No single- sex groups, no unaccompanied under-18s, no motorcycles. 2¼ miles NW of Filey, 5 miles SE of Scarborough on the A165, turn left then turn NE to site.*

Lebberston Touring Caravan Park
Home Farm, Lebberston, YO11 3PF.
☎ (0723) 582254
Open: May-September
Size: 7½ acres, 125 touring pitches. 8 hot showers, 24 WCs

From A64 or A165, take B1261 to Lebberston. Site signed.

PRIMROSE VALLEY HOLIDAY PARK RĀC A
YO14 9RF. ☎ (0723) 513771
Open: Easter-October
Size: 145 acres, 45 touring pitches, all level, all with elec, 190 static caravans. 12 hot showers, 12 cold showers, 12 WCs, 1 CWP

Charges on application.
Large family holiday park with organised entertainments. Extensive facilities and amenities. 50 yards from beach. Calor gas only. 190 caravans and 194 chalets for hire (own WCs).
Turn E off the A165 2 miles S of Filey. Site signposted.

Orchard Farm Holiday Village
Hunmanby, YO14 0PU. ☎ (0723) 891582
Open: March-October
Size: 14 acres, 85 touring pitches plus 30 for tents. 8 hot showers, 12 WCs. 6 static caravans, 8 cottages

Just off the A165 main Bridlington to Scarborough road then signposted.

FOLKESTONE *Kent* Map 3 B3

BLACK HORSE FARM CARAVAN & CAMPING PARK RĀC L
Canterbury Road, Densole-Swingfield, Hawkinge,

CT18 7BG.
☎ (030 389) 2665
Open: All year
Size: 2 acres, 30 touring pitches, all level, 10 with elec, 2 with hardstanding. 2 hot showers, 5 WCs, 1 CWP

(1991) Car & caravan, Motor caravan, Car & tent £1.90, M/cycle & tent £1.65; all plus £1.15 per adult, 55p per child; elec £1.15, awn 60p, dogs 55p; WS
Ideal base for exploring east Kent and Canterbury or stopover for Channel ports of Dover or Folkestone. Shop 50 metres: directly opposite park entrance. Swimming pool 4 miles. Pub food available 150 metres.
From Folkestone, travel N on A260 for 3½ miles to Densole, site on left, halfway between Black Horse Inn and Esso filling station on right.

Camping & Caravanning Club Site
The Warren, CT19 6PT. ☎ (0303) 55093
Open: 30 March-28 September
Size: 4 acres, 82 touring pitches. 6 hot showers, 17 WCs

Charges on application.
cc Access, Visa/B'card
Convenient for the coast, this site is only 1½ miles from the town centre.
From the A20 follow the Folkestone Harbour signs and then the international camping signs.

Little Satmar Holiday Park
Winehouse Lane, Capel-le-Ferne, CT18 7JF.
☎ (0303) 51188
Open: Easter-October
Size: 4 (9) acres, 64 touring pitches. Hot showers, WCs

From Folkestone, A20 to Dover through Capel-le-Ferne. Site in lane opposite petrol station.

LITTLE SWITZERLAND CARAVAN SITE RĀC L
Wear Bay Road. ☎ (0303) 52168
Open: March-October
Size: 18 touring pitches, 16 with hardstanding, 15 static caravans. 4 hot showers, 13 WCs, 1 CWP

Charges on application.
Quiet site in the cliffs East of town with magnificent views of Dover straits. Calor gas only.

 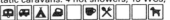

Shop 500 yards. Swimming pool 1½ miles.
From the end of the M20 travel E on the
A20 straight over first 2 roundabouts. At third
roundabout at foot of Folkestone Hill turn right
along A2033 (Hill Road), then ½ mile S further
continue ahead into Wear Bay Road for ¼ mile, site
on left. (Entrance to site is between Hollands
Avenue and the Martello Tower.)

White Cliffs Carapark
Capel-le-Ferne, CT18 7HY. ☎ (0303) 50192
Open: May-September
Size: 6½ acres, 100 touring pitches. 4 hot showers,
6 WCs. 46 static caravans

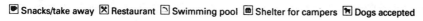

Site on N side of A20 between Dover and
Folkestone.

FOLKINGHAM *Lincolnshire*   Map 5 B3

LOW FARM CARAVAN TOURING PARK   RÁC A
Spring Lane, NG34 0SJ. ☎ (052 97) 322
Open: March 31/Easter-mid October
Size: 1½ acres, 18 touring pitches, all level, 12 with
elec. 4 hot showers, 6 WCs, 1 CWP

Car & caravan, Motor caravan, Car & tent £6, plus
£2 per person above 2; elec £1, awn £1
cc Some cards accepted
*Folkingham village is a conservation area. The
camp is well away from the main road. There is a
Post Office and general store in village and also
several places for eating out. Many places of
interest to visit. Peaceful camp in countryside. No
children except by special arrangement with
proprietor: it is a quiet camp for those wanting
absolute peace. No gas available.*
By A52 and then by A15 from Grantham area. By
A15 from N and also from S.

FORDINGBRIDGE *Hampshire*   Map 2 B3

NEW FOREST COUNTY HOLIDAYS   RÁC A
Sandy Balls Estate, Godshill, SP6 2JZ.
☎ (0425) 653042
Open: All year
Size: 15 (30) acres, 350 touring pitches, 300 level
pitches, 180 with elec, 30 with hardstanding,
200 static caravans (50 for hire), 42 chalets (40 for
hire). 30 hot showers, 60 WCs, 9 CWPs

Car & caravan, Motor caravan, Car & tent, M/cycle

& tent £8.50, plus £1.25 per person, 50p per child;
elec £1.50, awn 50p, dogs £1
*Beautiful wooded park with very a high standard of
facilities, all of which are open throughout the
year. New licensed bar and lounge opened July
1991 serving food and drinks. "Super Pitch"
standard due for 1992 season. New activity centre
for adults and children, including conference
seating for up to 150 delegates (lodge
accommodation). Large supermarket.*
From M27 Cadnam take B3078 to Fordingbridge.
From A338 Fordingbridge take B3078 Cadnam.
9 miles from motorway.

FOREST OF DEAN *Gloucestershire*   Map 2 A2

CHRISTCHURCH   RÁC A
Forestry Commission. ☎ (0594) 33376
Open: March-October
Size: 67 acres, 1300 touring pitches, 450 level
pitches, 72 with elec, 100 with hardstanding. 32 hot
showers, 67 WCs, 18 CWPs

Charges on application. WS
Attractive, wooded site. Restaurant ½ mile.
From the junction of the A4138 and B4228, N of
Coleford, travel N on the B4228 for ½ mile, turn left
and follow signs to site.

FOWEY *Cornwall*   Map 3 A1

Higher Lampetho Farm
☎ (072 683) 3247
Open: May-October
Size: 2 acres, 20 touring pitches. 4 hot showers,
6 WCs

1¾ miles NW of Fowey on A3082.

Penhale Caravan & Camping Site
☎ (072 683) 3425
Open: April-October
Size: 8½ acres, 94 touring pitches. 9 hot showers,
16 WCs. 16 static caravans

Next to coast road on A3082. Signed.

Polruan Holiday Centre
Polruan. ☎ (0726) 870263
Open: March-October
Size: 3 acres, 7 touring caravan pitches, 25 tent
pitches. 2 hot showers, 5 WCs. 11 static caravans

■ Snacks/take away ✖ Restaurant ◿ Swimming pool ▣ Shelter for campers ⛊ Dogs accepted

⬚ 🚐 🚙 ⛺ 🧺 ⬚ ⬚ ⬚ 🐕

A38 (W) left on to A390, continue to East Taphouse, turn left past petrol station. Follow signs to Polruan.

GARSTANG Lancashire — Map 4 B2

BRIDGE HOUSE MARINA & CARAVAN PARK RAC A
Nateby Crossing Lane, Nateby, PR3 0JJ.
☎ (0995) 603207
Open: March-October
Size: 5 acres, 50 touring pitches, all level, all with elec, 20 static caravans. 7 hot showers, 12 WCs, 1 CWP

⬚ 🚐 🚙 ⬚ 🧺 🛍 ⬚ ⬚ ⬚ 🐕

Car & caravan, Motor caravan £4.50; elec £1, awn 75p; WS
An attractive, level, sheltered, grassy site with children's play area, adjoining the canal. Boating and fishing nearby. Restaurant 300 yards. Swimming pool 1 mile. No motorcycles.
From the Chequered Flag Hotel (on the A6 W of Garstang), travel W along Longmoor Lane then turn right into Nateby Crossing Lane to site.

CLAYLANDS CARAVAN PARK RAC A
Claylands Farm, Cabus, PR3 1AJ.
☎ (0524) 791242
Open: March-August
Size: 6 (10) acres, 64 touring pitches, all level, 40 with elec, 10 with hardstanding, 22 static caravans. 5 hot showers, 5 cold showers, 1 CWP

🦽 🚐 🚙 ⛺ 🧺 🛍 ☕ ✕ ⬚ 🐕

Charges on application.
Quiet riverside site in wooded setting, with children's play area and clubhouse.
At 1¼ miles N of junction of the A6 and B6430 (N of Garstang), turn E off the A6 to site in ¼ mile.

Meadowcroft Caravan Park
Garstang Road, Little Eccleston, PR3 0ZQ.
☎ (0995) 70266
Open: March-October
Size: 2 acres, 4 touring pitches. 2 hot showers, 5 WCs. 40 static caravans

⬚ 🚐 🚙 ⬚ 🧺 ⬚ ⬚ ⬚ 🐕

From M6 junction 32, take A6 until A586 signposted Blackpool. Site 5½ miles, on left of A586.

SIX ARCHES CARAVAN PARK RAC L
Scorton, PR3 1AL. ☎ (0524) 791683
Open: 1 March-31 October
Size: 13 acres, 16 touring pitches, all level, all with elec, elec, all with hardstanding, 275 static caravans, 6 chalets. 5 hot showers, 11 WCs

⬚ 🚐 🚙 ⛺ 🧺 🛍 ⬚ ⬚ ↘ 🐕

(1991) Car & caravan, Motor caravan £6.75 inclusive
Situated just off the main A6 within easy reach of Blackpool, Morecambe and the Lake District. Offering family holidays at an affordable price. 50 caravans and 6 chalets for hire (own WCs). Calor gas only. Restaurant 500 yards. No motorcycles.
At 1¾ miles N of junction of A6 and B6430 (N of Garstang) turn E off A6 by Little Chef for 200 yards,

then turn left and pass under railway bridge to site.

GEDNEY BROADGATE Lincolnshire — Map 5 B3

LAUREL PARK RAC L
Huntsgate, Near Spalding, PE12 0DJ.
☎ (0406) 364369
Open: 1 April-31 December
Size: 15 touring pitches, all level. 2 hot showers, 3 WCs, 2 CWPs

⬚ 🚐 🚙 ⛺ 🧺 ⬚ ⬚ ⬚ 🏪 🐕

(1991) Adult £1.75, child £1 (12-18 years), under 12s free, fully inclusive (minimum charge £3)
Secluded, very conveniently situated for visitors wishing to see sights in north Norfolk, Lincolnshire and Cambridgeshire. Very popular, especially during May (Flower Festival time). Shop and restaurant 1½ miles. Swimming pool 11 miles. No minimum stay.
From the main A17 trunk road at Gedney take the road from the roundabout that is signposted "Gedney Hill". Signs for Laurel Park are on roundabout and also elsewhere en route from roundabout directly to site.

GISBURN Lancashire — Map 5 A2

Todber Caravan Park
BB7 4JJ. ☎ (0200) 445322
Open: March-October
Size: 25 acres, 100 touring pitches. 8 hot showers, 15 WCs

⬚ 🚐 🚙 ⛺ 🧺 🛍 ⬚ ⬚ 🏪 🐕

Site is 1½ miles S of Gisburn on the A682.

TWYN GHYLL CARAVAN PARK RAC A
Buck House, Paythorne, BB7 4JD.
☎ (0200) 445465
Open: 1 March-31 October
Size: 3 (16) acres, 42 touring pitches, all with elec, all with hardstanding, 28 level pitches. 208 static caravans. 5 hot showers, 6 WCs, 1 CWP

⬚ 🚐 🚙 ⬚ 🧺 🛍 ⬚ ⬚ ⬚ 🐕

Car & caravan, Motor caravan £8, includes 1 car, occupants, elec, awn
Peaceful park in Ribble Valley, on the edge of the Yorkshire Dales. Hair salon (unisex) and solarium on park. Restaurant 200 yards. Swimming pool 7 miles. No tents. No motorcycles. Calor gas only.
From Gisburn, travel N on A682 for almost 1¾ miles, turn left to Paythorne (¾ mile) to site on left.

GLASTONBURY Somerset — Map 2 A3

ASHWELL FARM RAC L
Ashwell Lane, BA6 8LB. ☎ (0458) 32313
Open: All year
Size: 4 acres, 46 touring pitches, 11 with elec, 8 level pitches. 2 hot showers, 8 WCs, 1 CWP

⬚ 🚐 🚙 ⛺ ⬚ ⬚ ⬚ ⬚ 🏪 🐕

(1991) Car & caravan, Motor caravan, Car & tent, M/cycle & tent all £2.50 per adult, £1.20 per child; awn £1
Attractive rural site with panoramic views, and in the lee of Glastonbury Tor. Shop and restaurant 1 mile. Swimming pool 3 miles.
From the centre of Glastonbury, take the A361 E for

1 mile, then turn left into Ashwell Lane for site.

ISLE OF AVALON TOURING CARAVAN PARK RAC A
Godney Road, BA6 9AF. ☎ (0458) 33618
Open: 1 March-31 October
Size: 6 (8) acres, 120 touring pitches, all level,
58 with elec, 58 with hardstanding. 12 hot showers,
17 WCs, 2 CWPs

Charges on application.
*Quiet, family-run site, well-landscaped with
individual pitches, beside river. Excellent facilities
including special self-contained units for disabled
people. Children's play area. Families and couples
only. Shop 400 yards. Swimming pool 3 miles.
From centre of Glastonbury (Market Cross), travel
NW along the B3151 for ½ mile, turn right, signed
Godney, for 100 yards to site on left.*

OLD OAKS TOURING PARK   RAC A
Wick Farm, Wick, BA6 8JS. ☎ (0458) 31437
Open: 1 March-30 October
Size: 4 acres, 40 touring pitches, 24 with elec,
20 level pitches, 14 with hardstanding. 6 hot
showers, 9 WCs, 2 CWPs

Car & caravan, Motor caravan, Car & tent, M/cycle
& tent £1.50-£2.50; all plus £1.50 per adult, £1 per
child; elec £1.25, awn 50p-£1
*Small, friendly park nestled ¾ mile NE of the
Glastonbury Tor in tranquil, unspoilt countryside
with beautiful views and walks and private coarse
fishing. Pets corner/farm animals. Restaurant
3 miles.*
Take the A361 NE from Glastonbury, after 1 mile
turn left signposted Wick. Follow caravan site
signs.

GLOUCESTER *Gloucestershire*   Map 2 A2

GABLES FARM CARAVAN & CAMP SITE   RAC L
Moreton Valence, GL2 7ND.
☎ (0452) 720331
Open: All year
Size: 3 (4) acres, 20 touring pitches, 9 with elec, all
level, 3 with hardstanding. 4 hot showers, 5 WCs, 1
CWP

Car & caravan £3.50-£4, Motor caravan, M/cycle &
tent £3.20-£3.50, Car 75p-£1, Tent 75p-£1; plus 30p-
50p per person, elec £1-£1.50, awn 75p-£1, dogs
10p; WS
*Park orchard with hedging for shelter. Open all
year but restricted facilities only November to
February. Milk available on farm. Shop and
restaurant 1½ miles. Swimming pool 6 miles.*
6 miles S of Gloucester on E side of A38.

RED LION CARAVAN & CAMPING PARK   RAC L
Wainlode Hill, Norton, GL2 9LW.
☎ (0452) 730251
Open: All year
Size: 12½ acres, 60 touring pitches, all level,
27 with elec. 6 hot showers, 7 WCs, 1 CWP

Car & caravan, Motor caravan, Car & tent, M/cycle
& tent £5; extra person per night 50p; elec £7, awn
50p

*Situated adjacent to River Severn, excellent
fishing, beautiful walks, including the Severn Way
walk. Swimming pool 6 miles. No groups of
motorcyclists.*
At 3¾ miles N of Gloucester on A38, turn W for
1½ miles. Signpost to Wainlode Hill.

GOATHLAND *North Yorkshire*   Map 5 B1

Brow House Farm
YO22 5NP. ☎ (0947) 86274
Open: March-October
Size: 2 acres, 50 touring pitches. 1 hot shower,
2 WCs

Turn W off A169 at ¼ mile N of Eller Beck Bridge.
Site 1 mile S of Goathland.

GOONHAVERN *Cornwall*   Map 1 A3

PENROSE FARM TOURING PARK   RAC L
TR4 9QF. ☎ (0872) 572287
Open: 1 April-31 October
Size: 6 acres, 120 touring pitches, all level, 43 with
elec. 7 hot showers, 10 WCs, 2 CWPs

(1991) Car & caravan, Motor caravan, Car & tent,
M/cycle & tent £3.75-£5.95, plus £1.25 per adult
above 2, child £1; extra car £1, elec £1.50, awn £1
*6 acres of level grassed site divided into
4 meadows. Restaurant 400 yards. Swimming
pools 1 and 5 miles. No groups of motorcyclists.
Dogs must be kept on leads at all times.*
Leave the A30 after the village of Mitchell on to the
B3285 signed Perranporth. Site 1½ miles on the left
hand side as you enter the village of Goonhaven.

Rose Hill Farm Tourist Park
TR4 9LA. ☎ (0872) 572448
Open: Easter-October
Size: 5 acres, 65 touring pitches. 7 hot showers,
9 WCs

From A30, take B3285 signposted Perranporth. Site
¼ mile past Goonhavern on B3285.

SILVERBOW PARK   RAC A
TR4 9NX. ☎ (0872) 572347
Open: May-Mid October
Size: 10 (14) acres, 90 touring pitches, 54 with elec,
54 level pitches, 4 with hardstanding, 14 static
caravans. 12 hot showers, 25 WCs, 2 CWPs

(1991) Car & caravan, Motor caravan, Car & tent
£4.70-£9.60, plus £2.50-£4.30 per adult above 2, 2-
13 years & over 60s £1.25-£2.50; elec £1.80-£2.20,
dogs up to £1
*A small, unashamedly upmarket park catering for
the more discerning. No noisy club or bars, just
immaculate facilities. Large, fully serviced touring
pitches in beautiful landscaped parkland.
Restaurant 1¼ miles. No motorcycles. Familes and
couples only.*
At 6 miles S of Newquay on A3075, pass through
Goonhavern village. Site is ½ mile further on left.

GORRAN *Cornwall* — Map 1 A3

TREGARTON FARM CARAVAN & CAMPING PARK
RAC L
PL26 6NF. ☎ (0726) 843666
Open: 1 April-31 October
Size: 8 acres, 150 touring pitches, 42 with elec, 85 level pitches. 10 hot showers, 15 WCs, 1 CWP

(1991) Car & caravan, Motor caravan, Car & tent, M/cycle & tent £5.65-£8.20; £1.35-£2.05 per adult above 2, child 75p-£1; elec £1.35, awn £1, dogs 75p
cc Access/M'card, Visa, Eurocheques
No club. No bar. No bingo. A quiet, family-run park with good amenities. Off licence. French and German spoken. Restaurant 1 mile.
At 4¼ miles S of St Austell on B3273 turn W on unclassified road at Tregiskey cross-roads as signed Gorran for 3¾ miles.

TRELISPEN CAMPING & CARAVAN PARK
RAC L
PL26 6NS. ☎ (0726) 843501
Open: Easter-31 October
Size: ½ (1½) acres, 40 touring pitches, 7 chalets. 2 hot showers, 7 WCs, 1 CWP

Charges on application.
cc Access, Visa/B'card
Level, well-screened, rural site with 7 chalets for hire. ¾ mile to safe, sandy beaches; coastal footpath nearby. Shop ¼ mile. Restaurant ½ mile.
At 4¼ miles S of St Austell on the B3273, turn W on unclassified road at Tregiskey crossroads as signed Gorran and Gorran Haven for 5½ miles to site.

TREVEOR FARM CARAVAN & CAMPING SITE
RAC L
PL26 6LW. ☎ (0726) 842387
Open: 1 April-End October
Size: 4 acres, 50 touring pitches, all level, 16 with elec. 4 hot showers, 4 cold showers, 12 WCs, CWP

Car & caravan, Motor caravan, Car & tent £4-£7; elec £1.50

Level, meadow site on working dairy farm. 2 ponds for coarse fishing. Telephone kiosk on site. Mobile shop visits the site. Shop and restaurant 1 mile. Swimming pool 9 miles. Gas available in village.
From St Austell, travel S on the B3273 for 3½ miles to Pentewan, 3¼ miles further turn right signed "Gorran" for 4½ miles, bear right and just over ¼ mile beyond, turn right to site on right.

GOSFORTH *Cumbria* — Map 4 B1

Church Stile Camp Site
Wasdale, Seascale. ☎ (09467) 26388
Open: March-November
Size: 4 acres, 50 touring pitches. 4 hot showers, 9 WCs

Off A595 Gosforth head 4 miles E to Wasdale.

National Trust Camp Site
Wasdale, Seascale.
☎ (09467) 26220
Open: Easter-October
Size: 8 acres, 120 touring pitches. 4 hot showers, 10 WCs

In Gosforth, turn E off A595, signposted Wasdale. Site 9 miles at NE end of Wastwater.

Seven Acres Holiday Park
Holmrook. ☎ (09467) 25480
Open: March-November
Size: 7 acres, 35 touring pitches. 8 hot showers, 14 WCs. 66 static caravans

200 yards off A595. 1 mile S of Gosforth.

GOSPORT *Hampshire* — Map 2 B3

Kingfisher Caravan Park
Browndown Road, Stokes Bay, PO12 2QR.
☎ (0705) 502611
Open: February-November

Size: 14 acres, 120 touring pitches. 12 hot showers, 18 WCs. 118 static caravans

⟨symbols⟩

Take M27 to junction 11 then A32 to Gosport. Seafront road into Browndown Road, Stokes Bay.

LAKELAND HOLIDAY PARK OS395 S582 RAC A
Moor Lane, Flookburgh. ☎ (044 853) 556 35
Open: Easter-End October
Size: 10 (75) acres, 102 touring pitches, all level, 18 with elec, 750 static caravans. 7 hot showers, 8 WCs

⟨symbols⟩

(1991) Car & caravan, Motor caravan, Car & tent £7, plus 85p per person; elec £3, dogs 85p (peak season prices); WS
cc Access, Visa/B'card
Holiday park with putting green, family entertainment, arcade, children's adventure playground. 350 caravans for hire (own WCs). Calor gas only. No motorcycles. No dogs 11 July to 16 August. No parties of all young people.
From Grange-over-Sands, travel S on the B5277 for 3½ miles to Flookburgh, turn left at crossroads to site on left in 1 mile.

Meathop Fell Caravan Club Site
Meathop. ☎ (044 84) 2912
Open: All year
Size: 10 acres, 150 touring pitches, all level, hardstanding. 8 hot showers, 12 WCs, CWP

⟨symbols⟩

From A590 towards Barrow, take exit for Lindale/ Grange at roundabout. Turn right immediately and follow international caravan signs.

OLD PARK WOOD CARAVAN SITE   RAC A
Cark-in-Cartmel, LA11 7PP.
☎ (053 95) 58266
Open: 1 March-31 October
Size: 2 acres, 22 touring pitches, all level, all with elec, all with hardstanding, 325 static caravans. 4 hot showers, 10 WCs, 2 CWPs

⟨symbols⟩

Charges on application.
Wooded site with access to beach. Magnificent views of Morecambe Bay and Cartmel hills. Play area on site. Restaurant 2 miles. Calor gas only.
At 4¾ miles W of Grange, or 1 mile N of Cark on B5277, turn W.

HAWKSWICK COTE FARM CARAVAN PARK   RAC L
Arncliffe, BD23 5PX. ☎ (0756) 770226
Open: 1 April-31 October
Size: 2 (12) acres, 40 touring pitches, all level, 75 static caravans. 4 hot showers, 4 cold showers, 8 WCs, 1 CWP

⟨symbols⟩

Car & caravan, Motor caravan, Car & tent £6.50; plus £2.20 per adult, child £1.10
Flat, grassy site with wonderful views all round. Restaurant and swimming pool 6 miles. No motorcycles.

From Skipton B6265 Dales road, then B6160 from Threshfield. Left past Kilnsey Crag into Littondale. 1½ miles on that road on left hand side.

Whinstone View Farm
☎ (0642) 723285
Open: March-October
Size: 4 acres, 60 touring pitches. 6 hot showers, 7 WCs

⟨symbols⟩

N of Great Ayton (A173), turn W on B1292. Site ½ mile (before A172).

SKIPSEA SANDS CARAVAN PARK   RAC L
Mill Lane, Skipsea Sands
☎ (026 286) 210
Open: March-October
Size: 3 (40) acres, 70 touring pitches, static caravans. 10 hot showers, 80 WCs

⟨symbols⟩

Charges on application.
cc Access, Visa/B'card
Spacious, well-organised site 100 yards from a sandy beach with children's play area, bar and evening social activities on the site. Caravans for hire (own WCs).
Skipsea is 11 miles SE of Driffield on B1249. From Skipsea follow signs E to Skipsea Sands.

BURGH CASTLE MARINA   RAC A
Burgh Castle, NR31 9PZ. ☎ (0493) 780331
Open: All year
Size: 2 (15) acres, 47 touring pitches, all level, 21 with elec, 165 static caravans. 10 hot showers, 18 WCs, 3 CWPs

⟨symbols⟩

(1991) Car & caravan, Motor caravan, Car & tent, M/cycle & tent £6; elec £1.50, awn £1.50
A small, quiet park set in open countryside next to the Norfolk Broads, with solar heated swimming pool.
From the roundabout, junction of the A12 and A143, S of Great Yarmouth, travel SW along A143 for 2 miles. Turn right for Belton/Burgh Castle, after ¾ mile turn right for ¾ mile. Turn left at Marina sign to site.

CHERRY TREE HOLIDAY PARK   RAC A
Mill Road, Burgh Castle, NR31 9QR.
☎ (0493) 780229
Open: Easter-end October
Size: 2 (24) acres, 24 touring pitches, all level, all with elec, all with hardstanding, 313 static caravans, 20 chalets. 12 showers, 21 WCs, 1 CWP

⟨symbols⟩

Car & caravan £6-£10; elec £1.50, awn £1.50, dogs £1.50
cc Major cards
Modern, all-facility holiday park run personally by owners. Indoor all-weather centre including swimming, licensed bars, entertainment, snooker, putting. 148 caravans and 20 chalets for hire (own

---

⟨symbol⟩ Snacks/take away ⟨symbol⟩ Restaurant ⟨symbol⟩ Swimming pool ⟨symbol⟩ Shelter for campers ⟨symbol⟩ Dogs accepted   **49**

WCs). Calor gas only. No motorcycles. Booking essential from late May to the end of September. From the roundabout, junction of the A12 and A143, S of Great Yarmouth, travel W on Burgh Road for 2 miles. Turn left to site on right in ½ mile.

THE GRANGE TOURING PARK   RAC L
Ormesby St Margaret, NR29 3QG.
☎ (0493) 730306
Open: Easter-End September
Size: 3½ acres, 70 touring pitches, 60 with elec, 70 level pitches. 8 hot showers, 16 WCs, 1 CWP

[icons]

(1991) Car & caravan, Motor caravan, Car & tent, M/cycle* & tent £5.50-£9.50; elec £1, awn £1
Level, grassy site. 5 Ticks (excellent) grading from Tourist Board, top class facilities. Shop ½ mile. Swimming pool 3 miles. 3 night minimum charge at Whitsun and August Bank Holiday weekends. The site is at the junction of the A149 and B1159, 3 miles N of Caister.

LIFFENS HOLIDAY PARK   RAC A
Burgh Castle, NR31 9QB. ☎ (0493) 780357
Open: Easter-October
Size: 12 (22) acres, 100 touring pitches, all level, 40 with elec, 90 static caravans, 4 chalets. 14 hot showers, 43 WCs, 1 CWP

[icons]

Car & caravan, Motor caravan, Car & tent, M/cycle & tent from £6, plus 75p per person above 4; extra car £1, elec £1.50, awn 75p-£1, dogs £1; WS
2 bars and entertainment, 2 heated pools, restaurant, chip shop, amusements, games room, children's play area. Friendly family holiday park in Broadland countryside but only 10 minutes by car from Great Yarmouth. 35 caravans and 3 chalets for hire (own WCs).
From the junction of the A12 and A143 S of Great Yarmouth, take A143 SW for 2 miles. Then turn right signposted Belton & Burgh Castle, after ¾ mile turn right for ¾ mile, where turn left into site on right.

ROSE FARM TOURING & CAMPING PARK   RAC L
Stepshort, Belton, ☎ (0493) 780896
Open: All year
Size: 5 acres, 30 touring pitches, all level, 18 with elec. 6 hot showers, 6 cold showers, 12 WCs, 3 CWPs

[icons]

(1991) Car & caravan, Motor caravan, Car & tent

£3-£4.75; extra person 50p; elec £1.25, awn 50p, dogs 20p; WS
A level holiday park with a family room with colour TV, pool tables and darts. Clean and quiet. Swings for young children. Open all year with limited facilities through winter. Restaurant 200 yards. Swimming pool 1½ miles. No motorcycles.
From the A12/A143 junction, S of Great Yarmouth, travel SW along the A143 for 2 miles. Turn right along an unclassified road for Belton/Burgh Castle. After ¾ mile, turn right for site.

Sunfield Caravan Site
Station Road, Belton, NR31 9NB.
☎ (0493) 780256
Open: Easter-September
Size: 30 acres, 200 touring pitches. 14 hot showers, 40 WCs. 7 static caravans

[icons]

On A143 towards Great Yarmouth, turn left at Belton crossroads. After ½ mile turn left into Station Road (south). Site in ½ mile.

VAUXHALL HOLIDAY PARK   RAC A
Acle New Road, NR30 1TB. ☎ (0493) 857231
Open: Easter then Mid May-End September
Size: 47 acres, 313 touring pitches, all level, 144 with elec and hardstanding, 405 static caravans, 48 chalets. 32 hot showers, 8 cold showers, 82 WCs, 4 CWPs

[icons]

(1991) Car & caravan, Motor caravan, Car & tent, M/cycle & tent £4.50-£11; elec £2
cc Access, Visa/B'card
Well-run, pleasantly landscaped park with facilities to fulfil all needs. Free entertainment, super games room, children's nursery and play area, shops and fast food outlets, bingo and arcade. 405 caravans and 48 chalets for hire (own WCs). Doctor's surgery.
Just outside Great Yarmouth on A47 from Norwich.

WILD DUCK CARAVAN PARK   RAC A
Belton, NR31 9NE. ☎ (0493) 780268
Open: Easter-October
Size: 15 (60) acres, 150 touring pitches, all level, 60 with elec, 230 static caravans, 21 chalets. 18 hot showers, 22 WCs, 2 CWPs

[icons]

Car & caravan, Motor caravan, Car & tent £4-£7.50;

car £1; elec £1, awn £1
cc Access, Visa/B'card
*Set in pinewoods, this large site has a games
room, licensed bars and entertainments. No
motorcycles. 21 caravans and 19 chalets for hire
(own WCs).
From the roundabout junction of the A12 and
A143, S of Great Yarmouth, travel SW along
Beccles Road (A143) for 3 miles. Turn right for
½ mile, turn left into Station Road South to site on
left in ½ mile.*

STRANGEWAYS CARAVAN PARK RAC L
Staithe Road, Repps-with-Bastwick, NR29 5JU.
☎ (0692) 670380
Open: March-November
Size: 2 acres, 40 touring pitches, all level, 5 with
elec. 2 hot showers, 5 WCs, 1 CWP

Charges on application.
*Secluded site, ideal touring centre for Broads.
Fishing and boating nearby. Shop and restaurant
½ mile. Swimming pool 3 miles.
In Repps-with-Bastwick (A149) take Ashby/Thurne
road. In ½ mile turn in to Staithe Road. Site ½ mile
on right.*

BURESIDE HOLIDAY PARK RAC A
Boundary Farm, Oby, NR29 3BW.
☎ (0493) 369233
Open: Whitsun-Mid September
Size: 12 acres, 85 touring pitches plus 85 for tents,
approx. 50 with elec, all level, all level. 6 hot
showers, 18 WCs, 2 CWPs

Car & caravan, Motor caravan, Car & tent, M/cycle*
& tent, all from £5, plus 60p per person above 2;
elec £1.50, awn £1, dogs free
*Level, sheltered, meadowland site with trees,
shrubs and hedges. Private fishing lake with carp
and tench (small daily charge) plus free fishing on
¾ mile river frontage running through park.
Launching slipway. Games room. Children's play
area. Sandy beach approx 7 miles. Restaurant/pub
10 minutes' walk. 1 week minimum stay on pitches
with electricity (peak season). Dogs on leads.
From junction A47/A1064 W of Acle, take A1064 N
to Billockby, keep left along B1152 for 1.4 miles,
then turn left at crossroads along unclassified road
(signed Oby) for 1.2 miles and take the second
road on left, then 0.2 miles further turn right to site.*

Camping & Caravanning Club Site
Grizedale Hall, Hawkshead, Ambleside, LA22 0GL.
☎ (022 984) 257
Open: 30 March-28 September
Size: 3 acres, 60 touring pitches. 2 hot showers,
5 WCs

Charges on application.
cc Access, Visa/B'card
*A non-commercialized site in grounds of Grizedale
Hall (demolished).
From the A5092 take the road signposted "Colton,
Oxen Park". Follow the road for about 5 miles, the
site is on the right opposite Grizedale Hall.*

MARGROVE PARK RAC L
Boosbeck, TS12 3BZ. ☎ (028 75) 0663
Open: 1 April-30 October
Size: 8 acres, 100 touring pitches. 5 hot showers,
10 WCs, 1 CWP

Charges on application.
*Landscaped meadowland site with a play area.
Shop and restaurant 1 mile. Swimming pool
5 miles. No gas available.
From Guisborough, travel E on the A171 for
3 miles, turn N on unclassified road for ½ mile to
site on right.*

Waveney River Centre
Burgh St Peter, Staithe. ☎ (050 277) 217
Open: Easter-October
Size: 12 acres, 40 touring pitches. 4 hot showers,
15 WCs

*From A143 go off at Haddiscoe and site signposted
from there.*

The Old Mill Caravan Park
Chalvington Road, Golden Cross
☎ (0825) 872532
Open: Easter-October
Size: 2 acres, 20 touring pitches. 2 hot showers,
5 WCs. 1 static caravan

Off A22 at Golden Cross, 4 miles NW of Hailsham.

Sandy Bank Caravan Park
Magham Down, BN27 1PW. ☎ (0323) 842488
Open: February-December
Size: 2 acres, 20 touring pitches. 4 hot showers,
7 WCs. 4 static caravans

*Going N from Hailsham, fork off A271 at Forge
Guest House and Restaurant.*

Camping & Caravanning Club Site
Clent Hills, Fieldhouse Lane, Romsey, B62 0NH.
☎ (0562) 710015
Open: 30 March-28 September
Size: 6½ acres, 150 touring pitches. 2 hot shower, 7
WCs

Charges on application.
cc Access, Visa/B'card
*Level, grassy site sheltered by wooded hills. Plenty
of nature trails and wildlife at nearby Clent Hills
Country Park.
Take the B4551 then take the road by the Sun
Hotel, turn left at the Bell End Broughton junction,
take the left turn after ¼ mile, the site is on the left.*

▣ Snacks/take away ⊠ Restaurant ◳ Swimming pool ▣ Shelter for campers ⋔ Dogs accepted

HALIFAX *West Yorkshire* — Map 5 A2

Pennine Camping & Caravan Site
High Greenwood House, Heptonstall, Hebden
Bridge, HX7 7AZ.
☎ (0422) 842287
Open: All year
Size: 5 acres, 50 touring pitches. 2 hot showers,
7 WCs. 4 static caravans

From Hebden Bridge (A646) take Heptonstall Road.
Site signed.

HALSTEAD *Essex* — Map 3 A2

Gosfield Lake Caravan & Camping Leisure Centre
Church Road, Gosfield, CO9 1UE.
☎ (0787) 475043
Open: March-December
Size: 7 acres, 25 touring pitches. 2 hot showers,
6 WCs

A131 from Braintree, into Gosfield, turn into
Church Road by Kings Head public house. Site
100 yards beyond church.

HALTWHISTLE *Northumberland* — Map 7 A3

Roam-n-Rest Caravan Park
Raylton House, Greenhead, CA6 7HA.
☎ (069 77) 47213
Open: March-October
Size: 1 acre, 20 touring pitches. 2 hot showers,
5 WCs. 1 static caravan

Leave A69 at Greenhead junction, direction
Greenhead. First left in approximately 400 yards.

Camping & Caravanning Club Site
Burnfoot, Park Village, NE49 0HZ.
Open: 30 March-26 October
Size: 3 acres, 70 touring pitches. 4 hot showers,
9 WCs

Charges on application.
From the A69 take the road signposted Alston
Whitfield, follow the road and then take the right
turn to Kellah, the site is on the right.

HARLESTON *Norfolk* — Map 3 B1

Little Lakeland
Wortwell. ☎ (098 686) 646
Open: All year
Size: 4½ acres, 35 touring pitches. 4 hot showers, 6
WCs. 2 static caravans

2¾ miles NE of Harleston off A143. Turn off and
follow signs to Wortwell. Through village,
250 yards past service station, turn right down lane
to site.

LONE PINE CAMPING — RAC L
Low Road, Wortwell, IP20 0HJ.
☎ (098686) 596
Open: 1 May-30 September
Size: 2 acres, 24 touring pitches. 2 hot showers,
4 WCs

(1991) Motor caravan, Car & tent, M/cycle & tent
£3.50, 25p per person above 2
*Quiet and clean with nice view across Waveney
valley. No crowding. Shop ½ mile. Restaurant
1 mile. Swimming pool 5 miles. Dogs on leads
always. No loud radios.*
Off A143 N of Harleston, turn to Wortwell at
roundabout. Turn right at Bell Inn. Site ½ mile on
right.

HARROGATE *North Yorkshire* — Map 5 A1

HIGH MOOR FARM PARK — RAC A
Skipton Road, HG3 2LT. ☎ (0423) 563637
Open: 1 April-31 October
Size: 15 (22) acres, 250 touring pitches, all level,
150 with elec, 5 with hardstanding, 160 static
caravans. 20 hot showers, 20 cold showers,
50 WCs, 2 CWPs

Car & caravan, Motor caravan, Car & tent, M/cycle
& tent £6.50, plus 75p per person above 2; elec
£1.50, awn £1
*Well-arranged, level, meadowland site with
excellent facilities. Large, heated, indoor
swimming pool, which adjoins an amusement
area, complete with pool tables, etc. Licensed bar
serving bar meals. 9-hole golf course (subject to
small fee). 5 caravans for hire (own WCs). No
unaccompanied youths/boys.*
Travel W from Harrogate on the A59 for 4 miles.
Site on left.

MAUSTIN CARAVAN PARK — RAC L
The Riddings, Spring Lane, Kearby-with-Netherby,
LS22 4DP.
☎ (0532) 886234
Open: 1 March-31 October
Size: 2 (6) acres, 13 touring pitches, all level, all
with elec, 73 static caravans. 4 hot showers,
12 WCs, 1 CWP

Car & caravan, Motor caravan, Car & tent £9,
including 2 persons and elec
*Quiet, select meadowland site in beautiful Lower
Wharfe Valley between Harrogate and Wetherby
and near to moors and dales. Tranquil setting for
people without family responsibilities.*
From A61 take first turn right after crossing
Harewood Bridge. Then turn right to Kearby and
right again to caravan park.

RIPLEY CARAVAN PARK — RAC A
Ripley, HG3 3AU. ☎ (0423) 770050
Open: Easter-31 October
Size: 12 (18) acres, 100 touring pitches, all level,
72 with elec, 5 with hardstanding. 10 hot showers,
13 WCs, 1 CWP

Charges on application. WS
*Quiet, family-run site close to village and castle.
Indoor pool, sauna and sunbed, children's dinghy
pool, nursery playroom and playground.
Restaurant ½ mile.*
From A61, 3¾ miles N of Harrogate at roundabout,
turn W on B6165 for ¼ mile to site on left.

⚹ Facilities for Disabled 🚒 Caravans accepted 🚑 Motor caravans △ Tents ▲ Laundry room ▪ Shop

RUDDING HOLIDAY PARK RAC A
Follifoot, HG3 1JH. ☎ (0423) 870439
Open: 20 March-1 November
Size: 20 acres, 141 touring pitches, all with elec,
120 level pitches, 4 with hardstanding, 79 static
caravans, 14 chalets. 16 hot showers, 34 WCs,
4 CWPs

Car & caravan, Motor caravan, Car & tent, M/cycle
& tent £9-£11, Tent £5; elec £1.50; WS
cc Access, Visa/B'card
*This pleasant, wooded site has a swimming pool,
pitch and putt course and children's playground on
site. Restaurant 1 mile.*
From A661, 1½ miles SE of Harrogate, turn W for ¾
mile, entrance to site on left.

SHAWS TRAILER PARK RAC A
Knaresborough Road. ☎ (0423) 884432
Open: All year
Size: 11 acres, 45 touring pitches, 30 with elec,
38 with hardstanding, all level, 146 static caravans.
4 hot showers, 24 WCs, 1 CWP

1991) Car & caravan, Motor caravan £5.50; Car &
tent, M/cycle* & tent £1, plus £1.50 per person, 75p
child; elec £1.50, awn £1.50; WS
*Town site planted with trees. Shop 500 yards.
Swimming pool ½ mile. Restaurant 1 mile. Calor
gas only.*
On A59 between Harrogate and Knaresborough,
opposite Harrogate General Hospital.

Village Farm
Old Bilton, HD1 4DH. ☎ (0423) 863121
Open: April-October
Size: 3 (10) acres, 25 touring pitches. 4 hot
showers, 17 WCs. Static caravans

Site 1 mile E of A59 at Dragon Hotel, Harrogate.

**YORKSHIRE HUSSAR INN
HOLIDAY CARAVAN PARK** RAC L
Markington, HG3 3NR. ☎ (0765) 677327
Open: 1 March-31 October
Size: 2 (6) acres, 20 touring pitches, all level,
16 with elec, 75 static caravans. 4 hot showers,
4 cold showers, 14 WCs, 1 CWP

(1991) Car & caravan, Car & tent, M/cycle & tent £4,
Motor caravan £3.50, plus 75p per person above 2,
child 50p; extra car £1, elec £1.20, awn £1; WS
*Situated in village at rear of old world pub in
garden setting. 8 caravans for hire (own WCs).
Shop 300 yards. Restaurant 1 mile. Swimming pool
5 miles. Calor gas only. Brochure available.*
At 7 miles N of Harrogate on A61, turn W at
Wormald Green to Markington. Site signed.

HARWICH *Essex* Map 3 B2

Dovercourt Haven Caravan Park
Low Road, Dovercourt Bay, CO12 3TZ.
☎ (0255) 243433
Open: Easter-November
Size: 1 acre, 60 touring pitches. 11+ hot showers,
11 WCs. 30 static caravans

Colchester-Harwich (A120), just outside Romsey,
follow signs to park.

HASTINGS *Sussex* Map 3 A3

Old Coghurst Farm
Rock Lane, Three Oaks. ☎ (0424) 753622
Open: March-September
Size: 5 acres, 60 touring pitches. 4 hot showers,
8 WCs

A21 on to A28 to Westfield. Left opposite New Inn
public house, 1¾ miles to site at bottom of lane.

SHEAR BARN HOLIDAY PARK RAC A
Barley Lane, TN35 5DX. ☎ (0424) 423583
Open: March-January
Size: 16 (34) acres, 150 touring pitches, 50 with
elec, all level, 210 static caravans. 16 hot showers,
50 WCs, 5 CWPs

(1991) Car & caravan £4.50-£9, Motor caravan
£3.50-£8, Car & tent £3-£9, plus 50p person above
6; extra car £1, elec £1.50, dogs £1; WS
cc Access, Visa/B'card
*Spacious, well-run park with good views.
Children's play area and evening social activities.
25 caravans for hire (own WCs). Swimming pool
3 miles. Bank Holiday only: stay to include Sunday
night, eg. Friday arrival minimum stay 3 nights,
Saturday arrival minimum stay 2 nights. No
motorcycles. Dogs must be kept on a lead.*
A259 from Hastings sea front, follow road to Rye
and Folkestone, travel inland a few hundred yards,
turn right into Harold Road, right into Gurth Road,
left at end into Barley Lane. Reception 200 yards on
right. A259 from Rye/Folkestone: through village of
Ore, turn left into Saxon Road, travel 1¼ miles to
crossroads, turn left into Gurth Road, left into
Barley Lane.

Stalkhurst Cottage
Ivyhouse Lane. ☎ (0424) 439015
Open: March-January
Size: 1½ acres, 33 touring pitches. 2 hot showers, 5
WCs. 6 static caravans

From A2, left on to B2093, in 2 miles turn left into
Ivyhouse Lane.

HATFIELD *South Yorkshire* Map 5 A2

HATFIELD MARINA WATERSPORTS CENTRE RAC L
DW7 6EQ. ☎ (0302) 841572
Open: March-September
Size: 10 acres, 60 touring pitches. 4 hot showers,
12 WCs, 2 CWPs

Charges on application.
*Grassy campsite by the side of the marina, where
most types of watersports are available.
Swimming strictly prohibited for safety reasons.*
From M180 junction 1, travel S on the A18 to
Hatfield and follow signs to site.

HATHERSAGE *Derbyshire* — Map 5 A2

North Lees Campsite
Birley Lane. ☎ (0433) 50838
Open: All year
Size: 1½ acres, 45 touring pitches. 2 hot showers, 5 WCs

1½ miles N of Hathersage, off A625.

Swallow Holme Caravan Park
Bamford. ☎ (0433) 50981
Open: April-October
Size: 3 acres, 60 touring pitches. 6 hot showers, 9 WCs

On A6013, 2 miles S of Ladybower Reservoir.

HAWES *North Yorkshire* — Map 5 A1

BAINBRIDGE INGS FARM   RAC L
DL8 3NU. ☎ (0969) 667354
Open: 1 April-31 October
Size: 5 (6) acres, 55 touring pitches, 10 with elec, 50 level pitches, 15 static caravans. 6 hot showers, 15 WCs, 1 CWP

(1991) Car & caravan £4.20, Motor caravan, Car & tent, M/cycle & tent £3.70, plus 50p per adult above 2, child 30p; extra car 25p, elec £1.20, awn 50p
Quiet family site with modern, clean toilets, set in beautiful countryside. Ideal for walking and visiting the Dales. Restaurant ½ mile, shop in Hawes. Swimming pool 2½ miles. 3 caravans for hire. All cars must be back on site by 11pm. Site to be quiet after 11pm. All dogs strictly on a lead on the site. No groups of motorcycles.
At ¼ mile E of Hawes on A684, turn S as signed Gayle, for 220 yards.

Brown Moor
DL8 3PS. ☎ (0969) 667338
Open: March-October
Size: 8 acres, 145 touring pitches. 8 hot showers, 14 WCs

Off A684, take the Muker road for ¼ mile.

Honeycott Caravan Site
Ingleton Road, DL8 3LH. ☎ (0969) 667310
Open: March-October
Size: 3 acres, 20 touring pitches. 4 hot showers, 10 WCs. 8 static caravans

¼ mile SW of Hawes on B6255.

Shaw Ghyll Farm Caravan & Camping Site
Simonstone. ☎ (0969) 667359
Open: March-October
Size: 2½ acres, 25 touring pitches. 2 WCs

2 miles N of Hawes on the Muker road.

HAWORTH *West Yorkshire* — Map 5 A2

Upwood Holiday Park
Blackmoor Road, Oxenhope, BD22 9SS.
☎ (0535) 43254
Open: April-October
Size: 10 acres, 70 touring pitches. 8 hot showers, 15 WCs. 2 static caravans

At Denholme (A629), turn W on to B6141. After 1¼ miles turn right on to Blackmoor Road. Site ¾ mile.

HAYFIELD *Cheshire* — Map 5 A2

Camping & Caravanning Club Site
Kinder Road, SK12 5LE. ☎ (0663) 45394
Open: 30 March-26 October
Size: 7 acres, 90 touring pitches. 6 hot showers, 12 WCs

Charges on application.
cc Access, Visa/B'card
A riverside site with fishing available. High in the Peak District, close to Kinder Scout. Calor gas only.
From the A624 follow the signs for Hayfield and then the international camping signs.

HAYLE *Cornwall* — Map 1 A3

ATLANTIC COAST CARAVAN PARK   RAC L
53 Upton Towans, TR27 5BL.
☎ (0736) 752071
Open: Early April-31 October
Size: 1½ (4) acres, 17 touring pitches, all level, 14 with elec, 33 static caravans. 5 hot showers, 15 WCs, 1 CWP

Charges on application.
cc Access, Visa/B'card
Family holiday park, on edge of St Ives Bay, close to beaches and countryside. All amenities including sauna and sunbed. 33 caravans for hire (own WCs). Restaurant and swimming pool approx 2 miles. Motorcycles accepted at management's discretion.
From the E end of the Hayle by-pass (A30) follow signs "Hayle" and 300 yards on turn right on the B3301 for 1¼ miles to site on left.

Beachside Leisure Holidays
TR27 5AW. ☎ (0736) 753080
Open: Easter-September
Size: 40 acres, 92 touring pitches. 4 hot showers, 12 WCs, 109 static caravans

---

Seasonal variation of prices

Where a single price is given it may be a low season minimum charge - rates can increase considerably at peak periods and for extra people or vehicles.
Please confirm prices with the site when booking.

🦽 Facilities for Disabled   🚐 Caravans accepted   🚙 Motor caravans   ⛺ Tents   🧺 Laundry room   🛒 Shop

From A30 take road to Hayle into town and straight through mini roundabouts until take right turn at recreation ground and then signposted.

CALLOOSE CARAVAN & CAMPING PARK RAC A
Leedstown, TR27 5ET. ☎ (0736) 850431
Open: 1 April-6 October
Size: 8½ acres, 120 touring pitches, all level, 70 with elec, 2 with hardstanding, 17 static caravans. 12 hot showers, 18 WCs, 2 CWPs

(1991) Car & caravan, Motor caravan, Car & tent, M/cycle & tent £4-£7; extra person 50p; elec £1.55, awn free, dogs from 50p
Quiet, secluded, friendly, family park in sheltered suntrap valley. Skittle alley, crazy golf, adventure playground, trout fishing. 17 caravans for hire (own WCs).
At 4 miles SE of Hayle on B3302, turn left at Leedstown village hall on unclassified road for ½ mile. Site signed on left.

Higher Travaskis Caravan & Camping Park
Station Road, Connor Downs, TR22 5DQ.
☎ (0209) 831736
Open: April-October
Size: 6 acres, 82 touring pitches. Hot showers, WCs

Take Camborne West exit from A30 Redruth-Hayle. Left on A3047, then right on to B3301 towards Connor Downs/Hayle. After 1½ miles turn left for Carnhell Green. Site ¾ mile.

Parbola Holiday Park
Wall, Gwinear. ☎ (0209) 831503
Open: Easter-October
Size: 17½ acres, 115 touring pitches. 9 hot showers, 15 WCs. 20 static caravans

Take Camborne West exit from A30. Left on to A3047 then right on to the B3301 towards Connor Downs/Hayle. After 1½ miles, and before Connor Downs, turn left into Gwinear Road. Continue to Carnhell Green, turn right at t-junction. Site ¾ mile.

St Ives Bay Holiday Park
73 Loggans Road, Upton Towans, TR27 5BH.
☎ (0736) 752274
Open: Easter (chalets)/May (tourers)-October
Size: 80 acres, 300 touring pitches. 38 hot showers, 45 WCs. 250 static caravans, 150 chalets

Leave A30 at Hayle exit and take B3301 coast road. Site 600 yards.

Sunny Meadow Caravan Park
Lelant Downs. ☎ (0736) 752243
Open: Easter-October
Size: 1 acre, 5 touring pitches. 2 hot showers, 4 WCs. 6 static caravans

Take Hayle by-pass then the St Ives road to mini roundabout. Take first left on to B3311 for ½ mile.

HAYLING ISLAND *Hampshire* Map 2 B3

Fleet Camp Site
Yew Tree Road. ☎ (0705) 463684

Open: March-October
Size: 3 acres, 75 touring pitches. 8 hot showers, 13 WCs

On A3023 towards Hayling Island, 2 miles S of bridge in Stoke, turn E into Copse Lane, then first right to site.

LOWER TYE FARM CAMP SITE RAC L
Copse Lane, PO11 0RQ. ☎ (0705) 462479
Open: 1 March-31 October
Size: 5 acres, 150 touring pitches, all level, 72 with elec. 15 hot showers, 17 WCs, 1 CWP

Car & caravan, Motor caravan, Car & tent, M/cycle* & tent £5, includes 2 people; elec £1, dogs 50p; WS
Level site, well marked-out, all pitches bookable. Restaurant ½ mile. Swimming pool 3 miles.
Follow A3023 from Havant, turn left into Copse Lane. Do not turn off until you see entrance of site.

The Oven Camping Site
Manor Road. ☎ (0705) 464695
Open: March-October
Size: 10½ acres, 330 touring pitches. 35 hot showers, 30 WCs

Site on A3023 from Havant, in 3 miles there is a roundabout: turn right and site is 450 yards on the left.

HEACHAM *Norfolk* Map 3 A1

HEACHAM BEACH HOLIDAY PARK RAC A
South Beach Road, PE31 7DD.
☎ (0485) 70270
Open: Easter-October
Size: 26 acres, 20 touring pitches, all level, 2 with elec, 20 static caravans. 12 hot showers, 20 WCs, 1 CWP

Charges on application.
This well-run site near the beach has its own tennis courts, clubhouse and children's play area.
20 caravans for hire (own WCs). Restaurant 300 yards.
On the A149 (N of King's Lynn) 1 mile N of Snettisham, turn left as signed Heacham Beach and ¾ mile on bear left to beach, site on right.

HEATHFIELD *East Sussex* Map 3 A3

GREENVIEWS CARAVAN PARK RAC L
Burwash Road, Broad Oak, TN21 8RT.
☎ (0435) 863531
Open: 1 April-31 October
Size: 1½ (3½) acres, 10 touring pitches, 51 static caravans, 2 chalets. 2 hot showers, 8 WCs, 2 CWPs

(1991) Car & caravan, Motor caravan £5, Car & tent, M/cycle & tent £2.50-£5; awn £3
This site is situated in delightful East Sussex. It is not a seaside site but is within easy reach of Eastbourne, Brighton, Bexhill and Hastings. Bar and clubhouse open at weekends. Shop on site at weekends and over Bank Holidays. Restaurant and shop 200 yards. Swimming pool 1 mile. We do not

● Snacks/take away ☒ Restaurant ◹ Swimming pool ▣ Shelter for campers ▨ Dogs accepted   55

accept young people under 18 years of age who are unaccompanied. No dogs.
From the junction of the A265 and A267 at Heathfield, travel E on the A265 for 1¾ miles to site on left.

Park Farm
Burwash, Etchington, TN19 7DR.
☎ (0435) 882358
Open: March-October
Size: 1 acre, 3+ touring pitches. No showers or WCs

Look for Batemans (National Trust signed), leave road and follow signs to Park Farm. South of Burwash.

HELMSLEY *North Yorkshire*   Map 5 A1

FOXHOLME TOURING CARAVAN PARK   RAC A
Harome, YO6 5JG. ☎ (0439) 70416/71696
Open: March-31 October
Size: 6 (10) acres, 60 touring pitches, all level, all with hardstanding. 6 hot showers, 2 cold showers, 16 WCs, 2 CWPs

Car & caravan, Motor caravan, Car & tent, M/cycle & tent £4.50-£5; elec £1.80-£2, awn £1.50; WS
All pitches are attractively situated amongst evergreen trees and are well-spaced to ensure quiet and privacy, with hard roads throughout the site giving good all weather access. The site is level and very well sheltered. Shop 1 mile. Restaurant 2 miles. Swimming pool 3 miles. Small shop on site. Centrally heated toilet and shower block. Dogs must be kept on a lead.
From Helmsley, travel E on the A170 for ½ mile, turn right on road to Harome 2 miles, turn left at church, ½ mile further keep left, then take first turning on left (sign on signpost) to site 350 yards on right.

GOLDEN SQUARE CARAVAN PARK   RAC A
Oswaldkirk, YO6 5YQ. ☎ (04393) 269
Open: 1 March-31 October
Size: 10 acres, 110 touring pitches, all level, 80 with elec, 20 with hardstanding. 14 hot showers, 6 cold showers, 16 WCs, 2 CWPs

(1991) Car & caravan, Motor caravan, Car & tent, M/cycle & tent £4.85, including 2 people, child 75p; elec £1.35, awn £1; WS
A quiet, secluded site hidden from the outside world with magnificent views of the North Yorks Moors. 2 luxury toilet blocks. Regional Winner of Loo of the Year 1988, '89, '90. Near York and coast. Restaurant and swimming pool 1 mile. Dogs must be kept on a lead, but a dog walk is provided.
Take the A168 E from the A1. Take the second turning marked Thirsk onto A19 for 3 miles S. Then take caravan route marked Coxwold. Follow signs to Ampleforth, past village fork left towards Helmsley. Site on left.

WRENS OF RYEDALE CARAVAN SITE   RAC L
Gale Lane, Nawton, YO6 5SD. ☎ (0439) 71260
Open: 1 April-17 October
Size: 3 acres, 45 touring pitches, all level, 6 with elec. 4 hot showers, 10 WCs, 1 CWP

(1991) Car & caravan, Motor caravan, Car & tent, M/cycle & tent £4; all plus 50p per person, children under 7 free; elec £1.25, awn £1.25, dogs free; WS
Attractive, level, sheltered site convenient for North York Moors, Dales, coast and York. Quiet, family-run site with recently improved facilities, now with 4 Ticks on British Tourist Board grading system. 2 caravans for hire (own WCs). Restaurant ¼ mile. Swimming pool 3 miles.
Take A170 to Pickering from Helmsley, 3 miles on you come to Beadlam village. Take right turn after White Horse Inn into Gale Lane. Site is 600 yards on right.

HELSTON *Cornwall*   Map 1 A3

Boscrege Caravan Park
Ashton, TR13 9TG. ☎ (0736) 762231
Open: April-October
Size: 6 acres, 12 touring pitches. 2 hot showers, 6 WCs. 26 static caravans

W of Helston, turn right off A394 on to B3302 at Hilltop Garage. In 2 miles, left for Godolphin. Left at Godolphin Arms public house. Site on right ¾ mile.

Camping & Caravanning Club Site
Trelowarren Chateau Park, Trelowarren, Mawgan, TR12 6AF.
☎ (032 622) 637
Open: 30 March-28 September
Size: 225 touring pitches. 15 hot showers, 27 WCs

Charges on application.
cc Access, Visa/B'card
In the grounds of a manor house. Licensed bar, entertainments and an on-site pottery.
From the A3083 take the B3293, turn right at the War Memorial then left at the "Trelowarren" sign. Follow the road round till the site is on the left.

Glenhaven Touring Caravan Park
Clodgey Lane, TR13 8PW. ☎ (0326) 572734
Open: May-September
Size: 3½ acres, 75 touring pitches. 10 hot showers, 12 WCs. 1 static caravan

On the main Helston to Lizard road, about ¾ mile out of town centre.

Gunwalloe Caravan Park
Gunwalloe. ☎ (0326) 572668
Open: April-October
Size: 2½ acres, 40 touring pitches. 4 hot showers, 9 WCs

2 miles S of Helston on Lizard road, turn right for Gunwalloe. Site 1 mile.

Lower Polladras Caravan & Camping Park
Carleen, Breage. ☎ (0736) 762220
Open: April-October
Size: 4 acres, 60 touring pitches. 6 hot showers, 12 WCs

1½ miles W of Helston (A394), turn N at Hilltop Garage on to B3303. After 1 mile, turn left to Carleen. Site ¼ mile N of village.

Pinetrees
Goonhilly Downs, Mawgan. ☎ (032 622) 310
Open: April-October
Size: 6 acres, 15 touring pitches. 4 hot showers, 7 WCs. 10 static caravans

From Helston take Lizard road, turn left to St Keverns on the B3293, 4 miles later site on left.

Poldown Caravan & Camping Park
Carleen, TR13 9NN. ☎ (0326) 574560
Open: Easter-October
Size: 2 acres, 12 touring pitches. 2 hot showers, 4 WCs. 5 static caravans

W of Helston, turn right off A394 on to B3302. Take second left for ¾ mile towards Carleen.

Camping & Caravan Park
Tregullas Farm, Penhale, Ruan Minor, TR12 7LJ. ☎ (0326) 240387
Open: April-October
Size: 1½ acres, 18 touring pitches. 2 hot showers, 3 WCs. 12 static caravans

Take A39 (A394) from Truro to Helston. From Helston take A3083 road to Lizard. Site approximately 7 miles, close to junction B3296 Mullion road.

Gwendreath Farm Caravan Park
Kennack Sands, TR12 7LZ. ☎ (0326) 290666
Open: Easter-October
Size: 7 acres, 10 touring pitches plus 25 for tents. 4 hot showers, 8 WCs. 30 static caravans

From Helston take the A3083 then turn left on to B3293, about 4 miles on take right turn after radar station then first left, turn right at end of lane over cattle grid, then through caravan site, sea view.

HEMSBY *Norfolk* — Map 3 B1

Long Beach Estate
NR29 4JD. ☎ (0493) 730023
Open: Easter-October
Size: 1½ acres, 18 touring pitches. 10 hot showers, 24 WCs

N on B1159, turn right at Beach Road then second left at Kings Loke.

Newport Caravan Park
☎ (0493) 730405
Open: April-October
Size: 16 acres, 90 touring pitches. 22 hot showers, 40 WCs. 33 static caravans

From A47 to Hemsby, signed to Newport (B1159).

HENFIELD *West Sussex* — Map 3 A3

DOWNSVIEW CARAVAN PARK — RAC L
Bramlands Lane, BN5 9TG. ☎ (0273) 492801
Open: Mid March-Mid November
Size: 1½ (3½) acres, 12+ touring pitches, all level, all with elec, 11 with hardstanding, 10 with waste water hook-up, 28 static caravans. 4 hot showers, 7 WCs, 2 CWPs

(1991) Car & caravan, Motor caravan £5, Car & tent £3.25-£4.25, plus £1 per adult, child 50p (under 8s); elec £1.50, awn £1.50, dogs 50p; WS
Quality, quiet park set in depth of countryside with only the birds to disturb you, with no clubs, pubs or playgrounds. Restaurant 1 mile. Swimming pool 1½ miles. Shop 2 miles, with limited supplies available on site. 3 caravans for hire (own WCs). Dogs must be kept on a lead. No motorcycles.
Signed off A281 in village of Woodmancote, 2 miles E of Henfield or W of A23.

Southdown Caravan Park
Henfield Road, Small Dole
☎ (0903) 814323/813665
Open: April-October
Size: 3 acres, 10 touring pitches. 4 hot showers, 8 WCs. 35 static caravans

From A23 at Bolney on to A272 to Cowfold, on A281 to Henfield. Site off A2037 S of Small Dole.

HENLEY-ON-THAMES *Oxfordshire* — Map 2 B2

Swiss Farm
☎ (0491) 573419
Open: March-October
Size: 7 (10) acres, 200 touring pitches. 10 hot showers, 21 WCs. Static caravans

Site ½ mile N of Henley, W side of A4155.

HEREFORD *Hereford & Worcester* — Map 2 A2

Hereford Racecourse Caravan Club Site
Roman Road. ☎ (0432) 272364
Open: April-September
Size: Touring pitches, all with elec. 4 hot showers, 15 WCs, CWP

1 mile N of Hereford (A49), turn W on to A4103. Site ½ mile.

Lucks'all Camp Site
Mordiford. ☎ (0432) 870213
Open: Easter-October
Size: 7 acres, 40 touring pitches. 4 hot showers, 9 WCs. 1 static caravan

From M50 take B4224 (Hereford and Ross-on-Wye), 5 miles from Hereford.

HERNE BAY *Kent* — Map 3 B2

Hillborough Caravan Park
Reculver Road, CT6 6SR. ☎ (0227) 374618
Open: Easter/April-October

◨ Snacks/take away ☒ Restaurant ◹ Swimming pool ▣ Shelter for campers ⚐ Dogs accepted

Size: 27 acres, 52 touring pitches. 46 hot showers, 60 WCs

[icons]

A299 towards Margate after Canterbury turn-off. Left at sign saying Sweechbridge Road, then first left.

Westbrook Farm Caravan Park
Sea Street, CT6 8BT. ☎ (0227) 375586
Open: Easter-October
Size: 5 acres, 100 touring pitches. 12 hot showers, 18 WCs

[icons]

Off A299 to B2205, site ¼ mile. (Left at fifth roundabout from M2 then left at traffic lights and site ½ mile on left).

HERTFORD *Hertfordshire* — Map 3 A2

Camping & Caravanning Club Site
Balls Park, Mangrove Road, SG13 8QL.
☎ (0992) 586696
Open: 30 March-26 October
Size: 32 acres, 150 touring pitches. 2 hot showers, 7 WCs

[icons]

Charges on application.
cc Access, Visa/B'card
Quiet meadowland site, close to the county town of Hertford. Shop 1 mile.
From the A414 follow the signs to "Simon Balle School, Balls Park College". The site is on the left.

HEXHAM *Northumberland* — Map 7 B3

Barrasford Park Caravan Site
Barrasford Park. ☎ (0434) 681210
Open: April-October
Size: 60 acres, 28 touring pitches. 4 hot showers, 6 WCs

[icons]

Site is 8 miles N of Corbridge just off A68. Turn W at signpost Barrasford Park.

Bensons Fell Farm
Causey Hill. ☎ (0434) 602834
Open: Easter-October
Size: 3 acres, 33 touring pitches. 12 hot showers, 24 WCs

[icons]

From Hexham centre take B6305 signposted Blanchland and racecourse. Follow international signs to site at top of hill.

Carts Bog Inn
Langley-on-Tyne. ☎ (0434) 684338
Open: March-September
Size: 1½ acres, 6 touring pitches. No hot showers, 3 WCs

[icons]

From A69 from Hexham to Haydon Bridge. Take A686 to Alston (signposted). Site on A686, 3 miles from Haydon Bridge.

Fallowfield Dene Caravan & Camping Park
Acomb, NE46 4RP. ☎ (0434) 603553
Open: March-October

Size: 17½ acres, 155 touring pitches. 8 hot showers, 14 WCs

[icons]

From A69 Penrith/Carlisle, turn left on to A6079. At Acomb, take second right turning. Follow signs.

HEXHAM RACECOURSE CARAVAN CLUB SITE — RAC L
High Yarridge, NE46 3NN. ☎ (0434) 606847
Open: Easter-September
Size: 4½ (5½) acres, 80 touring pitches, 40 level pitches, 26 with elec. 4 hot showers, 10 WCs, 2 CWPs

[icons]

Car & caravan, Motor caravan £3; Tent £1, Car £1, M/cycle 50p; all plus £1.90 per person, 90p child; elec £1, awn free, dogs free
Wonderful views over Tyne Valley. Very clean and peaceful. Pony trekking and walking. Good base for exploring Northumberland and Durham.
Restaurant and swimming pool 1½ miles.
Maximum stay 21 days.
In town centre, turn S on B6306, at ¼ mile on turn right and ¾ mile further turn right again for ¾ mile.

Riverside Leisure
Tyne Green. ☎ (0434) 604705
Open: March-October
Size: 1¼ (6) acres, 30 touring pitches. 14 hot showers, 26 WCs. 6 static caravans

[icons]

From A69 cross river bridge until Haugh Lane and at Shell garage turn right and at bottom of hill turn left. Site signed.

HEYSHAM *Lancashire* — Map 4 B1

Hawthorne House Farm
Carr Lane, Middleton Sands, LA3 3LL.
☎ (0524) 52074
Open: March-October
Size: 8 acres, 35 touring pitches. 4 hot showers, 6 WCs

[icons]

A589 Heysham to Middleton, then follow signs to Middleton Sands. Site 150 yards from beach.

MELBREAK CARAVAN PARK — RAC L
Carr Lane, Middleton, LA3 3LH.
☎ (0524) 852430
Open: 1 March-30 October
Size: 1½ (2) acres, 20+ touring pitches, all level, 8 with elec, 3 with hardstanding, 10 static caravans. 4 hot showers, 7 WCs, 1 CWP

[icons]

Car & caravan, Motor caravan £5-£5.50, Car & tent, M/cycle & tent £4.50-£5; elec £1.30, awn £1.30
A small, clean, grade 4 park with modern high grade facilities, 1 mile from sandy beach. Morecambe and Lancaster also within easy reach.
Restaurant and swimming pool 2 miles.
From Lancaster, travel W on the A589 for 1¼ miles, turn left on the B5273 as signed 'Heysham', at end turn left on the A5105 for 1¼ miles, then keep left for 1¼ miles to Middleton, keep right to village for ½ mile to site on left.

HIGH BENTHAM *Lancashire*   Map 4 B1

Riverside Caravan Park
Wenning Avenue, Bentham. ☎ (0468) 61272
Open: March-October
Size: 11 acres, 30 touring pitches. 6 hot showers,
12 WCs

Turn S on the B4680 at Black Bull Hotel in High
Bentham. Site signed.

HIGH WYCOMBE *Buckinghamshire*   Map 2 B2

Harleyford Estate
Harleyford, Marlow, SL7 2DX.
☎ (062 84) 71361
Open: March-October
Size: 3 (300) acres, 60 touring pitches. 10 hot
showers, 10 WCs

M4 on to A404(W) on to A4155(W) for 2 miles. Site
on left.

HINDERWELL *North Yorkshire*   Map 5 A1

Fern Farm
30 High Street. ☎ (0947) 840350
Open: March-October
Size: 3 acres, 5 touring pitches. 2 WCs

Site in centre of Hinderwell.

HODDESDON *Hertfordshire*   Map 3 A2

DOBB'S WEIR CARAVAN PARK   RAC L
Essex Road, EN11 0AS. ☎ (0992) 462090
Open: Easter-31 October
Size: 8 (24) acres, 100 touring pitches, 66 with elec,
100 static caravans. 19 hot showers, 19 WCs,
2 CWPs

Car & caravan, Motor caravan, Car & tent, M/cycle
& tent £4 per adult, £2 per child; elec £2; WS
*A secluded, riverside park with excellent facilities
plus angling, boating, walking and picnicking
within immediate surroundings. Shop 500 yards.
Restaurant and swimming pool 1½ miles.
Maximum stay 14 days.*
From the Hoddesdon interchange of the A10,
follow signs to Hoddesdon town centre. At second
roundabout, turn left into Essex Road to site on

right in 1 mile, signed.

HOLBEACH *Lincolnshire*   Map 5 B3

WHAPLODE MANOR CARAVAN PARK   RAC L
Saracen's Head, PE12 8AZ. ☎ (0406) 22837
Open: Easter-30 November
Size: 1 acre, 20 touring pitches, all level, all with
elec. 2 hot showers, 4 WCs, 1 CWP

(1991) Car & caravan £5, Motor caravan £4.50, Car
& tent, M/cycle & tent £4-£5; elec £1, awn £1
cc Access, Visa/B'card
*In the grounds of an 18th century manor house.
Grassy, level and sheltered, ideal base for
exploring the Fens. Shop ¼ mile. Restaurant
2 miles. Swimming pool 8 miles.*
From Long Sutton, travel W on the A17 to
Saracen's Head on right ¼ mile after Holbeach
village.

Matopos Touring Park
Main Street, Fleet Hargate
☎ (0406) 22910
Open: March-October
Size: 3 acres, 45 touring pitches. 4 hot showers,
7 WCs

A17 King's Lynn to Sleaford, turn left opposite
Happy Eater. From Spalding A151 to Fleet Hargate,
turn right just past Post Office.

HOLSWORTHY *Devon*   Map 1 B2

HEDLEY WOOD CARAVAN &
CAMPING PARK   RAC A
Bridgerule, EX22 7ED. ☎ (028 881) 404
Open: 1 March-30 November
Size: 6 (16½) acres, 120 touring pitches, 60 with
elec, 20 with hardstanding, 60 level pitches,
12 static caravans 15 hot showers, 26 WCs, 3 CWPs

Car & caravan, Motor caravan, Car & tent, M/cycle
& tent £4.50-£5.50, plus 75p-£1 per adult above 2,
child (under 3 years) free; elec £1.25, awn 75p,
dogs 25p; WS
*A quiet, country/woodland site, panoramic views,
children's adventure area, new clubroom and
facilities with licensed bar/off licence and children's
room. Restaurant 3 miles. Swimming pool 3 miles.
10 caravans for hire (own WCs).*
From M5 take junction 27, on new A361 Tiverton to

◙ Snacks/take away   ✖ Restaurant   ◩ Swimming pool   ▣ Shelter for campers   🐕 Dogs accepted   **59**

Barnstaple by-pass take A39 Bideford to Bude road to Kilkhampton, left on to B3254 across A3072 at Red Post for 2½ miles, turn right, 500 yards on right.

Sonventura
Bude Road, Pancrasweek. ☎ (0409) 253731
Open: All year
Size: 5 acres, touring pitches. 1 hot shower, 2 WCs

| 🛏 | 🚐 | 🚗 | 🅰 | | | | | | | 🐕 |

3 miles W of Holsworthy, on A3072.

Long Furlong Cottage Caravan Site
Long Lane, Wiveton, NR25 7DD.
☎ (0263) 740833
Open: All year
Size: 1½ acres, 24 touring pitches. 2 hot showers, 6 WCs

| 🚐 | 🚗 | 🅰 | 🔋 | | | | | | | 🐕 |

In Blakeney (A149), turn S signposted Saxlingham. Site 1½ miles.

TREVORNICK HOLIDAY PARK RAC A
Holywell Bay, TR8 5PW. ☎ (0637) 830531
Open: 1 May-30 September
Size: 30 acres, 500 touring pitches, 230 with elec, all level pitches, 5 with hardstanding. 50 hot showers, 70 WCs, 4 CWPs

| ♿ | 🚐 | 🚗 | 🅰 | 🔋 | 🛒 | 🛍 | ✕ | ⛵ | 🏪 | 🐕 |

(1991) £2.90-£4.25 per person, £1.70-£2.60 per child, plus 60p per Motor caravan, 60p per car; elec £2, dogs £1.30
cc Access, Visa/B'card
Cornwall's best holiday park. Excellent facilities, very high standards and offering far more entertainment and leisure pursuits than any other. Beach ½ mile. No motorcycles.
At 3½ miles S of Newquay on A3075, turn right on unclassified road for 2 miles towards Holywell Bay.

Camping & Caravanning Club Site
Otter Valley Park, Northcote, EX14 8SS.
☎ (0404) 44546
Open: 30 March-26 October
Size: 5 acres, 60 touring pitches. 6 hot showers, 8 WCs

| 🚐 | 🚗 | 🅰 | 🛒 | | | | | | | 🐕 |

Charges on application.
cc Access, Visa/B'card
Set in picturesque vale of the River Otter, 15 minutes' walk from the town centre.
From the A30 follow the "Honiton" signposts then follow the caravan and tent signs. Drive through the public site to reach the Club site.

FISHPONDS HOUSE CAMP SITE RAC A
Dunkeswell, EX14 0SH. ☎ (0404) 891287
Open: All year
Size: 40 acres, 15 touring pitches, 8 with elec, 5 level pitches, 3 camping cabins. 3 hot showers, 3 cold showers, 3 WCs, 1 CWP

| ♿ | 🚐 | 🚗 | 🅰 | 🔋 | 🛒 | 🛍 | ✕ | ⛵ | 🏪 | 🐕 |

Car & caravan, Motor caravan, Car & tent, M/cycle* & tent £2.85 per adult, £1.85 per child; elec £2
cc Visa/B'card
40 acres of tranquil wild life sanctuary. Some entertainment available at certain times. 3 camping cabins for hire. No gas available. Shop 2 miles. Maximum stay one month.
From the junction of the A30 and the A35 at Honiton, follow signs for Dunkeswell and Luppitt for 3 miles to Limers Cross, bear right for 2 miles, at cross-roads turn left to site on right in ½ mile. Site signed.

Fieldhead Campsite
Edale, S30 2ZF. ☎ (0433) 670386
Open: April-October (November-March weekends)
Size: 1¼ acres, 50 touring pitches. 4 hot showers, 6 WCs

| | | | 🅰 | | | | | | 🏪 | 🐕 |

In Hope (A625), take minor road N to Edale. Site ½ mile S of village. Turn left past railway station.

Hardhurst Farm
☎ (0433) 20001
Open: All year
Size: 3 acres, 37 touring pitches. 1 hot shower, 9 WCs

| | 🚐 | 🚗 | 🅰 | | 🛒 | | | | 🏪 | 🐕 |

Site N of A625 from Sheffield-Castleton, 1 mile E of Hope. Rear of Travellers Rest pub.

Laneside Caravan Site
Laneside Farm, S30 2RR. ☎ (0433) 20215
Open: April-October
Size: 5 acres, 60 touring pitches. 6 hot showers, 17 WCs

| | 🚐 | 🚗 | 🅰 | 🔋 | | | | | | 🐕 |

Site on A625, ½ mile E of Hope village.

Losehill Caravan Site
Castleton. ☎ (0433) 20636
Open: March-November
Size: 6 acres, 100 touring pitches. 6 hot showers, 16 WCs

| ♿ | 🚐 | 🚗 | 🅰 | 🔋 | | | | | | 🐕 |

Site 1 mile on right after passing through Hope on the A625.

New Fold Farm
Edale, S30 2ZD. ☎ (0433) 70372
Open: All year
Size: 10 acres, 135 touring pitches. 8 hot showers, 20 WCs

| | 🚐 | 🚗 | 🅰 | 🔋 | 🛒 | 🛍 | | | | 🐕 |

In Hope (A625), take minor road N for 4 miles to site on right.

Waterside Farm
Edale. ☎ (0433) 70215
Open: March-October
Size: 4 (7) acres, 55 touring pitches. 12 WCs

| | 🚐 | 🚗 | 🅰 | | | | | | | 🐕 |

On A625, take minor road N for 4½ miles.

HORAM *East Sussex* — Map 3 A3

HORAM MANOR TOURING PARK RAC L
Near Heathfield, TN21 0YD.
☎ (04353) 3662
Open: 1 March-31 October
Size: 6 (7) acres, 90 touring pitches, 20 with elec.
6 hot showers, 13 WCs, CWP

Car & caravan, Motor caravan, Car & tent, M/cycle
& tent £8; awn free
*An attractive, secluded, country site surrounded by
trees. Very well-kept. Nature trails and Sussex
Farm Museum on Horam Estate. Shop ¼ mile.
Restaurant ¼ mile. Old Barn Tea Rooms with
children's play area and horse riding 200 yards.
Coarse fishing on site.*
Site is on the A267, ½ mile S of Horam village,
3 miles from Heathfield.

HORNCASTLE *Lincolnshire* — Map 5 B2

Ashby Park
West Ashby, PE23 5DW.
☎ (0790) 53321
Open: All year
Size: 50 acres, 35 touring pitches. 4 hot showers,
6 WCs

1½ miles N of Horncastle between A153 and A158.

HORNSEA *Lincolnshire* — Map 5 B2

Four Acres Caravan Park
Atwick.
☎ (0964) 532428
Open: March-October
Size: 4 acres, 40 touring pitches. 3 hot showers,
10 WCs

Site on B1242, 2 miles N of Hornsea.

HORRABRIDGE *Devon* — Map 1 B3

MAGPIE LEISURE PARK RAC L
Bedford Bridge, PL20 7RY.
☎ (0822) 852651
Open: 15 March-15 November
Size: 2-3 (10) acres, 30 touring pitches, all level, 20+
with elec, 3 with hardstanding, 18 static caravans, 5
chalets. 4 hot showers, 8 WCs, 2 CWPs

Car & caravan, Motor caravan, Car & tent, M/cycle
& tent £4-£6.50, plus 75p per adult above 2, 50p
child; extra car 50p; elec £1, awn 75p, dogs £1; WS
*A spacious, sheltered, woodland site on the edge
of the Dartmoor National Park with separate
riverside caravan and camping field and new toilet
block. Adjacent to open moorland and ideally
placed for touring Devon and Cornwall. Shop and
restaurant less than a mile away. Swimming pool
2½ miles. Calor gas only. 5 chalets and 2 caravans
for hire (own WCs).*
Direct access from A386 Tavistock to Plymouth
road.

HORSEY *Norfolk* — Map 3 B1

Waxham Sands Holiday Park
Warren Farm, NR29 4EJ. ☎ (069 261) 325
Open: May-September
Size: 12 acres, 200 touring pitches. 1b hot showers,
4b WCs

Site 2 miles N of Horsey on E side of B1159.

HORSHAM *West Sussex* — Map 3 A3

RAYLANDS CARAVAN PARK RAC L
Jackrells Lane, Southwater
☎ (0403) 730218/731822
Open: 1 March-31 October
Size: 6 (8) acres, 60 touring pitches, all level,
40 with elec, 60 static caravans. 6 hot showers,
10 WCs, 1 CWP

(1991) Car & caravan, Motor caravan £6.25, Car &
tent, M/cycle & tent £4 (2 people); elec £1.25
*Picturesque parkland setting in the heart of the
Sussex countryside, landscaped and developed to
the highest standards. English Tourist Board grade
4 Ticks. Shop 2 miles. Swimming pool 3 miles.
Clearly signposted from main A24 S of Horsham.*

Wincaves Park Caravan & Camping
Dial Post, RH13 8WX. ☎ (0403) 710923
Open: March-January
Size: 9 acres, 100 touring pitches. 16 hot showers,
16 WCs

300 yards off A24. Follow international signs to
Ashurst ¼ mile S of Dial Post village.

HUDDERSFIELD *West Yorkshire* — Map 5 A2

Holme Valley Camping & Caravan Park
Thongsbridge, Holmfirth, HD7 2TD.
☎ (0484) 665819
Open: All year
Size: 4½ acres, 57 touring pitches. 4 hot showers, 8
WCs. 5 static caravans

Take A616 S from Huddersfield. At Honley, turn on
to A6024 towards Holmfirth. Site access midway
between Honley and Holmfirth.

HULL *Humberside* — Map 5 B2

BURTON CONSTABLE CARAVAN PARK RAC A
Sproatley, HU11 4LN. ☎ (0964) 562508
Open: 1 March-31 October
Size: 30 acres, 175 touring pitches, 36 with elec,
175 static caravans. 16 hot showers, 41 WCs,
3 CWPs

Car & caravan, Motor caravan £5.10, Car & tent,
M/cycle & tent £4.60; elec £1.35
*Access to 20 acres of lakes with fishing and
boating, clubhouse, shop, adventure playground.
Restaurant 1½ miles. Swimming pool 4 miles.*
At 4 miles NE of Hull on A165, turn E on B1238 for
3¾ miles and in Sproatley, fork left, Coniston Road,
site on right in ½ mile.

BURTON CONSTABLE
Caravan Park

Set in the park of Burton Constable Hall, this peaceful lakeside setting is the ideal site for all the family with clubhouse, shop, fishing and adventure playground. We welcome caravans and tents. Close by is a luxury holiday home site.

For more details write to:
The Warden, Old Lodges, Burton Constable Caravan Park, Sproatley, Nr. Hull HU11 4LN or telephone: 0964 562508

SEARLES, GATEWAY TO THE GLORIOUS NORFOLK COAST

EVERY MODERN AMENITY, HEATED SWIMMING POOLS, CLUBROOMS, LUXURY CARAVANS FOR HIRE, SUPERMARKET, HEALTH FACILITIES, INDOOR POOL OPENING EASTER 1992

DIAL A BROCHURE
0485 534211

NORFOLK TOURIST PARK

**HUNSTANTON** *Norfolk*   Map 3 A1

SEARLES HOLIDAY CENTRE   RAC L
3 South Beach Road, PE36 5BB.
☎ (0485) 534211
Open: Easter-October
Size: 12 (50) acres, 150 touring pitches, 76 with elec, all level pitches, 40 with hardstanding, 480 static caravans. 60 hot showers, 60 WCs, 3 CWPs

(1991) Car & caravan, Motor caravan £10, Car & tent, M/cycle & tent £7.25; elec £1.50, Awn £1.75 cc Access, Visa/B'card
Family holiday centre with plenty of room for tourers and tents on individual pitches and only 150 metres from a sandy beach. 200 caravans for hire (own WCs). Minimum stay 3 nights over Bank Holidays and 2 nights over peak weekends. 1 dog per unit.
Turn W off A149 on to B1161 on S outskirts of Hunstanton and then turn left as signed "South Beach".

HUNTINGDON *Cambridgeshire*   Map 3 A1

Houghton Mill Caravan & Camping Park
Mill Street, Houghton. ☎ (0480) 62413
Open: April-September
Size: 10 acres, 50 touring pitches. 6 hot showers, 8 WCs

Site halfway between St Ives and Huntingdon on A1123.

OLD MANOR CARAVAN PARK   RAC A
Church Lane, Grafham, PE18 0BB.
☎ (0480) 810264
Open: All year
Size: 6 acres, 74 touring pitches, all level, 48 with elec. 6 hot showers, 9 WCs, 1 CWP

(1991) Car & caravan, Motor caravan £8, Car & tent £5.50, plus £1 per person above 2; elec £1.50, awn 75p, dogs 50p
Picturesque country site with direct access to 75 acres of woods and near Grafham Water (sailing, fishing, windsurfing). Children's play area. Shop and restaurant ¼ mile. No motorcycles.
At 5 miles W of Huntingdon (2 miles W of junction with A1) on A604, turn S on unclassified road as signed Grafham Water, passing through Ellington to Grafham, 1¾ miles, site on right (International signs from A1 Buckden and A604).

PARK LANE TOURING SITE   RAC A
Park Lane, Godmanchester, PE18 8AF.
☎ (0480) 453740
Open: March-October
Size: 2½ acres, 50 touring pitches, all level, all with elec, 50 static caravans. 4 hot showers, 8 WCs, 1 CWP

Car & caravan, Motor caravan, Car & tent, M/cycle & tent £6, plus £1 per child; elec £1.50, awn £1, dogs free; WS
Parkland site with mature trees and shrubs, level pitches, children's play area. Shop 100 yards. Public house at entrance (serving meals). Swimming pool 5 miles.
Travelling N of Cambridge A604, turn off at

Huntingdon/ Godmanchester turn-off. Proceed through Godmanchester village to War Memorial and turn right.

QUIET WATERS CARAVAN PARK RAC A
Hemingford Abbots, PE18 9AJ.
☎ (0480) 63405
Open: April-October
Size: ½ (5) acres, 20 touring pitches, all level, 16 with elec, 9 static caravans. 6 hot showers, 7 WCs, 1 CWP

| | ⊞ | 🚐 | 🅰 | | 👤 | | | | 🐕 |

Car & caravan, Motor caravan, Car & tent, M/cycle* & £7, plus £1 per person above 2; elec £1.50, awn £1
cc Access/Mastercard, Visa, Eurocard
A riverside park in the centre of the picturesque village of Hemingford Abbots. 9 caravans for hire (own WCs). Restaurant 100 yards. Swimming pool 3 miles.
12 miles W of Cambridge on A604, turn left 1 mile into Hemingford Abbots. 3 miles E of Huntingdon, turn right into Hemingford Abbots and follow site signs for 1 mile.

HUTTOFT *Lincolnshire* **Map 5 B2**

Jolly Common
Sea Lane. ☎ (0507) 490236
Open: March-October
Size: 6¼ acres, 55 touring pitches. 6 WCs

| | ⊞ | 🚐 | 🅰 | | | | | 🏠 | 🐕 |

Take A52 N from Skegness and turn E 1 mile N of Huttoft. Site 1¼ miles.

HYDE *Cheshire* **Map 5 A2**

Camping & Caravanning Club Site
Crowden Camp Site, Crowden, Hadfield, SK14 7HZ.
☎ (04574) 66057
Open: 30 March-26 October
Size: 2 acres, 45 touring pitches. 2 hot showers, 6 WCs

| | | | 🅰 | | 👤 | | | | 🐕 |

Charges on application.
cc Access, Visa/B'card
Level site alongside Crowden Brook. Views of hills and moors of the Peak District National Park. Calor gas only. Shop in Crowden Youth Hostel.
Take the A628 in Crowden. Take the turning at the Hostel and then left at the telephone box, the site is on the left.

ILFRACOMBE *Devon* **Map 1 B2**

Baker's Lincombe Farm
Lee. ☎ (0271) 862304
Open: May-October
Size: 2½ acres, 3 touring pitches. No hot showers, 2 WCs

| | ⊞ | 🚐 | 🅰 | | | | | | 🐕 |

From Ilfracombe take Lee road, follow that to "Give Way" sign, turn right and site is 250 yards on left.

Berrynarbor Caravan Park
Sterridge Valley. ☎ (027 188) 2631
Open: Easter-October
Size: 9 acres, 15 touring pitches. 4 hot showers,

10 WCs. 16 static caravans

| | ⊞ | 🚐 | | ♿ | | | | | 🐕 |

3 miles E of Ilfracombe (A399), turn S signposted Berrynarbor and follow signs to Sterridge Valley. Site signed.

Big Meadow Caravan Site
Watermouth. ☎ (0271) 62282
Open: May-September
Size: 9 acres, 125 touring pitches. 4 hot showers, 18 WCs

| | | 🚐 | 🅰 | | 👤 | | | | 🐕 |

3 miles E of Ilfracombe on A399.

HELE VALLEY HOLIDAY PARK RAC L
Hele Bay, EX34 9RD. ☎ (0271) 862460
Open: April-November
Size: 7 (17) acres, 12 touring pitches, all level, 8 with elec, 83 static caravans. 12 hot showers, 12 cold cold showers, 18 WCs, 1 CWP

| | ⊞ | 🚐 | 🅰 | | 👤 | | | | 🐕 |

(1991) Car & caravan £5-£9.50, Motor caravan £4.50- £6.50, Car & tent, M/cycle & tent £6, plus £2 per adult above 2, child £1.50; elec £1.50, awn 80p, dogs £1.50
A level site in a picturesque, sheltered valley, a few minutes' walk to the beach. Children's play area. 23 caravans for hire (own WCs). Restaurant 300 yards (5 minutes' walk). Swimming pool 500 yards (10 minutes' walk).
At 1¼ miles E of Ilfracombe on A399, turn S as signed "Hele Village".

Little Meadow Camping Site
Lydford Farm. ☎ (0271) 862222
Open: Whitsun-September
Size: 6 acres, 5+ touring pitches. 4 hot showers, 5 WCs

| | ⊞ | 🚐 | 🅰 | | | | | | 🐕 |

Site at Watermouth, 3 miles E of Ilfracombe (A399).

Little Shelfin Farm
Mullacott Cross. ☎ (0271) 862449
Open: July-August
Size: 4 acres, 3+ touring pitches. 1 hot shower, 4 WCs

| | ⊞ | 🚐 | 🅰 | | | | | | 🐕 |

From Mullacott Cross roundabout, take Woolacombe road. Site is 500 yards on right hand side.

Mill Park Camping Site
Berrynarbor. ☎ (0271) 882647
Open: March-October
Size: 30 acres, 160 touring pitches. 12 hot showers, 20 WCs

| | ⊞ | 🚐 | 🅰 | ♿ | 👤 | ☕ | | 🏠 | 🐕 |

Site halfway between Ilfracombe and Combe Martin.

MULLACOTT CROSS HOLIDAY PARK RAC A
EX34 8NB. ☎ (0271) 862212
Open: Easter-End October
Size: 8 (20) acres, 65 touring pitches, 24 with elec, 13 with with hardstanding, 150 static caravans. 16 hot showers, 42 WCs, 1 CWP

🍴 Snacks/take away ❌ Restaurant 🌊 Swimming pool 🏠 Shelter for campers 🐕 Dogs accepted **63**

Car & caravan £5-£8, Motor caravan, Car & tent, M/cycle & tent £4-£7, plus £1 per adult above 2, child 50p; extra car 50p; elec £1.50, awn 50p
cc Access, Visa/B'card
Generally a quieter site between Ilfracombe and Woolacombe. A good centre for touring North Devon. 42 caravans for hire (own WCs). Swimming pool 2 miles. Dogs must be kept on a lead and exercised off the site.
On main A361 road, 2 miles S of Ilfracombe.

NAPPS CAMP SITE   RAC L
Old Coast Road, Berrynarbor, EX34 9SW.
☎ (0271) 882557
Open: Easter-30 October
Size: 6 acres, 100 touring pitches, 60 with elec, 90 level pitches, 10 with hardstanding, 1 static caravan. 10 hot showers, 18 WCs, 1 CWP

Car & caravan £5, Motor caravan £4, Car & tent, M/cycle & tent £5, plus 80p per person above 2; elec £1.50, awn £1, dogs 50p; WS
Quiet, family site right on beautiful North Devon coast. Glorious sea views, footpath to beach 200 yards, footpath to pub and beach 250 yards. Popular well-kept site. 1 caravan for hire.
From M5 leave at Exit 27, follow new North Devon Link Road (A361) to South Molton, turn off A361 following directions to Combe Martin, drive through Combe Martin (A399), site signposted after 1½ miles on right.

Stowford Farm Meadows
Combe Martin. ☎ (0271) 882476
Open: Easter-October
Size: 35 acres, 570 touring pitches. 62 hot showers, 108 WCs

2 miles SE of Combe Martin (A399), turn W onto B3343 for 3½ miles. Site ¾ mile along site road.

WATERMOUTH COVE HOLIDAY PARK   RAC A
Berrynarbor.
☎ (0271) 62504
Open: Easter-September
Size: 5½ (27) acres, 90 touring pitches. 4 chalets. 16 hot showers, 32 WCs

Charges on application.
A wooded site with a private beach, headland and harbour with slipway adjacent. Swimming, boating and fishing available, clubhouse and children's play area. 4 chalets for hire (own WCs).
2¼ miles E of Ilfracombe and 3 miles W of Combe Martin on A399.

HIDDEN VALLEY TOURING & CAMPING PARK   RAC A
West Down, EX34 8NU.
☎ (0271) 813831
Open: 15 March-15 November
Size: 4 (25) acres, 50 touring pitches, all level, 1 with hardstanding, 42 with elec. 7 hot showers, 9 WCs, 3 CWPs

Car & caravan £3-£7.50, Motor caravan, Car & tent, M/cycle & tent £3-£6; extra car £1; extra person £1, child 50p; elec £1.30, awn £1, dogs free-£1
Nestling in a beautiful, secluded, wooded valley where wild ducks often join our tame ones on the lake. Only a few minutes' drive to our famous golden coast or to Exmoor's National Park. Sheltered pitches terraced for privacy. Children's play area. Dog walking area. Lounge and restaurant, NOT clubroom. 4 acre field for rallies adjoins the park. Reduced rates for over 50s.
On A361, 2 miles from Branton village, travelling from Branton to Ilfracombe. From Ilfracombe the site lies 3 miles along the main road (A361) to Barnstaple, on the left.

ILMINSTER *Somerset*   Map 2 A3

Southfork Caravan Park
Parrett Works, Martock, TA12 6AE.
☎ (0935) 825661
Open: All year
Size: 2 acres, 30 touring pitches. 4 hot showers, 5 WCs

Halfway between Martock and South Petherton off the A303. Signed.

IPSWICH *Suffolk*   Map 3 B2

Orwell Meadows Caravan Park
Priory Farm, Nacton, IP10 0JS.
☎ (0473) 726666
Open: March-October
Size: 23 acres, 80 touring pitches. 10 hot showers, 12 WCs. 10 static caravans

From A45 Ipswich by-pass take first exit left after Orwell Bridge. Continue to roundabout, take first exit. Take left in 300 yards into Priory Lane for 1 mile. Site is past Tudor cottages.

PRIORY PARK   RAC A
Nacton Road, IP10 0JT.
☎ (0473) 727393
Open: All year
Size: 5 (85) acres, 75 touring pitches, 70 level pitches, all with elec, 10 with hardstanding, 20 static caravans, 15 chalets. 10 hot showers, 10 cold showers, 20 WCs

(1991) Car & caravan, Motor caravan, Car & tent, M/cycle & tent £5; all plus £2.50 per person; dogs £1
Superb, south-facing, 85-acre parkland stretching down with access to foreshore, beach and River Orwell estuary. Panoramic views. Very tranquil. 5 minutes to motorway, 7 minutes to Ipswich centre. Own private 9 hole golf course. Nature trail. Adventure playground. Tourist Board graded 4 Ticks. Shop 2 miles. 3 chalets for hire (own WCs). No single-sex groups.
Travelling E along the A45 Ipswich southern by-pass, take first exit after River Orwell road bridge. Turn left towards Ipswich following caravan/camping signs. 300 yards from by-pass on left is entrance to mile-long access road. Follow signs to Priory Park.

Facilities for Disabled   Caravans accepted   Motor caravans   Tents   Laundry room   Shop

KELSALL Cheshire · Map 4 B2

Northwood Hall
Lower Kelsall, Tarporley, CW6 0PR. ☎ (0829) 51305
Open: March-October
Size: 2½ acres, 30 touring pitches. 2 hot showers, 6 WCs

Site on A54, ¼ mile W of Kelsall.

KENDAL Cumbria · Map 4 B1

Millbrook Caravan Park
Endmoor, LA8 0HJ. ☎ (044 87) 624
Open: March-October
Size: 23 acres, 10 touring pitches. 5 hot showers, 8 WCs

Site signed from A65 to Kendal: ¼ mile.

Millness Hill
Preston Patrick, Milnthorpe, LA7 7NU.
☎ (044 87) 306
Open: March-October
Size: 2 (3) acres, 29 touring pitches. 2 hot showers, 7 WCs Static caravans

From M6 junction 36, take A65 towards Kirkby Lonsdale. Turn left signposted Endmoor.

Camping & Caravanning Club Site
Millcrest, Skelsmergh, Shap Road, LA9 6NY.
Open: 30 March-26 October
Size: 60 touring pitches. 4 hot showers, 6 WCs

Charges on application.
This site is directly off the A6.

KESSINGLAND Suffolk · Map 3 B1

Chestnut Farm
Gisleham, NR33 8EE. ☎ (0502) 740227
Open: March-October
Size: 3½ acres, 20 touring pitches. 2 hot showers, 4 WCs

A12 southern end of Kessingland by-pass, big roundabout, turn W signposted Rushmere/Mutford. Take second left for site.

Heathland Beach Caravan Park
London Road. ☎ (0502) 740337
Open: Easter-October
Size: 35 acres, 106 touring pitches. 32 hot showers, 50 WCs. 7 static caravans

1 mile N of Kessingland on B1437, turn E into site.

Whitehouse Farm
Gisleham, NR33 8DX. ☎ (0502) 740248
Open: Easter-October
Size: 4½ acres, 40 touring pitches. 2 hot showers, 5 WCs

In Kessingland (A12), turn W opposite Wildlife Park. Turn right at second junction. Site 250 yards.

Camping & Caravanning Club Site
Suffolk Wildlife Park, Whites Lane, NR33 7SL.
Open: 30 March-26 October
Size: 90 touring pitches. 10 hot showers, 9 WCs

Charges on application.
From the A12, follow the signs for the Wildlife Park.

KESWICK Cumbria · Map 4 B1

Burns Farm
St Johns-in-the-Vale, CA12 4RR.
☎ (076 87) 79225
Open: March-October
Size: 1½ acres, 37 touring pitches. 4 hot showers, 5 WCs

Off A66 coming from Penrith. Site 1 mile SW of Threlkeld.

Castlerigg
☎ (076 87) 72437
Open: April-November
Size: 5 (15) acres, 110 touring pitches. 6 hot showers, 16 WCs. Static caravans

Site off A591, 1½ miles SE of Keswick.

Dale Bottom Farm
☎ (076 87) 72176
Open: March-October
Size: 2 acres, 20 touring pitches. 5 hot showers, 12 WCs. 30 static caravans

Site off A591, 2½ miles SE of Keswick.

DERWENTWATER CARAVAN SITE RAC A
Crow Park Road, CA12 5EN.
☎ (07687) 72579
Open: 1 March-14 November
Size: 4 (19) acres, 60 touring pitches, all with elec, all level, all with hardstanding, 178 static caravans. 22 hot showers, 22 cold showers, 52 WCs, 1 CWP

(1991) £2.80-£3.40 per person; £1.40-£1.60 per pitch
Within walking distance of Keswick town centre (five minutes). Own lake frontage. Calor gas only. Restaurant 300 yards. Swimming pool 1 mile. No motorcycles.
½ mile W of town centre, leaving by Tithebarn Street.

NORTH LAKES CARAVAN & CAMPING PARK RAC A
Bewaldeth, CA13 9SY. ☎ (07687) 76510
Open: March-14 November
Size: 30 acres, 145 touring pitches, all level, 100 with elec, 37 static caravans. 24 hot showers, 30 WCs, 3 CWPs

Charges on application.
Tranquil site set in hilly countryside. Many pitches along two small streams running through site. Licensed bar, play area. 2 caravans for hire (own WCs). Restaurant 2 miles.
Site on W side of the A591, 3 miles S of Bothel and 9 miles N of Keswick.

◪ Snacks/take away ☒ Restaurant ◺ Swimming pool ▣ Shelter for campers ⌂ Dogs accepted **65**

England

Scotgate Caravan & Camping Site

Braithwaite. ☎ (059 682) 343
Open: March-October
Size: 4½ (5) acres, 175 touring pitches. 8 hot showers, 28 WCs. Static caravans, chalets

[icons]

Site on B5292, 2 miles W of Keswick, near junction with A66.

Camping & Caravanning Club Site

Derwentwater, CA12 5EP.
Open: 3 February-30 November
Size: 11 acres, 250 touring pitches. 17 hot showers, 25 WCs

[icons]

Charges on application.
From the A66/A591 junction take the A591 towards Keswick. Turn left at the roundabout, over the bridge take the second right and follow the road to the site.

KIDDERMINSTER *Hereford & Worcester Map 2 A1*

Shorthill Farm

Kidderminster Road, Crossway Green, Stourport, DY13 9SH.
☎ (0299) 250571
Open: All year
Size: 4 acres, 25 touring pitches. 4 hot showers, 4 WCs

[icons]

Site on A449 Kidderminster-Worcester road at rear of Little Chef. 2¾ miles SE of Stourport.

Camping & Caravanning Club Site

Brown Westhead Park, Wolverley, DY10 3PX.
Open: 30 March-26 October
Size: 8.2 acres, 130 touring pitches. 6 hot showers, 12 WCs

[icons]

Charges on application.
From the A371 follow the international camping signs.

KIELDER *Northumberland Map 7 A3*

KIELDER FORESTRY COMMISSION SITE RAC L

☎ (0434) 250291
Open: Easter-31 October
Size: 5 acres, 70 touring pitches, all level. 4 hot showers, 10 WCs, 1 CWP

[icons]

Car & caravan, Motor caravan, Car & tent, M/cycle & tent £6.50-£7.50; elec £1, awn 50p-£1
Flat site beside stream surrounded by woodland and fields. ¼ mile from Kielder village and Kielder Castle Visitor Centre. Small shop on site, Post Office and general store 400 yards in village. Restaurant ½ mile. Swimming pool 36 miles. No gas available.
From Newcastleton, take the B6357 to Saughtree, turn right for Kielder to site on left in 6 miles.

KINGSBRIDGE *Devon Map 1 B3*

Camping & Caravanning Club Site

Middle Ground, Slapton, TQ7 1QW.

☎ (0548) 580538
Open: 30 March-26 October
Size: 5.9 acres, 119 touring pitches. 4 hot showers, 12 WCs

[icons]

Charges on application.
cc Access, Visa/B'card
Site overlooks Start Bay and is only a few minutes' walk from the beach. Only 8 caravans accepted. Shop 400 yards.
From the A379 turn towards Slapton, the site is on the right.

Parkland Caravan & Camping Site

Sorley Green Cross, TQ7 4AF.
☎ (0548) 852723
Open: All year
Size: 3 acres, 45 touring pitches. 5 hot showers, 8 WCs

[icons]

From A381 Totnes/Kingsbridge, 12 miles down see Stumpy Post Cross and turn on to B3194 straight down road. 1 mile N of Kingsbridge.

KING'S LYNN *Norfolk Map 3 A1*

DIGLEA CAMPING & CARAVAN PARK RAC L

Beach Road, Snettisham, PE31 7RB.
☎ (0485) 41367
Open: 2 April-31 October
Size: 8 (32) acres, 200+ touring pitches, 30 with elec, all level pitches, 150 static caravans. 20 hot showers, 35 WCs, 5 CWPs

[icons]

(1991) Car & caravan, Motor caravan, Car & tent, M/cycle & tent from £3.50-£6.50, (+£3 for weekend stay) plus £2 per adult/£1 child above 2; elec £2, awn £1
Situated ¼ mile from the beach, surrounded by trees with large, open, grassed areas. Large clubhouse with 2 bars: 1 for parents and children, 1 for adults only. Children's activity play area. 5 caravans for hire. Fully-stocked shop on site, also ¼ mile away. Swimming pool 6 miles.
Turn to the sea off the A149 at Snettisham by-pass to beach. 1½ miles from by-pass.

Gatton Waters Caravan & Camping Site

Hillington. ☎ (0485) 600643
Open: April-October
Size: 22 acres, 90 touring pitches. 12 hot showers, 12 WCs

[icons]

8½ miles NE of King's Lynn on A148. Signposted.

PENTNEY PARK CAMPING & CARAVAN SITE RAC L

Gayton Road, Pentney, PE32 1HU.
☎ (0760) 337479
Open: All year
Size: 16 acres, 201 touring pitches, all level, 106 with elec. 14 hot showers, 44 WCs, 3 CWPs

[icons]

Charges on application. WS
cc Access, Visa/B'card
Well-maintained, attractive woodland site with swimming pool and children's play area. Restaurant 500 yards.

🖳 Facilities for Disabled 🚐 Caravans accepted 🚙 Motor caravans 🅰 Tents 🧺 Laundry room 🛒 Shop

At 9 miles SE of King's Lynn on A47 turn left on to B1153 to site on left.

One and a third miles from Junction 3 on M55.

KIRKBY LONSDALE *Cumbria*   Map 4 B1

Crabtree Farm
Lupton. ☎ (044 87) 288
Open: March-October
Size: 1 acre, 10 touring pitches. 2 WCs. 5 static caravans

From M6 junction 36, take A65 for Kirkby Lonsdale. In Lupton, turn into lane opposite Plough Inn. Site ½ in mile.

KIRKBY STEPHEN *Cumbria*   Map 4 B1

Bowber Head
Ravenstonedale. ☎ (05396) 23254
Open: All year
Size: 1 acre, 10 touring pitches. 2 hot showers, 3 WCs

4½ miles S of Kirkby Stephen on A683 opposite Fat Lamb Hotel.

Pennine View Caravan & Camp Site
Pennine View, Station Road
☎ (07683) 71717
Open: March-November
Size: 2½ acres, 38 touring pitches. 6 hot showers, 10 WCs

Site on S side of Kirkby Stephen, 1 miles from town centre, on A685.

KIRKHAM *Lancashire*   Map 4 B2

Whitmore Caravan Site
Bradshaw Lane, Greenhalgh, PR4 3HQ.
☎ (0253) 836224
Open: March-October
Size: 16 touring pitches. 2 hot showers, 4 WCs

KNARESBOROUGH *North Yorkshire*   Map 5 A1

Allerton Park
☎ (0423) 330569
Open: March-October (tourers)/January (static)
Size: 12 acres, 40 touring pitches. 10 hot showers, 20 WCs. 2 static caravans

From Knaresborough, travel E on A59. After 4 miles (and 800 yards after crossing A1) turn N on unclassified road. Site signposted and ¼ mile up the road.

LIDO CARAVAN PARK   RAC A
Wetherby Road, HG5 8LR. ☎ (0423) 865169
Open: 1 April-31 October
Size: 20 (64) acres, 400 touring pitches, 25 with elec, 200 level pitches. 300 static caravans. 10 hot showers, 60 WCs, 1 CWP

Charges on application.
Grassy site by River Nidd, part level, part sloping. Swimming, boating and fishing; children's play area. Pub serving bar meals. Family groups only. At ½ mile E of Knaresborough on A59, turn S on B6164 for ½ mile. Cross River Nidd and take second turn on right at top of hill.

Riverside Caravan Park
York Road. ☎ (0423) 711383
Open: March-October
Size: 1 (2½) acres, 20 touring pitches. 4 hot showers, 8 WCs. 35 static caravans

Site 1½ miles E of Knaresborough on A59.

Scotton Park Caravans
New Road, Scotton, HG5 9HH.
☎ (0423) 864413
Open: March-October

■ Snacks/take away   ✗ Restaurant   ◹ Swimming pool   ▣ Shelter for campers   ⵜ Dogs accepted   67

Size: 4 (5½) acres, 60 touring pitches. 6 hot showers, 6 WCs. Static caravans

1¾ miles W of Knaresborough (B6165), turn right to Scotton.

LACOCK *Wiltshire*　　Map 2 A2

PICCADILLY CARAVAN SITE　　RAC L
Folly Lane, SN15 2LP. ☎ (0249) 730260
Open: 1 April-31 October
Size: 2½ acres, 40 touring pitches, all level, 12 with elec, 11 with hardstanding. 4 hot showers, 6 WCs, 1 CWP

Car & caravan, Motor caravan, Car & tent, M/cycle & tent £5.50; elec £1
Level, grassy site, standing in open countryside, close to the National Trust village of Lacock. Shop and restaurant ½ mile. Swimming pool 4 miles. Turn right off A350 Chippenham/Melksham road signposted to Gastard and caravan symbol.

LAMPLUGH *Cumbria*　　Map 4 B1

Inglenook Caravan Park
CA14 4SH. ☎ (0946) 861240
Open: March-November
Size: 3½ acres, 42 touring pitches. 4 hot showers, 8 WCs. 5 static caravans

6 miles S of Cockermouth (A5086), turn E for ¾ mile to Lamplugh. Site signed near Pack of Hounds Inn.

LANCASTER *Lancashire*　　Map 4 B1

CROOK-O-LUNE CARAVAN PARK　　RAC L
Scarthwaite, Caton, LA2 9HS.
☎ (0524) 770216
Open: 1 March-31 October
Size: 32 acres, 23 touring pitches, 10 with elec, 152 static caravans. 6 hot showers, 8 WCs, 1 CWP

Charges on application.
Quiet country site on open parkland, surrounded by trees. Games room. Fishing on river across road. Shop ¾ mile. Swimming pool 2 miles. 3½ miles E of Lancaster or 1½ miles E of M6 exit 34, on A683.

Marina Caravan Park
Glasson Dock. ☎ (0524) 751787
Open: March-October
Size: 12 acres, 16 touring pitches. 4 hot showers, 5 WCs

From A6 Cockerham road (A588) follow signposts to Glasson Dock.

MOSS WOOD CARAVAN PARK　　RAC A
Crimbles Lane, Cockerham, LA2 0ES.
☎ (0524) 791041
Open: March-October
Size: 2 (20) acres, 25 touring pitches, 15 with elec, 143 static caravans. 2 hot showers, 4 WCs, 1 CWP

Charges on application.
Pleasant, spacious site lined with trees. Restaurant 1½ miles. Swimming pool 4½ miles. New ironing and laundry room for 1992.
Crimbles Lane is 1 mile W of Cockerham village on the A588.

LANGPORT *Somerset*　　Map 2 A3

Crest Leisure Caravan Park
Bowdens. ☎ (0458) 250553
Open: March-November
Size: 16 acres, 30 touring pitches. 4 hot showers, 8 WCs. 10 static caravans

Between Taunton, Bridgwater, Yeovil. 1½ miles N of Langport on the A372. Turn N into lane signposted Bowdens. Site in ½ mile.

LAUNCESTON *Cornwall*　　Map 1 B3

Launceston Rugby Football Club
Polson Bridge. ☎ (0566) 773406
Open: All year
Size: 13 acres, 25 touring pitches. 8 hot showers, many WCs

Towards Launceston from E, follow signposts for Callington/Tavistock then camping signs. Site 1 mile from town centre.

LECHLADE *Gloucestershire*　　Map 2 B2

Bridge House
GL7 3AG. ☎ (0367) 52348
Open: March-October
Size: 3¼ acres, 45 touring pitches. 4 hot showers, 8 WCs

Site ¼ mile S of Lechlade on A361.

ST JOHNS PRIORY PARK　　RAC L
Faringdon Road, GL7 3EZ. ☎ (0367) 52360
Open: 1 March-31 October
Size: 5 (25) acres, 35 touring pitches, all level, 16 with elec, 74 static caravans. 6 hot showers, 10 WCs, 1 CWP

(1991) Car & caravan, Motor caravan £6-£9, Car & tent, M/cycle & tent £3 per person; elec £1.75
100 yards from River Thames adjacent to famous Trout Inn. Flat, well-drained, grassy, sheltered holiday and touring park. Ideal for Cotswolds. 4 caravans for hire (own WCs). Shop and restaurant ½ mile. Swimming pool 6 miles. ½ mile outside Lechlade on A417 to Faringdon.

LEDBURY *Hereford & Worcester*　　Map 2 A2

RUSSELL'S END CARAVAN PARK　　RAC A
Bromesberrow, HR8 1PB. ☎ (0531) 650687
Open: 1 March-30 November
Size: 3 (3¾) acres, 60 touring pitches, all level, 43 with elec. 6 hot showers, 11 WCs, 1 CWP

　 🚾 Facilities for Disabled　🚐 Caravans accepted　🚍 Motor caravans　🅰 Tents　🅰 Laundry room　🔳 Shop

Car & caravan £5-£6, Motor caravan £4.50-£5.50, Car & tent, M/cycle* & tent £4, plus £2.50 per adult above 2, child £1.50; extra car £1.50; elec £1.50
Level and sheltered rural site. Play area for ball games, etc. Barbecues allowed. Ideal situation for touring. Shop 1 mile. Restaurant 1½ miles. Swimming pool 4 miles. 21 days maximum stay. Site on W side of A417, 150 yards S of M50 junction 2.

LEEDS *West Yorkshire* — Map 5 A2

Camping & Caravanning Club Site
Roundhay Park, Elmete Lane, off Wetherby Road, LS8 2LG.
☎ (0532) 659005
Open: 30 March-28 September
Size: 8 acres, 60 touring pitches. 4 hot showers, 7 WCs

Charges on application.
cc Access, Visa/B'card
Set in a vast country park which has a lake, golf course and tennis courts. 4 miles from Leeds city centre. Shop and restaurant 1 mile.
From the A52 turn into Wetherby Road, then right into Elmete Lane, the site is on the left.

LEEK *Staffordshire* — Map 5 A3

Blackshaw Moor
☎ (053 834) 203
Open: March-November
Size: 8½ acres, 96 touring pitches. 10 hot showers, 10 WCs

From Buxton take A53 towards Leek. Site 150 yards beyond Blackshaw Moor sign.

Glencote Caravan Park
Churnet Valley, Station Road, Cheddleton, ST13 7EE.
☎ (0538) 360745
Open: April-October
Size: 6 acres, 48 touring pitches. 4 hot showers, 6 WCs. 5 static caravans

Site off A520, 3½ miles S of Leek.

LEISTON *Suffolk* — Map 3 B1

CAKES & ALE PARK ㎂ A
Abbey Lane, IP16 4TE. ☎ (0728) 831655
Open: Easter/1 April-31 October
Size: 5 (45) acres, 75 touring pitches, all level, 50 with elec, 20 with hardstanding, 200 static caravans, 4 chalets. 20 hot showers, 20 cold showers, 20 WCs, 2 CWPs

(1991) Car & caravan, Motor caravan, Car & tent, M/cycle & tent £4; all plus £2 per person; elec £1, dogs £1
Very well-maintained, low-profile, quiet park ideally placed as a centre for access to the best of coastal Suffolk. Restaurant 2 miles. Swimming pool 2 miles. 4 chalets for hire (own WCs). English Tourist Board graded 4 Ticks.
Leave A12 Woodbridge/Lowestoft at Saxmundham

turning on to B1121. Go to Saxmundham, turn on to B1119 towards Leiston. 3 miles from Saxmundham leave B1119 turning on to minor road going over level crossing. Follow international caravan signs.

LEOMINSTER *Hereford & Worcester* — Map 2 A1

Nicholson Farm
Docklow. ☎ (056 882) 269
Open: Easter-October
Size: 1¾ acres, 8 touring pitches. 1 hot shower, 2 WCs

Midway between Leominster and Bromyard (A44), turn N ¾ mile E of Docklow. Farm signed.

LEYBURN *North Yorkshire* — Map 5 A1

AKEBAR PARK ㎂ A
Wensleydale. ☎ (0677) 50201
Open: March-October
Size: 10 (23) acres, 110 touring pitches, all level, 40 with elec, 180 static caravans. 23 hot showers, 50 WCs, 6 CWPs

Charges on application.
A wooded site with extensive facilities. Caravans for hire (own WCs). Family groups only.
5¼ miles E of Leyburn on A684.

CONSTABLE BURTON HALL CARAVAN PARK ㎂ A
DL8 5LJ. ☎ (0677) 50428
Open: April-October
Size: 10 acres, 120 touring pitches, 80 with elec, 20 level pitches. 9 hot showers, 14 WCs, 3 CWPs

Charges on application.
A wooded parkland site in the grounds of Constable Burton Hall (open April-August). Good spot for bird-watching. Shop 3 miles.
From intersection of A684 and A1, travel W on A684 for 9 miles. Site on right in grounds of Constable Burton Hall.

LINCOLN *Lincolnshire* — Map 5 B2

HARTSHOLME COUNTRY PARK ㎂ L
Skellingthorpe Road. ☎ (0522) 686264
Open: 1 March-31 October
Size: 3 acres, 50 touring pitches, all level, 20 with elec. 4 hot showers, 10 WCs, CWP

(1991) Car & caravan, Motor caravan £4.90, Car & tent, M/cycle & tent £2.20-£4.90; elec £1.10, awn 70p
Attractive camp site set within mature landscaped country park. Sheltered and level pitches. Shop 300 metres. Restaurant 1/2 miles. Swimming pool 500 metres. No gas available. Maximum stay 3 weeks.
2½ miles S of Lincoln on A46, turn right at Bracebridge into Rookery Lane and ½ mile on turn left for ¾ mile.

LISKEARD *Cornwall* — Map 1 B3

Colliford Lake Park
PL14 6PZ. ☎ (020 882) 335

Open: March-October
Size: 3¾ acres, 40 touring pitches. 4 hot showers, 7 WCs

[&] [caravans] [motor caravans] [tents] [laundry] [] [shop] [cafe] [X] [] [] [dog]

2 miles SW of Bolventor (A30), turn S signposted St Neot. Site signposted in ½ mile. 6 miles E of Bodmin.

GREAT TRETHEW MANOR CAMPSITE   RAC L
Horningtops, PL14 3PY. ☎ (050 34) 663
Open: March-October
Size: 3 (30) acres, 55 touring pitches, 30 level pitches. 4 hot showers, 8 WCs, CWP

[caravans] [motor caravans] [tents] [laundry] [shop] [] [cafe] [X] [] [] [dog]

Charges on application.
cc Visa/B'card
A sheltered site set amidst 30 acres of beautiful grounds. Tennis court, trout lake, ponies, playground, restaurant and bar.
From Liskeard, travel towards Plymouth on the A38 to the junction with the B3251, turn S on the B3251 for ¼ mile to site on left.

Kinrowan Park
Trerulefoot, Saltash, PL12 5BZ.
☎ (050 34) 446
Open: March-October
Size: 4 acres, 4 touring pitches. 2 WCs. 7 static caravans

[caravans] [motor caravans] [tents] [laundry] [] [] [] [] [] [dog]

Site 1 mile W of Trerulefoot roundabout (A38), 200 yards N of road.

PINE GREEN CARAVAN PARK   RAC L
Doublebois, PL14 6LD. ☎ (0579) 20183
Open: Easter-October
Size: 2 acres, 50 touring pitches. 4 hot showers, 6 WCs, 1 CWP

[caravans] [motor caravans] [tents] [laundry] [shop] [] [] [] [] [dog]

Charges on application.
A small, terraced site planted with young trees. Views over Bodmin Moor. Children's play area on site. Restaurant 1 mile. Swimming pool 4 miles.
From Liskeard, travel W on the A38 to Dobwalls. Keep right and ¾ mile further turn left on the B3360, site ¼ mile on right.

Trenant Caravan Park
St Neot. ☎ (0579) 20896
Open: April-October
Size: 1 acre, 8 touring pitches. 2 hot showers, 3 WCs. 4 static caravans

[caravans] [motor caravans] [tents] [laundry] [] [] [] [] [] [dog]

Come off A38 at Dobwalls, go past Family Adventure Park and come to junction, turn right, 200 yards later take left signposted St Neot and after crossing bridge, sharp right turn signposted Trenant, up to crossroads, turn right and site at bottom of hill.

LITTLEHAMPTON *West Sussex*   Map 3 A3

White Rose Touring Park
Mill Lane, Wick, BN17 7PH. ☎ (0903) 716176
Open: March-January
Size: 6¾ acres, 127 touring pitches. 8 hot showers, 17 WCs

[&] [caravans] [motor caravans] [tents] [laundry] [shop] [] [] [] [dog]

Turn off A27 on to A284 signposted Littlehampton. In 1½ miles turn left for site.

LITTLEPORT *Cambridgeshire*   Map 3 A1

Riverside Caravan & Camping Park
21 New River Bank. ☎ (0353) 860255
Open: March-October
Size: 3½ acres, 35 touring pitches. 4 hot showers, 8 WCs. 12 static caravans

[caravans] [motor caravans] [tents] [laundry] [] [] [] [] [] [dog]

On A10 (Ely-Littleport by-pass) take first left on Queen Adelaide roundabout. Site 1 mile down on your left.

LONDON, NORTH   Map 3 A2

Camping & Caravanning Club Site
Theobalds Park, Bulls Cross Ride, Waltham Cross, EN7 5HS.
☎ (0992) 20604
Open: 30 March-26 October
Size: 14 acres, 150 touring pitches. 4 hot showers, 6 WCs

[caravans] [motor caravans] [tents] [] [shop] [] [] [] [] [dog]

Charges on application.
cc Access, Visa/B'card
Level grass site screened by trees. Only 13 miles from Central London.
From the A10 follow "Crews Hill" signs, turn right over the M25, the site is on the right.

Debden House Campsite
Debden Green, Loughton, IG10 2PA.
☎ 081-508 3008
Open: April-October
Size: 48 acres, 225 touring pitches. 8 hot showers, 18 WCs

[&] [caravans] [motor caravans] [tents] [] [shop] [cafe] [] [] [] [dog]

M25 Junction 26, get on to A121 at Loughton 3/4 miles. Turn on to A1168 (Rectory Lane), second left into Pyrles Lane to a t-junction. Turn right and second left is the site.

EASTWAY CYCLE CIRCUIT   RAC L
Temple Mills Lane, Newham, E15.
☎ 081-534 6085
Open: April-October
Size: 4 acres, 70 touring pitches, 20 level pitches. 10 hot showers, 15 WCs, 1 CWP

[&] [caravans] [motor caravans] [tents] [] [] [] [] [] [dog]

HACKNEY CAMPING
Millfields Road, Hackney Marshes, London E5   ✆ **081-985 7656**

8m north of central London off A104. *Open Jun 18 – Aug 25.* 200 pitches. Level grass and hard standings. Snack bar, baggage store, laundry. ***£4.00 (inc. showers) per person a night.***

CAMP CLOSE TO THE HEART OF LONDON

Within easy reach of the centre of London, you'll discover a range of sites to suit all needs and tastes. All have access to the pleasures of Lee Valley Leisure Park . . . and excellent modern and varied facilities.

For a free colour brochure tel:
Lee Valley
(0992) 700766

Dobbs Weir (Hoddesdon)
Secluded park with 'on site' fishing. Good shopping facilities close by.
Tel: 0992 462090

Picketts Lock Centre (Edmonton)
Every kind of leisure activity on site, also bars, cafeteria and shop.
Tel: 081-803 4756

Eastway (Leyton)
Small friendly site in the heart of London. Close to the excellent Lee Valley sports facilities.
Tel: 081 534 6085

Sewardstone (Chingford)
Quickly reached from London and near M25 Shop and play area
Tel: 081-529 5689

LONDON

LeeValley *Leisure* **Park**

Lee Valley Leisure Park
PO Box 88
Enfield
Middx.

Car & caravan, Motor caravan, Car & tent, M/cycle & tent all £4 per adult, £2 per child
Situated within 40 acres of landscaped parkland only 4 miles from the City of London. Sport and leisure facilities available. Shop and restaurant ¼ mile. Swimming pool 2 miles. No gas available. Maximum stay 14 days.
Site located just off the S side of the A106 (Eastway), between Leyton and Hackney.

Hackney Camping
Millfields Road, Hackney, E5.
☎ 081-985 7656
Open: June-August
Size: 3 acres, 210 touring pitches. 14 hot showers, 13 WCs

Between Hackney and Leyton on A106, turn W into Homerton Road. Continue via Daubeney Road into Millfields Road.

PICKETTS LOCK LEISURE CENTRE
Picketts Lock Lane, Edmonton, N9 0AS.   RAC A
☎ 081-803 4756
Open: All year
Size: 1.82 acres, 150 touring pitches, all level, 60 with elec, 20 with hardstanding. 10 hot showers, 10 cold showers, 12 WCs, 1 CWP

Car & caravan, Motor caravan, Car & tent, M/cycle & tent, Backpackers all £3.60 per adult, £1.60 per child; minimum charge £5.20; elec £1.50
cc Access, Visa/B'card
Adjacent to large sports and leisure complex offering racquet sports, swimming, synthetic pitches, golf, putting, golf driving range, sauna, fitness suite, beauty salon, toning tables, indoor
bowls (winter). Maximum stay: off season 14 days, high season 21 days.
The Centre is off Meridian Way which runs between A406 North Circular Road and Lee Valley Road and is signposted (Picketts Lock Centre).

SEWARDSTONE CARAVAN PARK   RAC A
Sewardstone Road, Chingford, E4 7RA.
☎ 081-529 5689
Open: April-October
Size: 12 acres, 200 touring pitches, 100 level pitches, 72 with elec, 30 with hardstanding. 28 hot showers, 37 WCs, 3 CWPs

Car & caravan, Motor caravan, Car & tent, M/cycle & tent all £4 per adult, £1.60 per child; elec £1.50, awn free, dogs free
cc Access, Visa/B'card
Conveniently situated on outskirts of London, with easy public transport links to central London. Restaurant 1 mile. Swimming pool 3 miles. Maximum stay 14 nights. No single-sex groups, no unaccompanied under 18 year olds.
Leave M25 orbital motorway at Junction 26. Follow signs for Waltham Abbey. Turn left at traffic lights. Site 2 miles on right. (Signposted from motorway junction).

LONDON, SOUTH   Map 3 A2

Abbey Wood Caravan Club Site
Federation Road, Abbey Wood, SE2.
☎ 081-310 2233
Open: All year
Size: 9 acres, 330 touring pitches, 136 with elec, part level, some hardstanding. 3b hot showers, 3b

---

WCs, CWP

From A2, site signed via Danson Road (A221).

Camping & Caravanning Club Site
Bridge Road, Chertsey, Surrey, KT6 8JX.
☎ (0932) 562405
Open: All year (restrictions)
Size: 12 acres, 250 touring pitches, 84 with elec.
8 hot showers, 26 WCs, 2 CWPs

Charges on application.
cc Access, Visa/B'card
Situated on the banks of the Thames. Good rail connection to Central London. Children's play area.
From M25 junction 11 turn NW on to A317. After ½ mile at roundabout keep left. Fork right at school in ¼ mile. At t-junction turn right on to B375. Site on right.

Crystal Palace Caravan Site
Crystal Palace Parade, SE19.
☎ 081-778 7155
Open: All year
Size: 6 acres, 77 touring pitches. 10 hot showers, 15 WCs

Next to BBC transmitter. See A-Z of London.

LONG SUTTON *Lincolnshire*   Map 5 B3

Foremans Bridge Caravan Park
Sutton Road, Sutton St James, PE12 0HU.
☎ (094 585) 346
Open: March-December
Size: 3 acres, 40 touring pitches. 4 hot showers, 6 WCs. 6 static caravans

From A17 take B1390. Site 2 miles down on left.

LONGHORSLEY *Northumberland*   Map 7 B3

Tudor Lodge Caravan Park
☎ (067 088) 364
Open: March-October
Size: 6 (25) acres, 60 touring pitches. 2 hot showers, 9 WCs

Site signed from A697 in Longhorsley.

LONGRIDGE *Lancashire*   Map 4 B2

BEACON FELL VIEW CARAVAN PARK   RÁC A
110 Higher Road, RR3 2TY.
☎ (0772) 785434
Open: 23 March-19 October
Size: 32 acres, 44 touring pitches, 40 with elec. 290 static caravans. 10 hot showers, 18 WCs, 1 CWP

(1991) Car & caravan £5-£9, extra car £3
Inland, terraced park set in old sandstone quarry, overlooking Ribble Valley and views of Beacon Fell Country Park. Restaurant 1 mile. 20 caravans for hire (own WCs). No motorcycles. No under 21s and no all male/female groups.
From Broughton (3½ miles N of Preston on the A6), travel E on the B5269 to Longridge where at roundabout continue ahead, then ¼ mile further, keep left. 400 yards beyond, bear left (Higher Road) to site on right in ¾ mile.

LONGSTOWE *Cambridgeshire*   Map 3 A2

The Fox Inn
CB3 7UF. ☎ (0954) 719264
Open: All year
Size: 2½ acres, 32 touring pitches. 1 hot shower, 3 WCs

Site on A1198, about 11 miles from Cambridge at crossroads with B1046.

LONGTOWN *Cumbria*   Map 7 A3

Camelot Caravan Park
Sandysikes. ☎ (0228) 791248
Open: March-October
Size: 1½ acres, 20 touring pitches. 2 hot showers, 4 WCs

Leave M6 Junction 44, take A7 to Longtown. Site on right in 4 miles.

LOOE *Cornwall*   Map 1 B3

CAMPING CARADON   RÁC A
Trelawne Gardens, PL13 2NA.
☎ (0503) 72388
Open: 1 April-31 October
Size: 2 (3½) acres, 85 touring pitches, all level, 37 with elec, 1 static caravan. 4 hot showers, 13 WCs, 1 CWP

(1991) Car & caravan from £4.50, Motor caravan from £4, Car & tent, M/cycle & tent from £3.50; plus 60p per adult above 2, child 30p; elec £1.40; WS
A quiet, welcoming, family-run site on level ground with children's play area and evening social activities. 1 caravan for hire (own WC). No groups of motorcycles.
At 2¼ miles W of Looe on the A387, turn N on the B3359 and take first on right. Site ¼ mile on left.

POLBORDER HOUSE CARAVAN & CAMPING PARK   RÁC L
Bucklawren Road, PL13 1QR.
☎ (0503) 264265

Open: 1 April-31 October
Size: 3 acres, 36 touring pitches, all level, 28 with elec, 5 static caravans. 8 hot showers, 8 cold showers, 14 WCs, 2 CWPs

Car & caravan, Motor caravan, Car & tent, M/cycle & tent £5.50-£7, plus £1-£2 per person above 2; extra car or trailer 50p-£1; elec £1.60, awn 50p-£1, dogs 50p-£1
Quiet, rural site with good views. Children's play area. 5 caravans for hire (own WCs). Restaurant and swimming pool 1¼ miles.
From the junction of the A38 and A374 between Liskeard and Saltash, travel S down the A374 for 1¼ miles, turn right on the A387 for 3¼ miles to Widegate, turn left on the B3253 for 1¼ miles to No Man's Land, turn left for 3¼ miles to site.

Shillamill Lakes
Lanreath, PL13 2PE. ☎ (0503) 20271
Open: Easter-October
Size: 2 acres, 40 touring pitches. 4 hot showers, 6 WCs

From A390 take B3359 towards Looe and follow signs.

Talland Barton Caravan Park
Talland Bay. ☎ (0503) 72429
Open: Easter-October
Size: 3½ acres, 20 touring pitches. 6 hot showers, 16 WCs. 20 static caravans

From Looe on B road to Polperro, 1 mile turn left, 1¼ miles down road on right hand side.

TENCREEK CARAVAN PARK   RAC A
PL13 2JR. ☎ (0503) 262447
Open: All year
Size: 14 acres, 254 touring pitches, all level, 160 with elec, 45 static caravans. 24 hot showers, 46 WCs, 1 CWP

(1991) Car & caravan, Motor caravan, Car & tent, M/cycle & tent £5-£8.25; plus up to £1.35 per person above 2 (over 3 years); elec £1.60, awn free, dogs 75p; WS
cc Visa/B'card
Large holiday park with clubhouse and entertainment, cafe/takeaway, heated outdoor swimming pool, shop, adventure play area, laundry. 45 caravans for hire (own WCs). No single-sex groups, ie. families and couples only. 400 yards off A387 Looe-Polperro road, the nearest park to Looe.

TREBLE B HOLIDAY CENTRE   RAC A
Polperro Road, PL12 2JS. ☎ (0503) 262425
Open: Easter-End September
Size: 20 (22) acres, 450 touring pitches, all level, 170 with elec, 23 with hardstanding, 30 static caravans, 8 chalets. 36 hot showers, 100 WCs, 4 CWPs

(1991) Car & caravan, Motor caravan, Car & tent, M/cycle & tent £2.50-£4 per adult, £1.25-£2 per child, car 50p-70p; elec £1.50, dogs £1; WS
Set in countryside on main A387, ideal for touring the South West. Large site with all facilities. A family site, with shop, club and dancehall, games and TV rooms, hairdressing salon, outdoor

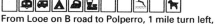 Snacks/take away ☒ Restaurant ◻ Swimming pool ▣ Shelter for campers ♞ Dogs accepted   73

swimming pool, laundry, crazy golf. 30 caravans and 8 chalets for hire (own WCs). No all male or all female parties.
At 2 miles W of Looe on A387. Observe site sign.

Tregoad Caravan & Camp Site
St Martins, PL13 1PB. ☎ (0503) 262718
Open: April-October
Size: 8 acres, 150 touring pitches. 9 hot showers, 23 WCs. 3 static caravans

| 🏠 | 📷 | 🚐 | Ⓐ | 🛁 | 🛍️ | ☕ | | | 🔌 | 🐕 |

E side of Looe. Approaching Looe from E on A387, at Widegates turn left on to B3253 for 1¾ miles. Site on left.

TRELAWNE MANOR HOLIDAY ESTATE   RAC A
☎ (0503) 72151
Open: 1 March-31 October
Size: 5 (40) acres, 47 touring pitches, 16 with elec, 4 with hardstanding, all level, 200 static caravans, 38 flats. 11 hot showers, 10 WCs

| 🏠 | 📷 | 🚐 | Ⓐ | 🛁 | 🛍️ | ☕ | ✕ | 🔌 | |

Charges on application.
Set in park of manor house, this holiday site has lots of amenities including tennis, two bars, a ballroom with nightly entertainment, games and TV rooms. 200 caravans and 38 flats for hire (own WCs).
At 2¼ miles W of Looe on the A387, turn N on the B3359 and take first turn on right, site 100 yards on right.

TRELAY FARMPARK   RAC L
Pelynt, by Looe, PL13 2JX. ☎ (0503) 20900
Open: Easter-end October
Size: 3 (5) acres, 35 touring pitches, all level, 8 with elec, 20 static caravans. 2 hot showers, 8 WCs, 1 CWP

| 🏠 | 📷 | 🚐 | Ⓐ | 🛁 | | | | | 🐕 |

(1991) Car & caravan, Motor caravan, Car & tent, M/cycle & tent from £4.60-£5.30, plus 70p per person above 2 (July & August only); elec £1.30, awn 50p
A friendly, pretty and tranquil park beautifully cared for. ETB and WCTB graded 4 Ticks (Very Good). Shop and restaurant ¼ mile. Swimming pool 10 miles (Liskeard). Sea 3 miles. No gas available. 4 caravans for hire (own WCs).
Motorcycles accepted at owner's discretion.
From the A387 Looe/Polperro road or the A390 Dobwalls/ Lostwithiel road take the B3359.
Park is ¼ mile S of village of Pelynt.

West Wayland Touring Park
West Wayland. ☎ (0503) 262418
Open: Easter-October
Size: 10 acres, 120 touring pitches. 6 hot showers, 14 WCs. 50 static caravans

| 🏠 | 📷 | 🚐 | Ⓐ | 🛁 | 🛍️ | | | | 🐕 |

Site on A387 from Looe to Polperro (2 miles W of Looe).

POWDERHAM CASTLE TOURIST PARK   RAC A
Lanlivery, PL30 5BU. ☎ (0208) 872277
Open: 1 April-31 October
Size: 7 (10) acres, 70 touring pitches, all level,

---

65 with elec, 38 static caravans. 8 hot showers, 20 WCs, 1 CWP

| 🏠 | 📷 | 🚐 | Ⓐ | 🛁 | 🛍️ | | | | 🔌 | 🐕 |

Car & caravan, Car & tent, M/cycle & tent from £2.10, Motor caravan from £1.70, all plus from £1.45 per adult and from 25p per child; elec £1.50; WS
Uncommercialised, quiet park in delightful surroundings with convenient access to all Cornwall. Wiiner of the AA Environmental Award. Highest rating BH&HPA and English Tourist Board. Indoor badminton. Children's activity centre. Restaurant ¼ mile. Swimming pool 2 miles.
At 1¼ miles SW of Lostwithiel, on A390 turn N, signposted to the site, 400 yards.

SPRINGS FARM CARAVAN PARK   RAC L
BD20 8HH. ☎ (0535) 632533
Open: Easter-End October
Size: 1 (3½) acres, 20 touring pitches, 8 with hardstanding, 8 with elec. 2 hot showers, 2 cold showers, 5 WCs, 1 CWP

| 🏠 | | | | 🛁 | | | | | |

(1991) Car & caravan, Motor caravan £4, Car & tent £5; extra car £1; extra person 70p; elec £1, awn £1; WS
Quiet, secluded site on the edge of Lothersdale village with wonderful views of the surrounding hills and own trout lake with fly fishing available, run by conservationists. Ideal position for touring Yorkshire Dales and Moors, Brontë Country and Pendle Hills, or a peaceful relaxing holiday. Shop & restaurant 1½ miles. Calor gas only. No dogs, no hikers. Booking essential.
Take the A629 NE from Keighley, turn W onto the A6068, after ½ mile turn right onto unclassified road to Lothersdale, turn left at crossroads through village, then fork left at derestriction signs, then first left, site in ½ mile.

Azure Sea Caravan Park
The Street, Corton. ☎ (0502) 731403
Open: April-October
Size: 7 acres, 49 touring pitches. 8 hot showers, 12 WCs

| 🦽 | 🏠 | 📷 | 🚐 | Ⓐ | 🛁 | | | | | 🐕 |

Site on A12, 2 miles N of Lowestoft.

HEDLEY HOUSE CARAVAN SITE   RAC L
Chapel Road, Carlton Colville, NR33 8BL.
☎ (0502) 566511
Open: Easter/1 April-October
Size: 8 acres, 90 touring pitches, all level, 48 with elec. 8 hot showers, 8 WCs, 3 CWPs

| 🏠 | 📷 | 🚐 | Ⓐ | 🛁 | | ☕ | ✕ | | 🔌 | 🐕 |

(1991) Car & caravan £5.50 (inc. 2 people), Motor caravan £6 (inc. 4), Car & tent £4.50 (inc. 2), plus £1.25 per extra person; elec £1.75, awn 80p, dogs 75p; WS
cc Access, Amex, Diners, Visa, Switch
Set in 8 acres of flat grass area with numerous mature trees, plus large natural spring-fed pond. Shop ¼ mile. Swimming pool 1 mile.
Approach from A12 or A146. Follow all signs to the

Transport Museum. Site is next door on B1384.

KESSINGLAND BEACH HOLIDAY VILLAGE   RAC A
Kessingland, NR33 7RN. ☎ (0502) 740636
Open: Easter-31 October
Size: 10 (65) acres, 90 touring pitches, all level,
30 with elec, 200 static caravans, 97 chalets. 6 hot
showers, 14 WCs, 1 CWP

(1991) Car & caravan, Motor caravan £10-£11.50,
Car & tent, M/cycle & tent £10; awn £2.50; WS
cc Access, Visa/B'card
*Full sports and day and evening entertainment
programme with nightly cabarets and live bands,
disco, three clubrooms. 103 caravans and
97 chalets for hire (own WCs). No all male or all
female parties under 25.*
At Kessingland, S of Lowestoft, turn E off the
A12 on to the B1437 to site.

North Denes Camping & Caravan Site
☎ (0502) 3197
Open: April-October
Size: 40 acres, 700 touring pitches. 30 hot showers,
65 WCs. Static caravans

From A12 in Lowestoft, turn into road called `The
Ravine'.

Taylors Farm
Corton. ☎ (0502) 730241
Open: All year
Size: 12½ acres, 5 touring pitches. 1 hot shower,
1 WC

Site on A12, 3 miles N of Lowestoft.

LYDFORD *Devon*   Map 1 B3

Pulborough Farm Caravan & Camping Park
The Croft, EX20 4AT. ☎ (082 282) 275
Open: March-September
Size: 5½ acres, 90 touring pitches. 8 hot showers,
18 WCs

A30 turn left follow Tavistock A308 up to Dartmoor
Inn, turn right, turn right at War Memorial in
Lydford, 100 yard up on right fork.

Camping & Caravanning Club Site
EX20 4BE.
Open: 30 March-28 September
Size: 4 acres, 90 touring pitches. 8 hot showers,
18 WCs

Charges on application.
From the A386 take the road signposted Lydford,
turn right at the war memorial and bear right at the
fork in the road. The site is on the left.

LYME REGIS *Dorset*   Map 2 A3

Cannington Farm Campsite
Uplyme. ☎ (0297) 443172
Open: March-October
Size: 4½ acres, 33 touring pitches. 2 hot showers, 6
WCs

A3052 (Lyme Regis-Exeter), 1½ miles out of Lyme
Regis, turn right. Follow signs.

HOOK FARM CAMPING & CARAVAN PARK   RAC L
Uplyme, DT7 3UU. ☎ (0297) 442801
Open: All year
Size: 5 (10) acres, 100 touring pitches, all level,
24 with elec, 15 static caravans. 5 hot showers,
29 WCs, 2 CWPs

Pitch per night £6 inc. 2 persons, VAT & transport;
extra car £1+VAT; Tent £1+VAT; M/cycle £1+VAT;
extra adult £1+VAT; elec £1.50
*Site set in ideal tourist area with outstanding
surrounding views. 2 caravans for hire. Restaurant
250 yards. Swimming pool 10 miles. Dogs must be
kept on a lead at all times. Charges are from
midday to midday or any part. Maximum stay is 21
days. No campfires.*
At 1¼ miles NW of Lyme Regis on A3070, turn left
opposite Talbot Arms, pass over cross-roads, site
in ¼ mile on right.

Shrubbery Caravan Park
Rousdon. ☎ (0297) 442227
Open: March-November
Size: 10½ acres, 90 touring pitches. 19 hot
showers, 27 WCs

3 miles W of Lyme Regis on the A3052.

Westhayes International Caravan Park
Sidmouth Road, Rousdon, DT7 3RD.
☎ (0297) 23456
Open: All year (limited facilities Dec-March)
Size: 7 acres, 150 touring pitches. 8 hot showers,
16 WCs

Site 3½ miles W of Lyme Regis on A3052.

LYMINGTON *Hampshire*   Map 2 B3

Lytton Lawn Camping & Caravan Park
Lymore, Milford-on-Sea. ☎ (0590) 643339
Open: Easter-October
Size: 9 acres, 138 touring pitches. 12 hot showers,
30 WCs

2½ miles SW of Lymington on A337, turn S onto
B3058. In ¼ mile, fork left. Site ½ mile.

SHOREFIELD COUNTRY PARK   RAC A
Shorefield Road, Downton, SO41 0LH.
☎ (0590) 642513
Open: Easter-31 October
Size: 5 (100) acres, 69 touring pitches, all level, all
with elec, all with hardstanding. 24 hot showers, 24
WCs, 2 CWPs

(1991) Car & caravan, Motor caravan from £5.50-
£15, all inclusive
cc Access, Visa/B'card
*Overlooking the Isle of Wight, Shorefield is near
the beach and the New Forest. Facilities on the
park are magnificent, as are the leisure club and
indoor pool. No motorcycles. No tents. Three*

weeks maximum stay.
At the Royal Oak public house on the A339, 3½ miles W of Lymington, or 8 miles E of Christchurch, turn S for ½ mile, turn left on Shorefield Road to site.

LYNTON *Devon*   Map 1 B2

Camping & Caravanning Club Site
Caffyns Cross, EX35 6JS. ☎ (0598) 52379
Open: 30 March-26 October
Size: 5½ acres, 105 touring pitches. 10 hot showers, 17 WCs

Charges on application.
cc Access, Visa/B'card
From the A39 take the road signposted "Six Acre", take the first right and then second left to the site.

CHANNEL VIEW CARAVAN PARK   RAC A
Manor Farm, Barbrook, EX35 6LD.
☎ (0598) 53349
Open: Easter-Mid October
Size: 6 (9) acres, 76 touring pitches, 16 with elec, 38 level pitches, 32 static caravans. 10 hot showers, 17 WCs, 2 CWPs

(1991) Car & caravan £6.50, Car & tent £6, Motor caravan £5.50, plus £1 per adult above 2, child 50p; elec £1.75, awn £1, dogs free
cc Access, Visa/B'card
A wooded site giving panoramic views of Lynton and the coast. Pub with family room on site. Boat trips from Lynmouth. 10 caravans for hire (own WCs). Swimming pool 18 miles. No motorcycles. Recommended route A39 N from Barnstaple, site

on left just past Barbrook Mill.

Lorna Doone Farm
Parracombe. ☎ (059 83) 262
Open: March-November
Size: 1½ acres, 50 touring pitches. 2 hot showers, 5 WCs

Site ½ mile E of Parracombe on A39.

Millslade House
Brendon. ☎ (059 87) 322
Open: All year
Size: 1½ acres, 5+ touring pitches. No hot showers or WCs

From Barbrook on A39 towards Simonsbath, left turn into Brendon. Site next to river.

SUNNY LYN CARAVAN PARK   RAC A
Lynbridge, EX35 6NS. ☎ (0598) 53384
Open: Easter-Beginning October
Size: 1½ (3½) acres, 7 touring pitches, all level, all with elec, all with hardstanding, 27 static caravans. 4 hot showers, 4 cold showers, 9 WCs, 1 CWP

(1991) Car & caravan, Motor caravan, Car & tent, M/cycle & tent £4-£5; all plus £1 per adult, 50p per child; elec £2, awn £2, dogs £1; all prices plus VAT
Small, secluded park in wooded valley on edge of trout stream, amidst beautiful scenery of Exmoor National park. 27 caravans for hire (own WCs). No groups of motorcyclists.
At ½ mile S of Lynton on B3234. Best approach from Taunton via Exford and Simonsbath.

LYTHAM ST ANNE'S *Lancashire*   Map 4 B2

EASTHAM HALL CARAVAN PARK   RAC A
Saltcotes Road, FY8 4LS. ☎ (0253) 737907
Open: 1 March-31 October
Size: 10 (25) acres, 140 touring pitches, most level,
85 with elec, 20 with hardstanding, 250 static
caravans. 10 hot showers, 52 WCs, 10 CWPs

(1991) Car & caravan, Motor caravan £4; all plus
£1.50 per person, £1 per child (over 5 years); elec
£1.50, awn £1.50; WS
*Well-maintained grassy and level site, with
children's play area. Shop open April-October.
Swimming pool 4 miles. No motorcycles.*
Head W on the A584 from Preston, turn right on to
B5259 and site is ¾ mile on right, signposted.

SEA VIEW CARAVAN PARK   RAC L
Bank Lane, Warton, Near Preston, PR4 1TD.
☎ (0772) 679336
Open: 1 March-31 October
Size: 2 (6) acres, 4 touring pitches, all level, all with
elec, 80 static caravans. 4 hot showers, 4 cold
showers, 5 WCs, 1 CWP

Car & caravan, Motor caravan £5.85; awn £1
*Flat, level site with easy access. Quiet, family site
within easy reach of Blackpool, Fleetwood and
West Coast resorts. 3 caravans for hire (own WCs).
Shop ½ mile. Restaurant 1 mile. Swimming pool
2 miles. Calor gas only.*
At 4¼ miles W of Preston on A583, bear left on
A584 for 4 miles. Pass through Warton and take
first turn S into Bank Lane.

MABLETHORPE *Lincolnshire*   Map 5 B2

Camping & Caravanning Club Site
Highfield, Church Lane, LN12 2NU.
☎ (0507) 72374
Open: 30 March-28 September
Size: 6 acres, 105 touring pitches. 4 hot showers,
11 WCs

Charges on application.
cc Access, Visa/B'card
Level, grassy site ¾ mile from sandy beaches.
From the A1104 turn into Church Lane, the site is
about ½ mile on the right.

Cherry Tree Cottage
Huttoft Road, Sutton-on-Sea
☎ (0507) 441626
Open: Easter-October
Size: 2¼ acres, 60 touring pitches. 4 hot showers, 7
WCs

Site on E side of A52, 2½ miles N of Huttoft.

GOLDEN SANDS HOLIDAY PARK   RAC A
Quebec Road, LN12 1QJ. ☎ (0507) 77871
Open: Easter-October
Size: 112 acres, 450 touring pitches, all level,
40 with elec, 1300 static caravans. 40 hot showers,
50 WCs, 2 CWPs

Charges on application.
*Large, well-maintained site, with adventure
playground, close to dunes and beach. Evening
social activities at site. 400 caravans for hire (own
WCs). Calor gas only.*
1 mile N of Mablethorpe.

Mermaid Caravan Site
Seaholme Road. ☎ (0507) 473273
Open: March-October
Size: 25 acres, 200 touring pitches. 13 hot showers,
40+ WCs

A16 turn to Alford from Ulceby. Follow to
Mablethorpe and then site signposted. Large water
tower is landmark.

South Farm
Huttoft Road, Sutton-on-Sea
☎ (0507) 441592
Open: April-September
Size: 1 acre, 30 touring pitches. 1 hot shower,
2 WCs

Site is on the A52, 4 miles S of Mablethorpe.

TRUSTHORPE SPRINGS LEISURE PARK   RAC L
Trusthorpe Hall, Trusthorpe, LN12 2QQ.
☎ (0507) 441384
Open: 3 March-3 November
Size: 1 (6) acres, 20 touring pitches, all with elec, all
level, 128 static caravans. 4 hot showers, 4 cold
showers, 24 WCs, 1 CWP

Car & caravan, Motor caravan £4; plus 50p per
adult above 4; extra car 50p; elec £1, awn £1, dogs
free
*Set in woodland with club on site, live
entertainment most nights. Families welcome.
Arcade and pool room. 5 caravans for hire (own
WCs). No motorcycles. No tents.*
Enter Mablethorpe on A1104, turn right at Cross
Inn public house, into Mile Lane. Site on corner,
approx 1 mile from Cross Inn.

MAIDSTONE *Kent*   Map 3 A3

Hogbarn Caravan Park
Hogbarn Lane, Harrietsham, ME17 1NZ.
☎ (0622) 859648
Open: March-October
Size: 25 acres, 100 touring pitches. 10 hot showers,
13 WCs

On the A20 between Maidstone and Charing.
Signposted from Harrietsham.

MALMESBURY *Wiltshire*   Map 2 A2

BURTON HILL CARAVAN & CAMPING PARK   RAC L
Burton Hill, SN16 0EJ. ☎ (0666) 822585
Open: Easter-30 November
Size: 2 acres, 30 touring pitches, all level, 8 with
elec. 2 hot showers, 4 WCs, 1 CWP

Charges on application. WS

⬛ Snacks/take away ☒ Restaurant ◩ Swimming pool ⬚ Shelter for campers ⊞ Dogs accepted   77

Simple site, with children's play area. Shop and restaurant ¼ mile. Swimming pool ¾ mile.
At 200 yards S of roundabout at junction of A429, B4014 and B4042, turn W off A429 opposite Malmesbury Hospital and observe site signs. 6 miles from M4 junction 17.

MALTON *North Yorkshire* — Map 5 A1

Flamingo Land Holiday Village
Kirby Misperton, YO17 0UX.
☎ (065 386) 300
Open: Easter-October
Size: 375 acres, 250 touring pitches. Hot showers, WCs. 140 static caravans

A64 on to A169 and site is midway between Pickering and Malton.

Willow Garth
Great Barugh. ☎ (065 386) 630
Open: March-October
Size: 2 acres, 15 touring pitches. 2 hot showers, 4 WCs

Enter Malton and follow signs to Amotherby. From village turn right until you arrive in Great Barugh. Site up on the hill.

MANNINGTREE *Essex* — Map 3 B2

STRANGERS HOME INN — RAC L
The Street, Bradfield, CO11 2US.
☎ (0255) 870304
Open: 1 March-31 October
Size: 2.2 acres, 65 touring pitches, all level, 14 with elec. 4 hot showers, 10 WCs, 1 CWP

(1991) £2.50 per adult per night, £1.50 per child
Situated within walking distance of River Stour, centrally located for Colchester, Ipswich, Constable Country and convenient stopover to and from Parkeston Quay. Shop ½ mile. Swimming pool 6 miles.
From A120 Colchester to Harwich road turn right at Horsley Cross on B1035 and follow brown tourist signs to campsite (opposite parish church).

MANSFIELD *Nottinghamshire* — Map 5 A2

SHERWOOD FOREST CARAVAN PARK — RAC A
Old Clipstone, NG21 9HW. ☎ (0623) 823132
Open: 1 April-30 September
Size: 20 acres, 130 touring pitches, 125 level pitches, 99 with elec, 12 static caravans. 16 hot showers, 20 WCs, 6 CWPs

Car & caravan, Motor caravan, Car & tent, M/cycle* & tent £8.50; plus 75p per child; elec £1.50, dogs 75p
Beautiful lakeside park in heart of Robin Hood Country with fishing and woodland walks. Restaurant 2 miles. 2 caravans for hire (own WCs).
At 2 miles N of Mansfield on A60, turn E on A6075 for 2½ miles and then turn SE as signed Clipstone for ¾ mile to site on right.

MANSTON *Kent* — Map 3 B3

MANSTON CARAVAN & CAMPING PARK — RAC A
Manston Court Road, Ramsgate, CT12 5AU.
☎ (0843) 823442
Open: Easter-31 October
Size: 4 (7) acres, 100 touring pitches, 40 with elec, 30 static caravans. 8 hot showers, 13 WCs, 1 CWP

(1991) Car & caravan, Motor caravan from £5, Car & tent M/cycle & tent from £4, plus £1 per person above 2; elec £1, awn £1, dogs 50p; WS
A quiet, family-run site, in pleasant countryside, with children's play area and evening social activities. Caravan for hire (own WC). No unaccompanied children under 18. Restaurant 2 miles. Swimming pool 1½ miles.
From junction of A256 and A253 (2 miles W of Ramsgate), turn N on the A256 for ½ mile, turn left on to the B2050 and in just over 1 mile turn right for 250 yards to site on right.

Pine Meadow Caravan Park
Spratling Court Farm, CT12 5AN.
☎ (0843) 587770
Open: March-October
Size: 2 acres, 40 touring pitches. 4 hot showers, 7 WCs

From A256 turn W on to B2050 signposted Manston. After 400 yards turn right (N) up private farm track. Site signed.

PRESTON PARKS — RAC L
Preston Road, CT10 2NB. ☎ (0843) 823346
Open: 1 March-31 October
Size: 20 acres, 6 touring pitches, all level, all with elec, 153 static caravans. 4 hot showers, 4 WCs

Charges on application.
Rural site, with children's play area. Restaurant and swimming pool 1½ miles. Very close to supermarket.
From junction of A256 and A253 (2 miles W of Ramsgate), turn N on the A256 for ½ mile, turn left on to the B2050 for ½ mile, then turn right to site on right in ½ mile.

MARAZION *Cornwall* — Map 1 A3

Trevair Touring Site
South Treveneague, St Hilary
☎ (0736) 740647
Open: Easter-October
Size: 3 acres, 30 touring pitches. 4 hot showers, 6 WCs. 1 static caravan

From Marazion on B3280, 3 miles.

WAYFARERS CAMPING SITE — RAC L
St Hilary, TR20 9EF. ☎ (0736) 763326
Open: April-November
Size: 5 acres, 60 touring pitches, all level, 14 with elec, 3 with hardstanding, 4 static caravans. 6 hot showers, 6 cold showers, 17 WCs, 1 CWP

(1991) Car & caravan, Motor caravan, Car & tent £2,

  Facilities for Disabled ⊞ Caravans accepted ⊡ Motor caravans ▲ Tents ⬚ Laundry room ⬛ Shop

M/cycle & tent £2.80; all plus £2 per adult, £1 per child; elec £1.20, awn £1, dogs £1
Level site in peaceful rural setting, 1½ miles from sea. Children's play area. 4 caravans for hire (own WCs). Restaurant 1 mile. Swimming pool 1½ miles. New toilet and shower block and pay phone.
From Marazion, travel E on the A394, turn NE on the B3280 for 1½ miles to site on left, or from Helston on the A394 turn right at Rosudgeon, at ½ mile on turn left, then right to the B3280, entrance to site on right.

Wheal Rodney Carapark
Gwallon, TR17 0HL. ☎ (0736) 710605
Open: Easter-October
Size: 5 acres, 45 touring pitches. 6 hot showers, 7 WCs. 10 holiday bungalows

A30 Crowlas crossroads, turn left, keep on for 1½ miles and site is on right.

MARGATE *Kent* Map 3 B2

Frost Farm Caravan Site
St Nicholas-at-Wade, Birchington
☎ (0843) 47219
Open: March-October
Size: 2½ acres, 12 touring pitches. 2 hot showers, 8 WCs

Site on A299, just before St Nicholas roundabout on London side.

St Nicholas Camping Site
Court Road, St Nicholas-at-Wade, Birchington
☎ (0843) 47245
Open: Easter-October
Size: 3½ acres, 75 touring pitches. 4 hot showers, 6 WCs

Site on A299, travelling from Herne Bay, turn right at end of A299 into village. Signposted.

Two Chimneys Caravan Park
Five Acres, Shottendane Road, Birchington, CT7 0HD.
☎ (0843) 41068
Open: March-October
Size: 8 acres, 70 touring pitches. 11 hot showers, 15 WCs. 5 static caravans

On A299 take A28 to Birchington Square, turn right at church into Park Lane (B2048). Left at Manston Road (B2050) then first left into Shottendene Road. Site 300 yards on right.

MARKET DEEPING *Lincolnshire* Map 5 B3

The Deepings Caravan & Camping Park
Outgang Road, Towngate East, PE6 8LQ.
☎ (0778) 344335
Open: February-January
Size: 4 acres, 70 touring pitches. 4 hot showers, 7 WCs. 9 static caravans

Off A16, 2½ miles NE of Market Deeping (Stamford to Spalding) turn left on unclassified road, site

½ mile on right.

Tallington Lakes Leisure Park
Tallington, Stamford, PE9 4RN.
☎ (0778) 347000
Open: All year
Size: 242 acres, touring pitches. 18 hot showers, 26 WCs

4½ miles E of Stamford on A16, after level crossing turn into Barholm Road and then first right. Site signed.

MARKET RASEN *Lincolnshire* Map 5 B2

MARKET RASEN RACECOURSE RAC L
Legsby Road, LN8 3EA. ☎ (0673) 843434
Open: 10 April-11 October
Size: 3 acres, 60 touring pitches, 27 with elec. 5 hot showers, 16 WCs, 1 CWP

(1991) Car & caravan, Motor caravan £3, Car & tent £2, M/cycle & tent £3.50; all plus £2.25 per adult, £1.05 per child; elec £1.20, awn free, dogs free
cc Access, Visa/B'card
A rural site, with pay phone, TV room, playground, games area, reduced admission to racing, 9 hole pay and play golf course. Shop and restaurant 1 mile. Swimming pool 15 miles.
Turn S as signed Legsby off A631 on E outskirts of Market Rasen. Site on left after ¾ mile.

The Rother Cafe
Middle Rasen, LN8 3JU. ☎ (0673) 842433
Open: March-October
Size: 2 acres, 45 touring pitches. 2 WCs

West side of Market Rasen (1½ miles) at junction of A46 and A631.

WALESBY WOODLANDS RAC A
Walesby, LN8 3UN. ☎ (0673) 843285
Open: 1 March-1 November
Size: 3 acres, 62 touring pitches, all level, 50 with elec. 4 hot showers, 10 WCs, 2 CWPs

Car & caravan, Motor caravan, Car & tent, M/cycle & tent £4.50, plus £1 per adult above 2, child 75p; elec £1.25, awn £1, dogs free; WS
A small, family-run site on well-drained land bordered by woodland. Well-appointed and clean. Children's play area. Restaurant 1½ miles. Swimming pool 12 miles.
From the centre of Market Rasen, travel N on the B1203 towards Tealby for ¾ mile, turn left for ¼ mile, turn left along track 150 yards to site on right.

MARLBOROUGH *Wiltshire* Map 2 B2

Hillview Caravan Park
Oare. ☎ (0672) 62271
Open: April-September
Size: 1 acres, 10 touring pitches. 4 hot showers, 3 WCs

Site on A345, at Sunny Hill between Marlborough

England

and Amesbury.

Little London Caravan Park
Torksey. ☎ (042 771) 322
Open: April-October
Size: 11 acres, 65 touring pitches. 12 hot showers,
19 WCs

🏕 ▢ 📷 🚐 🔺 🛏 　 🍴 ✕ ◥ 　 🐕

Site on A156, 200 yards S of junction with A1133. 3
miles S of Marton.

Fearby Caravan & Camping Site
Black Swan, Fearby. ☎ (0765) 689477
Open: March-October
Size: 3 acres, 50 touring pitches. 4 hot showers,
9 WCs. 2 static caravans

🦽 🚐 📷 🔺 🛏 🛒 ☕ 🍴 　 🎱 🐕

A6108 ¼ mile NW of Masham, turn right on to
unclassified road. Site at rear of Black Swan.

Middle Hills Farm
Grange Mill, DE4 4HY. ☎ (0629) 650368
Open: Easter-November
Size: 2 acres, 10 touring pitches. 3 WCs. 1 static
caravan

🏕 ▢ 🚐 📷 🔺 　 　 　 🐕

On A5012 4 miles heading W. Site ¼ mile W of
Holly Bush Inn.

PACKHORSE FARM　　　　　　RAC L
Matlock Moor, DE4 5LF. ☎ (0629) 582781
Open: All year
Size: 2 acres, 30 touring pitches, all level, 17 with
elec. 2 hot showers, 4 WCs, 1 CWP

🏕 ▢ 🚐 📷

Car & caravan, Motor caravan £4, plus 50p-£1 per
person above 2, child 50p; elec £1, awn £1
*Simple, level meadowland farm site. No gas
available. Shop and restaurant 1 mile. Swimming
pool 3 miles. RAC member motorcyclists only.
On A615 Alfreton-Matlock, turn right in Tansley
village.*

Peaceful Pines
Two Dales, Darley Dale. ☎ (0629) 732428
Open: All year
Size: 32 acres, 40 touring pitches. 8 hot showers,
14 WCs. 15 static caravans

🦽 🏕 📷 　 🛏 🛒 🛒 🛒 ✕ 　 🐕

B5057 heading W towards Darley Dale. Site 2 miles
down road. Signed.

PINEGROVES CARAVAN PARK　　RAC L
High Lane, Tansley, DE4 5GS.
☎ (0629) 534815
Open: 1 April/Easter-End October
Size: 10 (24) acres, 100 touring pitches, 85 level
pitches, 35 with elec. 6 hot showers, 10 WCs,
1 CWP

🦽 🏕 🚐 📷 🔺 🛏 　 　 　 🐕

(1991) Car & caravan, Motor caravan, Car & tent £5;
plus £1 per extra person; elec £1, awn £1
*Pinegroves Caravan Park is situated in
approximately 23 acres of mature woodland with a
wide variety of trees, rhododendrons and other
shrubs. Shop and restaurant 2 miles. Swimming
pool 3 miles. No motorcycles.
From M1 exit 28, via A38 and A615, through
Wessington, 2 miles to crossroads, turn left OR
From A6 and A615 from Matlock, through Tansley,
1 mile after garden centre to crossroads, turn right.*

Sycamore Caravan & Camping Site
Lant Lane, Matlock Moor. ☎ (0629) 55760
Open: March-October
Size: 7 acres, 20 touring pitches. 4 hot showers,
7 WCs

🏕 📷 🔺 　 　 　 　 🐕

A632 from Chesterfield towards Matlock.
A615 from Alfreton off M1. Site signed.

Magic Cove Touring Park
☎ (0637) 860263
Open: Easter-October
Size: 1 acre, 26 touring pitches. 4 hot showers,
5 WCs

🏕 ▢ 📷 🔺 　 　 　 🐕

Take Mawgan Porth to St Mawgan road and site is
300 yards on left hand side.

SUN HAVEN VALLEY CARAVAN PARK　RAC A
TR8 4BQ. ☎ (0637) 860373
Open: Easter-October
Size: 7 acres, 118 touring pitches, 24 with elec,
96 level pitches, 32 static caravans, 5 chalets.
10 hot showers, 20 WCs, 2 CWPs

🏕 ▢ 🚐 📷 🔺 🛏 🛒 　 　 🐕

Charges on application.
*Sheltered, grassy site with children's play area.
Caravans and chalets for hire (own WCs).
Restaurant ¾ mile. Swimming pool 1 mile.
From A30 Bodmin by-pass follow airport signs for
RAF St Mawgan, go past the airport, take the
Mawgan Porth road, over river bridge, right at BP
garage, park is ¾ mile on left.*

LARCHES CARAVAN PARK　　　RAC A
CA5 1LQ. ☎ (09657) 379
Open: 1 March-31 October
Size: 4 (18) acres, 73 touring pitches, 38 with elec,
20 level pitches, 38 with hardstanding, 177 static
caravans. 17 hot showers, 27 WCs, 2 CWPs

🦽 🏕 🚐 📷 🔺 🛏 🛒 　 ◥ 🎱 🐕

(1991) Car & caravan, Motor caravan, Car & tent,
M/cycle & tent £5.40, plus £1 per person above 2;
elec £1.30, awn 75p; WS
*Peaceful, meadowland site with particularly good
facilities, including brand new, heated indoor
swimming pool. TV room and campers' kitchen.
Familes and couples only. Restaurant ¼ mile.
From Keswick, travel N on A591 for 12 miles to
Bothel, turn right on A595 for 2 miles. Site on right.*

Skiddaw View Caravan Park
Bothel. ☎ (06973) 20919
Open: March-November
Size: 10 acres, 16 touring pitches. 12 hot showers,
14 WCs. 1 static caravan

	⚏	⌁	⚠	◪	⚏					⼧

On A591 just before Bothel junction on A595.
Follow signs.

MERSEA ISLAND *Essex*　　　Map 3 B2

Fen Farm Camping & Caravan Site
East Mersea. ☎ (0206) 383275
Open: April-October
Size: 6 acres, 20 touring pitches. 4 hot showers,
8 WCs

	⚏	⌁	⚠					▣	⼧

As you come to Mersea Island, take left fork past
Dog & Pheasant, site is first turning right after that.

Waldegraves Farm Holiday Park
West Mersea, CO5 8SE. ☎ (0206) 382898
Open: March-October
Size: 25 acres, 60 touring pitches. 10 hot showers,
13 WCs. 8 static caravans

♿	⚏	⌁	⚠	◪	⚏	▣			⼧

Take B1025 to Mersea. Fork left for East Mersea
and take second right. Follow signs.

MIDDLESBROUGH *Cleveland*　　Map 5 A1

PRISSICK CARAVAN PARK　　　RAC L
Morton Road. ☎ (0642) 300202
Open: Easter-1 October
Size: 5 acres, 22 touring pitches, all level. 4 hot
showers, 4 cold showers, 8 WCs, 1 CWP

	⚏	⌁	⚠					▣	⼧

Charges on application.
Grassy site adjacent to Sports Centre. Shop and
restaurant ½ mile. Swimming pool 2 miles. No gas
available.
Access from A172 (Morton Road), 50 yards N of
junction with B1380 (Ladgate Lane).

MIDDLETON-IN-TEESDALE *Co Durham* Map 5 A1

Daleview Caravan Park
☎ (0833) 40233
Open: March-October
Size: 3 acres, 52 touring pitches. 6 hot showers,
6 WCs. 8 static caravans

	⚏	⌁	⚠	◪	⚏	▣			⼧

Take A66 heading W, turn on to B6277 at Barnard
Castle and head to Middleton. Site is ¼ mile from
centre of Middleton.

MILLOM *Cumbria*　　　Map 4 B1

Silecroft Camping & Caravan Site
Silecroft. ☎ (0229) 85203
Open: March-October
Size: 12½ acres, 60 touring pitches. 12 hot
showers, 36 WCs

	⚏	⌁	⚠	◪					⼧

Turn W off A5093. Site by sea shore.

MILNTHORPE *Cumbria*　　　Map 4 B1

FELL END CARAVAN PARK　　　RAC A
Slackhead Road, Near Hale, LA7 7BS.
☎ (05395) 62122
Open: All year
Size: 8 (28) acres, 68 touring pitches, all with elec,
60 level pitches, 60 with hardstanding, 215 static
caravans. 13 hot showers, 44 WCs, 3 CWPs

♿	⚏	⌁	⚠	◪	⚏	⼧	☕			▣	⼧

(1991) Car & caravan £6.40, Motor caravan, Car &
tent from £5,75, M/cycle & tent from £6,75, plus
£1 per adult, child 60p; elec £1.30, awn £1; WS
cc Access, Amex, Visa/B'card
Rural park, area of outstanding natural beauty.
Tourist Board graded Excellent. Awarded Runner-
Up in Calor Most Improved Park contest 1991. Free
luxury facilities, TV and satellite hook-ups. Lakes,
Dales, historic houses and gardens, RSPB
sanctuary, sports facilities, etc. within easy reach.
Restaurant 1 mile. Swimming pool 10 miles. Well-
stocked shop on park.
Leave M6 at junction 35 and head N up A6 for
3½ miles. Turn left on to unclassified road at brown
"Sites" sign and follow road ¾ mile, pick up Fell
End Caravan Park signs.

Hall More Caravan Park
Hale, LA7 7BP. ☎ (05395) 63383
Open: March-October
Size: 7 acres, 40 touring pitches. 6 hot showers,
8 WCs. 2 static caravans

♿	⚏	⌁	⚠	◪					▣	⼧

M6 junction 35, A6 N for 4 miles. First left after first
garage on left. Keep left for a mile.

Low Sampool Caravan Park
Levens, Kendal. ☎ (044 852) 265
Open: March-October
Size: 2 acres, 30 touring pitches. 16 hot showers,
9 WCs

	⚏	⌁		◪	⚏					⼧

On A6 until Levens Bridge. Take A590 W. First left
is the site.

MINEHEAD *Somerset*　　　Map 1 B2

Camping & Caravanning Club Site
Hill Road, North Hill, TA24 5RY.
☎ (0643) 4138
Open: 30 March-28 September
Size: 3¾ acres, 60 touring pitches. 2 hot shower,
9 WCs

		⌁	⚠		⚏					⼧

Charges on application.
cc Access, Visa/B'card
Hilltop site with fine views over Minehead.
From the A39 turn into The Parade then take
Blenheim Road into Martlet Road. Follow this road
past the church into Moor Road then Hill Road,
the site is about ½ mile on the right.

MINEHEAD & EXMOOR CARAVAN &　　RAC L
CAMPING PARK
Porlock Road, TA24 8SN. ☎ (0643) 703074
Open: 1 March-1 November
Size: 1 (2½) acres, 50 touring pitches, all level,
30 with elec, 5 with hardstanding. 3 hot showers,

🍴 Snacks/take away 　 ✕ Restaurant 　 ◺ Swimming pool 　 ▣ Shelter for campers 　 ⼧ Dogs accepted 　　**81**

3 cold showers, 6 WCs, 1 CWP

Car & caravan, Motor caravan £4, Car & tent, M/cycle* & tent £3; all plus £1 per adult, 50p per child; elec £1, awn £1, dogs free; WS
cc Major cards
Small, family park, well-supervised with excellent facilities. 1 mile from centre of Minehead, we are a park to which lots of people return, to stay with us every season. Mobile shop calls at park. Restaurant, shop and swimming pool 1 mile. Dogs must be kept on a lead at all times and exercised off the park. Gate closes at 11pm.
Site on N side of the A39, 1½ miles W of Minehead town centre. Site signed.

MINSTER *Kent*   Map 3 B3

Plough Inn Leisure Park
Plough Road, ME12 4JF. ☎ (0795) 872419
Open: March-October
Size: 2 acres, 12+ touring pitches. 6 hot showers, 6 WCs

Off M2, take A249. Over Kingsferry Bridge, down to roundabout, turn right. Go 300 yards and turn left in Barton Hill Drive. At bottom turn right on to main Minster road. After Minster village ¼ mile, Plough Road forks to left. Signed.

MODBURY *Devon*   Map 1 B3

Broad Park Touring Caravan Site
Ivybridge, PL21 0SH. ☎ (0548) 830256
Open: 18 May-23 September
Size: 5 acres, 75 touring pitches. 4 hot showers, 15 WCs

From the junction of A38 and A385, travel SW on the A38 for 3 miles, then S on the B3210 for 1 mile to Kitterford Cross. Keep right on the B3207 and 400 yards and bear right for 1 mile to site on left.

Camping & Caravanning Club Site
California Cross, PL21 0SG.
☎ (054 882) 297
Open: 30 March-26 October
Size: 3.6 acres, 89 touring pitches. 6 hot showers, 11 WCs

Charges on application.
cc Access, Visa/B'card
A very clean and tidy grass site.
From Modbury take the B3207 for about 4 miles, the site is behind the filling station.

PENNYMOOR CAMPING & CARAVAN PARK   RAC L
PL21 0SB. ☎ (0548) 830269/830542
Open: 15 March-15 November
Size: 6 (12) acres, 154 touring pitches, 16 with elec, 120 level pitches, 70 static caravans. 15 hot showers, 31 WCs, 2 CWPs

Car & caravan, Car & tent £3.50-£7.50, Motor caravan £2.50-£6, all inc. 4 persons, from Easter; M/cycle £4; extra person 50p; elec £1.30, awn £1, dogs 80p
This peaceful, grassy site has lovely views. Children's equipped playground. Superb new toilet/shower block, fully tiled, with facilities for the disabled. 20 caravans for hire (own WCs). Restaurant 1 mile. Swimming pool 5 miles. No groups of motorcycles.
From Exeter, leave A38 at Wrangaton Cross. Turn left, then straight ahead at next crossroads. Continue for approx. 4 miles. Pass petrol garage on left, then take second left to site: 1 mile on right.

MORECAMBE *Lancashire*   Map 4 B1

Glen Holiday Caravan Park
Westgate, LA3 3EL. ☎ (0524) 423896
Open: March-October
Size: 3½ acres, 18 touring pitches. 5 hot showers, 8 WCs

From Lancaster enter Morecambe on the A589. First roundabout in the town take first left and site is 1½ miles down road. Signed.

REGENT LEISURE PARK   RAC A
Westgate, LA3 3DF. ☎ (0524) 413940
Open: 1 March-31 October
Size: 1½ (15) acres, 23 touring pitches, all level, all with elec, all with hardstanding, 300 static caravans. 7 hot showers, 7 WCs, 1 CWP;

Charges on application.
Level, grassy site in town, ½ mile from beach. Club, disco, family room and children's play area. 2 swimming pools. 120 caravans for hire (own WCs).

Travelling towards Morecambe on the A589, turn left at roundabout. Site 1½ miles on left.

RIVERSIDE CARAVAN PARK   RAC A
Oxcliffe Hill Farm, Heaton-with-Oxcliffe, LA3 3ER.
☎ (0524) 844193
Open: 1 March-31 October
Size: 2.2 acres, 50 touring pitches, all level, all with elec. 4 hot showers, 8 WCs, 1 CWP

(1991) Car & caravan, Motor caravan, Car & tent £4-£5; elec £1.25, awn £1
cc Access, Visa
Quiet site, but only 5-10 minutes from the centre of Morecambe or Lancaster. Old world pub next to site entrance. Restaurant 30 yards. Swimming pool 2 miles. Mobile shop calls at park, otherwise shop 1 mile away. Calor gas only. No motorcycles.
Leave M6 junction 34, follow signs for Morecambe. Cross over river and follow signs for Overton and Middleton. Site gate is next to Golden Ball Inn, where river and road run next to each other.

Sunnyside Camping Site
250 Oxcliffe Road, Greenlea
☎ (0524) 418373
Open: March-October
Size: 3 acres, 20 touring pitches. 6 hot showers, 10 WCs

From Westgate turn left on to Westcliff Drive. First left and site is first on left in 500 yards.

VENTURE CARAVAN PARK   RAC A
Langridge Way, Westgate, LA4 4TQ.
☎ (0524) 412986
Open: All year for touring vans
Size: 5½ (17½) acres, 56 touring pitches, all level, 50 with elec, 260 static caravans. 29 hot showers, 29 cold showers, 46 WCs, 2 CWPs

(1991) Car & caravan, Motor caravan, Car & tent, M/cycle & tent £5.15; elec £1.30, awn £1.30; WS
Level, grassy park. Disabled hire caravans available (14 caravans for hire in total). TV room, amusements. Launderette. Play area. Hairdrying facilities, etc. Restaurant 1 mile. Dogs to be kept on a lead.
M6 exit 34 signposted Morecambe. A589 at first roundabout. Straight forward at second roundabout, first left (Westgate). ¾ mile on right by school turn right (Langridge Way).

MORETON GLADE TOURING PARK   RAC L
Station Road, DT2 8BB. ☎ (0305) 853801
Open: March-31 October
Size: 7½ acres, 154 touring pitches, 80 with elec, 125 level pitches, 10 with hardstanding. 12 hot showers, 20 WCs, 3 CWPs

Charges on application. WS
Family site with children's adventure play area. Next door to pub. Swimming pool 2 miles.
From the junction of the A353 and the A352 and B3390, travel N on the B3390 for 3¼ miles, site on right after Moreton Station.

Ellington Caravan Park
Warkworth Lane, Ellington
☎ (0670) 861807
Open: April-November
Size: 20 acres, 24 touring pitches. 6 hot showers, 17 WCs. 10 static caravans

Site off A1068, ¼ mile N of Ellington village.

PERCY WOOD CARAVAN PARK   RAC L
Chesterhill, Swarland, NE65 9JW.
☎ (0670) 787649
Open: All year except February
Size: 20 (67½) acres, 39 touring pitches. 6 hot showers, 15 WCs, CWP

Car & caravan, Motor caravan, Car & tent, M/cycle & tent £5.50-£9.50
A secluded woodland site with plenty of wildlife; each pitch is in its own bay separated by trees; peace and quiet in a very rural site. Calor gas only.
Travelling from Morpeth proceed N on A1, at about 10 miles, turn left on to B6345, signposted Swarland. From Alnwick proceed S on A1, after about 7 miles turn right and proceed as above. Observe caravan site signs on A1.

MILL FARM HOLIDAY PARK   RAC L
Hughley, SY5 6NT. ☎ (074636) 208/255
Open: 1 March-31 October
Size: 4 (11) acres, 25 touring pitches, all level, 20 with elec, 6 with hardstanding, 45 static caravans. 6 hot showers, 11 WCs, 2 CWPs

(1991) Car & caravan, Motor caravan, Car & tent £6, plus £1 per adult above 2, 50p per child; elec £1, awn £1; WS
A remote and peaceful site with level pitches at different levels, surrounded by trees, skirted by a brook. Fishing available on site. Riding nearby. No motorcycles. No single-sex parties.
M6 to M54. At junction 4 (next roundabout) turn left on A464, keep following signs for Ironbridge Gorge Museum until randley (A442). At sign for A4169 head for Much Wenlock (A4169/B4380) turning left at end of new by-pass. Out of Much Wenlock turn right (A458) on to Shrewsbury road. Take B4371 Church Stretton road for 2 miles then bear right for Hughley.

Usha Gap
Muker, Richmond, DL11 6DW. ☎ (0748) 86214
Open: All year
Size: Touring pitches. 2 hot showers, 2 WCs

Site adjacent to B6270, between Muker and Thwaite.

CRIGGAN MILL   RAC L
TR12 7EU. ☎ (0326) 240496

▣ Snacks/take away   ☒ Restaurant   ◺ Swimming pool   ▥ Shelter for campers   ⚐ Dogs accepted   83

Open: 7 days before Easter-31 October
Size: ½ (3½) acres, 10 touring pitches, 2 with elec, 10 with hardstanding, 5 static caravans, 22 chalets. 4 hot showers, 5 WCs, 1 CWP

Car & caravan, Motor caravan, Car & tent, M/cycle & tent £6-£8; extra person £1; elec £1-£1.50 (these rates are for tourers)
Luxury timber lodges nestling in quiet, secluded SW facing valley 200 yards from Mullion Cove and harbour. Calor gas only. Shops 100 yards (has Camping Gaz) and 1 mile. Swimming pool ½ mile. 4 caravans and 22 lodges for hire (own WCs).
From Helston, travel S on the A3083 for 8 miles, turn W on the B3296 to Mullion, then left to Mullion Cove to site on left 200 yards before harbour.

Franchis Holidays
Cury Cross Lanes, Helston
☎ (0326) 240301
Open: Easter-September
Size: 16¾ acres, 70 touring pitches. 11 hot showers, 12 WCs. 7 static caravans, 5 bungalows

Site 6 miles S of Helston and 5 miles from Lizard on A3083 near Mullion.

MULLION HOLIDAY PARK   RAC A
Penhale Cross, Ruan Minor
☎ (0326) 240000
Open: Easter-October
Size: 8 (39) acres, 150 touring pitches, all level, 30 with elec, 20 with hardstanding, 289 static caravans, 54 chalets. 7 hot showers, 15 WCs, 1 CWP

Charges on application.
cc Access, Visa/B'card
Level park with plenty of facilities. Some chalets suitable for disabled people.
At 6 miles S of Helston on E side of A3083 by junction with B3296.

Sandy Gulls Clifftop Touring Park
Cromer Road, NR11 8DF. ☎ (0263) 720513
Open: March-November
Size: 20 acres, 50 touring pitches. 10 hot showers, 20 WCs. 100 static caravans, 4 chalets

On coast road from Mundesley, N of Mundesley village, 5 miles S of Cromer.

Woodland Caravan Park
Trimingham, NR11 8AL. ☎ (0263) 833301
Open: April-September
Size: 110 touring pitches. 14 hot showers, 48 WCs. 154 static caravans

On B1159, ¼ mile W of Trimingham church.

Brookfield Caravan Park
Shrewbridge Road. ☎ (0270) 583191
Open: Easter-September
Size: ½ acre, 25 touring pitches. 4 hot showers, 3 WCs

½ mile from Nantwich on Shrewbridge Road leading to A530. Site on river bank.

The Forestry Commission offers visitors the choice of eleven campsites in the historic and beautiful New Forest. The sites are all locally signposted and have facilities for tents, touring caravans and motor caravans. They have a range of on-site facilities, nearby recreational and sporting facilities. The sites are both wooded and open in type and range from fully equipped sites to sites with minimum facilities where campers must have their own chemical toilets.
Bookings possible for Spring Bank Holiday. Pre-booking advisable in July and August, for a minimum of 7 nights. Credit cards accepted for advance booking.
Information and Camping Leaflet available from the Forestry Commission. ☎ (042128) 3771. Information also available from the Tourist Information Caravan at Lyndhurst car park (Apr-Sept) ☎ (042128) 2269 and at Furlong car park, Ringwood (May-Sept) ☎ (0425) 470896.

FORESTRY COMMISSION ASHURST CAMPSITE   RAC L
Lyndhurst Road, Ashurst, Near Southampton, SO4 2AA.
☎ (0703) 283771
Open: Easter-End October
Size: 23 acres, 280 touring pitches, all level, 193 with hardstanding. 12 showers, 28 WCs, 4 CWPs

(1991) £6.75 maximum charge
cc Access, Visa/B'card, Connect
Level site, part wooded. Shop and restaurant ½ mile.
5 miles SW of Southampton on A35.

FORESTRY COMMISSION DENNY WOOD   RAC L
☎ (0703) 283771
Open: March-September
Size: 170 pitches. 1 CWP

Charges on application.
Grassland site with scattered oak trees. Minimum

facilities - campers must have their own chemical toilets. Calor gas available. No dogs.
Take the B3056 SW from Lyndhurst. Site on S side signposted.

FORESTRY COMMISSION HOLIDAYS HILL CAMPSITE ♛ RAC L
☎ (0703) 283771
Open: March-September
Size: 100 pitches. 1 CWP

Charges on application.
Secluded woodland site. Minimum facilities - campers must have their own chemical toilet. Calor gas available. No dogs.
On the A35 Lyndhurst to Bournemouth road, just S of Lyndhurst. Site signposted.

FORESTRY COMMISSION HOLLANDS WOOD CAMPSITE ♛ RAC L
Lyndhurst Road, Brockenhurst, SO42 7QH.
☎ (0703) 283771
Open: Easter-End September
Size: 3 (168) acres, 600 touring pitches, all level, 175 with hardstanding. 24 hot showers, 64 WCs, 3 CWPs

(1991) £7.15 maximum charge
cc Access, Visa/B'card, Connect
Level oak woodland site with children's play area. Shop and restaurant ½ mile.
½ mile N of Brockenhurst on A337.

FORESTRY COMMISSION HOLMSLEY CAMPSITE ♛ RAC L
Forest Road, Thorney Hill, Bransgore Near Christchurch, BH23 7EQ.
☎ (0703) 283771
Open: Easter-End September
Size: 89 acres, 700 touring pitches, 120 with elec, 600 level pitches, 200 with hardstanding. 30 hot showers, 69 WCs, 6 CWPs

(1991) £6.75 maximum charge; elec £1.50
cc Access, Visa/B'card, Connect
Level site, mainly open with woodland fringes.
Turn W 8 miles SW of Lyndhurst off A35 and follow Holmsley Campsite signs.

FORESTRY COMMISSION LONGBEECH CAMPSITE ♛ RAC L
☎ (0703) 283771
Open: March-September
Size: 400 pitches. WCs, 1 CWP

Charges on application.
Woodland site. Semi-equipped. Calor gas only.
From Lyndhurst take the A337 to Cadnam, turn NW on to B3079 and take first left. Site signposted on left.

FORESTRY COMMISSION MATLEY WOOD CAMPSITE ♛ RAC L
☎ (0703) 283771
Open: March-September
Size: 70 pitches. 1 CWP

Charges on application.

Small, secluded site in open forest. Permit required from Denny Wood site. Minimum facilities - campers must have their own chemical toilet.
Turn left off the B3056 Lyndhurst to Beaulieu road. Site signposted.

FORESTRY COMMISSION OCKNELL CAMPSITE ♛ RAC L
☎ (0703) 283771
Open: March-September
Size: 280 pitches. WCs, 1 CWP

Charges on application.
Level, open site with woodland fringes. Permit required from Longbeech site. Semi-equipped.
From Lyndhurst take the A337 to Cadnam, turn NW on to B3079, take first left. Site signposted on right.

FORESTRY COMMISSION PIPERS WAIT CAMPSITE ♛ RAC L
☎ (0703) 283771
Open: March-September
Size: 40 pitches. 1 CWP

Charges on application.
Secluded site. Caravan only. Minimum facilities - campers must have their own chemical toilet.
Permit required from Longbeech site. No running water.
From Lyndhurst take the A337 to Cadnam, turn NW on to B3079. Turn right to site, signposted.

FORESTRY COMMISSION ROUNDHILL CAMPSITE ♛ RAC L
☎ (0703) 283771
Open: March-September
Size: 700 pitches. WCs, 1 CWP

Charges on application.
Heathland with scattered pines. Semi-equipped. Calor gas available.
Take the A337 N from Brockenhurst then turn E on to B3055. Site signposted to S.

FORESTRY COMMISSION SETTHORNS CAMPSITE ♛ RAC L
Wootton, New Milton, BH25 5UA. ☎ (0703) 283771
Open: All year
Size: 60 acres, 320 touring pitches, 120 with elec, 200 level pitches, 170 with hardstanding. Water supply, 5 CWPs

(1991) £5.40 maximum charge; elec £1.50-£2
cc Access, Visa/B'card, Connect
Varied woodland site. Part remains open all year. Shop 2 miles. Minimum facilities - campers must have their own chemical toilet.
E off A35 at Holmsley Old Station, follow site signs for 2 miles.

NEW MILTON Hampshire   Map 2 B3

BASHLEY PARK ♛ RAC A
Sway Road, BH25 5QR. ☎ (0425) 612340
Open: 1 March-31 October
Size: 35 (100) acres, 420 touring pitches, all with elec, all with hardstanding, 320 level pitches, 380 static caravans. 40 hot showers, 102 WCs,

---

▣ Snacks/take away ⊠ Restaurant ◺ Swimming pool ▣ Shelter for campers 🐕 Dogs accepted   85

4 CWPs

🏕️🚐 | 🔌🧺💧✕🛶 | 🐕

(1991) Car & caravan, Motor caravan £5.50-£14; elec included, awn £1.50, dogs £1.50
Spacious park in a country setting on edge of New Forest. Facilities include licensed club and family lounge with seasonal entertainment, indoor leisure complex, 2 outdoor swimming pools and a new indoor pool, par 3 9-hole golf course, children's adventure playground, snooker, pool, table tennis, arcade. Calor gas only. No tents. 45 caravans for hire (own WCs).
At 1 mile N of New Milton on B3058, turn right on B3055. Site ¼ mile on left.

NEW ROMNEY *Kent* — Map 3 B3

Marlie Farm
Dymchurch Road. ☎ (0679) 63060
Open: March-October
Size: 20 acres, 450 touring pitches. 14 hot showers, 55 WCs

🏕️🚐 | 🔺🔌🧺☕💧 | 🐕

Site 1 mile E of New Romney, on A259.

New Romney Caravan Site
136 Coast Drive. ☎ (0679) 62247
Open: April-October
Size: 4 (11) acres, 50 touring pitches. 8 hot showers, 20 WCs. Static caravans

🏕️🚐 | 🔌 | 🐕

From A259 in New Romney, take B2071 to coast, then turn S for site.

NEWARK *Nottinghamshire* — Map 5 B3

MILESTONE CARAVAN PARK RAC L
Cromwell, NG23 6JE. ☎ (0636) 821244
Open: All year
Size: 2½ acres, 30 touring pitches, all level, 10 with elec, 4 with hardstanding. 4 hot showers, 4 cold showers, 7 WCs, 1 CWP

♿🏕️🚐 | 🔺 | 🐕

Car & caravan, Motor caravan, Car & tent £5, Tent £1, M/cycle 50p; elec £1, awn 50p, dogs free; WS
Rural site with 18 acres of fly fishing to rear and 6 acres of coarse fishing in village. Also close to River Trent. Shop and restaurant in Cromwell village. Swimming pool 5 miles in Newark. Under new ownership.
At 5 miles N of Newark on A1, turn off at Cromwell junction.

NEWBIGGIN-BY-THE-SEA *Northumberland* — Map 7 B3

SANDY BAY CARAVAN PARK RAC L
North Seaton, NE63 9YD. ☎ (0670) 815055
Open: March-October
Size: 3 (56) acres, 70 touring pitches, all level, 10 with elec, 600 static caravans, 3 chalets. Hot showers, 36 WCs, 1 CWP

♿🏕️🚐 | 🔌🧺☕ | 🛶 | 🐕

Charges on application.
cc Access, Visa/B'card
Attractive site on estuary of River Wansbeck and next to sandy beaches. Licensed clubroom. Indoor swimming pool. Excellent children's playground

(bought from Gateshead Garden Festival).
40 caravans for hire (own WCs). Calor gas only.
Restaurant 1 mile.
¾ mile S of Newbiggin on B1334 turn E towards sea.

NEWBY BRIDGE *Cumbria* — Map 4 B1

BIGLAND HALL CARAVAN PARK RAC A
Haverthwaite, LA12 8PJ. ☎ (053 95) 31702
Open: 1 March-31 October
Size: 30 acres, 36 touring pitches, all level, all with hardstanding, 30 static caravans. 12 hot showers, 24 WCs, 3 CWPs

🏕️🚐 | 🔌🧺 | 🐕

(1991) Car & caravan, Motor caravan £4; awn £1.25; WS
Pleasantly-situated wooded site 2 miles south of Lake Windermere. Calor gas only. Coarse and trout fishing and a riding school situated within the Bigland Estate. 20 caravans for hire (own WCs). Restaurant 2 miles.
3 miles W of Newby Bridge on A590, turn left on to B5278 (signposted 'Cark') for 1 mile to site.

BLACK BECK CARAVAN PARK RAC L
Bouth, Near Ulverston, LA12 8JN.
☎ (0229) 861274
Open: 1 March-31 October
Size: 3 (38) acres, 70 touring pitches, all level, 50 with elec, 235 static caravans. 10 hot showers, 10 cold showers, 25 WCs, 2 CWPs

♿🏕️🚐 | 🔺🔌🧺

Car & caravan, Motor caravan £7-£9, Car & tent, M/cycle & tent £6; elec £1, awn £1; WS
Exceptionally well-wooded site, in a totally natural location in a river valley teeming with wildlife within the Lake District National Park boundary. Restaurant ½ mile. Swimming pool 1½ miles.
M6 off at junction 36 - Barrow and South Lakes A590 - Haverthwaite. Past Haverthwaite Steam Railway on right - crossroads right - well-signposted at the crossroads.

Fell Foot Park
☎ (053 95) 31273
Open: March-October
Size: 1 acre, 26 touring pitches. 5 hot showers, 9 WCs. 19 static caravans

♿🏕️🚐 | 🔌🧺💧 | 🐕

1 mile N of Newby Bridge on A592.

NEWBY BRIDGE CARAVAN PARK RAC L
Canny Hill, LA12 8NF. ☎ (0253) 728891
Open: 1 March-31 October
Size: 25 acres, 20 touring pitches, all level, all with elec, all with hardstanding, 69 static caravans. 4 hot showers, 8 WCs, 1 CWP

♿🏕️🚐 | 🔌 | 🐕

Car & caravan, Motor caravan £6; elec £1.20, awn £1.20
Quiet, family-run park noted for its wildlife. Close to Lake Windermere. Superb recently modernised toilet facilities with private wash cubicles.
9 caravans for hire (own WCs). Restaurant ½ mile. Shop 100 yards. Swimming pool 6 miles. Calor gas only.
Leave M6 at junction 36, follow signs to Barrow

and Newby Bridge along A590. Just before Newby Bridge about 2¼ miles beyond High Newton, turn left at the signpost to Canny Hill. The Park entrance is about 200 yards on the right hand side.

Oak Head Caravan Park
Ayside, LA11 6JA. ☎ (053 95) 31475
Open: March-October
Size: 25 acres, 60 touring pitches. 8 hot showers, 24 WCs. 4 static caravans

From M6 junction 36 follow signs to Newby Bridge on A590. Travel for 14 miles and site is on left.

NEWCASTLE-UPON-TYNE *Tyne & Wear* Map 7 B3

NEWCASTLE RACECOURSE   RAC L
High Gosforth Park, NE3 5HP.
☎ (091) 236 3258
Open: 17 May-9 September
Size: 5 acres, 90 touring pitches, all level, 6 with elec, 4 with hardstanding. 8 hot showers, 8 cold showers, 33 WCs, 1 CWP

Charges on application.
cc Access
This sheltered site, in 900 acres of wooded parkland, has a children's play area and there's nearby golf and tennis. Calor gas only. Swimming pool 3 miles.
4 miles N of Newcastle on the E side of the A6125 and W side of the A1 and A189.

NEWHAVEN *Derbyshire* Map 5 A3

Barracks Farm
Beresford Dale, Hartington
☎ (029 884) 261
Open: All Year
Size: 6 acres, 30 touring pitches. 4 hot showers, 10 WCs

From A515, turn on to B5054 through Hartington. Take first left, then keep left for 1½ miles.

NEWHAVEN CARAVAN & CAMPING PARK   RAC A
SK17 0DT. ☎ (0298) 84300
Open: 1 March-31 October
Size: 10 (25) acres, 95 touring pitches, 58 with elec, 70 level pitches, 20 with hardstanding, 45 static caravans. 8 hot showers, 18 WCs, 1 CWP

Car & caravan, Motor caravan, Car & tent, M/cycle & tent £6-£6.75, plus 50p per person above 4; elec £1.25, 75p
Delightful site in the heart of the Peak District providing an excellent base for touring the area. Convenient for Alton Towers, Chatsworth, Haddon Hall, etc. Restaurant 100 metres. Swimming pool 9 miles. It is advisable to book (£1 per night deposit) for Bank Holidays.
At junction of A515 and A5012, midway between Ashbourne and Buxton. Opposite Newhaven Hotel.

Waterloo Inn
Biggin, SK17 0DH. ☎ (029 884) 284
Open: All year
Size: 1 acre, 10 touring pitches. 2 WCs

¾ mile S of Newhaven on A515, turn W signposted Biggin for ½ mile. Inn on right.

NEWMARKET *Suffolk* Map 3 A1

Barron Cove
Weirs Road, Burwell, CB5 0BP.
☎ (0638) 741547
Open: All year
Size: 14 acres, 100 touring pitches (plus 50 for tents). 5 hot showers, 14 WCs. 3 static caravans

B1102 from Cambridge or B1103 from Newmarket. Site signposted from Burwell.

Trax Campsite
Rowley Mile Racecourse
☎ (0638) 663235
Open: May-September
Size: Touring pitches. 6 hot showers, 6 WCs

Site off A1304, SW of Newmarket.

NEWPORT PAGNELL *Buckinghamshire* Map 2 B2

Emberton Park
Emberton, Olney. ☎ (0234) 711575
Open: April-October
Size: 9½ acres, 96 touring pitches. Hot showers, 2b WCs

Site 4 miles N of Newport Pagnell, to W of A509.

NEWQUAY *Cornwall* Map 1 A3

Camping & Caravanning Club Site
Tregurrian, Watergate Bay, TR8 4AE.
☎ (0637) 860448
Open: 30 March-28 September
Size: 4.2 acres, 100 touring pitches. 6 hot showers, 16 WCs

Charges on application.
cc Access, Visa/B'card
Site is ¾ mile from the sands of Watergate Bay.
From the B3059 take the road signed Airport, left at the B3276 then follow the signs for the site.

GWILLS HOLIDAY PARK   RAC L
Lane, TR8 4PE. ☎ (0637) 873617
Open: Easter-End October
Size: 10 (14) acres, 105 touring pitches, 23 with elec, 27 static caravans. 12 hot showers, 12 WCs, 1 CWP

Charges on application.
Level, well-sheltered site beside a small stream (fishing possible). Children's playground, games and TV room. 27 caravans for hire (own WCs). Families and couples only.
From the junction of the A392 and A3058 (Quintrell Downs), travel W on unclassified road for ¾ mile then turn left for ¾ mile to site on left.

▣ Snacks/take away ☒ Restaurant ◁ Swimming pool ▣ Shelter for campers ▶ Dogs accepted   87

Full colour brochure from: Hendra Holiday Park, Newquay, Cornwall TR8 4NY · Tel: 0637 875778

HENDRA HOLIDAY PARK
RAC A
TR8 4NY. ☎ (0637) 875778
Open: April-October
Size: 40 acres, 600 touring pitches, 200 with elec, 26 with hardstanding, 500 level pitches, 160 static caravans. 39 hot showers, 96 WCs, 4 CWPs

(1991) £2.66-£4.14 per adult, £1.79-£3.01 per child; Car/M/cycle* 56p-77p; elec £1.99, awn 56p-86p, dogs £1.33; WS
cc Access, Visa/B'card
Ideal family site with children's club and nursery, nightly entertainment. 160 caravans for hire (own WCs). Families and couples only, no single-sex parties.
On A392 to Newquay town centre.

NEWQUAY TOURIST PARK
RAC A
TR8 4HS. ☎ (0637) 871111
Open: Mid April-Mid October
Size: 23 acres, 200 touring pitches, 120 static caravans. 25 hot showers, 37 WCs, 4 CWP

Car & caravan, Motor caravan, Car & tent from £2.30 per adult, children free-£2.85, 70p per car; elec £1.75
cc Access, Visa/B'card
South-facing parkland in green countryside 2 miles from Newquay. 3 pool complex and giant water slide. Free family admission to and nightly entertainment in modern club. Graded "Excellent", Rose Award. 120 caravans for hire (own WCs). Restaurant 2 miles. No dogs. No all- male or all-female groups. No motorcycles.
At the end of A30 dual carriageway follow

A30 Newquay/ Redruth. Pass Little Chef on left and after passing under iron bridge turn right "RAF St Mawgan". After 3 miles, at roundabout, follow A3059 Newquay. After 4 miles look for signs indicative right turn at bottom of hill to Newquay Tourist Park.

PORTH BEACH TOURIST PARK
RAC A
Porth, TR7 3NH. ☎ (0637) 876531
Open: Early April-End October
Size: 7 acres, 201 touring pitches, all level, 150 with elec, 12 static caravans. 8 hot showers, 24 WCs

Charges on application.
cc Access, Visa/B'card
Quiet, grassy site, 100 yards from sandy beach, for family groups only. Play area. Shop, bar and restaurant 50 yards.
At 1 mile E of Newquay, turn N off A392 onto B3276. Site ½ mile on right.

Resparva House
Summercourt. ☎ (0872) 510332
Open: Easter-October
Size: 1 acre, 5 touring pitches (plus 15 for tents). 2 hot showers, 4 WCs

Site on old A30, ½ mile W of Summercourt. On new A30, opposite exit to Summercourt.

ROSECLISTON PARK
RAC A
Trevemper, TR8 5JT. ☎ (0637) 830326
Open: 15 May-15 September
Size: 7 acres, 126 touring pitches, all level, 50 with elec, 7 with hardstanding. 14 hot showers, 22 WCs, 2 CWPs

⬥ Facilities for Disabled ⬥ Caravans accepted ⬥ Motor caravans ⬥ Tents ⬥ Laundry room ⬥ Shop

Charges on application.
A meadowland site with outdoor and indoor pools as well as sauna and solarium. Children's play area. Restaurant 1½ miles.
From Newquay, travel S on the A3075 for 2 miles to site on left.

SUMMER LODGE TOURING CENTRE RAC L
Whitecross, TR8 4LW. ☎ (0726) 860415
Open: Easter-end October
Size: 2 (10) acres, 50 touring pitches, all level, 8 with elec, 111 static caravans, 17 chalets. 8 hot showers, 22 WCs, 1 CWP

Charges on application.
There is a children's play area and a clubhouse with bar and disco at this level, grassy site. 111 caravans and 17 chalets for hire. Shop open May to September.
From Indian Queens, junction of the A30 and A392, travel W on the A392 for 2 miles to Whitecross. Turn left under railway bridge, keep right to site on right in 300 yards.

Treguistick Farm Holiday Park
Porth. ☎ (0637) 872478
Open: April-October
Size: 1 (8) acres, 20 touring pitches. 4 hot showers, 10 WCs. 26 static caravans, 18 chalets

From A392, turn N on to B3276 past Porth Beach. Turn right to Treguistick (Trevelgue road) for site.

TREKENNING MANOR TOURIST PARK RAC A
TR8 4JF. ☎ (0637) 880462
Open: Easter-end October
Size: 4½ (6½) acres, 75 touring pitches, 35 with elec, 52 level pitches. 10 hot showers, 10 cold showers, 12 WCs, 1 CWP

Charges on application.
Family site with a swimming pool, play area, barbecue area, games and TV rooms and bar. Activity play area and games field. Tents and cycles for hire.
From Indian Queens, junction of the A30 and A392, travel towards Newquay on the A392 for just over ½ mile to crossroads, turn right on the A39 for 2 miles to roundabout. Turn left on the A3059, and immediately turn left to site.

TRELOY TOURIST PARK RAC A
TR7 4JN. ☎ (0637) 872063
Open: April-End September
Size: 10 (11½) acres, 119 touring pitches, 59 with elec, 20 with hardstanding. 12 hot showers, 26 WCs, 1 CWP

(1991) Car & caravan, Motor caravan, Car & tent £1.80- £2.80 per adult, children free (under 14s); elec £1.20- £1.50, dogs 50p; WS
cc Access, Visa/B'card
There's a swimming pool, paddling pool, adventure playground, sports competitions and a licensed clubhouse with games and TV rooms at this grassy site. Coarse fishing available. Families

and couples only.
From Bodmin take A30 for 8 miles. First turning on right after passing under bridge. Follow signs to RAF St Mawgan. Site signposted off A3059.

Trenance Caravan Park
Edgcumbe Avenue, TR7 2JY.
☎ (0637) 873447
Open: April-September
Size: 12 acres, 50 touring pitches. 22 hot showers, 45 WCs. 134 static caravans, 21 chalets

Site 1 miles S of town centre on A3075 (Edgcumbe Avenue). Site in leisure park.

TRENCREEK FARM HOLIDAY PARK RAC L
Trencreek, TR8 4NS. ☎ (0637) 874210
Open: 1 April-30 September
Size: 10 acres, 150 touring pitches, all level, 30 with elec, 8 with hardstanding, 26 chalets. 20 hot showers, 20 cold showers, 57 WCs, 2 CWPs

(1991) Car & caravan, Motor caravan, Car & tent, M/cycle & tent £2-£3.20 per adult, £1-£1.60 per child, plus 40p per car; elec £1.70
Family park only 1½ miles from Newquay town centre, a footpath walk to town. Coarse fishing ponds on site. 26 chalets for hire (own WCs). Families only - no all- male or all-female parties accepted.
A392 to Quintrell Downs roundabout, turn right over level crossing (direction Newquay East/Porth). Proceed to Porth Four Turnings (2 mini roundabouts ¾ mile to Newquay town centre), turn left at the corner of Newquay Tretherras School into Trevenson Road to Trencreek (¾ mile). The Park is in the village on the right. Reception is inside the entrance on your left.

TRETHIGGEY TOURING PARK RAC L
Quintrell Downs, TR8 4LG.
☎ (0637) 877672
Open: 1 March-31 December
Size: 6 (6½) acres, 157 touring pitches, 85 with elec, 120 level pitches, 20 with hardstanding. 6 hot showers, 18 WCs, 1 CWP

(1991) Car & caravan, Motor caravan, Car & tent, M/cycle & tent from £1.75 per adult, 80p per child; elec £1.60, awn 50p, dogs 60p; WS
A small, friendly, family-run site, peaceful location with wonderful country views. Tarmac site road and hard ground suitable for any weather. Restaurant 200 yards. Swimming pool 3 miles. No large groups of young people accepted.
From the junction of the A30 and A392 at Indian Queens, leave as for Newquay along the A392 to Quintrell Downs (4¾ miles), turn left on A3058 for ¼ mile to site on left.

TREVARRIAN HOLIDAY PARK RAC A
Trevarrian. ☎ (0637) 860381
Open: Easter-End October
Size: 5 acres, 125 touring pitches, 12 with elec, 105 level pitches. 12 hot showers, 26 WCs, 1 CWP

Charges on application.
Level, grassy site in the country not far from beach.

⬛ Snacks/take away ☒ Restaurant ◁ Swimming pool ▣ Shelter for campers ⌂ Dogs accepted   **89**

Swimming pool and children's play area. Shop open 5 May to end September.
4 miles N of Newquay on the B3276, site on left upon entering Trevarrian village.

TREVELGUE CARAVAN & CAMPING PARK RAC A
Porth. ☎ (063 73) 3475
Open: April-October
Size: 15 acres, 268 touring pitches. Hot showers, WCs

Charges on application.
Large site in a river valley leading to coast. Plenty of entertainment including swimming pool, whirlpool spa, disco, nightclub and playground. Caravans for hire (own WCs). No dogs.
At ¾ mile E of Newquay on A392, turn N onto B3276 for ¾ mile, where turn right. Site is in ½ mile.

WATERGATE BAY HOLIDAY PARK RAC A
Tregurrian, Watergate Bay, TR8 4AD.
☎ (0637) 860837
Open: 1 March-30 November
Size: 9½ (15) acres, 171 touring pitches, all level, 69 with elec, 2 with hardstanding, 3 chalets. 20 hot showers, 20 cold showers, 32 WCs, 6 CWPs

(1991) Car & caravan, Motor caravan, Car & tent, M/cycle & tent £2.04-£3.38 per adult, £1.02-£1.69 per child; elec £1.80, dogs 80p (July & August only); WS
cc Access, Visa/B'card
Family-run site for families. Situated in area of Outstanding Natural Beauty, ideal centre for touring. Free evening entertainment. Free mini bus

to sandy beach (½ mile away). Dog exercise area. 3 chalets for hire (own WCs). Motorcycles admitted at owners' discretion.
From Newquay, travel N on the B3276 for 2¼ miles to where Watergate Bay signposted.

NEWTON ABBOT *Devon*   *Map 1 B3*

LEMONFORD FARM CARAVAN AND CAMPING PARK RAC A
Bickington, TQ12 6JR. ☎ (0626) 821242
Open: Easter-End September
Size: 6 (7½) acres, 34 touring pitches, all level, 25 with elec, 12 static caravans. 6 hot showers, 9 WCs, 1 CWP

(1991) Car & caravan from £5, Motor caravan, Car & tent M/cycle & tent from £4.50, plus £1 per person above 2; elec £1.30, awn £1, dogs 60p
A very pretty riverside park with excellent facilities, close to Dartmoor National Park and Torbay. Level grass pitches with children's play area. Golf, fishing, swimming and riding nearby. 12 caravans for hire (own WCs). Restaurant 0.3 miles.
Swimming pool 3 miles.
From Exeter leave A38 at A382 junction and take third exit off Drumbridge roundabout, signposted Bickington. Follow road 3 miles, pass the Toby Jug Inn, then turn left on to A383, then first left, site entrance on left. From Plymouth take A383 for ½ mile.

COMPASS CARAVANS TOURING PARK RAC L
Higher Brocks Plantation, Teigngrace, TQ12 9QZ.
☎ (0626) 832792
Open: March-January
Size: 3 acres, 38 touring pitches, 36 with elec,

20 level pitches, 20 with hardstanding. 4 hot showers, 9 WCs, 2 CWPs

	📦	🚐	⛺		🐾					🐕

Charges on application.
A quiet, family-run site, well sheltered by trees with a children's play area. Opposite Stover Country Park.
From Exeter, follow the A38, turn left at signpost to Teigngrace, site 100 yards on left.

DORNAFIELD CARAVAN PARK   RAC A
Two Mile Oak, TQ12 6DD. ☎ (0803) 812732
Open: 23 March-31 October
Size: 8 acres, 75 touring pitches, all with elec, 72 level pitches. 13 hot showers, 20 WCs, 1 CWP

	📦	🚐	⛺	🚿	🐾	📮		🏠	🐕

(1991) Car & caravan, Motor caravan, Car & tent, M/cycle* & tent £1.40-£3.50 plus £2.25-£2.75 per adult, £1.15-£1.25 child; elec £1.50, awn £1.30-£1.40, dog 70p
Beautiful 14th century farmhouse location in quiet, sheltered, level valley with superb facilities to suit the discerning caravanner. Restaurant ½ mile. Swimming pool 2½ miles.
At 2 miles S of Newton Abbot on the A381 turn right at Two Mile Oak Inn, in ½ mile turn left at crossroads to site 150 yards on right.

STOVER INTERNATIONAL CARAVAN PARK   RAC A
Lower Staple Hill, TQ12 6JD.
☎ (0626) 821446
Open: 15 March-31 October
Size: 16 acres, 246 touring pitches, 200 with elec, 175 level pitches, 45 with hardstanding, 2 static caravans, 3 chalets. 35 hot showers, 66 WCs, 3 CWPs

♿	📦	🚐	⛺	🚿	🐾	☕	✖	🔲	🏠	🐕

Car & caravan, Motor caravan, Car & tent, M/cycle* & tent £4.75-£7.50, plus £1.75 per adult above 2, child £1.15; elec £1.70, awn £1.65, dogs £1.50; WS cc Access, Visa/B'card
A well-equipped, landscaped park planted with trees and shrubs. Miniature steam railway. Coarse fishing lakes. Children's play area. 3 chalets for hire (own WCs). 4 and 6 berth holiday homes for hire. Heated indoor swimming pool.
A38 to junction with A382 then turn towards Newton Abbot and in 600 yards (550 metres) turn right. If approaching from Torquay use A382 and turn left after Stover Golf Club.

Ware Barton
Kingsteignton. ☎ (0626) 54025
Open: Easter-September
Size: 4 acres, 60 touring pitches. 10 hot showers, 22 WCs.

	📦	🚐	⛺	🚿					🐕

Site ½ mile E of Kingsteignton on A381.

Wear Farm
Newton Road, Bishopsteignton, TQ14 9PT.
☎ (0626) 775249
Open: Easter-October
Size: 20 acres, 147 touring pitches. 20 hot showers, 50 WCs. 40 static caravans

	📦	🚐	⛺	🚿	🐾				🐕

Site 1 mile E of Kingsteignton on A381.

Kilworth Caravan Park
North Kilworth House, Lutterworth
☎ (0858) 880597
Open: April-October
Size: 10 acres, 50 touring pitches. 1 hot shower

	📦	🚐	⛺						🐕

Site on A427, 2¼ miles W of Husbands Bosworth.

PAMPAS CARAVAN PARK   RAC A
Old Yarmouth Road, NR28 9NA.
☎ (0692) 405829
Open: 20 March-31 October plus 10 days at Xmas
Size: 5¼ acres, 50 touring pitches, all level, 18 with elec, 4 with hardstanding, 2 static caravans. 4 hot showers, 9 WCs, 1 CWP

	📦	🚐	⛺	🚿	🐾				🐕

(1991) Car & caravan, Motor caravan £5-£6, Car & tent, M/cycle & tent £3-£6, plus 50p per person above 2 (under 5s free); elec £1.50, awn £1.25, dog 50p above 1
Centrally located for Broads, coast, Norwich City and countryside. Minimal entertainment on site other than children's play area, but with full use of facilities on nearby site, customers have complete choice of type of holiday. Tourist Board graded 3 Ticks. 2 caravans for hire (own WCs, 3 nights minumum stay). Restaurant 200 yards. Swimming pool 4 miles (free at sister site).
From the junction of the A149 and B1145 (just W of North Walsham town centre), proceed into the town centre, then S along the Old Yarmouth Road for 1 mile to site on left.

COTE GHYLL CARAVAN PARK   RAC L
Osmotherley, OL6 3AH. ☎ (060 983) 425
Open: 1 April-31 October
Size: 4 (7) acres, 57 touring pitches, 15 level pitches, 40 with elec, 17 static caravans. 10 hot showers, 10 cold showers, 17 WCs, 2 CWPs

	📦	🚐	⛺	🚿					🐕

Car & caravan £2.50, Motor caravan £1.25, Car & tent £2.25, M/cycle & tent £2, all plus £1 per adult, 50p per child; elec £1.50, awn 50p
Small, quiet, sheltered, ideal walking area. Shop and restaurant ½ mile. Swimming pool 7 miles. Motorcycles accepted at owners' discretion.
At junction of A684 and A19, 5¾ miles E of Northallerton, turn E for 1 mile to Osmotherley. Turn N at village cross to site on right.

HUTTON BONVILLE CARAVAN PARK   RAC A
Hutton Bonville, DL7 0NR. ☎ (0609) 81416
Open: 1 March-31 October
Size: 5 acres, 11 touring pitches, all level, 64 static caravans. 4 hot showers, 11 WCs, 1 CWP

	📦	🚐	⛺	🚿	🐾				🐕

(1991) Car & caravan, Motor caravan, Car & tent, M/cycle & tent £5.50; elec £1
A well-maintained meadowland site. Children's play area, TV room, and licensed clubhouse with family room. Shop supplies basic provisions (opening hours are limited). Shop 3 miles.

🔲 Snacks/take away   ✖ Restaurant   🔲 Swimming pool   🔲 Shelter for campers   🐕 Dogs accepted

Swimming pool 4 miles.
4½ miles N of Northallerton, on W side of the A167.

NORTHAMPTON *Northamptonshire*　　Map 2 B1

BILLING AQUADROME　　RAC A
Little Billing, NN3 4DA. ☎ (0604) 408181
Open: 23 March-1 November
Size: 100 (270) acres, 755 touring pitches, all level,
200 with elec, 1200 static caravans. 54 hot showers,
202 WCs, 14 CWPs

(1991) Car & caravan, Motor caravan, Car & tent,
M/cycle & tent £6.50-£7.50
*270 acres of parkland, woods and lakes. Coarse
fishing during season. Amusement centre for
children and adults. Free children's play area.
Snack bars, restaurants and licensed bars. Outdoor
swimming pool and children's paddling pool.
From the junction of the A45 and unclassified road
at Great Billing, 4 miles E of Northampton, travel S
on unclassified road for almost ½ mile to site on
right.*

NORTHWICH *Cheshire*　　Map 4 B2

Lamb Cottage
Dalefords Lane, Whitegate
☎ (0606) 882302
Open: March-October
Size: 3 acres, 24 touring pitches. 2 hot showers,
4 WCs

*Turn S off A556 in Sandiway, signposted
Whitegate, into Dalefords Lane. Site 1 mile.*

Woodbine Cottage Caravan Park
Acton Bridge, CW8 3QB. ☎ (0606) 852319
Open: March-October
Size: 2¼ acres, 30 touring pitches. 5 hot showers, 8
WCs. 4 static caravans

*Site on A49, next door to Rheingold Reservoir
Restaurant.*

NORWICH *Norfolk*　　Map 3 B1

Camping & Caravanning Club Site
Martineau Lane, Lakenham, NR1 2HX.
☎ (0603) 620060
Open: 30 March-28 September

Size: 2½ acres, 30 touring pitches. 4 hot showers,
6 WCs

Charges on application.
cc Access, Visa/B'card
*Site has direct access to the River Yare. Shop
2 miles.
From the A47 turn into Long John Hill (under the
low bridge 10' 6") left into Martineau Lane, the site
is on the right.*

HAVERINGLAND HALL CARAVAN PARK　　RAC A
Cawston, NR10 4PN. ☎ (0603) 871302
Open: 1 April-25 October
Size: 3 (15) acres, 20 touring pitches, all level,
6 with elec, 57 static caravans. 5 hot showers,
9 WCs, 1 CWP

(1991) Car & caravan, Motor caravan, Car & tent,
M/cycle & tent £6, plus 80p per person above 2,
child 80p; elec 80p, awn 80p, dogs 80p; WS
*Secluded site in park of Haveringland Hall (now
demolished). Beautiful trees and 14-acre lake -
fishing by permit. 2 caravans for hire (own WCs).
Shop 2 miles. Restaurant 1 mile. Swimming pool
4 miles.
From Norwich, travel N on the A140 for 3¾ miles,
fork left on the B1149 for 2¾ miles. 3 miles past
Horsford turn left into unclassified road, after
1¼ miles turn right to site on right in ½ mile.*

NOTTINGHAM *Nottinghamshire*　　Map 5 A3

National Water Sports Centre
Adbolton Lane, Holme Pierrepont
☎ (0602) 821212
Open: Easter-October
Size: 18 acres, 320+ touring pitches. 12 hot
showers, 16 WCs

Site off A52, ½ mile S of Nottingham. Site signed.

New Moor Farm Trailer Park
Calverton. ☎ (0602) 652426
Open: All year
Size: 18 acres, 80 touring pitches. 12 hot showers,
94 WCs. 2 static caravans

*5 miles N of Nottingham (A614), turn right on to
B6386 to Calverton. Site ½ mile E of town.*

THORNTONS HOLT CAMPSITE  L
Stragglethorpe, NG12 2JZ.
☎ (0602) 332125
Open: 1 April-1 November
Size: 7½ acres, 84 touring pitches, all level, 32 with elec. 5 hot showers, 11 WCs, 1 CWP

(1991) Car & caravan, Motor caravan, Car & tent, M/cycle & tent £4.50, extra tent £1,plus 50p per person above 2 (under 5s free); elec £1.20, awn 50p, dogs free; WS
A spacious, quiet site ideally situated for visits to Nottingham, Vale of Belvoir, Sherwood Forest and the National Water Sports Centre at Holme Pierrepont. The site has had a steady improvement of facilities over the last year with the addition of an indoor heated swimming pool, a small shop and refurbishment to other amenities. Restaurant 100 metres.
From A52: 3 miles E of Nottingham, turn S at traffic lights on road signposted to Cropwell Bishop. Site is ½ mile on the left. From A46: 4 miles SE of Nottingham, turn N at crossroads on road signposted Stragglethorpe.

NUNEATON *Warwickshire*   **Map 2 B1**

WOLVEY VILLA FARM CARAVAN & CAMP SITE L
Wolvey, LE10 3HF. ☎ (0455) 220493
Open: All year
Size: 5½ (7) acres, 110 touring pitches, 50 with elec, all level pitches, 10 with hardstanding. 4 hot showers, 14 WCs, 1 CWP

Car & caravan, Motor caravan £4.20, Car & tent, M/cycle* & tent £4.10, plus 80p per person above 2; elec £1.75, awn £1, dogs 40p
A quiet site situated on the borders of Warwickshire and Leicestershire, ideally located for exploring the many places of interest in the Midlands. Restaurant ½ mile. Swimming pool 5 miles.
M6 junction 2, then B4065, site signposted.
M69 junction 1, then follow signs for Wolvey. Site signposted.

OAKHAM *Leicestershire*   **Map 5 B3**

Ranksborough Hall
Langham. ☎ (0572) 722984
Open: All year
Size: 34 acres, 110 touring pitches. 14 hot showers, 26 WCs. 70 static caravans

Site in Langham, ¼ mile W of A606.

OKEHAMPTON *Devon*   **Map 1 B3**

Bridestowe Caravan Park
Bridestowe, EX20 4ER. ☎ (083 786) 261
Open: March-September
Size: 6 acres, 17 touring pitches. 8 hot showers, 8 WCs. Static caravans

Tavistock end of Okehampton by-pass. Road forks to Launceston and site between the forks. Head for Bridestowe village on A30. Site signed from village.

DARTMOOR VIEW CARAVAN & CAMPING PARK A
Whiddon Down, EX20 2QL. ☎ (064 723) 545
Open: 15 March-15 November
Size: 3½ (6) acres, 60 touring pitches, 27 with elec, 40 level pitches, 10 with hardstanding, 20 static caravans. 4 hot showers, 11 WCs, 1 CWP

Car & caravan, Motor caravan £4.75-£6.95, Car & tent, M/cycle* & tent £3.50-£6.95, plus £1 per adult above 2, child 75p; elec £1.50, awn free, dogs free; WS
cc Major cards
Clean site with commanding views, licensed club, takeaway foods available. Dartmoor National Park boundary. West Country Tourist Board graded 5 Ticks - Excellent. 14 caravans for hire (own WCs). Restaurant 400 yards. A warm welcome awaits you.
From M5 take A30 (junction 31) to first island (Merrymeet), turn left through Whiddon Down, park is approximately ½ mile on right hand side.

OLDITCH FARM CARAVAN PARK L
Sticklepath, EX20 2NT. ☎ (0837) 840734
Open: 14 March-14 November
Size: 2 (3) acres, 35 touring pitches, 12 with elec, 10 level pitches, 8 with hardstanding, 16 static caravans. 4 hot showers, 12 WCs, 1 CWP

Car & caravan, Motor caravan £5, Car & tent, M/cycle* & tent £4, plus 50p per person above 2 (under 3s free); elec £1.25, awn free, dogs free; WS
Quiet, privately-run site within easy reach of shops, tourist attractions, etc. Convenient for exploring Dartmoor and touring Devon and east Cornwall. Licensed restaurant. Games and TV room. 3 caravans for hire (own WCs). Shop 400 metres (mobile shop also calls at park). Swimming pool 4 miles.
Take Sticklepath road from either Merrymeet Roundabout, Whiddon Down, or Okehampton turn-off on A30. Site is ½ E of Sticklepath village.

Prewley Caravan & Camping Site
Sourton Cross. ☎ (0831) 324353
Open: March-October
Size: 4½ acres, 52 touring pitches. 4 hot showers, 14 WCs

Site access from Sourton Cross roundabout, 4 miles W of Okehampton.

'YERTIZ' CARAVAN PARK L
Exeter Road, EX20 1QF. ☎ (0837) 52281
Open: 1 March-15 January
Size: 1 acre, 15 touring pitches, all level, all with elec, 3 static caravans. 3 hot showers, 5 WCs, 1 CWP

(1991) Car & caravan £3.50, Motor caravan £3, Car & tent, M/cycle & tent from £2, plus 50p per person above 4; elec £1
Friendly, family site under personal supervision of owners. Children's play area. 3 caravans for hire

---

🝾 Snacks/take away ☒ Restaurant ◹ Swimming pool ▦ Shelter for campers 🐕 Dogs accepted

(own WCs). Shop 200 yards. Restaurant and swimming pool 50 yards.
From the direction of Exeter take B3260 from by-pass. Site is on left just past the motel, site approx 50 yards.

White Cat Park
Shaw Lane, PE22 9LQ. ☎ (0205) 870121
Open: April-October
Size: 2 acres, 40 touring pitches. 2 hot showers, 8 WCs. 4 static caravans

8 miles NE of Boston on A52.

ORLETON RISE CARAVAN PARK   RAC L
Green Lane, Orleton, SY8 4JE.
☎ (058 474) 617
Open: 1 March-30 September
Size: 1 (10) acres, 20 touring pitches, all level, all with elec, 75 static caravans. 4 hot showers, 7 WCs, 1 CWP

(1991) Car and caravan £6.50, Motor caravan £5.50, plus £1 per person above 2; elec £1.20, awn £1
A picturesque rural site, set amongst rolling hills. Calor gas only. Shop and restaurant ¾ mile.
From the junction of the A49, A456 and B4362 between Ludlow and Leominster, travel W on the B4362 for 2 miles, then turn left on the B4361 for ¼ mile. Turn right at Maidenhead Inn to site.

ABBEY FARM CARAVAN PARK   RAC L
Dark Lane, L40 5TX. ☎ (0695) 572686
Open: All year
Size: 3 (6) acres, 36 touring pitches, all level, all with elec, 10 with hardstanding, 8 static caravans. 13 hot showers, 20 WCs, 1 CWP

Car & caravan, Motor caravan £6, Car & tent, M/cycle & tent £4.95, Tent from £4.40, plus £1 per person above 2, child 75p; elec £1.50, awn £1.50; WS
Quiet, rural park with level, mown grass surrounded by mature trees, with pitches for touring and some static vans. Amenities include family bathroom with facilities for disabled, undercover washing-up area, adventure playground, dog exercise area. Shops in Ormskirk (1½ miles). Restaurant ¼ mile (5 minutes' walk). Swimming pool 2 miles.
At 1½ miles NE of Ormskirk, via Derby Street. Sign at entrance.

CRANBERRY MOSS CAMPING & CARAVAN PARK   RAC A
Kinnerley, SY10 8DY. ☎ (074 381) 444
Open: April-October
Size: 4 acres, 60 touring pitches, 50 level pitches, 32 with elec, 10 with hardstanding. 2 hot showers,

6 WCs, 1 CWP

(1991) Car & caravan, Motor caravan, Car & tent £3.95- £4.75, plus 90p-£1.25 per person above 2; Tent £1.15- £1.50, Car 95p-£1.15, M/cycle 90p-£1.25; elec £1-£1.20
Modern site in pastoral setting with easy access to A5 and B4396 roads. Restaurant 1½ miles. Swimming pool 8 miles.
From junction of A4083 at A5, 3¾ miles SE of Oswestry, travel SE on A5 for 4¼ miles. Turn W on B4396 for 300 yards to site on left.

Royal Hill Inn
Edgerley, Kinnerley, SY10 8ES.
☎ (074 381) 242
Open: April-October
Size: 2 acres, 20 touring pitches. 1 hot shower, 2 WCs. 4 static caravans

From A5 (Shrewsbury), left at Melverley sign, left out of Pentre at post office. Site 1 mile from Pentre next to Severn River.

GREEN PASTURES FARM   RAC L
SO51 6AJ. ☎ (0703) 814444
Open: 15 March-31 October
Size: 4 acres, 45 touring pitches, all level, 42 with elec. 4 hot showers, 7 WCs, 1 CWP

(1991) Car & caravan, Motor caravan, Car & tent, M/cycle* & tent £5; extra person £1; elec £1.50; WS
A family site, with space for children to play. Also ideal for ferries from Portsmouth, Southampton and Lymington. Close to Paultons Park. Restaurant 1 mile. Swimming pool 4 miles.
Signposted from junction 2 of M27 and off A31 and A36 between Romsey and Cadnam.

SANDYHOLME HOLIDAY PARK   RAC A
31 Moreton Road, DT2 8HZ.
☎ (0305) 852677
Open: 1 April/Easter-31 October
Size: 5 acres, 65 touring pitches, all level, 43 with elec, 35 static caravans. 8 hot showers, 18 WCs, 1 CWP

(1991) Car & caravan, Motor caravan, Car & tent, M/cycle* & tent £4.50-£8; elec £1.50, awn £1, dogs 50p
A quiet, family-run site situated in Hardy countryside, central for Weymouth, Lulworth Cove and Dorchester. 29 caravans for hire (own WCs). Swimming pool 1½ miles.
Turn through village of Owermoigne off A352 for 1 mile.

OXFORD CAMPING INTERNATIONAL   RAC L
426 Abingdon Road, OX1 4XN.
☎ (0865) 246551
Open: All year
Size: 5 acres, 129 touring pitches, all level, 85 with

elec. 10 hot showers, 21 WCs, 1 CWP

♿ 🏕️ 🚐 ⛺ 🛏️ 🔌 🧳   🐕

Car & caravan, Motor caravan, Car & tent £4, M/cycle & tent £3.40; all plus £1.25 per adult, 70p per child; elec £1.25; WS
cc Access, Amex, Visa/B'card
Situated on the edge of Oxford, 1½ miles from the city centre, ½ mile from the River Thames. This modern site makes an ideal touring centre. Pub meals 200 yards. Swimming pool ¼ mile.
On S side of Oxford, take A4144 to city centre from ringroad ¼ mile on left. Signposted on ringroad and A34.

CASSINGTON MILL CARAVAN PARK   RAC L
Eynsham Road, Cassington, OX8 1DB.
☏ (0865) 881081
Open: 1 April-31 October
Size: 4 acres, 83 touring pitches, all level, 40 with elec, 4 hot showers, 15 WCs, 1 CWP

♿ 🏕️ 🚐 ⛺   🧳   🐕

(1991) Car & caravan, Motor caravan, Car & tent £5.50, M/cycle & tent £4.50, plus £1.25 per person above 2, £1.25 per child; elec £1.25, awn free, dogs free
cc Access, Amex, Diners, Visa/B'card
A grassy site, quiet area, with River Evenlode running through park. Restaurant 2 miles. Swimming pool 7 miles.
From the junction of the A40 and A4144, N of Oxford, travel W on the A40 for 3 miles. Turn S for 175 yards and turn left just before river bridge.

DIAMOND FARM CARAVAN & CAMPING PARK   RAC L
Bletchingdon, OX5 3DR. ☏ (0869) 50909
Open: March-October
Size: 1½ (3) acres, 37 touring pitches, all level, 25 with elec, 2 with hardstanding. 4 hot showers, 8 WCs, 1 CWP

  🏕️ 🚐 ⛺ 🔌 🧳 🛒   🏊 📷 🐕

Car & caravan, Motor caravan, Car & tent, M/cycle & tent £6.50; plus from £1 per person, child from 50p; elec £1.25, awn 75p, dogs 50p
Buildings in Cotswold stone converted from former farm. Site is well-planted with trees and shrubs. Separate children's playground and cycle track. TV and games room. Bar and full size snooker table. Restaurant 1 mile.
From A34 2 miles NE of Kidlington, turn left on B4027. Site 1 mile on left. Signposted from main road.

Spring Farm
Faringdon Road, Cumnor, OX2 9QY.
☏ (0865) 863028
Open: March-October
Size: 3 acres, 3 touring pitches, 20 pitches for tents. 1 hot shower, 1 WC

  🏕️ 🚐 ⛺   🐕

Site on A420, S of Oxford at end of dual carriageway turn right.

PADSTOW Cornwall   Map 1 A3

Carnevas Caravan & Camping Park
St Merryn. ☏ (0841) 520230
Open: April-October

Size: 8 acres, 195 touring pitches. 10 hot showers, 21 WCs. 14 static caravans

  🏕️ 🚐 ⛺ 🔌 🧳   🐕

From Padstow head for St Merryn on B3276 road. After St Merryn follow road for 2 miles towards Porthcothan Bay, turn N at Tredrea Inn and head to Treyarnon. Site on that road.

Dennis Cove Camping
PL28 8DR. ☏ (0841) 532349
Open: Easter-September
Size: 4½ acres, 60 touring pitches (5 caravans). 7 hot showers, 15 WCs

  🏕️ 🚐 ⛺ 🔌   ☕ ✕ 🏊   🐕

A389 into Padstow, turn right along Sarah's Lane, then second right along Dennis Lane. Site at end.

Higher Harlyn Park
St Merryn. ☏ (0841) 520022
Open: Easter-September
Size: 15 acres, 200 touring pitches. 25 hot showers, 32 WCs. 45 static caravans

  🚐 🚐 ⛺ 🔌 🧳   🏊 📷 🐕

Take B3276 into Padstow. Turn right at St Merryn turn-off and site is ¼ miles.

MOTHER IVEY'S BAY CARAVAN PARK   RAC L
Trevose Head, PL28 8SL. ☏ (0841) 520990
Open: 4 April-25 October
Size: 12 (25) acres, 100 touring pitches, 77 with elec, 85 level pitches, 200 static caravans. 27 hot showers, 30 WCs, 5 CWPs

♿ 🏕️ 🚐 ⛺ 🔌 🧳   🐕

Car & caravan £7-£7.50, Motor caravan £4-£4.50, Car & tent, M/cycle & tent £4-£7.50; elec £1, awn £1.50-£1.75 dogs up to £1
cc Access, Visa/B'card
Gently sloping park, sea views, open aspect, private sandy beach. No clubs. No bars. 28 caravans for hire (own WCs). Restaurant 1 mile. Swimming pool 4 miles. No single-sex groups.
A389 to Padstow, take B3276 to Newquay 3½ miles, right at St Merryn to Trevose Head, 1 mile straight on to Trevose Head, a third of a mile turn right at Trevose Head, ½ mile park entrance.

MUSIC WATER TOURING SITE   RAC A
Rumford, PL27 7SJ. ☏ (0841) 540257
Open: March-October
Size: 7½ acres, 140 touring pitches, mostly level, 19 with elec, 7 static caravans, 1 chalet. 8 hot showers, 20 WCs, 2 CWPs

  🏕️ 🚐 ⛺ 🔌 🧳 ☕   🐕

Charges on application.
Quiet country site with a licensed club and children's play area. 7 caravans for hire. Restaurant 2 miles. Swimming pool 4 miles.
From the junction of the A39 and B3274 (N of St Columb Major), travel NW on the B3274 as signed "Padstow" for 2 miles, turn left to site on right in just over ½ mile.

MARIBOU HOLIDAY PARK   RAC L
St Merryn, PL28 8QA. ☏ (0841) 520520
Open: May-October
Size: 10 (22) acres, 100 touring pitches, all level, 10 with elec, 125 static caravans, 13 chalets. 12 hot showers, 24 WCs, 2 CWPs

---

■ Snacks/take away   ☒ Restaurant   □ Swimming pool   ▣ Shelter for campers   🐕 Dogs accepted   95

⬜🚐🚙🅰🛏🛒🖱⬜ ⬜🛶⬜ 🐕

Car & caravan, Motor caravan, Car & tent, M/cycle & tent £6 (March-May) to £8 (June-October); elec £1.50, awn £1-£1.50, dogs £1
Children's playground. Restaurant ½ mile. 125 caravans and 11 chalets for hire (own WCs). No parties of the same gender.
From Wadebridge travel SW on A39 to first roundabout. Turn right on to B3274. Take second left to St Merryn, over crossroads to site in ½ mile.

Seagull Tourist Park
Treginegar Farm, St Merryn
☎ (0841) 520117
Open: April-October
Size: 4 acres, 75 touring pitches. 4 hot showers, 12 WCs

⬜🚐🚙🅰🛏⬜⬜⬜⬜⬜ 🐕

West of Wadebridge (A39), turn S on B3274 to crossroads. Take St Merryn road. Site signed.

Trerethern Touring Park
Wadebridge Road, PL28 8LE.
☎ (0841) 532061
Open: Easter-October
Size: 13½ acres, 90 touring pitches. 4 hot showers, 10 WCs

♿🚐🚙🅰🛏🛒⬜⬜⬜🖱🐕

Site 1½ miles E of Padstow on A389.

Trethias Farm
St Merryn. ☎ (0841) 520323
Open: April-September
Size: 12 acres, 55 touring pitches. 6 hot showers, 20 WCs. 20 static caravans

⬜🚐🚙🅰🛏⬜⬜⬜⬜⬜ 🐕

From A30 Gosmore crossroads take road to Padstow, by-pass to St Merryn on B3276, through St Merryn crossroads and then third right. Follows signs.

Trevean Farm Caravan & Camping Site
St Merryn, PL28 8PR. ☎ (0841) 520772
Open: April-October
Size: 2 acres, 36 touring pitches. 4 hot showers, 7 WCs. 3 static caravans

⬜🚐🚙🅰🛏🛒⬜⬜⬜⬜ 🐕

S from Padstow on B3276, 1 mile S of St Merryn turn E for Rumford. Site ¼ mile at first farm on right.

Trevemedar Farm
St Eval. ☎ (0841) 520431
Open: April-October
Size: 16 acres, 100 touring pitches. 4 hot showers, 9 WCs

⬜🚐🚙🅰🛏⬜⬜⬜⬜⬜ 🐕

Site on B3276, halfway between Newquay and Padstow.

Treyarnon Bay Caravan Park
Treyarnon Bay, St Merryn, PL28 8JR.
☎ (0841) 520681
Open: Easter-September
Size: 22½ acres, 50 touring pitches. 12 hot showers, 46 WCs. About 100 static caravans

⬜🚐🚙🅰🛏⬜⬜⬜⬜⬜ 🐕

Take A389 W from Wadebridge and follow signposts for St Merryn and Treyarnon.

PAIGNTON *Devon*   Map 1 B3

BEVERLEY PARK HOLIDAY CENTRE   RAC A
Goodrington Road, TQ4 7JE.
☎ (0803) 843887
Open: 17 April-31 October
Size: 8 (21) acres, 210 touring pitches, 70 level pitches, 110 with elec, 212 static caravans. 16 hot showers, 55 WCs, 3 CWPs

♿🚐🚙🅰🛏🛒🖱✖🛶⬜⬜

(1991) Car & caravan, Motor caravan £8-£14, Car & tent £8-£12, plus £2 per person above 4; awn £1.50 cc Access, Visa/B'card
First class Rose Award holiday park with bars and entertainment. 212 caravans for hire (own WCs). No dogs or motorcycles.
Follow A380 Torbay ring road. 2 miles S of Paignton turn left into Goodrington Road.

BYSLADES TOURING PARK   RAC A
Totnes Road, TQ4 7PY. ☎ (0803) 555072
Open: April-October
Size: 8 (23) acres, 150 touring pitches, all level, 50 with elec. 17 hot showers, 24 WCs, 2 CWPs

♿🚐🚙🅰🛏🛒🖱✖⬜🛶🐕

(1991) Car & caravan £7, Motor caravan, Car & tent, M/cycle & tent £6; child 30p-£1; elec £1.50, awn £1, dogs £1.25
Friendly, well-run family park set in 23 acres of rolling Devon countryside. 7 acres of level, terraced pitches. Excellent amenities, award-winning site. Situated on the main A385 Paignton to Totnes road.

GRANGE COURT HOLIDAY CENTRE   RAC A
Grange Road, Goodrington, TQ4 7JP.
☎ (0803) 558010
Open: 1 March-31 October
Size: 10 (60) acres, 157 touring pitches, all with elec, 100 level pitches, 80 with hardstanding, 530 static caravans. 17 hot showers, 38 WCs, 3 CWPs

⬜🚐🚙⬜🛏🛒🖱✖🛶⬜⬜

Car & caravan, Motor caravan £6-£16 (estimated rates)
First-class family holiday park with panoramic views over Torbay. Licensed club with family entertainment, children's playground. 170 caravans for hire (own WCs). No all-male or all-female parties, no groups of unaccompanied teenagers.

From the junction of the A3022 (Paignton Ring Road) and the A385, travel S on the A3022 for 1 mile, turn left (Goodrington Road), after ¾ mile turn left into Grange Road and follow signs to site.

Higher Well Farm Holiday Park
Stoke Gabriel, TQ9 6RN. ☎ (080 428) 289
Open: April-October
Size: 3 acres, 45 touring pitches. 12 hot showers, 18 WCs. 18 static caravans

A380 turn (W) right on to A385. After ½ mile turn S at Parkers Arms. Continue for 1½ miles towards Stoke Gabriel then left to Wadderton and Brixham. Site 200 yards down road.

HOLLY GRUIT CAMP   RAC L
Brixham Road, TQ4 7BA. ☎ (0803) 550763
Open: End May-End September
Size: 3 acres, 70 touring pitches, all with hardstanding. 4 hot showers, 11 WCs

Charges on application.
Well-kept site for tents only. Children's play area and room, licensed bar and clubhouse. Swimming pool 1 mile.
From the junction of A3022 (Paignton Ring Road) and A385 (1 mile W of Paignton), travel S on A3022 for ¾ mile. Observe site signs.

LOWER YALBERTON CARAVAN & CAMPING PARK   RAC L
Long Road, Lower Yalberton, TQ4 7PH.
☎ (0803) 558127
Open: Easter- 30 September
Size: 23 (24) acres, 240 touring pitches, 70 with elec, 140 level pitches, 8 static caravans. 24 hot showers, WCs, 3 CWPs

(1991) Car & caravan £4.60-£8.70, Motor caravan, Car & tent, M/cycle & tent £4.10-£6.65, plus 77p-£1.53 per person above 2; elec £1.53, dogs £1.02 (rates approx)
A gently sloping grassy site in peaceful Devon countryside only 2½ miles from Paignton, 5 miles from Torquay and 3 miles from Brixham.
8 caravans for hire (own WCs).
At 1 mile S of intersection of A385 and A3022 (Paignton Ring Road) turn W off A3022 by ITT factory on to unclassified road for 1 mile.

MARINE PARK HOLIDAY CENTRE   RAC L
Grange Road, TQ4 7JR. ☎ (0803) 843887

Open: 12 May-31 October
Size: 1½ (4½) acres, 30 touring pitches, all with elec, 12 level pitches, 66 static caravans. 10 hot showers, 18 WCs, 1 CWP

(1991) Car & caravan £8-£12, plus £2 per person above 4; awn £1.50
cc Access, Visa/B'card
A small park with views over Torbay. Children's play area. No dogs. 66 caravans for hire (own WCs). Restaurant ½ mile. Swimming pool ½ mile.
Follow A380 Torbay ring road, 2 miles S of Paignton turn left into Goodrington Road then left into Grange Road.

Orchard Park
Totnes Road. ☎ (0803) 550504
Open: March-October
Size: 17 acres, 100 touring pitches. 12 hot showers, 12 WCs. 75 static caravans

Site 1 mile W of Paignton, on N side of A385.

PAIGNTON INTERNATIONAL CAMPING PARK   RAC A
Totnes Road, TQ4 7PY. ☎ (0803) 521684
Open: All year
Size: 14 (20) acres, 230 touring pitches, 191 with elec, all level pitches, 46 with hardstanding. 17 hot showers, 50 WCs, 3 CWPs

(1991) Car & caravan, Motor caravan, Car & tent, M/cycle & tent £5.10-£11.75, plus £1-£2.30 per person (14+) above 2, 75p-£1.55 child; elec £1.55, awn £1.20; WS
cc Visa/B'card
Landscaped park with good hedging for privacy and protection. Licensed bar and club with seasonal entertainment. Children's entertainment. Dogs admitted during low season only (1991 prices 75p-£1). Restaurant 200 yards. Heated swimming pool open from mid May until early September.
2 miles from Paignton on A385 Totnes to Paignton road. Well-signposted.

RAMSLADE TOURING PARK   RAC L
Stoke Road, Stoke Gabriel, TQ9 6QB.
☎ (080 428) 575
Open: Mid March-End October
Size: 8½ acres, 135 touring pitches, 135 with elec. 12 hot showers, 20 WCs, 3 CWPs

■ Snacks/take away ✕ Restaurant ◻ Swimming pool ▣ Shelter for campers ▦ Dogs accepted   **97**

PAIGNTON : SOUTH DEVON
WHITEHILL

HIRE A LUXURY CARAVAN ON OUR ROSE AWARD PARK
PITCHES FOR TOURING CARAVANS, TENTS AND DORMOBILES

This lovely park is beautifully situated amongst the rolling green Devonshire hills, yet within easy reach of the sea and the Dartmoor National Park.

Self-service shop - Children's playground - Colour television - Launderette - Free showers - Games room - Bus stop at the entrance - 2 telephones - Free hot water - Families & couples only - No dogs - Licensed bar - Heated swimming pool - Family room - Cafe - Adventure Playground.

How to find us – Turn off Paignton - Totnes Road (A385) at "Parkers Arms", ½ mile from Paignton Zoo. Signpost to Stoke Gabriel. Camping park 1 mile.

Send for 1992 prices and colour brochure

Whitehill Farm Holiday Parks

STOKE ROAD, PAIGNTON, SOUTH DEVON. TQ4 7PF
Tel: STOKE GABRIEL 338 (STD 080 428)

(1991) Car & caravan, Motor caravan, Car & tent £6-£8, plus £2.30-£2.75 per adult above 2, £1.20 per child; elec £1
A quiet, small site with good facilities for families. Playground, paddling pool, mother and baby room, and recreation field. No motorcycle groups. Restaurant 1 mile. Swimming pool 2½ miles.
At 1½ miles W of Paignton on the A385, turn left in Collaton St Mary by Parkers Arms Inn. Site on right in 1½ miles.

WHITEHILL FARM HOLIDAY PARK   RAC A
Stoke Road, TQ4 7PF. ☎ (080 428) 338
Open: May-September inclusive
Size: 25 (30) acres, 400 touring pitches, 85 with elec, 64 static caravans. 50 hot showers, WCs, 3 CWPs

(1991) Car & caravan £4.50, Motor caravan £3.50, Car & tent, M/cycle & tent £4; all plus £1.50 per adult, £1 per child under 14, 50p under 5s; elec £1-£2, awn £1-£2
Disco, licensed bar, playground, arcade, TV, family room, tarmac roads. Families or mixed couples only. No pets.
At 1½ miles W of Paignton on A385, turn left in Collaton St Mary by Parkers Arms Inn. Site in 1 mile. Well signposted.

WIDEND CAMPING PARK   RAC A
Berry Pomeroy Road, Marldon, TQ3 1RT.
☎ (0803) 550116
Open: 15 March-15 November
Size: 20 acres, 250 touring pitches, all level, 98 with elec. 16 hot showers, 26 WCs, 3 CWPs

Charges on application.

This landscaped holiday park has an outdoor swimming pool, a playground and TV and table tennis rooms. Restaurant 1 mile.
Travelling from the N; from the junction of the A380 and A3022, travel SW on the A3022 for 2½ miles to Marldon. Turn right (Five Lanes) for 1¼ miles to site on right.

PAR Cornwall   Map 1 A3

PAR SANDS HOLIDAY PARK   RAC L
Par Beach, PL24 2AS. ☎ (0726) 812868
Open: 1 April-31 October
Size: 12 (23) acres, 200 touring pitches, all level, 30 with elec, 200 static caravans. 12 hot showers, 30 WCs, 2 CWPs

(1991) Car & caravan, Motor caravan, Car & tent, M/cycle & tent £4-£8; elec £2, awn £1, dogs 50p; WS
cc Access, Visa/B'card
Sheltered position on a level, grassy site immediately behind Par Beach. Ideal for windsurfing, safe bathing for children. Alongside freshwater lake and bird sanctuary. 50 caravans for hire.
Turn right off A3082 Par to Fowey road, ½ mile E of Par. Signposted to park.

PATELEY BRIDGE North Yorkshire   Map 5 A1

Heathfield Caravan Park
Ramsgill Road, HG3 5PY. ☎ (0423) 711652
Open: April-October
Size: 8 acres, 4 touring pitches. 5 hot showers, 21 WCs

Ⓕ Facilities for Disabled   🚕 Caravans accepted   🚕 Motor caravans   🏕 Tents   🏢 Laundry room   🛒 Shop

From Pateley Bridge, turn N off B6265 at garage. After 1 mile turn left to site.

Studfold Farm
Lofthouse, HG3 5SG. ☎ (0423) 75210
Open: Easter-October
Size: 2 acres, 20 touring pitches. 8 hot showers, 15 WCS. 1 static caravan

From Pateley Bridge turn into Lofthouse Road. After Lofthouse, first left fork signposted Stean. Site in 200 yards.

Westfield Farm
☎ (0423) 711410
Open: April-October
Size: 3 acres, 25+ touring pitches. 2 hot showers, 12 WCs. 1 static caravan

NW of Pateley Bridge off B6265 on to Ramsgill-Lofthouse road. Left after Watermill Inn. Site in 1 mile.

PATTERDALE Cumbria　　　　Map 4 B1

Side Farm
CA11 0NP. ☎ (076 84) 82337
Open: All year
Size: 5 acres, 60 touring pitches. 5 WCs

Site in Patterdale, off A592.

PENRITH Cumbria　　　　Map 7 A3

Gill Head Farm
Troutbeck, CA11 0ST. ☎ (076 87) 79652
Open: Easter-October
Size: 2½ acres, 13 touring pitches. 4 hot showers, 8 WCs. 4 static caravans

Take A5091 off A66. After 300 yards turn right. Site is first on right in ¼ mile.

Hutton Moor End
Troutbeck. ☎ (076 87) 79615
Open: Easter-October
Size: 4 acres, 20 touring pitches, 15 pitches for tents. 4 hot showers, 11 WCs. 12 static caravans

M6 (Junction 40) W towards Keswick on A66 for 8 miles, bear left to Wallthwaite, site ½ mile down road.

Knotts Hill Caravan Site
Watermillock, Pooley Bridge
☎ (076 84) 86328
Open: March-October
Size: 47 acres, 15 touring pitches. 4 hot showers, 14 WCs. 4 static caravans, 6 chalets

¼ mile W of A592. At Texaco garage turn up to site, 2½ miles S of Pooley Bridge.

LOWTHER CARAVAN PARK　　　　RAC A
Eamont Bridge, CA10 2JB. ☎ (0768) 63631
Open: 23 March-1 November
Size: 10 (40) acres, 196 touring pitches, 100 with elec, 100 level pitches, 50 with hardstanding, 375 static caravans. 42 hot showers, 90 WCs, 3 CWPs

Car & caravan, Motor caravan £7.50, Car & tent, M/cycle & tent £2.50 per person; elec £1.50; WS
Close to the many attractions of the Lake District, ideal as a base for sightseers, walkers, sailors and fishermen. Swimming pool and tennis courts 2 miles.
From the roundabout (junction of the A6, A66 and A686) S of Penrith, travel on the A6 for just over ½ mile, turn right along the W bank of River Lowther to site.

Thacka Lea Caravan Site
CA11 9HX. ☎ (0768) 63319
Open: March-October
Size: 2 acres, 25 touring pitches. 2 hot showers, 7 WCs

Travelling N, fork left off A6 at Esso station at N end of Penrith.

Thanet Well Caravan Park
Greystoke, CA11 0XX. ☎ (085 34) 262
Open: March-October
Size: 10 acres, 20 touring pitches. 6 hot showers, 10 WCs. 1 static caravan

Take junction 41 off M6 on to B5305 for 6 miles to Wigton. Turn off to Lamonby and follow caravan signs.

Snacks/take away　☒ Restaurant　Swimming pool　Shelter for campers　Dogs accepted　　99

Troutbeck Head Caravan Park
Troutbeck. ☎ (07684) 83521
Open: March-October
Size: 8 (25) acres, 55 touring pitches. 8 hot showers, 16 WCs Static caravans

9 miles W of Penrith (A66), take A5091 for 1½ miles.

Ullswater Caravan, Camping & Marine Park
Watermillock, Pooley Bridge
☎ (07684) 86666
Open: March-October
Size: 14 acres, 40 touring pitches. 18 hot showers, 35 WCs. 8 static caravans, 7 flats

Site 2 miles S of Pooley Bridge, ½ mile from A592. Signposted Watermillock Church, Ullswater Lake. There is a telephone box at the bottom of the road.

Whitbarrow Hall Caravan Park
Berrier, CA11 0XB. ☎ (07684) 83456
Open: March-October
Size: 22 acres, 100 touring pitches. 10 hot showers, 17 WCs.

From M6 junction 40, take A66 towards Keswick for 8 miles. Turn N (right) at Sportsman Inn, on to minor road signed Hutton Roof. Site in ½ mile.

PENRYN *Cornwall* **Map 1 A3**

CALAMANKEY FARM RAC L
Longdowns, TR10 9DL. ☎ (0209) 860314
Open: Easter-31 October
Size: 2½ (3) acres, 60 touring pitches, a few level pitches, 4 static caravans. 3 hot showers, 13 WCs, 1 CWP

Motor caravan, Car & tent, M/cycle & tent £1.60 per adult, child 80p
Farm site on gentle slope. 4 caravans for hire. Shop and restaurant 200 yards. Gas available at shop. Swimming pool 5 miles.
Site is on the N side of the A394, 2½ miles W of Penryn.

PENTEWAN *Cornwall* **Map 1 A3**

MOLINGEY CARAVAN PARK RAC A
Pentewan Road, London Apprentice, PL26 7AP.
☎ (0726) 73533
Open: Easter/31 March-31 October
Size: 10 acres, 20 touring pitches, all level, 10 with elec, 40 static caravans. 6 hot showers, 6 cold showers, 11 WCs, 1 CWP

Car & caravan, Motor caravan, Car & tent, M/cycle & tent £5-£10, plus 60p-£1.20 per adult above 2; extra car £1.25; elec £1.80, dogs £1.25; WS
Small site in sheltered valley with children's playground. Dogs by prior arrangement. Restaurant 400 metres. Shop 100 metres. 40 static caravans for hire own WCs). Minimum stay 3 nights in hired caravans.
Site on E side of B3273 1½ miles S of St Austell.

PENHAVEN TOURING PARK RAC A
PL26 6DL. ☎ (0726) 843687
Open: Easter-31 October
Size: 13 acres, 105 touring pitches, all level, 48 with elec, 4 with hardstanding. 8 hot showers, 12 WCs, 1 CWP

Charges on application. WS
cc Access, Visa/B'card
Quiet, level, grassy site beside river in lovely countryside 1 mile from beach. Play area and recreation field. Take-away food in high season. Restaurant 1 mile.
2½ miles S of St Austell on the B3273, site on left.

PENTEWAN SANDS RAC A
PL26 6BT. ☎ (0726) 843485
Open: 1 April-31 October
Size: 24 (32) acres, 470 touring pitches, 450 level pitches, 175 with elec, 90 static caravans, 39 chalets. 30 hot showers, 71 WCs, 4 CWPs

(1991) Car & caravan, Motor caravan, Car & tent, M/cycle & tent £4.60-£10.25, plus 75p-£2.50 per adult above 2, 40p-£1.25 child (5-15) under 5s free; elec £2
Well-equipped park adjoining own safe, sandy beach. Clubhouse, games room, mini-golf and children's play area. 90 static caravans and 39 chalets for hire (own WCs). No dogs.
At 4 miles S of St Austell on B3273. 1½ miles from Mevagissey.

Sun Valley Holiday Park
Pentewan Road, PL26 6DJ. ☎ (0726) 843266
Open: April-October
Size: 20 acres, 22 touring pitches. 6 hot showers, 8 WCs. 75 static caravans, 10 apartments and 1 lodge house.

Site is 3 miles S of St Austell on the B3273.

PENZANCE *Cornwall* **Map 1 A3**

BONE VALLEY CARAVAN PARK RAC L
Heamoor, TR20 8UJ. ☎ (0736) 60313
Open: 1 March-7 January
Size: 1 acre, 17 touring pitches, all level, 10 with elec, 7 with hardstanding. 2 hot showers, 3 WCs, 1 CWP

Car & caravan, Motor caravan, Car & tent, M/cycle & tent £2; all plus £2 per adult, £1 per child; Car £1, M/cycle £1; elec £1, awn 50p
Small, friendly, clean site. Very sheltered and quiet, within easy walking distance of Penzance. Restaurant 5 minutes' walk. Swimming pool 10 minutes' walk.
From A30 at Heamoor roundabout, turn right for Heamoor. Continue through village to second camping sign on left. Site 200 yards on left.

KENNEGGY COVE HOLIDAY PARK RAC L
Higher Kenneggy, Rosudgeon, TR20 9AU.
☎ (0736) 763453
Open: 1 April-31 October
Size: 3 (3½) acres, 60 touring pitches, 13 with elec, 50 level pitches, 9 static caravans. 4 hot showers,

12 WCs, 1 CWP

[icons]

Car & caravan, Motor caravan, Car & tent, M/cycle*
& tent £3.50-£6.50, plus 50p per person above 2;
elec £1.30, awn 70p, dogs 70p
*Quiet, family site with spectacular sea views, set
back from the cliffs overlooking Kenneggy Cove.
Play area. 9 caravans for hire (own WCs).
Restaurant ½ mile. Swimming pool 3 miles.*
From the junction of the A30 and A394, travel E on
the A394 for just over 4 miles. Turn right as
signposted "Higher Kenneggy" for ½ mile to site
on left.

Mounts Bay Holiday Village
Eastern Green. ☎ (0736) 64160/6
Open: Easter-October
Size: 5 acres, several touring pitches. 15 hot
showers, 20 WCs. 20 holiday cottages

[icons]

Site is 1 mile NE of Penzance, off A30.

Cardinney Caravan & Camping Park
Crows-an-Wra, TR19 6HJ. ☎ (0736) 810880
Open: Easter-October
Size: 5 acres, 105 touring pitches. 6 hot showers,
10 WCs

[icons]

From Penzance take A30 to Land's End. Site on
right 2 miles past sign "The Drift".

PERRANPORTH *Cornwall*　　　　Map 1 A3

Perranporth Camping & Touring Park
Budnick Road. ☎ (0872) 572174
Open: Easter-September
Size: 7 acres, 200 touring pitches. 10 hot showers,
24 WCs. Static caravans

[icons]

Approaching Perranporth from E on B3285, follow
signs from Budnick Hill.

Tollgate
☎ (0872) 572130
Open: April-September
Size: 5½ acres, 140 touring pitches. 6 hot showers,
20 WCs

[icons]

From A30, take B3285. Site 1 mile before
Perranporth.

PETERCHURCH *Hereford & Worcester*　Map 2 A2

POSTON MILL CARAVAN & CAMPING PARK ♛ L
Near Hereford, HR2 0SF. ☎ (0981) 550225
Open: 1 April-31 October
Size: 4 (4½) acres, 64 touring pitches, all level,
18 with elec, 13 static caravans. 8 hot showers,
15 WCs, 1 CWP

[icons]

(1991) Car & caravan £5.20, Motor caravan, Car &
tent, M/cycle & tent £4.70, plus 50p per person
above 2; elec £1.20, awn 50p; WS
*Country site in Hereford's beautiful Golden Valley
near Black Mountains and Wye Valley. 4 caravans
for hire (own WCs). Swimming pool 11 miles. Take
away meals are available during High Season.
Well-stocked shop. Fishing on park in stream
running alongside.*
Midway between Vowchurch and Peterchurch on
the B4348.

PETWORTH *Sussex*　　　　　Map 3 A3

Camping & Caravanning Club Site
Great Bury, Graffham, GU28 0QJ.
☎ (07986) 476
Open: 30 March-26 October
Size: 20 acres, 60 touring pitches. 2 hot showers,
9 WCs

[icons]

Charges on application.
From A285 follow the signs for Graffham, the site
is about 1½ to 2 miles on the left.

PEVENSEY BAY *East Sussex*　　Map 3 A3

Bay View Caravans
Old Martello Road. ☎ (0323) 768688
Open: Easter-October
Size: 3 acres, 70 touring pitches. 6 hot showers,
12 WCs. 4 static caravans

[icons]

Site 1 mile S of Pevensey Bay, just E of A259.
Signed from A259.

Canon Camping
☎ (0323) 762022
Open: March-October
Size: 9 acres, 60 touring pitches. 4 hot showers,
14 WCs

[icons]

Site on A259 ½ mile from Pevensey Bay.

CASTLE VIEW CARAVAN SITE ♛ L
Eastbourne Road, BN24 6DT.
☎ (0323) 763038
Open: 1 March-31 October
Size: 15 acres, 100 touring pitches, 30 with elec,
30 with hardstanding, 32 static caravans. 14 hot
showers, 25 WCs, 1 CWP

[icons]

Charges on application.
cc Access, Visa/B'card
*Not far from the sea, a grassy site with children's
play area. Fishing on site. 32 caravans for hire
(own WCs). Restaurant ½ mile. Swimming pool
1 mile.*

[icon] Snacks/take away [icon] Restaurant [icon] Swimming pool [icon] Shelter for campers [icon] Dogs accepted　　101

Site on N side of A259, almost 1 mile SW of Pevensey Bay and 3½ miles NE of Eastbourne.

Fairfields Farm
Westham. ☎ (0323) 763165
Open: April-October
Size: 3 acres, 60 touring pitches. 6 hot showers, 12 WCs

Site on B2191 off the A27 from Westham.

Martello Beach Caravan Park
☎ (0323) 761424
Open: March-October
Size: 30 acres, 10 touring pitches. 20 hot showers, 30 WCs

Site ½ mile W of Pevensey Bay on A259.

The Rookery
Oak Tree Lane, Friday Street
☎ (0323) 762146
Open: April-September
Size: 2 acres, 50 touring pitches. 6 hot showers, 12 WCs

Site off B2104. Turn into Oak Tree Lane. S of Stone Cross.

Camping & Caravanning Club Site
Norman's Bay, BN24 6PP.
Open: 30 March-26 October
Size: 12 acres, 200 touring pitches. 8 hot showers, 22 WCs

Charges on application.
From the A259 follow the signs for "Beachlands".

PICKERING *North Yorkshire*   Map 5 B1

Black Bull Caravan Park
Malton Road. ☎ (0751) 72528
Open: March-October
Size: 7 acres, touring pitches. 4 hot showers, 6 WCs. Static caravans

Site behind Black Bull Inn, 1¼ miles S of Pickering (A169).

Old Ellers
Ellerburn, Thornton Dale. ☎ (0751) 74381
Open: March-October
Size: ½ acre, 14 touring pitches. 2 hot showers, 5 WCs. 1 static caravan

2¼ miles E of Pickering (A170), take Whitby road at Thornton Dale. Fork right in 400 yards then bear left along gated road.

SPIERS HOUSE CARAVAN & CAMPSITE   RAC L
(Forestry Commission), Cropton, YO18 8ES.
☎ (07515) 591
Open: 27 March-4 October
Size: 10 acres, 150 touring pitches, 6 level, 70 with elec. 13 hot showers, 14 WCs, 1 CWP

(1991)Car & caravan, Motor caravan, Car & tent, M/cycle & tent, all £4.50-£5.50 for 2 persons, extra persons over 5 years 50p-70p; elec £1.20
A south-facing site surrounded by forest, near the south boundary of the North York Moors National Park. Plenty of room for ball games. Restaurant 1½ miles. No motorcycle groups.
From Pickering, travel W on the A170 for 2½ miles to Wrelton. Turn right for 300 yards, then turn left to Cropton and in just over 1 mile turn right to site.

Upper Carr Touring Park
Lane View, Black Bull. ☎ (0751) 73115
Open: March-October
Size: 4 acres, 80 touring pitches. 6 hot showers, 9 WCs. 2 chalets

2 miles S of Pickering (A169), turn E opposite Black Bull Inn. Site 50 yards.

VALE OF PICKERING CARAVAN PARK   RAC A
Carr House Farm, Allerston, YO18 7PQ.
☎ (0723) 85280
Open: Mid March-End October
Size: 8 acres, 120 touring pitches, all level, 100 with elec, 30 with hardstanding, 1 static caravan. 7 hot showers, 12 WCs, 1 CWP

(1990) Car & caravan, Motor caravan, Car & tent, M/cycle & tent £3-£6; elec £1.20, awn £1; WS
One of the better sites in the country, immaculately clean at all times. Well-designed layout, superb show of flower beds. Friendly family-run business. Central for all areas. 1 caravan for hire. Restaurant 1 mile. Swimming pool 5 miles. Minimum stay 3 nights over Bank Holidays only.
Travel E from Pickering on the A170. 1 mile past Wilton turn S onto the B1415. Site in 1 mile.

PLYMOUTH *Devon*   Map 1 B3

Briar Hill Farm
Newton Ferrers, PL8 1AR. ☎ (0752) 872252
Open: Easter-October
Size: 2.1 acres, 25 touring pitches. 2 hot showers, 5 WCs

Enter Newton Ferrers from Plymouth, go to bottom of hill and turn right shortly after old-style telephone box. Site opposite village green.

Brixton Camping Site
Venn Farm, Brixton, PL8 2AX.
☎ (0752) 880378
Open: Easter-October
Size: 3½ acres, 45 touring pitches. 6 hot showers, 8 WCs

Site on A379, ½ mile W of Brixton.

RIVERSIDE CARAVAN PARK   RAC A
Longbridge Road, Marsh Mills
☎ (0752) 344122
Open: All year
Size: 10 (10½) acres, 300 touring pitches, all level, 80 with elec, 22 with hardstanding. 46 hot showers, 50 WCs, 2 CWPs

🦽 Facilities for Disabled 🚐 Caravans accepted 🚙 Motor caravans 🛖 Tents 🧺 Laundry room 🛒 Shop

Smithaleigh Caravan and Camping Park

Nr Plympton, Plymouth, South Devon PL7 5AX Tel: (0752) 893194

A quiet, happy site in beautiful countryside, only 2 minutes off the A38. Open all year. All modern facilities. Convenient for Brittany Ferries and Cornwall. RAC By Appointment

(1991) Car & caravan, Motor caravan, Car & tent, M/cycle & tent £4.50; all plus £1.25 per adult, £1 per child; elec £1.25-£1.40, awn £1, dogs 50p
cc Access, Visa/B'card
Very pleasant level site by the river and surrounded by woodland. Playground, bar, games room on site. River fishing available.
From end of M5 motorway at Exeter, travel S on A38 for 37¾ miles, turn E at roundabout as signed Plympton for 100 yards, turn left into Longbridge Road. Site on left.

SMITHALEIGH CARAVAN & CAMPING PARK RAC L
Near Plympton, PL7 5AX. ☎ (0752) 893194
Open: All year
Size: 2 acres, 120 touring pitches, 80 with elec. 5 hot showers, WCs, CWP

Car & caravan, Motor caravan, Car & tent, M/cycle & tent £4.75-£5.75, plus £1 per adult above 2, child 75p; extra car 50p; elec £1.50, awn 75p, dogs free; WS
Country site with orchard, meadow, duck pond and a stream. New toilet block and new shop/office. Games room, TV/video room, pool table, skittle alley, darts, and new licensed bar. Two swimming pools within 3 miles.

200 yards from Little Chef on A38 at Smithaleigh.

POLPERRO *Cornwall*   Map 1 B3

KILLIGARTH MANOR HOLIDAY ESTATE RAC A
PL13 2JQ. ☎ (0503) 72216
Open: 11 Aoril-3 October
Size: 15 (30) acres, 220 touring pitches, 74 with elec, 180 level pitches, 144 static caravans. 14 hot showers, 14 WCs, 1 CWP

Car & caravan, Motor caravan, Car & tent, M/cycle & tent £2.80; all plus £1.50 per adult, 70p per child; elec £1.75
cc Access, Visa/B'card
A family-run site in beautiful countryside close to picturesque Polperro and Talland Bay. Free luxurious showers. Outdoor swimming pool, children's play areas, children's entertainment. 144 caravans for hire (own WCs). Restaurant 1 mile.
At 3 miles W of Looe on A387, turn S by telephone box, signposted to Killigarth.

POOLE *Dorset*   Map 2 B3

BEACON HILL TOURING PARK RAC A
Blandford Road North, Near Poole, BH16 6AB.
☎ (0202) 631631
Open: 1 March-31 October

◨ Snacks/take away ☒ Restaurant ◹ Swimming pool ◨ Shelter for campers 🐕 Dogs accepted   103

Size: 30 acres, 120 touring pitches, all with elec, all level. 23 hot showers, 25 WCs, 2 CWPs

(1991) Car & caravan, Motor caravan £5.10, Car & tent, M/cycle & tent £4.09-£5.10, all plus £2.55 per adult, £1.02 per child; elec £1.79, awn £1.55, dogs £1.28

Immediate proximity to main routes, 3 miles from Poole and ferry, yet in quiet seclusion of partly wooded heathland with open grassy spaces, level pitches, excellent facilities. Restaurant 1½ miles. Groups of young people at management's discretion and subject to anti-complaints deposit (returnable on departure and currently £30 per head). Maximum stay 21 days.
From the junction of the A35 and A350, travel N on the A350 for 200 yards to site on right.

Huntick Farm
Lytchett Matravers. ☎ (0202) 622222
Open: April-September
Size: 3 acres, 30 touring pitches. 4 hot showers, 6 WCs

Head for Lytchett Matravers. Locate Rose & Crown pub and site is behind that.

Organford Manor
BH16 6ES. ☎ (0202) 622202
Open: March-October
Size: 8 acres, 50 touring pitches. 8 hot showers, 10 WCs. 4 static caravans

From A35/A351 junction, continue on A35 for ¼ mile towards Dorchester, and take first left and then first right.

PEAR TREE FARM
Organford, BH16 6LA. ☎ (0202) 622434   RAC L
Open: 1 April or Easter-15 October
Size: 5 (7) acres, 60 touring pitches, all level, all with elec, plus 45 tent pitches. 10 hot showers, 21 WCs, 1 CWP

(1991) Car & caravan, Motor caravan, Car & tent, M/cycle & tent £5.50, plus £1 per adult above 2, child 50p; elec £1.30, awn £1, dogs free; WS
Quiet country site with good facilities. Excellent centre for Bournemouth, Swanage, Sandbanks, Studland. Swimming pool 3 miles. Families and couples only.
Take A351 to Wareham from Lytchett Minster. Turn right in 1 mile, signposted Organford. Second right on left, 500 yards.

ROCKLEY PARK
Napier Road, Hamworthy, BH15 4LZ.   RAC A
☎ (0202) 679393
Open: 1 March-31 October
Size: 4 (88) acres, 100 touring pitches, 10 with elec, 999 static caravans. 18 hot showers, 22 WCs, 2 CWPs

Charges on application.
cc Access, Visa/B'card
A large, well-organised, holiday-camp-style site, surrounded by sea on three sides. Swimming and

paddle pools, plus children's play area. Evening social activities. Caravans for hire (own WCs). Calor gas only.
At 2 miles W of Poole on A350, turn S into Lake Road by Shell garage, and follow signs.

SOUTH LYTCHETT MANOR CARAVAN PARK   RAC L
Lytchett Minster, BH16 6JB.
☎ (0202) 622577
Open: 1 April-15 October
Size: 9 (10) acres, 150 touring pitches, 60 with elec, 150 level pitches, 1 with hardstanding. 23 hot showers, 23 cold showers, 27 WCs, 1 CWP

(1991) Car & caravan, Motor caravan, Car & tent, M/cycle & tent £2.70-£3.65, plus £1.40-£1.65 per adult, 80p-£1.10 child; elec £1.35, awn to £1.60, dogs to 85p; WS
cc Major cards
Pleasant, mostly level, country site on parkland, with children's play area and ample open spaces. TV lounge. Restaurant ½ miles. Swimming pool 3 miles. Take away foods available during High Season only.
From the junction of the A35 and A350, travel S on the A350 to Upton. Turn right on the B3067 for 1 mile to site on right.

SANDFORD PARK   RAC A
Holton Heath, BH16 6JZ. ☎ (0202) 622513
Open: May-October
Size: 20 (60) acres, 525 touring pitches, all level, 300 with elec, 126 static caravans, 29 chalets. 32 hot showers, 32 cold showers, 68 WCs, 2 CWPs

Charges on application.
cc Access, Visa/B'card
Large, well-organised, family site. Extensive amenities include swimming pool, clubhouse, 3 bars, ballroom, 2 restaurants, TV lounge, family room, children's swimming pool with 'beach', tennis courts, crazy golf, shortmat bowls, barbecues, adults' and children's entertainment, pony trekking. 126 caravans and 29 chalets. ETB graded 5 Ticks Excellent.
2½ miles NE of Wareham on A351, turn into Organford Road at Holton Heath crossroads. Site 50 yards on left.

PORLOCK *Somerset*   Map 1 B2

Burrowhayes Caravan & Camping Site
West Luccombe, TA24 8HU. ☎ (0643) 862463
Open: March-October
Size: 8½ acres, 54 touring pitches. 8 hot showers, 17 WCs. 19 static caravans

5 miles W of Minehead on A39 turn S signposted West Luccombe. Site ¼ mile on right.

PORLOCK CARAVAN PARK   RAC L
Near Minehead, TA24 8NS. ☎ (0643) 862269
Open: 16 March-31 October
Size: 3 (5) acres, 40 touring pitches, all level, 16 with elec, 55 static caravans, 1 chalet. 6 hot showers, 20 WCs, 2 CWPs

Car & caravan £5.50, Motor caravan, Car & tent,

M/cycle* & tent £5; extra person 50p, child 50p; elec £1.50, awn 50p
A grassy, level and sheltered site with children's play area. Convenient for the sea. 14 caravans and 1 chalet for hire (own WCs). Restaurant 150 yards. Swimming pool 6 miles. No single-sex groups. Minehead to Porlock: take B3225 turning to the right, signposted Porlock Weir. After 50 yards turn right signposted Porlock Caravan Park.

Sparkhayes Farm
☎ (0643) 862470
Open: Easter-September
Size: 3 (6) acres, 60 touring pitches. 4 hot showers, 9 WCs

		🍴	🅰							🐕

Site in centre of Porlock, signed.

PORTHTOWAN *Cornwall*　　Map 1 A3

Porthtowan Tourist Park
Mile Hill, TR4 8TY. ☎ (0209) 890256
Open: Easter-October
Size: 5 acres, 31 touring pitches. 4 hot showers, 5 WCs

From A30 take Redruth/Porthtowan turn-off. In Porthowan direction pass through North Country to t-junction. Turn right and site is on left after Woodlands Restaurant.

ROSEHILL TOURING PARK　　RAC A
TR4 8AR. ☎ (0209) 890802
Open: April-October
Size: 2½ acres, 40 touring pitches, all level, 20 with elec, 2 static caravans, 1 chalet. 4 hot showers, 7 WCs, 2 CWPs

Charges on application.
3 small fields in wooded valley near the beach. 2 caravans and 1 chalet for hire. Play area on site. Restaurant 400 yards. Swimming pool 5 miles. From the junction of the A30 and A3300 N of Redruth, travel N on unclassified road to Porthtowan. Site on right 100 yards before village.

Globe Vale Caravan & Touring Park
Radnor, Near Redruth
☎ (0209) 890083/891183
Open: February-November
Size: 12 acres, 28 touring pitches. 6 hot showers, 5 WCs. 53 static caravans

Off A30 take Redruth/Porthtowan turn-off, follow the signposts for Porthtowan, take third exit on left to crossroads, then turn right, then signposted.

PORTSMOUTH *Hampshire*　　Map 2 B3

HARBOUR SIDE CARAVAN & CAMPING SITE　RAC L
Eastern Road. ☎ (0705) 663867
Open: 21 March-25 October
Size: 2½ (4½) acres, 50 touring pitches, all level, 38 with elec, 75 static caravans. 12 hot showers, 24 WCs, 2 CWPs

(1991) Car & caravan, Motor caravan, Car & tent,

M/cycle & tent £6.65-£8.50, plus 60p per person above 2 (over 5 years); elec £1, awn £1, dogs free; WS
cc Access, Visa/B'card
This site is pleasantly situated alongside Langstone Harbour and has an 18-hole golf course, driving range, hotel and bars within ¼ mile. It is approximately 2½ miles from Southsea seafront and entertainment areas. Restaurant ¼ mile. Supermarket ½ mile. Swimming pool 2 miles. 15 caravans for hire. At the junction of A3 and A27 (4½ miles N of Portsmouth), turn E on A27 for 1½ miles and turn S on to A2030 for 1½ miles.

Southview Farm
Duck Pond Lane, Blendworth, PO8 0AP.
☎ (0705) 595805
Open: All year
Size: 1 acre, 10 touring pitches. 1 WC

S on A3 towards Horndean, turn left signposted Blendworth. Take first lane on right, follow down to t-junction, turn left (church on right). Site down on left.

POTTER HEIGHAM *Norfolk*　　Map 3 B1

Broadlands Caravan Park
Ludham, NR29 5NY. ☎ (0692) 630357
Open: Easter-October
Size: 9 acres, 126 touring pitches. 13 hot showers, 2 baths, 27 WCs. 2 static caravans

6 miles NE of Norwich on A1151, turn E on to A1062. Site 6 miles, by Ludham Bridge.

Causeway Cottage Caravan Park
Bridge Road, NR29 5JB. ☎ (0692) 670238
Open: March-October
Size: 0.3 acre, 5 touring pitches. 2 hot showers, 4 WCs. 9 static caravans

Site off A149 in Potter Heigham. At old bridge turn into Bridge Road.

White House Farm
High Road, Repps. ☎ (0692) 670403
Open: March-October
Size: 1 acre, 30 touring pitches. 2 hot showers, 5 WCs

Site 2½ miles E of Ludham on A149.

POYNTON *Cheshire*　　Map 5 A2

ELM BEDS CARAVAN PARK　　RAC L
Elm Beds Road, Higher Poynton, SK12 1TG.
☎ (0625) 872370
Open: 1 April-31 October
Size: 2 (8) acres, 20 touring pitches, 15 with elec, 15 level pitches, 8 with hardstanding, 55 static caravans. 4 hot showers, 9 WCs, 1 CWP

(1991) Car & caravan £4.50, Motor caravan £4.25, Car & tent £2.50-£4.50, plus £1 per person above 4; elec 85p, awn 50p

---

■ Snacks/take away　☒ Restaurant　⬭ Swimming pool　▣ Shelter for campers　🐕 Dogs accepted　　**105**

A quiet and peaceful park situated adjacent to the Macclesfield Canal, in a good walking area on the edge of the Peak District. Restaurant 2 miles. Shop ¼ mile. Swimming pool 1½ miles. No motorcycles. Families only.
At 5 miles SE of Stockport by A6, then A523, turn E at traffic lights in Poynton. At 1 mile on, keep right for 1 mile, then cross railway bridge.

PRAA SANDS *Cornwall* Map 1 A3

PRAA SANDS HOLIDAY VILLAGE RAC L
Pengersick, TR20 9SH. ☎ (0736) 762201
Open: All year
Size: 9 (14) acres, 200 touring pitches, 12 with elec, 86 static caravans. 7 hot showers, 39 WCs, 1 CWP

Charges on application.
Grassy site a few minutes from a long, sandy beach. Swimming and fishing from the beach. Children's play area on site. 80 caravans for hire (70 with own WCs). Shop adjoining site. Restaurant ¼ mile. Swimming pool 4 miles.
5½ miles W of Helston on A394, turn S as signposted "Pengersick & Praa Sands". Site on right in ½ mile.

PREESALL *Lancashire* Map 4 B2

Maaruig
71 Pilling Lane. ☎ (0253) 810404
Open: March-October
Size: 1 acre, 25 touring pitches. 4 hot showers, 7 WCs

From B5270 towards Knott End, turn right at Cross, ½ mile from Knott End.

ROSEGROVE CARAVAN PARK
77 Pilling Lane. ☎ (0253) 810866
Open: March-October
Size: 3 acres, 50 touring pitches. 4 hot showers, 7 WCs

From the N, travel S on the A588 through Cockerham and Stake Pool turning right on the B5270 through Preesall, and turn right into Pilling Lane to site on left.

Willowgrove Caravan Park
Sandy Lane, FY6 0EJ. ☎ (0253) 811306
Open: March-October
Size: 20 acres, 60 touring pitches. 12 hot showers, 12 WCs

M55 (junction 3) on to A585, turn right at third set of traffic lights on to A588, follow signs to Knott End for 5 miles, turn right at t-junction after Preesall into Sandy Lane.

RAVENGLASS *Cumbria* Map 4 B1

Walls Caravan & Camping Park
CA18 1SR. ☎ (0229) 717250
Open: February-November
Size: 5 acres, 50 touring pitches. 4 hot showers, 8 WCs

Off A595 into Ravenglass, down hill and turn left and signed.

REDRUTH *Cornwall* Map 1 A3

Caddys Corner Farm
Carnmenellis, TR16 6PH. ☎ (0209) 860275
Open: Easter-October
Size: 2½ acres, 5 touring pitches. 2 hot showers, 1 bath, 3 WCs. 5 static caravans

Redruth-Helston (B3297) 1 mile out turn left to Stithians, ignore next sign to Stithians and take turn to Carnmenellis. In Carnmenellis turn right to Porkellis and site ½ mile on left.

Cambrose Touring Park
Portreath Road. ☎ (0209) 890747
Open: April-October
Size: 3 acres, 50 touring pitches. 5 hot showers, 12 WCs. 2 static caravans

On B3300 W, towards Portreath, past golf course and take first right signposted Porthtowan. Site on left.

Lanyon Caravan Park
Loscombe Lane, Four Lanes, TR16 6LP.
☎ (0209) 216447
Open: April/Easter-October
Size: 1½ acres, 28 touring pitches. 8 hot showers, 17 WCs. 49 static caravans

On B3297 enter Four Lanes village, after petrol station take third turning right. Site in 100 yards.

Rose Cottage Caravan & Camping Site
Wheal Rose, Scorrier. ☎ (0872) 42338
Open: February-November
Size: 6 acres, 50 touring pitches. 10 hot showers, 12 WCs. 4 static caravans

A30 dual carriageway from Bodmin, after Chiverton roundabout take Scorrier turn into village.

Tehidy Holiday Park
Harris Mill, Illogen. ☎ (0209) 216489
Open: April-October
Size: 5 acres, 18 touring pitches. 2 hot showers, 3 WCs. 20 static caravans

A30 towards Redruth, leave dual carriageway at Redruth, Porthtowan exit, turn right at double roundabout, left at crossroads towards B3300, continue through 2 crossroads. Site 200 yards, past Cornish Arms on left.

TRESADDERN CARAVAN PARK RAC L
St Day, TR16 5JR. ☎ (0209) 820459
Open: Easter-October
Size: 2 (3) acres, 25 touring pitches, all level, 16 with elec, 10 static caravans, 4 chalets. 4 hot showers, 7 WCs, 1 CWP

Charges on application.
Quiet rural site with some trees. 10 caravans and 4 chalets for hire (own WCs). Restaurant 600 yards. Swimming pool 4 miles.
2 miles E of Redruth on A3047, turn S on B3298 for 1½ miles to site on right.

REJERRAH *Cornwall*　　Map 1 A3

MONKEY TREE FARM TOURIST PARK　RĀC A
TR8 5QL. ☎ (0872) 572032
Open: Easter-October
Size: 12 (18) acres, 245 touring pitches, all level, 84 with elec, 3 with hardstanding. 18 hot showers, 34 WCs, 1 CWP

(1991) Car & caravan, Motor caravan, Car & tent, M/cycle & tent £5, including 2 adults, plus £1 per child; elec £1.75, awn free, dogs free
Rural holiday site with sauna and solarium, games room, dog exercise area, all on a level site with children's play area.
Take A3075 from Newquay to Perranporth, after 4 miles turn left signed Zelah, site in 800 yards.

NEWPERRAN TOURIST PARK　RĀC A
TR8 5QJ. ☎ (0872) 572407
Open: Mid May-Mid September
Size: 15 acres, 270 touring pitches, 200 level pitches, 100 with elec, 6 with hardstanding. 18 hot showers, 50 WCs, 3 CWPs

(1991) Car & caravan, Motor caravan, Car & tent, M/cycle* & tent £2.25-£3.70 per adult, £1.10-£1.85 per child; cars 50p-75p; elec £1.60, dogs 85p
cc Access, Visa/B'card
Attractive, large site with flower beds and shrubs. Crazy golf, adventure playground, TV and games room.
5 miles SW of Newquay on A3075, turn right as signed "Newperran".

Perran Quay Tourist Park
Hendra Croft. ☎ (0872) 572561
Open: April-October
Size: 7 acres, 135 touring pitches. 18 hot showers, 22 WCs

Site 3 miles S of Newquay on A3075.

RELUBBUS *Cornwall*　　Map 1 A3

RIVER VALLEY CARAVAN PARK　RĀC A
TR20 9ER. ☎ (0736) 763398
Open: 1 March-1 November
Size: 18 acres, 90 touring pitches, all level, 60 with elec, 20 with hardstanding. 12 hot showers, 30 WCs, 1 CWP

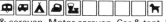

Car & caravan, Motor caravan, Car & tent, M/cycle

& tent £2, all plus £1.80 per adult, 50p per child; elec 80p, awn 60p, dogs 70p (all prices exclusive of VAT); WS
cc Access/Mastercard, Visa
In sheltered valley, 3 miles from south coast, 5 miles from north coast, with small stream. Surrounded by farmland, very quiet, no entertainments. All roads tarmaced, easy access. Free fishing. Tourist Board graded "Excellent" 5 Ticks. Restaurant 2½ miles. Swimming pool 4 miles. No parties of young persons, or single-sex groups.
From Hayle B3302 to Leedstown, turn right on to B3280 to Townsend and straight on to Relubbus. From Marazion B3280 through Goldsithney and straight on to Relubbus.

RICHMOND *North Yorkshire*　　Map 5 A1

BROMPTON-ON-SWALE CARAVAN PARK　RĀC A
Brompton, DL10 7EZ.
☎ (0748) 824629
Open: April (or Easter if in March)-31 October
Size: 10 acres, 150 touring pitches, all level, 92 with elec, 20 static caravans. 14 hot showers, 14 cold showers, 28 WCs, 2 CWPs

Car & caravan £4.80, Motor caravan £4.50, Car & tent, M/cycle & tent £3.95-£4.80, plus £1.15 per adult above 2, child 60p; elec £1.25, awn £1.30, dogs free
Situated on the banks of the River Swale in the heart of the Yorkshire Dales. River fishing. Scenic walks. Children's play area and TV room. 4 caravans for hire (own WCs). Restaurant 1½ miles. Swimming pool 2 miles. Dogs must be kept on leads. No unaccompanied youths without prior arrangement.
Exit A1 at Catterick A6136. Follow B6271 through Brompton-on-Swale. The park is on the left, 1½ miles out of Brompton-on-Swale on the road to Richmond.

SWALEVIEW CARAVAN PARK　RĀC L
Reeth Road, DL10 4SF. ☎ (0748) 823106
Open: 1 March-31 October
Size: 5 (12) acres, 50 touring pitches, all level, 25 with elec, 100 static caravans. 10 hot showers, 10 cold showers, 22 WCs, 1 CWP

Car & caravan, Motor caravan, Car & tent, M/cycle & tent from £1.40, Tent from 40p, all plus £1.80 per adult, child 20p-50p; extra car 30p; elec £1, awn 60p
Swaleview Caravan Park is situated in a beautiful valley in the Yorkshire Dales National Park beside the River Swale. 5 caravans for hire (own WCs). Restaurant and swimming pool 3 miles.
3 miles W of Richmond on A6108.

▣ Snacks/take away ☒ Restaurant ◠ Swimming pool ▣ Shelter for campers ⚏ Dogs accepted　　107

RINGWOOD Hampshire — Map 2 B3

Oakhill Farm Campsite
St Leonards.
☎ (0202) 876968
Open: Easter/April-October
Size: 10 acres, 100 touring pitches. 10 hot showers, 10 WCs

½ mile from A31, near St Leonards Hospital. Just off roundabout.

Red Shoot Camping Site
Linwood, BH24 3QT.
☎ (0425) 473789
Open: March-October
Size: 4 acres, 30 touring pitches. 6 hot showers, 19 WCs

Site off A338, 2 miles N of Ringwood, turn right and follow signs to Linwood. Site signed.

St Leonards Farm
Ringwood Road, West Moors
☎ (0202) 872637
Open: April-October
Size: 12 acres, 190 touring pitches. 12 hot showers, 33 WCs

Site 4 miles SW of Ringwood on A31.

Woolsbridge Manor Farm Caravan Park
Three Legged Cross, BH21 6RA.
☎ (0202) 826369
Open: Easter-October
Size: 7 acres, 60 touring pitches. 6 hot showers, 11 WCs

A31 W 1 mile past Ringwood, come to roundabout, turn right towards Three Legged Cross. Site 2 miles on left.

RIPLEY North Yorkshire — Map 5 A1

Chequers Inn
Bishop Thornton.
☎ (0423) 771544
Open: April-October
Size: 9 acres, 20+ touring pitches. 4 hot showers, 12 WCs. 14 chalets

Follow A61 N to Ripon and then take B6165 NW for ½ mile, take right signed Fountains Abbey and site 300 yards past crossroads.

Warren House Caravan Site
Warsill.
☎ (0765) 620683
Open: April-October
Size: 10 acres, 45 touring pitches. 6 hot showers, 12 WCs

From A61, take B6165. After ¼ mile turn right to Fountains Abbey. Straight over crossroads and keep left at following two junctions. Site opposite sign to for Warsill.

RIPON North Yorkshire — Map 5 A1

Newholme Caravan Site
Grewelthorpe. ☎ (0765) 658225
Open: April-October
Size: 3 acres, 5 touring pitches. 2 hot showers, 6 WCs

From Ripon, take minor road for Grewelthorpe. After 5 miles, just below village, turn left at site sign.

SLENINGFORD WATERMILL CARAVAN & CAMPING PARK — RAC A
North Stainley, HG4 3HQ. ☎ (0765) 635201
Open: 1 April or Easter if earlier-31 October
Size: 4 (14) acres, 25 touring pitches, all level, all with elec, all with hardstanding, 25 static caravans, 1 chalet. 10 hot showers, 18 WCs, 6 CWPs

Car & caravan, Motor caravan, Car & tent, M/cycle & tent £6-£8, plus £1 per adult above 2, child 50p; elec £2; WS
Beautiful, quiet, riverside park in the heart of the Dales, ideal for walking, bird- and wild flower-spotting, white water canoeing and fly fishing. One chalet for hire (own WC). Restaurant 1 mile. Swimming pool 5 miles.
Proceed N from Ripon on the A6108 for 5½ miles to site entrance on right.

URE BANK CARAVAN PARK — RAC L
☎ (0765) 2964
Open: 1 March-31 October
Size: 26 acres, 175 touring pitches, 60 with elec, 50 with hardstanding, 200 static caravans. 12 hot showers, 24 WCs, 2 CWPs

Charges on application. WS
This riverside site offers a children's play area, licensed bar, boating and fishing on the Ure. 4 caravans for hire (own WCs). Swimming pool 2 miles.
Leave Ripon N on A61. Cross River Ure and turn W and ahead bear right to site.

Winksley Banks Holiday Park
The Curlews, Winksley Banks, Galphay, HG4 3NS.
☎ (0765) 658439
Open: March-October
Size: 4 acres, 8 touring pitches. 2 hot showers, 5 WCs. 3 static caravans

1½ miles W of Ripon, turn N off B6265. In Galphay turn left, then follow signs.

WOODHOUSE FARM CARAVAN & CAMPING PARK — RAC A
Winksley, HG4 3PG. ☎ (0765) 658309
Open: 1 April-31 October
Size: 15 acres, 50 touring pitches, all level, all with elec, 35 with hardstanding, 10 static caravans, 1 chalet. 8 hot showers, 17 WCs, 2 CWPs

Car & caravan, Motor caravan £5.50, Car & tent, M/cycle & tent from £3; plus 50p per person above 2, child 50p; elec £1.35, awn £1; WS

  ⓖ Facilities for Disabled ⬛ Caravans accepted ⬛ Motor caravans Ⓐ Tents Ⓐ Laundry room ⬛ Shop

Attractive, secluded, well-equipped, family-run site, ideally situated for exploring the Yorkshire Dales. 2-acre lake adjacent to site for coarse fishing. 10 caravans for hire (9 with own WC). Restaurant 1¼ miles. Swimming pool 6 miles. No loose dogs. No unaccompanied children. Minimum 3 nights stay over Bank Holidays. Please send SAE for brochure.
Leave Ripon on the B6265 (Pateley Bridge) road. After 3½ miles turn right at the Winksley/Grantley signpost. Follow caravan site signs to site.

ROCHDALE Lancashire   Map 5 A2

Hollingworth Lake Caravan Park
Rakewood, Littleborough, OL15 0AT.
☎ (0706) 78661
Open: All year
Size: 5 acres, 50 touring pitches. 6 hot showers, 11 WCs

Off A58, follow signs to Hollingworth Country Park. Go past Fishermans Inn and turn right to Rakewood. Site signed.

ROCHESTER Kent   Map 3 A2

Woolmans Wood Tourist Caravan Park
Bridgewood. ☎ (0634) 867685
Open: All year
Size: 3 acres, 50 touring pitches. 6 hot showers, 12 WCs

From M2 junction 3, follow A229 to Rochester Airfield. Site behind.

ROTHBURY Northumberland   Map 7 B2

COQUETDALE CARAVAN PARK   RAC A
Whitton, Near Morpeth, NE65 7RU.
☎ (0669) 20549
Open: Easter-31 October
Size: 1½ (13) acres, 50 touring pitches, all level, 30 with elec, 200 static caravans. 10 hot showers, 30 WCs, 2 CWPs

(1991) Car & caravan, Motor caravan, Car & tent, M/cycle & tent from £6; elec £1.50
A beautiful country caravan park, ideal for walking and touring the Border Country. Shop and restaurant ½ mile. Swimming pool 1 mile. Strictly families and couples only.
½ SW of Rothbury on road to Newton.

ROTHERHAM South Yorkshire   Map 5 A2

Thrybergh Country Park
Doncaster Road, Thrybergh, S65 4NU.
☎ (0709) 850353
Open: April-October
Size: 6 acres, 37 touring pitches. 7 hot showers,

10 WCs

Site 3 miles NE of Rotherham on A630.

ROWLAND'S GILL Tyne & Wear   Map 7 B3

Derwent Park
☎ (0207) 543383
Open: April-September
Size: 4 acres, 45 touring pitches. 9 hot showers, 14 WCs

From A1, follow A694 signposted Consett. Site at junction of A694 and B6314 in Rowland's Gill.

ROYDON Essex   Map 3 A2

ROYDON MILL CARAVAN PARK   RAC L
Near Harlow, CM19 5EJ. ☎ (027979) 2777
Open: All year
Size: 9 (58) acres, 110 touring pitches, all level, 72 with elec, 8 with hardstanding, 106 static caravans. 8 hot showers, 14 WCs, 2 CWPs

(1991) Car & caravan, Motor caravan, Car & tent, M/cycle* & tent £4.60; extra person £1.80, child £1.30; elec £1.50, awn £1
cc Access, Visa
Roydon Mill Leisure Park is set in 58 acres of beautiful Essex countryside. Catering for families only, it is an ideal place in which to relax and unwind. However, if you want a more active holiday, there are numerous recreational pursuits for all tastes and ages. 3 caravans for hire (own WCs). No dogs. English Tourist Board graded 4 Ticks: Very Good.
Easily located from the north via the A1 or M1/M25/M11. Approaching from the south, take junction 7 off M11, follow signs to Harlow, then A414 and B181 to Roydon. Roydon Mill is located at end of High Street, just before level crossing at Roydon Station.

ROYSTON Hertfordshire   Map 3 A2

Appleacre Park
London Road, Fowlmere, SG8 7RU.
☎ (0763) 208229
Open: All year
Size: 2 acres, 15 touring pitches. 2 hot showers, 4 WCs. 3 static caravans

Turn left off A10 (Cambridge-Royston) on to B1368 signposted Fowlmere. Site on left through village, 4½ miles.

RUAN MINOR Cornwall   Map 1 A3

Chy Carne Camping
Kennack Sands. ☎ (0326) 290541

Seasonal variation of prices

Where a single price is given it may be a low season minimum charge - rates can increase considerably at peak periods and for extra people or vehicles.
Please confirm prices with the site when booking.

Open: Easter-October
Size: 6 acres, 14+ touring pitches (100 in peak season). 6 hot showers, 10 WCs. 18 static caravans, 12 chalets

Follow A3083 from Helston to Lizard for 2 miles until signpost to St Keverne. Turn left on B3293, past Goonhilly satellite station. Turn right signed Cadgwith and Kennack Sands. T-junction at Kuggar, turn left towards Kennack Sands. Site 50 yards on left.

SEA ACRES HOLIDAY PARK RAC A
Kennack Sands. ☎ (0326) 290064
Open: March-October
Size: 20 acres, 50 touring pitches, 20 with elec, 100 static caravans. 13 hot showers, 3 cold showers, 12 WCs, 1 CWP

(1991) Car & caravan, Motor caravan, Car & tent, M/cycle & tent £6;£9; elec £1.20, awn £1, dogs £1
cc Access, Visa/B'card
Owner-run, cliff-top site above lovely beach. Licensed club and TV room. 100 caravans for hire (own WCs).
At 1½ miles S of Helston on A3085, turn left on to B3293 for 4¾ miles. Turn right and 2¼ miles on at Kuggar turn left to site.

SILVER SANDS HOLIDAY PARK RAC L
Gwendreath, Kennack Sands, TR12 7LZ.
☎ (0326) 290631
Open: April-September
Size: 2½ (6) acres, 11 touring pitches, all with elec, 19 static caravans. 4 hot showers, 8 WCs, 1 CWP

(1991) Car & caravan, Motor caravan £3, Car & tent, M/cycle* & tent £2.40; all plus £1.30 per adult, £1 per child; elec £1.20, awn 50p, dogs £1.10
Quiet, sheltered, family park, individually marked touring and camping pitches set amongst flowers and shrubs, with a short woodland walk to safe, clean, sandy beach. 19 caravans for hire (own WCs). Shop 100 yards. Restaurant 1 mile. Swimming pool 10 miles. Families and couples only.
At 1½ miles S of Helston on A3083, turn left on to B3293. At 4¾ miles on turn right for 1 mile and observe site signs to left.

RUDSTON *North Humberside* Map 5 B1

Thorpe Hall Caravan & Camping Site
Thorpe Hall, YO25 OJE. ☎ (026 282) 393
Open: March-October
Size: 4½ acres, 90 touring pitches. 6 hot showers, 19 WCs

Site ½ mile E of Rudston on B1253.

RUGELEY *Staffordshire* Map 5 A3

Camping & Caravanning Club Site
Old Youth Hostel, Wandon, WS15 1QW.
☎ (088 94) 2166
Open: April-October
Size: 5 acres, 80 touring pitches. CWP

Charges on application.
cc Access, Visa/B'card
Situated in the heart of Cannock Chase. Minimum facilities - campers must have their own chemical toilet.

🕭 Facilities for Disabled ▣ Caravans accepted ▨ Motor caravans 🅰 Tents 🄰 Laundry room 🅛 Shop

Take the A460 SW for Rugeley, after 1¼ miles turn left on to unclassified road to Wandon, where turn SW to site on right in 200 yards.

SILVERTREES CARAVAN PARK   RAC A
Stafford Brook Road, WS15 2TX.
☎ (0889) 582185
Open: 1 April-31 October
Size: 10 (30) acres, 56 touring pitches, all with hardstanding, 43 with elec, 11 level pitches, 44 static caravans. 8 hot showers, 8 cold showers, 16 WCs, 2 CWPs

Car & caravan, Motor caravan £6, plus £1 per person above 4; elec £1, awn £1
Set in the heart of Cannock Chase, a quiet woodland site with video and games room, tennis court. 10 static caravans for hire (own WCs). Restaurant 2 miles. No motorcycles. No tents. 3 days minimum stay over Bank Holidays.
From A51 N through Rugeley. Turn left at traffic lights on to B5013 towards Penkridge. After 2 miles, turn right at bottom of hill by white fencing to site on left in 100 yards.

RYE *East Sussex*   Map 3 B3

Camber Sands Leisure Park
Lydd Road, Camber, TN31 7RX.
☎ (0797) 225282
Open: Easter- September
Size: 10 acres, 160 touring pitches. 16 hot showers, 12 WCs. 171 static caravans

1 mile NE of Rye (A259), turn right to Camber. Site in centre of village in 2 miles.

The Cock Inn
Peasmarsh. ☎ (079 721) 281
Open: March-October
Size: 2 acres, 8 touring pitches. 2 hot showers, 6 WCs

Site on A268 towards Rye.

Rye Bay Caravan Park
Pett Level Road, Winchelsea Beach
☎ (0797) 226340
Open: March-October
Size: 70 touring pitches. 8 hot showers, 14 WCs. 260+ static caravans

2 miles S of Rye (A259), turn E for Winchelsea Beach. Site 1½ miles on left.

SALCOMBE *Devon*   Map 1 B3

ALSTON FARM CARAVAN SITE   RAC L
TQ7 3BJ. ☎ (0548) 561260
Open: Easter-31 October
Size: 10½ (12) acres, 70 touring pitches, all level, 60 with elec, 41 static caravans. 14 hot showers, 33 WCs, 1 CWP

(1991) Car & caravan £5, Motor caravan, Car & tent, M/cycle* & tent £4; plus £1 per person above 2; elec 70p, awn 50p; WS

A quiet, rural farm site, with 4 caravans for hire. Children's play area. Restaurant, swimming pool and tennis courts 2 miles. No noise after 10.30pm.
At 1½ miles NW of Salcombe on A381, turn N and follow signs to site.

Higher Rew Farm
Malborough. ☎ (054 884) 2681
Open: Easter/April-October
Size: 5½ acres, 80 touring pitches. 8 hot showers, 10 WCs

From Malborough fork right on to road to Soar. After 1 mile, turn left to Combe. Site signed.

Karrageen Caravan & Camping Park
Bolberry, Malborough, TQ7 3EN.
☎ (0548) 561230
Open: Easter-October
Size: 7½ acres, 60 touring pitches. 4 hot showers, 9 WCs

3½ miles SW of Kingsbridge (A381), fork right through Malborough, after 0.9 mile turn right and site is on right.

SUN PARK CARAVAN & CAMPING PARK   RAC L
Soar, Malborough, TQ7 3DS. ☎ (0548) 561378
Open: Easter-1 October
Size: 3 (5½) acres, 75 touring pitches, all level, 31 static caravans. 8 hot showers, 14 WCs, 1 CWP

(1991) Motor caravan, Car & tent, M/cycle & tent £4; all plus £1.70 per person, 85p per child; awn 50p
Situated ¾ mile above Sandy Cove, 3 miles from the seaside town of Salcombe. It has a pay phone and a children's play area. 27 caravans for hire (own WCs). Shop and restaurant 1½ miles. Swimming pool 3 miles.
At 2¾ miles W of Salcombe on A381, turn W at Malborough and follow roads signed Soar.

SALISBURY *Wiltshire*   Map 2 B3

COOMBE NURSERIES TOURING CARAVAN PARK   RAC A
Race Plain, Netherhampton, SP2 8PN.
☎ (0722) 328451
Open: All year
Size: 3 acres, 50 touring pitches, all level, 48 with elec. 6 hot showers, 12 WCs, 2 CWPs

(1991) Car & caravan, Motor caravan, Car & tent, M/cycle & tent £1, all plus £2 per adult, 75p per child (3-12 years); car £1; elec £1.25, dogs 20p
Family-run site, children's bathroom, children's play area. Views over Chalke Valley. Restaurant 1½ miles. Swimming pool 5 miles.
Take A36 Salisbury to Wilton road, turn at traffic lights on to A3094, on bend take Stratford Tony road, second left at top of hill, site on right, behind Racecourse grandstand.

STONEHENGE TOURING PARK   RAC A
Orcheston, SP3 4SH. ☎ (0980) 620304
Open: All year
Size: 1½ (2) acres, 30 touring pitches, all level,

---

12 with elec, 12 with hardstanding. 4 hot showers, 5 WCs, 1 CWP

🐕	🚐	🚐	🔺		🛒	☕					🐕

(1991) Car & caravan, Motor caravan, Car & tent, M/cycle & tent £2.80; all plus £1.30 per adult, 50p per child; elec £1.40
A pretty, quiet site with a warm welcome. Children's play area. Restaurant 100 yards. Swimming pool 5 miles.
Take the A360 NW from Shrewton for just over ¾ mile, then turn right along an unclassified road to Orcheston. Site on right.

Camping & Caravanning Club Site
Hudson's Field, Castle Road, SP1 3RR.
Open: 30 March-28 September
Size: 4½ acres, 100 touring pitches. 4 hot showers, 12 WCs

	🚐	🚐	🔺		🛒						🐕

Charges on application.
From the A354 turn into Hudson's Field for the site.

SALTASH *Cornwall*　　　　Map 1 B3

DOLBEARE CARAVAN PARK　　RAC A
St Ive Road, Landrake, PL12 5AF.
☎ (0752) 851332
Open: All year
Size: 4½ acres, 60 touring pitches, 30 with elec, 40 level pitches, 15 with hardstanding. 4 hot showers, 4 cold showers, 6 WCs, 1 CWP

	🚐	🚐	🔺	🔋	🛒		✕			🐕

Car & caravan, Motor caravan, Car & tent, M/cycle* & tent £5-£6, plus £1 per adult above 2, child 50p; elec £1.50, awn £1.50; WS
4½ acres in pretty countryside, part sloping, part level. Good facilities in excellent order. Caravan storage and sales. Restaurant 1 mile. Swimming pool 4 miles.
From Saltash, travel W on the A38 to Landrake, turn N signed 'Pond Hill' for ¾ mile.

NOTTER BRIDGE CARAVAN & CAMPING PARK　　RAC A
Notter Bridge, PL12 4RW. ☎ (0752) 842318
Open: 1 April-30 November
Size: 4 (4½) acres, 50 touring pitches, all level, 12 with elec, 12 static caravans. 4 hot showers, 12 WCs, 2 CWPs

	🚐	🚐	🔺	🔋	🛒			🛶		🐕

(1991) Car & caravan, Moro caravan, Car & tent, M/cycle & tent £4.75-£6; plus 50p per person (over 5s); extra car £1; elec £1, awn 50p, dogs free
Small, quiet, family-run site, sheltered by trees, with a river running through it. Good for fishing. 12 static caravans for hire (own WCs). Restaurant opposite site.
At 3 miles W of Saltash (Tamar Bridge) on A38, opposite Notter Bridge Inn.

SALTBURN-BY-SEA *Cleveland*　　Map 5 A1

HAZELGROVE CARAVAN SITE　　RAC L
Milton Street. ☎ (0287) 22014
Open: 1 April-31 October
Size: 20 acres, 16 touring pitches, 16 with hardstanding. 20 hot showers, 47 WCs

🐕	🚐	🚐			🛒					🐕

Charges on application.
On a grassy cliff-top, this large and established site has panoramic coastal views. Footpath to beach; play area on site. No gas available. Shop and restaurant ½ mile.
From the S on A174, turn right into Milton Street.
From the N on A174, turn left by church into Hilda Place then first left after passing under railway bridge.

SANDBACH *Cheshire*　　　　Map 4 B2

Warmingham Craft Workshops
The Mill, Warmingham, CW11 9QW.
☎ (027077) 366
Open: All year
Size: 0.3 acres, 5 touring pitches. 1 hot shower, 2 WCs

	🚐	🚐	🔺			☕	✕			🐕

From Middlewich, take A533 for Sandbach.
200 yards past Kings Lock Inn, turn right then left.
Warmingham signposted.

SANDRINGHAM *Norfolk*　　　Map 3 A1

Camping & Caravanning Club Site
The Sandringham Estate, Double Lodges, PE35 6EA.
Open: 30 March-26 October
Size: 90 touring pitches. 6 hot showers, 9 WCs

🐕	🚐	🚐	🔺	🔋	🛒					🐕

Charges on application.
From the A42 turn right on to the A149. 1 mile after Babingley turn right, right again at the next crossroads, the site is on the left.

SANDWICH *Kent*　　　　　Map 3 B3

SANDWICH LEISURE PARK　　RAC A
Woodnesborough Road, CT13 0AA.
☎ (0304) 612681
Open: March-October
Size: 5 (10½) acres, 71 touring pitches, all level, all with elec, 103 static caravans. 8 hot showers, 16 WCs, 2 CWPs

	🚐	🚐	🔺	🔋	🛒					🐕

Car & caravan, Motor caravan, Car & tent, M/cycle & tent from £5.75; elec £1; WS
Situated ½ mile outside the mediaeval Cinque Port town itself, a quiet, secluded park, graded 4 Ticks, with children's play ground, phone, launderette and shop. 10 caravans for hire (own WCs). Restaurant ½ mile. Swimming pool 6 miles.
From Deal on the A258 follow the 'camping/caravan' signs on the approach to Sandwich.

SAXMUNDHAM *Suffolk*　　　Map 3 B1

Carlton Park Camping Site
78 Saxon Road, IP17 1EE. ☎ (0728) 603685
Open: April-October
Size: 3 acres, 50 touring pitches. 5 hot showers, 12 WCs

	🚐	🚐	🔺							🐕

Site on B1121, signed from A12. ½ mile N of

Saxmundham.

SCARBOROUGH *North Yorkshire* Map 5 B1

AROSA CAMPING & CARAVAN PARK RAC L
Ratten Row, Seamer, YO12 4QB.
☎ (0723) 862166
Open: 1 March-31 October
Size: 3 (5) acres, 50 touring pitches, all level, all with elec, 3 static caravans. 4 hot showers, 8 WCs, 1 CWP

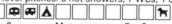

Charges on application.
Small grassland site, suitable for families. TV and games room; children's play area. 3 caravans for hire. Swimming pool 4 miles.
Approaching Scarborough on the A64 from York, take first turn left immediately on entering Seamer village. Site in 300 yards from the main road.

JACOBS MOUNT CARAVAN PARK RAC A
Stepney Road, YO12 5NL. ☎ (0723) 361178
Open: March-October
Size: 3 (7) acres, 44 touring pitches, all with elec, 12 level pitches, 44 static caravans. 4 hot showers, 4 cold showers, 14 WCs, 1 CWP

(1991) Car & caravan, Motor caravan, Car & tent from £4.50, plus £1.50 per adult above 2, child £1 (under 5s free); extra car £1.50; elec £1, awn £1.50, dogs 80p
A small, family-run park surrounded by mature woodland, yet only 2 miles from Scarborough. Facilities include licensed bar with new family room. Shop. Toilet block with launderette and showers. Pot wash area. Children's play park.

10 caravans for hire (own WCs). Swimming pool 2 miles.
The site is signposted 2 miles SW of Scarborough on the A170.

MERRY LEES CARAVAN PARK RAC L
Staxton, YO12 4NN. ☎ (0944) 70080
Open: 1 March-30 October
Size: 7½ acres, 60 touring pitches, all with elec, 60 level pitches. 6 hot showers, 7 WCs, 1 CWP

Car & caravan, Motor caravan, Car & tent, M/cycle* & tent £4-£8.50; elec £1.50, awn £1.40; WS
Central to coastal and National parks with its own wealth of wildlife (60 different species of birds). Shop 1½ miles. Restaurant ¾ mile. Swimming pool 6 miles.
On E side on A64 ½ N of the junction of the A64 and A1039.

SCALBY CLOSE CAMP RAC A
Burniston Road, YO13 0DA.
☎ (0723) 365908
Open: March-October
Size: 3 acres, 42 touring pitches, all level, 15 with elec, 5 with hardstanding, 5 static caravans. 4 hot showers, 4 cold showers, 9 WCs, 1 CWP

Car & caravan, Motor caravan, Car & tent, M/cycle & tent £3.75-£6.75; elec £1.20, awn £1.25
cc Major cards
Sheltered by mature trees, all pitches on level ground, ideal for touring North Yorks Moors, yet only 2 miles from Scarborough. 3 caravans for hire (own WCs). Restaurant ¼ mile. Swimming pool 1½ miles.
On the A165 2½ miles N of Scarborough.

SCALBY MANOR CARAVAN & CAMPING SITE · RAC A

Burniston Road. ☎ (0723) 366212
Open: 1 week before Easter-Last w/e in October
Size: 20 acres, 375 touring pitches, 100 with elec,
20 with hardstanding, 230 level pitches. 22 hot
showers, 40 WCs 1 CWP

⬜⬜⬜⬜⬜⬜⬜⬜⬜⬜⬜🐕

(1991) Car & caravan, Motor caravan, Car & tent,
M/cycle & tent £3.90-£7.15; awn £1-£1.50
cc Access, Visa/B'card
*Grassland site within short walking distance of
beach and popular family entertainments. Bus
service runs between site and town centre.
Children's playground and late arrival park.
Restaurant next to site. Swimming pool 1 mile.
Fish and chip shop on site.*
At 2¼ miles N of Scarborough on A165, turn W and
then take first left.

SPRING WILLOWS CARAVAN PARK · RAC A

Main Road, Staxton, YO12 4SB.
☎ (0723) 891505
Open: March-31 October
Size: 7 (8½) acres, 145 touring pitches, all level,
80 with elec, 6 with hardstanding. 13 hot showers,
29 WCs, 2 CWPs

⬜⬜⬜⬜⬜⬜⬜⬜⬜⬜⬜🐕

(1991) Car & caravan, Motor caravan, Car & tent,
M/cycle* & tent from £5.10, plus 50p per person
above 2; extra car 50p; elec £1.35, awn £1.35, dogs
£1; WS
*Pleasant, embanked site with separate play area,
dogs' walk, bar and lounge, sauna, solarium; well-
sheltered from coastal winds. Restaurant ½ mile
(bar meals on site). Minimum stay during Spring
Bank Holiday and August Bank Holiday.*
A64 towards Scarborough. Turn right at Staxton on
to A1039 to Filey. Site entrance on right.

St Helens in the Park

Wykeham, YO13 9QD. ☎ (0723) 862771
Open: All year
Size: 32 acres, 250 touring pitches. 22 hot showers,
55 WCs

⬜⬜⬜⬜⬜⬜⬜⬜⬜⬜🐕

On A170, 5 miles out of Scarborough, 10 miles E of
Pickering.

Lowfield

Down Dale Road, Staintondale
☎ (0723) 870574
Open: All year
Size: 2 acres, 5 touring pitches plus 20 for tents.
2 hot showers, 4 WCs. 1 bungalow

⬜⬜⬜⬜⬜⬜⬜⬜⬜🐕

A171 Whitby road to Cloughton then Ravenscar
road for 2 miles to site.

SCOTCH CORNER *North Yorkshire* — Map 5 A1

SCOTCH CORNER CARAVAN PARK · RAC A

☎ (0748) 822530
Open: Easter-mid October
Size: 7 acres, 96 touring pitches, all level, 23 with
elec. 6 hot showers, 14 WCs, 1 CWP

⬜⬜⬜⬜⬜⬜⬜⬜⬜🐕

(1991) Car & caravan £4.30, Motor caravan £2.80,
Car & tent £3.80, M/cycle & tent £3.30; all plus
£1 per adult, 60p per child; elec £1.20, awn £1,
dogs 50p
*Level, landscaped site, with extensive views, next
to hotel. Convenient overnight stop. Children's
play area on site. Family groups only. Swimming
pool 3 miles.*
Just S of Scotch Corner roundabout on the A6108.

SEA PALLING *Norfolk* — Map 3 B1

Golden Beach Holiday Centre

NR12 0AL. ☎ (069 261) 269
Open: March-November
Size: 7 acres, 50 touring pitches. 9 hot showers,
14 WCs. 26 static caravans

⬜⬜⬜⬜⬜⬜⬜⬜⬜🐕

At Stalham follow signs to Sea Palling. Turn N on
to Beach Road. Site in 300 yards.

SEAFORD *East Sussex* — Map 3 A3

Buckle Caravan & Camping Park

Marine Parade. ☎ (0323) 897801
Open: March-January
Size: 9 acres, 150 touring pitches. 12 hot showers,
19 WCs

⬜⬜⬜⬜⬜⬜⬜⬜⬜🐕

Site midway between Newhaven and Seaford on
A259. Signed.

SEATON *Devon* — Map 2 A3

Ashdown Touring Caravan Park

EX13 6HY. ☎ (0297) 21587
Open: April-October
Size: 9 acres, 90 touring pitches. 8 hot showers,
10 WCs

⬜⬜⬜⬜⬜⬜⬜⬜⬜🐕

3 miles W of Seaton at Stafford Cross (A3052), site
on turn for Colyton. Site ½ mile.

Manor Farm Camping & Caravan Site

☎ (0297) 21524
Open: April-October
Size: 20 acres, 104 touring pitches. 15 hot showers,
30 WCs. 6 static caravans

⬜⬜⬜⬜⬜⬜⬜⬜⬜🐕

Site 1 mile N of Seaton on A3052.

SEDBERGH *Cumbria* — Map 4 B1

Conder Farm

Dent. ☎ (058 75) 277
Open: All year
Size: 1 acre, 48 touring pitches. Hot showers,
3 WCs

⬜⬜⬜⬜⬜⬜⬜⬜⬜🐕

Site in Dent.

Cross Hall Caravan Site

Cautley, LA10 5LY. ☎ (053 96) 20668
Open: April-October
Size: 2 acres, 5+ touring pitches. Hot showers,
3 WCs. Static caravans

Site on A683, 2 miles N of A684 junction.

Harbergill Farm
Cowgill, Dent. ☎ (058 75) 392
Open: May-October
Size: 4 acres, 5 touring pitches, plus 20 pitches for tents. 2 WCs

Site 4 miles S off A684 at Garsdale Head.

High Laning Farm
Dent. ☎ (058 75) 239
Open: All year
Size: 1¼ acres, 15 touring pitches, plus 20 tent pitches. 4 hot showers, 7 WCs. 4 static caravans, 1 cottage

M6 Junction 37, A684 to Dent. Site in Dent.

Pinfold Caravan Park
LA10 5JL. ☎ (053 96) 20576
Open: March-October
Size: 7 acres, 38 touring pitches, plus 20 tent pitches. 4 hot showers, 9 WCs

Site ½ mile E of Sedbergh on A684.

SENNEN Cornwall   Map 1 A3

Lower Treave Caravan Park
Crows-an-wra. ☎ (0736) 810559
Open: April-October
Size: 4½ acres, 80 touring pitches. 4 hot showers, 12 WCs. 5 static caravans

Site is 6 miles from Penzance on A30 to Land's End.

Sea View Caravan Park
TR19 7AD. ☎ (0736) 871266
Open: Easter-September
Size: 10 acres, 100+ touring pitches. 14 hot showers, 14 WCs. 70 static caravans

Site on A30 just N of Land's End.

**TREVEDRA FARM CARAVAN &
CAMPING SITE**   RAC L
TR19 7BE. ☎ (0736) 871379
Open: 1 April-31 October
Size: 4 (6) acres, 30 touring pitches, all level. 8 hot showers, 17 WCs, 2 CWPs

Charges on application.
Farm meadow site close to beach. Restaurant ¼ mile. Swimming pool 3½ miles.
At 1½ miles NE of Sennen village on A30 just before junction with B3306.

SETTLE North Yorkshire   Map 4 B1

Knight Stainforth Hall
Stainforth. ☎ (0729) 822200
Open: March-October
Size: 7 acres, 100 touring pitches. 8 hot showers,

14 WCs. 60 static caravans

Go through Settle, cross River Ribble and take first right. After 2 miles go into Steakhouse Lane. Site on right.

Langsliffe Caravan Park
☎ (0729) 822387
Open: March-October
Size: 8 acres, 46 touring pitches. 4 hot showers, 16 WCs. 55 static caravans

¼ mile N of Settle on the B6479.

SEVENOAKS Kent   Map 3 A3

To The Woods Caravan Park
Botsom Lane, West Kingsdown, TN15 6BN.
☎ (0322) 863751
Open: All year
Size: 2½ acres, 70 touring pitches. 2 hot showers, 8 WCs

4 miles NW of Wrotham (A20), turn W into Botsom Lane.

SEVERN BEACH Avon   Map 2 A2

Salthouse Farm Caravan & Camping Park
BS12 3NH. ☎ (045 45) 2274
Open: April-October
Size: 8 acres, 40 touring pitches. 6 hot showers, 7 WCs

From M4 exit 21, take A403 S to Pilning. At traffic lights turn right on to B4064. In ½ mile turn left. Site in ½ mile on right.

SHEPTON MALLET Somerset   Map 2 A3

Greenacres Camping
Barrow Lane, North Wootton, BA4 4HL.
☎ (074 989) 497
Open: May-September
Size: 4½ acres, 30 touring pitches. 4 hot showers, 7 WCs

3 miles SW of Shepton Mallet (A361), site ½ mile out of North Wootton. Signed.

MANLEAZE CARAVAN PARK   RAC L
Cannards Grave, BA4 4LY. ☎ (0749) 342404
Open: All year
Size: 1 acre, 20 touring pitches, all level, 6 with elec, 3 static caravans. 2 hot showers, 2 cold showers, 4 WCs, 1 CWP

Car & caravan, Motor caravan, Car & tent, M/cycle & tent £3; elec £1, awn 80p
Flat, grassland site, open all year but facilities are reduced in winter. 3 caravans for hire (1 has own WC). Calor gas only. Restaurant 200 yards. Swimming pool 1 mile.
At ¾ mile S of town centre on A371 (¼ mile N of its junction with A37).

◗ Snacks/take away ✗ Restaurant ◺ Swimming pool ▦ Shelter for campers 🐕 Dogs accepted   115

Old Down Caravan & Camping Park
Emborough, BA3 4SA. ☎ (0761) 232355
Open: April-October
Size: 3½ (5¼) acres, 25 touring pitches, plus 10 tent pitches 4 hot showers, 5 WCs

5½ miles N of Shepton Mallet (A37), turn E on to B3139. Take turn to Midsummer Norton and site is opposite Old Down Inn.

SHERINGHAM *Norfolk* — Map 3 B1

KELLING HEATH CARAVAN PARK — RAC L
Weybourne, NR25 7HW. ☎ (026 370) 224
Open: 19 March-31 October
Size: 20 (250) acres, 300 touring pitches, all level, 100 with elec, 385 static caravans. 22 hot showers, 62 WCs, 8 CWPs

Charges on application.
In 250 acres of woodland and heather, this attractive site has plenty of space. Clubhouse with entertainments. Nature trail and adventure playground. 25 caravans for hire (own WCs). At 3 miles W of Sheringham on A149, turn S opposite Weybourne church, then turn left for 1 mile to top of ridge.

WOODLANDS CARAVAN PARK — RAC L
Holt Road, NR26 8TU. ☎ (0263) 823802
Open: 20 March-31 October
Size: 13 (21) acres, 286 touring pitches, all level, 166 with elec, 133 static caravans. 28 hot showers, 82 WCs, 4 CWPs

Car & caravan, Motor caravan £6-£6.50; elec £1-£1.20, awn £1.10-£1.50
A quiet, secluded park surrounded by woodland and fields in a very pleasant area. No motorcycles. No tents. 28 days maximum stay, no minimum. Entrance to site on N side of A148. 4 miles E of Holt.

SHOEBURYNESS *Essex* — Map 3 B2

EAST BEACH CARAVAN PARK — RAC L
SS3 9SG. ☎ (0702) 292466
Open: March-31 October
Size: 4 (9) acres, 45 touring pitches, all level, 10 with elec, 82 static caravans, 2 chalets. 17 hot showers, 17 cold showers, 24 WCs, 2 CWPs

Charges on application.
A well-organised, level site, 100 yards from beach. Family groups only. Restaurant ½ mile. Swimming pool 1 mile.
From Shoebury High Street, proceed via George Street to seafront, turn left through car park to site. Site signed.

The Bridge Inn
Dorrington, SY5 7ED. ☎ (0743) 73209
Open: All year
Size: 2½ acres, 6+ touring pitches. 1 WC

A49 towards Ludlow. Site 8 miles from Shrewsbury.

Cartref Caravan & Camping Site
Ford Heath, SY5 8QD. ☎ (0743) 821688
Open: May-October
Size: 1½ acres, 25 touring pitches. 4 hot showers, 5 WCs. 1 static caravan

Site 5 miles W of Shrewsbury on A458. Signed.

Severn House
Montford Bridge, SY4 1ED.
☎ (0743) 850229
Open: April-October
Size: ¼ acre, 5 touring pitches. Hot showers, 1 WC

5 miles NW of Shrewsbury (A5), turn E immediately after river bridge. Site 50 yards.

SIDMOUTH *Devon* — Map 2 A3

Hillside House
Newton Poppleford. ☎ (0395) 68210
Open: March-October
Size: 1 acre, 10 touring pitches. 2 hot showers, 4 WCs

Site 1 mile W of Newton Poppleford on A3052.

Kings Down Tall Farm
Salcombe Regis, EX10 0PD.
☎ (029 780) 313
Open: March-November
Size: 5 acres, 100 touring pitches. 10 hot showers, 14 WCs. 2 static caravans

Site 3 miles E of Sidford on A3052 opposite Branscombe water tower.

OAKDOWN TOURING PARK — RAC A
Weston, EX10 0PH. ☎ (029 780) 387
Open: April-October
Size: 9 acres, 120 touring pitches, all level, 80 with elec. 8 hot showers, 12 WCs, 1 CWP

(1991) Car & caravan, Motor caravan, Car & tent, M/cycle* & tent from £5.31, including 2 people; child £1.02; elec £1.63, awn £1.43, dogs 61p; WS
Level, closely mown, well-sheltered park with easy access. Centrally heated facilities with family bathrooms, dishwashing sinks and use of deep freeze. Fully serviced super pitches and field trail to world-famous Donkey Sanctuary. Restaurant

2 miles. Swimming pool 2½ miles. Dogs must be kept on a lead at all times on the park.
2½ miles E of Sidford on the A3052. Clearly signposted "Oakdown" with international signs.

SALCOMBE REGIS CAMPING & CARAVAN PARK
RAC L
Salcombe Regis, EX10 0JH.
☎ (0395) 514303
Open: Easter-October
Size: 16 acres, 100 touring pitches, all level, 44 with elec, 10 static caravans. 7 hot showers, 7 cold showers, 14 WCs, 2 CWPs

[icons]

(1991) Car & caravan, Motor caravan, Car & tent, M/cycle & tent from £4.75, plus £1.25 per adult above 2, child 90p; elec £1.45, awn £1
A low density rural park in an Area of Outstanding Natural Beauty, within walking distance of the sea. 10 caravans for hire (own WCs). Restaurant 1½ miles. Swimming pool 10 miles.
From Honiton travel S on the A375 to Sidmouth, where turn E onto A3052 for 1½ miles. At the top of Trow Hill, turn sharp right for ½ mile.

SILLOTH *Cumbria* Map 7 A3

HYLTON PARK HOLIDAY CENTRE
RAC L
Eden Street, CA5 4AY. ☎ (069 73) 31707
Open: 15 March-31 October
Size: 4 (20) acres, 45 touring pitches, all level, 213 static caravans. 4 hot showers, 4 cold showers, 8 WCs, 2 CWPs

[icons]

(1991) Car & caravan, Motor caravan, Car & tent, M/cycle & tent £4; all plus 90p per person; dogs £1.20
Meadowland site close to town, sharing entertainment and amenities with Stanwix Park. Calor gas only. Shop, restaurant and swimming pool ½ mile.
¼ mile S of Silloth on B5300.

Seacote Caravan Park
Skinburness Road. ☎ (06973) 31121
Open: March-November
Size: 4½ acres, 20 touring pitches. 8 hot showers, 17 WCs, 80 static caravans

[icons]

From Silloth, take coast road to Skinburness for ¾ mile and site is on right.

Solway Village Holiday Park
The Lido Centre. ☎ (06973) 31236
Open: March-October
Size: 110 acres, 125 touring pitches. 9 hot showers, 20 WCs. 54 static caravans, 69 chalets

[icons]

Accessible from B5302 in Silloth. Site well-signposted from Silloth.

STANWIX PARK HOLIDAY CENTRE
RAC A
Greenrow, CA5 4HH. ☎ (06973) 31671
Open: 1 March-31 October
Size: 6 (20) acres, 121 touring pitches, all level, 90 with elec, 186 static caravans, 28 chalets. 15 hot showers, 15 cold showers, 20 WCs, 2 CWPs

[icons]

Car & caravan, Motor caravan, Car & tent, M/cycle && tent from £4.40; all plus £1 per person; elec £1.65, awn 60p, dogs £1.20; WS
cc Access, Visa/B'card
A large, well-run holiday site, with ballroom, disco, bar, play park and riding school. Boating, tennis and golf available nearby. 80 caravans and 28 chalets for hire (own WCs).
1 mile S of Silloth on B5300.

Tanglewood Caravan Park
Causeway Heath, CA5 4PE. ☎ (06973) 31253
Open: March-October
Size: 7 acres, 31 touring pitches. 4 hot showers, 12 WCs. 6 static caravans

[icons]

Site 4 miles W of Abbeytown on B5302 on left hand side.

SILSDEN *West Yorkshire* Map 5 A2

Dales Bank Caravan Park
Low Lane, BD20 9JH. ☎ (0535) 653321
Open: April-October
Size: 5 acres, 52 touring pitches. 4 hot showers, 11 WCs

[icons]

In Silsden on A6034, turn left at police station, then right up Bradley Road. Continue up hill for 1 mile and turn right. Site third entrance on right.

SKEGNESS *Lincolnshire* Map 5 B2

Beacon Way Caravan Park
Beacon Way. ☎ (0754) 67950

Snacks/take away X Restaurant Swimming pool Shelter for campers Dogs accepted **117**

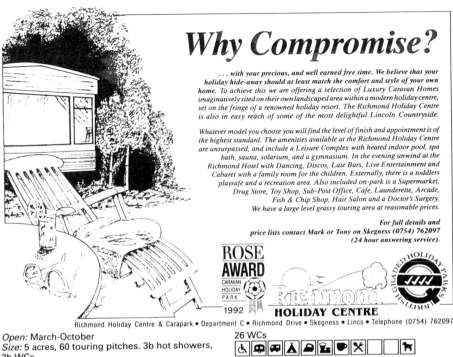

Why Compromise?

... with your precious, and well earned free time. We believe that your holiday hide-away should at least match the comfort and style of your own home. To achieve this we are offering a selection of Luxury Caravan Homes imaginatively sited on their own landscaped area within a modern holiday centre, set on the fringe of a renowned holiday resort. The Richmond Holiday Centre is also in easy reach of some of the most delightful Lincoln Countryside.

Whatever model you choose you will find the level of finish and appointment is of the highest standard. The amenities available at the Richmond Holiday Centre are unsurpassed, and include a Leisure Complex with heated indoor pool, spa bath, sauna, solarium, and a gymnasium. In the evening unwind at the Richmond Hotel with Dancing, Discos, Late Bars, Live Entertainment and Cabaret with a family room for the children. Externally, there is a toddlers playsafe and a recreation area. Also included on-park is a Supermarket, Drug Store, Toy Shop, Sub-Post Office, Cafe, Launderette, Arcade, Fish & Chip Shop, Hair Salon and a Doctor's Surgery. We have a large level grassy touring area at reasonable prices.

For full details and price lists contact Mark or Tony on Skegness (0754) 762097 (24 hour answering service).

ROSE AWARD CARAVAN HOLIDAY PARK 1992

Richmond HOLIDAY CENTRE

Richmond Holiday Centre & Carapark • Department C • Richmond Drive • Skegness • Lincs • Telephone (0754) 762097

Open: March-October
Size: 5 acres, 60 touring pitches. 3b hot showers, 3b WCs

1 mile W of Skegness on A158, left into Oldburgh Road and left again into Beacon Way.

Croft Bank Caravan Site
☎ (0754) 3887
Open: Easter-September
Size: 4 acres, 10 touring pitches. 2 hot showers, 19 WCs

Site 1¾ miles SW of Skegness on A52.

DAINVILLE CARAVAN PARK RAC L
Church Lane, PE25 1EW. ☎ (0754) 3679
Open: March-October
Size: ½ (4½) acres, 10 touring pitches, all level, 90 static caravans, 2 chalets. 6 hot showers, 6 cold showers, 10 WCs, 1 CWP

Car & caravan, Motor caravan £3; awn 50p
Quiet, small, family-run park on level ground, with children's play area and games room, near the sea. 4 caravans and 2 chalets for hire (own WCs). Calor gas only. Shop 100 yards. Restaurant and swimming pool 1 mile.
1 mile N of Skegness on A52, turn left for 300 yards.

Greenacres
Bolton's Lane, Ingoldmells, PE25 1JJ.
☎ (0754) 72263
Open: March-October
Size: 8 acres, 200 touring pitches. 8 hot showers,

26 WCs

At southern end of Ingoldmells on A52.

Pine Trees Park
Croft Bank. ☎ (0754) 810866
Open: March-October
Size: 3½ acres, 80 touring pitches. 4 hot showers, 10 WCs. 8 static caravans

Site 1 mile W of Skegness on A52.

Retreat Farm
Croft Bank. ☎ (0754) 2092
Open: March-November
Size: 2 acres, 12 touring pitches. 2 hot showers, 3 WCs

Site 1 mile S of Skegness on A52.

RICHMOND HOLIDAY CENTRE RAC A
Richmond Drive, PE25 3TQ.
☎ (0754) 762097
Open: 1 March-30 November
Size: 12 (50) acres, 210 touring pitches, all level, 100 with elec, 620 static caravans. 28 hot showers, 98 WCs, 3 CWPs

Car & caravan, Motor caravan £6-£8; elec £1.20, awn £1, dogs £5 refundable deposit; WS
cc Access/Mastercard, Visa
Live entertainment for adults and children, heated indoor pool, sauna, sunbeds, whirlpool spa and gymnasium. Nice flat site, no steps or hills, close to town centre with regular bus service. 100 caravans

for hire. No single-sex groups.
Just S of Skegness town centre at end of Richmond Drive, well-signposted.

Riverside Caravan Park
Wainfleet Bank, Wainfleet ☎ (0754) 880205
Open: March-October
Size: 1¼ acres, 30 touring pitches. 2 hot showers, 6 WCs

1½ miles W of A52. Take B1195 to Wainfleet and All Saints. Site signed.

Southview Leisure Park
Burgh Road. ☎ (0754) 4893
Open: Easter-September
Size: 5 acres, 100 touring pitches. 4 hot showers, 10 WCs. 12 static caravans

Site ½ mile W of Skegness on A158.

Valetta Farm
Mill Lane, Addlethorpe. ☎ (0754) 3758
Open: March-October
Size: 2½ acres, 35 touring pitches. 2 hot showers, 4 WCs

In Burgh-le-Marsh on A158, turn N for Ingoldmells. Follow Ingoldmells signpost to Addlethorpe Mill. Turn right for site.

Beach Bank Caravan Park
South Field Lane, Ulrome, YO25 8TU.
☎ (026 286) 491
Open: March-October
Size: 2½ acres, 60 touring pitches. 4 hot showers, 13 WCs. Static caravans

From A165 at Beeford, turn E on B1249 to Skipsea. Turn N to Cross Street and continue into Mill Lane. Site 1½ miles.

Far Grange Park
☎ (026 286) 248
Open: March-November
Size: 60 acres, 200 touring pitches. 20 hot showers, 75 WCs. 16 static caravans

Site 1½ miles S of Skipsea on B1242.

Overdale Trailer Park
Harrogate Road. ☎ (0756) 793480
Open: Closed January
Size: 1 acre, 20 touring pitches. 4 hot showers, 4 WCs

Site is 1 mile NE of Skipton on A59.

Tarn Caravan Park
Stirton, BD23 3LQ. ☎ (0756) 795309
Open: March-October
Size: 5 (15) acres, 32 touring pitches. 8 hot showers, 22 WCs

Site on B6265 signed from Grassington road roundabout, 1¾ miles NW of Skipton.

Old Hall Farm
Sudbrook, Near Ancaster, NG32 3RY.
☎ (0400) 30262
Open: All year
Size: 2½ acres, 10 touring pitches (including 5 for tents). 1 WC

From A1 at Colsterworth, take B6403 through Ancaster for 1 mile. At crossroads turn left for Sudbrook, and then right in 1 mile.

TUDOR ARMS CARAVAN & CAMPING PARK ʀᴀ̃ᴄ A
Shepherds Patch, GL2 7BP. ☎ (0453) 890483
Open: All year
Size: 7½ acres, 75 touring pitches, all level, 30 with elec, 6 with hardstanding. 4 hot showers, 12 WCs, 1 CWP

Charges on application.
Behind a pub in farming country, this orchard site is bordered by the Gloucester-Sharpness canal, with the Wild Fowl Trust on the far bank. Fishing in canal. Family groups only.
From junction of A4135 and A38, 11 miles SW of Gloucester, take road through Slimbridge towards Wild Fowl Trust for 1½ miles. Site on left immediately before canal bridge.

Camping & Caravanning Club Site
Railway Street, YO6 7AA. ☎ (065 382) 335
Open: 30 March-26 October
Size: 3½ acres, 70 touring pitches. 4 hot showers, 9 WCs

Charges on application.
cc Access, Visa/B'card
Level site with simple facilities. Shop 1 mile.
From the A170 take the B1257 towards Slingsby, at the crossroads in Slingsby turn right and the site is on the right.

Amerden Caravan Park
Old Marsh Lane, Taplow. ☎ (0628) 27461
Open: April-October
Size: 3 acres, 20 touring pitches. 3 hot showers, 6 WCs. 2 static caravans

A4 E from Maidenhead, turn right at Taplow Station towards Dorney Reach. Right again after 1 mile. Signed. Right before motorway.

Jasmine Caravan Park
Low Road, YO13 9BE. ☎ (0723) 859240

⬛ Snacks/take away ☒ Restaurant ◺ Swimming pool 🏠 Shelter for campers 🐦 Dogs accepted   119

EDESWELL FARM CARAVAN PARK
RATTERY, SOUTH BRENT, DEVON. Tel: 0364 72177
Picturesque country park convenient for Torbay, Dartmoor, Plymouth and Exeter. 22 static caravans, colour TVs, bar, playgrounds, shop and laundrette. Tourers, tents and pets welcome.

Open: March-January
Size: 6 acres, 30-40 touring pitches. 4 hot showers, 14 WCs. 1 static caravan

Site in Snainton, ¾ mile S of A170.

SOUTH BRENT *Devon* — Map 1 B3

EDESWELL FARM COUNTRY CARAVAN PARK RAC L
Rattery, TQ10 9LN. ☎ (0364) 72177
Open: Easter-End October
Size: 5 (18) acres, 45 touring pitches, all level, 18 with elec, 22 static caravans. 10 hot showers, 11 WCs, 2 CWPs

Car & caravan, Motor caravan, Car & tent, M/cycle* & tent £6.50; extra person 50p, child 50p maximum; elec £1, awn free, dogs free; WS
A family-run country site, close to main railway line. Children's adventure area, TV/bar lounge, trout fishing, games and table tennis rooms. 20 caravans for hire (own WCs). Swimming pool 4 miles. Minimum stay 3 nights in static caravans during High Season. No minimum stay for tourers. From the junction of the A38 and A385, follow signs 'Totnes A385' for ½ mile to site on right.

Great Palstone Caravan Park
☎ (036 47) 2227
Open: March-November
Size: 5½ acres, 100 touring pitches. 6 hot showers, 9 WCs

½ mile from Marley Head. Leave A38 at signpost to South Brent.

WEBLAND FARM HOLIDAY PARK RAC A
Avonwick, TQ10 9EX. ☎ (0364) 73273
Open: 15 March-15 November
Size: 5½ (24) acres, 35 touring pitches, 4 with elec, 15 level pitches, 49 static caravans. 4 hot showers, 4 WCs, 1 CWP

(1991) Car & caravan, Motor caravan, Car & tent, M/cycle & tent £4.30, plus £1.20 per adult above 2, child 70p; elec £1.20, awn free, dogs free; WS
Quiet country park, gently sloping with beautiful views of Dartmoor. Children's play area. 5 caravans for hire (own WCs). Restaurant ½ mile. Swimming pool 3 miles.
Leave A38 at South Brent (Marley Head) exit. Follow Webland signs for 1½ miles.

Whiteoaks of Ivybridge
Daveys Cross, Filham, Ivybridge
☎ (0752) 892340
Open: Easter-October
Size: 1 acre, 24 touring pitches. 2 hot showers, 6 WCs

From A38 S at Bittaford junction, continue through Bittaford towards Ivybridge. 1 mile after Bittaford, turn left for site. Signed from A38.

SOUTH MOLTON *Devon* — Map 1 B2

Black Cock Pub & Camping Park
Molland, EX36 3NW. ☎ (076 97) 297
Open: March-November
Size: 7 acres, 64 touring pitches. 12 hot showers, 20 WCs. 2 static caravans, 2 holiday cottages

Site signed from A361, 4 miles E of South Molton.

Romansleigh Holidays
Odam Hill, Romansleigh, EX36 4NB.
☎ (076 97) 259
Open: March-October
Size: 1 acre, 5 touring pitches. 6 hot showers, 9 WCs. 10 static caravans

Site halfway between Alswear and Mesham on the B3137. Follow signs.

SOUTH SHIELDS *Tyne & Wear* — Map 7 B3

LIZARD LANE CARAVAN & CAMPING SITE RAC L
Marsden, NE34 7AB. ☎ (091) 454 4982
Open: Easter-October
Size: 4¼ acres, 45 touring pitches, all level, 70 static caravans. 6 hot showers, 14 WCs, 1 CWP

Charges on application. WS
Quiet grassy site. Shop and restaurant 200 yards. Swimming pool 2 miles.
2 miles S of South Shields on A183.

SANDHAVEN CARAVAN PARK RAC L
Sea Road. ☎ (091) 454 5594
Open: 1 March-26 October
Size: 6½ acres, 35 touring pitches, all level, 20 with elec, 45 static caravans. 10 hot showers, 13 WCs, 1 CWP

Charges on application.
Holiday site 300 yards from sandy beach. Caravans for hire. Shop ½ mile. Restaurant ¼ mile. Swimming pool 2 miles.
Site ¾ mile E of town centre on coast road (Sea Road).

SOUTHAM *Warwickshire* — Map 2 B1

Holt Farm
CV33 0NJ. ☎ (092 681) 2225
Open: March-October
Size: 1½ acres, 45 touring pitches. 4 hot showers, 6 WCs

□ 🏕 🚐 ▲ □ □ □ □ □ 🐕
3 miles SE of Southam. Site signed.

SOUTHAMPTON Hampshire — Map 2 B3

DIBLES PARK CARAVAN SITE ⚓ RAC L
Dibles Road, Warsash, SO3 9SA.
☎ (0489) 575232
Open: April-End October
Size: 1 (5) acres, 22 touring pitches, all level,
16 with elec, 41 static caravans. 4 hot showers,
7 WCs, 1 CWP

□ 🏕 🚐 □ □ 🛏 □ □ □ □ □ 🐕

(1991) Car & caravan, Motor caravan £6; elec £1.40,
awn 80p; WS
*Small local authority site with facilities for tourers.
Quiet location about 1 mile from the River Hamble
and Warsash village. Well-maintained facilities.
Shop ½ mile. Pub ¼ mile, restaurant ¾ mile.
Swimming pool 5½ miles. Dogs to be exercised off
site. No tents. No motorcycles.
Turn S off A27 at Sarisbury Green to Warsash
village. Turn left at village centre and right after
500 yards into Dibles Road (signposted).*

Riverside Park
Satchells Lane, Hamble. ☎ (0703) 453220
Open: March-October
Size: 2½ acres, 60 touring pitches. 6 hot showers,
11 WCs. 8 static caravans

□ 🏕 🚐 ▲ 🛏 □ □ □ □ □ 🐕

M27 Junction 8, second left on to Hamble Lane.
Through until third roundabout, first right and
second left. Site signed.

SOUTHBOURNE Hampshire — Map 2 B3

CHICHESTER CAMPING ⚓ RAC L
343 Main Road, PO10 8JH. ☎ (0243) 373202
Open: 1 February-30 November
Size: 3 acres, 60 touring pitches, all level, all with
elec. 6 hot showers, 8 WCs, 1 CWP

□ □ 🚐 ▲ □ □ □ □ □ □ 🐕

Car & caravan, Motor caravan £7-£8, Car & tent £4-
£7; elec £1-£1.50, awn £1
*Part orchard site, quiet family site. Dogs welcome
with dog walk through public footpath to the sea.
Facilities include kitchen with freezer and washing
machine. Shop approximately 300 yards.
Restaurant approximately 50 yards. Swimming
pool 8 miles. No gas available (local caravan*

---

*accessories shop has it). No motorcycles. 28 days
maximum stay.
Site entrance off A259.*

SOUTHMINSTER Essex — Map 3 B2

BEACON HILL LEISURE PARK RAC L
St Lawrence Bay, CM10 7LS.
☎ (0621) 779248
Open: 1 April-31 October
Size: 10 (25) acres, 50 touring pitches, all level,
20 with elec, 88 with hardstanding, 88 static
caravans. 10 hot showers, 24 WCs, 2 CWPs

□ 🏕 🚐 ▲ 🛏 🖳 □ □ □ □ 🐕

Car & caravan, Motor caravan, Car & tent, M/cycle
& & tent, all £3.25 per adult, child £1.20; extra adult
£2.50; elec £1.75; WS
*Beside River Blackwater, level ground, quiet park,
own slipway to river, lake for children's boating
and fishing, excellent for sailing, water skiing,
windsurfing and bird watching. Restaurant ¼ mile.
Swimming pool 13 miles.
B1010 to Latchingdon, mini roundabout take
Bradwell Road, at St Lawrence take left turn at sign
St Lawrence Bay, ¼ mile down road on right hand
side.*

SOUTHPORT Lancashire — Map 4 B2

LEISURE LAKES CARAVAN PARK ⚓ RAC A
Mere Brow, Tarleton, PR4 6LA.
☎ (0772) 813446
Open: All year
Size: 90 acres, 63 touring pitches, 50 with elec,
6 with hardstanding. 6 hot showers, 7 WCs, 1 CWP

♿ 🏕 🚐 ▲ 🛏 □ □ ✕ □ □ 🐕

(1991) Car & caravan, Motor caravan, Car & tent,
M/cycle & frame tent £6; elec £1.30, awn £1.30
*90 acre picnicking park with 2 lakes and sandy
beaches. Windsurfing, canoeing and sailing, pub
with children's room and golf driving range. Shop
1 mile. Swimming pool 8 miles.
From Southport, take the A565 N for 3½ miles, then
turn right onto the B5246, site entrance ¼ mile past
Mere Brow on right.*

Riverside Touring & Leisure Centre
Southport New Road, Banks, PR9 8DF.
☎ (0704) 28886
Open: March-January
Size: 40 acres, 250 touring pitches. 24 hot showers,
6b WCs

🍴 Snacks/take away ✕ Restaurant ◺ Swimming pool ▣ Shelter for campers 🐕 Dogs accepted   **121**

[icons] Site 4 miles NE of Southport on A565.

SOUTHSEA Hampshire   Map 2 B3

Southsea Activity Caravan Park
Melville Road, PO4 9TB. ☎ (0705) 735070
Open: All year
Size: 12 acres, 166 touring pitches plus 22 for tents.
Hot showers, WCs. 45 static caravans

[icons]

From M27 take A2030 S for 3 miles, then left on to
A288, following caravan signs, turn left into
Bransbury Road. Site on left and signposted.

SOUTHWOLD Suffolk   Map 3 B1

Southwold Caravan & Camping Site
Ferry Road. ☎ (0502) 722486
Open: Easter-October
Size: 40+ touring pitches. 19 hot showers, 42 WCs

[icons]

Turn off A12 at Boythburgh and follow signs to
Southwold. Site next to harbour.

SPALDING Lincolnshire   Map 5 B3

LAKE ROSS CARAVAN PARK   RAC A
Dozens Bank, West Pinchbeck, PE11 3NA.
☎ (0775) 761690
Open: 1 April-31 October
Size: ¼ (2½) acres, 20 touring pitches, all level,
8 with elec, 6 static caravans. 2 hot showers, 2 cold
showers, 4 WCs, 1 CWP

[icons]

(1991) Car & caravan, Motor caravan, Car & tent,
M/cycle & tent £6, plus 50p per person above
2 (under 5s free); elec £1.40, awn 50p
*Small, family-run, quiet site in Lincolnshire
Fenland. Coarse fishing on site. Lake. Licensed
club. 6 caravans for hire. Restaurant ¼ mile.
Swimming pool 2½ miles. Dogs to be kept on
leads.*
2½ miles W of Spalding on A151, site on left just
after crossing Pode Hole Bridge.

ST AGNES Cornwall   Map 1 A3

Beacon Cottage Farm
Beacon Drive, TR5 0NU. ☎ (087 255) 2347
Open: Easter-October
Size: 2½ acres, 55 touring pitches. 4 hot showers, 7
WCs

[icons]

From A30 on to B3275, on entering St Agnes site
signed on left.

Chapel Porth Caravan Park
Chapel Porth. ☎ (087 255) 2720
Open: Easter-October
Size: ½ (2¼) acres, 10 touring pitches. 2 hot
showers, 6 WCs. 16 static caravans

[icons]

From B3277 to St Agnes, turn SW for Chapel Porth.
Site 1 mile.

CHIVERTON CARAVAN & TOURING PARK   RAC L
Blackwater, Near Truro, TR4 8HS.
☎ (0872) 560667
Open: Easter-October
Size: 2 (4½) acres, 30 touring pitches, 8 with elec,
40 static caravans. 4 hot showers, 10 WCs, 1 CWP

[icons]

Charges on application.
*Family-run site. Level, well-drained touring area
separate from statics. Children's play area. Shop
open Spring Bank Holiday-mid September.*
Take the A30 SW towards Redruth. 5 miles before
Redruth, at large traffic island, turn on to B3277 to
St Agnes. Take first left, site entrance 100 yards on
left.

Presingoll Farm
TR5 0PB. ☎ (087 255) 2333
Open: April-October
Size: 3½ acres, 90 touring pitches. 4 hot showers, 8
WCs

[icons]

Site on B3277 to St Agnes, 3 miles on right after
leaving A30.

TREVARTH HOLIDAY PARK   RAC A
Blackwater, Near Truro, TR4 8HR.
☎ (0872) 560266
Open: Easter-31 October
Size: 2 (4½) acres, 35 touring pitches, all level,
16 with elec, 20 static caravans. 2 hot showers,
5 WCs, 1 CWP

[icons]

Charges on application. WS
*Trees enhance this level meadowland site.
Children's playground. 20 caravans for hire (own
WCs). Shop and restaurant 300 yards. Swimming
pool 5 miles.*
200 yards W of Chiverton roundabout, A30, 4 miles
NE of Redruth.

ST AUSTELL Cornwall   Map 1 A3

SEA VIEW INTERNATIONAL   RAC A
Boswinger, Gorran, PL26 6LL.
☎ (0726) 843425
Open: 1 April-30 September
Size: 7 (16) acres, 172 touring pitches, all level,
135 with elec, 4 with hardstanding, 42 static
caravans, 2 chalets. 13 hot showers, 32 WCs,
1 CWP

[icons]

(1991) Car & caravan, Motor caravan, Car & tent
£6.13, plus £1.83 per adult above 2, child £1.53;
extra car £1.22; caravan to hire £12.77; elec £1.53,
dogs £2.04
cc Access, Visa/B'card
*Peaceful, landscaped, level park close to beautiful
beaches. Acres of recreational space, badminton,
volley ball, putting green. 42 static caravans and
2 chalets for hire (own WCs). Restaurant 1 mile. No
motorcycles. In July and August all stays must be
multiples of 7 nights, starting on a Saturday or a
Sunday.*
From St Austell take B3273 towards Mevagissey;
1 mile before Mevagissey turn right at Gorran
signpost and continue for 5 miles, then turn right
at camp signs.

CARLYON BAY CAMPING PARK RAC L
Cypress Avenue, Bethesda, PL25 3RE.
☎ (0726) 812735
Open: Easter-October
Size: 14 (32) acres, 180 touring pitches, 30 with
elec, 140 level pitches, 6 with hardstanding, 2 static
caravans, 1 chalet. 12 hot showers, 2 cold showers,
24 WCs, 1 CWP

(1991) Car & caravan, Car & tent, M/cycle* & tent
£5.20 -£9.20, Motor caravan £4.20-£8.20; plus
£1 per extra person; elec £1.50, awn £1, dogs £1;
WS
cc Major cards
*Award-winning family park with footpath to golf
course and European Blue Flag Award sandy
beach. 2 caravans and 1 chalet for hire (own WCs).
Restaurant 500 yards.
Midway between St Blazey and St Austell (A390),
turn S at the Britannia Inn roundabout.*

TRENCREEK FARM HOLIDAY PARK RAC A
Hewaswater, PL26 7JG. ☎ (0726) 882540
Open: April-October
Size: 20 (56) acres, 139 touring pitches, 66 with
elec, 70 level pitches, 27 static caravans, 11 chalets.
10 hot showers, 18 WCs, 2 CWPs

Car & caravan, Motor caravan, Car & tent, M/cycle*
& tent £7, plus £1 per extra adult, 60p per child;
elec £1.40, awn 80p, dogs 50p
*Trencreek is a small working farm with plenty of
children's activities including tame animals.
27 caravans and 11 chalets for hire (own WCs).
Restaurant 1 mile.
4 miles SW of St Austell on the A390, fork left on to
the B3287, Trencreek is 1 mile on, on the left.*

TREWHIDDLE HOLIDAY ESTATE RAC L
Trewhiddle, Pentowan Road, PL26 7AD.
☎ (0726) 67011
Open: 1 January-30 November
Size: 5 (16) acres, 105 touring pitches, 22 with elec,
76 static caravans. 9 hot showers, 18 WCs, 1 CWP

(1991) Car & caravan, Motor caravan, Car & tent,
M/cycle & tent £5-£9.50, plus £1.50 per adult above
2, child £1; extra car £1.50; boat £1; awn £1, dogs
£1
*Site consists of several fields partially enclosed by
hedges, with some mature trees, and is in a
sheltered position. Reception and shop are housed
in the old coach house of the former Trewhiddle
Estate. Children's play area. Golf, tennis, sea
fishing and horse riding all within 2 miles. Calor
gas and Camping Gaz should be available for 1992.
From St Austell turn S on to B3273, signed
Pentowan and Mevagissey, to site entrance ¾ mile
on the right. Site signed.*

ST BURYAN *Cornwall*   Map 1 A3

Camping & Caravanning Club Site
Sennen, Higher Tregiffian Farm, TR19 6JB.
☎ (0736) 871588
Open: 30 March-28 September
Size: 4 acres, 75 touring pitches. 6 hot showers,
9 WCs

Charges on application.
cc Access, Visa/B'card
*Easy access to the beach at Sennen Cove. Shop
2 miles.
Take the A30, turn on to the B3306, the site is on
the left.*

ST GENNYS *Devon*   Map 1 A3

Edmore Tourist Park
Wainhouse Corner, Jacobstowe, EX23 0BJ.
☎ (084 03) 467
Open: Easter-October
Size: 2½ acres, 28 touring pitches. 2 hot showers,
3 WCs. 2 static caravans

*S of Bude on A39, turn into Wainhouse Corner and
site is 250 yards down Jacobstowe Road.*

Hentervene Caravan & Camping Park
Crackington Haven, EX23 0LF.
☎ (084 03) 365
Open: All year
Size: 8½ acres, 35 touring pitches. 6 hot showers,
6 WCs. 20 static caravans

*Turn off A39 opposite Otterham Garage,
signposted Marshgate/Boscastle. Turn left after
2½ miles. (Park is approximately 10 miles SW of
Bude).*

ST IVES *Cornwall*   Map 1 A3

AYR HOLIDAY PARK RAC A
TR26 1EJ. ☎ (0736) 795855
Open: 1 April-31 October
Size: 2 (4) acres, 40 touring pitches, 35 with elec, 10
level pitches, 3 with hardstanding, 43 static
caravans, 16 chalets. 9 hot showers, 11 WCs,
1 CWP

Charges on application.
*Small, family site close to coastal footpath, ½ mile
from town and beaches. Play area on site.
43 caravans and 16 chalets for hire (own WCs). No
single-sex groups. Restaurant ½ mile.
½ mile W of St Ives on B3306, turn N onto Carnellis
Road, then follow signs to `Ayr District'.*

Balnoon Camp Site
Halsetown, TR26 3JA. ☎ (0736) 795431
Open: April-September
Size: 1 acre, 25 touring pitches. 2 hot showers,
2 WCs

From A30, take A3074 for St Ives. At second
roundabout turn left signposted Towednack for
1¼ mile, then second right for site.

Carbis Bay Holiday Centre
Laity Farm, Carbis Bay. ☎ (0736) 797580
Open: Easter-October
Size: 25 acres, 200 touring pitches. 16 hot showers,
16 WCs. 70 static caravans, 70 bungalows

From A30, take A3074 for St Ives. In Carbis Bay, site signed.

CHY AN GWEAL HOLIDAY PARK   RAC A
Carbis Bay, TR26 2RS. ☎ (0736) 976257
Open: 1 April-31 October
Size: 3 (5) acres, 50 touring pitches, 20 with elec, 35 static caravans. 8 hot showers, 17 WCs

Charges on application.
Sheltered site ¾ mile from town with bar, children's play area and mother and baby room. 35 caravans for hire (own WCs). ¾ mile S of St Ives on A3074.

Hellesveor Caravan & Camping Site
TR26 3AD. ☎ (0736) 795738
Open: Easter-October
Size: ½ acre, 20 touring pitches. 4 hot showers, 5 WCs. 10 static caravans

Site 1 mile W of St Ives on B3306.

POLMANTER FARM TOURING
CARAVAN PARK   RAC A
Halsetown, TR26 3LX. ☎ (0736) 795640
Open: April-October
Size: 12 acres, 240 touring pitches, 85 with elec, 200 level pitches. 28 hot showers, 42 WCs, 5 CWPs

Charges on application.
Family-run park with bar lounge, games room, sports field and a children's play area. No single-sex groups.
From A30 follow H.R. route to St Ives. Signposted.

TREVALGAN FAMILY CAMPING PARK   RAC L
TR26 3BJ. ☎ (0736) 796433
Open: 1 May-30 September
Size: 4.9 acres, 120 touring pitches, all level, 10 with elec, 8 chalets. 6 hot showers, 12 WCs, 1 CWP

Car & caravan, Motor caravan, Car & tent, M/cycle & tent all £1 plus £2-£3.50 per adult, children £1-£2.50; elec £2
Family, friendly park, superb views and walks to the clifftops in our fields. Farm Pets Corner. Lots of space to play. Run entirely by the Osborne Family.
Turn right off B3306 1½ miles W of St Ives, signed Trevalgan Farm; right again in ½ mile.

ST JUST *Cornwall*   Map 1 A3

Bosavern House
TR19 7RD. ☎ (0736) 788301
Open: March-October
Size: 2 acres, 12 touring pitches. 2 hot showers, 3 WCs

From A3071 in St Just, turn left on to B3306 towards land and site is on left in ¼ mile.

KELYNACK CARAVAN & CAMPING PARK   RAC L
Kelynack, TR19 7RE. ☎ (0736) 787633
Open: April-October
Size: 1½ (2½) acres, 7 touring pitches, all level, 4 with elec, 6 with hardstanding, 11 static caravans. 2 hot showers, 6 WCs, 1 CWP

Car & caravan, Motor caravan, Car & tent, M/cycle & tent £3.50, plus 75p per person above 2; elec £1,

awn 75p; WS
Sheltered, level and secluded rural site alongside a stream. Public telephone and campers' wash-up available. Restaurant and swimming pool 1 mile. 11 caravans for hire (own WCs).
A3071 from Penzance towards St Just. After 6 miles, left on B3306 towards Land's End. Park signposted left after ½ mile.

Levant Caravan & Camping Site
Levant Road, Trewellard, Pendeen, TR19 7SX.
☎ (0736) 788795
Open: August-September
Size: 2 acres, 44 touring pitches. 6 hot showers, 11 WCs

2 miles N of St Just on B3306, turn W at Trewellard Chapel. Site 300 yards.

ST LEONARDS *Dorset* — Map 2 B3

CAMPING INTERNATIONAL 🏰 A
229 Ringwood Road, BH24 2SD.
☎ (0202) 872817
Open: 1 March-31 October
Size: 9 acres, 170 touring pitches, all level, 130 with elec, 6 with hardstanding. 16 hot showers, 16 cold showers, 48 WCs, 2 CWPs

(1991) Car & caravan, Motor caravan, Car & tent, M/cycle* & tent £4.20-£6.40; all plus £1-£1.20 per person; elec £1.30, awn £1-£1.30; WS
cc Access, Visa/B'card
Quiet, family-run park for families and couples only, for those who deserve superior facilities. Minimum ADVANCE booking is 3 nights.
3 miles SW of Ringwood on left of A31.

OAKDENE HOLIDAY PARK 🏰 A
BH24 2RZ. ☎ (0202) 875422
Open: 1 March-31 October
Size: 20 (50) acres, 400 touring pitches, all level, 161 with elec, 200 static caravans. 50 hot showers, 90 WCs, 5 CWPs

(1991) Car & caravan, Motor caravan, Car & tent, M/cycle* & tent £4.60-£11.25; elec £6.15-£12.75, awn £1, dogs £1; WS
cc Access, Visa/B'card
A family site with riding stables, bike hire, sauna, solarium, gym and full entertainment for both adults and children. 90 caravans for hire (own WCs).
The park is adjacent to St Leonards Hospital on the A31 road W of Ringwood.

ST MABYN *Cornwall* — Map 1 A3

ST MABYN HOLIDAY PARK 🏰 A
Longstone Road, BL30 3BY.
☎ (020 884) 236
Open: Easter-End September
Size: 8 acres, 150 touring pitches, all level, 7 with elec, 7 with hardstanding, 20 static caravans, 2 chalets. 12 hot showers, 32 WCs, 1 CWP

Charges on application.
A family site with good facilities. Games room, bar

and adventure playground. 20 caravans and 2 chalets for hire (own WCs).
Turn W off B3266 (Bodmin-Camelford road) at Longstone Cross, signed `St Mabyn'. Site ¼ mile.

ST MAWES *Cornwall* — Map 1 A3

TRETHEM MILL CARAVAN PARK 🏰 A
St Just-in-Roseland, TR2 5JF.
☎ (087 258) 504
Open: 1 April-31 October
Size: 3¾ acres, 84 touring pitches, 28 with elec, 20 level pitches. 8 hot showers, 8 cold showers, 16 WCs, 1 CWP

(1991) Car & caravan, Motor caravan, Car & tent, M/cycle & tent £6.10, plus £2.20 per adult above 2, child £1.10; car 50p; elec £1
Trethem Mill is situated in the beautiful Roseland Peninsula, only 3 miles from the lovely village of St Mawes, surrounded by safe, sandy beaches and ideal for sailing, boating, etc. Restaurant 3 miles. Swimming pool 10 miles.
At 2½ miles N of St Mawes on A3078, turn W at Trethem Mill.

Trewince Manor
Portscatho. ☎ (0872) 580289
Open: March-October
Size: 25 acres, 50 touring pitches. 6 hot showers, 12 WCs. 22+ static caravans

From St Austell take A390 towards Truro, pass through Hewaswater, bear left on to B3287 to Tregony, from Tregony follow signs to St Mawes for 7 miles to Trewithian, turn left to Gerrans and Portscatho, stay on road following signs for St Anthony to Trewince Manor.

ST NEOTS *Cambridgeshire* — Map 3 A1

Camping & Caravanning Club Site
Rush Meadow, PE19 2UD.
☎ (0480) 74404
Open: 30 March-26 October
Size: 10 acres, 180 touring pitches. 8 hot showers, 12 WCs

Charges on application.
cc Access, Visa/B'card
Site borders the River Ouse, which provides good fishing.
On A45 travel towards St Neots, take the left turn by the Hare & Hounds public house. Follow the road round to the site.

ST OSYTH *Essex* — Map 3 B2

Hutleys Caravan Park
St Osyth Beach, CO16 8TB.
☎ (0255) 820712
Open: March-October
Size: 1 acre, 18 touring pitches. 12 hot showers, 60 WCs

On B1027 to St Osyth. Through village and continue following signs to beach.

⬛ Snacks/take away ✗ Restaurant ◲ Swimming pool ▣ Shelter for campers 🐕 Dogs accepted **125**

POINT CLEAR HOLIDAY PARK   RAC L
CO16 8LJ. ☎ (0255) 820651
Open: March-October
Size: 2 (119) acres, 31 touring pitches, 1278 static
caravans. 20 hot showers, 60 WCs

[icons: caravan, motor caravan, laundry, shop, restaurant, swimming, dog]

Charges on application.
cc Access, Visa/B'card
Adjacent to a Holiday Park complex, this well-kept
site offers windsurfing and water-skiing as well as
a swimming pool, club with entertainments, and a
children's play area. Caravans for hire (own WCs).
Site 2¼ miles W of St Osyth.

STANDLAKE *Oxfordshire*   Map 2 B2

LINCOLN FARM PARK   RAC A
High Street, OX8 7RH.
☎ (0865) 300239
Open: 1 April-30 October
Size: 4 (6) acres, 63 touring pitches, all level,
40 with elec, 1 with hardstanding, 1 static caravan,
11 chalets 6 hot showers, 10 WCs, 2 CWPs

[icons: caravan, motor caravan, tents, laundry, shop, dog]

(1991) Car & caravan, Motor caravan, Car & tent,
M/cycle & tent £7.50, plus £1 per adult above 2,
child 75p; elec £1.50, awn £1, dogs 50p; WS
Award-winning park situated in the heart of the
classic Oxfordshire village of Standlake. Private
leisure club on the park with swimming pool, spa
pool and sauna. 1 caravan for hire (own WC).
Restaurant 100 yards. Minimum stay over Bank
Holidays is 3 nights (4 nights over Easter).
At Standlake, turn N off A415 (Witney-Abingdon
road) on road signed 'Village Only' to site on right.

HARDWICK PARK   RAC L
Downs Road, Off Witney Road (A415), OX8 7PZ.
☎ (0865) 300501
Open: 1 April-31 October
Size: 25 (180) acres, 150 touring pitches, all level,
55 with elec, 91 static caravans. 16 hot showers,
33 WCs, 1 CWP

[icons: caravan, motor caravan, tents, laundry, shop, restaurant, dog]

(1991) Car & caravan, Motor caravan, Car & tent,
M/cycle & tent £5.50-£7.25; plus £1.10 per person
above 4; extra car £1; elec £1.50, awn £1.10; WS
cc Access, Visa/B'card
Large, open park, surrounded by willows. Two
lakes, windsurfing, water skiing, sailing, fishing,
swimming. 3 caravans for hire (own WCs).
Swimming pool 5 miles (at Witney Leisure Centre).
Off A415 between Witney and Abingdon, at
Standlake.

STANLEY *Co Durham*   Map 7 B3

Harperley Country Park
Near Tanfield Lea.
☎ (0207) 234168
Open: April-October
Size: ½ acre, 5 touring pitches. 4 hot showers,
6 WCs

[icons: caravan, motor caravan, laundry, shop, restaurant, dog]

From Stanley, follow B6173 to Tanfield Lea, turn
left for 1 mile. Site signed.

STEYNING *West Sussex*   Map 3 B3

Steyning's Caravan & Camping Park
The White House, Newham Lane, BN44 3LR.
☎ (0903) 813737
Open: March-August
Size: 3 (4½) acres, 50+ touring pitches. 1 WC

[icons: caravan, motor caravan, tents, dog]

From Steyning, look for the White Horse public
house, turn directly into Sheep Pen Lane and then
into Newham Lane. (Site is signposted from the
White Horse and is ½ mile up Newham Lane from
the High Street, on the left hand side).

STOKE FERRY *Norfolk*   Map 3 A1

Grange Farm
Whittington, PE33 9TF. ☎ (0366) 500307
Open: March-October
Size: 3 acres, 25 touring pitches. 2 hot showers,
2 WCs

[icons: caravan, motor caravan, tents, dog]

Site on A134 at junction with B1106. Site midway
between King's Lynn and Thetford.

STOKESLEY *North Yorkshire*   Map 5 A1

Toft Hill Farm
Kirkby-in-Cleveland. ☎ (0642) 712469
Open: April-October
Size: 2 acres, 26 touring pitches. 2 hot showers,
6 WCs. Static caravans

[icons: caravan, motor caravan, tents, laundry, dog]

Site 3 miles S of A172, signposted Kirkby.

White House Farm
Little Broughton, TS9 5JE.
☎ (0642) 778238
Open: March-October
Size: 1½ (10) acres, 30 touring pitches. 4 hot
showers, 7 WCs

[icons: disabled, caravan, motor caravan, tents, laundry, dog]

From B1257 into Great Broughton, turn E in ½ mile
towards Ingleby Greenhow. Site signed.

STOKE-ON-TRENT *Staffordshire*   Map 5 A3

Trentham Caravan & Camping Park
Trentham, ST4 8AX. ☎ (0782) 657341
Open: All year
Size: 35 acres, 250 touring pitches. 24 hot showers,
92 WCs

[icons: disabled, caravan, motor caravan, tents, laundry, shop, restaurant, dog]

From M6 junction 15 on to A500, then take first slip
road, signposted A34 to Stone and Stafford, 1 mile
site on right.

STOW-ON-THE-WOLD *Gloucestershire*   Map 2 B2

The New Inn
Nether Westcote, Kingham, OX7 6SD.
☎ (0993) 830827
Open: All year
Size: 3 acres, 25 touring pitches. 2 hot showers,
5 WCs

[icons: caravan, motor caravan, tents, laundry, restaurant, shop, dog]

4½ miles SE of Stow-on-the-Wold on A424, midway between Stow-on-the-Wold and Burford.

STRATFORD-UPON-AVON *Warwickshire* Map 2 B2

Cottage of Content Inn
Barton, Bidford-on-Avon, B50 4NP.
☎ (0789) 772279
Open: March-October
Size: 2½ acres, 25 touring pitches. 4 WCs

At Bidford (A439), turn S on B4085. After ¾ mile, turn left to Barton. Site on S-bend just before village centre.

DODWELL PARK RAC L
Evesham Road, CV73 9ST. ☎ (0789) 204957
Open: All year
Size: 2 (17) acres, 50 touring pitches, 25 with elec, 20 level pitches, 4 with hardstanding. 6 hot showers, 6 cold showers, 7 WCs, 1 CWP

(1991) Car & caravan, Motor caravan, Car & tent, M/cycle & tent £6.50, plus £1 per adult above 2, child 50p; elec £1.25, awn £1, dogs free
A quiet family site in Shakespeare countryside, near Stratford-upon-Avon. Country walks. Large additional area for ball games, etc. Restaurant 1 mile. Swimming pool 2 miles.
Site on S side of the B439. 2½ miles W of Stratford town centre.

Longbarn
The Elms Camp, Tiddington, CV37 7AG.
☎ (0789) 292312
Open: April-October
Size: 4 acres, 28 touring pitches, plus 20 tent pitches. 8 hot showers, 24 WCs

Site on B4086, 1¼ miles NE of Stratford.

STREET *Somerset* Map 2 A3

Bramble Hill Camping Site
Bramble Hill, Walton. ☎ (0458) 42548
Open: Easter-September
Size: 3 acres, 60 touring pitches. Hot showers, WCs

Site set on W side of Street on A39.

SUDBURY *Suffolk* Map 3 A2

Willowmere Caravan Park
Bures Road, Little Cornard
☎ (0787) 75559
Open: Easter-October
Size: 3 acres, 40 touring pitches. 4 hot showers, 8 WCs

Site 1½ miles S of Sudbury on the B1508.

SUTTON COLDFIELD *West Midlands* Map 2 B1

Camping & Caravanning Club Site
Kingsbury Water Park, Bodymore Heath, B76 0DY.
☎ (0827) 874101
Open: 30 March-26 October

Size: 10 acres, 60 touring pitches. 4 hot showers, 6 WCs

Charges on application.
Site set in 600 acres of landscaped park. Minimum facilities - campers must bring their own chemical toilet. Camping Gaz only. Shop 1½ miles.
From the A4097 turn towards Kingsbury Water Park. Do not take the main entrance but pass over the M42, take the turning right just before the canal, follow the road to the site.

SWAFFHAM *Norfolk* Map 3 A1

Breckland Meadows Touring Park
Lynn Road, PE37 7AY. ☎ (0760) 721246
Open: March-October
Size: 2½ acres, 25 touring pitches. 2 hot showers, 7 WCs

Site ½ mile W of Swaffham on the old A47.

SWALLOWCLIFFE *Wiltshire* Map 2 B3

The Lancers Inn
Sutton Mandeville (A30)
☎ (072 270) 220
Open: All year
Size: 1¾ acres, 46 touring pitches. WCs

1 mile NE of Swallowcliffe on A30.

SWANAGE *Dorset* Map 2 B3

Acton Fields
Langton Matravers. ☎ (0929) 424184
Open: Spring Bank Holiday week-July/August
Size: 7 acres, 80 touring pitches. 2+ hot showers, 6 WCs. 1 static caravan

On B3069 to Langton Matravers. Site 70 yards after sign to village.

Burnbake Campsite
Rempstone, Corfe Castle. ☎ (0929) 480317
Open: April-September
Size: 12½ acres, 130 touring pitches. 8 hot showers, 13 WCs

E of Corfe Castle on B3351, take third left signed Rempstone. Follow camp signs.

Flower Meadow Caravan Park
Haycrafts Lane, Harman's Cross, BH19 3EB.
☎ (0929) 480358
Open: April-October
Size: 3 acres, 10 touring pitches. 4 hot showers, 6 WCs

From A351 towards Swanage, turn S at Harman's Cross. Site 200 yards.

Westacre Farm
Harman's Cross. ☎ (0929) 480276
Open: July-August
Size: 3 acres, 3+ touring pitches. 2 hot showers,

■ Snacks/take away ☒ Restaurant ◲ Swimming pool ▣ Shelter for campers ⊓ Dogs accepted   127

3 WCs

☐ ☐ 🚐 🚗 🏕 ☐ ☐ ☐ ☐ ☐ ☐ 🐕

On A351 midway between Swanage and Corfe Castle.

Woodyhyde Farm
☎ (0929) 480274
Open: April-October
Size: 13 acres, 10 touring pitches. 8 hot showers, 15 WCs

☐ ☐ 🚐 🚗 🏕 ☐ ☐ 🧺 ☐ ☐ ☐ 🐕

Site 1 mile on A351 from Corfe Castle.

White Cote
Ryther Road, Ulleskelf. ☎ (0937) 835231
Open: March-January
Size: 2 acres, 18 touring pitches. Hot showers, 4 WCs. Static caravans

☐ ☐ 🚐 🚗 🏕 ☐ ☐ ☕ ☐ ☐ 🏠 🐕

Site ½ mile E of Ulleskelf.

DRAYTON MANOR PARK   ⚓ RAC L
Fazeley, B78 3TW. ☎ (0827) 287979
Open: Easter-end October
Size: 4 acres, 75 touring pitches. 9 hot showers, 9 WCs, 1 CWP

🦽 🚐 🚗 🏕 🚿 🧺 ☕ ✕ ☐ 🏠 🐕

Charges on application.
Pleasant site within 160-acre leisure park and zoo, with children's play area. Families only. No telephone bookings. No gas available. Shop open at weekends. Swimming pool 4 miles.
2½ miles S of Tamworth (or 1 mile S of A5) on A4091, entrance at Drayton Manor Gardens.

Orchard Caravans
Chapel Hill, LN4 4PZ. ☎ (0526) 42414
Open: February-December
Size: 7½ acres, 33 touring pitches. 6 hot showers, 14 WCs. 50 static caravans

🦽 🚐 🚗 🏕 🚿 🧺 ☕ ✕ 🛶 🏠 🐕

2½ miles SW of Coningsby (A153), turn left at Tattershall Bridge. Site 1½ miles.

TATTERSHALL PARK COUNTRY CLUB   ⚓ RAC A
Sleaford Road, LN4 4LR. ☎ (0526) 43193
Open: 1 March-31 October
Size: 35 (365) acres, 400 touring pitches, all level, 50 with elec, all with hardstanding. 30 static caravans. 16 hot showers, 47 WCs, 5 CWPs

🦽 🚐 🚗 🏕 🚿 🧺 ☕ ✕ ☐ 🏠 🐕

Car & caravan, Motor caravan, Car & tent £7.50;

elec £2, awn £1.50, dogs £1; WS
cc Access, Visa/B'card
Site with range of leisure activities including horse riding, pony trekking, windsurfing, water skiing, canoeing, rowing, squash, snooker, gymnasium, saunas, jet ski, island adventure playground, nature walks, lake swimming. Licensed bars. Swimming pool 4 miles (at Woodhall Spa). No motorcycles.
Site on SE side of the A153, ½ mile SW of Tattershall, adjacent to Tattershall Castle.

ASHE FARM CAMPING & CARAVAN SITE   ⚓ RAC L
Thornfalcon, TA3 5NW.
☎ (0823) 442567
Open: 1 April-31 October
Size: 6 acres, 40 touring pitches, all level, 30 with elec, 2 static caravans. 3 hot showers, 9 WCs, 1 CWP

☐ 🚐 🚗 🏕 🛁 🧺 ☐ ☐ 🏠 🐕

(1991) Car & caravan, Motor caravan, Car & tent, M/cycle* & tent £2 per adult, £1 per child; elec £1, awn 50p; WS
Quiet farm site in sheltered, mown meadow, with hot water in all basins, telephone, daily delivery of milk, bread, newspapers, etc. Restaurant ¼ mile. Swimming pool 4 miles. Shop 2 miles. 2 caravans for hire.
Leave M5 at junction 25. Take A358 SE for 2½ miles. Turn right at Nags Head towards West Hatch. Site in ¼ mile.

Holly Bush Park
Culmhead, TA3 7EA.
☎ (082 342) 515
Open: All year
Size: 2 acres, 40 touring pitches. 6 hot showers, 9 WCs

☐ 🚐 🚗 🏕 🛁 🧺 ☐ ☐ ☐ ☐ 🐕

6½ miles S of Taunton (B3170), at crossroads turn right towards Wellington. Site 50 yards past public house.

ST QUINTIN HOTEL CARAVAN & CAMPING PARK   ⚓ RAC A
Bridgwater Road.
☎ (0823) 259171
Open: All year
Size: 5½ (6) acres, 125 touring pitches. 12 hot showers, 18 WCs

☐ 🚐 🚗 🏕 🧺 🧺 ☕ ✕ ☐ ☐ 🐕

Charges on application.
Level, grassy site adjacent to an inland waterways canal, with boating, fishing and cycle hire, plus a children's play area. Caravans for hire.
2 miles NE of Taunton on A38, 1 mile from junction 25 of the M5.

TAVISTOCK *Devon* — Map 1 B3

HARFORD BRIDGE PARK RAC L
Peter Tavy, PL19 9LS. ☎ (0822) 810349
Open: 20 March-6 November
Size: 10 (16) acres, 120 touring pitches, all level, 20 with elec, 38 static caravans, 7 chalets. 6 hot showers, 14 WCs, 1 CWP

Car & caravan £2-£4.50, Motor caravan, Car & tent, M/cycle* & tent £2-£3.50; plus £1.50-£2 per extra person, child £1-£1.50; elec £1.40, awn £1, dogs 55p
Flat, sheltered, rural site with an abundance of trees and shrubs. Set on the River Tavy with beautiful views of the moors. 8 caravans and 7 chalets for hire (own WCs). Restaurant 1 mile. Swimming pool 2 miles. No groups.
At 2 miles N of Tavistock on A386, turn right at Peter Tavy sign for 100 yards.

HIGHER LONGFORD FARM RAC A
Moorshop, PL19 9LQ. ☎ (0822) 613360
Open: All year
Size: 3 (6) acres, 52 touring pitches, all level, 20 with elec, 2 chalets. 5 hot showers, 10 WCs, 3 CWPs

Car & caravan, Motor caravan, Car & tent £6, M/cycle* tent £3.50, plus 50p per person above 2; elec £1; WS
Ideal for touring, situated in Dartmoor National Park, good base for walking, horse riding, fishing. 2 chalets for hire (own WCs). Swimming pool 2½ miles.
Take B3357 Tavistock to Princetown road, 2½ miles from Tavistock.

LANGSTONE MANOR CAMPING & CARAVAN PARK RAC A
Moortown, PL19 9JZ. ☎ (0822) 613371
Open: 15 March-15 November
Size: 3 (5) acres, 40 touring pitches, all level, 6 with elec, 30 static caravans. 6 hot showers, 6 cold showers, 8 WCs, 1 CWP

Motor caravan, Car & tent, M/cycle & tent £4-£7, plus 50p per person above 2, child 50p; elec £1.50, awn 50p, dogs 40p
A small, family-run site situated in the Dartmoor National Park at the foot of Pew Tor. Lounge bar

and play area. Swimming pool 2 miles. 19 caravans for hire.
2 miles E of Tavistock, on B3357, turn S and ½ mile on bear left.

The Plume of Feathers Inn
Princetown. ☎ (082 289) 240
Open: All year
Size: 2½ acres, 80 touring pitches. 4 hot showers, 7 WCs

From B3212, site access in Princetown main square.

WOODOVIS CARAVAN & CAMPING PARK RAC A
Gulworthy, PL19 8NY.
☎ (0822) 832968
Open: 1 March-31 December
Size: 4½ acres, 54 touring pitches, 12 with elec, 3 level pitches, 3 with hardstanding, 9 static caravans. 6 hot showers, 6 cold showers, 12 WCs, 1 CWP

Car & caravan, Motor caravan, Car & tent, M/cycle & tent £5-£6, plus £1 per adult above 2, 50p per child (5-16 years); elec £1, awn 50p, dogs free; WS
Quiet countryside park, ideally situated for Dartmoor, Bodmin Moor, north and south coast. 2 caravans for hire (own WCs). Restaurant ½ mile. Swimming pool 3 miles.
On A390 Tavistock-Liskeard road after 3 miles turn right at Gulworthy Cross (signpost Lamerton, chip shop, caravan park) in 1 mile on left is caravan park. Down ½ mile drive.

TEBAY *Cumbria* — Map 4 B1

TEBAY CARAVAN PARK RAC A
Orton, CA10 3SB.
☎ (05874) 482
Open: 14 March-31 October
Size: 3½ acres, 70 touring pitches, all level, 40 with elec, all with hardstanding. 6 hot showers, 10 WCs, 1 CWP

Car & caravan, Motor caravan £5; elec £1
Wooded site useful as base for touring the Lakes. Swimming pool 4 miles. No tents or motorcycles.
From junction 38 on the M6, travel N to Tebay Service Area, site on left.

Snacks/take away · Restaurant · Swimming pool · Shelter for campers · Dogs accepted

129

TEIGNMOUTH *Devon* — Map 1 B3

Coast View Country Club
Torquay Road, Shaldon, TQ14 0BG.
☎ (0626) 872392
Open: Easter-September
Size: 13 acres, 110 touring pitches. 6 hot showers,
12 WCs. 50 static caravans

[icons]

From M5 Junction 31, follow signs for Torbay and
Teignmouth. Cross Shaldon Bridge. Site overlooks
village.

TELFORD *Shropshire* — Map 4 B3

Camping & Caravanning Club Site
Ring Bank, Ebury Hill, Haughton, TF6 6BU.
☎ (0743) 77334
Open: 30 March-26 October
Size: 18 acres, 160 touring pitches

[icons]

Charges on application.
cc Access, Visa/B'card
*This site commands splendid views over the
Severn Valley. Fish pond. Children's play area.
Minimum facilities - campers must have their own
chemical toilet. Shop 1½ miles.*
From the A53 follow the signs towards Haughton,
Upton Magna. The site is approximately 1 mile on
the right.

Severn Gorge Caravan Park
Bridgnorth Road, Tweedale
☎ (0952) 684789
Open: All year
Size: 2 acres, 80 touring pitches. 6 hot showers,
18 WCs

[icons]

From M54, follow A442 for Tweedale.

TENTERDEN *Kent* — Map 3 B3

WOODLANDS PARK   RAC A
Tenterden Road, Biddenden, TN27 8BT.
☎ (0580) 291216
Open: 1 March (weather permitting)-31 October
Size: 9 (24) acres, 100 touring pitches, all level,
36 with elec, 13 static caravans. 4 hot showers,
16 WCs, 1 CWP

[icons]

(1991) Car & caravan, Motor caravan, Car & tent,
M/cycle & tent £5.60-£6.95, plus £1.75-£2.15 per
person above 2, child £1.25-£1.75; elec £1.50, awn
80p-£1.20
*Woodlands caters for tents, caravans and motor
caravans on level, grassy land, with clubhouse
(licensed bar). Children welcome. Camping
accessories sales. Now graded ETB 4 Ticks.
Restaurant 1½ miles. Swimming pool 3 miles.
Holidaymakers only (no workmen).*
At 1¾ miles N of Tenterden on A28, turn left on to
A262 for ¾ mile, site entrance next to Woodlands
Cafe and filling station.

TEWKESBURY *Gloucestershire* — Map 2 A2

Sunset View Touring Tent & Caravan Park
Church End Lane, Twyning, GL20 6EH.
☎ (0684) 292145
Open: All year
Size: 2 acres, 40 touring pitches. 4 hot showers,
6 WCs

[icons]

2 miles N of Tewkesbury (A38), turn E near Crown
Inn. Site 200 yards.

Three Counties Caravan Park
Sledge Green, Berrow. ☎ (068 481) 439
Open: Easter-October
Size: 8 acres, 35 touring pitches. 4 hot showers,
10 WCs

[icons]

Site 6 miles W of Tewkesbury on A438.

THETFORD *Norfolk* — Map 3 A1

The Dower House Touring Park
East Harling, NR16 2SE. ☎ (0953) 717314
Open: March-October
Size: 20 acres, 190 touring pitches. 6 hot showers,
18 WCs

[icons]

Site ¾ mile in Thetford Forest. 5 miles E of
Thetford (A1066).

Puddledock Farm
Great Hockham. ☎ (0953) 498455
Open: All year
Size: 4 acres, 24+ touring pitches. 2 hot showers,
8 WCs

[icons]

¾ mile W of Great Hockham (A1075), turn N along
lane to site.

THORPE WOODLAND CAMP SITE   RAC L
Forestry Commission, IP24 2RX.
☎ (0842) 761248
Open: 22 March-29 September
Size: 50 acres, 191 touring pitches, all level, 36 with
elec. Water supply, no WCs, 12 CWPs

[icons]

(1991) Car & caravan, Motor caravan, Car & tent,
M/cycle & tent £2.95-£3.95
*This simple, quiet, woodland site offers fishing in
the River Thet and a children's play area. Visitors
must have their own chemical toilets. Restaurant
and swimming pool 5 miles.*
At 5 miles E of Thetford on A1066, continue ahead
on road signed East Harling. Site entrance ¼ mile
on left.

THIRSK *North Yorkshire* — Map 5 A1

Carlton Miniott Park
Carlton Miniott. ☎ (0845) 523106
Open: April-October
Size: 5 acres, 20 touring pitches. 2 hot showers,
5 WCs

[icons]

1½ miles W of Thirsk (A61), take road signposted
Sandhutton. Site 400 yards.

Nursery Caravan Park
Rainton, YO7 3PG. ☎ (0845) 577277
Open: (1991) 1 March-31 October

Size: 2 (5) acres, 30 touring pitches. 4 hot showers, 6 WCs. 44 static caravans

	⌂🚐		🚃					🏠	🐕

From the junction of the A1 and A168 (E of Ripon), travel NE on the A168 towards Thirsk for 1 mile, then filter left on unclassified road towards Asenby, at crossroads turn left to site on right in ½ mile.

Quernhow Caravan & Camp Site
Great North Road, Sinderby
☎ (0845) 567221
Open: All year
Size: 4 acres, 50 touring pitches. 4 hot showers, 8 WCs. Static caravans

	🏕️🚐	🅰		🎿	♥	✗		🏠	🐕

Site 9 miles N of Boroughbridge, to W of A1.

Thirkleby Hall Caravan Site
Thirkleby, YO7 3AR. ☎ (0845) 401360
Open: March-October
Size: 3 acres, 50 touring pitches. 2 hot showers, 4 WCs

	🏕️🚐	🅰		🎿				🏠	🐕

Site 3 miles S of Thirsk on A19.

THIRSK RACECOURSE CARAVAN CLUB SITE RAC A
Station Road, YO7 1QL. ☎ (0845) 25266
Open: April-Mid September
Size: 3 acres, 60 touring pitches, all level, 10 with elec, 6 with hardstanding. 6 hot showers, 8 WCs, 1 CWP

🏕️🚐	🅰							🏠	🐕

Charges on application.
cc Access, Visa/B'card
Level site bounded by woods and the racecourse. Shop and restaurant 5 minutes' walk. Milk available at site office.
500 yards from Thirsk on the A61 (Thirsk to Ripon).

YORK HOUSE CARAVAN PARK RAC A
Balk, YO7 2AQ.
☎ (0845) 597495
Open: 1 April-31 October
Size: 2½ (12) acres, 80 touring pitches, 30 with elec, 60 level pitches, 200 static caravans. 10 hot showers, 10 cold showers, 22 WCs, 1 CWP

	🏕️🚐	🅰	🚃	🎿				🏠	🐕

(1991) Car & caravan, Motor caravan £5.65, Car & tent £3.85-£5.65, M/cycle & tent £3.85; elec £1, awn free, dogs free; WS
The park is situated on the edge of the North Yorkshire National Park. Quiet family site, central to major tourist attractions. Trout stream runs through site with private fishing rights. Restaurant 2 miles. Swimming pool 3 miles.
From Thirsk, travel E on the A170 for 2 miles, turn S for 1 mile, turn left to site on left in ½ mile.

White Rose Farm
Hutton, Sessay.
☎ (0845) 401215
Open: March-October
Size: 12 acres, 100 touring pitches. 12 hot showers, 24 WCs. 150 static caravans

♿	🏕️🚐	🅰	🚃	🎿		✗	🏊	🏠	🐕

5 miles outside Thirsk on A19 to York.

THRAPSTON *Northamptonshire* Map 3 A1

Mill Marina Caravan Park
Midland Road, NN14 4JR. ☎ (080 12) 2850
Open: April-December
Size: 4 acres, 30 touring pitches, plus 12 tent pitches. 4 hot showers, 5 WCs. 5 static caravans

	🏕️🚐	🅰	🚃						🐕

In Thrapston, take A605 S for 500 yards.

THRESHFIELD *North Yorkshire* Map 5 A1

Threaplands House Farm
Cracoe. ☎ (075 673) 248
Open: April-October
Size: 6 acres, 30 touring pitches. 2 hot showers, 4 WCs

♿	🏕️🚐	🅰							🐕

From Skipton, take B6265 towards Grassington through Cracoe and cross main road to lane. Site 200 yards.

WOOD NOOK CARAVAN SITE RAC L
Skirethorns, BD23 5NU. ☎ (0756) 752412
Open: 1 March-31 October
Size: 2 (6) acres, 40 touring pitches, all with elec, all level, 28 with hardstanding, 10 static caravans. 8 hot showers, 9 WCs, 2 CWPs

	🏕️🚐	🅰	🚃	🎿					🐕

Car & caravan, Motor caravan, Car & tent, M/cycle & tent £2.05; all plus £2.05 per adult, 51p per child; elec £1.53, awn £1.03
Our park is small and quiet and surrounded by woodland which has an abundance of wild flowers and wildlife. 10 caravans for hire (own WCs). Restaurant 1 mile. Swimming pool 2 miles. No groups - family camping only.
From Skipton take B6265 signposted Grassington. In 9 miles at Threshfield take B6160 for 50 yards, turn left into "Skirethorns Lane". Follow signposts 600 yards and 300 yards. Park entrance on left.

THURSTATON *Merseyside* Map 4 B2

Wirral Country Camping & Caravan Club
Station Road, L61 0HN. ☎ (051) 648 5228
Open: March-November
Size: 1½ acres, 107 touring pitches. 6 hot showers, 9 WCs

	⌂🚐		🚃						🐕

Access from A540 through village.

TILSHEAD *Wiltshire* Map 2 B3

BRADES ACRE CARAVAN SITE RAC A
Near Salisbury, SP3 4RX. ☎ (0980) 620402
Open: 1 April-31 October
Size: 1½ acres, 25 touring pitches, all level, 19 with elec. 2 hot showers, 4 WCs, 1 CWP

	🏕️🚐	🅰	🚃						🐕

Car & caravan, Motor caravan, Car & tent, M/cycle & tent £5.50, plus 50p per person above 4; elec £1, awn £1; WS
Flat grass site, central to most sightseeing places, surrounded by trees and scenic views, nice walks. Shop 200 yards, restaurant 300 yards. Swimming pool 8 miles. Maximum stay 28 days.

▣ Snacks/take away ✗ Restaurant ◺ Swimming pool 🏠 Shelter for campers 🐕 Dogs accepted   131

10 miles S of Devizes on the A360, site on right at far side of village.

BOSSINEY FARM CARAVAN SITE   RAC L
PL34 0AY. ☎ (0840) 770481
Open: April-October
Size: 2 (3) acres, 30 touring pitches, 12 with elec, 20 level pitches, 20 static caravans. 4 hot showers, 8 WCs, 1 CWP

(1991) Car & caravan, Motor caravan, Car & tent, M/cycle* & tent all £2.50 per adult, £1.40 per child; elec £1.50, awn £1
Small, sheltered, farm site with flat terraces and electric hook-ups. 19 caravans for hire (own WCs). Restaurant ½ mile. Swimming pool 4 miles.
Site on the S side of the B3263, ¾ mile NE of Tintagel.

The Headland
☎ (0840) 770239
Open: Easter-October
Size: 5 acres, 62 touring pitches. 5 hot showers, 13 WCs. 28 static caravans

Site ½ mile NW of Tintagel off B3263.

OCEAN COVE CARAVAN PARK   RAC L
☎ (0840) 770325
Open: 1 April-30 September
Size: 1 (7½) acres, 20 touring pitches, all level, 12 with elec, 130 static caravans, 9 chalets. 6 hot showers, 32 WCs, 1 CWP

Charges on application.
Pleasant site with sea views. Family groups only. Children's play area and licensed bar on site. Caravans and chalets for hire. Restaurant 50 yards.
At ¾ mile NE of Tintagel on B3263.

MINNOWS CAMPING & CARAVAN PARK   RAC L
Sampford Peverell, EX16 6LD.
☎ (0884) 252652
Open: 1 April-31 October
Size: 2 acres, 41 touring pitches, 8 with elec, 36 level pitches. 4 hot showers, 6 WCs, 1 CWP

Car & caravan from £4.90, Motor caravan from £4.40, Car & tent, M/cycle & tent from £3.10; plus 75p per person above 2 (under 5 years free); elec from £1.45, awn £1
Small touring park with modern facilities. Fishing in Grand Western Canal which borders the park. Pleasant canal towpath walk to village. Easy to find but with lovely countryside views. No gas available (shop in village, ½ mile). Restaurant ½ mile. Swimming pool 6 miles.
From M5 Junction 27 take A361, take first exit left and follow brown signs.

West Middlewick Farm
Nomansland, EX16 8NP. ☎ (0884) 860286
Open: All year
Size: 3 acres, 15 touring pitches. 1 hot shower, 2 WCs

Site 8 miles W of Tiverton, to N of B3137 (formerly A373).

CARBEIL CARAVAN & CAMPING PARK   RAC L
Downderry. ☎ (05035) 636
Open: Easter-October
Size: 1¼ acres, 20 touring pitches, part level, 7 static caravans. 4 hot showers, 7 WCs, 1 CWP

Charges on application.
Newly recognised by the RAC for 1992.
From A387, turn S on to B3247 for Seaton, and continue towards Downderry. Turn left at St Nicholas Church for site.

Whitsand Bay Holiday Park
Millbrook, PL10 1JZ. ☎ (0752) 822597
Open: April-October
Size: 20 acres, 80 touring pitches. 12 hot showers, 12 WCs. 100 static caravans

At Antony (A374), turn S on to B3247 for 1¼ miles. At t-junction, turn left for ¼ mile, then right on to Cliff Road. Site 2 miles.

WIDDICOMBE FARM CARAVAN PARK   RAC A
Ring Road (A380), Compton, TQ3 1ST.
☎ (0803) 558325
Open: Easter-Mid October

Size: 8 (38) acres, 200 touring pitches, all level, 62 with elec, 3 static caravans. 20 hot showers, 28 WCs, 4 CWPs

(1991) Car & caravan, Motor caravan, Car & tent, M/cycle & tent from £4.50, plus £1.50 per person above 2; elec £1.25, awn 50p, dogs 50p; WS
Family-run site on working farm with children's play area. Restaurant ½ mile. Swimming pool 2 miles.
From Exeter follow signs to Torbay and A380. After 15 miles turn right at roundabout on to A3022 (new dual-carriageway opened in 1991).

Manor Farm Camp Site
Manor Farm, Daccombe, TQ12 4ST.
☎ (0803) 328294
Open: June-September
Size: 3 acres, 75 touring pitches. 8 hot showers, 15 WCs

On A380 Newton Abbot-Torquay, turn left after roundabout on outskirts of Torquay. Take second left for site.

TORRINGTON *Devon*   Map 1 B2

Greenways Valley Holiday Park
☎ (0805) 22153
Open: March-October
Size: 8 acres, 8 touring pitches. 2 hot showers, 5 WCs. 5 static caravans, 14 chalets

E of Torrington, turn S off B3227 into Borough Road. Follow Tourist Board signs.

SMYTHAM MANOR HOLIDAYS   RAC L
Little Torrington, EX38 8PU.
☎ (0805) 22110
Open: 15 March-31 October
Size: 2 (14) acres, 30 touring pitches, 10 with elec, 20 level pitches, 3 with hardstanding, 40 static caravans, 7 chalets .4 hot showers, 12 WCs, 1 CWP

(1991) Car & caravan, Motor caravan, Car & tent, M/cycle & tent from £4.50, plus 50p per person above 4; elec £1, awn 50p, dogs £1; WS
cc Access, Visa/B'card
A wooded country park with children's play area, TV room and bar. 20 caravans and 7 chalets for hire (own WCs). One chalet designed and equipped for disabled people.
2 miles S of Torrington on A386, between Barn Cross Garage and Gribble Inn.

TRURO *Cornwall*   Map 1 A3

CARNON DOWNS CARAVAN & CAMPING PARK   RAC L
Carnon Downs, TR3 6JJ. ☎ (0872) 862283
Open: 1 April-31 October
Size: 10 acres, 150 touring pitches, all level, 84 with elec, 6 with hardstanding. 8 hot showers, 18 WCs, 2 CWPs

Car & caravan, Motor caravan, Car & tent, M/cycle* & tent £5-£7.50, plus £1.25 per person (child under

5 years free); Tent £2, M/cycle* £3.50; elec £1.25; WS
10 acres of short-cut grass and 4 acres of woodland, 84 electric hook-ups, situated in attractively landscaped pitches. Excellent facilities and plenty of space for everyone. Special facilities for babies and children: baths, etc, in own heated room. Restaurant 2 miles. Swimming pool 3 miles. Single-sex parties not encouraged.
On the A39 2½ W of Truro.

Cosawes Caravan Park
Perranarworthal. ☎ (0872) 863724
Open: All year
Size: 100 acres, 40 touring pitches. 2 hot showers, 6 WCs

6 miles S of Truro (A39), site signed near Norway Inn.

LEVERTON PLACE CARAVAN & CAMPING PARK   RAC A
Green Bottom, TR4 8QW. ☎ (0872) 560462
Open: All year
Size: 9½ acres, 120 touring pitches, 70 with elec, all level, 15 static caravans, 7 chalets. 25 hot showers, 40 WCs, 3 CWPs

(1991) Car & caravan, Motor caravan, Car & tent, M/cycle* & tent £5.50-£11, plus £1.75 per adult above 2, child £1; elec £1.50, dogs £1; WS
cc Access, Visa/B'card
A 9½ acre park, 3 miles west of the beautiful city of Truro. An excellent location for touring and exploring Cornwall. 15 caravans and 7 chalets for hire (own WCs).
From A30 take A390 to Truro. 2 miles at roundabout turn right, take road to Chalewater from Threemile Stone. Leverton Place is on right.

LISKEY TOURING PARK   RAC L
Green Bottom, Chacewater, TR4 8QN.
☎ (0872) 560274
Open: 1 April-30 September
Size: 4 (8) acres, 68 touring pitches, 29 with elec, 40 level pitches, 11 with hardstanding. 4 hot showers, 8 WCs, 1 CWP

Car & caravan, Motor caravan, Car & tent, M/cycle & tent £4.50-£7, plus £1.40 per adult above 2, child 80p; extra car £1; elec £1.30, first dog free then £1
Quiet meadowland site for family groups. Adventure playground and colour TV lounge. Restaurant 600 yards. Swimming pool 3 miles. No skateboards, bicycles, roller skates to be used on site. No single-sex groups.
From A30, turn left onto A390 (5 miles W of Truro). At next roundabout turn right signposted Threemile Stone, then right at mini-roundabout. Site 600 yards on right.

RINGWELL HOLIDAY PARK   RAC A
Bissoe Road, Carnon Downs, TR3 6LQ.
☎ (0872) 862194
Open: Easter-31 October
Size: 4 (12) acres, 45 touring pitches, 16 with elec, 30 level pitches, 2 with hardstanding, 30 static caravans. 30 hot showers, 16 WCs, 1 CWP

⬛ Snacks/take away ☒ Restaurant ◺ Swimming pool ▣ Shelter for campers ⵍ Dogs accepted   **133**

Charges on application.
Grassy site in quiet, sheltered, rural valley, only a short drive from both the north and south coasts. Facilities include pool room, Biergarten overlooking heated swimming pool, licensed club bar, games room, children's playground, toddlers' sandpit. 28 caravans for hire (own WCs). ETB graded 4 Ticks and Rose Award.
A39 to Truro and then Falmouth road for approximately 2 miles. Playing Place Garage on left, then 1 mile further on you enter Carnon Downs. Take the Bissoe Road which is on the right just before the traffic lights. Continue for ¾ mile along this road and our entrance is on the right.

SUMMER VALLEY TOURING PARK   RAC L
Shortlanesend, TR4 9DW.
☎ (0872) 77878
Open: 1 April-31 October
Size: 3 acres, 60 touring pitches, 20 with elec, 20 level pitches. 4 hot showers, 7 WCs, 1 CWP

(1991) Car & caravan, Motor caravan, Car & tent, M/cycle & tent from £4-£5.50, plus £1.25 per adult above 2, child 60p; elec £1.25; WS
An attractive and secluded family site personally run by the owners. Play area on site. Shop open May-September. Restaurant and swimming pool 2 miles.
From Truro town centre, travel NW on the B3284 for 2¾ miles, turn left to site.

TUXFORD *Nottinghamshire*   Map 5 A2

Greenacres
Lincoln Road, NG22 0JN.
☎ (0777) 870264
Open: April-October
Size: 3½ acres, 75 touring pitches. 4 hot showers, 9 WCs. 6 static caravans

Site 1 mile E of Tuxford, N of A6075.

Longbow Caravan Park
Milton Road, Markham Moor, Retford
☎ (0777) 871450
Open: All year
Size: 1 acre, 20 touring pitches. 5 hot showers, 5 WCs

2 miles N of Tuxford, leave A1 at Markham Moor roundabout and take Milton/Walesby exit. Site in 200 yards.

UFFCULME *Devon*   Map 2 A3

The Waterloo Inn Camping & Caravan Park
The Waterloo Inn.
☎ (0884) 40317
Open: March-November
Size: 5 acres, 50 touring pitches. 6 hot showers, 10 WCs

From M5 junction 27, turn E on Willand/Wellington road. Site 500 yards.

ULLSWATER *Cumbria*   Map 4 B1

COVE CARAVAN & CAMPING PARK   RAC A
Watermillock, CA11 0LS. ☎ (07684) 86549
Open: March-31 October
Size: 2½ (5) acres, 50 touring pitches, 12 with elec, 20 level pitches, 2 with hardstanding, 38 static caravans. 4 hot showers, 4 cold showers, 8 WCs, 1 CWP

Car & caravan, Motor caravan £2.50-£3, Car & tent, M/cycle & tent £2.20-£2.40; all plus £1.10-£1.20 per person; elec £1.10-£1.20, awn £1.10-£1.20, dogs 50p
cc Major cards
Peaceful park, sheltered by nearby fells, overlooking Lake Ullswater. Super toilet block, hand dryers, hair dryers, dish washing area, freezer for ice-packs, shop nearby, children's play area, telephone, electric hook-ups. Convenient for walking, fishing, boating, pony trekking, windsurfing. 1 caravan for hire (own WC). Restaurant 1½ miles. Swimming pool 4½ miles.
From M6 junction 40 take A66 to Keswick, at next roundabout take A592 to Ullswater. Turn right at t-junction, then right at Brackenrigg Hotel. Park is 1½ miles on the left hand side.

HILLCROFT PARK   RAC L
Pooley Bridge, CA10 2LT. ☎ (07684) 86363
Open: 9 March-28 October
Size: 7 (21) acres, 200 touring pitches, 45 with elec, 100 level pitches, 190 static caravans, 29 chalets. 20 hot showers, 36 WCs, 3 CWPs

Car & caravan, Motor caravan, Car & tent £1-£2, all plus £2 per person; awn £1
Level, well-drained site (nearest to Pooley Bridge village), with modern toilet blocks and showers (hot water free). Elevated site with lake views offering quiet family camping only. Restaurant 200 yards. Swimming pool 3 miles. No motorcycles. No groups.
In Pooley Bridge village centre, turn right by church (signed Howtown), at crossroads go straight across up Roe Head Lane. Site is on left hand side.

PARK FOOT CARAVAN & CAMPING PARK   RAC L
Howtown Road, Pooley Bridge, CA10 2NA.
☎ (07684) 86309
Open: Mid March-31 October
Size: 25 (100) acres, 300 touring pitches, 150 level pitches, 57 with elec, 6 with hardstanding, 124 static caravans, 12 chalets. 24 hot showers, 40 WCs, 1 CWP

Car & caravan £4.50, Motor caravan, Car & tent, M/cycle & tent £3; all plus £1.75 per adult, 75p per child (5-14 years); elec £2, awn £1.50, dogs free
Free access to Lake Ullswater. Licensed bar and restaurant. Adventure and 2 children's play areas, pony trekking. Public telephones. Mountain bike hire. Tourist Board grade 4 Ticks (Very Good). 12 chalets for hire (own WCs). Indoor swimming pool 6 miles, outdoor 3 miles.
M6 junction 40, A66 Keswick/Ullswater, take A592 to Ullswater, at t-junction left to Pooley Bridge, right at church and right at crossroads,

1 mile on Howtown road, park is on left.

THE QUIET SITE RĀC A
Watermillock, CA11 0LS. ☎ (07684) 86337
Open: 1 March-31 October
Size: 5 (6) acres, 60 touring pitches, 30 with elec, 50 level pitches, 10 with hardstanding, 23 static caravans. 8 hot showers, 15 WCs, 1 CWP

Car & caravan, Motor caravan, Car & tent, M/cycle & tent £5, plus 50p per person above 2 (under 4 years free); elec £1.25, awn £1.25, dogs 25p; WS *Idyllic setting amongst the fells. English Tourist Board grading: Excellent. Large adventure playground and "probably" the best campsite bar in Britain. Family run site. Help with siting touring caravans always extended. Quiet after 10pm, ie. no loud TV or radios or talking. TV and games room. 2 caravans for hire (own WCs). Restaurant 1¼ miles (bar food available on site).*
From junction 40 of the M6 SW of Penrith, follow signs "Keswick" on the A66 for ¾ mile to roundabout, turn left on A592 for 5 miles, turn right at Brackenrigg Hotel for 1½ miles to site, signposted on right.

WATERFOOT CARAVAN PARK RĀC L
Pooley Bridge, CA11 0JF. ☎ (07684) 86302
Open: 1 March-31 October
Size: 4 (20) acres, 65 touring pitches, 45 with elec, 45 level pitches, 115 static caravans. 12 hot showers, 12 WCs, 1 CWP

Charges on application.
Peaceful, partially wooded site overlooking Lake Ullswater. Licensed bar and children's play area. Calor gas only. Restaurant 2 miles. Swimming pool 5 miles.
From junction 40 of the M6 near Penrith, follow signs 'A66 Keswick' and after ¾ mile to roundabout, turn left on the A592 for 3¼ miles to site on right.

Bardsea Leisure Caravan Park
Priory Road. ☎ (0229) 54712
Open: All year
Size: 10 acres, 80 touring pitches, 6 hot showers, 20 WCs. 75 static caravans

Site 1 mile S of Ulverston on A5087.

Cavendish Garage
Doveridge, DE6 5JR. ☎ (0889) 562092
Open: All year
Size: 2 acres, 15 touring pitches. 1 WC

Site in Doveridge on A50.

TRETHEAKE MANOR TOURIST PARK RĀC L
Near Truro, TR2 5PP. ☎ (0872) 501658
Open: Easter-31 October
Size: 8 (9) acres, 175 touring pitches, 53 with elec, 100 level pitches. 8 hot showers, 20 WCs, 1 CWP

Charges on application.
cc Access, Visa/B'card
Quiet, rural site with shrubs and partly bounded by mature trees. Some of site gently sloping. Children's play area, games and TV rooms. Coarse fishing lake adjacent. Restaurant 1 mile.
From St Austell take the A390 towards Truro. Turn left on to the B3287 at Hewas Water. At Tregony turn left on to the A3078 for 1½ miles, where turn left on to unclassified road, past garage. Follow signs to site.

The Bridge Inn
Michaelchurch Escley, HR2 0JW. ☎ (098 123) 646
Open: April-October
Size: 2½ acres, 8 touring pitches. 2 hot showers, 2 WCs

In Vowchurch (B4348), turn W on minor road signposted Michaelchurch Escley. At t-junction near village turn left, then left 300 yards after church.

Carlyon Farm
St Minver. ☎ (020 886) 3429
Open: April-October
Size: 7 acres, 40 touring pitches. 4 hot showers, 7 WCs

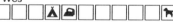

Site NW of Wadebridge, on banks of Camel Estuary.

■ Snacks/take away ✗ Restaurant ◣ Swimming pool ▣ Shelter for campers ⊞ Dogs accepted   135

DINHAM FARM CARAVAN & CAMPING PARK 🏢 L

St Minver, PL27 6RH.
☎ (0208) 880564/812878
Open: 1 April-31 October
Size: 3 acres, 40 touring pitches, 30 level pitches, 15 with elec, 8 "super" pitches, 20 static caravans. 4 hot showers, 12 WCs, 1 CWP

Car & caravan, Motor caravan, Car & tent, M/cycle & tent all £5-£6 for 2 persons, £1.50 per adult above 2, 50p per child; elec £1,50, awn 50p, dogs 80p; WS
Luxury caravans on secluded park with trees and shrubs overlooking the River Camel. Heated outdoor swimming pool. New "super" pitches. Free hot water/showers. 7 caravans for hire (all with own WCs and showers). Shop 2 miles. Restaurant 1½ miles.
At ½ mile E of Wadebridge on A39, turn N on B3314 for 2¼ miles, then turn W for 200 yards.

GUNVENNA TOURING CARAVAN & CAMPING PARK 🏢 L

St Minver. ☎ (0208) 862405
Open: April-October
Size: 9 (10) acres, 75 touring pitches. 6 hot showers, 22 WCs

Charges on application.
A well-kept, family-run site on level grassland. Children's play area and indoor games room.
From Wadebridge, travel N on the B3314 for 4½ miles to site on right.

Lanarth Hotel Caravan Park

St Kew Highway.
☎ (0208) 84215
Open: April-October
Size: 10 acres, 86 touring pitches. 4 hot showers, 9 WCs

Site 3 miles NE of Wadebridge on A39.

The Laurels

Whitecross, PL27 7JQ.
☎ (0208) 813341
Open: April-October
Size: 2½ acres, 30 touring pitches. 4 hot showers, 8 WCs

Site ½ mile S of Whitecross at A39/A389 junction.

LITTLE BODIEVE HOLIDAY PARK 🏢 A

Bodieve, PL27 6EG. ☎ (0208) 812323
Open: Easter-31 October
Size: 15 (22½) acres, 195 touring pitches, all level, 51 with elec, 42 static caravans. 24 hot showers, 24 cold showers, 20 WCs, 3 CWPs

(1991) Car & caravan, Motor caravan, Car & tent £2.55 per adult, £1.15 per child; elec £1.50, awn 75p, dog £1; WS
Family site run by a family. Graded 5 Ticks by British Tourist Board. Rose Award 1991, 1992. Pay phone. Battery charging. Mother and baby room. Play area. Launderette. Crazy golf. 16 caravans for hire (own WCs). Restaurant ½ mile (bar meals available on park). No minimum stay restrictions. No motorcycles. No groups of single-sex persons.
At ½ mile E of Wadebridge on A39, turn N on B3314 and follow signs.

Lundynant Caravan Park

St Minver. ☎ (0208) 862268
Open: April-October
Size: 5 acres, 25 touring pitches. 3 hot showers, 14 WCs. Static caravans

From A39, turn NW on to B3314, fork left towards Polzeath. Site on road to New Polzeath.

Ponderosa Caravan Park

St Issey, PL27 7QA. ☎ (0841) 540359
Open: Easter-October
Size: 4 acres, 60 touring pitches. 2 hot showers, 6 WCs

Site on A389 near St Issey village.

ST MINVER HOLIDAY PARK 🏢 A

St Minver, PL27 6RR. ☎ (020 886) 2305
Open: Easter-October
Size: 45 acres, 75 touring pitches, all level, 24 with elec, 118 static caravans, 26 chalets. 22 hot showers, 28 WCs, CWPs

Charges on application.
Holiday park in grounds of former manor house. Playground, evening entertainment, bars, TV lounges and games rooms. 114 caravans and 26 chalets for hire (own WCs).
½ mile E of Wadebridge on A39, turn N on B3314 for 3 miles where turn W as signed 'Pityme-Rock Trebetherick' for 300 yards.

Southwinds Camping Site
Polzeath, St Minver. ☎ (0208) 863267
Open: Easter-October
Size: 5 acres, 100 touring pitches. 4 hot showers, 15 WCs

From A39, turn NW on to B3314, fork left towards Polzeath. Site ¾ mile E of Polzeath.

TREWINCE HOLIDAY PARK　　　　　RAC A
St Issey, PL27 7RL. ☎ (0208) 812830
Open: Easter-31 October
Size: 8 acres, 80 touring pitches, all level, 24 with elec, 4 with hardstanding, 21 static caravans. 11 hot showers, 15 WCs, 2 CWPs

Car & caravan, Motor caravan, Car & tent, M/cycle & tent all £2.25-£3.25 per adult, £1-£1.50 per child; extra car 50p; elec £1.50; WS
A rural wooded park with games room, crazy golf and children's play area. Terraced, south-facing slope. 21 caravans for hire (own WCs). Restaurant ½ mile. Polzeath, Constantine Bay, Halyn Bay and Treyarnon Bay are all within easy reach and have been given prestigious awards.
From Wadebridge, travel W on the A39 for 2½ miles, turn right on the A389 for 1¼ miles, turn left on unclassified road to site on right in 200 yards.

WAKEFIELD *West Yorkshire*　　　　Map 5 A2

NOSTELL PRIORY HOLIDAY PARK　　RAC L
Nostell, WF4 1QD. ☎ (0924) 863938
Open: 1 April-1 October
Size: 3 (30) acres, 60 touring pitches, all level, all with elec, 7 with hardstanding, 80 static caravans. 8 hot showers, 12 WCs, 1 CWP

(1991) Car & caravan, Motor caravan, Car & tent, M/cycle* & tent £5.50, plus 50p per person above 2, under 5 years free; elec £1, awn £1
Beautiful woodland park on the estate of one of Yorkshire's most loved stately homes, Nostell Priory. Grassy, level and sheltered. Amenities to a high standard. Well-equipped holiday homes for hire. Shop 1½ miles. Restaurant ½ mile. Swimming pool 5 miles. Saturday to Saturday bookings only in holiday homes.
From Wakefield, travel on the Doncaster road A638 for 5 miles. From the junction of the A1 (M), A1 and A638, travel NW along A638 for 7 miles.

WALLINGFORD *Oxfordshire*　　　Map 2 B2

Benson Cruisers
Benson, OX10 6SJ. ☎ (0491) 38304
Open: Easter-October
Size: 3 acres, 25 touring pitches. 4 hot showers, 6 WCs. Static caravans

Site 1½ miles NE of Wallingford on A423.

BRIDGE VILLA INTERNATIONAL CAMPING & CARAVAN PARK　　RAC L
Crowmarsh Gifford, DX10 8HB.
☎ (0491) 36860
Open: 1 March-31 October

Size: 2 (4) acres, 120 touring pitches, all level, all with elec. 4 hot showers, 4 cold showers, 13 WCs, 2 CWPs

(1991) Car & caravan, Motor caravan, Car & tent, M/cycle & tent £3.50, plus 75p per person above 4; extra car 75p; elec £1.50, awn 75p; WS
A country site, recently landscaped, within 5-7 minutes' walking distance of the River Thames and old market town of Wallingford (oldest borough) with all facilities. Site not commercialised. Restaurant 500 metres. Swimming pool 600 metres. No minimum stay.
At ¼ mile E of Wallingford on A4130.

RIVERSIDE PARK　　　　　　RAC L
Crowmarsh. ☎ (0491) 35351
Open: May-September
Size: 1 acre, 25 touring pitches. 6 hot showers, 6 WCs

(1991) Car & caravan, Motor caravan, Car & tent, M/cycle & tent £4-£6
Site is well-situated with an air of rural spaciousness and is ideal for touring picturesque villages of the Thames Valley and Chiltern Hills. Restaurant 300 yards. 14 days maximum stay. No dogs.
Approach Riverside from the E (the A423) as the access is at the end of Wallingford Bridge which is walled, narrow, and has lights controlling a single file of traffic.

WAREHAM *Dorset*　　　　　Map 2 A3

Wareham Forest Tourist Park
North Trigon, BH20 7NZ. ☎ (0929) 551393
Open: All year
Size: 42 acres, 100 touring caravan pitches, 100 tent pitches. 10 hot showers, 25 WCs

Site is off the A35 on Bere Road between Bere Regis and Wareham.

East Creech Farm
☎ (0929) 480519
Open: March-October
Size: 2 acres, 60 touring pitches. 4 hot showers, 6 WCs

Site 3½ miles S of Wareham.

HUNTER'S MOON CARAVAN & CAMPING PARK　　　　　　RAC L
Cold Harbour, BH20 7PA. ☎ (0929) 556605
Open: Easter-31 October
Size: 5 acres, 90 touring pitches, most level, all with elec. 8 hot showers, 14 WCs, 4 CWPs

Car & caravan, Motor caravan, Car & tent, M/cycle & tent £5-£6, plus £1 per person above 2, child 50p; elec 31.30, awn 50p-£1, dogs 50p
A quiet, wooded, family-run site with a children's play area. Restaurant ½ mile. Swimming pool 2½ miles. No large single-sex groups. Dogs to be kept on leads at all times.
From Bere Regis travel E on the A35 for 1 mile then

◼ Snacks/take away ☒ Restaurant ◠ Swimming pool ▣ Shelter for campers 🐕 Dogs accepted　　137

turn SE onto unclassified road, signposted
'Wareham' and with brown and white site signs for
3½ miles to site on right.

THE LOOKOUT CARAVAN PARK RAC A
Stoborough, BH20 5AZ. ☎ (0929) 552546
Open: 1 April-31 October
Size: 7 (15) acres, 150 touring pitches, all level,
80 with elec, 50 with hardstanding, 50 static
caravans. 10 hot showers, 14 WCs, 2 CWPs

Car & caravan, Motor caravan, Car & tent, M/cycle
& tent £6.50-£8; elec £1.50, awn £1.50; WS
*A neat and tidy family site, with games room and
children's play area. 50 caravans for hire (own
WCs). Restaurant and swimming pool 1 mile. No
dogs.*
Take new Wareham by-pass and turn off for
Stoborough at the roundabout. Park is on right
hand side.

MANOR FARM CARAVAN PARK RAC L
East Stoke, BH20 6AW. ☎ (0929) 462870
Open: Easter-30 September
Size: 2½ acres, 40 touring pitches, all level, 20 with
elec. 4 hot showers, 8 WCs, 1 CWP

Charges on application. WS
*Flat, clean, grassy site, family-run and quiet. Ideal
for all areas of Dorset. Seasonal pitches available.
Restaurant 2 miles, pub 1 mile. Swimming pool
4 miles. No groups, singles or motorcycles.*
Take A352 from Wareham, turn left on to B3070. At
second crossroads turn right, next crossroads turn
right to site on left.

Ridge Farm Caravan Park
Barnhill Road, BH20 5BG. ☎ (0929) 552347
Open: May-September
Size: 3½ acres, 60 touring pitches. 6 hot showers,
12 WCs

Site adjacent to Marina.

WARMWELL *Dorset* **Map 2 A3**

WARMWELL TOURING PARK RAC A
DT2 8JE. ☎ (0305) 852313
Open: Mid March-December
Size: 15 acres, 190 touring pitches, 120 with elec.
12 hot showers, 30 WCs, 2 CWPs

Charges on application.
*Family-run site situated in an old quarry and
divided up by trees. Extensive facilities in adjacent
leisure resort available to campers.*
Take A35 W from Bere Regis, turn left after
1½ miles on to B3390. Site on left in 7 miles.

WARRINGTON *Cheshire* **Map 4 B2**

HOLLYBANK CARAVAN PARK RAC A
Warburton Bridge Road, Rixton, WA3 6HU.
☎ (061) 775 2842
Open: All year
Size: 4½ (8½) acres, 60 touring pitches, all level,
44 with elec, 50 with hardstanding. 4 hot showers,
9 WCs, 1 CWP

(1991) Car & caravan, Motor caravan £3.50, Car &
tent, M/cycle* & tent £2.50; all plus £1.50 per adult,

£1 per child; elec £1.75, awn £1, dogs free; WS
Situated in open countryside between Manchester and Warrington. Ideal base for touring North West, Peak District, Yorkshire Dales, North Wales. Convenient night halt off M6, M62, M56. Restaurant ¼ mile. Swimming pool 3 miles. Maximum stay 28 days. ETB graded 4 Ticks. From junction 21 of the M6 E of Warrington travel E on A57 for 2¼ miles, turn right on unclassified road, entrance to site 100 yards on left.

WARWICK Warwickshire — Map 2 B1

Warwick Racecourse Caravan Club Site
☎ (0926) 495448
Open: March-October
Size: 40 touring pitches. Hot showers, 4b WCs

Site on B4095 to W of Warwick.

WATCHET Somerset — Map 2 A3

DONIFORD HOLIDAY PARK RAC A
TA23 0TJ. ☎ (0984) 32423
Open: Easter-October
Size: 4 (49) acres, 100 touring pitches, 37 with elec, 70 level pitches, 288 static caravans, 134 chalets. 12 hot showers, 24 WCs, 2 CWPs

Charges on application.
cc Access, Visa/B'card
Organised holiday village with excellent leisure facilities including sports hall and heated indoor pool. Children's indoor adventure playground. 63 caravans and 134 chalets for hire (own WCs). Restaurant 1½ miles.
Take the A39 from Bridgwater towards Minehead. At Williton turn N on to B3191 then NE signposted Doniford. Cross railway then turn right at t-junction. Site signposted.

Sunnybank Caravan Park
Doniford. ☎ (0984) 32237
Open: March-October
Size: 2½ acres, 16 touring pitches. 4 hot showers, 4 WCs. 30 static caravans

From A39, turn N to Doniford/Watchet. Turn right at bottom of hill, then right to site.

WARREN BAY CARAVAN & CAMPING PARK RAC A
☎ (0984) 31460
Open: March-End October
Size: 11 (22) acres, 75 touring pitches, static caravans. 6 hot showers, 45 WCs

Charges on application.
A gently sloping site overlooking the sea with access to the beach. Caravans for hire.
1 mile W of Watchet on B3191.

Warren Farm
Blue Anchor. ☎ (0984) 31220
Open: Easter-September
Size: 12 acres, 100 touring pitches. 10 hot showers, 23 WCs

Site 1½ miles W of Watchet on B3191.

WATERBEACH Cambridgeshire — Map 3 A1

Landbeach Marina Park
Ely Road. ☎ (0223) 860019
Open: April-October
Size: 120 acres, 600 touring pitches. 12 hot showers, 4b WCs

Site 2 miles N of Waterbeach, to W of A10.

WELLINGTON Somerset — Map 2 A3

GAMLINS FARM CARAVAN SITE RAC A
Greenham, TA21 0LZ. ☎ (0823) 672596
Open: 1 March-31 October
Size: 3 acres, 25 touring pitches 4 hot showers, 5 WCs, 1 CWP

(1991) Car & caravan, Motor caravan £6, Car & tent £5, plus £1 per adult above 2, child 75p; elec £1.50, awn £1, dogs 50p; WS
A pleasant, quiet site with excellent views. Children's play area. Coarse fishing available nearby.
From Wellington, travel SW on the A38 for 5 miles, turning right at sign for Greenham Caravan Park.

WELLS Somerset — Map 7 A3

Beaconsfield Farm
Easton, BA5 1DU. ☎ (0749) 870308
Open: All year
Size: 4 acres, 5 touring pitches. 1 WC

Site 2½ miles NW of Wells on A371.

Beechbarrow Camping & Caravanning
Pen Hill. ☎ (0749) 76387
Open: All year
Size: 2 acres, 3+ touring pitches. 1 WC

Site 3 miles N of Wells, to E of A39.

Ebborlands
Wookey Hole. ☎ (0749) 72550
Open: Easter-October
Size: 2 acres, 20 touring pitches. 5 WCs

Site 1 mile E of Easton.

HOMESTEAD PARK RAC A
Wookey Hole, BA5 1BW. ☎ (0749) 73022
Open: Easter-31 October
Size: 2 acres, 50 touring pitches, all level, 6 with elec, 1 static caravan. 2 hot showers, 2 cold showers, 13 WCs, 1 CWP

(1991) Car & caravan £7, Motor caravan £6.50, Car & tent, M/cycle & tent £7.20, plus £1.20 per person above 2; Car £1; Tent £1.30; elec £1.60, awn £1.30, dogs 70p
The touring area is bounded by the River Axe and is composed of level grassland with metalled roads, with screening and shelter provided by

---

■ Snacks/take away　⊠ Restaurant　◩ Swimming pool　▣ Shelter for campers　⋔ Dogs accepted　　**139**

hedges and trees. It is pleasantly secluded and offers a peaceful haven for those wanting a quiet holiday located within easy reach of many interesting places inland as well as north and south coasts. Restaurant 100 yards. Dogs on leads.
Leave Wells to W on A371 and then turn N as signed Wookey Hole. Site in 1¼ miles.

MENDIP HEIGHTS CAMPING & CARAVAN PARK   RAC A
Townsend, Priddy, BA5 3BP. ☎ (0749) 870241
Open: 1 March-31 October
Size: 4½ acres, 90 touring pitches, 6 with elec, 5 with hardstanding, 2 static caravans. 4 hot showers, 11 WCs, 1 CWP

Charges on application.
A quiet family site, with children's play area, in peaceful, open country on the Mendip Hills. Close to Cheddar Gorge. Riding and caving. 2 caravans for hire. Swimming pool 4 miles.
At 3½ miles NE of Wells on the A39, turn W on the B3135 for 4½ miles, turn S as signed to site.

WELLS-NEXT-THE-SEA Norfolk   Map 3 B1

High Sand Creek Camping Site
Stiffkey. ☎ (0328) 830479
Open: April-October
Size: 2 acres, 80 touring pitches. 8 hot showers, 3b WCs

Turn N off A149 ½ mile W of Stiffkey.

Pinewoods Caravan & Camping Holiday Park
Beach Road. ☎ (0328) 710439
Open: April-October
Size: 75 acres, 200 touring pitches. 66 hot showers, 143 WCs. 600 static caravans

Turn N off A149 in Wells and follow signs to beach.

WEM Shropshire   Map 4 B3

LOWER LACON CARAVAN PARK   RAC A
Lerdene, Crabtree Lane, Wemsbrook Road, SY4 5RP. ☎ (0939) 32376
Open: All year
Size: 36 acres, 270 touring pitches, all level, 100 with elec, 30 with hardstanding, 50 static caravans. 16 hot showers, 24 WCs, 4 CWPs

Car & caravan, Motor caravan, Car & tent, M/cycle & tent £6.70-£7.20
cc Major cards (minimum £20)
Spacious site, with a children's play area, mini- and crazy golf and dancing in the Dutch barn. Lounge bar. 4 caravans for hire (own WCs). Restaurant 1 mile. Families and couples only. Payment for electric hook-up must be made in full with booking.
From Shrewsbury, travel N on the A49 for 8¾ miles, turn left on the B5063 to Wem, turn right on the B5065 for 1½ miles to site on left.

WEST WITTERING West Sussex   Map 2 B3

Gee's Camp
127 Stocks Lane, East Wittering, PO20 8MY.

☎ (0243) 670223
Open: March-October
Size: 1 acre, 25 touring pitches. 2 hot showers, 4 WCs

On B2179 W from Bracklesham, site on right opposite British Legion.

Nunnington Farm
☎ (0243) 514013
Open: Easter-October
Size: 4½ acres, 112 touring pitches. 4 hot showers, 16 WCs

Approaching West Wittering from NE (B2179), turn left for site.

Red House Farm
Bookers Lane, Earnley, PO20 7JG.
☎ (0243) 512959
Open: April-October
Size: 4 acres, 100 touring pitches. 4 hot showers, 12 WCs

From A286, turn S on B2198 to Bracklesham Bay for ½ mile, then left into Bookers Lane.

Scotts Farm
PO20 8ED. ☎ (0243) 672185
Open: March-October
Size: 25 acres, 650 touring pitches. 16 hot showers, 3b WCs. 230 static caravans

From East Wittering, site third turning on right after village centre on B2179.

WICKS FARM CARAVAN PARK   RAC L
Redlands Lane, PO20 8QD.
☎ (0243) 513116
Open: 7 March-31 October inclusive
Size: 4 (14) acres, 40 touring pitches, all level, all with elec, 67 static caravans. 8 hot showers, 11 WCs, 1 CWP

(1991) Motor caravan, Car & tent, M/cycle* & tent £7, plus 50p per person above* ; elec £1
Peaceful, rural park with all modern facilities, sheltered by trees within landscaped grounds. Camping Gaz only. Restaurant 400 yards. Swimming pool 5 miles. No cats.
From Chichester take A286 which changes to B2179 to West Wittering. Redlands Lane is second on right after The Lamb pub, opposite West Wittering boundary name sign.

WESTBURY Wiltshire   Map 2 A3

The Woodland Park
Brokerswood.
☎ (0373) 822238
Open: All year
Size: ½ acre, 24 touring pitches. 3 WCs

Turn off A36 at Standerwick and follow signposts to Woodland Park. Take minor road by garage. In Rudge, turn right and straight over at crossroads for site.

WESTON-SUPER-MARE *Avon* — Map 2 A3

Airport View Caravan Site
Moor Lane, Worle. ☎ (0934) 622168
Open: March-October
Size: 12½ acres, 135 touring pitches. 8 hot showers, 27 WCs.

Opposite Airport (A371), turn into Moor Lane. Site 100 yards.

Country View Caravan Park
Sand Road, Sand Bay. ☎ (0934) 627595
Open: March-October
Size: 8 acres, 120 touring pitches. 8 hot showers, 20 WCs. 66 static caravans

Site 3½ miles N of Weston.

DULHORN FARM CAMPING SITE
RAC A
Weston Road, Lympsham, BS24 0JQ.
☎ (0934) 750298
Open: February-January
Size: 2 acres, 48 touring pitches, all level, 11 with elec, 4 chalets. 2 hot showers, 2 cold showers, 5 WCs, 1 CWP

Car & caravan £4.50-£5.50, Motor caravan, Car & tent, M/cycle & tent £3-£4.50; elec £1
On working farm. Ideal for touring and fishing, country surroundings, beaches approximately 4 miles. Easy access to motorway. Restaurant 1 mile. Swimming pool 4 miles. Shop 1½ miles. 4 chalets for hire (own WCs).
On A370, 6 miles S of Weston-super-Mare.

Norton Farm
Kewstoke. ☎ (0934) 623030
Open: Spring Bank Holiday/July-September
Size: 3 acres, 5 touring pitches, 400 pitches for tents. 2 hot showers, 4 WCs

Site 1½ miles NW from A370.

Oak Farm Touring Park
Congresbury. ☎ (0934) 833246
Open: March-October
Size: 2 acres, 20 touring pitches. 4 hot showers, 6 WCs

Site ¼ mile W of Congresbury.

OAK TREE & WEST END FARM TOURING PARK
RAC A
Locking, BS24 8RH. ☎ (0934) 822529
Open: All year
Size: 10 acres, 75 touring pitches, all level, all with elec, 10 with hardstanding. 4 hot showers, 4 cold showers, 15 WCs, 1 CWP

Car & caravan, Motor caravan, Car & tent from £5.50, plus from 80p per person above 4, extra from 60p; extra car from 75p; elec from £1.40; awn from £1; dogs 60p
Quiet, family site, good views of surrounding country. Guaranteed peaceful stay - no club. Restaurant 1½ miles and swimming pool 2½ miles.

No motorcycles. Families and couples only. Latest arrival time 10pm.
2½ miles W of junction 21 of the M5, or 2 miles E of Weston-super-Mare on A370, turn S by Heron Hotel on A371 for 1 mile, turn right, follow signs. Otherwise follow signs to International Helicopter Museum, as entrance to park is 20 yards away.

Purn International Holiday Park
Bridgwater Road, Bleadon, BS24 0AN.
☎ (0934) 812342
Open: March-October
Size: 10 acres, 139 touring pitches. 6 hot showers, 20 WCs. 140 static caravans

3 miles S of Weston on A370.

WESTON GATEWAY TOURIST PARK
RAC A
West Wick, BS24 7TF. ☎ (0934) 510344
Open: All year
Size: 15 acres, 375 touring pitches, all level, 60 with elec, 10 with hardstanding. 18 hot showers, 60 WCs, 1 CWP

(1991) Car & caravan, Motor caravan, Car & tent, M/cycle & tent £5.50; elec £1.25, awn £1.25
Amenities on this level, grassy site include a club with bar, restaurant and TV lounge, and children's play area. Swimming pool 3 miles. Families and couples only.
From junction 21 on M5, turn W on A370 for ¼ mile. Turn S on unclassified road signed West Wick to site on right after ¼ mile.

Willowmead Caravan Park
Moor Lane, Locking. ☎ (0934) 622423
Open: March-October
Size: 4 acres, 30+ touring pitches. 4 hot showers, 9 WCs. 22 static caravans

From M5 junction 21, take A370 for Weston. After 1 mile, at first traffic lights, turn left into Moor Lane.

WESTWARD HO! *Devon* — Map 1 B2

ATLANTIC SANDS TRAILER PARK
RAC L
Cornborough Road, EX39 1AA.
☎ (0237) 474774
Open: April-October
Size: 1½ (10) acres, 20 touring pitches, 12 with elec, 10 level pitches, 130 static caravans. 16 hot showers, 24 WCs, 1 CWP

Car & caravan, Motor caravan £6-£9, Car & tent, M/cycle & tent £5-£9; elec £2, awn £3-£4; WS
cc Access, Visa/B'card
Family-run park, spectacular coastal views. 45 caravans for hire, all with own shower, toilet, colour TV - no meters. On site shops, launderette, games room, play area, barbecue, indoor heated swimming pool, sauna and solarium. Restaurant 600 yards. No dogs.
Take A386 N from A39 to Northam, turn W into Bay View Road for ¾ mile. At `Halt' sign, continue ahead for 200 yards.

Pusehill Farm
Buckleigh. ☎ (023 74) 74295

☑ Snacks/take away ☒ Restaurant ◲ Swimming pool ▣ Shelter for campers ⊞ Dogs accepted   **141**

Open: Easter-September
Size: 5 acres, 60 touring pitches. 3 hot showers, 8 WCs

From Bideford, take A386 N. After 1¾ miles, turn W into Bay View Road, and continue on Cornborough Road to site.

WETHERBY *West Yorkshire*   Map 5 A2

MOOR LODGE CARAVAN PARK   RAC L
Blackmoor Lane, Bardsey, LS17 9DZ.
☎ (0937) 572424
Open: All year
Size: 3 (15) acres, 12 touring pitches, all with elec, 3 with hardstanding, 9 level pitches, 60 static caravans. 4 hot showers, 10 WCs, 1 CWP

Car & caravan, Motor caravan £5.50; plus 50p per person above 2; elec £1.50, awn 50p
4 Ticks Award. Immaculate, owner-managed, rural site, very peaceful. Suits couples rather than families. Shop 1 mile. Restaurant ½ mile. Swimming pool 2 miles. Non- residential holiday and recreational site.
From A1, turn off at Wetherby sign. Take A58 for Leeds, after 5 miles turn right after Harvester pub (on right hand side) on to Ling Lane, turn right at crossroads and we are on the right.

Wetherby Racecourse Caravan Club Site
☎ (0937) 62035
Open: May-September
Size: 5 acres, 90 touring pitches. 8 hot showers, 4b WCs

Site ¾ mile E of Wetherby, off B1224.

WEYMOUTH *Dorset*   Map 2 A3

BAGWELL FARM TOURING PARK   RAC L
Chickerell, DT3 4EA. ☎ (0305) 782575
Open: 16 March-31 October
Size: 14 acres, 150 touring pitches, all level, 114 with elec. 13 hot showers, 1 cold shower, 38 WCs, 1 CWP

(1991) Car & caravan, Motor caravan £4.10-£7.20, Car & tent £3.10-£5.20, plus £1.10 per person above 2, child 60p above 2; extra car 60p; elec £1.60, awn £1.60
Quiet, family-run site situated ideally for touring Dorset. Bathroom. Wet suit wash. Small pets and farm animals. Restaurant and swimming pool 1½ miles. No motorcycles.
On main coast road, B3157. Site signed.

East Fleet Touring Park
Fleet, DT3 4DW.
☎ (0305) 785768

Open: March-October
Size: 20 acres, 210 touring pitches. 16 hot showers, 32 WCs

3 miles NW of Weymouth (B3157), turn left at TA Centre. Site signed.

LITTLESEA HOLIDAY PARK   RAC L
Lynch Lane, DT4 9DT. ☎ (0305) 774414
Open: Easter-October
Size: 5 (46) acres, 100 touring pitches, all level, 20 with elec, 119 static caravans. 26 hot showers, 33 WCs, 1 CWP

Charges on application.
cc Access, Visa/B'card
A large site, with club, games room. Suitable for families. 119 caravans for hire (own WCs).
At 1¼ miles W of Weymouth Bay on B3157, turn S by Swiss Cottage into Lynch Lane.

Osmington Mills Holidays
Osmington Mills, DT3 6HB.
☎ (0305) 832311
Open: Easter-October
Size: 18 acres, 225 touring pitches. 24 hot showers, 24 WCs. 62 static caravans

4½ miles NE of Weymouth (A353), turn SE to Osmington Mills. Site ½ mile.

WEST FLEET HOLIDAY FARM   RAC L
Fleet, DT3 4EF.
☎ (0305) 782218
Open: Easter-31 October
Size: 12 (20) acres, 250 touring pitches, 18 with elec, 200 level pitches. 20 hot showers, 40 WCs, 1 CWP

(1991) Motor caravan, Car & tent, M/cycle & tent £7, plus £1.50 per person above 2, child £1; dogs 50p
Beautiful situation on Dorset Heritage coast, yet close to Weymouth. Ideal for touring Dorset countryside. Children welcome. Clubhouse, pool. No all-male groups without prior arrangement. Family site.
From Weymouth take B3157 towards Bridport, after 3 miles turn left at the only mini-roundabout to Fleet. Park 1 mile on right. Signposted MoT signs.

WHALEY BRIDGE *Cheshire*   Map 5 A2

Ringstones Caravan Park
Yeardsley Lane, Furness Vale, SK12 7EB.
☎ (0663) 732152
Open: March-October
Size: 7 acres, 50 touring pitches. 3 hot showers, 10 WCs. Static caravans

☐ 🏕 🚐 🛆 ☐ ☐ ☐ ☐ ☐ 🐕

Take A6 from Whaley Bridge for 1½ miles to
Furness Vale. Turn left at pelican crossing for site.

WHATSTANDWELL Derbyshire · Map 5 A3

Birchwood Farm
Wirksworth Road, DE4 5HF. ☎ (0629) 2280
Open: March-October
Size: 2 (4) acres, 12+ touring pitches. 1 hot shower,
6 WCs. Static caravans

☐ 🏕 🚐 🛆 🔌 ☐ ☐ ☐ ☐ 🐕

From A6 in Whatstandwell, take road for
Wirksworth for 1 mile. Site on right off B5035.

HAYTOP COUNTRY PARK RAC L
DE4 5HP. ☎ (0773) 852063
Open: All year
Size: 15 (65) acres, 20 touring pitches, all with elec,
10 with hardstanding. 4 hot showers, 10 WCs,
1 CWP

🚐 🏕 🛆 ☐ ☐ ☐ ☐ ☐ ☐ 🐕

Car & caravan £8, Motor caravan £6, Car & tent £7,
M/cycle & tent £6.50; extra person £1, child 50p;
extra car £1, elec £1.50, awn £1, dogs 50p-75p
*This small estate of 65 acres is a country park with
meadows, 2 streams, mixed woodland and 1 mile
of river bank. Shop 1 mile. Restaurant ½ mile.
Swimming pool 5 miles.*
From Cromford, travel SE on A6 to bridge over
River Derwent then turn left along private road to
site.

MEREBROOK CARAVAN PARK RAC L
DE4 5HH. ☎ (0773) 852154
Open: All year
Size: 1 (11) acres, 75 touring pitches, all level,
28 with elec, 116 static caravans. 14 hot showers,
28 WCs, 3 CWPs

☐ 🏕 🚐 🛆 🔌 🛒 ☐ ☐ ☐ 🐕

Car & caravan £6, Motor caravan £5, Tent £2 per
person, M/cycle £1; elec £1.25, awn £1, dogs free
*A pleasant, level, grassy site occupying a position
along the river bank in the lovely Derwent Valley.
Devoted entirely to holiday caravanners and
campers, the park is maintained to the high
standard necessary in such a magnificent location.
Ideal as a centre for exploring the Derbyshire Dales
and the Peak National Park. Restaurant 1,500 yards.
Swimming pool 5 miles.*
From the junction of the A38 and A610 (NW of
Ripley), travel W on the A610 to Ambergate. Turn
N on the A6 to Whatstandwell, cross River Derwent
and turn right to site on right in ½ mile.

WHITBY North Yorkshire Map 5 B1

BURNT HOUSE CARAVAN SITE RAC A
Ugthorpe, YO21 2BG. ☎ (0947) 840448
Open: April-31 October
Size: 7½ acres, 99 touring pitches, some with elec,
40 static caravans. 12 hot showers, 20 WCs, 1 CWP

☐ 🏕 🚐 🛆 🔌 🛒 ☐ ☐ ☐ 🐕

Charges on application.
*A well-planned site, with children's play area,
views over moors. 2 caravans for hire (own WCs).
Family groups only. Restaurant ¼ mile.*

8½ miles N of Whitby on A171, turn E for 275 yards
and turn right to site.

Grouse Hill Caravan Park
Flask Bungalow Farm, Fylingdales
☎ (0947) 880543
Open: April-October
Size: 12 acres, 300 touring pitches. 4 hot showers,
3b WCS

♿ 🏕 🚐 🛆 🔌 🛒 ☐ ☐ 🏠 🐕

Site 8 miles S of Whitby, behind Flask Inn (A171).

Manor House Farm
Hawsker. ☎ (0947) 603107
Open: March-October
Size: 2 acres, 20 touring pitches. 2 hot showers,
5 WCs

☐ 🏕 🚐 🛆 🔌 ☐ ☐ ☐ ☐ 🐕

Site 2 miles S of Whitby, off A171.

MIDDLEWOOD FARM HOLIDAY PARK RAC L
Fylingthorpe, Robin Hood's Bay, YO22 4UF.
☎ (0947) 880414
Open: 1 March-31 October
Size: 3½ acres, 50 touring pitches, all level, 30 with
hardstanding, 30 static caravans. 10 hot showers,
18 WCs, 1 CWP

☐ ☐ 🚐 🛆 🔌 ☐ ☐ ☐ ☐ 🐕

Charges on application.
*Small field camping site with luxury toilet facilities
and free hot showers, private bathrooms for hire.
Hairdryers, laundry, under cover washing-up area,
adventure playground, telephone. Short walk to
beach. Set in delightful countryside with
panoramic sea and moorland views. 25 caravans
for hire (own WCs) Shop 300 yards. Restaurant 600
yards. Swimming pool 6 miles.*
5 miles S of Whitby on A171, turn E on B1447; at
1½ miles on turn right, then left to Fylingthorpe.
Continue ahead to site.

NORTHCLIFFE HOLIDAY PARK RAC A
High Hawsker, YO22 4LL. ☎ (0947) 880477
Open: Mid March-End October
Size: 8 (26) acres, 36 touring pitches, most level, 18
with elec, 161 static caravans. 6 hot showers,
9 WCs, 1 CWP

♿ 🏕 🚐 🛆 🔌 🛒 ☐ ☐ ☐ ☐

Car & caravan, Motor caravan, Car & tent, M/cycle*
& tent from £5; elec £1.50, awn free
*A well-planned, quiet site, set in the North York
Moors National Park. Facilities include children's
play areas, junior football pitch, games room, and
a shop with off licence. 11 caravans for hire (own
WCs). Pub ½ mile. Restaurant/cafe 2½ miles.
Swimming pool 3½ miles. No groups of
motorcycles.*
From High Hawsker (3 miles S of Whitby on the
A171), take the B1447 E for ½ mile, then turn left.
Site in ¾ mile.

Sandfield House Farm
Sandsend Road. ☎ (0947) 602660
Open: March-October
Size: 12 acres, 50 touring pitches. 12 hot showers,
12 WCs

☐ 🏕 🚐 🛆 🔌 ☐ ☐ ☐ ☐ 🐕

Site 1 mile N of Whitby on A174, opposite golf

🔲 Snacks/take away ☒ Restaurant ◻ Swimming pool 🏠 Shelter for campers 🐕 Dogs accepted 143 course.

Ugthorpe Caravan Site
Ugthorpe. ☎ (0947) 840518
Open: April-October
Size: 8 acres, 40 touring pitches. 12 hot showers,
18 WCs. 70 static caravans

Site 2 miles W of Ugthorpe, to E of A171.

Whitby Holiday Village
YO22 4JX.
☎ (0947) 602664
Open: May-October
Size: 6 acres, 140 touring pitches. 6 hot showers,
15 WCs

From A171 in Whitby, take Hawsker Abbey `B'
road.

York House Caravan Park
Hawsker.
☎ (0947) 880354
Open: March-October
Size: 2½ acres, 60 touring pitches. 8 hot showers,
14 WCs

3 miles S of Whitby, off A171.

WHITCHURCH *Shropshire*   Map 4 B3

Brook House Farm
Grindley Brook, SY13 4QJ. ☎ (0948) 2349
Open: March-October
Size: 3 (4) acres, touring pitches. 2 hot showers,
2 WCs. Static caravans

Site 1 mile NW of Whitchurch on A41.

WHITEPARISH *Wiltshire*   Map 2 B3

HILLCREST CAMP SITE   RAC L
Southampton Road, SP5 2QW.
☎ (0794) 884471
Open: All year
Size: 2 acres, 35 touring pitches, 12 with elec,
12 level pitches. 3 hot showers, 5 WCs, 1 CWP

Car & caravan, Motor caravan, Car & tent, M/cycle
& tent £2.25 per adult, £1 per child, 50p per car or
M/cycle; elec £1.50, awn 50p
*Small, family-run site surrounded by mature trees
with easy access and very convenient for New
Forest and Salisbury/Romsey area. No gas
available. Shop and restaurant 1 mile. Swimming
pool 8 miles.*
From junction 2 of the M27, travel NW on the
A36 for 7 miles to site on right.

WHITSTABLE *Kent*   Map 3 B2

LIMBERLOST PARK   RAC L
Church Lane, Seasalter. ☎ (0227) 272270
Open: All year
Size: 2½ acres, 77 touring pitches, all level, 33 with
elec. 6 hot showers, 10 WCs, 1 CWP

(1991) Car & caravan, Motor caravan, Car & tent,
M/cycle & tent from £4; elec £1, awn 50p; WS
*Attractive, small site near beach, with children's
play area and evening social activities. No gas
available. Shop 150 yards. Swimming pool 1 mile.*
From the junction of the M2, A2 and A299, travel
on the A299 towards Whitstable. At 4½ miles on,
turn left into Church Lane to site on right.

WIGTON *Cumbria*   Map 7 A3

CLEA HALL HOLIDAY PARK   RAC L
Westward, CA7 8NQ. ☎ (0965) 42880
Open: March-November
Size: 10 acres, 50 touring pitches, 12 with elec,
80 static caravans. 2 hot showers, 13 WCs, 1 CWP

Car & caravan, Motor caravan, Car & tent, M/cycle
& tent £5.50; elec £1, awn £1; WS
*A family site in rural setting, within easy reach of
walking, climbing, touring the Lakes and Borders.
Games room and children's play area. 4 caravans
for hire (own WCs). Calor gas only. Restaurant
2 miles.*
From the junction of the A595 and B5304 (S of
Wigton), travel S for 1½ miles to cross-roads, turn
right and ½ mile further keep left to site on left in ¾
mile.

WILLINGHAM *Cambridgeshire*   Map 3 A1

ALWYN TOURIST PARK   RAC A
Over Road, CB4 5PE. ☎ (0954) 60977
Open: 1 March-30 October
Size: 4.7 acres, 85 touring pitches, all level, 36 with
elec. 6 hot showers, 11 WCs, 2 CWPs

(1991) Car & caravan, Motor caravan, Car & tent,
M/cycle & tent £5.50, plus £1.50 per adult above 2,
child £1; elec £1.50, awn £1; WS
*Level pasture enclosed by hedges, conifers and
trees offering a play area, a small licensed bar and
club room. Restaurant ¼ mile. Swimming pool
9 miles.*
Travel NW off the M11 onto the A604 for 2¾ miles
to Bar Hill. Turn NE onto the B1050 to Longstanton,
then on entering Willingham, turn left on
unclassified road (to Over), site on left in ¼ mile.

WILLITON *Somerset*   Map 2 A3

HOME FARM HOLIDAY CENTRE   RAC L
St Audries Bay, TA4 4DP. ☎ (0984) 32487
Open: All year
Size: 2 (35) acres, 35 touring pitches, 18 with elec,
17 level pitches, 184 static caravans, 10 chalets.
11 hot showers, 18 WCs, 3 CWPs

Car & caravan, Motor caravan, Car & tent, M/cycle
& tent £5; elec £1
*Quiet and secluded park with own private beach,
lying between Quantock Hills and the sea.
4 caravans and 10 chalets for hire (own WCs).
Licensed bar. Restaurant 1½ miles. Swimming
pool 17 miles.*
At 1¼ miles E of Williton on A39 turn N for
600 yards, where turn right as signed `Home Farm

MERLEY COURT TOURING PARK

AWARD WINNING PARK: IDEAL FOR BOURNEMOUTH, POOLE, SANDBANKS, NEW FOREST

- SWIMMING POOL ● TENNIS COURT ● CRAZY GOLF ● ADVENTURE PLAYGROUND
- GAMES ROOM ● LICENSED CLUB *(with family room)* ● SHOP ● TAKE-AWAY
- ELECTRIC HOOK-UPS and much, much more . . .

Families & Couples only. Regret no dogs peak season. Tourers & Campers welcome (no statics).
Advance booking advised. Send stamp only for brochure to:-

MERLEY COURT TOURING PARK, MERLEY,
WIMBORNE, Nr. POOLE, DORSET BH21 3AA. Tel: (0202) 881488
(off A31 Wimborne by-pass follow signs for Merley Bird Gardens)

RAC APPOINTED

OPEN March 1st – Jan 7th

Holiday Centre'.

Quantock Orchard Caravan Park
Flaxpool, Crowcombe.
☎ (098 48) 618
Open: All year
Size: 3½ acres, 55+ touring pitches 5 hot showers, 9 WCs

On A358 from Taunton, site signed before village of Crowcombe.

WIMBORNE MINSTER *Dorset* — Map 2 B3

CHARRIS CAMPING AND CARAVAN PARK   RAC L
Candy's Lane, Corfe Mullen, BH21 3EF.
☎ (0202) 885970
Open: 1 March-30 October
Size: 2 (3) acres, 45 touring pitches, all with elec, 28 level pitches. 4 hot showers, 8 WCs, 1 CWP

(1991) Car & caravan, Motor caravan, Car & tent, M/cycle & tent £3.85-£4.70, plus £1 per adult above 2, child 75p; elec £1.25, awn 50p, dogs free; WS
On rising ground overlooking Stour Valley, pleasantly screened with mature trees and shrubs. Caravan parking in 4 separate areas. Convenient for Bournemouth, Poole, Purbeck and the New Forest, also for Poole-Cherbourg ferries. Restaurant 600 yards. Swimming pool 2 miles. From Wimborne Minster, take B3073 SW to A31 roundabout, then take the A31 W for ¾ mile. Turn left into Candy's Lane signposted 'Camping' (after Esso garage), site entrance 250 yards on left.

MERLEY COURT TOURING PARK   RAC A
Merley, BH21 3AA.
☎ (0202) 881488
Open: 1 March-7 January
Size: 15 acres, 160 touring pitches, all level, 120 with elec, 20 with hardstanding. 17 hot showers, 35 WCs, 3 CWPs

(1991) Car & caravan, Motor caravan, Car & tent, M/cycle & tent £1-£6; all plus £2-£2.30 per adult, £1-£1.30 per child; elec £1-£4; elec £1.40, dogs 80p
Family park with up-to-date facilities. Clubhouse with family room, games room, adventure playground, crazy golf. 5 acres of woodland. Shop open March-October. No dogs accepted during High Season. No motorcycle groups. Minimum stay 7 nights over Spring Bank Holiday and High

Season.
Site entrance signposted from the junction of the A31 and A349, S of Wimborne Minster.

WILKSWORTH FARM CARAVAN PARK   RAC A
Cranborne Road, BN21 4HW.
☎ (0202) 883769
Open: 1 March-30 October
Size: 5 (11) acres, 85 touring pitches, all level, 68 with elec, 20 with hardstanding, 77 static caravans. 10 hot showers, 15 WCs, 1 CWP

(1991) Car & caravan, Motor caravan, Car & tent, M/cycle & tent £4.60-£6.90, plus £2.10 per adult above 2, child up to £1.05 (age 3-16); elec £1.30, dogs £1.05
Country park, with tennis courts, games room, outdoor heated swimming pool and children's play area, in a peaceful setting. 2 caravans for hire (own WCs). Restaurant ½ mile. Barbecue and activity area on site. Dog exercise paddock. Wilksworth is an ideal base from which to visit Wimborne Minster and Model Village, the New Forest, Hardy country and miles of golden beaches. 1 mile N of Wimborne on B3078 to Cranborne,

---

WINCANTON *Somerset* — Map 2 A3

Sunnyhill Farm
☎ (0963) 33281
Open: May-September
Size: 3 acres, 10 touring pitches. 4 hot showers, 6 WCs. 5 static caravans

Site 1¾ miles E of Wincanton, off A303.

WINCANTON RACECOURSE   RAC L
BA9 8BJ.
☎ (0963) 34276
Open: 27 April-21 September
Size: 2 acres, 50 touring pitches, all level, 18 with elec. 2 hot showers, 8 WCs, 1 CWP

Car & caravan, Motor caravan, Car & tent, M/cycle & tent £1 (members) or £3 (non-members), plus £2.20 per person, child £1 (peak rates); elec £1.20 cc Access, Visa/B'card
Well-kept site with children's play area. Shop and restaurant 1 mile. Swimming pool 7 miles. ½ mile N of Wincanton on B3081. Site signed from A303.

● Snacks/take away   ✗ Restaurant   Swimming pool   Shelter for campers   Dogs accepted   **145**

England

 **WINDERMERE** *Cumbria*   **Map 4 B1**

ASHES LANE CARAVAN PARK

Staveley, LA12 8NL. ☎ (0539) 821119   RĀC A
Open: 1 March-14 November
Size: 18 (22) acres, 150 touring pitches, all level,
130 with elec, 150 with hardstanding, 68 static
caravans. 30 hot showers, 60 WCs, 2 CWPs

(1991) Car & caravan £3.35, Motor caravan £1.90,
Car & tent, M/cycle & tent £3.10; all plus £1.80 per
adult, 95p per child; elec £1.35
*A family-run site, a good centre for hill walking.
Licensed bar, TV and games room, children's play
area. 7 caravans for hire (own WCs). Restaurant
½ mile. Swimming pool 2½ miles.
From junction 36 of M6 take A591 NW to
roundabout where take second left signed
'Windermere and the Lakes'. Continue on A591 to
site on left before Staveley by-pass.*

FALLBARROW PARK

Rayrigg Road, Bowness, LA23 3DL.   RĀC A
☎ (05394) 44428
Open: 15 March-31 October
Size: 3 (32) acres, 81 touring pitches, all level, all
with elec, all with hardstanding, 245 static
caravans, 5 chalets. 9 hot showers, 9 cold showers,
15 WCs, 2 CWPs

(1991) Car & caravan, Motor caravan £8.75-£12.10;
elec included, awn £2.90, dogs free; WS
cc Major cards
*Situated in parkland on shore of Lake Windermere.
Boat launching facilities. Licensed bar with meals
and family lounge. Games and TV room and
adventure play area. 70 caravans for hire (own
WCs). Swimming pool 5km. No motorcycles.
From Windermere take B5284. At Bowness turn
right on to road signposted Ambleside. Park
300 yards left.*

HILL OF OAKS & BLAKEHOLME CARAVAN ESTATE ⚐ RÅC A
LA23 3PJ. ☎ (05395) 31417
Open: March-October inclusive
Size: 4 (69) acres, 43 touring pitches, all level, 30 with elec, all with hardstanding, 209 static caravans. 24 hot showers, 24 WCs, 2 CWPs

(1991) Car & caravan, Motor caravan £10; elec £1
69 acre woodland site with over a mile of private lake frontage. Facilities for sailing, power and rowing boats. Restaurant 2 miles. Swimming pool 1 mile. Calor gas only. No motorcycles. No tents. Between Newby Bridge and Bowness-on-Windermere on the A592.

Ings Caravan Park
Grassgarth Lane, Ings, Kendal, LA8 9QF.
☎ (0539) 821426
Open: March-November
Size: 5 acres, 20 touring pitches. 6 hot showers, 14 WCs. 50 static caravans

1 mile W of Staveley on A591, turn right and follow signs.

LIMEFITT PARK ⚐ RÅC A
LA23 1PA. ☎ (05394) 32300
Open: Week before Easter-31 October
Size: 15 (115) acres, 110 touring pitches, all with elec, 80 level pitches, 30 with hardstanding. 16 hot showers, 28 WCs, 1 CWP

(1991) Car & caravan, Motor caravan, Car & tent £3.20- £4; all plus £1.60-£2 per adult, 80p-£1 per child; elec £1, awn £1.60-£2, dogs £1.60-£2
Situated in spectacular Lakeland valley only 10 miniutes' drive from Lake Windermere. Licensed bar. Pony trekking, grass skiing, trail riding. Families and couples only. Swimming pool 3 miles.
At ½ mile NW of Windermere on A591, turn N on A592 (road to Ullswater) for 2¼ miles. Site on right.

PARK CLIFFE CAMPING & CARAVAN ESTATE ⚐ RÅC A
Birks Road, Tower Wood, LA23 3PG.
☎ (05395) 31344
Open: 1 March-31 October
Size: 15 (25) acres, 65 touring pitches, 30 with elec, 55 level pitches, 10 with hardstanding, 50 static caravans. 16 hot showers, 17 WCs, 1 CWP

Car & caravan £4.50, Motor caravan, Car & tent, M/cycle & tent £3.50; all plus £1.75 per adult, child £1.20; elec £1.20, dogs £1.20
cc Access, Visa/B'card
Flat and gently sloping, grass and hardstanding, rural site with magnificent views over surrounding countryside. The highest tent pitches have commanding views over Lake Windermere and Langdale. Restaurant 2 miles. Swimming pool 4 miles.
Junction 36 of M6, take A591 heading towards Kendal. Then take A590 to Barrow. On reaching Newby Bridge turn right on to A592 towards Bowness. Go 4 miles, turn right into Birks Road. In ½ mile caravan and camp site is on the right hand side.

White Cross Bay Caravan Park
Ambleside Road, LA23 1LF.
☎ (05394) 43937
Open: March-October
Size: 72 acres, 120 touring pitches. 45 hot showers, 80 WCs. 250 static caravans

At 2 miles NW of Windermere and 3 miles S of Ambleside. Site on W side of A591.

WINDSOR *Berkshire*   Map 3 A2

WILLOWS RIVERSIDE PARK ⚐ RÅC L
Maidenhead Road, SL4 5TR.
☎ (0753) 861785
Open: All year
Size: 15 acres, 40 touring pitches, all level, all with elec, 20 with hardstanding. 4 hot showers, 8 WCs, 2 CWPs

Charges on application.
cc Access, Visa/B'card
A licensed club with children's room is one feature of this popular Thames-side site. Swimming pool 2 miles.
2 miles W of Windsor on A308, site on right.

WINKLEIGH *Devon*   Map 1 B2

Wagon Wheels Holiday Village
☎ (083 783) 456
Open: March-October
Size: 9½ acres, 20 touring pitches. 6 hot showers, 12 WCs. 106 static caravans

Site ½ mile W of Winkleigh on B3220.

WISBECH *Lincolnshire*   Map 3 A1

ORCHARD VIEW CARAVAN & CAMPING PARK ⚐ RÅC L
Sutton St Edmund, PE12 0LT.
☎ (0945) 700482
Open: Easter-End October
Size: 2 (6) acres, 30 touring pitches, all level, 8 with elec, 2 static caravans. 2 hot showers, 3 WCs, 1 CWP

Charges on application.
Small, level site with licensed clubhouse, children's play area and BBQ area. 2 caravans for hire (own WCs). Restaurant 2 miles.
Turn N off the A47 on to the B1187 ½ mile before bridge over River Nene. After 4 miles turn right to Broadgate, signposted Sutton St Edmund (second turning over bridge). Site on right in ¾ mile.

WITTON-LE-WEAR *Co Durham*   Map 5 A1

WITTON CASTLE CARAVAN SITE ⚐ RÅC L
DL14 0DE. ☎ (038 888) 230
Open: 1 April-31 October
Size: 8 (30) acres, 186 touring pitches, 60 level pitches, 280 static caravans. 10 hot showers, 48 WCs, 1 CWP

(1991) Car & caravan, Motor caravan, Car & tent,

📋 Snacks/take away ✖ Restaurant 🖾 Swimming pool 📧 Shelter for campers 🐕 Dogs accepted   **147**

M/cycle & tent £4.60-£5, plus 40p per adult, child 30p; WS
Set in 150 acres of parkland. Licensed bars, snack bar, games rooms, playground and all usual camping facilities. Periodic special events, eg. scrambling, horse racing, horse trials, etc. Signposted on A68 between Toft Hill and Witton-le-Wear.

WIVELISCOMBE Somerset — Map 2 A3

Bouchers Farm
Waterrow. ☎ (0984) 23464
Open: April-October
Size: 3 acres, 25 touring pitches. 2 WCs

3 miles SW of Wiveliscombe on A361, turn first left after Waterrow.

WOKINGHAM Berkshire — Map 2 B2

CALIFORNIA CHALET & TOURING PARK   RAC L
Nine Mile Ride, Finchampstead, RG11 3NY.
☎ (0734) 733928
Open: 1 March-30 October
Size: 5½ acres, 29 touring pitches, all level, 20 with elec, 27 with hardstanding, 13 chalets. 3 hot showers, 4 WCs, 28 CWPs

Car & caravan, Motor caravan, Car & tent £7-£8.50, including 2 adults and 2 children
An attractive lakeside setting amid trees and rhododendrons, some lakeside pitches; level hardstandings with electricity, water, disposal points. 9 chalets for hire (own WCs). No gas available. Restaurant 1½ miles. Swimming pool 5 miles. No motorcycles.
From Wokingham, travel S on the A321 for 1½ miles, bear right on the B3016 for ¾ mile, then turn right on to unclassified road. Site on right after ½ mile.

WOLSINGHAM Co Durham — Map 7 B3

Bradley Hall
☎ (0388) 527280
Open: April-October
Size: 2 acres, 12 touring pitches. 2 hot showers, 3 WCs. Static caravans

Site 2 miles E of Wolsingham on A689.

WOODBRIDGE Suffolk — Map 3 B2

THE MOON & SIXPENCE   RAC A
Newbourn Road, Waldringfield, IP12 4PP.
☎ (0473) 727393
Open: 1 April or Easter-31 October
Size: 5 (85) acres, 75 touring pitches, all with elec, all level, 150 static caravans. 12 hot showers, 25 WCs, 1 CWP

(1991) Car & caravan, Motor caravan, Car & tent, M/cycle & tent £5; all plus £2.50 per person; dogs £1
Located in beauty spot occupying both sides and floor of a valley. Very attractive, sheltered, terraced sites. 2 acre lake with sandy beach in centre of park. Adventure play areas. Plenty of walks and trails. Tourist Board graded 4 Ticks. Swimming pool 3 miles.
A12 Ipswich eastern by-pass. Take turning signposted Waldringfield and Newbourn. Follow international caravan signs, after 1½ miles turn left at crossroads.

ST MARGARET'S HOUSE CARAVAN SITE   RAC L

Shottisham, IP12 3HD. ☎ (0394) 411247
Open: 1 April or Easter-31 October
Size: 1½ (2½) acres, 25 touring pitches, all level, 2 with elec. 2 hot showers, 4 WCs, 1 CWP

(1991) Car & caravan, Motor caravan, Car & tent, M/cycle* & tent £3.20, plus 20p per person above 2, child 10p; elec £1, awn 20p
Level, grass site, plenty of trees, large playing field. Shop 200 yards. Restaurant ½ mile. Swimming pool 6 miles. Dogs must be kept on a lead.
From the junction of the A12 and A1152 (N of Woodbridge), travel E on the A1152 for 1¾ miles. Turn right on the B1083 for 4 miles, turn E through Shottisham to site on left 200 yards past the Sorrel Horse public house.

THE SANDLINGS CENTRE   RAC L

Lodge Road, Hollesley, IP12 3RR.
☎ (0394) 411202
Open: 1 March-14 January
Size: 6 (10) acres, 22 touring pitches, 12 with elec, 8 static caravans, 4 chalets. 6 hot showers, 8 WCs,

Car & caravan, Motor caravan, Car & tent £6.50, M/cycle & tent £6; elec £1.50, awn 50p
Thickly-wooded site in rural surroundings, with children's play area. 4 chalets for hire (own WCs). Shop and restaurant 1 mile. Swimming pool 6 miles.
From the junction of the A12 and A1152 (N of Woodbridge), travel E on the A1152 for 1¾ miles. Turn right on the B1083 for 4 miles, turn E through Shottisham to site on left in 2 miles.

TANGHAM CAMPSITE   RAC L

Butley, IP12 3NP. ☎ (0394) 450707
Open: 1 April-12 January
Size: 7 acres, 90 touring pitches, all level, 35 with elec. 6 hot showers, 12 WCs, 6 CWPs

Car & caravan, Motor caravan, Car & tent, M/cycle* & tent £7 up to 4 persons
Clearing in centre of Forestry Commission forest, sandy soil, well-drained. 1 mile off main road B1084: safe for children. Restaurant 2½ miles. Swimming pool 7 miles.
Turn off A12 Woodbridge by-pass looking for Orford sign (B1084). 6 miles along A1084 turn into forest.

WOODHALL SPA Lincolnshire — Map 5 B2

BAINLAND COUNTRY PARK   RAC A
Horncastle Road, LN10 6UX.
☎ (0526) 52903
Open: All year
Size: 12 (50) acres, 100 touring pitches, all with elec, all level, 30 with hardstanding, 10 static caravans, 25 chalets. 8 hot showers, 14 WCs,

2 CWPs

[icons]

Car & caravan, Motor caravan £4.65-£7.25; elec £2, awn £2; WS
cc Access
Amenities at this sheltered site include an indoor swimming pool, children's play area, bowling greens and croquet lawns. 10 caravans and 25 chalets for hire (own WCs). Calor gas only. No tents.
1½ miles NE of Woodhall Spa on the B1191, site on right.

Camping & Caravanning Club Site
Wellsyke Lane, Kirkby on Bain, LN10 6YU.
☎ (0526) 52911
Open: 30 March-26 October
Size: 6 acres, 100 touring pitches

[icons]

Charges on application.
cc Access, Visa/B'card
Wooded site next to a nature reserve. Minimum facilities - campers must have their own chemical toilet. Shop 3 miles.
From the B1191 turn on to Kirkby Lane, then left into Wellsyke Lane, the site is on the left.

JUBILEE PARK CARAVAN SITE RAC L
Stixwould Road, LN10 6QH. ☎ (0526) 52448
Open: Easter or 1 April-October
Size: 5 (7) acres, 90 touring pitches, all level, all with elec. 4 hot showers, 19 WCs, 2 CWPs

[icons]

(1991) Car & caravan, Motor caravan £4.50-£6.50, Car & tent £2.10-£4.25, M/cycle & tent £2.70-£5.50; elec £1.35, awn £1.35; WS
Located in public landscaped park, very close to village centre. Park has swimming pool, bowling, tennis, putting and cycle hire facilities. No gas available. Shop ¼ mile.
At ¼ mile N of Woodhall Spa.

Willow Holt Caravan Park
Lodge Road, Tattershall. ☎ (0526) 43111
Open: March-October
Size: 25 acres, 60 touring pitches. 4 hot showers, 10 WCs

[icons]

From A153 in Tattershall, turn N on Lodge Road for Woodhall Spa. Site 1½ miles.

Durdle Door Camp
West Lulworth. ☎ (092 941) 200
Open: March-October
Size: 45 acres, 32 touring pitches. 30 hot showers, 120 WCs. Static caravans

[icons]

At Wool on A352, turn S on B3071 to West Lulworth. Site 1 mile W of village.

WHITEMEAD CARAVAN PARK RAC L
East Burton Road, BH20 6HG.
☎ (0929) 462241
Open: 1 April-30 October
Size: 4½ (5) acres, 95 touring pitches, 88 level

pitches, 32 with elec, 1 chalet. 6 hot showers, 2 cold showers, 13 WCs, 1 CWP

[icons]

(1991) Car & caravan, Motor caravan, Car & tent, M/cycle & tent £4-£4.80; all plus 30p per person; elec £1.25-£1.40, awn 40p-50p
Owner-supervised, friendly, clean, family site in the River Frome valley. One chalet for hire (own WC). Restaurant 100 yards. Swimming pool 4½ miles. Return to be constant with comfort of other "campers".
From Wool, travel N on the A352 for 200 yards, turn W to site on right.

Woodlands Camping Park
Bindon Lane, East Stoke. ☎ (0929) 462327
Open: Easter-September
Size: 3 acres, 40 touring pitches. 4 hot showers, 8 WCs

[icons]

Site 2 miles E of Wool.

Borough Cross Camping & Riding
Higher Warcombe Farm, Mortehoe
☎ (0271) 870501
Open: Easter-October
Size: 19 acres, 5 touring pitches, plus 135 for tents. 8 hot showers, 12 WCs

[icons]

4½ miles SW of Ilfracombe, turn NW off B3343 at Turnpike Cross. First right to site.

EASEWELL FARM RAC L
Mortehoe. ☎ (0271) 870225
Open: Easter-September
Size: 3 (12) acres, 62 touring pitches, 27 with elec, 30 level pitches, 27 with hardstanding. 28 hot showers, 44 WCs, 1 CWP

[icons]

Charges on application.
cc Access, Amex, Diners, Visa/B'card
Family site with sea views on a working sheep farm. TV, games room, club and children's play area. Restaurant ½ mile. 9 hole golf course and covered swimming pool on site.
At Mullacott Cross on A361, turn W on to B3343 for 1¾ miles, and keep right signed `Mortehoe' for 1½ miles. Site on right.

GOLDEN COAST HOLIDAY VILLAGE
& TOURIST PARK RAC A
EX34 7HJ. ☎ (0271) 870343
Open: Easter-31 October
Size: 6 (10) acres, 240 touring pitches, all level, 70 with elec, 6 with hardstanding, 21 static caravans, 66 chalets. 30 hot showers, 50 WCs, 2 CWPs

[icons]

(1991) Car & caravan, Motor caravan, Car & tent £7, plus £2.90 per adult, £1.45 per child; elec £1.75, awn free, dogs £1.50
cc Access, Visa/B'card
All the indoor and outdoor pleasures of a holiday park with full entertainment programme during main holiday season. 21 caravans and 66 chalets

---

⬛ Snacks/take away ✗ Restaurant ◰ Swimming pool ▣ Shelter for campers ⌧ Dogs accepted **149**

for hire (own WCs). Dogs accepted during low season only.
From Mullacott Cross (the junction of the A361 and B3343), travel W on the B3343 towards Woolacombe for 2¼ miles, where road turns left, site on left in ¼ mile.

Little Roadway Farm Camping Park
☎ (0271) 870313
Open: Easter-October
Size: 23 acres, 3 touring pitches, plus 200 for tents. 5 hot showers, 8 WCs

Site 1 mile SE of Woolacombe, at junction of Challacombe Hill/B3231.

NORTH MORTE FARM CARAVAN PARK   RAC L
Mortehoe, EX34 7EG. ☎ (0271) 870381
Open: Easter-30 September
Size: 17 acres, 24 touring pitches, 17 with elec, 73 static caravans. 14 hot showers, 21 WCs, 3 CWPs

(1991) Car & caravan £5.10, Motor caravan, Car & tent, M/cycle* & tent £4.50; extra person 50p; elec £1, awn 50p; WS
Quiet, family-run site in lovely countryside, 500 yards from beach. 25 caravans for hire (most with own WCs) and new children's play area. Restaurant 500 yards. Swimming pool 1 mile.
At Mullacott Cross on A361, turn W on B3343 for 1¾ miles, and keep right for 2 miles to Mortehoe. Turn right, site in ½ mile.

TWITCHEN HOUSE & MORTEHOE CARAVAN PARK   RAC A
Mortehoe, EX34 7ES. ☎ (0271) 870476
Open: April-End October
Size: 6 (45) acres, 51+ touring pitches, all with elec, most level, all with hardstanding, 295 static caravans, 4 flats. 20 hot showers, 53 WCs, 2 CWPs

(1991) Car & caravan, Motor caravan £7-£14, Car & tent £6-£12; plus 50p per person above 6
Approximately 1 mile from sandy beaches at Mortehoe and Woolacombe. Licensed club with seasonal entertainment, adventure playground, games field, snooker, pool, table tennis. 100 caravans and 4 flats for hire (own WCs). Family groups only. 1 week minimum stay during peak season.
Travel N on A361 from Barnstaple to the junction with the B3343 at Mullacott Cross. Travel W on the B3343 for 1¾ miles, keep right signed Mortehoe. Park is 1½ miles on left.

WOOLACOMBE BAY HOLIDAY VILLAGE   RAC L
Sandy Lane, EX34 7BW. ☎ (0271) 870221
Open: Mid May-30 September
Size: 11 (50) acres, 10 touring pitches, 220 static caravans, 3 chalets 12 hot showers, 20 WCs, 1 CWP

Charges on application.
cc Access, Visa/B'card
Good facilities at this attractive family park including children's play area, tennis, bar, sauna, solarium and crazy golf. 200 caravans and 3 chalets for hire (own WCs).
At Mullacott Cross on A361, turn W on to B3343 for 1¾ miles over bridge, and keep right for ½ mile, turn left into Sandy Lane. Site ½ mile on left.

Woolacombe Sands Holiday Park
Station Road. ☎ (0271) 870569
Open: Easter-October
Size: 30 acres, 200 touring pitches. 35 hot showers, 40 WCs

At Mullacott Cross on A361, take B3343 to Woolacombe. Site on left.

WOOLER *Northumberland*   Map 7 B2

RIVERSIDE CARAVAN PARK   RAC A
Brewery Road, NE71 6QG.
☎ (0668) 81447
Open: 1 March-31 October
Size: 6 (80) acres, 100 touring pitches, all level, 55 with elec, 150 static caravans. 6 hot showers, 6 WCs, 1 CWP

Charges on application.
cc Access, Visa/B'card
Site by river with private lake stocked with rainbow trout. Clubhouse, heated indoor pool and family room. Ideal for walking, fishing, horse riding or exploring the local area - Riverside is on the edge of the Northumbrian National Park.
Approaching Wooler from the S on the A697, site on left just before Wooler Bridge.

WORCESTER *Hereford & Worcester*   Map 2 A2

Holt Fleet Farm
Holt Fleet, Holt Heath. ☎ (0905) 620512
Open: April-October
Size: 9 acres, 150 touring pitches. 10 hot showers, 15 WCs. 99 static caravans

Site 1¼ miles W of Ombersley roundabout, off A4133. 7 miles N of Worcester.

Mill House
Hawford, WR3 7SE.
☎ (0905) 51283
Open: Easter-October
Size: 7½ acres, 150 touring pitches. 2 hot showers, 10 WCs

Site 3 miles N of Worcester, to E of A449.

Worcester Racecourse
Pitchcroft, WR1 3NZ. ☎ (0905) 25364
Open: May-October
Size: 74 touring pitches. 2 hot showers, 7 WCs

From M5 junction 7, follow A44.

Camping & Caravanning Club Site
The Walled Garden, Clumber Park, S80 3BA.
☎ (0909) 482303
Open: 30 March-28 September
Size: 4½ acres, 60 touring pitches. 2 hot showers, 6 WCs

Charges on application.
cc Access, Visa/B'card
Level, grass site in the centre of Clumber Park. Camping Gaz only.
From the A841 follow the Clumber park signs. After 2½ miles take the left turn at the crossroads. Follow the signs for the Estate Office. Right at the Estate Office, the site is on the left.

Crookford Caravan & Camping Park
Crookford Hill, Elkesley, Retford
☎ (077 783) 641
Open: April-November
Size: 3 acres, 30 touring pitches. 6 hot showers, 6 WCs

On A1 between Worksop roundabout and Markham Moor roundabout, turn off signposted Elkesley. Site signed.

Riverside Caravan Park
Worksop Cricket Club, Central Avenue, S80 1ER.
☎ (0909) 474118
Open: March-January
Size: 4½ acres, 45 touring pitches. 4 hot showers, 5 WCs

On Worksop by-pass (A57), at junction with A60, take B6040 for town centre. Then first left, first right, and first left to site.

GREENSPRINGS HOLIDAY PARK   RAC L
Rockley Abbey, S75 3DS.
☎ (0226) 288298
Open: 1 April-October
Size: 4 acres, 65 touring pitches, 17 with elec. 8 hot showers, 11 WCs, 2 CWPs

(1991) Car & caravan, Motor caravan, Car & tent, M/cycle* & tent £5, plus 50p per person above 4; elec £1.30, awn £1
Secluded, grassy site set amidst woodland and farmland. Very quiet. Good walks, wildlife, peaceful. Shop 2 miles. Restaurant and swimming pool 3 miles.
From junction 36 on M1, travel N on A61 for ¼ mile, turn left signed 'Pilley' for 1 mile. Site on left at bottom of hill, by pond.

Brook Lane Caravan Park
Brook Lane, Ferring, BN12 5JD.
☎ (0903) 42802
Open: March-October
Size: 5 acres, 6 touring pitches. 2 hot showers, 5 WCs. 76 static caravans

Site W of Worthing, S from A259.

Washington Caravan & Camping Park
Washington. ☎ (0903) 892869
Open: All year
Size: 5 acres, 20+ touring pitches. 4 hot showers, 5 WCs

7 miles N of Worthing on A24, turn E on to A283. Site first left.

Cotswold Gate Caravan Park
Canons Court Farm, Bradley, GL12 7PN.
☎ (0453) 843128
Open: March-October
Size: 6 acres, 55 touring pitches. 6 hot showers, 10 WCs

E on B4509 for 2½ miles, turn left on B4058 for 2½ miles. Bear left at Bushford Bridge. Site ¾ mile on left.

Ropes Hill Farm
Horning, NR12 8LB. ☎ (0692) 630554
Open: April-October
Size: 2 acres, 3+ touring pitches. 1 WC

E from Wroxham on A1062, turn left at Horning crossroads. Site 100 yards.

Camping & Caravanning Club Site
Bracken Hill, Sheriff Hutton, YO6 1QG.
☎ (03447) 660
Open: 30 March-26 October
Size: 6 acres, 90 touring pitches. 6 hot showers, 9 WCs

Charges on application.
cc Access, Visa/B'card
Level, grassy site with children's play area. Shop 1 mile.
From York take the A64 N. After 5 miles, just before Little Chef, turn left towards Sheriff Hutton. At West Lilling turn left to site in ½ mile.

CAWOOD HOLIDAY PARK   RAC A
Ryther Road, Cawood, Near Selby, YO8 0TT.
☎ (0757) 268450
Open: 1 March-31 January
Size: 3 (8) acres, 60 touring pitches, all with elec, all level pitches, 10 static caravans, 9 chalets. 10 hot showers, 13 WCs, 1 CWP

⬛ Snacks/take away ☒ Restaurant ◣ Swimming pool ▣ Shelter for campers 🐕 Dogs accepted

Car & caravan, Motor caravan, Car & tent, M/cycle*
& tent from £8.50, plus £1 per person above 4; elec
from £1.50, awn £1.50
*Twixt York and Selby, country site ideal for York
and Dales, approximately 1 hour from the coast.
Fishing (coarse/trout). Lakeside bar with family
entertainment. Kiddies boating, climbing
frame/slide. Disabled bungalows to rent.
5 caravans for hire (own WCs). Swimming pool
5 miles. Minimum 3 nights stay in rented
bungalows/caravans (& tourers over Bank Holidays
only).*
From the A1 or York take the B1222 to Cawood and
turn at traffic lights on B1223 for 1 mile towards
Tadcaster and then site is on left.

CHESTNUT FARM CARAVAN PARK   RAC
Acaster Malbis, YO2 1UQ. ☎ (0904) 704676
Open: April-October
Size: 2 (5) acres, 25 touring pitches, all level,
20 with elec, 3 with hardstanding, 56 static
caravans. 6 hot showers, 14 WCs, 1 CWP

(1991) Car & caravan, Motor caravan, Car & tent,
M/cycle & tent £5, plus 75p per person; elec £1,
awn £1
*Family-run site 3½ miles from centre of York in
pretty village by River Ouse. Ideal for touring York,
Dales and coast. Level pitches, well-screened with
hedges and shrubs. Modern facilities. 5 caravans
for hire (own WCs). Restaurant 100 yards.
Swimming pool 3 miles. Dogs on leads at all times.*
At 4 miles SW of York on A64, turn E on road
signed Copmanthorpe and Acaster Malbis for
2 miles.

GOOSEWOOD CARAVAN PARK   RAC A
Sutton-on-the-Forest, YO6 1ET.
☎ (0347) 810829
Open: 1 March-31 October
Size: 10 (20) acres, 75 touring pitches, all level, all
with elec, 4 with hardstanding. 6 hot showers,
12 WCs, 1 CWP

Car & caravan, Car & tent £7-£8.50, Motor caravan
£6- £7.50, M/cycle & tent £6.50-£8; plus £1 per
person above 2, child 50p (aged 2-14); elec £1.50,
awn £1
*Level site surrounded by woodland with its own
fishing lake. Children's play area. Good, modern
facilities. Restaurant 1 mile. Swimming pool
3 miles.*
From York take the B1363 N. Cross the A1237 ring
road and continue N past the Haxby turning. Take
next right and follow signs to site.

MOOR END FARM   RAC L
Acaster Malbis, YO2 1UQ. ☎ (0904) 706727
Open: Easter-31 October
Size: 0.3 acre, 10 touring pitches, all level, all with
elec, 5 static caravans. 2 hot showers, 3 WCs,
1 CWP

Car & caravan, Motor caravan, Car & tent, M/cycle
& tent £5; plus 50p-75p per person above 2
*Small, friendly park on working dairy farm.
Children's play area. 4 caravans for hire (own
WCs). No gas available. Shop 100 metres.
Restaurant ¼ mile. Swimming pool 2 miles. Dogs
on leads.*
At Copmanthorpe, on the A64 between York and
Tadcaster, travel S as signed `Acaster Malbis' for
2 miles to site.

MOUNT PLEASANT CARAVAN VILLAGE   RAC A
Acaster Malbis, YO2 1UW. ☎ (0904) 707078
Open: 1 April-31 October
Size: 5 (18) acres, 125 touring pitches, all level,
46 with elec, 180 static caravans. 16 hot showers,
38 WCs, 4 CWPs

(1991) Car & caravan, Motor caravan £5.75-£7; Car
& tent, M/cycle* & tent £4-£5.50 plus 50p-70p per
person above 2; elec £1.50, awn up to £1.50
*Quiet country situation 400 yards from river fishing
and boating. Washing-up room for campers. Mains
electric plug-ins in ladies ablutions blocks for*

hairdryers and curlers. *Restaurant 200 yards. Swimming pool 4 miles.*
At 2¾ miles SW of York on A64, turn E to Bishopthorpe, 1 mile, where bear right towards Acaster Malbis; at 1¼ 1¼ miles on continue ahead and 1 mile further, turn left then left again after 200 yards. Site in ¼ mile.

NABURN LOCK CARAVAN & CAMPING PARK RAC L
Naburn, YO1 4RO. ☎ (0904) 87697
Open: March-October
Size: 4 (4½) acres, 50 touring pitches, all level, 30 with elec. 6 hot showers, 14 WCs, 2 CWPs

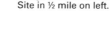

Car & caravan £7, Motor caravan £6.50, Car & tent, M/cycle & tent £6.50, plus £1 per adult above 2, child 50p; elec £1.20, awn £1
Small rural site, with nearby facilities for fishing and horse riding. Restaurant 200 yards. Swimming pool 4 miles.
Take the A19 S from York. Approaching by-pass (A64), turn right on to the B1222. Site 2½ miles.

Poplar Farm Caravan Park
Acaster Malbis. ☎ (0904) 706548
Open: April-September
Size: 8 acres, 80 touring pitches. 10 hot showers, 23 WCs. 70 static caravans

Turn S off A64 at Copmanthorpe. Site 2½ miles.

Post Office Caravan and Camping Park
Acaster Malbis, YO2 1UL. ☎ (0904) 706288
Open: Easter-October
Size: 1 acre, 37 touring pitches. 8 hot showers, 17 WCs

Turn S off A64 at Copmanthorpe. Site 2½ miles.

RAWCLIFFE CARAVAN PARK RAC A
Manor Lane, Shipton Road, YO3 6TZ.
☎ (0904) 624422
Open: All year
Size: 4½ acres, 120 touring pitches, all level, all with elec, 27 with hardstanding. 7 hot showers,

22 WCs, 2 CWPs

Car & caravan £7-£9, Motor caravan £6-£7, Car & tent, M/cycle* & tent £4-£9; plus £1.30 per person above 2, child 90p-£1.10; extra car £1.20; awn £1.10, dogs 80p; WS
cc Access, Visa/B'card
A flat, well-run, modern site with luxury facilities, with electricity on all pitches, satellite TV, water and drainage on most. Large supermarket, shopping complex, 10-screen cinema, bowling alley adjacent to site. Swimming pool 3 miles. Two thirds of the site is non-bookable, bookings taken for minimum 3 nights stay only.
Situated on the A19 York to Thirsk road on the outskirts of York, on the York side of the junction with the A1237 (northern York by-pass).

Weir Caravan Park
Stamford Bridge, YO4 1AN. ☎ (0759) 71377
Open: March-October
Size: 6 acres, 50 touring pitches. 2b hot showers, 2b WCs. 8 static caravans

8 miles E of York on A166, keep left on entering Stamford Bridge.

YOULGREAVE *Derbyshire*   Map 5 A2

Camping & Caravanning Club Site
Hopping Farm, DE1 1NA. ☎ (0629) 636555
Open: March-September
Size: 12 acres, 100 touring pitches. 10 hot showers, 15 WCs

Charges on application.
Gently sloping farm site in the heart of the Peak District National Park. Minimum facilities - campers must have their own chemical toilet.
From Matlock take the A6 NW. Turn SW on to A524. In Youlgreave turn left beside church. Cross bridge over River Bradford, then take first right. Site in ½ mile on left.

Seasonal variation of prices
Where a single price is given it may be a low season minimum charge - rates can increase considerably at peak periods and for extra people or vehicles.
Please confirm prices with the site when booking.

▼ Snacks/take away ✕ Restaurant ◺ Swimming pool ▥ Shelter for campers ⊓ Dogs accepted   153

ISLE OF MAN

Trailer caravans are not permitted on the Island and there are no touring or static caravans available for hire.

The RAC will be pleased to make the necessary ferry reservations on behalf of campers. The service from Heysham to Douglas operates throughout the year and the services from Belfast, Dublin and Fleetwood to Douglas, only during the summer months.

DOUGLAS   Map 4 A1

GLEN DHOO CAMPING SITE   RAC L
Hillberry, Onchan.
☎ (0624) 621254
Open: April-October
Size: 4 acres, 57 touring pitches, 8 with elec, 14 level pitches, 12 with hardstanding, 2 chalets. 11 hot showers, 12 WCs, 1 CWP

Motor caravan, Car & tent 90p, M/cycle & tent 80p; all plus £2.20 per adult, £1 per child; elec £1.10
Site in a sheltered wooded valley, 2½ miles from Douglas beach. Games room on site. Shop open from May. 2 chalets for hire (own WCs). Restaurant 1 mile. Swimming pool 2 miles. Pool table and table tennis available. On A18 and TT Course, 100 yards before Hillberry Corner, 2½ miles from car ferry.
3 miles N of Douglas centre on main Douglas to Ramsey inland road (A18). Site is just N of Cronkny-Mona.

Glenlough Farm
Union Mills.
☎ (0624) 851326
Open: April-October
Size: 10 acres, unlimited tent pitches. 3 hot showers, 10 WCs

1 mile N of Union Mills on A1.

Nobles Park Campsite
☎ (0624) 621132
Open: June-September
Size: 3 acres, 30 touring pitches. 5 hot showers, 12 WCs

Adjacent to Nobles Park, to rear of TT Grandstand.

LAXEY   Map 4 A1

QUARRY ROAD CAMPSITE   RAC L
Quarry Road, Off Minorca Hill
☎ (0624) 861241
Open: 1 May-30 September
Size: ½ acre, 30 touring pitches. 2 hot showers, 5 WCs

Car & caravan, Motor caravan, Car & tent, M/cycle & tent all £1.50-£2 per adult, 75p-£1 per child, plus £1 per car, 50p per m/cycle; elec free
Half acre site, very peaceful, ½ mile from Promenade, ½ mile from village and the famous Laxey Wheel. Amenities nearby include tennis, bowls, putting, cafe.
From the pier in Old Laxey, cross river and ascend hill towards Ramsey, for ½ mile, where turn left into Quarry Road.

PEEL   Map 4 A1

PEEL CAMP SITE   RAC L
Derby Road.
☎ (0624) 842341
Open: Mid May-Mid September
Size: 4 acres, 100 touring pitches, all level. 4 hot showers, 12 WCs

(1991) Motor caravan, Car & tent, M/cycle & tent all £2.50 per adult, £1.25 per child
Level, rural site on edge of small seaside town. Much historic interest - Castle, Cathedral, replica Viking longship. Golf course nearby. TT Course 2 miles. Shop 100 metres. Restaurant 400 metres. Swimming pool 10 miles.
On the N side of the A20, ¼ mile E of Peel town centre, site signed.

The Country Code
Enjoy the countryside and respect its life and work;
Guard against all risk of fire;
Fasten all gates;
Keep your dogs under close control;
Keep to public paths across farmland;
Use gates and stiles to cross fences, hedges and walls;
Leave livestock, crops and machinery alone;
Take your litter home;
Help to keep all water clean;
Protect wildlife, plants and trees;
Take special care on country roads;
Make no unnecessary noise.

ISLE OF WIGHT

Details of ferry services from Southampton to Cowes are available from: Red Funnel Ferries, Car Reservations & Passenger Enquiries, 12 Bugle Street, Southampton SO9 4LJ. ☎ (0703) 330333.

BEMBRIDGE   Map 2 B3

WHITECLIFF BAY HOLIDAY PARK   RAC L
Hillway, PO35 5PL. ☎ (0983) 872671
Open: Easter-31 October
Size: 21 (42) acres, 400 touring pitches, 128 with elec, 33 with hardstanding, 12 static caravans, 210 chalets. 38 hot showers, 68 WCs, 10 CWPs

Charges on application.
cc Access, Visa/B'card
A fine cliff-top site overlooking Whitecliff Bay. Indoor leisure centre, spa bath and sauna, children's play area and evening entertainment in main season.
1½ miles west of Bembridge on B3395, opposite Bembridge Airport.

CHALE   Map 2 B3

Chine Farm
Military Road, Atherfield Bay
☎ (0983) 740228
Open: May-October
Size: 5 acres, 80 touring pitches. 4 hot showers,

9 WCs. 2 static caravans

Midway between Chale and Brightstone on A3055.

Grange Farm
Military Road, Brightstone
☎ (0983) 740296
Open: easter-October
Size: 3 acres, 60 touring pitches. 7 hot showers, 15 WCs. 9 static caravans, 1 cabin

1 mile SW of Brightstone on A3055.

Tuttons Hill Cottage
Southdown. ☎ (0983) 79277
Open: All year
Size: 5 acres, 5 touring pitches, plus 30 for tents. 2 hot showers, 4 WCs

From Blackgang on A3055, through Chale then first right. Right again for site.

COWES   Map 2 B3

Comforts Farm
Pallance Road, Northwood
☎ (0983) 293888
Open: March-October
Size: 9½ acres, 50 touring pitches. 6 hot showers, 10 WCs

1½ miles S of Cowes (A3020), turn W at Radar Test Site into Three Gates Road, then left into Place Road. After ¼ mile, bear right for site.

Thorness Bay Holiday Park
Thorness Bay. ☎ (0983) 523109
Open: Easter-September
Size: 120 acres, 200 touring pitches. 12 hot showers, 3b WCs. 30 static caravans

S of Cowes on A3020, turn SW for 2¾ miles.

Waverly Park Holiday Centre
Old Road, East Cowes.
☎ (0983) 293452
Open: March-September
Size: 10 acres, 50 touring pitches. 10 hot showers, 24 WCs. Static caravans

From Red Funnel ferry terminal, turn left then first right. Site 300 yards.

RYDE — *Map 2 B3*

Beaper Farm
☎ (0983) 615210
Open: April-October
Size: 13 acres, 100 touring pitches. 12 hot showers, 24 WCs. 12 static caravans

2½ miles S of Ryde on A3055.

Carpenters Farm
St Helens. ☎ (0983) 872450
Open: June-September
Size: 12½ acres, 70 touring pitches. 4 hot showers, 8 WCs

3 miles S of Ryde (A3055), turn E on to B3330. Site in 1 mile.

Nodes Point Holiday Village
St Helens.
☎ (0983) 872401
Open: May-September
Size: 10 acres, 230 touring pitches. 10 hot showers, 32 WCs

S of Ryde (A3055), turn E on to B3330. Site on headland.

Pondwell Caravan & Camping Park
Pondwell Hill. ☎ (0983) 612100
Open: April-October
Size: 9 acres, 50 touring pitches. 15 hot showers, 24 WCs. 36 bungalows

2 miles SE of Ryde on B3330, adjacent to Wishing Well Inn.

SANDOWN — *Map 2 B3*

ADGESTONE CAMPING PARK RAC L
Lower Road, Adgestone, PO36 0HL.
☎ (0983) 403432
Open: Easter-September inclusive
Size: 7½ and 5½ (15½) acres, 200 touring pitches, all level, 170 with elec. 12 hot showers, 26 WCs, 2 CWPs

(1991) Car & caravan, Motor caravan, Car & tent, M/cycle & tent from £1.30; all plus from £2.30 per adult, from £1.30 per child; elec £1.40, dogs £1.20
cc Access, Visa/B'card
Set in beautiful country surroundings, but only a short distance to the island's safest sandy beaches. Well-stocked shop with extensive range of camping accessories and off licence. Adventure play area and private coarse fishing. Special Spring/Autumn/Mid Season package deals including ferry. No scooterists.
Turn off A3055 at Manor House pub in Lake, which is between Sandown and Shanklin. Go past golf course to t-junction, turn right, park is 200 yards on right.

Cheverton Copse Caravan & Camping Park
Newport Road, PO36 0JP. ☎ (0983) 403161
Open: April-September
Size: 5 acres, 26 touring pitches. 5 hot showers, 7 WCs. 57 static caravans

From Sandown, in Newport direction via Lake, site ½ mile beyond traffic lights in Lake (A3056).

Queen Bower Dairy Caravan Park
Alverstone Road, Queen Bower
☎ (0983) 403840
Open: May-October
Size: 2½ acres, 20 touring pitches. 1b WCs

2 miles W of Sandown (A3056), opposite Apse Heath P.O., turn N for site.

ADGESTONE CAMPING PARK
(OPEN EASTER TO SEPTEMBER)

SPECIAL PACKAGE HOLIDAYS
SPRING/AUTUMN - MID SEASON
Packages include park fees, return ferry fares for cars, motorhomes, trailers, touring caravans and up to 6 passengers.

Send for brochure and booking form to:
ADGESTONE CAMPING PARK
LOWER ADGESTONE, Nr. SANDOWN
ISLE OF WIGHT, PO36 0HL
Telephone: (0983) 403432/403989
RALLIES ARE WELCOME EARLY & LATE SEASON

Set in beautiful country surroundings but only a short distance to the island's safest sandy beaches. Pleasant, quiet park with marked pitches for tents, touring caravans and motorhomes. Excellent toilet facilities with free showers, private wash cubicles, baby/toddler bathing sinks and facilities for the disabled. Electric razor and hair-dryer points. Laundrette, ironing and dishwashing facilities. Well stocked shop with extensive range of camping accessories and off-licence. Take away meals. Ice-pack service. Public telephone. Camping Gaz/Calor Gas supplies. 10 amp electric hook-ups. Pets welcome. Any day arrival and departure.

CHILDREN'S ADVENTURE PLAY AREA
PRIVATE COARSE FISHING
PADDLING POOL AND HEATED SWIMMING POOL

Facilities for Disabled ⊞ Caravans accepted ⊠ Motor caravans △ Tents ⊿ Laundry room ⊾ Shop

SOUTHLAND CAMPING PARK  RĂC A
Newchurch, PO36 0LZ. ☎ (0983) 865385
Open: April-30 September inclusive
Size: 5½ acres, 100 touring pitches, all level,
46 with elec. 6 hot showers, 15 WCs, 1 CWP

(1991) Car & caravan, Motor caravan, Car & tent all
70p, plus £1.75-£2.40 per adult, £1.10-£1.30 per
child; elec £1.30, dogs 75p
cc Major cards
*Secluded, landscaped park, level and well-drained,
with good access. All pitches individually marked
and numbered. Pub ½ mile, restaurant ¾ mile.
Swimming pool 3 miles. No motorcycles.
From the junction of the A3055 and the A3056 (S of
Sandown), travel W on the A3056 for 2 miles. Turn
right for ½ mile to site on left.*

Village Way
Newport Road. ☎ (0983) 863279
Open: March-October
Size: 2 acres, 18 touring pitches. 4 hot showers,
5 WCs

1½ miles W of Sandown on A3056.

SHANKLIN Map 2 B3

LANDGUARD CAMPING PARK RĂC A
Landguard Manor Road, PO37 7PH.
☎ (0983) 867028
Open: 16 April-25 September
Size: 5 acres, 150 touring pitches, 140 level pitches,
80 with elec, 6 with hardstanding. 10 hot showers,
20 WCs, 1 CWP

(1991) Car & caravan, Motor caravan, Car & tent,
M/cycle & tent £2.50-£3.75 per adult, £1.50-
£2.10 per child; elec £1.50
cc Access, Visa/B'card
*Countryside setting only ½ mile from town centre.
Roads to all level, marked pitches. Free hot water
for showers, wash basins and dishwashing sinks.
No single-sex groups.
A3056 from Newport. ½ mile before Lake town sign
turn right up Whitecross Lane. 400 yards to site.*

HAVEN CHARACTER VILLAGE RĂC A
Landguard Road, PO37 7LL.
☎ (0983) 866131
Open: May-September
Size: 10 (50) acres, 150 touring pitches, 32 with
elec, 60 level pitches, 12 with hardstanding,
198 static caravans, 29 chalets. 16 hot showers,
16 cold showers, 20 WCs, 2 CWPs

(1991) Car & caravan, Motor caravan, Car & tent,
M/cycle* & tent £13.50; elec £2.20
cc Access, Visa/B'card
*Holiday village with entertainment complex and all
facilities. Families and couples only. 198 static*

caravans and 29 chalets for hire (own WCs). No
dogs.
In Shanklin, travel N from the A3055 along Regent
Street, take second turning left then first right and
follow signs to site.

Ninham Country Holidays
PO37 7PL.
☎ (0983) 864243
Open: Easter-September
Size: 20 acres, 150 touring pitches. 16 hot showers,
25 WCs. 3 static caravans

W of Sandown on A3056 at Temperature Ltd, turn
S into Whitecross Lane. Site 1 mile via Landguard.

VENTNOR Map 2 B3

APPULDURCOMBE HOLIDAY CENTRE RĂC A
Wroxall, PO38 3EP.
☎ (0983) 852597
Open: 1 March-31 October
Size: 5 (12) acres, 50 touring pitches, 44 with elec,
all level pitches, 40 static caravans. 12 hot showers,
12 cold showers, 12 WCs, 1 CWP

Car & caravan, Motor caravan, Car & tent, M/cycle*
& tent 90p-£2.20, all plus £1.40-£3.50 per adult,
75p-£2 per child; elec £1.70, dogs 50p
cc Access, Visa/B'card
*Set in rural surroundings - family site. 10 minutes
from Shanklin, Sandown or Ventnor. Dogs
restricted during high season. Take away foods
available during July and August only. 40 caravans
for hire (own WCs). Restaurant 500 yards.
Approach from Newport travelling S on the
A3020 through Rookley and Godshill to Whiteley
Bank, turn right on the B3327 for ¾ mile, turn right
on unclassified road for ¼ mile to site.*

YARMOUTH Map 2 B3

**THE ORCHARDS HOLIDAY CARAVAN
& CAMPING PARK** RĂC A
Newbridge, PO41 0TS.
☎ (0983) 78331
Open: March-October
Size: 8 (15) acres, 175 touring pitches, 144 with
elec, 50 level pitches, 5 with hardstanding, 56 static
caravans. 15 hot showers, 35 WCs, 2 CWPs

Charges on application.
cc Access, Visa/B'card
*Well-cared-for, family-run site in peaceful country
setting. Outdoor swimming pool and children's
play area. 56 caravans for hire (own WCs). No
motorcycle groups. Restaurant 1 mile. Package
deals on site fees and ferry tickets.
At ½ mile E of Yarmouth on A3054, turn S on to
B3401 for 4 miles to Newbridge, where turn left
into private road opposite Post Office.*

Seasonal variation of prices

Where a single price is given it may be a low season minimum charge - rates can increase
considerably at peak periods and for extra people or vehicles.
Please confirm prices with the site when booking.

💿 Snacks/take away ☒ Restaurant ◨ Swimming pool ▣ Shelter for campers 🐾 Dogs accepted

SCOTLAND

ABERCHIRDER *Grampian* Map 9 B2

McRobert Park Caravan Site
McRobert Park, Huntly Abous, AB5 5TT.
☎ (046 62560) 510
Open: (1991) 1 May-30 September
Size: 1 (4) acres, 9 touring pitches. 5 hot showers, 3 WCs. 6 static caravans

| | 🏕 | 🚐 | 🅰 | 🛄 | | | | 🏕 | 🐕 |

Turn N off the A97 in Aberchirder South Street, 9 miles SW of Banff, on to the B9023. Turn right after ¼ mile to site.

ABERDEEN *Grampian* Map 9 B3

HAZELHEAD CARAVAN & CAMPING SITE RAC L
Groat's Road, AB9 1XJ. ☎ (0224) 642121
Open: 1 April-30 September
Size: 6 acres, 165 touring pitches, mostly level, 165 with hardstanding. 22 hot showers, 33 WCs, 8 CWPs

| 🅰 | 🏕 | 🚐 | 🅰 | 🛄 | 🛍 | | | | 🐕 |

Charges on application.
A wooded site within 400 acres of Hazelhead Park and ornamental gardens. Two golf courses, pitch and putt, play park, summer season outdoor entertainment and summer season restaurant all within the park. Calor gas only.
3 miles W of city centre on A944 via Union Street, Albyn Place and Queens Road. Site is ¾ mile W of ring road (A947) on A944.

ABERFELDY *Tayside* Map 7 A1

ABERFELDY MUNICIPAL CARAVAN PARK RAC L
Dunkeld Road. ☎ (0887) 20662
Open: April-October
Size: 5 acres, 96 touring pitches, all level. 18 hot showers, 18 cold showers, 36 WCs, 1 CWP

| 🅰 | 🏕 | 🚐 | 🅰 | 🛄 | | | | | 🐕 |

Charges on application.
A neatly kept site beside the River Tay on the outskirts of the town. Children's play area. No gas available. Shop and restaurant 150 yards. Swimming pool 300 yards.
Accessible from A827 just E of the town.

Glengoulandie Caravan & Deer Park
Foss, by Pitlochry, PH15 6NL.
☎ (088 73) 261
Open: Easter-October
Size: 1 (3) acres, 10 touring pitches. 2 hot showers, 9 WCs. 38 static caravans

| | 🏕 | 🚐 | 🅰 | 🛄 | 🛍 | | | | 🐕 |

Site 4 miles S of Foss on B846.

ABERFOYLE *Central* Map 6 B1

COBLELAND CARAVAN & CAMPING SITE RAC L
(Forestry Commission), by Aberfoyle, FK8 3UX.
☎ (08772) 392
Open: 11 April-3 October
Size: 8 (12) acres, 100 touring pitches, all level, 44 with elec, 8 with hardstanding. 5 hot showers, 14 WCs, 2 CWPs

| 🅰 | 🏕 | 🚐 | 🅰 | 🛄 | 🛍 | | | | 🐕 |

(1991) £2-£2.50 per adult, £1-£1.20 per child; elec £1.40, awn 70p
Level site on the bank of the River Forth, surrounded by woodland. Swimming, fishing and cycle hire on site. Camping Gaz only. Restaurant 200 metres. Swimming pool 18 miles.
At 2 miles S of Aberfoyle on A81 turn W. Observe signs.

TROSSACHS HOLIDAY PARK RAC A
FK8 3SA.
☎ (08772) 614
Open: 15 March-31 October
Size: 6 (15) acres, 24 touring pitches, all with elec, 18 level pitches, 18 with hardstanding, 40 holiday caravans. 4 hot showers, 9 WCs, 2 CWPs

| | 🏕 | 🚐 | 🅰 | 🛄 | 🛍 | | | | 🐕 |

Car & caravan, Motor caravan, Car & tent, M/cycle* & tent £5.25-£5.50, plus £1-£1.50 per adult above 2, 50p-75p per child; elec £1.25-£1.50, awn £1
cc Major cards
This award-winning park is one of the finest privately owned caravan parks in Scotland. Excellent quality graded, superb situation, surrounded by mountains, lochs, rivers, forests. Outdoor adventure activities and mountain bike hire. 12 holiday caravans for hire (own WCs). Restaurant 1 mile. Swimming pool 16 miles.
Park is on the E side of the A81, 3 miles S of Aberfoyle.

ABOYNE *Grampian* Map 9 B3

ABOYNE LOCH CARAVAN PARK RAC A
AB34 5BR.
☎ (03398) 86244
Open: 1 April-31 October
Size: 4 (8) acres, 60 touring pitches, all with hardstanding, 40 with elec, 40 level pitches, 43 static caravans, 6 chalets. 8 hot showers, 8 cold showers, 18 WCs, 2 CWPs

| | 🏕 | 🚐 | 🅰 | 🛄 | 🛍 | | | | 🐕 |

Car & caravan, Motor caravan £7, Car & tent £4.50, plus 50p per adult above 2, child 25p; elec on meter (50p), awn £1; WS
Situated in 8 acres of mixed woodland with Loch Aboyne on three sides. Playground and swimming, boating and fishing on site. 3 caravans and 6 chalets for hire (own WCs). No single-sex groups. Restaurant and swimming pool ½ mile.
Site on N side of the A93, 1 mile E of Aboyne.

Drummie Hill Caravan Park
Tarland, AB3 4UP.
☎ (033 981) 388
Open: April-October
Size: 2 (8) acres, 45 touring pitches. 4 hot showers, 12 WCs. 60 static caravans

| 🅰 | 🏕 | 🚐 | 🅰 | 🛄 | 🛍 | | | 🏕 | 🐕 |

Approaching Tarland from SW (B9119), bear left before bridge for site in 600 yards.

🅰 Facilities for Disabled 🏕 Caravans accepted 🚐 Motor caravans 🅰 Tents 🛄 Laundry room 🛍 Shop

Resipole Farm Caravan and Camping Park

Loch Sunart, Acharacle, Argyll, PH36 4HX   Telephone: 0967 85 617/235

This small family run Park enjoys some of the most beautiful views in Scotland. Situated on the Ardnamurchan peninsula on the shores of Loch Sunart, Resipole has provided unforgettable holidays for the outdoor enthusiast and for those who require no more than a little peace and quiet. The Park is spacious, level and grassy with modern well maintained facilities which include free hot showers, laundry, deep sinks, hook up points, licensed shop and telephone. Opposite the park entrance is a private slipway for launching small boats and the Bar/Restaurant situated adjacent serves excellent food and drink. Holiday caravans and chalets for hire and for sale. Free colour brochure on request.

ACHARACLE *Highland*　　　Map 6 A1

Loch Sunart
Resipole. ☎ (096 785) 235
Open: Easter-October
Size: 8 acres, 45 touring pitches. 4 hot showers, 9 WCs

Site 7 miles W of Strontian on A861.

ALFORD *Grampian*　　　Map 9 B3

HAUGHTON CARAVAN PARK　　RAC A
Montgarrie Road, AB33 8NA.
☎ (09755) 62107
Open: April-September
Size: 18 acres, 135 touring pitches, all level, 42 with elec, 95 with hardstanding, 42 static caravans, 1 chalet. 20 hot showers, 37 WCs, 2 CWPs

(1991) Car & caravan, Motor caravan, Car & tent, M/cycle & tent £5.62; elec £1.30, awn £2.05
Set within sheltered woodlands of Haughton Country Park. Children's playground, putting, woodland and riverside walks, games rooms, picnic tables. 2 caravans and 1 chalet for hire (own WCs). Shop, restaurant and swimming pool ½ mile. No advance bookings.
½ mile N of Alford on road signed Montgarrie.

ALLOA *Central*　　　Map 7 A2

Diverswell Farm
Fishcross, FK10 3HL. ☎ (0259) 62802
Open: April-October
Size: 20 acres, 60 touring pitches. 6 hot showers, 13 WCs

6 miles E of Stirling, turn right off A91, S to St Andrews Road, ½ mile past B908 junction signpost to Fishcross, site on right ¾ mile.

ANNAN *Dumfries & Galloway*　　　Map 7 A3

GALA BANK CARAVAN SITE　　RAC L
North Street. ☎ (04612) 3311
Open: April-August
Size: 1 acre, 30 touring pitches, all level. 2 hot showers, 6 WCs

Charges on application.
A level grassy site next to River Annan. Children's play area, swimming and fishing on site. No gas available. Shop and restaurant ½ mile. Swimming pool 1 mile.
Turn N off A75 in Annan on to B722, Lady Street, continue into Thomas Street and North Street. Site on left ½ mile from A75.

Gemmell's Caravan Site
Central Road, Eastriggs. ☎ (0461) 304
Open: March-October
Size: 2 acres, 30 touring pitches. 4 WCs

Site entrance faces Eastriggs School, 3 miles E of Annan.

Queensberry Bay Caravan Park
Powfoot, DG12 5PU.
☎ (04617) 205
Open: April-October
Size: 11 acres, 60 touring pitches. 8 hot showers, 13 WCs

W of Annan on B724, turn S to Powfoot.

APPLECROSS *Highland*　　　Map 8 B2

Applecross Camp Site
via Loch Carron, Wester Ross
☎ (05204) 284
Open: Easter-September
Size: 6 acres, 60 touring pitches. 8 hot showers, 12 WCs

Access via high level road (not suitable for caravans) from 2 miles N of Kishorn (A896), or low level road from ½ mile S of Shieldaig (A896).

ARISAIG *Highland*　　　Map 8 B3

Camusdarach Camping Site
PH39 4NT.
☎ (068 75) 221
Open: April-September
Size: 3 acres, 25 touring pitches. 2 hot showers, 6 WCs

Follow A830 through Arisaig towards Morar. Site 4 miles further on.

⬛ Snacks/take away　☒ Restaurant　◻ Swimming pool　▣ Shelter for campers　🐕 Dogs accepted　159

GORTEN SANDS CARAVAN SITE RAC L
Gorten Farm, PH39 4NS. ☎ (06875) 283
Open: Easter-30 September
Size: 6 acres, 41 touring pitches, all level, 8 with elec, 4 static caravans. 2 hot showers, 10 WCs, 1 CWP

	🚐	🚙	⛺							🐕

(1991) Car & caravan, Motor caravan £5.50, Car & tent, M/cycle* & tent from £5; elec £1.50, awn 75p
Coastal farm site - private sandy beaches - water safe for bathing and boating. Views to Skye and the Isles. 30 acre tidal island, undisturbed bird, sea and wildlife. Abundance of wild flowers. Shop and restaurant ¾ mile. No gas available (stocked at shop). Swimming pool 38 miles. No minimum stay.
At 1¼ miles N of Arisaig on A830, turn W as signed `Back of Keppoch' for ¾ mile.

Kinloid Farm
PH39 4NT. ☎ (06875) 666
Open: Easter-October
Size: 2 acres, 4 touring pitches. 2 hot showers, 4 WCs. 6 static caravans, 2 chalets

	🚐	🚙	⛺	🧺						

½ mile N of Arisaig on A830 towards Mallaig, pass chapel on left, then take first right to site.

Portnadoran
PH39 4NT. ☎ (06875) 267
Open: March-October
Size: 2½ acres, 30 touring pitches. 4 hot showers, 9 WCs. 8 static caravans, 1 chalet

	🚐	🚙	⛺	🧺						🐕

Site 2 miles N of Arisaig, off A830.

Silver Beach
Bunnacaimbe, PH39 4NT. ☎ (06875) 630
Open: May-September
Size: 2 acres, 35 touring pitches. 2 hot showers, 4 WCs

	🚐	🚙	⛺							🐕

Site 2 miles N of Arisaig, off A830.

Skye View
PH39 4NT. ☎ (068 75) 209
Open: April-October
Size: ¾ acre, 20 touring pitches. 2 hot showers, 4 WCs

	🚐	🚙	⛺							🐕

Site 1 mile N of Arisaig, off A830.

ARROCHAR *Strathclyde* Map 6 B1

ARDGARTAN CARAVAN & CAMP SITE RAC L
Forestry Commission, Ardgartan, G83 7AL.
☎ (03012) 293
Open: 24 March-4 October
Size: 8 (9) acres, 160 touring pitches, all level, 40 with elec, 120 with hardstanding, 40 static caravans. 8 hot showers, 22 WCs, 3 CWPs

♿	🚐	🚙	⛺	🧺	🛒				🎣	🐕

Car & caravan, Motor caravan, Car & tent, M/cycle & tent £2.60 per adult, £1.30 per child; elec £1.35; WS
A level, easily accessible site extending into Loch Long, with launching facilities for small boats,

children's play area and dog exercise area. Adjacent to forest and forest walks. Restaurant 3 miles/5km. Swimming pool 10 miles/16km.
2½ miles W of Arrochar on A83.

AUCHENBLAE *Grampian* Map 9 B3

Brownmuir Caravan Park
by Laurencekirk, AB3 1SJ. ☎ (05612) 552
Open: April-October
Size: 6½ acres, 20 touring pitches. 2 hot showers, 8 WCs

	🚐	🚙	⛺	🧺	🛒					🐕

4 miles N of Laurencekirk at Fordoun (A94), turn NW for site.

AVIEMORE *Highland* Map 9 A3

AVIEMORE CENTRE CARAVAN PARK RAC L
PH22 1PF.
☎ (0479) 810751
Open: 1 December-31 October
Size: 6 acres, 90 touring pitches, all level, 72 with elec, all with hardstanding. 4 hot showers, 18 WCs, 1 CWP

	🚐	🚙		🧺						🐕

Car & caravan, Motor caravan £5.50-£6.50, plus 60p per person above 2 (under 5 years free); elec £1.30
cc Access/Mastercard, Visa, Eurocard
A wooded site attached to the Centre and adjoining the Craigellachie National Nature Reserve. Golf, tennis, fishing, riding, skiing, evening entertainment and a children's play area. No gas available. Single-sex groups by prior arrangement only. Discounts given to all caravanners on ice skating, adult cinema tickets. Bookings for 3 nights or more. Latest arrival 22.00hrs.
Off A9 in Aviemore village, next to entrance to Aviemore Centre.

Dalraddy Caravan Park
PH22 1QB. ☎ (0479) 810330
Open: All year
Size: 25 acres, 90 touring pitches. 10 hot showers, 42 WCs. 80 static caravans

	🚐	🚙	⛺	🧺	🛒					🐕

Site 4 miles SW of Aviemore on B9152.

GLENMORE CAMPING & CARAVAN PARK RAC A
Forestry Commission, Glenmore, PH22 1QU.
☎ (047986) 271
Open: 9 December-2 November
Size: 17 acres, 220 touring pitches, all level, 101 with elec, 100 with hardstanding. 20 hot showers, 26 WCs, 2 CWPs

♿	🚐	🚙	⛺	🧺		🍴	✖			🐕

(1991) Car & caravan, Motor caravan, Car & tent, M/cycle & tent £5-£6.15; elec £1.35
cc Major cards
Situated in superb scenery with many recreational and sporting facilities available nearby summer and winter. Good touring centre. Gas available 200 yards. Shop and restaurant 200 yards. Swimming pool 15 miles.
From the A9 turn on to the B9152 (S of Aviemore), at Aviemore take the B970 for 1¾ miles to Coylumbridge, keep right for 4¼ miles to site on right.

AYR *Strathclyde* — Map 6 B2

Crofthead Caravan Park
KA6 6EN. ☎ (0292) 263516
Open: March-October
Size: 3 (8½) acres, 80 touring pitches. 4 hot showers, 10 WCs. 35 static caravans

Travelling E from Ayr on A70, after roundabout junction with A77 take first right. Site ¾ mile.

MIDDLEMUIR HOLIDAY PARK RAC A
Tarbolton, Mauchline, KA5 5NR.
☎ (0292) 541647
Open: Easter-October
Size: 3 (16) acres, 20 touring pitches, all with elec, al level, 5 with hardstanding, 40 static caravans, 2 chalets. 4 hot showers, 9 WCs, 1 CWP

Car & caravan, Motor caravan, Car & tent £5-£8, plus £1 per person above 2; elec £1.50, awn £1-£1.50, dogs £1.25; WS
Quiet, family-run site with children's play area. 25 caravans for hire (own WCs). Shop and restaurant 1½ miles (mobile shop visits park). Swimming pool 6 miles.
On main B743 Ayr to Mauchline road.

SKELDON CARAVAN PARK RAC L
Hollybush, KA6 7ED. ☎ (029256) 202
Open: 1 April-30 September
Size: 2½ (3) acres, 20 touring pitches, all level, 6 with elec, 10 static caravans. 2 hot showers, 7 WCs

(1991) Car & caravan, Motor caravan, Car & tent, M/cycle & tent £5.50; elec £1.75, awn 50p, dogs free; WS
Flat area, very sheltered, pleasantly situated on bank of River Doon. Children's play area. Restaurant ½ mile. Swimming pool 6 miles.
Leave A74 at border on to A75 to Castle Douglas and then on to A713 (marked with a Thistle Recommended Tourist Route to Ayrshire) and observe caravan park signs on A713; site 6 miles from Ayr.

SUNDRUM CASTLE HOLIDAY PARK RAC A
Coylton, KA6 6HB. ☎ (0292) 570057
Open: 22 March-31 October
Size: 5 (23) acres, 52 touring pitches, all level, 24 with elec, all with hardstanding, 240 static caravans. 4 hot showers, 10 WCs, 2 CWPs

Charges on application. WS
cc Access, Visa/B'card
Well-organised site with games room, adventure playground, and nightclub. Suitable for families. 103 caravans for hire (own WCs).
4 miles E of Ayr on A70 turn N, site signposted on left.

BALLOCH *Strathclyde* — Map 6 B2

TULLICHEWAN CARAVAN PARK RAC A
Old Luss Road, G83 8QP. ☎ (0389) 59475
Open: 1 December-31 October
Size: 13½ acres, 140 touring pitches, 100 with elec, 80 with hardstanding, 70 level pitches, 29 static caravans, 6 chalets. 10 hot showers, 30 WCs, 3 CWPs

Car & caravan, Motor caravan, Car & tent, M/cycle & tent £7.50-£9.50, extra person £1; elec £1.50, awn £1.50
cc Access, Visa/B'card
A very attractive park, with a mix of touring and holiday let units. Excellent facilities on site. 6 caravans and 6 chalets for hire (own WCs). Swimming pool ¼ mile.
From the (roundabout) junction of the A82 and the A811, SW of Balloch, travel E on the A811 for just over ¼ mile, turn left to site on left.

BALMACARA *Highland* — Map 8 B3

BALMACARA WOODLAND CAMP SITE RAC L
Forestry Commission, Balmacara Square, IV40 8DN.
☎ (059986) 321
Open: 18 April-30 September
Size: 4 (10) acres, 53 touring pitches, all level, all with hardstanding, 8 with elec. 10 WCs, 2 CWPs

(1991) Car & caravan, Motor caravan, Car & tent, M/cycle & tent £2.50-£3.50; elec £1
An attractive woodland site beside Loch Alsh, offering superb views over to Skye. Two forest walks are on the doorstep, or orienteering for the more energetic. Do not leave food about, or the pine martens will take it! Shop and restaurant 2 miles. Swimming pool 35 miles. No gas available. Arrivals to be before 10pm.
3 miles E of Kyle of Lochalsh, off the A890.

RERAIG CARAVAN SITE RAC L
IV40 8DH.
☎ (059986) 215
Open: 1 May-30 September
Size: 2 acres, 45 touring pitches, 40 level pitches, 28 with elec, 7 with hardstanding. 4 hot showers, 9 WCs, 1 CWP

(1991) Car & caravan, Motor caravan, Car & tent £4.30, M/cycle & tent £3.50; elec £1, awn £1
A level, family-run site next to a sea loch, sheltered by wooded hills. Balmacara Hotel next door. Calor gas only. Shop 60 metres. Restaurant 25 metres. An ideal base from which to tour Wester Ross and the Isle of Skye. 5 days maximum stay on same pitch for awnings or tents.
From the junction of the A87 and A890, 3 miles W of Dornie, continue towards Kyle of Lochalsh for 1¾ miles, turn into lane adjacent to Balmacara Hotel.

BANCHORY *Grampian* — Map 9 B3

Banchory Lodge Caravan Site
Dee Street, AB3 3HY.
☎ (03302) 2246
Open: April-October
Size: 6 acres, 25 touring pitches. 10 hot showers, 38 WCs, 153 static caravans

Site off A93, near Bridge of Dee.

Feughside Caravan Site
Strachan, AB3 3NT. ☎ (033 045) 669
Open: April-October
Size: 3 acres, 16 touring pitches. 6 hot showers,
9 WCs. 45 static caravans

Site 5 miles W of Banchory (B976), behind
Feughside Inn.

BANFF *Grampian*　　　　　Map 9 B2

LINKS CARAVAN SITE　　　　RAC L
☎ (02612) 2228
Open: 1 April-September
Size: ¾ (4) acres, 33 touring pitches, static
caravans. 12 hot showers, 30 WCs

Charges on application. WS
*A good seaside site situated along the magnificent
sands of Banff Bay. Swimming, boating, fishing
and children's playground on site. Calor gas only.
Caravans for hire.*
1 mile W of Banff on A98, turn N on to B9139. Site
300 yards on right.

BARGRENNAN *Dumfries & Galloway*　Map 6 B3

Merrick Caravan Park
Near Newton Stewart, DG8 6RN.
☎ (067 184) 280
Open: March-October
Size: 6½ acres, 10 touring pitches. 4 hot showers, 9
WCs. Static caravans

From Newton Stewart, take A714 to Bargrennan.
Site ½ mile from road near Glentrool village.

BARRHILL *Strathclyde*　　　　Map 6 B3

WINDSOR HOLIDAY PARK　　　RAC L
KA26 0PZ. ☎ (046582) 355
Open: 1 March-31 October
Size: 2 (6) acres, 30 touring pitches, 10 with elec, 20
level pitches, 10 with hardstanding, 50 static
caravans. 2 hot showers, 14 WCs, 2 CWPs

Charges on application. WS
*This pleasant country site has a children's play
area. Shop open May-August. 3 caravans for hire
(own WCs). Calor gas only. Restaurant 100 yards.*
From the SE on the A714 travel through Barrhill to
site on right in 1½ miles.

BEATTOCK *Dumfries & Galloway*　Map 7 A3

BEATTOCK CARAVAN PARK　　　RAC L
DG10 9QX. ☎ (06833) 460
Open: 1 April-31 October
Size: 3 (3½) acres, 30 touring pitches, all level, with
elec, static caravans. 4 hot showers, 5 WCs

Charges on application.
*A level, grassy site with games room and
gymnasium. 4 caravans for hire.*
In the centre of Beattock village, ¼ mile from
junction of A74 and A701 and 2 miles S of Moffat.

BEATTOCK HOUSE CARAVAN PARK　RAC L
DG10 9QB. ☎ (06833) 402
Open: All year
Size: 2 acres, 15 touring pitches, all level, 12 with
elec. 2 hot showers, 3 WCs, 1 CWP

(1991) Car & caravan, Motor caravan, Car & tent,
M/cycle & tent £6, plus £1.25 per person above 2;
elec £1; WS
*A parkland site in the grounds of an hotel close to
the river; fishing possible. Children's play area.
Calor gas only. Shop 200 yards.*
At junction of A74 and A701, take unclassified road
to Beattock, site on left in grounds of Beattock
House Hotel.

BEAULY *Highland*　　　　　Map 9 A2

Cruivend Caravan & Camping Site
IV4 7BE. ☎ (0463) 782367
Open: March-October
Size: 2 acres, 30 touring pitches. 6 hot showers,
8 WCs

Site in Beauly, near Lovat Bridge.

BETTYHILL *Highland*　　　　Map 9 A1

CRAIGDHU CARAVAN & CAMPING SITE　RAC L
by Thurso, KW14 7SP. ☎ (06412) 273
Open: 1 April-31 October
Size: 5 (6) acres, 90 touring pitches, several level,
6 with elec, 4 static caravans, 4 hot showers,
7 WCs, 1 CWP

Car & caravan £5-£6, Motor caravan £5, Car & tent
£4.50 M/cycle & tent £3; elec £1.50, awn 50p; WS
*Sheltered, rural site facing beautiful, clean, sandy
beach. Picturesque scenery. 4 caravans for hire
(2 with own WCs). Calor gas only. Shop 200 yards.
Restaurant 300 yards.*
Adjacent to A836, Bettyhill village.

BLAIR ATHOLL *Tayside*　　　Map 7 A1

BLAIR CASTLE CARAVAN PARK　　RAC A
Near Pitlochry, PH18 5SR. ☎ (079681) 263
Open: 1 April- Mid October
Size: 35 acres, 330 touring pitches, 100 level
pitches, 100 with elec, 12 with hardstanding,
100 static caravans. 28 hot showers, 90 WCs,
3 CWPs

(1991) Car & caravan £7, Motor caravan £6, Car &
tent, M/cycle & tent £5; elec £1.50, awn £1.50, dogs
50p
*Extensive open spaces and walking/recreation
areas. Coffee Shop and take away available during
high season. Children's play area. 26 caravans for
hire (own WCs).*
Turn N on the A9 to Blair Atholl and follow signs to
site.

River Tilt Caravan Site
Bridge of Tilt, PH18 5TE.
☎ (079 681) 467
Open: All year
Size: 4 (14) acres, 34 touring pitches. 4 hot

showers, 16 WCs. 90 static caravans

🏕️🚐🛳️⛺🛏️ ❌ 🏠🐕

Site behind Glen Tilt Hotel in Blair Atholl.

BLAIRGOWRIE *Tayside*   *Map 7 A1*

BALLINTUIM HOTEL & CARAVAN PARK   RAC L
Bridge of Cally, PH10 7NH.
☎ (025086) 276
Open: All year
Size: 2½ (18) acres, 30 touring pitches, all level, all with elec, 10 with hardstanding, 34 static caravans. 7 hot showers, 6 WCs, 2 CWPs

♿🏕️🚐⛺🛏️ 🌂❌ 🐕

(1991) Car & caravan, Motor caravan, Car & tent, M/cycle & tent £3.50; elec £1.25, awn £1; WS cc Access, Visa/B'card
A well-managed site in the grounds of a small hotel. Children's play area. Mountain bikes for hire. 12 caravans for hire (own WCs). Shop 400 yards. From Blairgowrie travel N on the A93 for 6 miles to Bridge of Cally, turn left on the A924 for 3½ miles to site on right.

BOAT OF GARTEN *Highland*   *Map 9 A3*

Campgrounds of Scotland
PH24 3BN. ☎ (047983) 652
Open: All year
Size: 6 acres, 37 touring pitches. 6 hot showers, 2b WCs. 5 static caravans

♿🚐🛳️⛺🛏️📷 🐕

2 miles N of Aviemore, turn off A9 on to A95 N, following Boat of Garten signs, then caravan site signs.

BONCHESTER BRIDGE *Borders*   *Map 7 A2*

Bonchester Bridge Caravan Site
☎ (045086) 676
Open: April-October
Size: 3 acres, 25 touring pitches. 4 hot showers, 10 WCs

🚐🛳️⛺🛏️📷 🐕

Site 8 miles SE of Hawick on A6088.

BRECHIN *Tayside*   *Map 7 A1*

East Mill Road Caravan Site
DD9 7AL. ☎ (03562) 2810
Open: April-September
Size: 10 acres, 65 touring pitches. 4 hot showers, 9 WCs

🏕️🛳️⛺🛏️📷🌂 🐕

S off A935 in Brechin. Site signed.

BRIDGE OF CALLY *Tayside*   *Map 7 A1*

Corriefodly Hotel Caravan Site
PH10 7JG. ☎ (025 086) 236
Open: All year
Size: 4 acres, 38 touring pitches. 4 hot showers, 12 WCs. 72 static caravans

🏕️🚐⛺🛏️ 🌂❌ 🐕

Site on A924, ¼ mile from junction with A93.

BRORA *Highland*   *Map 9 A2*

Riverside Croft Caravan Site
Stone-House, Doll. ☎ (0408) 2189
Open: May-October
Size: 2 acres, 21 touring pitches. 1 hot shower, 4 WCs. Static caravans

🚐🛳️⛺🛏️ 🐕

Site 2 miles S of Brora, off A9.

BURGHEAD *Grampian*   *Map 9 A2*

Burghead Caravan Site
☎ (0343) 45121
Open: (1991) April-September
Size: 40 touring pitches. Hot showers, WCs. Static caravans

♿🏕️🚐⛺🛏️ 🐕

Turn S off B9089 on outskirts of Burghead.

Red Craig Hotel
IV30 2XX. ☎ (0343) 835663
Open: April-October
Size: 4½ acres, 38 touring pitches. 4 hot showers, 6 WCs. 7 static caravans

🏕️🚐⛺🛏️ ☕❌ 🐕

Off B9012 Burghead to Hopeman road, opposite radio mast.

Station Caravan Park
Hopeman, IV30 2RU. ☎ (0343) 830880
Open: April-October
Size: 4½ acres, 40 touring pitches. 8 hot showers, 20 WCs. 35 static caravans

🏕️🚐⛺🛏️ 🐕

In Hopeman (B9012), turn N towards harbour. Site on left.

CALLANDER *Central*   *Map 6 B1*

Callander Holiday Park
Invertrossachs Road, FK17 8HW.
☎ (0877) 30265
Open: March-October
Size: 35 acres, 40 touring pitches. 8 hot showers, 20 WCs. 110 static caravans

🏕️🚐 🛏️ 🐕

S from Callander on A81, turn right on to A892. Site ½ mile.

Gart Caravan Park
FK17 8HW. ☎ (0877) 30002
Open: April-October
Size: 25 acres, 130 touring pitches. 6 hot showers, 20 WCs

♿🏕️🚐 🛏️ 🐕

Site 1 mile E of Callander on A84.

CANNICH *Highland*   *Map 9 A3*

Campgrounds of Scotland
☎ (045 65) 364
Open: December-October
Size: 7 acres, 40 touring pitches. 4 hot showers, 9 WCs

🔲 Snacks/take away   ❌ Restaurant   🔵 Swimming pool   🏠 Shelter for campers   🐕 Dogs accepted

On A831 in Cannich.

CARGILL *Tayside* — Map 7 A1

Beech Hedge Caravan Park
PH2 6DU. ☎ (025083) 249
Open: March-October
Size: 3 acres, 12 touring pitches. 2 hot showers,
6 WCs. 8 static caravans, 1 chalet

Site 1 mile N of Cargill on A93.

CARNOUSTIE *Tayside* — Map 7 A1

WOODLANDS CARAVAN PARK   RĀC A
Newton Road, DD7 6HR. ☎ (0241) 54430
Open: Easter-October
Size: 4½ acres, 83 touring pitches, all level, 65 with
elec, 14 with hardstanding, 19 static caravans.
12 hot showers, 23 WCs, 2 CWPs

Charges on application.
*In the grounds of former Carnoustie House, a
wooded site with a children's play area. No gas
available. Shop 20 yards. Restaurant and
swimming pool ¼ mile.*
At E end of High Street in town centre, turn inland
(Carlogie Road) and take fifth turn left at sign.

CARRADALE *Strathclyde* — Map 6 A2

CARRADALE BAY CARAVAN SITE   RĀC L
The Steading. ☎ (05833) 665
Open: Easter-End September
Size: 9 acres, 60 touring pitches, 30 with elec. 4 hot
showers, 16 WCs, 2 CWPs

Charges on application.
cc Access, Visa/B'card
*Well-kept, grassy dune site on the edge of
Carradale Bay's safe sandy beach. Children's play
area on site. Shop and restaurant ½ mile.*
Travel to Campbeltown from Tarbert on A83, turn
N on B842 for 14½ miles, turn E on B879 for
½ mile, site on right. NB. These roads are
extremely narrow and hilly with sharp bends.
Caravanners intending to use this site should
exercise extreme caution.

CARSTAIRS *Strathclyde* — Map 7 A2

Newhouse Caravan Park
Ravenstruther, ML11 8NP.
☎ (055 587) 0228
Open: All year
Size: 4 acres, 45 touring pitches. 4 hot showers,
10 WCs

Site 3 miles E of Lanark on A70.

CASTLE DOUGLAS *Dumfries & Galloway* — Map 6 B3

Lochside Caravan Park
DG7 1EZ. ☎ (0556) 2949
Open: March-October
Size: 6 acres, 160 touring pitches. 13 hot showers,

29 WCs

In Castle Douglas (A75), by Carlingwark Loch.

COCKBURNSPATH *Borders* — Map 7 A2

Chesterfield Caravan Park
The Neuk, TD13 7YH. ☎ (03683) 226
Open: April-October
Size: 5 acres, 40 touring pitches. 10 hot showers,
17 WCs. 40 static caravans

Just S from Cockburnspath on A1, fork right into
Abbey St Bathans road. Site ½ mile.

COLDINGHAM *Borders* — Map 7 B2

Coldingham Caravan Park
Eyemouth, TD14 5NT. ☎ (08907) 71316
Open: March-November
Size: 10½ acres, 25 touring pitches. 10 hot
showers, 30 WCs. 165 static caravans

Site on W side of Coldingham (A1107).

COMRIE *Tayside* — Map 6 B1

Twenty Shilling Wood Caravan Park
PH6 2JY. ☎ (0764) 70411
Open: 1 April-mid October
Size: 3 (10½) acres, 21 touring pitches. 4 hot
showers, 14 WCs. 29 static caravans, 1 chalet

½ mile W of Comrie on A85, observe site sign.

WEST LODGE CARAVAN SITE   RĀC L
PH6 2LS. ☎ (0764) 70354
Open: 1 April-31 October
Size: 3 acres, 20 touring pitches, all level, 10 with
elec, 30 static caravans. 6 hot showers, 6 cold
showers, 13 WCs, 1 CWP

(1991) Car & caravan, Motor caravan, Car & tent,
M/cycle & tent £3-£4; all plus 50p per adult, 25p per
child; elec £1.25, awn 60p; WS
*Small, sheltered site with good facilities. Quiet and
friendly, family-run. 6 caravans for hire (own WCs).
Restaurant 1 mile. Swimming pool 5 miles.
Minimum stay in static caravan is 1 night.*
1 mile E of Comrie on A85.

CONNEL *Strathclyde* — Map 6 B1

Barcaldine Garden Caravan Park
Barcaldine, PA37 1SG. ☎ (063172) 348
Open: March-October
Size: 4 acres, 75 touring pitches. 4 hot showers,
17 WCs

6 miles N of Connel Bridge on A828.

North Ledaig Caravan Site
PA37 1RT. ☎ (063171) 291
Open: Easter-October
Size: 13 acres, 140 touring pitches. 18 hot showers,
27 WCs

[icon row]

In Connel, leave A85 and turn N over Connel Bridge, signposted Fort William (A828). Site 1½ miles.

Tralee Bay Holiday Park
Benderloch. ☎ (063 172) 255
Open: April-October
Size: 10 acres, 47 touring pitches. 8 hot showers, 15 WCs. 60 static caravans

[icon row]

Site 3½ miles N of Connel on A828.

Camping & Caravanning Club Site
Barcaldine, PA37 1SG.
Open: 30 March-26 October
Size: 6 acres, 75 touring pitches. 4 hot showers, 17 WCs

[icon row]

Charges on application.
From the A828 take the turning at the "Kelko" plant sign, the site is on the right.

Aberlour Gardens Caravan Park
Aberlour-on-Spey, AB3 9LD.
☎ (034 05) 586
Open: April-October
Size: 5½ acres, 20+ touring pitches. 2 hot showers, 5 WCs 26 static caravans

[icon row]

Just S of Craigellachie, off A95. Site signed.

Elchies Caravan & Camping Park
Elchies, AB3 9SL. ☎ (034 06) 414
Open: April-October
Size: 3 acres, 20 touring pitches. 2 hot showers, 8 WCs

[icon row]

From A941, turn W on to B9102. Site 2½ miles on left.

Ashburn House
St Andrews Road, KY10 3UL.
☎ (0333) 50314
Open: March-October
Size: 3 acres, 6 touring pitches. 3 hot showers, 6 WCs 64 static caravans

[icon row]

Near town centre on A917.

Sauchope Links Caravan Park
☎ (0333) 50460
Open: April-October
Size: 12 acres, 50 touring pitches. 4 hot showers, 10 WCs. 85 static caravans

[icon row]

1 mile E of Crail on road to Fife Ness.

Crawford Caravan & Camp Site
Murray Place, Carlisle Road, ML12 6TW.

☎ (08642) 258
Open: April-October
Size: 2 acres, 25 touring pitches. 2 hot showers, 6 WCs

[icon row]

Site in Crawford, off A74.

CASTLE CARY HOLIDAY PARK   RAC A
DG8 7DQ. ☎ (067182) 264
Open: 1 March-31 October
Size: 15 acres, 54 touring pitches, all level, 32 with elec, 10 with hardstanding, 20 static caravans. 10 hot showers, 16 WCs, 1 CWP

[icon row]

Car & caravan, Motor caravan, Car & tent, M/cycle & tent £5.50-£7.70, plus 80p per person above 2; extra car £1; elec £1.50, awn £1, dogs free; WS cc Visa/B'card
Superbly laid-out holiday park with beautiful natural parkland setting and first class facilities. Boating pond. Castle with Laird's Inn. Lounge bar/restaurant.
Directly off main A75 Euroroute on right hand side, ½ mile S of Creetown village.

CREETOWN CARAVAN PARK   RAC L
Silver Street, DG8 7JF. ☎ (067182) 377
Open: 1 March-end October
Size: 3½ (4) acres, 25 touring pitches, all level, 20 with elec, 51 static caravans. 7 hot showers, 7 cold showers, 15 WCs, 2 CWPs

[icon row]

(1991) Car & caravan, Motor caravan, Car & tent, M/cycle & tent £5;£6; elec £1
Small family-run site. 10 caravans for hire (own WCs). Calor gas only. Shop and restaurant 200 yards.
In Creetown on A75, turn W by the clock tower for 200 yards.

Glen Dochart Caravan Park
Luib, FK20 8QT. ☎ (05672) 637
Open: March-October
Size: 15 acres, 45 touring pitches. 4 hot showers, 10 WCs. 60 static caravans

[icon row]

Site 6 miles E of Crianlarich on A85.

CRIEFF HOLIDAY VILLAGE   RAC A
Turret Bank, PH7 4JN. ☎ (0764) 3513
Open: All year
Size: 2½ (4½) acres, 56 touring pitches, all level, 36 with elec, all with hardstanding, 40 static caravans, 3 chalets. 8 hot showers, 13 WCs, 1 CWP

[icon row]

(1991) Car & caravan, Motor caravan £5.50-£7.15, Car & tent, M/cycle & tent £4.50-£6; elec £1.20, awn £1; WS
cc Major cards
Bordered by River Turret and beautiful public parks: quietly situated. Easy walking distance from

---

town centre. Ideal for touring the Highlands.
10 caravans and 3 chalets for hire (own WCs).
Restaurant 300 yards. Swimming pool ¾ mile.
½ mile W of Crieff on A85, turn left at crossroads,
site 300 yards on left. Well-signposted.

Thorn Hill Lodge Tenting Park
Monzievaird, PH7 4JU. ☎ (0764) 2453
Open: Easter-October
Size: 1 acre, 15 touring pitches. 2 hot showers,
3 WCs

3 miles W of Crieff on A85, turn S at telephone box
on to small side road. Camp site 600 yards on left.

CROCKETFORD Dumfries & Galloway   Map 7 A3

PARK OF BRANDEDLEYS   RAC A
Near Dumfries, DG2 8RG. ☎ (055669) 250
Open: 1 March-31 October
Size: 7 (16) acres, 80 touring pitches, all with elec,
45 level pitches, 20 with hardstanding, 27 static
caravans, 4 chalets. 13 hot showers, 25 WCs,
2 CWPs

Car & caravan, Motor caravan, Car & tent £7,
M/cycle & tent £6; all plus £1.50 per adult, £1.20 per
child; extra car £1; elec £1.75, awn £2
cc Access, Mastercharge, Visa, Eurocard
Well-landscaped with views to Auchenreoch Loch
and the Galloway Hills, the park has "Excellent"
grading. Toilets include en suite shower/WHB/WC
units, bath and hair care facilities. Washing-up and
laundry rooms. 12 caravans and 4 chalets for hire
(own WCs). No groups, no singles parties.
Turn S off A75 in Crocketford (9 miles W of
Dumfries) at international sign for 100 yards.

CULLEN Grampian   Map 9 B2

Logie Caravan Site
☎ (0343) 45121
Open: (1991) April-September
Size: 6 acres, 40 touring pitches. Hot showers,
WCs. Static caravans

Signposted to the E of Cullen from A98.

CULZEAN CASTLE Strathclyde   Map 6 B2

Camping & Caravanning Club Site
Glenside, KA19 8JX. ☎ (06556) 627
Open: 30 March-26 October
Size: 6 acres, 90 touring pitches. 4 hot showers,
9 WCs

Charges on application.
In Culzean Castle Country Park, with views over the
Firth of Arran and the Mull of Kintyre. Plenty of
wildlife to see.
From the A719 follow the sign to Culzean Castle
and Country Park, take the right fork for the site.

CUMNOCK Strathclyde   Map 6 B2

WOODROAD CARAVAN PARK   RAC L
☎ (0290) 22111
Open: Easter-September

Size: 11 acres, 100 touring pitches. Hot showers,
WCs

Charges on application.
A neatly kept site, with children's play area. Open
air swimming pool, tennis courts and putting green
adjacent to park.
On NW outskirts of Cumnock on A76, turn right
just after crossing River Lugar. Signposted.

CUPAR Fife   Map 7 A1

CLAYTON CARAVAN PARK   RAC A
KY16 9YA. ☎ (0334) 870242
Open: Easter-October
Size: 2 acres, 26 touring pitches, 20 level pitches,
all with elec, 20 with hardstanding, 215 static
caravans. 5 hot showers, 10 WCs, 1 CWP

(1991) Car & caravan, Motor caravan £6.50-£8.50;
elec £1, awn free
cc Access, Visa/B'card
Rural, undulating park, sheltered by trees. Pitches
are flat and where grass-surfaced are well-
maintained. Play park, pool room, TV room, club
room, restaurant and licensed bar on site.
Swimming pool 4½ miles.
Site on S side of the A91 4½ miles NW of Cupar,
5½ miles W of St Andrews.

DALBEATTIE Dumfries & Galloway   Map 7 A3

Barlochan Caravan Park
Palnackie, by Castle Douglas
☎ (055660) 256
Open: April-October
Size: 9 acres, 45 touring pitches. 6 hot showers,
9 WCs. 35 static caravans

Take A711 W from Dalbeattie. In ½ mile bear left at
t-junction signposted Auchencairn. Site 2 miles.

Castle Point Caravan Park
Rockcliffe, by Dalbeattie
☎ (055663) 248
Open: April-September
Size: 2 acres, 38 touring pitches. 2 hot showers,
4 WCs

Take A710 from Dalbeattie. After 8 miles turn right
to Rockcliffe. Site signed after 1 mile.

Doonpark Caravan Park
Kippford, DG5 4LF. ☎ (055662) 259
Open: March-October
Size: 7 acres, 20 touring pitches. 4 hot showers,
7 WCs

Site 3 miles S of Dalbeattie on A710.

Islecroft Caravan Site
Colliston Park, Mill Street, DG5 4HE.
☎ (0556) 610012
Open: Easter-September
Size: 3 acres, 74 touring pitches. 4 hot showers,
10 WCs. 74 static caravans

⑤ Facilities for Disabled ⊞ Caravans accepted ⊞ Motor caravans ⊠ Tents ⊟ Laundry room ⊞ Shop [icons] In Dalbeattie, next to Colliston Park.

Kippford Caravan Park
Kippford, by Dalbeattie. ☎ (055662) 636
Open: March-October
Size: 16 acres, 45 touring pitches. 4 hot showers,
10 WCs. 90 static caravans, 23 chalets

[icons] Site 4 miles S of Dalbeattie on A710.

Sandyhills Bay Leisure Park
Sandyhills, by Dalbeattie
☎ (038778) 257
Open: April-October
Size: 6 acres, 40 touring pitches. 4 hot showers,
13 WCs. 30 static caravans

[icons] In Sandyhills village, near golf course.

DALRYMPLE *Strathclyde* — Map 6 B2

Doon Valley Caravan Park
Burnton Road. ☎ (029256) 849
Open: All year
Size: 11 acres, 20 touring pitches. 8 hot showers,
12 WCs. 45 static caravans

[icons] From A77, turn E on B7034 to Dalrymple. After
1½ miles turn left, taking B742 in village. Site
500 yards.

DAVIOT *Highland* — Map 9 A2

AUCHNAHILLIN CARAVAN &
CAMPING PARK RAC A
Daviot East, IV1 2XQ. ☎ (0463) 85286
Open: Mid March-Mid October
Size: 4/5 (10) acres, 65 touring pitches, all level,
24 with elec, 6 with hardstanding, 22 static
caravans. 6 hot showers, 12 WCs, 1 CWP

[icons] Pitch £1.25, Caravan £2, Motor caravan £2.50, Car
£1, Tent £1-£2, M/cycle 50p, all plus 75p-£1.25 per
adult, 35p per child; elec £1.50, awn £1.25; WS
*Ideally situated for touring, only 5 minutes from
the centre of Inverness, yet in unspoiled
surroundings of hills and forests with a vast range
of places to visit and sights to see. 20 caravans and
1 chalet for hire (own WCs). Swimming pool
6 miles.*
Take the B9154 loop 5 miles S of Inverness off the
A9. North end signposted "Daviot East" and the
south end signposted for "Moy".

DINGWALL *Highland* — Map 9 A2

Camping & Caravanning Club Site
Jubilee Park, IV15 9QZ. ☎ (0349) 62236
Open: 30 March-26 October
Size: 6½ acres, 110 touring pitches. 4 hot showers,
11 WCs

[icons] Charges on application.
cc Access, Visa/B'card
On the shores of Cromarty Firth. Fishing, riding,

*and the town sports centre and recreation park is
nearby. Shop 1 mile.*
Follow the A862, follow the town centre signs
down Tulloch Street into High Street, into Ferry
Road turning left into Jubilee Park Road for the
site.

DOLLAR *Central* — Map 7 A1

Riverside Caravan Park
FK14 7LF. ☎ (02594) 2896
Open: April-September
Size: 5 acres, 30 touring pitches. 4 hot showers,
14 WCs. 30 static caravans

[icons] In Dollar on B913, ½ mile S off A91.

DORNOCH *Highland* — Map 9 A2

Dornoch Caravan & Camping Site
The Links. ☎ (0862) 810423
Open: March-October
Size: 25 acres, 125 touring pitches. 16 hot showers,
38 WCs. 75 static caravans

[icons] From town centre leave S along Church Street and
River Street to site.

GRANNIE'S HEILAN' HAME RAC A
Embo, IV25 3QP. ☎ (0862) 810383
Open: 31 March-31 October/all year for tourers
Size: 30 (32) acres, 224 touring pitches, 200 level
pitches, 110 with elec, 66 static caravans. 14 hot
showers, 46 WCs, 1 CWP

[icons] (1991) Car & caravan, Motor caravan, Car & tent,
M/cycle* & tent £7.15-£10.70; elec £1
cc Access, Visa/B'card
*Seaside holiday park where the general facilities
also include sauna, spa bath, children's games
room. Right close to beautiful sandy beach, also in
one of Scotland's lowest rainfall areas. 66 caravans
for hire (own WCs), minimum stay in hired
caravans is 2 nights, available 31 March to
31 October. Park is open to tourers all year round.*
Turn N in Dornoch and follow unclassified road for
2 miles to Embo.

Pitgrudy Caravan Site
☎ (086282) 253
Open: Easter-September
Size: 9 acres, 40 touring pitches. 4 hot showers,
8 WCs. 8 static caravans

[icons] Site 1 mile N of Dornoch on B9168.

DOUGLAS *Strathclyde* — Map 7 A2

Crossburn Caravan Park
ML11 0QA. ☎ (0555) 851029
Open: All year
Size: 4 acres, 60 touring pitches. 5 hot showers,
14 WCs. 2 static caravans

[icons] Turn W off M74 on to A70 to Ayr. Site 2 miles.

[icon] Snacks/take away [icon] Restaurant [icon] Swimming pool [icon] Shelter for campers [icon] Dogs accepted 167

DRUMMORE Dumfries & Galloway — Map 6 B3

Clashwhannon Caravan Site
DG9 9PS. ☎ (077684) 374
Open: March-October
Size: 1 acres, 6 touring pitches. 2 hot showers,
6 WCs. 6 static caravans

[icons: caravan, motor caravan, tent, laundry, shop, cup, restaurant, games, dog]

Site ½ mile N of Drummore on A716.

DRUMNADROCHIT Highland — Map 9 A3

Bearnock
Glen Urquhart. ☎ (04564) 353
Open: March-November
Size: 4 acres, 10 touring pitches. 1 WC

[icons: caravan, motor caravan, tent, shop, cup, restaurant, dog]

6½ miles W of Drumnadrochit (A831).

Borlum Farm
☎ (04562) 220
Open: May-September
Size: 2 acres, 40 touring pitches. 2 hot showers,
6 WCs

[icons: caravan, motor caravan, tent, laundry, dog]

Site ¼ mile S of Lewiston village on A82.

DRYMEN Central — Map 6 B2

Camping & Caravanning Club Site
Milarrochy Bay, Balmaha, G63 0JQ.
☎ (036087) 236
Open: 30 March-26 October
Size: 9 acres, 150 touring pitches. 6 hot showers,
11 WCs

[icons: disabled, caravan, motor caravan, tent, laundry, shop, dog]

Charges on application.
Site is on the shores of Loch Lomond, and has its own landing stage. Children's play area.
From the A811 take the B837 to Balmaha, the site is ½ mile N of Balmaha.

CASHEL CARAVAN & CAMP SITE ⚓ L
Forestry Commission, Rowardennan, G63 0AW.
☎ (036087) 234
Open: 11 April-3 October
Size: 12 (20) acres, 120 touring pitches, all level,
40 with elec. 8 hot showers, 20 WCs, 2 CWPs

[icons: disabled, caravan, motor caravan, tent, laundry, shop, dog]

(1991) Car & caravan, Motor caravan, Car & tent,
M/cycle & tent all £2-£2.50 per adult, £1-£1.20 per child; elec £1.40, awn 70p, dogs 10p
Adjacent to a beach on Loch Lomond with scattered trees. Swimming, boating, fishing and play area on site. Camping Gaz only. Restaurant 3 miles.
N from Drymen follow B837 for 4 miles and continue on unclassified road for 2¼ miles.

DUMFRIES Dumfries & Galloway — Map 7 A3

Craigsview Caravan Site
296 Annan Road. ☎ (0387) 53812
Open: Easter-October
Size: 2 acres, 20 touring pitches. 2 hot showers,
8 WCs

[icons: caravan, motor caravan, dog]

Site 1 mile E of Dumfries on A75.

Mouswald Caravan Park
Mouswald Place. ☎ (038783) 226
Open: Easter-October
Size: 5½ acres, 50 touring pitches. 6 hot showers, 8
WCs. 5 static caravans

[icons: caravan, motor caravan, tent, laundry, cup, dog]

From A75 NW of Annan, follow international signs.

Newfield Caravan Park
Annan Road, DG1 3SE. ☎ (038775) 228
Open: All year
Size: 3 acres, 10 touring pitches. 2 hot showers,
8 WCs. 10 static caravans

[icons: caravan, motor caravan, laundry, dog]

2½ miles E of Dumfries on A75. Next to Little Chef.

DUNBAR Lothian — Map 7 A2

Battleblent Hotel Caravan Park
West Barns, EH42 1TS.
☎ (0368) 62234
Open: April-October
Size: 1 acre, 10 touring pitches. 2 hot showers,
4 WCs

[icons: caravan, motor caravan, cup, restaurant, dog]

Leave A1 at Dunbar roundabout (W of by-pass) and turn E on to A1087. Site 1 mile.

Camping & Caravanning Club Site
Barns Ness, EH42 1QP.
☎ (0368) 63536
Open: 30 March-28 September
Size: 8 acres, 100 touring pitches. 4 hot showers,
9 WCs

[icons: disabled, caravan, motor caravan, tent, laundry, shop, dog]

Charges on application.
A quiet site on the foreshore, overlooking the Wild Bird Reserve and Barns Ness Lighthouse. Shop 2 miles.
From the A1 follow the signs for East Barns Skateraw and then the signs for Barns Ness.

WINTERFIELD CARAVAN SITE ⚓ L
Winterfield.
☎ (0368) 63353
Open: July-August
Size: 2¾ acres, 10 touring pitches, all level. 9 hot showers, 16 WCs, 2 CWPs

[icons: caravan, motor caravan, tent, shop, dog]

Charges on application.
Simple site by the beach with children's play area, in a public park on the edge of town. No gas available. Shop and restaurant 1 mile.
At N end of Dunbar High Street, bear left into Bayswell Road, ¼ mile on turn right just past the tennis courts, and continue to the sea.

DUNBEATH Highland — Map 9 A1

Inver Guest House
Inver.
☎ (05933) 252
Open: April-October
Size: 1½ acres, 15 touring pitches. 2 hot showers, 3

[&] Facilities for Disabled [⌐] Caravans accepted [⊡] Motor caravans [▲] Tents [◧] Laundry room [▣] Shop

WCs

[symbols]

½ mile N of Dunbeath Harbour on A9.

DUNDEE Tayside — Map 7 A1

CAMPERDOWN CARAVAN PARK RAC L
Liff Road. ☎ (0382) 621995
Open: March-October
Size: 2½ acres, 80 touring pitches, 40 level pitches.
12 hot showers, 15 WCs, 3 CWPs

[symbols]

Charges on application.
A well-tended site, with children's play area, located within a spacious public park. Calor gas only. Shop and restaurant 5 minutes' walk. Swimming pool 4 miles.
Site is 3 miles NW of Dundee city centre, located in Camperdown Park. Entrance from Kingsway, via Myrekirk Road and Liff Road.

DUNKELD Tayside — Map 7 A1

ERIGMORE HOUSE HOLIDAY PARK RAC A
Birnam, PH8 9XX.
☎ (03502) 236
Open: 1 April-31 October
Size: 4 (20) acres, 58 touring pitches, all with elec, 48 level pitches, 186 static caravans. 5 hot showers, 21 WCs, 1 CWP

[symbols]

(1991) Car & caravan, Motor caravan, Car & tent, M/cycle* & tent £9.20; elec £1.50, awn £2; WS
cc Access, Visa/B'card
Set in the grounds of a most imposing Scottish baronial mansion, only 12 miles north of Perth, overlooking the village of Birnam. The grounds are a wonderful tribute to the treeplanting exploits of its Scottish ancestry - there are over 50 different varieties - as well as a wealth of shrubbery and rhododendron to enhance your holiday surroundings. 65 caravans hire (own WCs)
From the junction of the A9 and A923 travel SE on the A9 for just over 1 mile. Turn N as signed Birnam for ¼ mile to site on right.

DUNOON Strathclyde — Map 6 B2

Cot House Caravan Park
Cot House, by Dunoon, PA23 8QS.
☎ (036984) 351
Open: Easter-October
Size: 3 acres, 25 touring pitches. 4 hot showers, 4 WCs. 23 static caravans

[symbols]

Site off A815, near junction with A880.

Invereck Caravan Park
Near Sandback.
☎ (036984) 208
Open: Easter-October
Size: 8½ acres, 20 touring pitches. 4 hot showers, 6 WCs. 12 static caravans

[symbols]

Site 4½ miles N of Dunoon on A815. At head of Holy Loch.

DURNESS Highland — Map 9 A1

Sango Sands Camping & Caravan Site
Sangomore. ☎ (097181) 222
Open: April-October
Size: 11 acres, 75 touring pitches. 6 hot showers, 22 WCs

[symbols]

Site overlooks Sango Bay, adjacent to A838.

ECCLEFECHAN Dumfries & Galloway — Map 7 A3

HODDOM CASTLE CARAVAN PARK RAC A
Hoddom, Lockerbie, DG11 1AS. ☎ (05763) 251
Open: Easter-31 October
Size: 10 acres, 170 touring caravans, 100 with elec, all level pitches, all with hardstanding. 15 hot showers, 40 WCs, 1 CWP

[symbols]

Car & caravan, Motor caravan, Car & tent £5.50-£9.50; WS
Rural family site with nature trails in surrounding woodland and guided walks. Also mountain bike trail, 9-hole golf course, salmon and seatrout fishing (own water on River Annan), and coarse fishing available within 3 miles. Swimming pool 5 miles.
From Ecclefechan, travel SW on B725 as signed "Dalton" for 2¼ miles, cross River Annan and follow signs to site.

EDINBURGH Lothian — Map 7 A2

Little France Caravan Site
Old Dalkeith Road, EH16 4SU.
☎ (031) 666 2326
Open: April-October
Size: 8½ acres, 285 touring pitches. 12 hot showers, 42 WCs

[symbols]

Site 3 miles S of city centre on A68.

MORTONHALL CARAVAN PARK RAC A
36 Mortonhall Gate, Frogston Road East, EH16 6TJ.
☎ (031) 664 1533
Open: Late March-31 October
Size: 22 (25) acres, 250 touring pitches, 75 with elec, 20 with hardstanding, 30% level pitches, 18 static caravans. 18 hot showers, WCs, 2 CWPs

[symbols]

(1991) Car & caravan, Motor caravan, Car & tent, M/cycle & tent £6.10-£8.20; elec £1.55, awn £1.80, dogs 50p
cc Access, Visa/B'card
In a sheltered bowl with southerly views to Pentland Hills, Mortonhall House and stable block, designed in classical style, set the character of the park. An old woodland garden with specimen trees from all over the world flanks the western end of the estate, providing delightful secluded walks. Ideally situated with easy access to the by-pass and the main roads into the city.
Follow new city by-pass (A720) to junction with A701 or A702; leave as for city centre to Frogstone Road East (B701) junction. Site lies on B701 between A701 and A702. Look for signs to Mortonhall.

[●] Snacks/take away [✕] Restaurant [�—] Swimming pool [▥] Shelter for campers [⊓] Dogs accepted   169

Forestry Commission
Touring Sites

Balmacara
Glenmore
Glencoe
Kilvrecht
Ardgartan
●Cobleland
●Cashel

Kielder
Caldons●
●Talnotry

Spiers House

●Beddgelert
●Tackeroo

Thorpe Woodland

●Dean(4 sites)

Savernake

New Forest (10 sites)

Free colour brochure from:
Forest Holidays (RAC)
Forestry Commission
231 Corstorphine Road
EDINBURGH EH12 7AT
Tel: 031 334 0303/2576
or 031 334 0066
(24 hour answerphone)

MUIRHOUSE MUNICIPAL CAMPING SITE RAC L
Marine Drive. ☎ (031) 336 6874
Open: April-September
Size: 9 acres, 300 touring pitches. Hot Showers, WCs

Charges on application with sae.
A well-kept site on the shores of the Firth of Forth.
Site is signposted from the A90, the NW exit from the city.

EDZELL *Tayside* | Map 7 A1

Glenesk Caravan Site
Glenesk, by Edzell. ☎ (03564) 565
Open: April-October
Size: 8 acres, 45 touring pitches. 6 hot showers, 8 WCs. 8 static caravans

1½ miles NE of Edzell turn off B966 to Glenesk site on RHS within ¾ mile.

ELGIN *Grampian* | Map 9 A2

NORTH ALVES CARAVAN PARK RAC A
Alves, IV30 3XD. ☎ (034385) 223
Open: 1 April-31 October
Size: 8 (12) acres, 75 touring pitches, 20 with elec. 4

hot showers, 8 WCs, 1 CWP

Car & caravan, Motor caravan, Car & tent, M/cycle
& tent £4.50-£6.50 up to 2 people; elec £1.50; WS
*Rural, tree-lined park with level, grassy ground.
Restaurant 1 mile. Swimming pool 6 miles.*
At 5½ miles W of Elgin on A96, turn N in Alves at
international sign for 1 mile.

Riverside Caravan Park
West Road, IV30 3UN. ☎ (0343) 542813
Open: April-October
Size: 5 acres, 44 touring pitches. 6 hot showers,
12 WCs. 10 static caravans

Site ½ mile W of Elgin, off A96.

ELIE *Fife* | Map 7 A1

Shell Bay Caravan Site
KY9 1HB. ☎ (0333) 330283
Open: April-October
Size: 36 acres, 125 touring pitches. 14 hot showers,
30 WCs. Static caravans

4½ miles NW of Elie (A917), turn S on to single
track road.

GLENESK CARAVAN PARK
EDZELL, ANGUS DD9 7YP   Tel: 03564 565
Situated amidst woodland surrounding a small lake. 1½ miles NW Edzell.
All amenities for tourers and campers. *Open April–October*

SHELL BAY CARAVAN PARK
ELIE, FIFE   Tel: 0333 330 283

A superb holiday centre set in lovely countryside with its own sandy beach and extensive sandhills. Ideal for both children and adults, it is an unrivalled centre for touring and visiting the many local places of interest. Amenities include a lounge bar for drinks and inexpensive meals; shop; laundry; and excellent toilets with free showers and washing-up facilities. 75 electric hook-up points available for tourers. Dogs allowed on lead only.

ETTRICK *Borders*   Map 7 A2

ANGECROFT CARAVAN PARK   RAC A
TD7 5HY. ☎ (0750) 62310/62251
Open: 1 March-1 November
Size: ½ (2½) acres, 4 touring pitches, all level, all with elec, 35 static caravans, 2 chalets. 2 hot showers, 7 WCs, 1 CWP

(1991) Car & caravan, Motor caravan £4-£6, Car & tent, M/cycle* & tent £4-£6; elec £1, awn 50p; WS
Small, high standard, family-run park in very quiet and peaceful country surroundings. A natural haven for the wildlife enthusiast. 2 chalets for hire (own WCs). Restaurant 3 miles. Swimming pool 4 miles. Calor gas only.
From the A7 at Langholm take B709 to park OR from A74 at Lockerbie take B723 to Boreland and Eskdalemuir, then left on B709 to park.

HONEY COTTAGE CARAVAN PARK   RAC L
Hope House, Ettrick Valley, TD7 5HU.
☎ (0750) 62246
Open: All year
Size: 3 (7) acres, 30 touring pitches, all level, 8 with elec, 50 static caravans. 8 hot showers, 16 WCs

(1991) Car & caravan, Motor caravan £4.75, Car & tent £4, M/cycle or cyclist or walker & tent £1.70 per person; elec £1, awn 75p
Peaceful, rural family-run site on the banks of Ettrick Water with swimming, boating and fishing available. 2 caravans for hire. Restaurant 1 mile. Swimming pool 3 miles.
Site 1¾ miles NE of Ettrick on the B709, or from Tushielaw Inn (junction of the B709 and B711), travel SW on the B709 for 1 mile to site on left.

EVANTON *Highland*   Map 9 A2

Black Rock Caravan & Camping Park
☎ (0349) 830867
Open: Easter-October
Size: 4 acres, 45 touring pitches. 6 hot showers, 9 WCs. 6 static caravans

From A9 N, fork left on to B817. Site ¾ mile.

FINDHORN *Grampian*   Map 9 A2

Findhorn Bay Caravan Park
Near Forres, IV36 0TY. ☎ (0309) 30203
Open: April-October
Size: 6 acres, 150 touring pitches. 12 hot showers, 20 WCs. 20 static caravans

On B9011, site on right just before village.

Findochty Caravan Site
Buckie. ☎ (0343) 45121
Open: (1991) April-September
Size: 3 acres, 18 touring pitches. Hot showers, WCs. Static caravans

Just W of harbour in Findochty on A942.

FOCHABERS *Grampian*   Map 9 B2

BURNSIDE CARAVAN SITE   RAC A
The Nurseries, IV32 7ES. ☎ (0343) 820362
Open: 1 April-30 October
Size: 8 (10) acres, 120 touring pitches, 18 with elec, 100 level pitches, 20 with hardstanding. 8 hot showers, 30 WCs, 2 CWPs

Car & caravan, Motor caravan, Car & tent, M/cycle & tent £5; WS
This level site, situated in woodland, has an indoor swimming pool, TV room and children's play area. No gas available. Shop and restaurant 200 yards.
From junction on A96 and A98 travel S on A96 for ¼ mile. Site on right.

FORFAR *Tayside*   Map 7 A1

LOCHSIDE CARAVAN SITE   RAC L
Forfar Country Park, DD8 1BT.
☎ (0307) 64201
Open: April-Mid October
Size: 4 acres, 48 touring pitches, all level, all with elec. 4 hot showers, 12 WCs, 1 CWP

Car & caravan, Motor caravan £4.80-£5.60, Car & tent, M/cycle & tent £2.80-£3.75; elec £1.25, awn £1.65
Situated on east shore of Forfar Loch, adjacent to Lochside Leisure Centre, within Forfar Country Park. No gas available. Shop ¼ mile. Swimming pool ½ mile. Dogs must be kept on leads.
E of the A94/A929 follow signs to Leisure Centre.

FORRES *Grampian*   Map 9 A2

RIVERVIEW CARAVAN PARK   RAC A
Mundole Court, IV36 0SY. ☎ (0309) 73932
Open: 1 April-31 October
Size: 10 (50) acres, 60 touring pitches, all level, 36 with elec, 36 static caravans. 6 hot showers, 6 cold showers 12 WCs, 1 CWP

(1991) Car & caravan, Motor caravan £5, Car & tent, M/cycle & tent £4; elec £1.50; WS
cc Major cards
A large, level site, beautifully landscaped and a huge children's play park. A bar and beer garden next to play park. 300-seater nightclub, all

---

▣ Snacks/take away ☒ Restaurant ◹ Swimming pool ▣ Shelter for campers ⌘ Dogs accepted   171

entertainments available, every sport available including salmon fishing. *30 caravans for hire (own WCs). Swimming pool 1 mile.*
A96 from Forres to Inverness, take first left after Little Chef, then second right.

FORT AUGUSTUS *Highland*　　Map 9 A3

Fort Augustus Caravan & Camping Park
Market Hill, PH32 4DH. ☎ (0320) 6360
Open: Easter-October
Size: 3¼ acres, 50 touring pitches. 4 hot showers, 10 WCs

Site ¼ mile S of Fort Augustus on A82.

FORT WILLIAM *Highland*　　Map 8 B3

GLEN NEVIS CARAVAN & CAMPING PARK　RAC A
Glen Nevis, PH33 6SX.
☎ (0397) 2191
Open: 15 March-31 October
Size: 19 acres, 150 touring pitches, all level, 91 with elec, 100 with hardstanding, 30 static caravans, 12 cottages. 23 hot showers, 63 WCs, 2 CWPs

Charges on application.
cc Access, Visa/B'card
This wooded site by the river and overlooked by Ben Nevis has children's play area and fishing. 30 caravans and 12 cottages for hire (own WCs). No motorcycle groups. Swimming pool 2 miles.
Just N of Fort William on A82, turn E at international sign at the S end of Bridge of Nevis. Site at 2 miles on.

LINNHE CARAVAN PARK　RAC A
Corpach, PH33 7NL. ☎ (039772) 376
Open: Early March-Late October
Size: 5 (20) acres, 75 touring pitches, all level, all with hardstanding, 57 with elec, 90 static caravans. 8 hot showers, 2 baths, 15 WCs, 1 CWP

Car & caravan, Motor caravan from £5; elec from £1, awn from 50p; WS
One of the best and most beautiful lochside parks in Scotland. Magnificent views, hardstanding, private beach, launching slipway, free fishing, playground. Graded "Excellent". 85 caravans for hire (own WCs). Restaurant 1½ miles. Swimming pool 5 miles.
On A830, approximately 1 mile W of Corpach village, 5 miles from Fort William.

LOCHY CARAVAN & CAMPING PARK　RAC A
Camaghael, PH33 7NF. ☎ (039770) 3446
Open: December-Mid October
Size: 6 acres, 90 touring pitches, 38 with elec, 30 level pitches, 8 with hardstanding, 16 static caravans, 7 chalets. 10 hot showers, 12 WCs, 1 CWP

Charges on application.
cc Access, Visa/B'card
A secluded, family-run site, sloping down to a river and with Ben Nevis in the background. 16 caravans and 7 chalets for hire (own WCs). No single-sex groups. Restaurant 1 mile. Swimming pool 1½ miles.
2 miles N of Fort William on A82 turn W on A830 for 500 yards and take first turn on right past Lochaber High School.

GAIRLOCH *Highland* — Map 8 B2

SANDS HOLIDAY CENTRE   RAC A
IV21 2DL. ☎ (0445) 2152
Open: 1 April-20 October
Size: 49 (50) acres, 360 touring pitches, 20 with
elec, 20 static caravans. 22 hot showers, 56 WCs,
1 CWP

Car & caravan £7, Motor caravan £6.65, Car & tent,
M/cycle & tent £6.15; elec £1.50, awn £1
*Site adjoining sandy beach, water sports available,
sailboarding, canoeing, waterskiing. 5 caravans for
for hire (own WCs). Restaurant 3 miles. Swimming
pool 7 miles.*
At Gairloch take the B8021 to Melvaig through
village and on to site by sandy beach.

GATEHOUSE OF FLEET *Dumfries & Galloway* — Map 6 B3

Anwoth Caravan Site
Garden Street, DG7 2JU. ☎ (0557) 814333
Open: April-September
Size: 4 acres, 30 touring pitches. 6 hot showers,
12 WCs. 40 static caravans

Site signed off A75, at W end of town.

Auchenlarie Holiday Farm
DG7 2EX. ☎ (055724) 251
Open: March-October
Size: 20 acres, 287 touring pitches. 10 hot showers,
50 WCs. 163 static caravans

Site 5 miles SW of Gatehouse (A75).

Mossyard Caravan Site
Mossyard. ☎ (055724) 226
Open: April-October
Size: 5 acres, 15 touring pitches. 4 hot showers,
6 WCs

Site 5 miles SW of Gatehouse, ¾ mile from A75.

GIRVAN *Strathclyde* — Map 6 B3

Jeancroft Holiday Park
Dipple, KA26 9JW. ☎ (0655) 31288
Open: March-October
Size: 11 acres, 30 touring pitches. 2 hot showers,
10 WCs. Static caravans

3½ miles N of Girvan, E off A77.

GLASGOW *Strathclyde* — Map 6 B2

CRAIGENDMUIR PARK   RAC A
3 Campsie View, Stepps, G33 6AF.
☎ (041) 779 2973
Open: All year
Size: 2½ acres, 20 touring pitches, all level, all with
elec, 15 static caravans, 4 chalets. 6 hot showers,
9 WCs, 1 CWP

(1991) Car & caravan, Motor caravan, Car & tent,
M/cycle & tent £4, plus 50p per person above 2;
elec £1
*Convenient for Glasgow. Good overnight stopping
place en route to West of Scotland. 15 caravans
and 4 chalets for hire (own WCs). Calor gas only.
Restaurant 1 mile. Swimming pool 4 miles.*
Leave M8 at junction 11. Turn N on to B7053 for
½ mile, where turn NE on to A80 towards Stirling,
Cross railway bridge, turn right at traffic lights into
Cardowan Road (before start of dual carriageway).
Take third right into Clayhouse Road to site on left.

GLENCOE *Highland* — Map 6 B1

GLENCOE CAMPSITE   RAC A
Forestry Commission. ☎ (08552) 397
Open: Easter-End September
Size: 15 (30) acres, 100 touring pitches, all level, all
with hardstanding, 28 with elec. 6 hot showers,
6 cold showers, 15 WCs, 1 CWP

(1991) Car & caravan, Motor caravan £6.30, Car &
tent, M/cycle & tent £4.70; extra car £1.30; Tent
£3.40; elec £1.30
*Set in a partially wooded glen with spectacular
views of surrounding mountains. Restaurant
1 mile.*
1 mile SE of Glencoe village on A82.

INVERCOE CARAVANS   RAC A
Argyll, PA39 4HP. ☎ (08552) 210
Open: Easter-October
Size: 5 acres, 60 touring pitches, all level, 36 with
elec, 5 static caravans. 8 hot showers, 12 WCs,
3 CWPs

(1991) Car & caravan, Motor caravan, Car & tent,
M/cycle & tent £5; all plus 50p per person; elec

£1.50, awn £1.50
Small, family-owned and run park on the shores of Loch Leven. Separate toilet and shower for disabled. 5 caravans for hire (own WCs). Restaurant ¼ mile. No noise after 11pm. Dogs on leads.
From the junction of the A82 and B863 at Glencoe, travel N on the B863 for ½ mile to site on left.

GLENDARUEL *Strathclyde*   Map 6 B2

GLENDARUEL CARAVAN PARK   RAC A
by Colintraive, PA22 3AB. ☎ (036982) 267
Open: April-October
Size: 3 (22) acres, 25+ touring pitches, all level, all with elec, 25 static caravans. 4 hot showers, 10 WCs, 1 CWP

(1991) Car & caravan, Motor caravan, Car & tent, M/cycle & tent £5.65-£6.15, plus 50p per adult above 2, child 25p; extra car £1; elec £1.30, awn £1.30; WS
Peaceful, secluded country park with sea trout and salmon fishing. Sea (Kyles of Bute) 5 miles. Play area and indoor games room. Bicycles for hire. Thistle Award caravans for hire (own WCs). Discount Clyde Ferry fares. Restaurant 2 miles.
For campers, travel N on the A815 from Dunoon to Dalinlongart then W on the B836 and N on the A886 to site on left. For caravans approach from the N. From the junction of the A815 and A886 at Strachur, travel SW on the A886 for 12¾ miles to site on right.

GLENLUCE *Dumfries & Galloway*   Map 6 B3

THE COCK INN CARAVAN PARK   RAC A
Auchenmalg, DG8 0JT. ☎ (05815) 227
Open: 1 March-31 October
Size: 1 (5) acres, 30 touring pitches, 32 with elec, 15 level pitches, 4 with hardstanding, 60 static caravans, 1 chalet. 6 hot showers, 6 cold showers, 15 WCs, 3 CWPs

Car & caravan, Motor caravan, Car & tent, M/cycle & tent £5.60-£6; elec £1.50-£1.75, awn 85p-£1; WS
A quiet site overlooking Luce Bay. Swimming, boating and sea fishing available on site. The inn is close to the site (across A747) and provides food as well as drinks. 5 caravans and 1 chalet for hire (own WCs). No motorcycle groups.
½ mile E of Glenluce on A75, turn S on A747 for 5 miles.

Glenluce Caravan Park
DG8 0QR. ☎ (05813) 412
Open: April-October
Size: 5 acres, 45 touring pitches. 4 hot showers, 14 WCs. Static caravans

On main street in Glenluce.

Whitecairn Farm Caravan Park
DG8 0NZ. ☎ (05813) 267
Open: March-October
Size: 6 acres, 10 touring pitches. 4 hot showers, 4 WCs. 40 static caravans

1½ miles N of Glenluce, off A75.

GLENROTHES *Fife*   Map 7 A1

Balbirnie Park Caravan Club Site
Markinch, KY7 6NR. ☎ (0592) 759130
Open: April-October
Size: 6 acres, 110 touring pitches. 10 hot showers, 10 WCs

Site 2 miles E of Glenrothes.

GRANTOWN-ON-SPEY *Highland*   Map 9 A3

GRANTOWN-ON-SPEY CARAVAN PARK   RAC A
Seafield Avenue, PH26 3JQ. ☎ (0479) 2474
Open: March-30 September
Size: 10 (23) acres, 60 touring pitches, all with elec, 30 level pitches, 30 with hardstanding, 50 static caravans. 16 hot showers, 20 WCs, 2 CWPs

(1991) Car & caravan, Motor caravan £6.15, Car & tent, M/cycle & tent £5.10, plus 50p per person above 2, 50p per child; elec £1, awn £1; WS
cc Access, Visa/B'card
A quiet site in an attractive wooded setting. Play area and games room on site. 10 caravans for hire (own WCs). Restaurant and shop a third of a mile away. Graded "Excellent". Gates closed 10.30pm to 7.30am.
From square in town centre, turn N by Bank of Scotland. Park clearly seen.

GREENLAW *Borders*   Map 7 A2

Greenlaw Caravan Park ☎
Bank Street, TD10 6XX. ☎ (036 16) 341
Open: March-November
Size: 1 (5) acres, 16 touring pitches. 6 hot showers, 8 WCs. 58 static caravans

In Greenlaw, turn N on A6105. Site signed 50 yards.

GRETNA *Dumfries & Galloway*   Map 7 A3

The Braids Caravan Park
Annan Road, CA6 5DQ. ☎ (0461) 37409
Open: All year
Size: 5 acres, 70 touring pitches. 4 hot showers, 10 WCs. 3 static caravans

From A74 N, take A75, first left into Gretna. Site 500 yards.

OLD TOLL CARAVAN SITE   RAC L
Gretna. ☎ (0461) 37439
Open: Easter-End September
Size: 5 acres, 100 touring pitches, 36 with elec. 2 hot showers, 9 WCs, 1 CWP

Charges on application.
Riverside site which claims to have the first building in Scotland on it. Children's play area. Restaurant 50 yards. New, enlarged toilet block for 1992.
Adjacent to the England-Scotland border on

B721 to the S of Gretna village.

MONKSMUIR CARAVAN PARK RAC A
EH41 3SB. ☎ (0620) 860340
Open: All year
Size: 5½ acres, 23 touring pitches, 26 with elec,
18 level pitches, 10 with hardstanding, 7 static
caravans. 6 hot showers, 13 WCs, 2 CWPs

| 🚐 | 🚐 | ⚠ | 🔌 | 🏪 | 🍵 | | | 🐕 |

(1991) Car & caravan, Motor caravan £5.30-£6.60,
Car & tent £4.20-£5.50, M/cycle & tent £3.40-£4;
elec £1.20- £1.40, awn £1.20; WS
*A pleasant, secluded rural site, with children's play
area. 5 caravans for hire (own WCs). Shop
(seasonal) 2½ miles. Restaurant and swimming
pool 3 miles.*
3 miles E of Haddington on A1.

RIVERSIDE CARAVAN PARK RAC A
Hornshole Bridge, TD9 8SY.
☎ (0450) 73785
Open: 1 April-10 September
Size: 2 (10) acres, 25 touring pitches, all level,
6 with elec, 4 with hardstanding, 52 static caravans.
4 hot showers, 9 WCs, 1 CWP

| ♿ | 🚐 | 🚐 | ⚠ | 🔌 | 🏪 | 🍵 | | | |

Car & caravan, Motor caravan, Car & tent, M/cycle*
& tent £2, plus £1.50 per adult, 75p per child; WS
*Level, well-sheltered site on banks of River Teviot.
Children's play area, river fishing and swimming
on site. 1 caravan for hire (own WC). Swimming
pool 2 miles.*
Site 2½ miles NE of Hawick on the A698.

Crakaig Caravan Site
Loth Beach, Loth, KW8 6HP. ☎ (0408) 21260
Open: Easter-September
Size: 7 acres, 15 touring pitches. 2 hot showers,
2 WCs

| 🚐 | 🚐 | ⚠ | | | | | | 🐕 |

Site 6 miles N of Brora, ½ mile from A9.

Courthill Caravans
Auldgirth, DG2 0RR. ☎ (038774) 336
Open: All year
Size: 1 acre, 5 touring pitches. 2 hot showers,
7 WCs, 24 static caravans

| 🚐 | 🚐 | ⚠ | | | ✗ | | | 🐕 |

Site 2 miles N of Holywood on A76.

ARGYLL CARAVAN & CAMPING PARK RAC A
PA32 8XT. ☎ (0499) 2285
Open: 1 April-31 October
Size: 8 (50) acres, 60 touring pitches, all level,
16 with elec, 16 with hardstanding, 200 static
caravans. 16 hot showers, 80 WCs, 6 CWPs

| ♿ | 🚐 | 🚐 | ⚠ | 🔌 | 🏪 | 🍵 | 🍴 | ✗ | | | 🐕 |

(1991) Car & caravan, Motor caravan £5.50-£6.50,
Car & tent, M/cycle & tent £4.40-£5.50; Bivouac tent
£2.75; extra car £1; elec £1.40, awn £1; WS
*A well-maintained site, with children's play area,
on the shores of Loch Fyne. 11 caravans for hire
(own WCs), 1 specially fitted for disabled persons.
Restaurant 1½ miles.*
2½ miles S of Inveraray on A83, in direction of
Campbeltown.

Faichemard Highland Holiday Park
☎ (080 93) 276
Open: Easter-October
Size: 42 acres, 40 touring pitches. 2 hot showers,
6 WCs. Static caravans

| | 🚐 | 🚐 | ⚠ | | | | | | 🐕 |

Take A87 W from Invergarry. After 2 miles turn
right signposted Faichem. Site signed `A & D
Grant'.

Faichem Park
Faichem. ☎ (080 93) 226
Open: March-October
Size: 3 acres, 30 touring pitches. 2 hot showers,
6 WCs

| | 🚐 | 🚐 | ⚠ | | | | | | 🐕 |

Take A87 W from Invergarry. After 1 mile turn right
signposted Faichem, then follow signs.

Caravan Club Site
Morvich, by Kyle of Lochalsh, IV40 4HQ.
☎ (059981) 354
Open: April-September
Size: 5 acres, 75 touring pitches. 4 hot showers,
6 WCs

| | 🚐 | 🚐 | ⚠ | 🔌 | | | | | 🐕 |

SE from Inverinate on A87, turn left 2 miles past
Esso garage, signposted Morvich. Cross bridge
and turn left for site.

LOCH NESS CARAVAN PARK RAC L
☎ (0320) 51207
Open: 15 March-15 October
Size: 5 (8½) acres, 50 touring pitches, all level,
18 with elec, 6 with hardstanding, 5 static caravans.
6 hot showers, 15 WCs, 3 CWPs

| | 🚐 | 🚐 | ⚠ | 🔌 | | | | | 🐕 |

Charges on application.
*There's fishing, boating and swimming at this
wooded site by the banks of the River Moriston
facing Loch Ness. Play area. 5 caravans for hire
(own WCs). Shop 1¼ miles. Restaurant ½ mile.*
1 mile S of Invermoriston on A82.

Bught Park
☎ (0463) 236920
Open: Easter-October
Size: 9 acres, 250 touring pitches. 16 hot showers,
36 WCs

🍴 Snacks/take away ✗ Restaurant Swimming pool 🏠 Shelter for campers 🐕 Dogs accepted

Coulmore Bay Camping & Caravan Park

Kessock, Inverness. Tel: (046 373) 322

A peaceful country site near the Beauly Firth and facing South. Children's play ground. Restaurant, launderette and shop. Inverness 4 miles.

Site in Inverness on A82.

Bunchrew Caravans
Bunchrew. ☎ (0463) 237802
Open: April-October
Size: 20 acres, 100 touring pitches. 8 hot showers, 14 WCs. 14 static caravans

Site 3 miles W of Inverness on A862.

COULMORE BAY SITE   RAC L
North Kessock. ☎ (046 373) 322
Open: April-September
Size: 3 acres, 30 touring pitches, 8 with elec, 1 static caravan. 4 hot showers, 4 WCs

Charges on application.
A level farm site beside shingle/rock beach and next to a water sports centre. Children's playground. Small shop open 1 June-1 September, other shops 3 miles. Calor gas only. Caravans for hire (own WCs). Pony trekking.
3 miles W of North Kessock.

Dochgarroch Caravan Site
Dochgarroch. ☎ (046386) 218
Open: Easter-September
Size: 2½ acres, 90 touring pitches. 5 hot showers, 20 WCs

5 miles SW of Inverness on A82.

Torvean Caravan Park
Glen Urquhart, IV3 6JL. ☎ (0463) 220582
Open: Easter-October
Size: 3 acres, 50 touring pitches. 7 hot showers, 12 WCs. 8 static caravans

Off A9 follow signs for A82 signed for Fort William, turn right after crossing Tomnahurich canal bridge. Caravan park to rear of caravan sales area.

Camping & Caravanning Club Site
Elliot Park, Edinburgh Road, TD8 6ED.
☎ (0835) 63393
Open: 30 March-26 October
Size: 2 acres, 60 touring pitches. 12 hot showers, 9 WCs

Charges on application.
cc Access, Visa/B'card
Site is in the Jed Valley, and sheltered by wooded hills. Shop 1 mile.
From the A68 take the turning opposite the Edinburgh Woollen Mills buildings.

Lilliardsedge Park
TD8 6TZ. ☎ (08353) 271
Open: April-September
Size: 25 acres, 60 touring pitches. 10 hot showers, 28 WCs. 82 static caravans

6¼ miles N of Jedburgh on A68, look for signs.

JOHN O'GROATS CARAVAN SITE   RAC L
KW1 4YS. ☎ (095581) 329
Open: 1 April-31 October
Size: 2 acres, 45 touring pitches, all level, 12 with elec, 2 with hardstanding. 4 hot showers, 4 cold showers, 10 WCs, 1 CWP

(1991) Car & caravan, Motor caravan, Car & tent £4, Tent £2-£3, M/cycle £3; awn £1
At end of A9, on seafront, beside last house in Scotland. Booking office for day trips to Orkney Islands on site, public telephones, hotel, snack bar, harbour, cliff scenery. Sea birds 1½ miles. Shop 1km. Restaurant 100 metres.
Accessible from N of A9.

STROMA VIEW CAMPING SITE   RAC L
Huna, KW1 4YL. ☎ (095581) 313
Open: April-October
Size: ½ (¾) acre, 20 touring pitches, all level, 8 with elec, 5 with hardstanding, 1 static caravan. 2 hot showers, 2 cold showers, 3 WCs, 1 CWP

Charges on application.
cc Access, Visa/B'card
This popular and busy site overlooks the island of Stroma - a bird watcher's paradise. Access to beach for swimming and fishing, also boats to the island and for fishing can be hired. 1 caravan for hire (own WC). Camping gaz only. Souvenir shop only; shop 1½ miles. Restaurant 1 mile.
From the junction of A9 and A836, at John O'Groats travel W on A836 for 1¼ miles.

Beach Road Caravan Site
DD10 0EP. ☎ (0561) 62395
Open: April-October
Size: 6½ acres, 30 touring pitches. 4 hot showers, 12 WCs. 52 static caravans

Site by the sea.

Keith Caravan Site
Dunnyduff Road. ☎ (05422) 7289
Open: (1991) April-September
Size: 2½ acres, 17 touring pitches. Hot showers,

WCs. 20 static caravans.

⌨🏕🚐⛺🛁 ☐☐☐☐☐ 🐕

¼ mile S of Keith on A96.

KELSO *Borders* Map 7 B2

SPRINGWOOD CARAVAN PARK RAC A
Springwood Estate, TD5 8LS.
☎ (0573) 24596
Open: 1 April or Easter-14 October
Size: 4 (30) acres, 40 touring pitches, 25 with elec,
270 static caravans. 12 hot showers, 38 WCs,
1 CWP

🚐🏕 ⛺🛁 ☐☐☐☐ 🐕

Car & caravan, Motor caravan £6.50, plus 60p per
adult above 2, child 40p; elec £1.50, awn from
£1.10
*Well-kept park set in wooded countryside adjacent
to River Teviot. Spacious surroundings offering
plenty of walks. Lots to see and do within 20 mile
radius in largely undiscovered Scottish Border
Country. Restaurant and swimming pool 1 mile.
Leave Kelso to S, cross River Tweed and turn W on
A699 for ½ mile, where turn left just before
crossing River Teviot.*

KENMORE *Tayside* Map 6 A1

KENMORE CARAVAN & CAMPING PARK RAC A
Aberfeldy, PH15 2HN. ☎ (08873) 226
Open: Easter-October
Size: 10 (12) acres, 160 touring pitches, 70 with
elec, 60 static caravans, 3 chalets. 10 hot showers,
36 WCs, 3 CWPs

🏕🚐⛺🛁🛒✉✕ ☐ 🏠🐕

(1991) Car & caravan £3.50, Motor caravan £3.50,
Car & tent, M/cycle & tent £2.50; all plus £1 per
adult, 50p per child; second tent 50p; elec £1, awn
50p
cc Major cards taken in site shop only
*Family site with 3 children's play areas. Ideal
touring centre. Walking, golfing and all water
activities in area. Owner-supervised. 1 caravan and
3 chalets for hire (own WCs). W on A827 from
Ballinluig to Aberfeldy. E on
A827 from Killin.*

KILBERRY *Strathclyde* Map 6 A2

Port Ban Caravan Site
☎ (08803) 224
Open: April-September
Size: 11 acres, 42 touring pitches. 4 hot showers,
11 WCs. 50 static caravans

☐🏕🚐⛺🛁🛒✉ ☐🏠🐕

SW of Tarbert via B8024. Site by sea.

KILLIN *Central* Map 6 B1

Cruachan Caravan & Camping Site
FK21 8TY. ☎ (05672) 302
Open: March-October
Size: 6 acres, 60 touring pitches. 2 hot showers,
15 WCs. 8 static caravans

🏕🚐⛺🛁 ☐☐☐☐ 🐕

3½ miles E of Killin on A827.

High Creagan Caravan Site
FK21 8TX. ☎ (05672) 449
Open: Easter-October
Size: 4 acres, 15 touring pitches. 2 hot showers,
6 WCs. 3 static caravans

☐🏕🚐⛺🛁🛒 ☐☐ 🏠🐕

2 miles NE of Killin on A827.

KILMARNOCK *Strathclyde* Map 6 B2

**CUNNINGHAMHEAD ESTATE
CARAVAN PARK** RAC L
Irvine, KA3 2PE. ☎ (029485) 238
Open: 1 April-30 September
Size: 3 (6) acres, 50 touring pitches, all level,
14 with elec, 40 static caravans. 6 hot showers,
14 WCs, 1 CWP

☐🏕🚐⛺🛁 ☐☐☐☐ 🐕

Car & caravan, Motor caravan £5-£6, Car & tent £4-
£5, M/cycle & tent £6-£7; elec £1.30, awn £1.30; WS
*Grounds of mansion house (now gone) with
commanding views of surrounding countryside.
Peaceful yet convenient for surrounding resorts
and Glasgow. Magnum Leisure Centre at Irvine
(Scotland's No. 1 attraction). 6 caravans for hire
(own WCs). Shop 2 miles. Restaurant 3 miles.
Swimming pool 4 miles. No gas available.
From S take A78 to Irvine by-pass. From Newhouse
interchange take A736 Glasgow Road (Long Drive)
through Oldhall roundabout until you reach
Stanecastle roundabout. Turn E (right) on to
B769 Stewarton Road. The park is 2½ miles on the
left.*

KILMELFORD *Strathclyde* Map 6 B1

Arduaine Caravan & Camping Park
☎ (08522) 288
Open: March-October
Size: 2¼ acres, 30 touring pitches. 4 hot showers, 6
WCs

⌨🏕🚐⛺🛁 ☐☐☐🏊 🐕

4 miles SW of Kilmelford on A816.

KILNINVER *Strathclyde* Map 6 A1

GLEN GALLAIN CARAVAN PARK RAC L
Scamadale, PA34 4UU. ☎ (08526) 200
Open: April-Mid October
Size: 4¼ acres, 30 touring pitches, all level, 4 with
elec, 30 with hardstanding. 4 hot showers, 6 WCs,
1 CWP

⌨🏕🚐⛺🛁🛒 ☐☐☐☐ 🐕

(1991) Car & caravan, Motor caravan £6, Car & tent,
M/cycle & tent £5; elec £2, awn £1
*A quiet site situated on a farm among wooded hills
beside River Euchar - fishing possible. Children's
play area. Site shop open July/August only. Gas
available July/August only. Shop 5 miles.
Restaurant 3 miles.
Travel S from Oban on A816 for 9½ miles, site on
left.*

KINGHORN *Fife* Map 7 A2

PETTYCUR BAY CARAVAN PARK RAC A
Kinghorn Road, KY3 9YE. ☎ (0592) 890321
Open: 1 March-28 October

🛒 Snacks/take away ✕ Restaurant 🏊 Swimming pool 🏠 Shelter for campers 🐕 Dogs accepted 177

KINGHORN, FIFE   Tel: (0592) 890321 & 890913

Luxury Caravans for hire and sale.
Excellent site facilties.
Licensed restaurant, cocktail lounge
TV lounge, shop etc.
Tourers and tents welcome.

Size: 42 acres, 100 touring pitches, 70 with elec,
60 level pitches, 60 with hardstanding, 400 static
caravans, 20 chalets. 12 hot showers, 100 WCs,
4 CWPs

(1991) Car & caravan, Motor caravan £4.50, Car &
tent, M/cycle* & tent £3.50; elec £1, awn £1
*A terraced site overlooking the Firth of Forth. On-
site entertainment, licensed bar and cocktail
lounge, children's play park and snooker room.
Calor gas only. 40 caravans for hire (own WCs).
Swimming pool 2 miles.*
Site on the N side of the A92, ¾ mile W of the
centre of Kinghorn and 1¾ miles E of Burntisland.

KINLOCH RANNOCH *Tayside*   Map 6 A1

KILVRECHT CAMPING & CARAVAN SITE   RAC L
Forestry Commission, Lochend, PH16 5QA.
☎ (08822) 335
Open: 30 March-25 October
Size: 4 acres, 90 touring pitches, all level. 8 WCs,
1 CWP

(1991) Car & caravan, Motor caravan, Car & tent,
M/cycle & tent £4.50
*Woodland setting ½ mile from Loch Rannoch.
Peaceful and quiet. Shop, restaurant and
swimming pool 3½ miles. No gas available.*
3½ miles W of Kinloch Rannoch on unclassified
road on S bank of Loch Rannoch.

KINLOCHEWE *Highland*   Map 8 B2

Kinlochewe Caravan Club Site
Achnasheen, IV22 2PA. ☎ (044584) 239
Open: April-October
Size: 5 acres, 60 touring pitches. 4 hot showers,
9 WCs

Site in Kinlochewe on A832.

KINLOCHLEVEN *Highland*   Map 6 B1

Caolasnacon Caravan & Camping Park
☎ (08554) 279
Open: April-October
Size: 7½ acres, 50 touring pitches. 8 hot showers,
14 WCs. 17 static caravans

Site 3 miles E of Glencoe on B863. On S side of
Loch Leven.

KINROSS *Tayside*   Map 7 A1

Granada Motorway Services
KY13 7NQ. ☎ (0577) 63123
Open: All year
Size: 7 acres, 20 touring pitches. 4 hot showers,
20 WCs

Site on A977, ¼ mile W of M90 junction 6.

KINTORE *Grampian*   Map 9 B3

HILLHEAD CARAVAN PARK   RAC A
AB51 0YX. ☎ (0467) 32809
Open: 27 March-1 November
Size: 1½ acres, 25 touring pitches, all level, 18 with
elec, 2 with hardstanding, 4 static caravans. 4 hot
showers, 6 WCs, 1 CWP

Car & caravan, Motor caravan, Car & tent, M/cycle
& & tent £4.50-£5.60; elec £1.15; WS
cc Access, Visa/B'card
*Small, family-run park, ideally situated for the
Castle and Whisky Trails, near Aberdeen. Disabled
facilities. Near new alternative tourist route from
Aberdeen to Inverness. 4 caravans for hire (own
WCs) Restaurant 1 mile. Swimming pool 4 miles.*
1 mile W of Kintore.

KIRKCALDY *Fife*   Map 7 A2

DUNNIKIER CARAVAN & CAMPING SITE   RAC A
Dunnikier Way, KY1 3ND. ☎ (0592) 267563
Open: March-October
Size: 5 acres, 80 touring pitches, all level, 6 with
elec, all with hardstanding. 12 hot showers,
20 WCs, 1 CWP

Charges on application.
*A well-landscaped, sheltered site. Children's play
park on site. Restaurant ¼ mile. Swimming pool
2½ miles. Calor gas only.*
On the N outskirts of Kirkcaldy on A988, midway
between its junctions with A92 and A910.

KIRKCOWAN *Dumfries & Galloway*   Map 6 B3

THREE LOCHS HOLIDAY PARK   RAC A
Balminnoch, DG8 0EP. ☎ (067183) 304
Open: 1 April-31 October
Size: 14 (22) acres, 45 touring pitches, 27 level
pitches, 21 with elec, 27 with hardstanding,
100 static caravans. 8 hot showers, 8 cold showers,
14 WCs, 1 CWP

(1991) Car & caravan, Motor caravan, Car & tent,
M/cycle* & tent £6; elec £1; WS
*Gently sloping park in area of outstanding scenic
beauty, overlooking our own stocked lochs. Indoor
swimming pool. Children's play area, TV and
games rooms. 9 caravans for hire (own WCs).
Restaurant 2 miles.*
From Newton Stewart travel W on the A75 for
6¾ miles, turn right at crossroads for 3½ miles,
turn left for 1¼ miles to site on right.

KIRKCUDBRIGHT *Dumfries & Galloway Map 6 B3*

BRIGHOUSE BAY HOLIDAY PARK　RAC A
Borgue, DG6 4TS. ☎ (05577) 267
Open: 1 April-31 October
Size: 15 (30) acres, 120 touring pitches, all with
elec, 100 level pitches, 7 with hardstanding,
120 static caravans, 2 chalets. 17 hot showers,
36 WCs, 2 CWPs

Car & caravan, Motor caravan, Car & tent, M/cycle*
& tent £6-£9 (provisional) including 2 persons; elec
£1.75-£2.25; awn £1.40; WS
*Spacious 30 acre park on a 600 acre farm next to
sandy beach. Facilities include en suite shower
rooms, bathrooms, launderette, dish wash-ups, TV
aerial hook-up. Watersports school with sailing,
windsurfing, jet skiing, canoeing, water skiing.
Guided farm tours and ornithological walks.
Mountain bikes. Pony-trekking. Boats on pond.
30 caravans for hire. Dogs on lead.*
At 1 mile W of Kirkcudbright on A755 turn S on
B727 for 3½ miles, turn left as signed Brighouse
Bay. At first fork (¾ mile) bear right and at second
fork (½ mile) bear right. Site behind wood.

Seward Caravan Park
☎ (0557) 31079
Open: March-October
Size: 10 acres, 30 touring pitches. 4 hot showers,
10 WCs

½ mile W of Kirkcudbright (A755), turn S on to
B727. Site 2 miles.

KIRKGUNZEON *Dumfries & Galloway Map 7 A3*

Beeswing Caravan Park
DG2 8JL. ☎ (038776) 242
Open: March-October
Size: 5½ acres, 30 touring pitches. 4 hot showers,
6 WCs. Static caravans

1½ miles N of Kirkgunzeon on A711.

Mossband Caravan Park
DG2 8JP. ☎ (038776) 208
Open: March-October
Size: 4 acres, 25 touring pitches. 2 hot showers,
8 WCs

8 miles SW of Dumfries on A711.

KIRKPATRICK FLEMING *Dumfries & Galloway Map 7 A3*

Cove Estate Caravan & Camping Site
☎ (04618) 285
Open: All year
Size: 21 acres, 50 touring pitches. 4 hot showers,
4 WCs

Turn off A74 signposted Kirkpatrick. In village,
follow signs to Bruce's Cave.

KIRKTON OF SKENE *Grampian　Map 9 B3*

Mains of Kier
AB3 6YA. ☎ (0224) 743282
Open: April-October
Size: 1½ acres, 10 touring pitches. 2 hot showers, 3
WCs. 9 static caravans

7 miles W of Aberdeen (A944), turn N on
B979 signposted Kirkton of Skene. Follow signs.

KIRRIEMUIR *Tayside　Map 7 A1*

DRUMSHADEMUIR CARAVAN PARK　RAC A
Roundyhill, DD8 1QT. ☎ (0575) 73284
Open: Mid March-End October
Size: 4½ (7½) acres, 80 touring pitches, all level,
40 with elec, 40 with hardstanding, 1 chalet. 6 hot
showers, 14 WCs, 2 CWPs

Car & caravan, Motor caravan £5.25-£5.75, Car &
tent, M/cycle* & tent £4-£4.50; elec £1.15-£1.50,
awn £1-£1.50; WS
*Clean and tidy family-run site, 2 miles north of the
historic village of Glamis and 2 miles south of
Kirriemuir (Peter Pan Country), the Angus Glens
being only a 10 minute car journey from the site.
Licensed premises on site. Swimming pool 2 miles.*
Site on E side of the A928, 2 miles S of Kirriemuir,
or 2¾ miles N of Glamis.

THE GLENS CARAVAN & CAMPING PARK　RAC L
Memus, by Forfar, DD8 3TY. ☎ (030786) 258
Open: 15 March-31 October
Size: ½ (1½) acres, 15 touring pitches, 10 level
pitches, 10 with elec, 24 static caravans. 2 hot
showers, 5 WCs, 1 CWP

Car & caravan, Motor caravan, Car & tent, M/cycle*
& tent £5.40; elec £1.50, awn 75p; WS
*Quiet rural site. 1 caravan for hire. Popular licensed
restaurant 300 yards. Suitable base for all types of
outdoor activities and an ideal area for hill walking,
cycling and fishing. Dogs are welcome but must be
kept on a lead within the park and exercised
outside the grounds.*
At 3 miles E of Kirriemuir on B957, turn N and
follow signs to Memus, 3 miles.

LAIRG *Highland　Map 9 A2*

Kenny's Caravan Site
Main Street.
☎ (0549) 2181
Open: May-September
Size: 2 acres, 20 touring pitches. 2 hot showers,

■ Snacks/take away ☒ Restaurant ◳ Swimming pool ▣ Shelter for campers ☝ Dogs accepted　　179

5 WCs. 5 static caravans

Entrance by Lairg Frozen Food Centre (A839).

Woodend Caravan & Camping Site
Achnairn.
☎ (0549) 2248
Open: April-September
Size: 4 acres, 53 touring pitches. 4 hot showers,
11 WCs. 7 static caravans

N from Lairg on A836, turn left on to A838. After
¼ mile, turn right into loop road. Site 2½ miles.

CLYDE VALLEY CARAVAN PARK   RAC L
Kirkfieldbank, ML11 9JW.
☎ (0555) 3951
Open: 1 April-31 October
Size: 5 (10) acres, 50 touring pitches, all level,
28 with elec, 50 static caravans, 50 chalets. 2 hot
showers, 14 WCs, 1 CWP

Charges on application.
*Situated in Clyde Valley's orchard land with two
fishing rivers running by it, this site has a
children's play area. Restaurant and shop adjacent.*
½ mile W of Lanark on A73 turn left A72, at ½ mile
on, turn right just before River Clyde bridge.

THIRLESTANE CASTLE CARAVAN &
CAMPING PARK   RAC L
TD2 6RU.
☎ (05782) 542
Open: Easter-1 October
Size: 4½ acres, 60 touring pitches, 30 level pitches,
12 with elec. 6 hot showers, 10 WCs, 1 CWP

Car & caravan, Motor caravan, Car & tent, M/cycle
& tent £6, plus £1 per person above 2; elec £1.50
*Set in beautiful parklands of Thirlestane Castle,
near River Leader. No gas available. Shop and
restaurant 500 metres (5 minutes' walk).*
At ½ mile S of Lauder on the A68, turn E on the
A697 for ¼ mile to site on left.

DOVECOT CARAVAN PARK   RAC L
Northwaterbridge, AB30 1QL.
☎ (067484) 630
Open: April-October
Size: 3 acres, 25 touring pitches, all level, 15 with
elec, 18 static caravans. 6 hot showers, 9 WCs,
2 CWPs

Car & caravan, Motor caravan, Car & tent £4; elec
£1, awn £1; WS
*Site on banks of River North Esk. Children's play
area. 2 caravans for hire (own WCs). Calor gas
only. Restaurant 1 mile. Swimming pool 8 miles.*
Turn off A94 at RAF base, Edzell junction. Site is
500 yards on the left.

Bennane Hill Caravan Park
☎ (046589) 233
Open: March-October
Size: 7 acres, 12 touring pitches. 4 hot showers,
16 WCs. 45 static caravans

1¾ miles S of Lendalfoot on A77.

LETHAM FEUS CARAVAN PARK   RAC A
Letham Feus, KY8 5NT.
☎ (0333) 350323
Open: 1 April-30 September
Size: 1 (7) acres, 15 touring pitches, all with elec,
100 static caravans. 6 hot showers, 14 WCs, 1 CWP

(1991) Car & caravan £5, Motor caravan £4; elec
50p
*Country site sheltered by woodland and with good
views. Children's playground. Restaurant 1½ miles.
Swimming pool 3½ miles.*
From the junction of B927 and A916 (N of Leven)
travel SW on A916 for ½ mile.

WOODLAND GARDENS CARAVAN &
CAMPING SITE   RAC L
Lundin Links, KY8 5QG.
☎ (033336) 319
Open: March-October inclusive
Size: ½ (1) acre, 20 touring pitches, all level,
18 with elec, 9 with hardstanding, 5 static caravans.
2 hot showers, 7 WCs, 1 CWP

Car & caravan, Motor caravan, Car & tent, M/cycle
& tent £1.50; all plus £1.50 per adult, 75p per child;
elec £1.50, awn £1.50; WS
*Small, quiet, peaceful site on level ground.
Sheltered. TV/games room. Children's play area on
site. 5 caravans for hire (own WCs). Restaurant
½ mile. Swimming pool 3 miles.*
At E end of Lundin Links turn N off A915. ½ mile
from A915. International signs from main road.

Lochgilphead Caravan Park
Bank Park, PA31 8NE.
☎ (0546) 2003
Open: April-October
Size: 5 acres, 30 touring pitches. 4 hot showers,
17 WCs. 10 static caravans

Site by A83/A816 junction.

Achmelvich Caravan Site
☎ (05714) 262
Open: Easter-October
Size: 1 acre, 12 touring pitches. 2 hot showers,
3 WCs. 6 static caravans

½ mile N of Lochinver (A837), turn W on to B869.
After 1½ miles, turn left at bridge. Site 1½ miles.

LOCHMABEN Dumfries & Galloway   Map 7 A3

HALLEATHS CARAVAN PARK   RAC L
DG11 1NA.
☎ (0387) 810321
Open: 1 April-31 October
Size: 8 acres, 60 touring pitches, all with elec, some with hardstanding, 2 static caravans. 8 hot showers, 12 WCs, 1 CWP

Charges on application. WS
Wooded site adjacent to loch. Children's play area and paddling pool on site, also fishing and boating. No gas available. Restaurant 1 mile.
From the junction of the A74 and A709 at Lockerbie, travel W on the A709 for 2¾ miles, turn right to site on right.

KIRK LOCH CARAVAN SITE   RAC L
Castle Hill Gate, DG11 1NQ.
☎ (0387) 810265
Open: April-27 September
Size: ½ acre, 30 touring pitches, all level, 10 with hardstanding, 6 with elec. 4 hot showers, 6 WCs, 1 CWP

Charges on application.
A small, level, council-run lochside site, part grass, part tarmac. Children's play area on site with golf course adjacent. No gas available. Shop and restaurant 100 metres. Swimming pool 8 miles. New signposts on approach roads.

LOCKERBIE Dumfries & Galloway   Map 7 A3

Dinwoodie Lodge Hotel
DY11 2SL.
☎ (05764) 289
Open: Easter-October
Size: 2 acres, 12 touring pitches. 6 WCs

5 miles N of Lockerbie, off A74.

LOCKERBIE CARAVAN SITE   RAC L
Glasgow Road.
☎ (05762) 2115
Open: 1 March-30 September
Size: 1 acre, 30 touring pitches, all level. 2 hot showers, 11 WCs, 1 CWP

Charges on application.
A level grassy site situated on the outskirts of Lockerbie. No gas available. Shop and restaurant ¼ mile.
Turn off A74 into Lockerbie. Site in Glasgow Road just to the N of the town.

LOSSIEMOUTH Grampian   Map 9 A2

Seatown Caravan Site
☎ (0343) 45121
Open: (1991) April-September
Size: 2 (4) acres, 32 touring pitches. Hot showers, WCs. Static caravans

Turn E off A941 on S outskirts of Lossiemouth.

LUSS Strathclyde   Map 6 B2

Camping & Caravanning Club Site
Loch Lomond, Near Glasgow, G83 8NT.
☎ (0436) 86658
Open: 30 March-26 October
Size: 15 acres, 90 touring pitches. 4 hot showers, 12 WCs

Charges on application.
cc Access, Visa/B'card
This site on the banks of Loch Lomond has a private beach, children's play area, and a boat ramp. Game fishing permits available from the warden. Camping Gaz only.
The site is directly accessible from the A82.

INVERBEG HOLIDAY PARK   RAC L
G83 8PD. ☎ (043686) 267
Open: 1 March-31 October
Size: 2 (17) acres, 55 touring pitches, all level, 30 with elec, 100 static caravans, 15 chalets. 6 hot showers, 13 WCs, 1 CWP

(1991) Car & caravan, Motor caravan, Car & tent, M/cycle & tent £7-£10, plus £1 per person above 2; elec £1.50, awn £1.50
Quiet site ideal for boating, fishing, walking and as a touring base. Licensed shop. Pets welcome, but must be kept under strict control. 20 static caravans and 1 chalet for hire (own WCs). Restaurant 200 yards. Swimming pool 12 miles.
3¼ miles N of Luss on A82.

MACDUFF Grampian   Map 9 B2

Myrus Caravan Park
AB4 3QP. ☎ (02612) 2845
Open: April-October
Size: 3½ acres, 24 touring pitches. 8 hot showers, 21 WCs. 36 static caravans

S of Macduff, site near A947/B9026 junction.

Wester Bonnyton
Gamrie, AB4 3EP. ☎ (0261) 32470
Open: Easter-October
Size: 1 acre, 8 touring pitches. 4 hot showers, 6 WCs. 22 static caravans, 3 chalets

2 miles E of Macduff on B9031.

MACHRIHANISH Strathclyde   Map 6 A2

Camping & Caravanning Club Site
East Trodigal, Campbeltown, PA28 6PT.
☎ (058681) 366
Open: 30 March-28 September
Size: 6 acres, 90 touring pitches. 4 hot showers, 9 WCs

Charges on application.
cc Access, Visa/B'card
A well-kept site with children's play area. Within a few minutes' walk of the beach.
Take the A83 from Campbeltown, then the B843, the site is on the right 200 yards past the square

◼ Snacks/take away ✕ Restaurant ◲ Swimming pool ◳ Shelter for campers 🐕 Dogs accepted   **181**

chimney.

MAIDENS *Strathclyde*   Map 6 B2

Ardlochan House
Culzean, KA19 8JZ. ☎ (06556) 208
Open: Easter-October
Size: 5 acres, 10 touring pitches. 4 hot showers,
8 WCs. 45 static caravans

| 🦽 | 🚐 | 🚙 | | 🧺 | | | | 🛏 | 🐕 |

1 mile N of Maidens (A719), turn W on Ardlochan
Road to site.

Old Mill Caravan Park
Ardlochan Road. ☎ (06556) 254
Open: April-October
Size: 1½ acres, 12 touring pitches. 1b hot showers,
1b WCs. 12 static caravans

| 🚐 | 🚙 | 🏕 | | | 🍴 | | | | 🐕 |

1 mile N of Maidens (A719), adjacent to Culzean
Estate.

MAYBOLE *Strathclyde*   Map 6 B2

Camping & Caravanning Club Site
The Gardens, Kilkerran Estate, KA19 7SJ.
☎ (06554) 323
Open: 30 March-28 September
Size: 3 acres, 80 touring pitches. 4 hot showers,
9 WCs

| 🚐 | 🚙 | 🏕 | 🧺 | 🛒 | | | | | 🐕 |

Charges on application.
cc Access, Visa/B'card
*Most of the site is located in the walled garden of
Kilkerran Estate, in the valley of the Waters of
Girvan. TV and games room. Ornamental walks
through estate.*
From the A77 take the B7023 to Cross Hill, keep on
the B7023 till the fork, bear right on to the B741,
after just over ¾ mile turn left, after a further
½ mile turn right. The site is on the left.

MELROSE *Borders*   Map 7 A2

Gibson Park Caravan Site
TD6 9RY. ☎ (089682) 2969
Open: April-October
Size: 3 acres, 80 touring pitches. 4 hot showers,
9 WCs

| 🚐 | 🚙 | 🏕 | | | | | | | 🐕 |

In Melrose High Street (A6091), turn off at
Riverside Garage for site.

MINTLAW *Grampian*   Map 9 B2

ADEN CARAVAN PARK   RAC L
Aden Country Park. ☎ (0771) 23460
Open: 1 April-30 September
Size: 3½ (4¼) acres, 50 touring pitches, all level,
39 with elec, 10 static caravans. 6 hot showers,

12 WCs, 1 CWP

| 🦽 | 🚐 | 🚙 | 🏕 | 🧺 | | | | | 🐕 |

(1991) Car & caravan £5.25, Motor caravan £4.75,
Car & tent, M/cycle & tent £2.30-£4.75; elec £1, awn
£2.30
*A good wooded site within a country park.
Children's play area on site. No gas available. Shop
½ mile. Restaurant ¼ mile.*
From the junction of the A92 and A950 (at
Mintlaw), travel W on the A950 for 1 mile to site on
left.

MOFFAT *Dumfries & Galloway*   Map 7 A2

Camping & Caravanning Club Site
Hammerland's Farm, DG10 9QL.
☎ (0683) 20436
Open: 30 March-26 October
Size: 12 acres, 200 touring pitches. 8 hot showers,
20 WCs

| 🦽 | 🚐 | 🚙 | 🏕 | 🧺 | 🛒 | | | | 🐕 |

Charges on application.
cc Access, Visa/B'card
*A level site by the river in the heart of the town.
Children's play area.*
At junction of A74 and A701 SE of Moffat (just N of
Beattock) travel NE on A701 to Moffat. Turn E in
town centre on A708 for 200 yards, turn right at
Silver Birches pub, then first left, then left again
across bridge to site.

MONIFIETH *Tayside*   Map 7 A1

RIVERVIEW CARAVAN SITE   RAC L
☎ (0382) 532837
Open: April-October
Size: 10 acres, 180 touring pitches. 18 hot showers,
36 WCs

| 🦽 | 🚐 | 🚙 | 🏕 | | 🛒 | | | 🎮 | |

Charges on application.
*A level grassy site near sea and beach. Children's
play area and games room. Calor gas only.*
Follow signs in the village from A930 (headroom
limit to site 10ft 4in).

MONREITH *Dumfries & Galloway*   Map 6 B3

KNOCK SCHOOL CARAVAN PARK   RAC L
Near Newton Stewart, DG8 8NJ.
☎ (09887) 409 or 414
Open: Easter-October
Size: 1 acre, 15 touring pitches. 1 hot shower,
4 WCs

| 🚐 | 🚙 | 🏕 | | 🛒 | | | | 🎮 | 🐕 |

Charges on application.
*A pleasant, quiet site with level grass overlooking
sea. Golf, safe sea bathing, sea and loch fishing,
and bowls all close to site. Camping Gaz only.
Restaurant ½ mile.*
Site on N side of A747, 3¼ miles S of Port William.

Seasonal variation of prices

Where a single price is given it may be a low season minimum charge - rates can increase
considerably at peak periods and for extra people or vehicles.
Please confirm prices with the site when booking.

🦽 Facilities for Disabled 🚐 Caravans accepted 🚙 Motor caravans 🏕 Tents 🧺 Laundry room 🛒 Shop

One of Scotland's leading Centres for outdoor recreation, with a wide range of activities to choose from, offers **Something for everyone. Top class facilities for Land and Water Sports, Countryside Ranger Service, Visitor Centre – Sandy Beaches, Play Areas – Caravan & Camping Site – Programme of Special Events.**

All enquiries are welcomed:
Strathclyde Country Park
366 Hamilton Road
Motherwell ML1 4ED
Telephone: Motherwell 66155

STRATHCLYDE COUNTRY PARK
Strathclyde REGIONAL COUNCIL

MONTROSE *Tayside* — Map 7 A1

SOUTH LINKS CARAVAN PARK RAC L
Traill Drive, DD10 8SW. ☎ (0674) 72044
Open: 1 April-9 October
Size: 9 acres, 160 touring pitches, 140 level pitches, 46 with elec. 14 hot showers, 34 WCs, 3 CWP

Charges on application.
Close to the sea and a good safe beach, this well-maintained site, with children's play area, makes an excellent choice for families. No gas available. Shop open July-August. Restaurant ½ mile. From A92 in town centre, follow signs to the beach.

MOTHERWELL *Strathclyde* — Map 6 B2

Strathclyde Country Park
366 Hamilton Road, ML1 4ED.
☎ (0698) 66155
Open: April-October
Size: 20 acres, 150 touring pitches. 32 hot showers, 36 WCs

From M74 junction 5, turn on to A725 (Belshill). Park signed off roundabout, also off motorway.

MUASDALE *Strathclyde* — Map 6 A2

Muasdale Caravan Site
☎ (05832) 234
Open: April-October
Size: 3 acres, 12 touring pitches. 2 hot showers,

3 WCs

Follow A83 S from Tarbert for 22½ miles.

MUIR OF ORD *Highland* — Map 9 A2

DRUIMORRIN CARAVAN & CAMPING PARK RAC L
Orrin Bridge, Urray, IV6 7UL.
☎ (09973) 252
Open: 1 April-End October
Size: 5½ acres, 60 touring pitches, 40 level pitches, 6 with elec, 4 with hardstanding, 3 static caravans. 4 hot showers, 13 WCs, 1 CWP

(1991) Car & caravan, Car & tent, M/cycle & tent £5.50, Motor caravan £5; elec £1
Approximately 5½ acres of mainly level, well-drained grass. Trees and bushes have been retained to provide shelter and privacy. 3 caravans for hire (own WCs). Restaurant 2½ miles. Swimming pool 7 miles.
Take A9 N from Inverness to Tore roundabout, then take A832 W through Muir of Ord. Park situated on the A832 W of Muir of Ord.

MUSSELBURGH *Lothian* — Map 7 A2

DRUM MOHR CARAVAN PARK RAC A
Levenhall, EH21 8JS.
☎ (031) 665 6867
Open: 1 March-31 October
Size: 10 acres, 120 touring pitches, 100 level pitches, 100 with elec, 30 with hardstanding. 12 hot showers, 24 WCs, 2 CWPs

---

🔲 Snacks/take away ☒ Restaurant ◻ Swimming pool ▣ Shelter for campers 🔳 Dogs accepted

[&][⊞][⊞][▲][⊟][�&][ ][ ][ ][🐕]

Car & caravan, Motor caravan, Car & tent, M/cycle
& tent from £6.50, plus 50p per person above 2;
elec £1.25, awn £1
*Grassy with hardstanding, level, sheltered and
sloping. Within easy reach of Edinburgh, beaches
and countryside. Restaurant 1½ mile. Swimming
pool 4 miles.
1½ miles E of Musselburgh, between the
B1348 Preston Pans road and the B1361 North
Berwick road, beside mining museum.*

NAIRN *Highland*   Map 9 A2

DELNIES WOOD TOURING PARK   RAC L
IV12 5NX. ☎ (0667) 55281
Open: 15 March-31 October
Size: 3 (4) acres, 50 touring pitches, all level,
12 with elec, 90 with hardstanding. 6 hot showers,
6 WCs, 1 CWP

[ ][⊞][⊞][ ][ ][ ][ ][ ][ ][🐕]

Charges on application. WS
cc Visa/B'card
*A quiet and secluded site surrounded by
woodland. Children's play area on site. Shop,
restaurant and swimming pool 1 mile.
Site located on the S side of the A96, 3 miles W of
Nairn.*

LOCH LOY HOLIDAY PARK   RAC A
IV12 4PH. ☎ (0667) 53764
Open: 15 March-31 October
Size: 3 (20) acres, 100 touring pitches, all level,
48 with elec, 155 static caravans, 21 chalets. 6 hot
showers, 12 WCs, 1 CWP

[⊞][⊞][▲][⊟][�&][ ][ ][≈][ ]

Charges on application. WS
cc Access, Visa/B'card
*Swimming, boating and fishing from beach just in
front of this site. Golf course adjacent and play
area on site. 54 caravans and 15 chalets for hire
(own WCs). Families only unless confirmed pre-
booking. Restaurant 250 yards.
To the E of the town on A96, cross river bridge and
take first turn N towards the beach.*

Spindrift Caravan Park
Little Kildrummie, IV12 5QU.
☎ (0667) 53992
Open: April-October
Size: 3 acres, 30 touring pitches. 4 hot showers,
8 WCs

[ ][⊞][⊞][▲][ ][ ][ ][ ][ ][🐕]

From A96, turn S on to B9090. After 1½ miles at left
hand bend, turn sharp right into minor road. Site
400 yards.

NEWTON STEWART *Dumfries & Galloway* Map 6B3

CALDONS CARAVAN & CAMP SITE   RAC L
Forestry Commission, Glentrool, Bargrennan
☎ (067 184) 218
Open: Easter-October
Size: 25 acres, 160 touring pitches, 40 with elec,
154 level pitches, 6 with hardstanding. 8 hot
showers, 36 WCs, 2 CWPs

[&][⊞][⊞][▲][⊟][�&][☕][ ][⊟][🐕]

Charges on application. WS
*A pleasant, completely uncommercialised site by
Loch Trool. Advance bookings to be made to
Newton Stewart District Office, telephone: (0671)
2420. Good spot for hill walkers. Calor gas only.
Restaurant 3 miles.
9 miles NW of Newton Stewart on A714, turn E at
Bargrennan. At 1¼ miles on, bear right and
2¼ miles further turn right to site.*

CREEBRIDGE CARAVAN PARK   RAC A
Minnigaff, DG8 6AJ.
☎ (0671) 2324
Open: 1 March-31 October
Size: 2 (4½) acres, 25 touring pitches, all level,
20 with elec, 12 with hardstanding, 40 static
caravans, 1 chalet. 4 hot showers, 15 WCs, 2 CWPs

[ ][⊞][⊞][▲][⊟][�&][ ][ ][ ][🐕]

(1991) Car & caravan £3, Motor caravan £2.50, Car
& tent, M/cycle & tent £2, plus £1.20 per adult,
70p per child; elec £1.20, awn 70p; WS
*Quietly secluded site 5 minutes' walk from town
centre. Golf, fishing, hill walking, swimming pool
all nearby. Security street lights. 5 caravans and
1 chalet for hire (own WCs). Restaurant 200 yards.
No single-sex groups.
From A75, 1 mile E of Newton Stewart, turn off for
Minnigaff. Caravan park is ½ mile from turn off.
Through Newton Stewart and over old bridge to
Minnigaff. Caravan park is 250m on right from
bridge.*

TALNOTRY CAMP SITE   RAC L
Forestry Commission, Queensway
☎ (0671) 2170
Open: Easter-End September
Size: 15 acres, 60 touring pitches, all level. Wash
basins, 6 WCs, 2 CWPs

[&][⊞][⊞][▲][ ][�&][ ][ ][ ][🐕]

Charges on application.
*Grassy, forest site situated on the scenic
Queensway. Fishing and forest and hill walking
available with swimming and paddling in the
Palnure Burn. Calor gas only.
7 miles NE of Newton Stewart on A712.*

NEWTONMORE *Highland*   Map 9 A3

Invernahavon Caravan Park
Glentrium.
☎ (05403) 534
Open: Easter-October
Size: 13 acres, 100 touring pitches. 8 hot showers,
2b WCs

[ ][⊞][⊞][▲][⊟][�&][ ][ ][ ][🐕]

3 miles S of Newtonmore (A9), turn W signposted
Glentrium/Laggan. Site ½ mile.

Spey Bridge Caravan Site
PH20 1BB.
☎ (05403) 275
Open: Easter-October
Size: 3 acres, 45 touring pitches. 4 hot showers,
7 WCs

[ ][⊞][⊞][▲][⊟][ ][ ][ ][ ][🐕]

On B9150, by river bridge, just S of Newtonmore.

NORTH BERWICK *Lothian*   Map 7 A2

RHODES CARAVAN PARK   RAC L
Tantallon Road, EH39 5NJ.
☎ (031) 665 3711
Open: April-September
Size: 10 acres, 350 touring pitches, 20 with elec.
20 hot showers, 59 WCs, 5 CWPs

▢🚐🚙▲🛢▢▢▢▢▢▢🐕

(1991) Car & caravan, Motor caravan, Car & tent,
M/cycle & tent £6.40; elec £1.15, awn £1.55
*Simple site, with children's play area, by the beach
on the edge of town. No gas available. Shop,
restaurant and swimming pool 1 mile. Maximum
stay 28 days.*
1¼ miles E of North Berwick on A198.

OBAN *Strathclyde*   Map 6 B1

Gallanachmore Farm
Gallanach Road, PA34 4QH.
☎ (0631) 62425
Open: Easter-October
Size: 9 acres, 145 touring pitches. 4 hot showers,
12 WCs. 15 static caravans

▢🚐🚙▲🛢🛎▢▢▢▢🐕

From Oban, follow signposts for Gallanach. Site 2½
miles on coast road.

**GANAVAN SANDS TOURING
CARAVAN PARK**   RAC L
Ganavan, PA34 5TU.
☎ (0631) 62179
Open: Easter-October
Size: 2 (2½) acres, 80 touring pitches, 35 with elec.
60 level pitches, 80 with hardstanding. 4 hot
showers, 18 WCs, 1 CWP

♿🚐🚙▢🛢🛎♥✕▢▢🐕

Charges on application.
cc Access, Visa/B'card
*Small site beside a sandy beach with boat
launching slip, donkey rides and swimming.
Children's play area, putting, indoor games/TV
room. Calor gas only. Swimming pool 2 miles.*
Travel N from Oban town centre, after ¾ mile
follow coast road left (past Cathedral on right),
signposted Ganavan. Site in ¾ mile.

Oban Divers
PA34 4QJ. ☎ (0631) 62755
Open: March-November
Size: 4 acres, 52 touring pitches. 6 hot showers,
12 WCs

♿🚐🚙▲🛢▢▢♥▢▢🏠

In High Street, pass tourist office on right, then first
left. Site 1½ miles.

OLDSHOREMORE *Highland*   Map 8 B1

Oldshoremore
by Lairg. ☎ (097182) 281
Open: April-September
Size: 1 acre, 15 touring pitches. 1 hot shower,
4 WCs

▢🚐🚙▲▢▢▢▢▢▢🐕

From B801 in Kinlochbervie, take minor road N for
2 miles.

ONICH *Highland*   Map 6 B1

Corran Caravans
Moss Cottage. ☎ (08553) 208
Open: March-October
Size: 2 acres, 25 touring pitches. 4 hot showers,
5 WCs. 10 static caravans

▢🚐🚙▲🛢▢▢▢▢▢🐕

4 miles N of Ballachulish Bridge (A82).

PARTON *Dumfries & Galloway*   Map 6 B3

Loch Ken Holiday Centre
by Castle Douglas, DG7 3NE.
☎ (06447) 282
Open: Easter-October
Size: 7 acres, 50 touring pitches. 6 hot showers,
10 WCs. 33 static caravans

♿🚐🚙▲🛢🛎▢▢▢▢🐕

7 miles NW of Castle Douglas, adjacent to A713.

PEEBLES *Borders*   Map 7 A2

Crossburn Caravan Park
Edinburgh Road, EH45 8ED. ☎ (0721) 20501
Open: April-October
Size: 2 (12) acres, 30 touring pitches. 9 hot
showers, 17 WCs. Static caravans

♿🚐🚙▲🛢🛎▢▢▢🏠🐕

½ mile N of Peebles on A703.

ROSETTA CARAVAN PARK   RAC A
Rosetta Road, EH45 8PG. ☎ (0721) 20770
Open: 1 April-End of October
Size: 27 (60) acres, 140 touring pitches, 100 level
pitches, 50 with elec, 29 static caravans. 8 hot
showers, 24 WCs, 4 CWPs

▢🚐🚙▲🛢🛎☕▢▢▢🐕

(1991) Car & caravan, Motor caravan £6.50, plus
£1 per person above 2, Car & tent, M/cycle & tent
£2.50 per adult, 50p per child; elec £1.25, awn £1
*Quiet, family-run site in beautiful wooded grounds
of "Rosetta House". Bowling green, putting green
and lounge bar, also adjacent to 18 hole golf
course, fishing available on River Tweed.
Restaurant and swimming pool 1 mile. 7 caravans
for hire (own WCs).*
Turn right off the A72 in Peebles into Young Street.
Continue into Rosetta Road to site on left in
300 yards. From Edinburgh on the A703, turn right
at outskirts of town signposted Rosetta.

PENPONT *Dumfries & Galloway*   Map 7 A3

PENPONT CARAVAN & CAMPING PARK   RAC L
Penpont, Thornhill, DG3 4BH.
☎ (0848) 30470
Open: 1 April-31 October
Size: 1 (2) acres, 20 touring pitches, 6 with elec,
10 level pitches, 1 static caravan. 6 hot showers,
9 WCs, 1 CWP

▢🚐🚙▲🛢▢▢▢▢▢🐕

(1991) Car & caravan £4.25, Motor caravan £4, Car
& tent, M/cycle & tent from £3, all plus 50p per
adult, 25p per child; elec £1.25, awn 50p, dogs free;
WS
Situated in beautiful countryside. Excellent for

📷 Snacks/take away ✕ Restaurant ◩ Swimming pool ▣ Shelter for campers 🏠 Dogs accepted   185

cycling, walking and touring. Play area on site. Shop 500 yards. Restaurant 2 miles. 1 caravan for hire (own WC).
Site on S side of the A702, ¼ mile E of Penpont.

PERTH Tayside — Map 7 A1

CLEEVE CARAVAN PARK — RAC L
Glasgow Road, PH2 0PH. ☎ (0738) 39521
Open: Late March-Late October
Size: 5¼ acres, 100 touring pitches, 50 with elec. 11 hot showers, 20 WCs, 4 CWPs

(1991) Car & caravan, Motor caravan £5.70 plus £1.10 per person above 4; Car & tent, M/cycle & tent £1 plus £1.25 per person; elec £1.20, awn £1.25; WS
Quiet, well-screened, wooded site with high standard of facilities and good reputation. Children's play area. Easy access to centre of Perth. Tourist Board graded 5 Ticks, Caravan Club listed 3 Pennants. Off-season discount for OAPs; sports discount for stays of 1 week or more. Restaurant 200 yards. Swimming pool ¾ mile.
½ mile E of A9/M90, on W side of Perth (A93).

PETERCULTER Grampian — Map 9 B3

LOWER DEESIDE CARAVAN PARK — RAC A
Maryculter. ☎ (0224) 733860
Open: April-November
Size: 4 (10) acres, 30 touring pitches, static caravans. 5 hot showers, 15 WCs

Charges on application.
Pleasant country site in woodland near a river, next door to a hotel and restaurant. Play area, games and TV rooms on site. Calor gas only.
Site on N side of the B9077, 7½ miles SW of Aberdeen city centre.

PITLOCHRY Tayside — Map 7 A1

FASKALLY HOME FARM CARAVAN SITE — RAC A
☎ (0796) 2007
Open: 15 March-31 October
Size: 23 acres, 250 touring pitches, 20 with elec, 60 static caravans. 18 hot showers, 78 WCs

Charges on application.
Level grassy site, well sheltered by trees, in a picturesque setting. Children's playground. There's

fishing on Loch Faskally and the Rivers Tummel and Garry. 40 caravans for hire (own WCs).
2 miles N of Pitlochry on A924 (A9), signposted.

Milton of Fonab Caravan Site
PH16 5NA. ☎ (0796) 2882
Open: Easter-October
Size: 15 acres, 130 touring pitches. 1b hot showers, 4b WCs. 36 static caravans

½ mile S of Pitlochry (A9), turn on to A924.

POOLEWE Highland — Map 8 B2

INVEREWE CAMPING & CARAVAN PARK — RAC L
Achnasheen, IV22 2LQ. ☎ (044586) 249
Open: April-September
Size: 3 (4½) acres, 50 touring pitches, all level, all with hardstanding. 4 hot showers, 10 WCs, 1 CWP

Charges on application.
cc Access, Visa/B'card
A level but stony site on the shores of the sea loch Ewe. Salmon fishing very popular. Collection of sub-tropical plants at Inverewe House Gardens nearby. Shop ½ mile. Restaurant 300 yards.
Site on A832, halfway between Inverewe Gardens and the junction of the A832 and B8057, in the centre of Poolewe.

PORT WILLIAM Dumfries & Galloway — Map 6 B3

West Barr Farm Caravan Park
DG8 9QS.
☎ (09887) 367
Open: March-October
Size: 1 acre, 10 touring pitches. 2 hot showers, 6 WCs. 20 static caravans

2 miles NW of Port William on A747.

PORTKNOCKIE Grampian — Map 9 B2

Moray District Council Caravan Site
☎ (0542) 40132
Open: April-September
Size: 1½ acres, 20 touring pitches. 2 hot showers, 7 WCs

Turn off A98 on to A942 for 1 mile towards Portknockie. Site signed.

Portknockie Site
McLeod Park. ☎ (0343) 45121
Open: (1991) June-September
Size: 1 acre, 14 touring pitches. Hot showers, WCs.
Static caravans

	🅿	🚐	⚠	🛏							🐕

At 1¼ miles W of Cullen on A98, turn N on
A942 and then turn right at primary school, along
Seafield Terrace to site in 250 yards.

Castle Bay Caravan Park
DG9 9AA. ☎ (077681) 462
Open: March-October
Size: 12½ acres, 45 touring pitches. 2b hot
showers, 2b WCs. 65 static caravans

	🅿	🚐	⚠	🛏	🔧				🏠	🐕

Into Portpatrick on A77, turn left opposite Old Mill
Restaurant. Continue for ¾ mile, under railway
bridge, site on right.

GALLOWAY POINT HOLIDAY PARK   RAC L
Portree Farm, DG9 9AA. ☎ (077681) 561
Open: Mid March-End October
Size: 6 (18) acres, 30 touring pitches, all with elec,
all level pitches, 5 with hardstanding, 60 static
caravans. 7 hot showers, 24 WCs, 1 CWP

	🅿	🚐	⚠	🛏		☕	✖		🏠	🐕

Car & caravan £7-£8, Motor caravan, Car & tent £6-
£8, M/cycle & tent £5; elec £1.50; WS
*A quality graded family park overlooking the sea,
offering a quiet holiday with fishing, golf (9 and
18 holes), bowling, all close by. The Barn Inn offers
meals and take aways each night. Shop ½ mile.
Swimming pool ¼ mile. 6 caravans for hire (own
WCs).*
A77 from Glasgow. A75 from Dumfries. First left on
entering Portpatrick. Park ½ mile on the right, park
office on the left beside the Barn public house.

Sunnymeade Caravan Park
DG9 8LN. ☎ (077681) 293
Open: Easter-October
Size: 3½ acres, 16 touring pitches. 4 hot showers,
11 WCs. Static caravans

	🅿	🚐	⚠	🛏						🐕

8 miles SW from Stranraer on A77, take first left in
Portpatrick.

PORTSOY CARAVAN PARK   RAC L
☎ (0261) 42695
Open: 1 April-30 September
Size: 2 acres, 31 touring pitches, 6 with elec,
10 level pitches, 16 static caravans. 4 hot showers,
10 WCs, 1 CWP

	🅿	🚐	⚠	🛏						🐕

Car & caravan, Motor caravan £4.85-£5.25, Car &
tent £4.30-£4.50; elec £1.25-£1.30, awn £2.15-£2.30
*Seaside site on the edge of town. Swimming,
boating and fishing from beach. Play area on site.
Shop 300 yards. Restaurant ¼ mile. Scottish
Graded Caravan and Camping Parks graded
4 Ticks.*
Turn N off A98 in Portsoy (6 miles W of Banff) into
Church Street for 100 yards and turn right along
Institute Street.

PRESTWICK HOLIDAY PARK   RAC A
KA9 1UH. ☎ (0292) 79261
Open: March-October
Size: 12 acres, 40 touring pitches, all level, all with
elec, 168 static caravans. 4 hot showers, 10 WCs,
1 CWP

	🅿	🚐	⚠	🛏	🔧					🐕

Car & caravan, Motor caravan, Car & tent all £7-
£8 per person; awn £1
*Immaculate park with lovely walks, in a beach
location surrounded by golf courses. Bar.
Restaurant ½ mile. Swimming pool 1 mile.
Bookings taken for a minimum of 1 week.*
At 1 mile N of Prestwick on A79, turn W opposite
Prestwick Airport, for ¼ mile.

Dunvegan Caravan Site
KW14 7RQ. ☎ (084781) 405
Open: June-October
Size: 1 acre, 25 touring pitches. 2 hot showers,
4 WCs

	🅿	🚐	⚠	🛏						🐕

In Reay on A836.

Rosehearty Caravan & Camping Park
Shore Street. ☎ (0346) 24557
Open: April-September
Size: 1½ acres, 30 touring pitches. 6 hot showers, 9
WCs

♿	🅿	🚐	⚠	🛏				🏊		🐕

In Rosehearty, off B9031.

Camping & Caravanning Club Site
Fortrose, IV10 8UW. ☎ (0381) 21117
Open: 30 March-28 September
Size: 5 acres, 60 touring pitches. 4 hot showers,
12 WCs

	🅿	🚐	⚠	🛏	🔧					🐕

Charges on application.
cc Access, Visa/B'card
*Level site in small seaside village overlooking the
Moray Firth. Calor gas only. Shop 1 mile.*
From the A832 take the road opposite the police
house into Ness Road, take the left turn on to Ness
Road East, the site is on the right after the golf
club.

ROSEMARKIE CARAVAN SITE   RAC L
The Shore, Rosemarkie. ☎ (0381) 21117
Open: March-September
Size: 7 acres, 50 touring pitches. 4 hot showers,
16 WCs

♿	🅿	🚐	⚠	🛏						🐕

Charges on application.
cc Access, Visa/B'card
The site is close to the beach. Calor gas only.

💬 Snacks/take away ✖ Restaurant 🏊 Swimming pool 🏠 Shelter for campers 🐕 Dogs accepted

Almost 1 mile N of Fortrose on A832, turn E to the sea where turn right.

ROY BRIDGE *Highland* — Map 8 B3

Bunroy Holiday Park
PH31 4AG. ☎ (039781) 332
Open: December-October
Size: 7 acres, 20 touring pitches. 4 hot showers, 6 WCs. 10 chalets

[icons]

At 300 yards E of Roy Bridge Hotel on A86 turn right and over railway bridge for 300 yards.

Glenspean Holiday Park
PH31 4AW. ☎ (039781) 432
Open: All year
Size: 4½ acres, 20 touring pitches. 2 hot showers, 8 WCs. 7 static caravans

[icons]

In Roy Bridge, access by Roy Bridge Hotel.

Stronreigh Campsite
☎ (039781) 275
Open: March-October
Size: 2 acres, 20 touring pitches. 2 hot showers, 5 WCs. 20 static caravans

[icons]

¾ mile W of Roy Bridge on A86.

SANDHEAD *Dumfries & Galloway* — Map 6 B3

Sandhead Caravan Park
☎ (077683) 296
Open: April-October
Size: 10 acres, 40 touring pitches. 8 hot showers, 22 WCs. 90 static caravans

[icons]

3 miles W of Glenluce (A75), turn S on to A716. Site on approach to Sandhead.

Sands of Luce Caravan Park
DG9 9JR. ☎ (077683) 456
Open: March-October
Size: 12 acres, 26 touring pitches. 4 hot showers, 8 WCs. 34 static caravans

[icons]

¼ mile S of A715/A716 junction.

SANQUHAR *Dumfries & Galloway* — Map 6 B2

Castleview Caravan Park
DG4 6AX. ☎ (0659) 291
Open: April-September
Size: 2 acres, 15 touring pitches. 1 hot shower, 3 WCs. Static caravans

[icons]

At S end of Sanquhar on A76.

SCONE *Tayside* — Map 7 A1

Camping & Caravanning Club Site
Scone Racecourse, PH2 6BB.
☎ (0738) 52323
Open: 30 March-26 October
Size: 14 acres, 150 touring pitches. 8 hot showers, 27 WCs

[icons]

Charges on application.
cc Access, Visa/B'card
An attractively landscaped site in quiet, well-kept surroundings. Children's play area.
On the A93 from Perth, drive past the entrance to Scone Palace, after 9 miles turn left, then follow the signs to the Racecourse.

SCOTLANDWELL *Tayside* — Map 7 A1

The Well Caravan Site
KY13 7JE. ☎ (059284) 289
Open: April-October
Size: 3½ acres, 60 touring pitches. 2 hot showers, 8 WCs. 2 static caravans

[icons]

In Scotlandwell on A911.

SCOURIE *Highland* — Map 8 B1

SCOURIE CARAVAN PARK RAC L
Harbour Road, IV27 4TG.
☎ (0971) 2060 or 2217
Open: Easter-30 September
Size: 4 acres, 60 touring pitches, all level, 18 with elec. 8 hot showers, 17 WCs, 1 CWP

[icons]

Car & caravan, Motor caravan, Car & tent £7, M/cycle & tent £3.50; extra person £1; elec £1.50, awn £1.50
This terraced, grassy site overlooks Scourie Bay with access to the beach. Loch fishing round the area and Handa Island bird sanctuary nearby. Good spot for hill walkers. Gas available at shop 200 yards away. Absolutely no noise between 11pm and 7am.
Site on the W side of the A894 at Scourie.

SELKIRK *Borders* — Map 7 A2

VICTORIA PARK CARAVAN SITE RAC L
Victoria Park, TD7 5DN. ☎ (0750) 20897
Open: 1 April-31 October
Size: 3 acres, 60 touring pitches, all level, 18 with elec, 8 with hardstanding. 6 hot showers, 11 WCs, 1 CWP

[icons]

(1991) Car & caravan, Motor caravan, Car & tent, M/cycle & tent £4.60-£5.25; elec £1.25
Town site in open parkland by River Ettrick. Children's playground and mini-gym available. Indoor swimming pool adjacent. No gas available. Shop ¼ mile. Restaurant ½ mile.
A7 N, signposted from Selkirk market place, right turn immediately before bridge over river. A7 S, take A72 (Peebles)/A708 (Moffat) turn off at entrance to town (site signposted at turn off); thereafter follow signs. From Peebles or Moffat, follow road in to Selkirk, turn left immediately after bridge over river.

SKELMORLIE *Strathclyde* — Map 6 B2

Mains Caravan Site
☎ (0475) 520794
Open: April-September

[🦽] Facilities for Disabled [🚐] Caravans accepted [🚙] Motor caravans [⛺] Tents [🔲] Laundry room [🏪] Shop

Size: 3 acres, 90 touring pitches. 6 hot showers,
8 WCs. Static showers

[icons]

Turn off A78, 4 miles N of Largs.

SOUTHEND *Strathclyde*   Map 6 A2

Machribeg
by Campbeltown. ☎ (058683) 249
Open: Easter-September
Size: 7 acres, 70 touring pitches. 7 hot showers,
18 WCs. Static caravans

[icons]

½ mile W of Southend on B842.

SOUTHERNESS *Dumfries & Galloway* Map 7 A3

SOUTHERNESS HOLIDAY VILLAGE   RAC A
DG2 8AZ. ☎ (038788) 256
Open: 1 March-31 October
Size: 8 (80) acres, 200 touring pitches, all level,
70 with elec, 10 with hardstanding, 300 static
caravans, 20 chalets. 25 hot showers, 36 WCs, ·
1 CWP

[icons]

Charges on application. WS
*A spacious, level site beside a safe, sandy beach.
Indoor swimming pool, evening entertainment and
play area. Restaurant ¼ mile. 50 caravans for hire
(own WCs).*
At 1 mile S of Kirkbean on A710 turn S for
2½ miles.

SPEAN BRIDGE *Highland*   Map 8 B3

Gairlochy Caravan Park
☎ (039 782) 229
Open: April-October
Size: ¾ acre, 20 touring pitches. 2 hot showers,
4 WCs. Static caravans

[icons]

1 mile N of Spean Bridge (A82), take
B8004 signposted Gairlochy. Site 2 miles.

ST ANDREWS *Fife*   Map 7 A1

Cairnsmill Caravan Site
KY16 8NN. ☎ (0334) 73604
Open: April-October
Size: 20 acres, 80 touring pitches. 8 hot showers,
10 WCs. 185 static caravans

[icons]

1 mile S of St Andrews on A915.

CRAIGTOUN MEADOWS HOLIDAY PARK   RAC A
Mount Melville, KY16 8PQ. ☎ (0334) 75959
Open: 1 March-31 October
Size: 6 (32) acres, 98 touring pitches, all level, all
with elec, all hardstanding, 136 static caravans,
6 chalets. 11 hot showers, 22 WCs, 2 CWPs

[icons]

Car & caravan, Motor caravan £9.20-£10.20, Car &
tent £7.15-£8.15, plus 50p per person above 2; awn
£2; WS
cc Access, Amex, Visa/B'card
*A well-maintained, level site in landscaped
woodland, 1½ miles from the coast. Play area,
barbecue, games and TV rooms, and tennis court
on site. 36 caravans for hire (own WCs). Swimming
pool 1½ miles.*
From St Andrews bear left opposite University
Playing Fields, park is 1¼ miles from playing fields
fork, coinciding initially with the east drive to
Craigtoun Hospital. A90 Junction 8 to A91 through
Cupar, Dairsie, to Guardbridge. 400 yards on turn
right (Strathkinness and St Andrews) and go
through Strathkinness, over crossroads, left at next
crossroads, park is in ¾ mile.

Kinkell Braes Caravan Site
KY16 8PX. ☎ (0334) 74250
Open: March-October
Size: 4 acres, 100 touring pitches. 11 hot showers,
21 WCs. 398 static caravans

[icons]

½ mile S of St Andrews on A918.

ST MONANS *Fife*   Map 7 A1

Abbeyford Caravans
The Common. ☎ (03337) 778
Open: March-October
Size: 8 acres, 15 touring pitches. 6 hot showers,
10 WCs. 90 static caravans

[icons]

Off A917, on E side of St Monans.

STIRLING *Central*   Map 6 B2

Auchenbowie Caravan Site
by Bannockburn, FK7 8HE. ☎ (0324) 822142
Open: April-October
Size: 3½ acres, 60 touring pitches. 6 hot showers,

◪ Snacks/take away ☒ Restaurant ◲ Swimming pool ▣ Shelter for campers 🐕 Dogs accepted   **189**

14 WCs. 8 static caravans

From M80/M9 junction 9, take A872 for Denny.
Take first right. Site ¾ mile.

Cornton Caravan & Camping Park
Cornton Road. ☎ (0786) 74503
Open: All year
Size: 2½ acres, 50 touring pitches. 4 hot showers,
12 WCs. 10 static caravans

From A9 Stirling towards Bridge of Allan, cross
bridge and left at traffic lights to B823 Cornton
Road. Site ½ mile.

STONEHAVEN *Grampian*   Map 9 B3

QUEEN ELIZABETH CARAVAN PARK   RAC L
Viewmount, Ardathie Road. ☎ (0569) 62001
Open: 1 April-Mid October
Size: 6 acres, 34 touring pitches, all level, 76 static
caravans. 5 hot showers, 20 WCs, 2 CWPs

Charges on application.
*This site is incorporated into a seaside leisure
centre with access to the beach. The centre offers a
swimming pool, basket ball, volley ball,
badminton, table tennis and 5-a-side football.
15 caravans for hire. Shop and restaurant ½ mile.*
Site on E side of the B979, ½ mile N of Stonehaven
town centre.

STRACHUR *Strathclyde*   Map 6 B1

STRATHLACHLAN CARAVAN PARK   RAC L
PA27 8BU. ☎ (036 986) 300
Open: 1 April-31 October
Size: 1 (8) acres, 6 touring pitches, 3 with elec,
6 with hardstanding, 70 static caravans. 4 hot
showers, 9 WCs, 2 CWPs

Charges on application.
*Simple little well-sheltered site close to Loch Fyne.
Restaurant ¼ mile.*
At 4 miles SW of Strachur on A886, turn W on the
B8000 for 3 miles to site on right.

STRANRAER *Dumfries & Galloway*   Map 6 B3

AIRD DONALD CARAVAN PARK   RAC A
off London Road, DG9 8RN. ☎ (0776) 2025
Open: All year
Size: 12 acres, 100 touring pitches, all level, 35 with
elec, 50 with hardstanding. 7 hot showers, 28 WCs,
3 CWPs

Charges on application.
*This woodland meadowland site is adjacent to the
beach. On-site play area. Restaurant and
swimming pool ¼ mile.*
Access from A75 (London Road). Opposite the new
school.

CAIRNRYAN CARAVAN & CHALET PARK   RAC A
DG9 8QX. ☎ (05812) 231
Open: 1 April-31 October
Size: 7 acres, 24 touring pitches, all level, 5 with

elec, 82 static caravans, 10 chalets. 4 hot showers,
32 WCs, 1 CWP

Charges on application.
*Overlooking Loch Ryan and the ferry terminal, this
site has a swimming pool, billiards room, disco,
licensed bar with TV, and a play area. 10 chalets
and 10 caravans for hire (own WCs). Calor gas
only. Restaurant 50 yards.*
5 miles N of Stranraer on A77. Observe sign.

DRUMLOCHART CARAVAN PARK   RAC A
Leswalt, DG9 0RN. ☎ (077687) 232
Open: 1 March-31 October
Size: 5 (22) acres, 30 touring pitches, 25 with elec,
25 level pitches, 25 with hardstanding, 80 static
caravans, 2 chalets. 4 hot showers, 10 WCs, 1 CWP

Car & caravan £7.50, Motor caravan £6.50; awn £1
*Off the beaten track in an outstandingly beautiful
glen, amidst 22 acres of rhododendron and birch,
yet only 4 miles from Stranraer and 8 miles from
Portpatrick. 7 caravans and 2 chalets for hire (own
WCs). No tents or motorcycles. Minimum 3 nights
stay over Bank Holidays.*
From Stranraer travel NW on the A718 for
2¾ miles to roundabout, take B798 to Leswalt. At
church turn left on the B7043 for 1¾ miles to site
on right.

Ryan Bay Caravan Park
Innermessan Croft. ☎ (0776) 3346
Open: March-October
Size: 12 acres, 40 touring pitches. 6 hot showers,
16 WCs

1½ miles NE of Stranraer on A77.

WIG BAY HOLIDAY PARK   RAC A
Loch Ryan, DG9 0PS.
☎ (0776) 853233
Open: 1 March-31 October
Size: 3 (7.7) acres, 24 touring pitches, all level,
16 with elec, 6 with hardstanding, 88 static
caravans, 2 chalets. 6 hot showers, 6 cold showers,
19 WCs, 1 CWP

Car & caravan, Motor caravan, Car & tent, M/cycle
& tent £4-£5; elec £1, awn £1; WS
*The site is on the west coast of Loch Ryan, well-
sheltered by a hill and woodland to the west,
panoramic views over the Rhins Peninsula.
7 caravans for hire (own WCs). Minimum stay in
static caravans is no less than 2 nights.*
From Stranraer travel NW on the A718 for 4¼ miles
to site on left.

STRATHYRE *Central*   Map 6 B1

Immervoulin Caravan & Camping Park
FK18 8NJ.
☎ (08774) 285
Open: April-October
Size: 30 acres, 40 touring pitches. 2 hot showers,
8 WCs

Just S of Strathyre on A84.

STRONTIAN *Highland* — Map 6 A1

Glen View Caravan Site
PH36 4HZ. ☎ (0967) 2401
Open: April-October
Size: 1 acre, 10 touring pitches. 2 hot showers, 7 WCs

[icons] 🐕

In Strontian, off A861.

TAIN *Highland* — Map 9 A2

MEIKLE FERRY CARAVAN PARK RAC A
Meikle Ferry, IV19 1JX. ☎ (0862) 2292
Open: 15 January-15 December
Size: 2 (3½) acres, 30 touring pitches, 15 with elec, all level pitches, 11 static caravans. 4 hot showers, 8 WCs, 1 CWP

[icons] 🐕

Car & caravan, Motor caravan £5, Car & tent, M/cycle & tent £4, plus 50p per person above 2; elec £1, awn £1; WS
Park is set in the country, 2 miles from Tain, with extensive views across Dornoch Firth and Kyle of Sutherland. There are golf courses at Tain and Dornoch (18 hole). Safe, sandy beaches at Portmahomack at Dornoch. The park is a good centre for touring the North and West. 11 caravans for hire (own WCs, minimum let 3 days). Restaurant 400 yards. Mac-Gas only.
2 miles N of Tain, straight on at new roundabout. Access to new bridge across Dornoch Firth. Park access is 500 yards on right.

TARBERT *Strathclyde* — Map 6 B2

West Tarbert Ventures
Rhu House, PA29 6YF. ☎ (088 02) 231
Open: All year
Size: 2 acres, 24 touring pitches. 4 hot showers, 6 WCs

[icons] 🐕

4 miles SW of Tarbert on A83.

TARBET *Strathclyde* — Map 6 B1

LOCH LOMOND HOLIDAY PARK RAC L
Inveruglas, G83 7DN. ☎ (03014) 224
Open: 1 April-31 October
Size: 1½ (13½) acres, 12 touring pitches, all with elec, 6 level pitches, 6 with hardstanding, 39 static caravans. 4 hot showers, 6 WCs, 1 CWP

[icons] 🐕

Charges on application. WS
A delightfully situated site, terraced and sloping down to shores of Loch Lomond. 8 caravans for hire (own WCs). Calor gas only. Shop 3 miles. Restaurant 5½ miles.
3 miles N of Tarbet on A82.

TAYINLOAN *Strathclyde* — Map 6 A2

POINT SANDS CARAVAN PARK RAC A
PA29 6XG. ☎ (05834) 263
Open: 1 April-31 October
Size: 14 (24) acres, 65 touring pitches, 36 with elec, 75 static caravans. 7 hot showers, 15 WCs, 2 CWPs

[icons] 🐕

Car & caravan, Motor caravan £5.60, Car & tent, M/cycle* & tent £4.60; elec £1.50, awn £1.50; WS
cc Access, Visa/B'card
Peaceful park, superb sandy beach, magnificent scenery, in area of outstanding beauty. Opposite Isle of Gigha. Ideal for family holidays. 12 caravans for hire (own WCs). Restaurant 2 miles.
From Tarbert, travel S on the A83 for almost 17 miles, turn right to site (in ½ mile).

TAYNUILT *Strathclyde* — Map 6 B1

Crunachy Caravan & Camping Site
Bridge of Awe. ☎ (08662) 612
Open: March-November
Size: 9 acres, 80 touring pitches. 8 hot showers, 16 WCs. 8 static caravans

[icons] 🐕

2 miles SE of Taynuilt on A85.

TAYPORT *Fife* — Map 7 A1

Tayport Caravan Park
☎ (0382) 552334
Open: March-October
Size: 7 acres, 30 touring pitches. 6 hot showers, 13 WCs. 80 static caravans

[icons] 🐕

Site SE of town centre on coast.

TAYVALLICH *Strathclyde* — Map 6 A2

Tayvallich Camping Site
Leachive Farm. ☎ (036986) 300
Open: March-October
Size: 7 acres, 10 touring pitches. 4 hot showers, 10 WCs. 107 static caravans

[icons] 🐕

12 miles W of Lochgilphead.

THORNHILL *Central* — Map 6 B1

Mains Farm Camping Site
FK8 3QB. ☎ (078685) 605
Open: All year
Size: 4 acres, 40 touring pitches. 2 hot showers, 10 WCs

[icons] 🐕

In Thornhill (A873), turn on to B822 signposted Kippen. Site 100 yards.

THURSO *Highland* — Map 9 A1

Lady Janets Wood Caravan Site
☎ (0847) 62611
Open: April-September
Size: 5 acres, 75 touring pitches. 4 hot showers, 11 WCs. Static caravans

[icons] 🐕

1 mile E of Thurso on A836.

THURSO CARAVAN & CAMPING SITE RAC L
Scrabster Road, KW14 7JY.
☎ (0955) 3761 ext. 241
Open: 1 May-1 September

💽 Snacks/take away ✖ Restaurant ◺ Swimming pool ⊞ Shelter for campers 🐕 Dogs accepted   191

Size: 4 (4½) acres, 105 touring pitches, all level, 12 with elec, 10 static caravans. 10 hot showers, 10 cold showers, 22 WCs, 1 CWP

[icons]

Charges on application.
Busy and popular meadowland site adjacent to the beach and with panoramic views. Children's play area adjoining. No gas available. 10 caravans for hire (own WCs). Shop 200 yards.
Just to the W of Thurso on A882.

TONGUE *Highland*   Map 9 A1

Kincraig Caravan & Camping Site
☎ (080 05) 218
Open: Easter-October
Size: 2 acres, 15 touring pitches. 2 hot showers, 4 WCs. Static caravans

[icons]

In Tongue, off A838.

TOWN YETHOLM *Borders*   Map 7 B2

Kirkfield Caravan & Camping Park
TD5 8RA. ☎ (057 382) 346
Open: April-October
Size: 1½ acres, 34 touring pitches. 2 hot showers, 9 WCs

[icons]

8 miles SE of Kelso on B6352.

TUMMEL BRIDGE *Tayside*   Map 6 B1

TUMMEL VALLEY HOLIDAY PARK   RAC A
PH16 6SA. ☎ (08824) 221
Open: 20 March-31 October
Size: 7.4 acres, 101 touring pitches, 90 level pitches, 72 with elec, 65 with hardstanding, 106 static caravans, 30 chalets. 8 hot showers, 21 WCs, 1 CWP

[icons]

(1991) Car & caravan, Motor caravan, Car & tent, M/cycle & tent £8-£9.50; awn £1.50-£2; WS
cc Access, Visa/B'card
Magnificent scenery, crazy golf, entertainment nightly (June to August), entertainment weekends (early and late season), bars, video, games room. 84 caravans and 30 chalets for hire (own WCs). No all-male or all- female parties under 25 years.
A9 N from Perth. Left to B8019 N of Pitlochry, 11 miles.

TURNBERRY *Strathclyde*   Map 6 B3

Balkenna Camp Site
☎ (0655) 31692
Open: April-September
Size: 1 acre, 15 touring pitches. 4 WCs

[icons]

½ mile S of Turnberry on A77.

TURRIFF *Grampian*   Map 9 B2

TURRIFF CARAVAN PARK   RAC L
Station Road. ☎ (0888) 62205
Open: 1 April-30 September
Size: 5 acres, 35 touring pitches, all level, all with elec, 10 static caravans. 9 hot showers, 9 WCs, 1 CWP

[icons]

Car & caravan, Motor caravan £5.50-£5.80, Car & tent £4.75-£5; elec £1.25-£1.30, awn £2.35-£2.50
cc Major cards
A town site next to a river. Boating round, paddling pool and recreation area in adjacent park. No gas available. Shop and restaurant 300 yards. Swimming pool 200 yards. Graded by Scottish Caravan and Camping Parks as 4 Ticks.
Site to the E side of the A947 just S of Turriff.

ULLAPOOL *Highland*   Map 8 B2

Ardmair Point Caravan Site
☎ (0854) 612054
Open: Easter-September
Size: 4 acres, 50 touring pitches. 10 hot showers, 22 WCs

[icons]

3½ miles N of Ullapool on A835, in Ardmair village.

Broomfield Holiday Park
☎ (0854) 612664
Open: April-September
Size: 12 acres, 300 touring pitches. 20 hot showers, 50 WCs. 100 static caravans

[icons]

Site entrance 100 yards from pier.

WHITHORN *Dumfries & Galloway*   Map 6 B3

BURROWHEAD CARAVAN & CHALET PARK   RAC L
DG8 8OA. ☎ (09885) 252
Open: 1 March-31 October
Size: 4 (100) acres, 40 touring pitches, 12 with elec, all level pitches, 10 with hardstanding, 180 static caravans, 10 chalets. 6 hot showers, 12 WCs, 2 CWP

[icons]

Car & caravan, Motor caravan, Car & tent, M/cycle & tent £5-£6; elec £1.25-£1.35
Large area, country coastal park situated on a major headland. Family orientated. Play areas, large pool with slide, bars, snooker. Calor gas only. 2 caravans and 10 chalets for hire (own WCs). Motorcycle groups by prior arrangement only.
Just S of Whithorn on A746, bear left on to A750 for 3 miles. Just before entering Isle-of-Whithorn village turn right and continue for 2 miles to Burrow Head.

⬙ Facilities for Disabled ⬙ Caravans accepted ⬙ Motor caravans ⬙ Tents ⬙ Laundry room ⬙ Shop

Castlewigg Caravan Park
DG8 8DP. ☎ (09885) 616
Open: March-October
Size: 2 acres, 15 touring pitches. 2 hot showers, 4 WCs

1½ miles N of Whithorn on A746.

Riverside Caravan Club Site
Janetstown, KW1 5SR. ☎ (0955) 5420
Open: May-September
Size: 6 acres, 90 touring pitches. 10 hot showers, 20 WCs

From Thurso on A882, pass "Welcome to Wick" sign and turn left in 400 yards.

The Country Code

Enjoy the countryside and respect its life and work;
Guard against all risk of fire;
Fasten all gates;
Keep your dogs under close control;
Keep to public paths across farmland;
Use gates and stiles to cross fences, hedges and walls;
Leave livestock, crops and machinery alone;
Take your litter home;
Help to keep all water clean;
Protect wildlife, plants and trees;
Take special care on country roads;
Make no unnecessary noise.

Seasonal variation of prices

Where a single price is given it may be a low season minimum charge - rates can increase considerably at peak periods and for extra people or vehicles.
Please confirm prices with the site when booking.

◨ Snacks/take away ☒ Restaurant ◹ Swimming pool ▣ Shelter for campers 🐾 Dogs accepted   193

ISLE OF ARRAN — Map 6 B2

BREADALBANE LODGE CARAVAN & CAMPING PARK   RAC L
Kildonan, KA27 8SE.
☎ (077082) 210
Open: All year
Size: 4½ (9½) acres, 60 touring pitches, most level, 6 with elec. 2 hot showers, 3 WCs, 1 CWP

Car & caravan, Motor caravan, Car & tent, M/cycle & tent all £2.50 per adult, £1.50 per child
In a beautiful bay with views of the Ayrshire coast. Noted for the seals, many birds and flowers. Fishing and boating arranged. Baby-sitting service. Full laundry service. Suitable for persons looking for a peaceful holiday away from it all. Restaurant next door. Swimming pool 12 miles.
Turn left at the ferry terminus, carry on through Lamlash and Whiting Bay and 3 miles outside Whiting Bay turn left at turning signposted Kildonan. 1.6 miles down road on the right hand side is the Breadalbane Lodge Caravan & Camping Park.

MIDDLETON CARAVAN & CAMPING PARK   RAC A
Lamlash, KA27 8NN.
☎ (07706) 251
Open: 1 April-31 October
Size: 3½ (7) acres, 70 touring pitches, 12 with elec, 40 level pitches, 49 static caravans. 4 hot showers, 11 WCs, 2 CWPs

Car & caravan £1.25, Motor caravan 75p, Car & tent £1- £2, M/cycle & tent 50p-£1.50, all plus £1.75 per adult, 75p per child (5-10 years); elec £1.50, awn 75p
This is a flat and grassy site, well-sheltered and close to all amenities. 5 minutes from beach. Popular with families. 7 static caravans for hire (own WCs). Shop and restaurant ¼ mile. Swimming pool 4 miles. Minimum stay in static caravans 3 nights (low season) and 1 week (high season).
Travelling from Ardrossan take ferry to Brodick, Isle of Arran, take A841 S to Lamlash, then first left past Police Station. From Kintyre take ferry to Lochranza, Isle of Arran, then A841 to Brodick, then Lamlash, then proceed as above. There is a camping and caravan sign on the left at the S end of the village.

LOCHRANZA GOLF & CARAVAN SITE   RAC A
Lochranza, KA27 8HL.
☎ (077083) 273
Open: Easter-31 October
Size: 60 touring pitches, all level. 4 hot showers, 6 WCs

Charges on application.
A quiet, rural, caravan and camping site near the sea, and with its own golf course (golf equipment for hire). New amenity block for 1992 season. Swimming pool 15 miles. No motorcycles.
Site on E side of village at side of A841.

  Facilities for Disabled   Caravans accepted   Motor caravans   Tents   Laundry room   Shop

ISLE OF LEWIS — Map 8 B1

BROAD BAY CARAVAN SITE — RAC L
Coll Sands. ☎ (0851) 2053
Open: 1 April-30 September
Size: ¾ (1½) acres, 10 touring pitches, 5 with elec,
static caravans. 2 hot showers, 7 WCs

🏕	🚐	⛺		🛁						🐕

Charges on application.
*An attractively situated sandy site near the beach.
Caravans for hire. Bus stop 20 yards.*
5 miles N of Stornoway on N Tolsta Road.

LAXDALE CARAVAN & CAMPING SITE — RAC L
Laxdale, Stornoway, PA86 0DR.
☎ (0851) 3234
Open: All year
Size: 2 acres, 30 touring pitches, static caravans.
2 hot showers, 3 WCs

🏕	🚐	⛺								🐕

Charges on application.
*This simple, rural site is surrounded by trees. Golf
and fishing available nearby. Shop ½ mile.*

At 1 mile N of Stornoway, turn left into Laxdale
Lane, which is second lane left after crossing cattle
grid.

ISLE OF SKYE — Map 8 B2

STAFFIN CARAVAN & CAMPING SITE — RAC L
Grenicle, Staffin, IV51 9JX.
☎ (047 062) 213
Open: 1 April-30 September
Size: 2 acres, 18 touring pitches, all level, all with
hardstanding, 2 static caravans, 2 chalets. 2 hot
showers, 1 cold shower, 8 WCs, 1 CWP

🚐	🚐	⛺		🛁						🐕

(1991) Car & caravan £4.50, Car &
tent £4, M/cycle & tent £3, including 2 adults
*Quiet, peaceful site 1 mile from Staffin Bay. Sea,
loch and river fishing nearby. 2 static caravans and
2 chalets for hire. Shop and restaurant ½ mile.
Swimming pool 15 miles. Plenty of scope for
climbing and hill walking on the doorstep. Family-
run site.*
On S side of Staffin village, sign at entrance.

ORKNEY AND SHETLAND ISLANDS

ORKNEY — Map 8 B1

Details of ferry services from Scrabster (near
Thurso) to Stromness (Orkney) are available from
P&O Ferries, Stromness, Orkney ☎ (0856) 850655.
This is a purpose-built roll-on/roll-off ferry capable
of carrying 100 cars and 400 passengers.

British Airways operate services daily, except
Sundays, from London, Birmingham, Manchester,
Glasgow, Edinburgh, Aberdeen and Inverness to
Kirkwall (Orkney). Daily air services, except
Sunday, are operated by Loganair Ltd, between
Edinburgh, Wick and Kirkwall (Orkney). Services
operate on Tuesdays, Wednesdays and Thursdays
between Inverness and Kirkwall. ☎ (0856) 3457

The mainland of Orkney has two sites for caravans
and tents which are open from May to September.

Ness Point Caravan & Camping Site, Stromness.
30 touring pitches. Facilities include flush toilets,
showers, hot water, shaving points and chemical
toilet disposal point.

Pickaquoy Park Caravan & Camping Site, Kirkwall.
Facilities include flush toilets, showers, hot water,
shaving points and chemical toilet disposal point.

Enquiries and bookings to Orkney Islands Council,
Kirkwall, Orkney, KW15 1NX.
☎ (0856) 3535 ext 2417

General tourist information on Orkney is available
from Orkney Tourist Board, Broad Street, Kirkwall,
KW15 1NX ☎ (0856) 2856

SHETLAND — Map 9 B1/2

Details of the ferry services from Aberdeen to
Lerwick (Shetland) are available from P&O Ferries,
PO Box 5, Jamiesons Quay, Aberdeen.
☎ (0224) 572615

British Airways operate services daily (one flight
on Sunday) from London, Birmingham, Glasgow,
Edinburgh, Aberdeen, Orkney, Inverness and
Manchester. For details apply to British Airways
Booking Office ☎ 081 - 897 4000

There are three campsites on the Shetlands.

Levenwick Camp & Caravan Site on A970 Lerwick
to Sumburgh road, about 18 miles S of Lerwick.
Open April-September.

Clickhimin Leisure Centre, Lerwick.
☎ (0595) 4555

Brae, at Valley Field Guest House. Open all year.
☎ (0806) 22365

ISLAND OF FETLAR — Map 9 B1/2

Garths Camping & Caravan Site
Miss A Hughson, Warden, Leagarth.
Open May-September.

Camping is forbidden on the Tresta Links in Fetlar.
Camping is usually permitted outside Lerwick
providing the camper asks permission from the
owner or occupier of the land before pitching a
tent.

Details of campsites and caravans to rent are
available from the Shetland Tourist Organisation
Information Centre, Lerwick, ZE1 0LU
☎ (0595) 3434

FAIR ISLE

Written permission for camping on Fair Isle MUST
be obtained from Mr N Thomson, Lower
Stoneybrek, Fair Isle. ☎ (03512) 228

🍴 Snacks/take away ✕ Restaurant ⌂ Swimming pool 🏠 Shelter for campers 🐕 Dogs accepted

WALES

ABERAERON *Dyfed* — Map 1 B1

Brynarian Caravan Park
Cross Inn, Llanon, SY23 5NA.
☎ (0974) 272231
Open: March-October
Size: 5 acres, 60 touring pitches. 2 hot showers, 6 WCs

5 miles NE of Aberaeron, off B4337.

Hafod Brynog
Ystrad Aeron, Felinfach. ☎ (0570) 470084
Open: April-October
Size: 8 acres, 30 touring pitches. 4 hot showers, 7 WCs. 7 static caravans

6 miles SE of Aberaeron on A482.

Tan-yr-allt Farm
Ciliau-Aeron, SA48 8BU. ☎ (0570) 470211
Open: All year
Size: 3 acres, 12 touring pitches. 4 WCs

In Ciliau-Aeron on A482.

Wide Horizons Caravan & Chalet Park
SA46 0ET. ☎ (0545) 570043
Open: 1 April-31 October
Size: 1½ (7) acres, 25 touring pitches. 7 hot showers, 10 WCs. 62 static caravans, 8 chalets

Travel S from Aberaeron on the A487 for ¾ mile to site on right.

ABERCARN *Gwent* — Map 2 A2

Forest Drive Campsite
Cwmcarn Forest Drive Visitor Centre, Cwmcarn
☎ (0495) 272001
Open: All year
Size: 3 acres, 40 touring pitches. 6 hot showers, 6 WCs

From Cwmcarn, follow signs for Cwmcarn Forest Drive.

ABERCRAVE *Powys* — Map 1 B1

DAN-YR-OGOF CAMPING SITE RAC L
Abercraf, SA9 1GJ.
☎ (0639) 730284/730693
Open: Week before Easter-31 October
Size: 1 (5) acres, 30 touring pitches, 10 level pitches, all with hardstanding. 6 hot showers, 9 WCs, 1 CWP

(1991) Car & caravan, Motor caravan £5, Car & tent, M/cycle & tent both £2 per person, £1 per child; extra person £1
Pony trekking centre and dry ski slope. River on one side of site, set in beautiful, mountainous, tree-covered area. No gas available. Shop 1 mile. Dogs must be kept on a lead.
Midway between Brecon and Swansea on A4067. In the Brecon Beacons National Park.

ABERDARON *Gwynedd* — Map 4 A3

Brynffynnon Caravan Park
Rhydlios, Rhoshirwaun. ☎ (075 883) 643
Open: March-October
Size: 1 acre, 10+ touring pitches. 3 WCs

½ mile N from Aberdaron (B4413), turn right on minor road to Rhydlios.

Caerau Farm
LL55 8BG. ☎ (075 886) 237
Open: March-October
Size: 1½ acres, touring pitches. 2 hot showers, 6 WCs

Take B4413 to Aberdaron.

Dwyros
LL53 8BS. ☎ (075886) 295
Open: Easter-October
Size: 3 acres, 60 touring pitches. 2 hot showers, 9 WCs

Towards Aberdaron on B4413, turn right in village. Site ¼ mile.

Pen-y-Bont Bach
Llangwnnadl, LL53 8NS. ☎ (075887) 252
Open: April-October
Size: 1 acre, 10 touring pitches. 1 hot shower, 2 WCs

3 miles SW of Tudweiliog.

Ty Mawr Caravan Park
Bryncroes, Sarn. ☎ (0248) 351537
Open: Easter-October
Size: 2 acres, 15 touring pitches. 2 hot showers, 4 WCs

SW from Sarn on B4413, after 1½ miles turn right for site. Site signed from B4413.

Ty-Newydd
Uwchmynydd. ☎ (075886) 302
Open: April-October
Size: 1 acre, 30 touring pitches. 3 WCs

From Aberdaron take St Mary's Well Road and follow road signposted Uwchmynydd. Site 1½ miles from Aberdaron.

ABERGAVENNY *Gwent* — Map 2 A2

Aberbaiden Caravan & Camping Park
Gilwern, NP7 0EF. ☎ (0873) 830157
Open: April-October
Size: 10 acres, 50 touring pitches. 8 WCs

  Facilities for Disabled   Caravans accepted   Motor caravans   Tents   Laundry room   Shop

CLYDACH GORGE CARAVAN SITE

Within the Brecon Beacons National Park and well signposted off A465(T) Heads of the Valley Road, between Abergavenny and Brynmawr. An excellent base for industrial heritage and scenic beauty.
Enquiries to: Claire Jenkins, Tourism Officer, Borough of Blaenau Gwent, Municipal Offices, Civic Centre, Ebbw Vale, Gwent NP3 6XB Tel: (0495) 350555

3 miles W of Abergavenny, adjacent to A465.

Clydach Gorge
Station Road, Clydach, Near Gilwern, NP7 0HD.
☎ (0495) 350555
Size: 2 acres, touring pitches. 2 hot showers, 4 WCs

Off A465 between Abergavenny and Brynmawr. Signed Clydach Gorge South and caravan sign.

Neuadd Farm
Cwmyoy. ☎ (0873) 890276
Open: Easter-November
Size: 5 acres, 30 touring pitches. 1 WC

4½ miles N from Abergavenny (A465), turn left at inn on to B4423. Site 2½ miles.

Pyscodlyn Farm
☎ (0873) 3271
Open: Easter-October
Size: 4½ acres, 30 touring pitches. 4 hot showers, 6 WCs. 2 static caravans

2½ miles W of Abergavenny on A40.

Rising Sun Inn
Pandy. ☎ (0873) 890254
Open: All year
Size: 1¾ acres, 28 touring pitches. 2 hot showers, 6 WCs. 13 static caravans

5 miles N of Abergavenny on A465.

ABERGELE *Clwyd*   Map 4 B2

Gwrych Towers Camp
☎ (0745) 832109
Open: July-September
Size: 3 acres, 50 touring pitches. 1 hot showers, 5 WCs

Site at main entrance to Gwrych Castle Park on B5443.

Manorafon Farm
☎ (0745) 823237
Open: Whitsun-October
Size: 6 acres, 83 touring pitches. 12 WCs

W of Abergele on A55, take main entrance to Gwrych Castle.

Sirior Bach
☎ (0745) 833265
Open: March-October
Size: 2 acres, 20 touring pitches. 2 hot showers,

3 WCs

2½ miles S of Abergele (A548), turn E on to B5381. Site 100 yards, at rear of petrol station.

ABERPORTH *Dyfed*   Map 1 B1

Arthen Caravan Park
Glynarthen, Llandysul. ☎ (023975) 333
Open: March-October
Size: 2 acres, 3+ touring pitches. 2 hot showers, 4 WCs

At Brynhoffnant (A487), turn S on to B4334. After 2 miles, turn right signposted Arthen Caravan Site. Right in ½ mile for site in 50 yards.

Brynawelon Caravan Park
Sarnau, Llandysul, SA44 6RE.
☎ (023 978) 584
Open: March-October
Size: 1½ acres, 30+ touring pitches. 4 hot showers, 7 WCs

On A487, 1 mile W of junction with B4334, turn SE signposted Rhydlewis at crossroads. Site ½ mile.

CAERFELIN CARAVAN PARK   ℞ L
SA43 2BY. ☎ (0239) 810540
Open: 1 April-30 October
Size: 2 (11) acres, 15 touring pitches, 10 with elec, 80 static caravans. 2 hot showers, 7 WCs, 1 CWP

(1991) Car & caravan, Motor caravan, Car & tent, M/cycle* & tent £5; elec £1, awn £1
A spacious, well-maintained site, with children's play area, near the beach. Calor gas only. Shop 300 yards. Restaurant 200 yards. Swimming pool 1 mile.
Turn N off A487 at Blaenannerch on to B4333. Enter Aberporth turn right by St Cynwyls Church, site 100 yards on left.

Dolgelynen Farm
☎ (0239) 811095
Open: Easter-September
Size: 5 acres, 24 touring pitches. 6 hot showers, 8 WCs. 15 static caravans

1 mile SE of Aberporth on B4333.

Helygfach Farm
☎ (0239) 810317
Open: Easter-October
Size: 16 acres, 50 touring pitches. 10 hot showers, 12 WCs. 12 static caravans

SE of Aberporth (A487), turn N on to B4333 for

⬛ Snacks/take away   ✕ Restaurant   � Swimming pool   🅱 Shelter for campers   🐕 Dogs accepted

1½ miles, then turn right for site.

Manorafon
Sarnau, Llandysul, SA44 6QH.
☎ (0239) 810564
Open: Easter-October
Size: 6 acres, 50 touring pitches. 2 hot showers,
6 WCs. Static caravans

At Sarnau on A487, turn NW towards Penbryn
Beach.

Pen-y-Graig
Felinwynt, Verwig, SA43 1QQ.
☎ (0239) 810664
Open: April-October
Size: 17 acres, touring pitches. 2 hot showers,
5 WCs

At Blaenannerch on A487, turn N on to B4333.
After ½ mile, fork left towards Verwig. Continue for
1¾ miles then turn right before phone box. Site
1 mile.

PILBACH CARAVAN PARK   RAC A
Bettws Ifan, Rhydlewis, SA44 5RT.
☎ (0239) 75434
Open: 1 March-31 October
Size: 2+ (14½) acres, 65 touring pitches, 28 with
elec, 57 level pitches, 2 with hardstanding, 70 static
caravans. 4 hot showers, 4 cold showers, 11 WCs,
1 CWP

(1991) Car & caravan, Motor caravan, Car & tent,
M/cycle* & tent £6.65-£7.65; elec £1.20, awn 90p,
dogs 90p; WS
*A friendly welcome awaits you at our family-run
park. Set in glorious countryside, 3½ miles from
safe, sandy beaches, our 14½ acre park is divided
by trees and hedging into close-mown areas.
Separate children's playing field and room.
7 caravans for hire (own WCs). No loud radios.
Dogs on lead. Last arrival 10pm prompt.*
From the junction of the A487 and the
B4333 (2 miles SE of Aberporth), travel on
B4333 towards Newcastle Emlyn for 1 mile, first
left to crossroads, turn right, first left to site on
right.

Talywerydd
Penbryn, Sarnau, Llandysul, SA44 6QY.
☎ (0239) 810322
Open: All year
Size: 4 acres, 25 touring pitches. 2 hot showers,
3 WCs

Travelling W on A487, after Sarnau crossroads,
take first right.

Treddafydd Private Caravan Site
Sarnau, Llandysul.
☎ (023 978) 551
Open: Easter-October
Size: 6+ touring pitches. 2 hot showers, 5 WCs.
Static caravans

At Sarnau crossroads on A487, turn NW, then take
first left. Site ¼ mile.

ABERSOCH *Gwynedd*   Map 4 A3

BRYN CETHIN BACH CARAVAN PARK   RAC A
Lon Garmon, LL53 7UL. ☎ (075881) 2719
Open: March-October
Size: 2 (12) acres, 15 touring pitches, 14 with elec,
14 level pitches, 48 static caravans, 6 chalets. 6 hot
showers, 6 cold showers, 7 WCs, 1 CWP

Car & caravan, Motor caravan £7-£9; elec £1.50
*Small, privately-owned park, set in lovely, well-
maintained grounds with excellent toilet, shower
and laundry facilities. Additional secluded area
including lake. Shop and swimming pool 1 mile.
Restaurant ¼ mile. Calor gas only. No groups of
unaccompanied youngsters.*
Travel on the A499 W from Pwllheli to Abersoch
(6½ miles), fork right on unclassified road at Land
& Sea Garage in Abersoch harbour for ½ mile to
site on right.

Deucoch Camp Site
Sarn-bach. ☎ (075881) 3293
Open: March-October
Size: 5 acres, 3 touring pitches. 8 hot showers,
6 WCs

From Abersoch, follow Sarn-bach road to wine
shop. Keep right up lane and turn left for site.

Fron Heulog Farm
Cilan, Sarn-bach, LL53 7LL.
☎ (075881) 2728
Open: Easter-October
Size: 5 acres, 50 touring pitches. 2 hot showers,
8 WCs

Take A499 to Abersoch and continue S to Sarn-
bach.

Sarn Farm
Sarn-bach. ☎ (075881) 2144
Open: Easter-October
Size: 2 acres, 53 touring pitches. 4 hot showers,
6 WCs

Take A499 to Abersoch and continue S to Sarn-
bach. Site at first farm on left in Sarn-bach.

Tai'r Lon
Cilan.
☎ (075881) 2600
Open: All year
Size: 1 acre, 3 touring pitches. 2 hot showers,
3 WCs

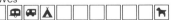

Take A499 to Abersoch and continue S for 1 mile
on Sarn-bach road.

Tan-y-Bryn Farm
Sarn-bach.
☎ (075881) 2093
Open: May-September
Size: 2 acres, 40 touring pitches. 4 hot showers,
8 WCs

Take A499 to Sarn-bach. Site at first farm on left.

⑤ Facilities for Disabled ⊞ Caravans accepted ⊞ Motor caravans Ⓐ Tents ⊟ Laundry room Ⓛ Shop

CAMPING OR CARAVANNING IN WALES?

RAC   **Aberystwyth Holiday Village**

The centre with all your requirements. Just a few minutes walk from the town and beach. On-park facilities include heated swimming pool, lounge bar, family night club, amusements, play area, fishing and much more. A great place for a family holiday. Call us for a colour brochure.

Penparcau Road, Aberystwyth, Dyfed.
Tel: (0970) 624211

Tyn-y-Mur Touring & Camping Site
Lon Garmon. ☎ (075 881) 2328
Open: March-October
Size: 3 acres, 43 touring pitches. 10 hot showers, 12 WCs

Approaching Abersoch from N on A499, turn right at Land and Sea Garage. Site ¾ mile.

ABERYSTWYTH *Dyfed*   Map 4 A3

ABERYSTWYTH HOLIDAY VILLAGE   RAC A
Penparcau Road, SY23 1BP.
☎ (0970) 624211
Open: 1 March-31 October
Size: 15 (30) acres, 152 touring pitches, 70 with elec, 152 level pitches, 25 with hardstanding, 152 static caravans, 1 chalet. 16 hot showers, 30 WCs, 4 CWPs

(1991) Car & caravan, Motor caravan, Car & tent, M/cycle & tent £6, plus £6 per adult, (under 5s free); extra person £1; elec £1, awn £1, dogs 50p; WS
Level site near town and beach, ideal for family holidays. 24 caravans and 1 chalet for hire (own WCs, no dogs in hired caravans). Motorcycles accepted with prior booking only.
¼ mile SE of Aberystwyth on the A487.

Bryncarnedd Caravan Park
Clarach Road. ☎ (0970) 615271
Open: April-October
Size: 4 acres, 100 touring pitches. 6 hot showers, 16 WCs. 2 static caravans

Take A487 N from Aberystwyth, take B4572 to Clarach. Site ½ mile on left.

GLAN-Y-MOR LEISURE PARK   RAC A
Clarach Bay, SY23 3DT. ☎ (0970) 828900
Open: March-November
Size: 3 (12) acres, 50 touring pitches, all level, 42 with elec, 160 static caravans. 10 hot showers, 9 WCs, 1 CWP

Car & caravan, Motor caravan, Car & tent, M/cycle & tent £7.50, plus £1 per person above 2; elec £1.55, awn £2.50, dogs £1.55
cc Access, Visa/B'card
Licensed club with nightly family entertainment.

Indoor leisure complex includes swimming pool, fitness gym, steam room, sauna, jacuzzi, sunbeds. Dragon award 5 Quality Ticks. Free hot showers and basins. 55 static caravans for hire (own WCs). Dogs not allowed over Bank Holidays or between July 20 and 31 August.
From Bow Street (just N of the junction of the A487 and A4159) NE of Aberystwyth, travel W to Clarach Bay to site on right.

Midfield Caravan Park
Southgate. ☎ (0970) 612542
Open: March-October
Size: 6 acres, 75 touring pitches. 14 hot showers, 15 WCs. 57 static caravans

1½ miles SE of Aberystwyth on A4120.

Morfa Bychan
Llanfarian, SY23 4QQ. ☎ (0970) 617254
Open: Easter-October
Size: 6 acres, 100 touring pitches. 12 hot showers, 11 WCs. Static caravans

2 miles S from Aberystwyth on A487, turn right at Rhydyfelin and follow minor road SW for 1¾ miles. Turn right along very narrow approach road.

Rhoslawdden Farm
Moriah, Capel Seion, SY23 4EA.
☎ (0970) 612585
Open: April-October
Size: 2 acres, 3+ touring pitches. 1 WC

3 miles E of Aberystwyth on A4120.

AMLWCH *Gwynedd*   Map 4 A2

Plas Eilian
Llaneilian, LL68 9LS. ☎ (0407) 830323
Open: Easter-September
Size: 2½ acres, 12 touring pitches. 1 hot shower, 2 WCs. 2 static caravans

2 miles E of Amlwch on coast road. 2 miles N of Penysarn.

Tyn Rhos Farm
Penysarn. ☎ (0407) 830574
Open: Easter-October
Size: 2 acres, 32 touring pitches. 2 hot showers,

⬛ Snacks/take away   ✕ Restaurant   � Swimming pool   ⬛ Shelter for campers   🐕 Dogs accepted   199

4 WCs. 1 static caravan

¼ mile S of Penysarn, to E of A5025.

BALA *Gwynedd* Map 4 B3

BRYN GWYN FARM CARAVAN PARK RAC L
Godre'r Aran Llanuwchllyn, LL23 7UB.
☎ (06784) 687
Open: Easter-October
Size: 3½ (6) acres, 10 touring pitches, 6 with elec,
static caravans. 2 hot showers, 6 WCs

Charges on application.
A peaceful, riverside farm site with lovely views.
Children's play area. Trout fishing. Calor gas only.
Farm produce sold on site every morning. Shop
1 mile.
At 4½ miles SW of Bala on A494, turn W on
Trawsfynedd Mountain Road for ½ mile.

BRYN MELYN LEISURE PARK RAC A
Llandderfel, LL23 7RA.
☎ (06783) 212
Open: March-October
Size: 6 (40) acres, 32 touring pitches, all with elec,
all level, 75 static caravans. 6 hot showers, 7 WCs,
1 CWP

Car & caravan £7, Motor caravan £6, Car & tent,
M/cycle* & tent £4-£5; awn £1
Pond for coarse fishing, and all newly developed,
up-to-date facilities, but the park is very quiet.
Panoramic views of Dee Valley. 5 caravans for hire
(own WCs, minimum stay in hired caravans
1 week). Calor gas only.
A5 at Corwen turn on to B4401, continue 7½ miles.
Entrance on left.

Camping & Caravanning Club Site
Crynierth Caravan Park, Cefn-ddwysarn, LL23 7IN.
☎ (06783) 324
Open: 30 March-28 September
Size: 4 acres, 50 touring pitches. 6 hot showers,
14 WCs

Charges on application.
cc Access, Visa/B'card
Site is adjacent to the River Tryweryn, a leading
European canoe slalom course. Sheltered by trees.
Shop 3 miles.
4 miles from Bala on A494 towards Corwen turn
left at telephone box in Cefn-ddwysarn.

Glanllyn
☎ (06784) 227
Open: Easter-September
Size: 14 acres, 84 touring pitches. 18 hot showers,
34 WCs

2½ miles SW of Bala on A494.

PENYBONT TOURING PARK RAC L
Llangynog Road, LL23 7PH.
☎ (0678) 520549
Open: 1 April-31 October
Size: 6 (8) acres, 75 touring pitches, 18 with elec, 25
level pitches, 25 with hardstanding. 2 hot showers,
9 WCs, 1 CWP

Car & caravan £1.70, Motor caravan £1, Car & tent,
M/cycle & tent from £1.40; all plus 70p per person;
Car 70p, M/cycle 70p; elec £1.20, awn 70p, dogs
free; WS
Penybont is a small, privately-owned touring park
for caravans, motorvans, tents, 300 yards from
Llyn Tegid and ¾ mile from the town of Bala.
Penybont has lovely views of the local mountains
and is an ideal base for touring North Wales. The
landscaped park has separate areas for caravans
and tents, each with hardstanding parking strip.
Restaurant ¾ mile.
¾ mile S of Bala on B4391.

PEN-Y-GARTH CARAVAN & CAMPING PARK RAC L
Rhos-y-Gwaliau, LL23 7ES.
☎ (0678) 520485
Open: 1 March-31 October
Size: 10 (20) acres, 48 touring pitches, 15 with elec,
40 level pitches, 10 with hardstanding, 45 static
caravans. 10 hot showers, 12 WCs, 1 CWP

Car & caravan, Motor caravan, Car & tent, M/cycle
& tent £5-£6; elec £1.50, awn £1
A quiet site with magnificent views amd modern
facilities. Well-spaced pitches in well-kept grounds.
5 acre recreation field and play area. Tourist Board
graded "Very Good". AA 3 Pennants. 6 caravans
for hire (own WCs).
From Bala travel S on the B4391 for 1 mile, turn
right on unclassified road as signed Rhos-y-
Gwaliau to site on right.

Ty Isaf Farm
☎ (0678) 520574
Open: April-October
Size: 4 acres, 30 touring pitches. 2 hot showers,
6 WCs

From Bala, take B4391. Cross head of lake and bear
left up hill for 2 miles. Site after phone box.

Tytanderwen
☎ (0678) 520273
Open: Easter-October
Size: 3½ acres, 45 touring pitches. 3 hot showers,
10 WCs

Take B4391 from Bala towards Llangynog for
2½ miles.

BANGOR *Gwynedd* Map 4 A2

Treborth Hall Farm Caravan Park
Treborth.
☎ (0286) 4949
Open: March-October
Size: 2½ acres, 24 touring pitches. 4 hot showers, 4
WCs

Leave A55 just before Britannia Bridge and take
A487 for Bangor. Site ¾ mile.

BANGOR-ON-DEE Clwyd — Map 4 B3

Camping & Caravanning Club Site
The Racecourse, LL13 0DA.
☎ (0978) 780740
Open: 30 March-28 September
Size: 2 acres, 100 touring pitches. 6 hot showers,
10 WCs

Charges on application.
cc Access, Visa/B'card
Level, grass site adjacent to racecourse. No gas available. Shop 5 miles.
From Bangor-on-Dee take the B5069 towards Shrewsbury. The site is on the racecourse ½ mile on the right.

BARGOED Mid Glamorgan — Map 1 B2

PARC CWM DARRAN CARAVAN & CAMPING SITE   RAC L
Cwn Lwydrew Farm, CF8 9AB.
☎ (0443) 875557
Open: 1 April-30 September
Size: 2 acres, 30 touring pitches, all level, 30 static caravans. 4 hot showers, 4 WCs, 1 CWP

(1991) Car & caravan, Motor caravan £3, Car & tent, M/cycle & tent £2.50
Sited in wooded Darran Valley close to large man-made lake well-stocked with fish. Shop ¼ mile. Swimming pool 5 miles.
From Bargoed take the A469 N for 1¼ miles, then turn left on to unclassified road for 3¼ miles to site on right.

BARMOUTH Gwynedd — Map 4 A3

Ballaport Farm
Tal-y-Bont, LL43 2BX. ☎ (03417) 338
Open: March-October
Size: ½ acre, 15 touring pitches. 1 hot shower, 4 WCs

N from Barmouth on A496, turn right at 30mph sign leaving Tal-y-Bont village to top of lane.

BENAR BEACH CAMPING & TOURING SITE   RAC L
Tal-y-Bont, LL43 2AR. ☎ (034 17) 571
Open: March-October
Size: 9 acres, 30 touring pitches (plus 125 for tents), all level, 22 with elec. 2 hot showers, 8 WCs, CWP

Car & caravan £5-£10, Motor caravan £4-£6, Car & tent £5-£6, M/cycle & tent £3-£4
Newly recognised by the RAC, this site is close to a wide, safe, sandy beach. Extra facilities available in high season. Restaurant ¼ mile. Shop ½ mile. Golf, tennis, sea fishing, canoeing, boating, horse riding, all within 5 miles.
Turn W off the A496 along unclassified road at Llanddwywe church, Tal-y-Bont 4½ miles N of Barmouth, 3 miles S of Llandbedr. Signs on main road (A496).

Dalar Farm
Tal-y-Bont, LL43 2RX. ☎ (034 17) 221
Open: Easter-September
Size: 1 acres, 5 touring pitches. 2 hot showers, 2 WCs. 3 static caravans

At Tal-y-Bont, turn W off A496, then turn right before railway bridge. Continue along for site.

DYFFRYN SEASIDE ESTATE   RAC L
Dyffryn Ardudwy, LL44 2HD.
☎ (034 17) 220
Open: 1 April-30 September
Size: 12 (600) acres, 3 touring pitches, all level, 248 static caravans, 3 chalets. 8 hot showers, 8 cold showers, 20 WCs

Car & caravan £6, Motor caravan, Car & tent, M/cycle & & tent £5
There's a level area for campers at this huge holiday site next to a wide sandy beach. Pub and children's play area on site; new indoor swimming pool. 18 caravans and 12 chalets for hire (own WCs).
Turn W off the A496 along unclassified road at Llanddwywe 4½ miles N of Barmouth, 3 miles S of Llanbedr.

HENDRE MYNACH CARAVAN PARK   RAC A
Llanaber Road, LL42 1YR. ☎ (0341) 280262
Open: 1 March-31 October
Size: 1 (10) acres, 60 touring pitches, all with elec, all level pitches, 5 with hardstanding. 13 hot showers, 22 WCs, 2 CWPs

(1991) Car & caravan £6-£9, Motor caravan £5.50-£9, Car & tent £4-£8, M/cycle* & tent £4-£6.50; elec £1.75, awn £1-£1.50, dogs 50p
This site is an ideal centre for touring Mid and North Wales and is also 100 yards from the beach, a pleasant 15 minutes' walk from the town centre. Restaurant adjacent. Swimming pool 12 miles.
½ mile N of Barmouth on A496 Barmouth to Harlech road, on the sea side of the road.

Islawrffordd Caravan & Camping Site
Tal-y-Bont, LL43 2BQ. ☎ (034 17) 269
Open: April-October
Size: 22 acres, 220 touring pitches. 6 hot showers, 14 WCs

At Tal-y-Bont, turn W off A496. Site second left turn.

Parc Isa
Cors-y-Gedol Drive, Dyffryn Arudwy
☎ (034 17) 447
Open: Easter-September
Size: 4 acres, 14 touring pitches. 2 hot showers, 4 WCs

At Tal-y-Bont, turn NE off A496. Site at second farm on right.

Rowen Farm & Benar Isa Farm
Tal-y-Bont, LL43 2AD. ☎ (034 17) 336
Open: April-October
Size: 20 acres, 50 touring pitches. 4 hot showers, 14 WCs

⬛ Snacks/take away ⊠ Restaurant ◩ Swimming pool ▣ Shelter for campers ⌂ Dogs accepted   **201**

N from Barmouth on A496, turn W at 30mph sign leaving Tal-y-Bont village.

BARRY *South Glamorgan* — Map 1 B2

FONTYGARY BAY CARAVAN PARK   RÁC A
Rhoose, CF6 9ZT. ☎ (0446) 710386
Open: 1 March-31 October
Size: 30 acres, 15 touring pitches, all with elec, 484 static caravans. 16 hot showers, 14 WCs, 2 CWPs

Charges on application.
Cliff-top site in Vale of Glamorgan. Extensive leisure facilities, which include indoor swimming pool, members health club (weekly membership available), bars, restaurants and shop. Calor gas only. 36 caravans for for hire (own WCs).
From the junction of the A48, A4050 and A4232 (W of Cardiff) take the A4050 S for 2½ miles, at roundabout turn right and ½ mile further take the A4226, 2 miles beyond bear left towards Cardiff airport. At roundabout take first road to Rhoose, continue for ¾ mile, then turn left under railway to site.

Vale Touring Caravan Park
Port Road (West). ☎ (0446) 736604
Open: Easter-September
Size: 2½ acres, 40 touring pitches. 4 hot showers, 6 WCs

Take A4226 W from Barry Island.

BEAUMARIS *Gwynedd* — Map 4 A2

Kingsbridge Caravan Park
Llanfaes, LL58 8LR. ☎ (024878) 636
Open: March-October
Size: 14 acres, 48 touring pitches. 6 hot showers, 13 WCs

Take the A545 to Beaumaris, at the Castle continue along the B5109 for 1½ miles, turn left for ¼ mile.

BEDDGELERT *Gwynedd* — Map 4 A3

SNOWDONIA NATIONAL FOREST PARK CAMPING SITE   RÁC L
Forestry Commission, LL55 4UU.
☎ (076 686) 288
Open: All year

Size: 25 acres, 140 touring pitches, all level, 14 with elec, 140 with hardstanding. 11 hot showers, 32 WCs, 2 CWPs

Charges on application.
In the heart of the National Park, this large forest site with terraced camping area stands 5 miles from the summit of Snowdon.
1 mile NW of Beddgelert on A4085.

BENLLECH *Gwynedd* — Map 4 A2

Bodafon
Benllech Bay. ☎ (0248) 852417
Open: March-October
Size: 2 acres, 33 touring pitches. 2 hot showers, 8 WCs

½ mile N of Benllech on A5025.

PLAS UCHAF CARAVAN & CAMPING PARK   RÁC L
Benllech Bay, LL74 8NU.
☎ (0407) 763012
Open: March-October
Size: 8 acres, 38 touring pitches, 100 tent pitches, all level, 24 with elec, 24 static caravans. 6 hot showers, 15 WCs, 1 CWP

Car & caravan, Motor caravan, Car & tent, M/cycle* & tent £4-£5; elec £1, awn £1; WS
A spacious, popular, quiet, rural holiday park, well-sheltered, close mown, tarmacadam roads, children's play area, swings, pay phone, safe beach less than a mile away. Shop ½ mile (mobile shop visits park). Restaurant ½ mile. Swimming pool 7 miles. Limited gas supplies available on site. Motorcycles accepted with couples or families only. Dogs on leads.
½ mile from Benllech, off A5025. Signposted on B5108.

BETHESDA *Gwynedd* — Map 4 A2

Dinas Farm
Halfway Bridge. ☎ (0248) 364227
Open: Easter-October
Size: 3 acres, 35 touring pitches. 2 hot showers, 6 WCs

From Bangor towards Bethesda on A5, bear right at bridge towards Tregarth. Site ½ mile.

Beddgelert Forest Campsite 🏕

THE WARDEN, FORESTRY COMMISSION,
BEDDGELERT, GWYNEDD, LL55 4UU
TELEPHONE: (076 686) 288

Mountain camping in a sheltered woodland environment.

Situated in the heart of Snowdonia National Park – 5 miles South West of Snowdon – climbing – fishing – easy access to North Wales beaches, Caernarfon Castle, Portmeirion Italian style village, Ffestiniog railway.

Facilities include flush toilets, hot and cold water, showers, phone coin boxes, shop and cafe, well levelled pitches, electrical hook-ups, fire precautions, resident warden.

Open all year round, reduced facilities in winter. No Bookings taken. Reduced rates for OAPs and large groups. Prices available on request.

  🦽 Facilities for Disabled 🚐 Caravans accepted 🚍 Motor caravans 🛆 Tents 🅰 Laundry room 🛒 Shop

OGWEN BANK CARAVAN PARK & COUNTRY CLUB
RAC A

Ogwen Bank, LL57 3LQ. ☎ (0248) 600486
Open: March-October
Size: 5½ (13½) acres, 66 touring pitches, all level, all with elec, all with hardstanding, 100 static caravans. 66 hot showers, 66 cold showers, 66 WCs, 1 CWP

Charges on application.
cc Access, Visa/B'card
A well-equipped site on the River Ogwen in the Nantffrancon pass. All pitches have their own shower, WC, washbasin, electric hook-up and TV aerial socket. Children's play area, licensed clubhouse and pony trekking station on site. 95 caravans for hire (own WCs). Swimming pool 5 miles.
½ mile S of Bethesda on A5.

BETWS-Y-COED *Gwynedd*   Map 4 A3

Bryn-Tirion
Dolwyddelan. ☎ (06906) 366
Open: Easter-October
Size: 4 acres, 6 touring pitches. 2 hot showers, 4 WCs

Site in grounds of Dolwyddelan Castle.

BLAENAU FFESTINIOG *Gwynedd*   Map 4 A3

Llechwrd Farm
Maentwrog. ☎ (076 685) 240
Open: March-October
Size: 4½ acres, 8+ touring pitches. 3 WCs

2 miles W of Ffestiniog on A496.

BORTH *Dyfed*   Map 4 A3

BRYNOWEN HOLIDAY PARK
RAC L

SY24 5LS. ☎ (0970) 871366
Open: Easter-Mid October
Size: 50 acres, 14 touring pitches, all with elec, 416 static caravans, 3 chalets. 4 hot showers, 4 cold showers, 5 WCs

(1991) Car & caravan £7-£11
Set in a valley among woodlands rising to 300 feet, with the beach approximately 150 metres away from the nearest gate. Some roads to certain sites are fairly steep. 124 caravans and 3 chalets for hire (own WCs). No under 21s. No all-male or all-female groups.
The entrance to Brynowen is on the B4353, 100 yards from the southern end of Borth seafront. The B4353 is off the A487 between Aberystwyth and Machynlleth.

CAMBRIAN COAST CARAVAN PARK
RAC A

Ynyslas, SY24 5JU. ☎ (0970) 871233
Open: March-November
Size: 4 (12) acres, 60 touring pitches, all level, 46 with elec, 144 static caravans. 9 hot showers, 13 WCs, 1 CWP

Car & caravan, Motor caravan, Car & tent, M/cycle & tent £7.50, plus £1 per extra person; elec £1.55, awn £2.50, dogs £1.55
cc Access, Visa/B'card
Licensed club with family entertainment. Outdoor children's fun pool (up to 11 years). Use of indoor pool at sister park 5 miles. Free hot showers, basins and washing-up facilities. Central barbecue area. 35 caravans for hire (own WCs).
From the S on the A487, turn W on B4353 1 mile N of Bow Street to coast where turn right and continue through Borth for just over 2 miles. Turn right, site just past level crossing.

Glanlerry Caravan Park
☎ (097 081) 413
Open: Easter-October
Size: 7 (15) acres, 100 touring pitches. 10 hot showers, 24 WCs. Static caravans

5 miles NE of Aberystwyth (A487), turn N on B4353. Site 2 miles.

Mill House Caravan & Camping Park
Dol-y-Bont, SY24 5LX. ☎ (0970) 871481
Open: Easter-October
Size: 4½ acres, 30 touring pitches. 2 hot showers, 5 WCs. Static caravans

N of Aberystwyth on A487, turn W on to B4353 through Llandre. After 1 mile, fork right under railway bridge for Dol-y-Bont. Site first right before hump-back bridge.

Riverside Caravan Park
Llandre. ☎ (0970) 820070
Open: March-October
Size: 14 acres, 24 touring pitches. 8 hot showers, 7 WCs. 2 static caravans, 3 chalets

N from Aberystwyth on A487, pass B4353 turning, and turn left 1 mile further, signposted Llandreon.

Ty Craig Holiday Park
Llancynfelin, SY20 8PU. ☎ (097086) 339
Open: March-October
Size: 3 acres, 70 touring pitches. 2 hot showers, 5 WCs

Turn W off A487 at Tre'r-ddol on to B4353. 200 yards past Llancynfelin church, turn left at Rock House. Site 100 yards.

Ty Mawr Caravan & Camping Park
Ynyslas, SY24 5LB. ☎ (0970) 871327
Open: March-October
Size: 9 acres, 20 touring pitches. 9 hot showers, 9 WCs. 51 static caravans

Turn W off A487 at Tre'r-ddol on to B4353. Site in 3 miles.

BRECON *Powys*   Map 1 B1

Aberbran Fawr
Penpont, LD3 9NG. ☎ (0874) 623301
Open: Easter-October
Size: 2 acres, 3+ touring pitches. 1 WC

● Snacks/take away ⊠ Restaurant ⌢ Swimming pool ▣ Shelter for campers 🐕 Dogs accepted   **203**

[☐][🚐][🚙][⛺][☐][☐][☐][☐][🐕]

4 miles W of Brecon (A40), turn W for Aberbran. Site 100 yds.

[♿][🚐][🚙][⛺][🚙][☐][☐][🍵][🍴][🛶][🏠][☐]

½ mile N of Talgarth on the A479, opposite Bronllys Castle.

BRYNICH CARAVAN PARK   RAC A
LD3 7SH. ☎ (0874) 623325
Open: Easter-October
Size: 5 acres, 60+ touring pitches, all level, 30 with elec, 5 with hardstanding, 6 hot showers, 12 WCs, 2 CWPs

[♿][🚐][🚙][⛺][🚙][🛒][☐][☐][☐][🐕]

Car & caravan £5.50-£6, Motor caravan £5-£5.50, plus £1.50 per adult above 2, child £1 (4-16), Car & tent, M/cycle & tent £2.50-£2.75; elec £1.50, awn £1, dog 25p; WS
Easy access to level, well-maintained site with cleanliness a top priority. Beautiful views. Ideally situated for walking and touring Mid Wales. Restaurant and swimming pool 1½ miles. From the roundabout junction of the A40 and A470 E of Brecon, travel NE on A470 for 200 yards and turn right to site.

BRYNSIENCYN *Gwynedd*   Map 4 A2

FRON CARAVAN & CAMPING SITE   RAC A
LL61 6TX. ☎ (0248) 430310
Open: Easter or 1 April-30 September
Size: 5½ acres, 69 touring pitches, 30 with elec, 5 with hardstanding, 1 static caravan. 4 hot showers, 6 WCs, 1 CWP

[☐][🚐][🚙][⛺][🚙][🛒][☐][☐][🛶][🏠][🐕]

(1991) Car & caravan, Motor caravan, Car & tent, M/cycle & tent £5.50, plus £1.50 per person above 2; elec £1, awn £1
Quiet, family site with mown grass and tarmac roads throughout. Ideal for beaches, attractions and touring Anglesey and Snowdonia. 1 caravan for hire (own WC). Restaurant 1 mile. From A5 (Britannia Bridge) follow signs to Llanfairpwllgwyngyll, at crossroads turn left (A4080) to Brynsiencyn, continue for ½ mile to site on right.

The Royal Oak Inn
Pencelli. ☎ (087486) 621
Open: All year
Size: 1 acre, 12 touring pitches, plus 15 tent pitches. 2 hot showers, 3 WCs

[☐][🚐][🚙][⛺][☐][☐][🍴][☐][🐕]

3 miles E of Brecon on B4558.

BRIDGEND *Mid Glamorgan*   Map 1 B2

CANDLESTON CAMP SITE   RAC L
Merthyr Mawr, CF32 0LR. ☎ (0656) 652038
Open: April-September inclusive
Size: 5 acres, 70+ touring pitches. 4 hot showers, 12 WCs, 1 CWP

[♿][☐][🚙][⛺][🛒][☐][☐][🏠][🐕]

Motor caravan, Car & tent, M/cycle & tent, all £2.50-£2.80 per adult, £1.25-£1.40 per child
Sheltered, rural site, part wooded, 1 mile across sandhills to beach. Covered cooking and games area, separate covered barbecue. Children's play area. Gower, Brecon Beacons, and the Valleys are all within a day's range. Restaurant and swimming pool 2½ miles. No unaccompanied under 18s. Travelling from the E, at the junction of the A48, A473 and A4063, travel W on the A48 for 1¼ miles. Turn left and ¼ mile on turn right then left to Merthyr Mawr. Site on left.

BRONLLYS *Powys*   Map 2 A2

Riverside International Caravan & Camping Park
Talgarth, Near Brecon, LD3 0HL.
☎ (0874) 711320
Open: Easter-October
Size: 10 acres, 100 touring pitches. 9 hot showers, 17 WCs

BRYNTEG *Gwynedd*   Map 4 A2

Ad Astra Caravan Park
LL78 7JH. ☎ (0248) 853283
Open: March-October
Size: 4 acres, 12 touring pitches. 4 hot showers, 8 WCs. 12 static caravans

[☐][🚐][🚙][⛺][🚙][☐][☐][☐][🐕]

B5108 for Llangefni. Left at crossroads on to B5110. Site ½ mile.

Garnedd Touring Site
LL78 8QA. ☎ (0248) 853240
Open: March-October
Size: 5 acres, 20 touring pitches. 2 hot showers, 8 WCs. 1 static caravan, 1 chalet

[☐][🚐][🚙][⛺][🚙][☐][☐][☐][☐]

On A5025 from Menai Bridge, after Pentraeth turn W at lay-by signposted Llanbedrgoch. After 2 miles, turn left at a t-junction sign Llanerchymedd. Take next lane on left for site.

Glan Gors Caravan Park
☎ (0248) 852334
Open: March-October
Size: 14 acres, 55+ touring pitches. 6 hot showers, 15 WCs. 260 static caravans

[☐][☐][🚙][⛺][🚙][🛒][🍵][☐][☐]

At Benllech crossroads turn W on B5108. Site signed after 1 mile.

NANT NEWYDD CARAVAN PARK   RAC A
LL78 8JH. ☎ (0248) 852842
Open: 1 March-31 October

NANT NEWYDD CARAVAN PARK
Brynteg, Benllech Bay, Anglesey. *Telephone: Tynygongl (0248) 852842 or 852266*
New luxury caravans for hire on totally uncommercialised site 2½ miles from Benllech Bay. Games room, play area, washers and dryers, licensed shop, heated swimming pool all available on site. Various sports within 3 miles. Disabled toilets.
TENTS AND TOURERS ESPECIALLY WELCOME – *Send SAE for brochure*   *Runners-up, Best Park in Wales*

Size: 4 (9) acres, 45 touring pitches, all with elec, 25 level pitches, 25 with hardstanding, 83 static caravans. 9 hot showers, 14 WCs, 2 CWPs

Car & caravan, Motor caravan, Car & tent £5.75-£7; elec £1.25, awn £1; WS
Laundry room with washers and dryers, play area, games room, TV room, licensed bar, telephone, outdoor heated swimming pool, doggie walk.
6 caravans for hire (own WCs). Restaurant ½ mile. No motorcycles.
After leaving Britannia Bridge take the A5025 Amlwch to Benllech. Turn left at the square and take B5108 towards Llangefni for approximately 2 miles. At crossroads turn left on to the B5110. We are 1 mile from here on the right.

BUILTH WELLS *Powys*   Map 1 B1

LLEWELYN LEISURE PARK   R&AC L
Cilmery, LD23 3NW. ☎ (0831) 101052
Open: Easter-31 October
Size: ¾ (2.14) acres, 17 touring pitches, all with elec, 10 level pitches, 5 with hardstanding, 30 static caravans. 2 hot showers, 2 cold showers, 4 WCs, 2 CWPs

Car & caravan, Motor caravan, Car & tent, M/cycle & tent £5-£7; elec £1.50, awn £1; WS
cc Mastercard, Visa, Eurocard
Panoramic southerly views, rural tranquility, adjacent to an inn with a restaurant. Nearby fishing, golf, riding, theatre, sports, bowls. Luxury accommodation £98-£298 weekly for 6 people, some with microwave, video, duvets.
Hardstandings, water and drainage hook-ups. Bus and rail services. Function/conference room. WTB 3 Ticks. Restaurant 20 yds. Swimming pool 2 miles.
Site at Cilmery, 2½ miles W of Builth Wells on the A483. Site behind Prince Llewelyn Inn.

Pont-ar-lthon
Newbridge-on-Wye. ☎ (059 789) 203
Open: April-October

Size: 2 (4) acres, 20 touring pitches. 3 WCs. Static caravans

5 miles N of Builth Wells on A470.

CAERNARFON *Gwynedd*   Map 4 A2

BRYN GLOCH CARAVAN & CAMPING PARK   R&AC A
Betws Garmon, LL54 7YY.
☎ (028685) 216
Open: All year
Size: 18 acres, 98 touring pitches, 92 level pitches, 52 with elec, 6 with hardstanding, 11 static caravans. 9 hot showers, 18 WCs, 1 CWP

(1991) Car & caravan, Motor caravan, Car & tent, M/cycle* & tent £5, plus £1 per adult above 2, child 80p (up to 14 years); elec £1.50, awn £1, dogs 50p
A well-kept site beside the River Gwyrfrai, where campers can swim, canoe and fish. Bus stop at gate. 11 caravans for hire (own WCs). Swimming pool 5 miles.
4½ miles SE of Caernarfon on A4085, site on right opposite Betws Garmon church.

BRYN TEG CARAVAN PARK   R&AC A
Llanrug, LL55 6ER. ☎ (0286) 871374
Open: 1 March-31 October
Size: 7 (39) acres, 68 touring pitches, all with elec, 50 level pitches, 286 static caravans. 8 hot showers, 45 WCs, 2 CWPs

Charges on application. WS
cc Access, Visa/B'card
Spacious, well-kept site beside a lake (fishing possible), with its own indoor swimming pool, 2 licensed bars and children's play area.
28 caravans for hire (own WCs). Restaurant 2 miles.
At 3½ miles E of Caernarfon on A4086, pass through Llanrug and ½ mile on turn S by Glyntwrog Hotel. At ¼ mile on turn left and ¼ mile further bear right under arch of Bryn Bras Castle.

◗ Snacks/take away ☒ Restaurant ◺ Swimming pool ⊡ Shelter for campers 🐕 Dogs accepted   205

CADNANT VALLEY CARAVAN PARK   RAC L
Llanberis Road, LL55 2DF.
☎ (0286) 673196
Open: 1 April-31 October
Size: 4 (4½) acres, 90 touring pitches, all level,
26 with elec, 4 with hardstanding, 8 hot showers,
12 WCs, 1 CWP

Car & caravan, Motor caravan, Car & tent, M/cycle
& tent £2.80-£3.20 per adult, £1.05-£1.30 per child;
elec £1.50
*Situated in a beautiful wooded valley, with a
stream. Within ½ mile of Caernarfon Castle, town
centre shops, Leisure Centre and Menai Straits, but
enjoying the peace and tranquility of a country
setting. Restaurant ½ mile. Swimming pool less
than ½ mile away.*
Less than a third of a mile from Caernarfon town
centre on A4086, Llanberis Road. Turn left just
before fire station.

Cynefin
Betws Garmon, LL54 7YR. ☎ (028 685) 294
Open: All year
Size: 1 acre, 13 touring pitches. 2 hot showers,
3 WCs

In Betws Garmon on A4085.

DINLLE CARAVAN PARK   RAC A
Dinas Dinlle, LL54 5TW. ☎ (0286) 830324
Open: 1 March-31 October
Size: 5 (23) acres, 100 touring pitches, all level,
80 with elec, 10 with hardstanding, 138 static
caravans. 22 hot showers, 35 WCs, 2 CWPs

Charges on application.
cc Access, Visa/B'card
*Near the beach, this large, level site has lovely
mountain and sea views. Amenities include a
licensed club and children's play area. Restaurant
¼ mile. 35 caravans for hire (own WCs). Shop open
Easter-October.*
5½ miles S of Caernarfon on A487 then A499, turn
right as signposted "Dinas Dinlle", continue to
Beach Road and take first turn right, signed.

Glan Gwna Holiday Park
Caeathro. ☎ (0286) 3456
Open: Easter-September
Size: 200 acres, 100 touring pitches. 7 hot showers,
20 WCs. 145 static caravans

1 mile S of Caernarfon, off A4085.

Greuor Farm
Llanrug. ☎ (0286) 2275
Open: March-September
Size: 4 acres, 37 touring pitches. 4 hot showers,
14 WCs

2½ miles E of Caernarfon on A4086.

Hendy Farm
☎ (0286) 2785
Open: Easter-October
Size: 2 acres, 5 touring pitches. 1 hot shower, 1 WC

½ mile S of Caernarfon on A487 at Seiont Bridge,
follow Pant Road towards Llanfaglan. In 500 yards
turn right over disused railway crossing to farm.

LLYN-Y-GELE FARM CARAVAN PARK   RAC L
Pontllyfni, LL54 5EL. ☎ (0286) 86283
Open: Easter-October
Size: 2 (5) acres, 6 touring pitches, all level, all with
elec. 24 static caravans, 2 hot showers, 7 WCs,
2 CWPs

Car & caravan £4, Motor caravan £3.50, both plus
£1.75 per adult, 50p per child; elec £1, awn 50p
*Quiet, family site, short walk to the sea along
private footpath from the site. In Area of
Outstanding Natural Beauty. Central for touring
Snowdonia, Lleyn Peninsula and Anglesey. Calor
gas only. 2 caravans for hire (own WCs). Shop at
site entrance. Restaurant 2 miles. Swimming pool
7 miles.*
Site is at Pontllyfni on the NW side of the A449,
7½ miles SW of Caernarfon.

MORFA LODGE CARAVAN &
CAMPING PARK   RAC A
Dinas Dinlle, LL54 5TP. ☎ (0286) 830205
Open: 1 March-31 October
Size: 12 (28) acres, 70 touring pitches, all level,
40 with elec, all with hardstanding, 150 static
caravans. 15 hot showers, 33 WCs, 2 CWPs

(1991) Car & caravan, Motor caravan £4.50-£7, Car
& tent, M/cycle & tent £1-£1.50 plus £1-£1.50 per
person; elec £1.50, awn £1, dogs 50p; WS
cc Major cards

*A well-maintained, level site with new luxury 12'
and 10' wide caravans for hire (own WCs). No
minimum stay for tourers or tents. Short breaks for
caravan hire available on application.*
5½ miles S of Caernarfon on A487 then A499 turn
right as signposted "Dinas Dinlle Beach", 1 mile on
keep left. Site is at far end of beach.

Rhyd-y-Galen Caravan Park
Bethel Road, LL55 3PS. ☎ (0248) 670110
Open: Easter-October
Size: 2 acres, 25 touring pitches. 2 hot showers,
5 WCs

2 miles NE of Caernarfon on B4366.

Riverside Camping
Caer Glyddyn, Pontrug. ☎ (0286) 2524
Open: Easter-October
Size: 4½ acres, 50 touring pitches. 2 hot showers,
6 WCs

2 miles E of Caernarfon on A4086.

Twll Clawdd Caravan Site
Llanrug. ☎ (0286) 2838
Open: Easter-October
Size: 2½ acres, 40 touring pitches. 2 hot showers,
4 WCs

3 miles E of Caernarfon on A4086.

Tyn Rhos Farm Caravan Site
Saron, Llanwnda, LL54 5UH. ☎ (0286) 830362
Open: March-October
Size: 2 acres, 20 touring pitches. 2 hot showers,
4 WCs

S from Caernarfon on A487, turn right after river
bridge signposted Saron/Llanfaglan. After 3 miles,
on right-hand bend, proceed through gateway to
site.

Ty'n-yr-Onnen Caravan Park
Waunfawr. ☎ (028 685) 281
Open: Easter-October
Size: 4 acres, 20 touring pitches. 3 hot showers, 2b
WCs. 2 static caravans, 1 chalet

SE from Caernarfon on A4085. At Waunfawr P.O.
fork left on No Through Road. Site at third farm on
left.

CAERSWS *Powys*   Map 4 B3

Carno Caravan Park
Carno. ☎ (0686) 420259
Open: April-October
Size: 7 acres, 45 touring pitches. 4 hot showers,
9 WCs. 35 static caravans

6 miles NW from Caersws (A470), in Carno turn left
at village shop and bear right over bridge. Site
½ mile.

Tyncwm Camping Site
Aberhafesp, SY16 3JF. ☎ (0686) 651
Open: May-October
Size: 5 acres, touring pitches. 2 hot showers,
3 WCs. Static caravans

From Caersws take B4569 signposted Aberhafesp.
Cross over B4568 and continue to next crossroads.
Turn left signposted Bwlch-y-Garreg. Site 1 mile.

CARDIFF *South Glamorgan*   Map 2 A2

PONTCANNA CARAVAN SITE   RAC A
☎ (0222) 398362
Open: All year
Size: 1¾ (2½) acres, 43 touring pitches, all level, all
with elec, all with hardstanding. 8 hot showers,
10 WCs, 2 CWPs

Charges on application.
*Site within Pontcanna fields, which has numerous
leisure facilities. Close to city centre. Shop,
restaurant and swimming pool ¼ mile.*
Site NW of Cardiff city centre. Entrance on E side of
A4119 Cathedral Road, via Sophia Close.

CARDIGAN *Dyfed*   Map 1 B1

Blaenwaun Farm
Mwnt. ☎ (0239) 612165
Open: Easter-September
Size: 10 acres, 100 touring pitches. 2 hot showers,
3 WCs

2 miles NE of Cardigan (A487), turn NW on to
minor road. Site 3 miles.

Penralltllyn Farm
Cilgerran, SA43 2PJ. ☎ (023 987) 350
Open: Easter-October
Size: 1 acre, 20 touring pitches. 1 hot shower,
4 WCs

3 miles SE of Cardigan on A484, at Llechryd turn S
over bridge and continue for 1 mile to crossroads.
Site straight on, second entrance to right.

Plas-y-Bridell
☎ (0792) 207194
Open: All year
Size: 3 (6) acres, 10+ touring pitches. 2 hot
showers, 9 WCs. Static caravans

2 miles S of Cardigan on A478.

Snacks/take away   ✕ Restaurant   Swimming pool   Shelter for campers   Dogs accepted   207

CEMAES *Gwynedd* Map 4 A2

Park Lodge
Cemaes Bay. ☎ (0407) 710103
Open: Easter-October
Size: 3 acres, 33 touring pitches. 2 hot showers,
4 WCs

| | ⌂ | ⊡ | Ⓐ | | | | | | | 🐕 |

In Cemaes, off A5025.

CHEPSTOW *Gwent* Map 2 A2

Chepstow Racecourse Caravan Club Site
St Arvans, NP6 6EH. ☎ (02912) 3710
Open: April-September
Size: 4 acres, 70 touring pitches. 6 hot showers,
20 WCs

| | ⌂ | ⊡ | Ⓐ | 🔲 | | | | | | 🐕 |

Entrance 1½ miles N of Chepstow on A466.

Howick Farm
Howick. ☎ (02912) 2590
Open: All year
Size: 2 acres, 40 touring pitches. 2 hot showers,
2 WCs

| | ⌂ | ⊡ | Ⓐ | | | | | | | 🐕 |

½ mile N of Chepstow (B4235), at A466 roundabout
take minor road signposted Itton. Site 2 miles.

The Severn Bridge Caravan Park
Beachley. ☎ (029 12) 2591
Open: All year
Size: 1 (4) acres, touring pitches. 2 hot showers,
9 WCs. Static caravans

| | ⌂ | ⊡ | Ⓐ | 🔲 | 🏪 | | | | | 🐕 |

2 miles SE of Chepstow, off B4228.

CHURCH STOKE *Powys* Map 4 B3

Bacheldre Watermill
SY15 6TE. ☎ (0588) 620489
Open: Easter-October
Size: 2 acres, 16 touring pitches. 2 hot showers,
8 WCs

| | ⌂ | ⊡ | Ⓐ | | 🏪 | | | | | 🐕 |

2½ miles W of Church Stoke (A489), turn S
signposted Bacheldre Watermill.

MELLINGTON HALL CARAVAN PARK RAC L
SY15 6HX. ☎ (05885) 456
Open: 1 March-31 October
Size: 2 (20) acres, 10 touring pitches, all level,
6 with elec, 3 with hardstanding, 120 static
caravans, 15 chalets. 4 hot showers, 16 WCs,
1 CWP

| | ⌂ | ⊡ | | | 🏪 | ♥ | ✕ | | |

(1991) Car & caravan, Motor caravan £6.50; elec
50p; WS
*The site is set in parkland in grounds of hotel with
bar, bar meals and take away food. Situated
among trees and shrubs. Shop 2 miles. Swimming
pool 10 miles. No tents or motorcycles.*
At 1½ miles W of Church Stoke on A489, turn S on
B4385 for 200 yards. Site entrance through
archway.

CLYNNOG-FAWR *Gwynedd* Map 4 A3

Aberafon Gyrn Goch
LL54 5PN. ☎ (028686) 295
Open: All year
Size: 15 acres, 150 touring pitches. 4 hot showers,
14 WCs

| | ⌂ | ⊡ | Ⓐ | 🏪 | | | | | | 🐕 |

Site 1 mile S of Clynnog-Fawr on A499.

Cappas Lwyd
Trevor. ☎ (028686) 682
Open: Easter-September
Size: 1 acre, 3+ touring pitches. 1 WC, CWP

| | ⌂ | ⊡ | Ⓐ | | | | | | | 🐕 |

12 miles S from Caernarfon (A499), turn right for
Trevor. Site ¼ mile at first farm on right.

Lyn-y-Gele Farm & Caravan Park
Pontlyfni, LL54 5EL. ☎ (028 686) 283
Open: Easter-September
Size: 2-5 acres, touring pitches. 2 hot showers,
7 WCs. Static caravans

| | ⌂ | ⊡ | Ⓐ | 🔲 | | | | 🏠 | | 🐕 |

7½ miles S from Caernarfon (A499), in Pontlyfni
take first right by petrol station.

Parsal Farm
LL54 5PS. ☎ (028686) 222
Open: March-October
Size: 5 acres, 5 touring pitches. 4 hot showers
9 WCs

| | ⌂ | ⊡ | Ⓐ | | | | | | | 🐕 |

11½ miles S of Caernarfon, off A499.

COLWYN BAY *Clwyd* Map 4 B2

WESTWOOD CARAVAN PARK RAC L
Llysfaen, LL29 8SD. ☎ (0492) 517410
Open: 1 April or Easter-31 October
Size: 6 acres, 84 touring pitches, 15 with elec. 2 hot
showers, 7 WCs, 1 CWP

| | ⌂ | ⊡ | | 🔲 | | | | | | 🐕 |

Car & caravan, Motor caravan £4.11-£4.70; awn £1
*Quiet site with panoramic views of sea and
countryside. Calor gas only. Shop 100 yards.
Restaurant ½ mile. Swimming pool 1¼ miles. No
tents or motorcycles.*
From A55 leave at Llanddulas A547 and follow
signs for Old Colwyn and turn into Highlands
Road.

CONWY *Gwynedd* Map 4 A2

CONWY TOURING PARK RAC A
Bwlch Manor, LL32 8UX. ☎ (0492) 592856
Open: April-October
Size: 50 (80) acres, 300 touring pitches, all level,
200 with elec, 100 with hardstanding. 100 hot
showers, 72 WCs, 7 CWPs

| ♿ | ⌂ | ⊡ | Ⓐ | 🔲 | 🏪 | ♥ | ✕ | | | 🐕 |

(1991) Car & caravan, Motor caravan, Car & tent
£4.45- £8.15; elec £1, awn £1.25-£1.40
*Landscaped park with views over the Conwy
estuary. Children's playground, club with games
room and beer garden. Swimming pool 5 miles.*

Ⓐ Facilities for Disabled ⌂ Caravans accepted ⊡ Motor caravans Ⓐ Tents 🔲 Laundry room 🏪 Shop

7 nights minimum stay over Bank Holidays, 3 nights minimum stay over high season weekends. No all-male or all-female groups. On E side of B5106 1¼ miles S of Conwy.

Tyn Terfyn Caravan Park
Tal-y-Bont. ☎ (049 269) 525
Open: March-October
Size: 2 acres, 15 touring pitches. 2 hot showers, 3 WCs. 1 static caravan

5½ miles S of Conwy on B5106.

CORWEN *Clwyd*   *Map 4 B3*

Afon Ro
Glyndyfrdwy. ☎ (049 083) 649
Open: May-September
Size: ¾ acre, 8 touring pitches. 1 hot shower, 2 WCs

5 miles E of Corwen on A5.

Disgarth Isaf
Ty-nant, LL21 0PS. ☎ (049 081) 366
Open: April-October
Size: 4 acres, 8+ touring pitches. 1 WC

6 miles W from Corwen on A5, take first right turn after Disgarth Isaf farmhouse.

HENDWR CARAVAN PARK   RAC A
Llandrillo, LL21 0SN. ☎ (049084) 210
Open: 1 April-31 October
Size: 3 (10) acres, 40 touring pitches, all level, 20 with elec, 80 static caravans, 6 chalets. 8 hot showers, 10 WCs, 2 CWPs

(1991) Car & caravan, Motor caravan £5.50, Car & tent, M/cycle* & tent £5, plus £1 per person above 2, 75p per child; elec £1, awn £1; WS
Select site, established and run by the Hughes family for 25 years. Set in the Dee Valley, the site has a small trout stream passing through. Excellent venue for walking in the Berwyn Mountains. 4 chalets for hire. Restaurant 1 mile. Swimming pool 4 miles.
4 miles SW of Corwen on B4401, turn right at sign Hendwr Caravan Park.

LHAWR-BETTWS FARM   RAC L
Lhawr-Bettws, LL21 0HD. ☎ (049081) 224
Open: March-October
Size: 5 (10) acres, 35 touring pitches, 25 with elec, 20 level pitches, 3 with hardstanding, 72 static caravans. 4 hot showers, 14 WCs, 1 CWP

Car & caravan £6, Motor caravan, Car & tent £5, M/cycle* & tent £4, all plus £1 per person, child 50p; elec £1, awn £1, dogs free; WS
Very quiet and peaceful, enabling you to enjoy the countryside. Good walks, etc. Children's play room and climbing frame, fishing in the trout pond. 3 caravans for hire (own WCs). Restaurant ½ mile. Shop and swimming pool 4 miles.
At 2¼ miles W of Corwen on A5, turn left on to A494 for 1¼ miles, where turn right; site ¼ mile.

Saracens Head Hotel
Cerrig-y-Drudion, LL21 9SY.
☎ (049 082) 684
Open: All year
Size: 21 touring pitches. 5 WCs

10 miles N of Corwen on A5.

COWBRIDGE *South Glamorgan*   *Map 1 B2*

LLANDOW TOURING CARAVAN PARK   RAC A
Llandow, CF6 9ZG. ☎ (0446) 794527/792462
Open: March-October
Size: 5 acres, 100 touring pitches, all level, 60 with elec. 8 hot showers, 12 WCs, 1 CWP

Car & caravan, Motor caravan £3.50-£4.50; extra adult £1, child 60p; Car £1, M/cycle 60p; elec £1.30, awn £1, dogs 50p
Situated in the heart of the rural Vale of Glamorgan, 3 miles from the Heritage Coast and with easy access to Cardiff, Swansea and seaside resorts. Public house 2 miles (bar meals). Swimming pool 3 miles (in Llantwit Major). Calor gas only. Pets on lead.
M4 junction 33, A4232, A48 to Pentre Meyrick, left B4268 - B4270 towards Llantwit Major. Right turn off B4270 marked Marcross, first right turn off this road (approximately 2 miles), site entrance on right.

CRICCIETH *Gwynedd*   *Map 4 A3*

Camping & Caravanning Club Site
Tyddyn Sianel, Llanystumdwy, LL52 0LS.
☎ (0766) 522855
Open: 30 March-26 October
Size: 4 acres, 70 touring pitches. 6 hot showers, 9 WCs

Charges on application.
cc Access, Visa/B'card
Site on Lleyn Peninsula with views of sea and mountains.
Take the A497 from Criccieth, take the second turning to Llanystumdwy, the site is on the right.

Eisteddfa
Pentrefelin. ☎ (076 671) 2104
Open: Easter-October
Size: 15 acres, 150 touring pitches. 6 hot showers, 2b WCs

1½ miles NE of Criccieth on A497.

Gell Farm
☎ (0766) 2781
Open: March-October
Size: 5 acres, 50 touring pitches. 4 hot showers, 12 WCs. Static caravans

1 mile N of Criccieth on B4411.

LLWYN BUGEILYDD FARM   RAC L
LL52 0PN. ☎ (0766) 522235
Open: Easter-31 October
Size: 6 acres, 45 touring pitches, all level, 12 with

---

elec. 2 hot showers, 6 WCs, 1 CWP

(1991) Car & caravan, Motor caravan, Car & tent, M/cycle & tent from £4; elec £1.20, awn 50p, dogs free
This is small, select, touring caravan site and camping ground, situated in an elevated position above Criccieth with fine views of Cardigan Bay and Snowdonia. Very quiet and peaceful. Shop and restaurant 1 mile. Swimming pool 9 miles.
Within easy walking distance of town, first site on B4411, 1 mile N of Criccieth, off A497 Porthmadog-Pwllheli road. Turn S off A487 Porthmadog-Caernarfon road on to B4411, site on left in 3½ miles.

Maes Meillion
Llwyn Mafon Isaf, LL52 0RE.
☎ (076 675) 205
Open: April-October
Size: 2½ acres, 20+ touring pitches. 1 hot shower, 3 WCs

3½ miles N of Criccieth, off A487.

Muriau Bach
Rhoslan, LL52 0PN. ☎ (076675) 642
Open: March-October
Size: 7 acres, 20+ touring pitches. 2 hot showers, 6 WCs. Static caravans

NW of Porthmadog (A487), turn S on to B4411. Site fourth left turning over cattle grid.

Mynydd-du
LL52 0PS. ☎ (076 671) 2533
Open: April-October
Size: 6 acres, 10+ touring pitches. 2 hot showers, 9 WCs

3 miles W of Porthmadog on A497.

OCEAN HEIGHTS CARAVAN PARK   RAC L
Pen-y-Bryn. ☎ (0766) 810519
Open: 1 March-31 October
Size: 2 (6) acres, 16 touring pitches, all level, all with elec, all with hardstanding, 76 static caravans. 4 hot showers, 8 WCs, 1 CWP

(1991) Car & caravan, Motor caravan, Car & tent, M/cycle* & tent £3-£6; elec £1.50, awn £1.25, dogs 40p; WS
Spacious, well-kept site, with children's play area and nearby golf, fishing and riding. 8 caravans for hire (own WCs). Calor gas only. Shop ¼ mile. Restaurant 1 mile. Swimming pool 3 miles.
4 miles W of Criccieth on the A497, turn N as signed Chwilog for ½ mile to site on left.

Trefan Farm
☎ (0766) 2782
Open: April-October
Size: 2 acres, 10 touring pitches. 5 WCs

Follow B4411 from Criccieth for 1½ miles, turn left before river bridge. Site ½ mile.

Tyddyn Cethin Farm
☎ (0766) 2149
Open: March-October
Size: 3 (10) acres, 20+ touring pitches. 4 hot showers, 13 WCs. Static caravans

1½ miles N of Criccieth, off B4411.

Tyddyn Heilyn
Chwilog, LL53 6SW. ☎ (0766) 88441
Open: May-September
Size: 2 acres, 25 touring pitches. 2 hot showers, 4 WCs. Static caravans

In Chwilog, turn into road opposite Butchery. Site 1½ miles.

CRICKHOWELL *Powys*   *Map 2 A2*

The Bell Hotel
Glangrwyney. ☎ (0873) 810247
Open: March-October
Size: 1 acre, 12 touring pitches. 3 WCs

1½ miles E of Crickhowell on A40.

Cwmdu Caravan & Camping Site
Cwmdu. ☎ (0874) 730441
Open: March-October
Size: 4½ acres, 12 touring pitches. 4 hot showers, 10 WCs

At 1¾ miles NW of Crickhowell on A40, turn N on to A479 (A470) for 3 miles to Farmers Arms Cwmdu, where turn E and then S for ¼ mile.

RIVERSIDE CARAVAN & CAMPING PARK   RAC L
New Road, NP8 1AY.
☎ (0873) 810397
Open: 1 March-31 October
Size: 3 (3½) acres, 25 touring pitches, all level, all with elec, 20 static caravans. 8 hot showers, 7 cold showers, 15 WCs, 1 CWP

Car & caravan from £4.50, Motor caravan from £4, Car & tent, M/cycle & tent from £2; child £1 (over 5 years); elec £1.50, awn £1-£2
Grassy, level site in National Park. Town 5 minutes' walk. Mountain and canal walks. Pony trekking, fishing, golf. 2 caravans for hire. Shop 400 yards. Restaurant 200 yards. Swimming pool 6 miles. No hang gliders.
On NW bank of River Esk on the A4077 at Crickhowell.

CRYMMYCH *Dyfed*   *Map 1 B1*

Trefach Manor
Clynderwen, SA66 7RU.
☎ (0994) 419225
Open: March-October
Size: 16 acres, 70 touring pitches. 4 hot showers, 4b WCs. Static caravans

8 miles N from Narberth (A478), fork left at Cross Inn. Site 1¾ miles.

🅰 Facilities for Disabled 🔲 Caravans accepted Motor caravans 🅰 Tents 🅰 Laundry room 🅰 Shop

DENBIGH *Clwyd* — Map 4 B2

STATION HOUSE CARAVAN PARK RAC L
Bodfari, LL16 4DA. ☎ (074575) 372
Open: 1 April-31 October
Size: 2 acres, 26 touring pitches, 18 with elec,
20 level pitches. 2 hot showers, 4 WCs, 1 CWP

▢|⊞|☮|Ⓐ▢▢▢▢▢|🐕

(1991) Car & caravan, Motor caravan £4-£4.50, Car
& tent, M/cycle & tent £2-£4, plus 50p per person
above 2; extra Car or M/cycle 50p; elec £1, awn £1,
dogs free; WS
*Quiet, friendly caravan park in a declared Area of
Outstanding Natural Beauty. Very convenient
centre for touring N Wales coast, Snowdonia and
Chester. Shop and restaurant 300 yards.
Swimming pool 4 miles. Calor gas only.
Enter Bodfari on the A541, turn left on to
B5429 signed Tremerichion, site immediately on
left.*

Vale of Clwyd Caravan Site
☎ (0745) 813211
Open: Easter-October
Size: 6 acres, 40 touring pitches. 4 hot showers,
9 WCs

▢|⊞|☮|Ⓐ|⊟▢▢▢▢|🐕

Site just N of Denbigh, to right of A543.

DEVIL'S BRIDGE *Dyfed* — Map 4 A3

Bronceiro
Pontrhydfendigaid, Ystrad Meurig, SY25 6EP.
☎ (09745) 236
Open: All year
Size: 1 acre, 15 touring pitches. 1 hot shower,
2 WCs

▢|⊞|☮|Ⓐ▢|🔒▢▢▢|🐕

Site off B4343 on minor road to Strata Florida
Abbey.

Erw Barfe Farm
☎ (097085) 665
Open: March-October
Size: 5 acres, 30 touring pitches. 8 hot showers,
5 WCs. 50 static caravans

▢|⊞|☮|Ⓐ|⊟▢▢▢▢|🐕

1 mile NE of Devil's Bridge on A4120.

Pantmawr
Pisgah, Capel Seion. ☎ (097084) 449
Open: Easter-October
Size: 3 acres, 25 touring pitches. 2 WCs

▢|⊞|☮|Ⓐ▢▢▢▢▢|🐕

3½ miles W of Devil's Bridge on A4120.

Tyllwyd
Cwmystwyth. ☎ (097422) 216
Open: All year
Size: 4 acres, 3+ touring pitches. 1 hot shower,
3 WCs

▢|⊞|☮|Ⓐ|⊟▢▢▢|🏊|🐕

2½ miles E of Cwmystwyth on B4574.

Woodlands Caravan Park
SY23 3JW. ☎ (097085) 233
Open: Easter-October

Size: 6 acres, 50 touring pitches. 4 hot showers,
9 WCs

▢|⊞|☮|Ⓐ|⊟|🔒|🍴▢▢|🐕

In Devil's Bridge on A4120.

DINAS-MAWDDWY *Gwynedd* — Map 4 B3

Celyn-Brithion
☎ (06504) 344
Open: April-1 November
Size: 3 acres, 8 touring pitches. 3 WCs. 14 static
caravans

▢|☮|☮|Ⓐ▢▢▢▢▢|🐕

½ mile S of Dinas-Mawddwy on A470.

Tyn-y-Pwll
☎ (065 04) 326
Open: All year
Size: 4 acres, 10+ touring pitches. 5 hot showers,
12 WCs. Static caravans

▢|⊞|☮|Ⓐ|⊟▢▢▢▢|🐕

At Dinas-Mawddwy on A470, turn E on to minor
road to Bwlch-y-Groes pass. Site at first farm on
left after bridge.

DOLGELLAU *Gwynedd* — Map 4 A3

Bryn-y-Gwin Farm
Cader Road. ☎ (0341) 422733
Open: All year
Size: 3 acres, 10+ touring pitches. 1 WC

▢|⊞|☮|Ⓐ▢▢▢▢▢|🐕

¼ mile W of Dolgellau centre leading to
A493 (Tywyn Road), turn S on minor road opposite
Cader Idris garage. Site ½ mile along farm lane.

Cwmrhwyddfor Farm
Talyllyn, Tywyn. ☎ (0654) 761286/761380
Open: Tents all year/Caravans April-October
Size: 6 acres, 60 touring pitches. 4 hot showers,
9 WCs

▢|⊞|☮|Ⓐ▢▢▢▢▢|🐕

E of Dolgellau (A470), fork right on A487 at Cross
Foxes Hotel. Site 3½ miles.

Dolgamedd
Bontnewydd, LL40 2DG. ☎ (034141) 221
Open: Easter-October
Size: 7 acres, 15 touring pitches plus 30 for tents.
2 hot showers, 10 WCs. 20 static caravans

▢|⊞|☮|Ⓐ▢▢▢▢▢|🐕

3 miles NE of Dolgellau on A494, turn S on B4416.
Site first left.

Dolserau Uchaf
LL40 2DE. ☎ (0341) 422639
Open: April-September
Size: 1¼ acres, 25 touring pitches. 2 hot showers, 4
WCs

▢|☮|☮|Ⓐ|⊟▢▢▢▢|🐕

2½ miles E of Dolgellau on A494.

Llwyn-yr-Helm
Brithdir. ☎ (034141) 254
Open: Easter-October
Size: 2 acres, 20 touring pitches. 2 hot showers,

🍴 Snacks/take away ✖ Restaurant 🏊 Swimming pool 🏠 Shelter for campers 🐕 Dogs accepted   **211**

4 WCs

2 miles E of Dolgellau (A470), turn on to
B4416 signposted Brithdir. Fork right by phone box
in village. Site ½ mile.

Tanyfron
LL40 2AA. ☎ (0341) 422638
Open: All year
Size: 2 acres, 13 touring pitches. 3 hot showers,
5 WCs. 12 static caravans

In Dolgellau on A470, site E of bridge by 30mph
sign.

Vanner Abbey Farm Site
☎ (0341) 422854
Open: Easter-October
Size: 10 acres, 25 touring pitches. 2 hot showers,
10 WCs. 60 static caravans

Take A470 W from Dolgellau for 1½ miles. Turn
right into minor road before bridge.

FAIRBOURNE *Gwynedd*   Map 4 A3

Borthwen Farm
Llwyngwril. ☎ (0341) 250322
Open: April-October
Size: 8 acres, 3+ touring pitches. 4 hot showers,
6 WCs. 80 static caravans

¼ mile W of A493 in Llwyngwril, turn towards
railway station. Site access over level crossing.

Garthyfog
Arthog, LL39 1AX. ☎ (0341) 250338
Open: All year
Size: 5 acres, 20 touring pitches. 1 hot shower,
2 WCs. 2 static caravans

6½ miles W from Dolgellau on A493, turn left up
narrow road near derestriction sign.

Hendre Hall
Llwyngwril. ☎ (0341) 250999
Open: April-October
Size: 6 acres, 10+ touring pitches. 2 hot showers,
2b WCs

In Llwyngwril, opposite petrol station (A493).

FISHGUARD *Dyfed*   Map 1 A1

FISHGUARD BAY CARAVAN PARK   RAC L
Penrhyn, Dinas Cross, SA42 0YD.
☎ (03486) 415
Open: 1 March-10 January
Size: 2 (6) acres, 20 touring pitches, all level, all
with elec, 50 static caravans 4 hot showers, 9 WCs,
1 CWP

Charges on application.
cc Access, Visa/B'card
*Magnificent sea-views are a feature of this well-
kept headland site. It offers a children's play area*

and TV room. 15 caravans for hire (own WCs).
Restaurant and swimming pool 3 miles.
At 2 miles E of Fishguard on A487, turn N for
1 mile to site.

Gwann Vale Caravan Park
Ddolwen Farm. ☎ (0348) 873154
Open: All year
Size: 4½ acres, 5 touring pitches plus 40 for tents. 2
hot showers, 4 WCs

From Fishguard Square (A40), turn E on B4313.
Site 1½ miles.

GARTH *Powys*   Map 1 B1

Irfon River Caravan Park
Upper Chapel Road. ☎ (059 12) 310
Open: Easter-October
Size: 3 (7) acres, 75 touring pitches. 7 hot showers,
13 WCs. Static caravans

At Garth on A483, turn SE on B4519. Site
500 yards.

Riverside Caravan Park
Llangammarch Wells. ☎ (05912) 629
Open: April-October
Size: 3 acres, 40 touring pitches. 2 hot showers,
6 WCs

6 miles W from Builth Wells (A483), in Garth take
second left to Llangammarch Wells. Site opposite
council depot.

HARLECH *Gwynedd*   Map 4 A3

Cae Cethin
Llanfair. ☎ (0766) 780247
Open: Easter-November
Size: 4 acres, 8 touring pitches plus 30 for tents.
2 hot showers, 5 WCs

1 mile S of Harlech, off A496.

Gwyndy Stores
Ynys. ☎ (0766) 780449
Open: All year
Size: 1½ acres, 23 touring pitches. 1 hot shower,
3 WCs

3 miles N of Harlech, off A496.

Hendy
Llanbedr. ☎ (034123) 263
Open: March-October
Size: 2½ acres, 20 touring pitches. 3 WCs

½ mile S of Llanbedr (A496), 50 yards E of road.

Min-y-Don
Beach Road. ☎ (0766) 780286
Open: Easter-October
Size: 3 acres, 20+ touring pitches. 12 hot showers,
40 WCs

ⓐ Facilities for Disabled ⊞ Caravans accepted ⊞ Motor caravans ⒜ Tents ⊡ Laundry room ⒣ Shop

Turn W off A496 into Beach Road.

Shell Island
Llanbedr. ☎ (034123) 217
Open: Easter-October
Size: 462 acres, 1400+ touring pitches. 19 hot showers, 50 WCs. Chalets

[icons: tent, caravan, etc.]

2½ miles W of Llanbedr.

Brandy Brook Caravan Site
Haycastle, SA62 5PT. ☎ (0348) 840272
Open: Easter-September
Size: 8 acres, 65 touring pitches. 2 hot showers, 6 WCs. 20 static caravans

[icons]

7 miles NW from Haverfordwest, at Roch (A487), turn right on to minor road for 1½ miles. Fork left and continue for ½ mile. Site signed 1¼ miles.

BROAD HAVEN CARAVAN PARK　　RAC A
Broad Haven, SA62 3JD. ☎ (0437) 81277
Open: 18 May-10 September
Size: 4+ (17+) acres, 40 touring pitches, 25 static caravans. 8 hot showers, 16 WCs, 1 CWP

[icons]

(1991) Motor caravan, Car & caravan, M/cycle & caravan £3-£4, plus £1.25-£1.50 per adult, 60p-£1 child; elec £2, awn 90p, dogs free-£1.50 cc Access, Visa/B'card
This spacious site is 300 yards from the beach and has 25 caravans for hire (own WCs). Restaurant ½ mile. Swimming pool 6 miles.
Take B4341 from Haverfordwest for 6 miles, Broad Haven Holiday Park is on right hand side at bottom of hill.

Cream Pots Touring Caravan & Camping Park
Near Broad Haven, SA62 3TU.
☎ (0437) 781776
Open: March-October
Size: 5 acres, 70 touring pitches. 4 hot showers, 8 WCs. Static caravans

[icons]

Take B4341 from Haverfordwest for 4½ miles. Site signed from B4341.

HASGUARD CROSS CARAVAN PARK　RAC A
Hasguard, Little Haven, SA62 3SL.
☎ (0437) 781443
Open: All year
Size: 2 (3¼) acres, 25 touring pitches, all level, 24 with elec, 35 static caravans. 6 hot showers, 10 WCs, 1 CWP

[icons]

(1991) Car & caravan, Motor caravan £4-£6; elec £1; WS
Set in 3¼ acres of level ground tastefully screened with trees, with views overlooking the Milford Haven and St Brides Bay. Licensed club serving good selection of bar food. 7 caravans for hire (own WCs). Calor gas only. Swimming pool 5 miles.
At 7 miles SW of Haverfordwest on Dale Road, B4327, turn right at Hasguard Cross for 70 yards.

Site first entrance on right, at shop.

Howelston Farm
Little Haven. ☎ (0437) 781253
Open: April-September
Size: 5 acres, 6+ touring pitches. 4 hot showers, 10 WCs

[icons]

8 miles SW of Haverfordwest, at Hasguard Cross (B4327), turn N signposted Little Haven. Site 1¼ miles.

Pelcomb Cross Farm
Pelcomb Cross, SA62 6AB. ☎ (0437) 710431
Open: March-January
Size: 2 acres, 30 touring pitches. 4 hot showers, 7 WCs

[icons]

3 miles NW of Haverfordwest (A487), site just beyond Pelcomb Cross Inn.

REDLANDS TOURING CARAVAN PARK　RAC A
Little Haven, SA62 3UU. ☎ (0437) 781301
Open: Easter-Mid September
Size: 5 acres, 60 touring pitches, all level, 52 with elec. 4 hot showers, 12 WCs, 1 CWP

[icons]

(1991) Car & caravan, Motor caravan £5-£6; elec £1
A small site exclusively for touring caravans set in the Pembrokeshire National Park, within easy reach of superb sandy beaches and coastal path. Shop 200 yards. Restaurant 2 miles. Swimming pool 5 miles. No gas available.
Site on N side of the B4327, 6½ miles SW of Haverfordwest.

Rising Sun Inn
Pelcomb Bridge, SA62 2EA. ☎ (0437) 5171
Open: March-October
Size: 2½ acres, 12+ touring pitches. 2 hot showers, 4 WCs

[icons]

2 miles NW of Haverfordwest on A487.

SOUTH COCKETT CARAVAN & CAMPING PARK　RAC L
Broadway, Little Haven, SA62 3TW.
☎ (0437) 781296/781760
Open: Easter-October
Size: 6 acres, 42 touring pitches, all level, 28 with elec, 1 static caravan. 2 hot showers, 6 WCs, 1 CWP

[icons]

(1991) Car & caravan, Car & tent, M/cycle & tent £2.50- £5.25, Motor caravan £2-£4.75; elec £1, awn 75p
South Cockett is a small, family-run site, in pleasant rural surroundings. The site is level and free draining with good access. It is centrally positioned for all the beautiful scenic areas of Pembrokeshire. 1 caravan for hire (own WC). Shop and restaurant 1 mile. Swimming pool 8 miles.
From Haverfordwest, travel W on the B4341 as signposted Broad Haven for 4¾ miles, turn left signposted Milford Haven to site in 300 yards.

Camping & Caravanning Club Site
Dwr Cwmdig, Berea St David's, SA62 6DW.
☎ (03483) 376

[●] Snacks/take away　[X] Restaurant　[◺] Swimming pool　[🏠] Shelter for campers　[🐕] Dogs accepted　　213

Open: 30 March-28 September
Size: 4 acres, 40 touring pitches. 4 hot showers,
7 WCs

[⊞][⊞][▲][⊟][⊠][ ][ ][ ][🐕]

Charges on application.
cc Access, Visa/B'card
*Level, grass site 1 mile from the sea. Camping Gaz
only. Shop 1 mile.*
From the A487 take the road signposted Abereiddy
and with a Club sign. At the fork in the road, turn
right towards Abereiddy, left at the crossroads, the
site is on the left.

HAY-ON-WYE *Powys*   *Map 2 A2*

Radnors End
HR5 5RS. ☎ (0497) 820780
Open: March-October
Size: 1 acre, 15 touring pitches. 2 hot showers,
3 WCs

[ ][ ][ ][▲][ ][ ][ ][ ][ ][🐕]

In Hay-on-Wye (B4350), turn W over bridge on
B4351. After 300 yards, turn right into Boatside
Lane. Site on left.

HOLYHEAD *Gwynedd*   *Map 4 A2*

Bagnol Caravan Park
Trearddur Bay. ☎ (0407) 860223
Open: Easter-October
Size: 11 acres, 10+ touring pitches. 16 hot showers,
3b WCs

[ ][⊞][⊞][▲][⊟][ ][ ][ ][🐕]

From A5 in Valley, turn SW on B4545 for Trearddur
Bay. After Beach Hotel, turn left into Ravenspoint
Road.

Silver Bay Caravan Park
Rhoscolyn. ☎ (0407) 860374
Open: Easter-October
Size: 20 acres, 414 touring pitches. 16 hot showers,
24 WCs. Static caravans

[ ][⊞][⊞][▲][⊟][⊠][♥][✕][◢][⊞][ ]

4 miles S of Holyhead (A5), turn SW on B4545.
Turn S at Four Mile Bridge for 1½ miles, then
follow signs.

Tyn-Rhos
Trearddur Bay. ☎ (0407) 860369
Open: March-October
Size: 20 acres, 50+ touring pitches. 9 WCs

[ ][⊞][⊞][▲][⊟][⊠][♥][ ][ ][🐕]

From A5 in Valley, turn SW on B4545 for
Trearddur. Turn left at Ravenspoint entrance.

HOLYWELL *Clwyd*   *Map 4 B2*

Barlow Caravan Park
Caerwys, CH7 5DY.
☎ (0352) 720273
Open: March-October
Size: 85 acres, 50+ touring pitches. 10 hot showers,
4b WCs. 305 static caravans

[♿][⊞][⊞][▲][⊟][⊠][ ][ ][ ][🐕]

4 miles W of Holyhead on A55, turn S signposted
Caerwys. Site signed in 1½ miles.

KILGETTY *Dyfed*   *Map 1 A1*

THE CROFT CARAVAN PARK   ♿ A
Reynalton.
☎ (0834) 860315
Open: 1 April-30 September
Size: 5 (12) acres, 85 touring pitches, all level,
65 with elec, 60 static caravans, 1 chalet. 14 hot
showers, 20 WCs, 1 CWP

[ ][⊞][⊞][▲][⊟][⊠][ ][ ][ ][🐕]

Charges on application.
*Evening social activities are part of this level, well-
maintained site's amenities. There's a children's
play area. Chalet for hire (own WC). Restaurant
2 miles.*
At ½ mile W of Kilgetty on A477, turn N on
A478 for 2¾ miles to beginning of Templeton,
where turn sharp left and take second left (after
1¼ miles) for ¾ mile to site.

Hoyles
Redberth. ☎ (064 67) 789
Open: All year
Size: 3 acres, 3+ touring pitches. 1 WC

[ ][⊞][⊞][▲][ ][ ][ ][ ][ ][🐕]

¼ mile W of Redberth on A477.

Little Kings Park
Amroth, Narberth, SA67 8PG. ☎ (083483) 330
Open: Easter-October
Size: 12 acres, 35 touring pitches plus 40 for tents.
4 hot showers, 9 WCs. 19 static caravans

[ ][⊞][⊞][▲][⊟][⊠][ ][ ][◢][🐕]

On A477 St Clears-Pembroke, turn S signposted
Amroth/Ludchurch. After ½ mile turn right at farm.
Site up hill.

**MASTERLAND FARM TOURING
CARAVAN PARK**   ♿ L
Broadmoor, SA68 0RH. ☎ (0834) 813298
Open: Easter-31 October
Size: 8 acres, 13 touring pitches, all level, all with
elec, all with hardstanding, 1 static caravan,
1 chalet. 3 hot showers, 3 cold showers, 8 WCs,
1 CWP

[ ][⊞][⊞][▲][⊟][ ][ ][ ][⊞][🐕]

Car & caravan £3-£7, Motor caravan, Car & tent,
M/cycle & tent £3-£6; extra person 50p; extra car
£1; elec £1.25, awn £1, 1 dog free, extra dog £1
*Quiet, family-run site, games room, baby
bathroom, washing-up and food preparation
facilities, TV room, play area. Shop 200 yards.
Restaurant 300 yards. Swimming pool 3 miles.
1 caravan and 1 chalet for hire (own WCs).*
From the junction of the A477 and A478 N of
Tenby, travel W on the A477 for 1½ miles to
Broadmoor, where turn right on to the B4586 for
300 yards to site on right.

Mill House
Stepaside, Narberth, SA67 8LN.
☎ (0834) 812069
Open: Easter-September
Size: 2 acres, 5+ touring pitches. 2 hot showers,
6 WCs

[ ][⊞][⊞][ ][ ][ ][ ][ ][ ][🐕]

Site 1 mile E of Kilgetty.

[♿] Facilities for Disabled   [⊞] Caravans accepted   [⊞] Motor caravans   [▲] Tents   [⊟] Laundry room   [⊠] Shop

Mountain Park Farm
Lawrenny. ☎ (0834) 620
Open: All year
Size: 4 acres, 3+ touring pitches. 2 WCs

⬜ 🏕️🚐⛺ ⬜⬜⬜⬜⬜ 🐕

Site in Pembroke National Park.

Ryelands Caravan Park
Ryelands Lane. ☎ (0834) 812369
Open: March-October
Size: 6 acres, 35 touring pitches. 6 hot showers,
9 WCs

⬜ 🏕️🚐⛺ ⬜⬜⬜⬜⬜ 🐕

From A477, turn N on to A478. Right at next
roundabout, pass railway bridge after ½ mile, then
turn left into Ryelands Lane. Site ¾ mile.

Springfield
Marros, Pendine, SA33 4PW. ☎ (09945) 428
Open: April-October
Size: 1 acre, 25+ touring pitches. 1 WC

⬜ 🏕️🚐⛺ ⬜⬜⬜⬜⬜ 🐕

At Red Roses (A477), turn S on B4314. After
2½ miles, turn right at crossroads. Site 1 mile W of
Marros.

Stone Pitt
Begelly, SA68 0XE. ☎ (0834) 811086
Open: March-October
Size: 2 acres, 22 touring pitches. 3 hot showers,
5 WCs. Self-contained cottages

⬜ 🚐⛺⛺🚿 ⬜⬜⬜⬜ 🐕

Site ½ mile N of A477/A478 junction.

The Village Touring & Caravan Park
Summerhill, Amroth, SA67 8NS.
☎ (0834) 811051
Open: April-October
Size: 2½ acres, 10 touring pitches. 4 hot showers, 5
WCs. 22 static caravans

⬜ 🏕️🚐⛺⛺🚿 ⬜⬜⬜⬜

From A477, turn S signposted Amroth/Wisemans
Bridge. Site 1 mile.

WOODLAND VALE CARAVAN PARK   RAC L
Ludchurch, SA67 8JE. ☎ (083483) 319
Open: 1 March-31 October
Size: 1 (9) acres, 25 touring pitches, all level,
18 with elec, 80 static caravans. 4 hot showers,
7 WCs, 1 CWP

⬜ 🏕️🚐⛺ ⬜🚿🛋️💽 ⬜🏠🐕

Charges on application. WS
*Well-appointed site with licensed clubhouse and
children's play area. Fishing available nearby.*
Static caravans for hire.
At Red Roses on the A477, turn NW onto the
B4314. In Tavernspite, turn left then keep left along
unclassified road for 2¾ miles. Turn left at
crossroads. Site on right in ¼ mile.

LAMPETER *Dyfed*   **Map 1 B1**

Lleinau
Cwmann. ☎ (0570) 422753
Open: April-September
Size: 1½ acres, 20 touring pitches. 1 WC

On A482, 1¼ miles SE of junction with A475.

⬜ 🏕️🚐⛺ ⬜⬜⬜⬜⬜ 🐕

Maesbach Farm
Farmers Village, Pumpsaint
☎ (05585) 413
Open: April-October
Size: 4½ acres, 15 touring pitches. 2 hot showers, 5
WCs. 6 static caravans

♿ 🏕️🚐⛺🚿🛋️💽 ⬜⬜⬜ 🐕

1¾ miles NW of Pumpsaint (A482), turn N for
1½ miles to Farmers. Turn right opposite Drovers
Arms. Site ¾ mile.

Moorlands Caravan Park
Llangybi, SA48 8NN. ☎ (057045) 543
Open: March-October
Size: 5 acres, 15+ touring pitches. 4 hot showers,
8 WCs. Static caravans

⬜ 🏕️🚐⛺🚿🛋️💽☕✖️⬜ 🐕

4 miles NE of Lampeter (A485), turn NW at
Llangybi. Site 2 miles.

Red Lion Caravan Park
Pencarreg, Llanybyther, SA40 9QG.
☎ (0570) 480018
Open: March-October
Size: 2½ acres, 30+ touring pitches. 4 hot showers,
6 WCs

⬜ 🚐⛺🚿🛋️💽📺✖️ ⬜⬜ 🐕

1 mile NE of Llanybyther on A485.

LAUGHARNE *Dyfed*   **Map 1 B1**

ANTS HILL CARAVAN & CAMPING PARK   RAC A
SA33 4QN. ☎ (099421) 293
Open: Easter-October
Size: 8½ (9) acres, 60 touring pitches, 40 with elec,
40 level pitches, 60 static caravans. 8 hot showers,
22 WCs, 1 CWP

⬜ 🏕️🚐⛺🚿🛋️💽☕⬜ ⬜🐕

Charges on application.
*A well-appointed site, with children's play area, a
games room, and a large clubhouse.*
From the junction of A40, A477 and A4066, at St
Clears, travel S on A4066 for 3¼ miles and turn E
as signed.

Laugharne Holiday Park
☎ (099 421) 332
Open: April-October
Size: 12 acres, 150 touring pitches. 8 hot showers,
11 WCs

⬜ 🚐⛺🚿🛋️💽📺⬜ ⬜🏠🐕

In Laugharne on A4066, turn E at Mariner's Arms.
Site ¼ mile.

LLANBEDROG *Gwynedd*   **Map 4 A3**

Bodwrog
☎ (0758) 740341
Open: Easter-October
Size: 2 acres, 30 touring pitches. 1 hot shower,
3 WCs

⬜⬜ 🚐⛺ ⬜⬜⬜⬜⬜ 🐕

In Llanbedrog (A499), turn W on B4413 for 1 mile.

💽 Snacks/take away ✖️ Restaurant ⬜ Swimming pool 🏠 Shelter for campers 🐕 Dogs accepted

Site on left.

Bron-Rug
Mynytho, LL53 7PS. ☎ (0758) 740713
Open: Easter-September
Size: ¼ acre, 3 touring pitches. 1 WC

| | ⊕ | ⊞ | | | | | | | 🐴 |

In Llanbedrog (A499), turn W on B4413 for
1½ miles. Right at village school, then after 1 mile
turn left at t-junction. Site ½ mile.

Brynhunog Farm
Rhoshirwaen. ☎ (075887) 245
Open: May-September
Size: 3 acres, 5 touring pitches. 1 WC

| | ⊕ | ⊞ | Ⓐ | | | | | | 🐴 |

In Llanbedrog (A499), turn W on B4413 for 9 miles.
Fork right on minor road signposted Whistling
Sands. Site ¼ mile.

CRUGAN CARAVAN PARK   RẴC L
☎ (075881) 2043
Open: 1 March-31 October
Size: 9 acres, 20 touring pitches, all level, all with
elec, 90 static caravans. 6 hot showers, 14 WCs,
1 CWP

| | ⊕ | ⊞ | | 🅰 | | | | | |

Charges on application.
cc Access, Visa/B'card
*A well-kept site near the beach. 5 caravans for hire
(own WCs). No gas available. Families only. Shop
and restaurant ½ mile. Swimming pool 1 mile.*
1 mile NE of Llanbedrog and 3 miles SW of
Pwllheli on A499.

Haulfryn Camping Site
Abersoch. ☎ (075881) 2045
Open: March-October
Size: 4 acres, 90 touring pitches. 12 hot showers,
14 WCs

| | | | Ⓐ | 🅰 | | | | | |

1½ miles S of Llanbedrog on A499.

REFAIL CARAVAN & CAMPING SITE   RẴC L
Refail, LL53 7NP. ☎ (0758) 740511
Open: 1 April-30 September
Size: 2½ acres, 33 touring pitches, 20 with elec,
26 level pitches. 6 hot showers, 6 cold showers,
6 WCs, 1 CWP

| ♿ | ⊕ | ⊞ | Ⓐ | 🅰 | | | | 🏠 | 🐴 |

Car & caravan, Motor caravan, Car & tent, M/cycle
& tent £6; elec £1.35; WS
*A rural site, yet in a village. Welsh Tourist Board
awarded 4 Ticks for 1992, and we hope to increase
our standard to 5 Ticks. Shop 150 yards.
Restaurants 150 yards and 300 yards away.
Swimming pool 3½ miles.*
Take the B4413 Aberdaron Road from Llanbedrog.
Site in 200 yards on right.

LLANDDULAS *Clwyd*   Map 4 B2

BRON-Y-WENDON CARAVAN PARK   RẴC L
Wern Road, LL22 8HG. ☎ (0492) 512903
Open: 21 March-31 October
Size: 8 acres, 75 touring pitches, 55 with elec,
50 level pitches, 4 with hardstanding. 7 hot

showers, 3 cold showers, 16 WCs, 1 CWP

| ♿ | ⊕ | ⊞ | | 🅰 | | | | | 🐴 |

(1991) Car & caravan, Motor caravan £4.50, both
plus £1 per adult, 50p per child; elec £1, awn £1
cc Access, Visa/B'card
*A new purpose-built park designed for the
caravanner of the 90s. Graded by Welsh Tourist
Board 5 Ticks. Shop and restaurant 300 yards.
Swimming pool 3 miles. Calor gas only.*
Leave the A55 at Llanddulas (A547) and follow
tourist information signs to the park.

LLANDISSILIO *Dyfed*   Map 1 A1

TREFACH COUNTRY CLUB &   RẴC L
CARAVAN PARK
Mynachlog-Ddu, SA66 7RU. ☎ (09947) 225
Open: 1 March-31 October
Size: 7 (16) acres, 20 touring pitches, mostly level,
6 with elec, 50 static caravans. 4 hot showers,
15 WCs, 1 CWP

| | ⊕ | ⊞ | Ⓐ | 🅰 | 🏊 | ☕ | ✖ | ⬚ | 🏠 | 🐴 |

Charges on application.
*A spacious country site with a children's play area,
children's farmyard, pony trekking, cycles for hire,
games room, licensed bar. 5 caravans for hire (own
WCs).*
From the junction of the A40 and A478 travel N on
the A478 through Llandissilio to the Cross Inn, bear
left for 1½ miles on right.

LLANDOVERY *Dyfed*   Map 1 B1

Camping & Caravanning Club Site
Rhandirmwyn, SA20 0NT. ☎ (05506) 257
Open: 30 March-26 October
Size: 11 acres, 90 touring pitches. 6 hot showers,
9 WCs

| ♿ | ⊕ | ⊞ | Ⓐ | | 🏊 | | | | 🐴 |

Charges on application.
cc Access, Visa/B'card
*Close to the Brecon Beacons National Park. Details
of tours and walks available from the warden.*
From the A483 take the road signposted
Rhandirmwyn, in Rhandirmwyn turn left opposite
the Post Office. The site is on the left after the
church.

Clynmawr Farm
Rhandirmwyn. ☎ (0550) 20462
Open: March-October
Size: 4 acres, 10 touring pitches. 1 hot shower,
1 WC

| | ⊕ | ⊞ | Ⓐ | | | | | | 🐴 |

From A40, W of Llandovery, take minor road N for
4 miles towards Rhandirmwyn.

ERWLON CARAVAN & CAMPING PARK   RẴC L
SA2 0RD. ☎ (0550) 20332
Open: All year
Size: 8 acres, 20 touring pitches, all level, 10 with
elec, 5 with hardstanding. 6 hot showers, 6 cold
showers, 12 WCs, 2 CWPs

| ♿ | ⊕ | ⊞ | Ⓐ | 🅰 | | | | 🏠 | 🐴 |

Car & caravan, Motor caravan, Car & tent, M/cycle*
& tent £4; elec £1, awn 50p; WS
Exceptionally well-situated in a delightful park and

---

setting. *Well-sheltered by beautiful trees. The whole area is delightful for rambling through, the park being set in the lovely Towy Valley. Shop and restaurant ½ mile. Swimming pool 6 miles. Calor gas only.*
Set beside the A40 between Brecon and Llandovery and 1 mile from Llandovery town.

Henblas
Llanwrda. ☎ (0550) 777263
Open: April-October
Size: ½ acre, 5 touring pitches. 2 WCs

[icons: caravan, motor caravan, tent, dog]

4 miles SW of Llandovery (A40), take A482 N for ½ mile. Site in village.

Disserth Farm Caravan Park
Disserth, Howey, LD1 6NL. ☎ (059789) 277
Open: March-October
Size: 3¼ acres, 25 touring pitches. 6 hot showers, 8 WCs. 21 static caravans

[icons: caravan, motor caravan, tent, shelter, snacks, restaurant, dog]

At Newbridge on Wye (A470), turn NE on B4358, then first right signposted Disserth/Howey. Site 1 mile.

Nantymynach
Nantmel. ☎ (0597) 810491
Open: Easter-October
Size: 1½ acres, 10 touring pitches. 4 WCs. 17 static caravans

[icons: caravan, motor caravan, tent, dog]

At Crossgates roundabout, 3½ miles NE of Llandrindod Wells, take A44 W for 5 miles. Turn left for site.

THE PARK MOTEL CARAVAN &
CAMPING PARK   RAC L
Rhayader Road, Crossgates, LD1 6RF.
☎ (059787) 201
Open: 1 March-31 October
Size: ½ (3) acres, 15 touring pitches, 5 with elec, 14 level pitches, 15 static caravans, 7 chalets. 2 hot showers, 4 WCs, 1 CWP

[icons: caravan, motor caravan, tent, shelter, snacks, restaurant, swimming pool, dog]

(1991) Car & caravan, Motor caravan, Car & tent, M/cycle* & tent £1.70; all plus £1.60 per adult, 80p per child; Tent 90p (cyclist/hiker); elec £1, awn £1; WS
A family-run site set in quiet, rural countryside on A44. Ideal for touring. Licensed restaurant, lounge bar, takeaway food, games room. Self-contained caravans and chalets for hire.
From Crossgates roundabout, N of Llandrindod Wells, travel W on A44 for ½ mile. Site on left.

Camping & Caravanning Club Site
Llwynhelyg, Cross Inn, Cardigan Bay, SA44 6LW.
☎ (0545) 560029
Open: 30 March-28 September
Size: 13½ acres, 90 touring pitches. 4 hot showers, 10 WCs

[icons: disabled, caravan, motor caravan, tent, swimming pool, shelter, dog]

Charges on application.
A well-run and beautifully situated site. Camping Gaz only. Shop 1 mile.
From the A486 towards New Quay, turn left after the public house (Penrhiw Galed Arms). The site is about 1 mile on the right.

Penrhyn Farm
LL65 4YG. ☎ (0407) 730496
Open: March-October
Size: 30 acres, 40 touring pitches. 8 hot showers, 16 WCs. 90 static caravans

[icons: disabled, caravan, motor caravan, tent, shelter, dog]

Take A5025 N from Valley, turning W for Llanfwrog. Fork left in village and keep left for site.

Sandy Beach Camping Site
☎ (0407) 730302
Open: March-October
Size: 12 acres, 40 touring pitches. 4 hot showers, 16 WCs. 83 static caravans

[icons: caravan, motor caravan, tent, shelter, dog]

Take A5025 N from Valley for 3 miles, then turn W to Sandy Beach. Site 3 miles.

PARC FARM CARAVAN SITE   RAC L
☎ (069 174) 204
Open: Easter-End October
Size: 1 (4) acres, 15 touring pitches, 8 level pitches, 65 static caravans, 1 chalet. 4 hot showers, 12 WCs, 1 CWP

[icons: caravan, motor caravan, shelter, dog]

Charges on application.
This tranquil, neatly kept site lies in delightful surroundings on the edge of a river. Children's play area. 3 caravans and 1 chalet for hire (own WCs). Shop 300 yards.
From A5 going NW, turn left for Knockin on B4396. Proceed on B4396 via Llangedinn to Penybontfawr. Turn right on to B4391. Site ¼ mile on right.

ABERMARLIAS CARAVAN PARK   RAC A
SA19 9NG. ☎ (0550) 777868
Open: March-December
Size: 8 (16) acres, 88 touring pitches, 60 level pitches, 30 with elec, 6 with hardstanding. 8 hot showers, 14 WCs, 1 CWP

[icons: caravan, motor caravan, tent, shelter, dog]

Charges on application.
Pleasant, level site next to woodland and with the River Morlais running through it. Walled garden of mansion house (demolished after a fire) is a feature of the site. Restaurant 1 mile.
Site on W side of the A40, ¾ mile N of the junction with the A4069 and 1½ miles SW of the junction with the A482.

CROSS INN & BLACK MOUNTAIN
CARAVAN PARK   RAC L
Llanddeusant, SA19 9YG. ☎ (0550) 4621
Open: All year
Size: 5 (7) acres, 40 touring pitches, 6 with elec,

⬛ Snacks/take away ☒ Restaurant ◹ Swimming pool ▣ Shelter for campers ☗ Dogs accepted   217

2 with hardstanding, 20 level pitches, 16 static caravans. 3 hot showers, 10 WCs, 1 CWP

⊞⊞▲ 🎍💧✖

Car & caravan, Motor caravan, Car & tent, M/cycle* & tent £4-£5.50; elec £1, awn £1
Family-run site in the beautiful Brecon Beacons National Park. Glorious views, unique wildlife, good walking country, good base for Mid and South Wales. 11 caravans for hire (own WCs).
From Llangadog, take the A4069 S. At the Three Horse Shoes public house, turn left, cross river, then turn right. Site on left in 3¼ miles.

LLANGOLLEN *Clwyd* Map 4 B3

Glan Llyn
Glyn Ceiriog, LL20 7AB. ☎ (069172) 320
Open: Easter-September
Size: 1 acre, 8 touring pitches. 1 hot shower, 4 WCs

⊞⊞▲ 🐕

Turn off A5 at Chirk and take B4500 W for 6 miles. Site on approach to Glyn Ceiriog.

Tower Camping & Caravan Site
Tower Farm, LL20 8TE. ☎ (0978) 860798
Open: Easter-October
Size: 7 acres, 70 touring pitches. 2 hot showers, 6 WCs. 5 static caravans

⊞⊞▲ 🐕

E towards Llangollen on A539, turn right at Bridge Hotel, and left after canal bridge. Site ¼ mile.

Ty-Ucha Farm
Maesmawr Road. ☎ (0978) 860677
Open: Easter-October
Size: 4 acres, 40 touring pitches. 4 hot showers, 8 WCs

⊞⊞ 🎍 🐕

1 mile E of Llangollen, S of A5.

Wern Isaf Farm
LL20 8DU. ☎ (0978) 860632
Open: Easter-September
Size: 4 acres, 20 touring pitches. 4 hot showers, 11 WCs. Static caravans

⊞⊞▲ 🐕

In Llangollen (A539), turn N by Bridge End Hotel. Over canal bridge then turn right. Site ½ mile.

Abbey Farm
☎ (0978) 860283/861297
Open: March-October
Size: 14 acres, 40 touring pitches. 6 hot showers, 20 WCs. 95 static caravans

⊞⊞▲🎍🐕

On A5942 1½ miles outside Llangollen at foot of Horseshoe Pass, by ruins of Abbey along main road.

LLANGORSE *Powys* Map 2 A2

LAKESIDE CARAVAN PARK RAC A
Llangorse Lake, LD3 7TR. ☎ (087484) 226
Open: April-October
Size: 2 (14) acres, 40 touring pitches, all level, 10 with elec, 75 static caravans. 12 hot showers, 17 WCs, 1 CWP

⊞⊞▲🎍💧✖☐ 🐕

(1991) Car & caravan, Motor caravan, Car & tent, M/cycle & tent £2.75-£3.60 per adult, £1.75 per child; elec £1.50; WS
cc Access, Visa/B'card
Friendly site, flat and well-sheltered. Fishing, canoeing, sailing, windsurfing, waterskiing, boats for hire, launching, tuition. 10 caravans for hire (own WCs).
From Crickhowell, travel NW on the A40 to Bwlch 5¾ miles, where turn right on the B4560 to Llangorse. Turn left for 300 yards, turn left to site.

LLANGRANOG *Dyfed* Map 1 B1

Gilfach Caravan Park
Blaencelyn. ☎ (023978) 250
Open: Easter-October
Size: 4 acres, 90 touring pitches. Hot showers, WCs

⊞⊞▲🎍

At 1¼ miles E of Llangranog on B4321 turn NE as for Llwyndafydd, for ½ mile.

Greenfields Caravan & Camping Park
Plwmp, SA44 6HF. ☎ (023978) 333
Open: 1 February-31 December
Size: 9 (34) acres, 50 touring pitches. 4 hot showers, 17 WCs. 95 static caravans, 1 chalet

⊞⊞▲🎍 ☐📷

At 12 miles E of Cardigan on the A487, turn N on the B4321, site on right in 200 yards.

Maes Glas Caravan Park
Penbryn, Sarnau, SA4 6QE. ☎ (023 978) 268
Open: Easter-October
Size: 4 (9) acres, 20 touring pitches. 2 hot showers, 5 WCs

⊞⊞▲ 🎍💧 🐕

Travelling S on A487, after Brynhoffnant Inn turn right signposted Penbryn. Site 1½ miles.

LLANGYNOG *Powys* Map 4 B3

Glendower Caravan Park
Berwyn Street. ☎ (069 174) 304
Open: Easter-December
Size: 1¼ (3¼) acres, 15 touring pitches. 2 hot showers, 5 WCs. 31 static caravans

⊞⊞▲🎍 💧 🐕

In centre of Llangynog on B4391. Site behind petrol station.

LLANIDLOES *Powys* Map 4 B3

Dol-llys Farm Caravan Site
☎ (05512) 2694
Open: Easter-October
Size: 3 acres, 20 touring pitches plus 10 tent pitches. 2 hot showers, 4 WCs

⊞⊞▲🎍 🐕

From Llanidloes, take B4569 over bridge and past hospital. Fork right into Oakley Park Road. Site first right turn.

Leylands Caravan Park
Dolwen, SY18 6LQ. ☎ (05512) 2668

Open: Easter-October
Size: 10 acres, 6 touring pitches. 4 hot showers,
6 WCs. 52 static caravans

2 miles E of Llanidloes (A470). Access via Dolwen
Garage.

LLANMADOC *West Glamorgan*   Map 1 B1

Llanmadoc Camping Site
☎ (0792) 386202
Open: April-October
Size: 13 acres, 250 touring pitches. 6 hot showers,
20 WCs

Follow signposts from Swansea or Gorseinon.

LLANRHYSTYD *Dyfed*   Map 1 B1

Greenacres Caravan Park
SY23 5AY. ☎ (0974) 202236
Open: April-October
Size: 6½ acres, 15 touring pitches. 4 hot showers,
10 WCs. 135 static caravans

Take B4337 from Llanrhystyd for ¼ mile.

PENGARREG CARAVAN PARK   RAC A
☎ (0974) 202247
Open: 1 March-31 October
Size: 17 (27) acres, 100 touring pitches, 40 with
elec. 9 hot showers, 48 WCs

Charges on application.
*A spacious, level farm site adjoining a shingle
beach, with licensed clubhouse and children's play
area. Restaurant 400 yards.*
At S end of Llanrhystyd on A487, turn W opposite
Lloyd Motor Garage. Site well signposted.

Woodlands Caravan Park
Llanon, SY23 5LX. ☎ (0974) 202342
Open: March-October
Size: 10 acres, 40 touring pitches. 6 hot showers,
14 WCs. Static caravans

2½ miles S of Llanrhystyd (S of
Llansantffraid)\(A487), turn W for site.

LLANRIAN *Dyfed*   Map 1 A1

Prendergast Camping Site
Cartlett Lodge, Trefin, SA62 5AL.
☎ (0348) 368
Open: April-October
Size: 2 acres, 18 touring pitches. 2 hot showers,
8 WCs. Static caravans

Site in Trefin, 1¾ miles NE of Llanrian.

LLANRWST *Gwynedd*   Map 4 A2

BODNANT CARAVAN PARK   RAC L
Nebo Road, LL26 0PT. ☎ (0492) 640248
Open: 1 March-31 October
Size: 2½ acres, 30 touring pitches, all level, all with

elec, 2 static caravans, 2 chalets. 6 hot showers,
9 WCs, 1 CWP

(1991) Car & caravan, Motor caravan £4-£5, plus
25p per person 2; elec £1, awn £1
*Sheltered, level site, within walking distance of
Llanrwst, many times winner of "Wales in Bloom".
Quiet, pretty site with lots of flowers. Shop,
restaurant and swimming pool ¼ mile. 2 caravans
and 2 chalets for hire (own WCs). Calor gas only.
Dogs must be kept on a lead at all times. No
ground sheets in awnings.*
Turn off A470 at Llanrwst for B5427. Site by 30mph
sign.

KERRY'S ORCHARD CAMPING SITE   RAC L
School Bank Road. ☎ (0492) 640248
Open: Easter-September
Size: 2 acres, 24 touring pitches, all level, 2 static
caravans, 2 cottages. 2 hot showers, 7 WCs

(1991) Motor caravan £3.50, Car & tent £3, plus 25p
per person; Tent £2.75; Car 25p
*Level, sheltered site, within walking distance of
town. Close to all local attractions and amenities.
Calor gas only. Shop and swimming pool
200 yards. Restaurant 300 yards. 2 caravans and
2 cottages for hire (own WCs). Dogs on lead only.*
Access off School Bank Road, W of Llanrwst town.

MAENAN ABBEY CARAVAN PARK   RAC L
Maenan. ☎ (0492) 69630
Open: 1 March-31 October
Size: 2 (6) acres, 28 touring pitches, all level,
20 with elec, all with hardstanding, 71 static
caravans, 7 chalets. 4 hot showers, 7 WCs, 1 CWP

(1991) Car & caravan, Motor caravan £3;£6; elec
£1.50, awn £1.25, dogs 40p
*There are plenty of trees and shrubs at this
pleasant site with a children's play area. 7 chalets
for hire (own WCs). Calor gas only. Shop 2 miles.
Swimming pool 3 miles.*
At 3 miles N of Llanrwst on A470, by the Maenan
Abbey Hotel.

PLAS MEIRION CARAVAN PARK   RAC L
Gower Road, LL27 0RZ. ☎ (0492) 640247
Open: Easter-End October
Size: ½ (2) acres, 11 touring pitches, all level, 6 with
elec, 4 with hardstanding, 16 static caravans,
2 flats. Hot showers, WCs

Charges on application. WS
*A most attractive, level, garden-like site in the
Conwy Valley. Children's play area. Swimming
pool 2 miles. 16 caravans and 2 flats for hire. Calor
gas only. Shop and restaurant 200 yards.*
From Llanrwst, leave on B5106 crossing River
Conwy to Trefriw. Camp site 300 yards on right.

Rynys Farm
☎ (069 02) 218
Open: Easter-October
Size: 2 acres, 3 touring pitches. 4 hot showers,
2 WCs

📷 Snacks/take away   ✗ Restaurant   ⌂ Swimming pool   📷 Shelter for campers   🐕 Dogs accepted   219

Turn E off A5 at Conwy Falls. 4½ miles NW of Pentrefoelas.

LLANSANTFFRAID *Powys*   Map 4 B3

Vyrnwy Caravan Park
SY22 6SY.
☎ (069 181) 217
Open: April-October
Size: 17 acres, 20 touring pitches. 4 hot showers, 5b WCs. Static caravans

6 miles S of Oswestry (A483), turn W on to B4398. After 1 mile, fork right on B4393. Site ½ mile.

LLANTEG *Dyfed*   Map 1 A1

Rose Park Farm
Amroth Road, Llanteg, Narbeth
☎ (083483) 203
Open: May-October
Size: 3½ acres, 40 touring pitches. 2 hot showers, 4 WCs. 1 static caravan, 1 chalet

1 mile W of Llanteg on the A477, 8 miles W of St Clears.

The Valley
Amroth Road, SA67 8QJ.
☎ (083483) 226
Open: Easter-October
Size: 3 acres, 3+ touring pitches. 2 WCs

Site 1¼ miles W of Llanteg on A477.

LLANTWIT MAJOR *South Glamorgan*   Map 1 B2

ACORN CAMPING & CARAVAN SITE   RAC L
Ham Lane South, CF6 9RP.
☎ (0446) 794024
Open: Easter/1 April-31 October
Size: 4½ acres, 90 touring pitches, 32 with elec, 4 level pitches, 13 static caravans. 8 hot showers, 8 cold showers, 17 WCs, 1 CWP

Car & caravan, Motor caravan, Car & tent, M/cycle & tent £3.50; all plus 75p per adult, 50p per child; elec £1-£1.30, awn free-50p, dogs 50p
A family-run site on Heritage Coast 1 mile from beach, 1 mile from historic town of Llantwit Major. On site: public phone, dishwashing sinks, children's play area, games room, NO gaming/video machines. 2 caravans for hire (own WCs). Restaurant 1 mile.
From the centre of Llantwit Major follow signs to the beach along Colhugh Street for ½ mile, then turn left.

Rosedew Camping Site
☎ (0446) 773333
Open: April-October
Size: 3 acres, 100 touring pitches. 8 hot showers, 12 WCs

In Llantwit Major, turn S past school. In Ham Lane, E through Ham Manor Residential Site. Continue down Beach Road for ½ mile, then follow signs.

LLIGWY BAY *Gwynedd*   Map 4 A2

CAPEL ELEN CARAVAN PARK   RAC L
Lligwy, Dulas, LL90 9PQ. ☎ (024888) 524
Open: 1 March-31 October
Size: 2 (7) acres, 10 touring pitches, 5 with elec, 8 level pitches, 45 static caravans. 2 hot showers, 7 WCs, 1 CWP

(1991) Car & caravan £6, Motor caravan £5.50, Car & tent £5; elec £1, awn 50p
Small, family-run site. Public telephone. Very well maintained and grass kept short. Calor gas only. Shop ½ mile. Restaurant 1 mile. Swimming pool 4 miles. Dogs must be kept on leads at all times. 10mph speed limit.
From roundabout at junction of the A5025 and A5108 (road to Moelfre), travel W on the A5025 for 2 miles, turn right 300 yards to site on left.

MELIN RHOS FARM CARAVAN & CAMPING SITE   RAC L
Dulas, LL70 9BQ. ☎ (024888) 213
Open: All year
Size: 15 acres, 15 touring pitches, all level, 6 with elec, 58 static caravans. 4 hot showers, 4 cold showers, 19 WCs, 3 CWPs

Charges on application; WS
cc Major cards
Pleasant, quiet, close to lovely, sandy beach; sheltered with plenty of space. 4 caravans for hire (own WCs). Shop and restaurant ½ mile. Swimming pool 4 miles.
From roundabout at junction of A5025 and A5108 (road to Moelfre) travel W on A5025 for 1½ miles and turn right for ¼ mile.

TYDDYN ISAF CAMPING & CARAVAN SITE   RAC A
Dulas, LL70 9PQ. ☎ (024888) 203
Open: 1 March-31 October
Size: 6½ (16) acres, 60 touring pitches, 30 level pitches, 21 with elec, 12 with hardstanding, 50 static caravans. 4 hot showers, 4 cold showers, 16 WCs, 1 CWP

(1991) Car & caravan from £7.15, Motor caravan, Car & tent, M/cycle* & tent from £5.50, plus from 75p per adult, child from 50p; elec £1.20-£1.35, awn from 85p; WS
Superior, family-run park overlooking Lligwy's fine beach. This sloping park is in an Area of Outstanding Natural Beauty, a Dragon Award park. 12 caravans for hire (own WCs). Swimming pool 3 miles. No groups - families and couples only.
From roundabout at junction of the A5025 and A5108 (road to Moelfre) travel W on A5025 for 2 miles. Turn right at telephone box for ½ mile to site on right.

Tyn Rhos Caravan & Camping Site
Moelfre, LL72 8NL. ☎ (024888) 808
Open: All year
Size: 15 acres, 13+ touring pitches. 8 hot showers, 20 WCs. 71 static caravans

On A5108 to Moelfre. Keep left on the Lligwy Road to site on right in 1¼ miles.

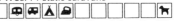

MACHYNLLETH Powys — Map 4 A3

Furnace Farm
Furnace.
☎ (0654) 781264
Open: Easter-September
Size: 7 acres, 50 touring pitches. 1 WC

[icons]

In Furnace (A487), 5½ miles S of Machynlleth.

Garth Farm Caravan Site
☎ (0654) 2194
Open: March-October
Size: 5 (10) acres, 5+ touring pitches. 2 hot showers, 8 WCs. Static caravans

[icons]

Approaching Machynlleth from E on A489, turn right at Chest Hospital, then right again. In 100 yards, turn left into road with 20mph sign. Site ½ mile.

Llwyngwern Farm
SY20 9RB.
☎ (0654) 2492
Open: March-October
Size: 2 acres, 30 touring pitches. 2 hot showers, 4 WCs

[icons]

3 miles N from Machynlleth, turn right off A487. Site adjacent to Alternative Technology Centre.

WARREN PARC CARAVAN PARK RAC L
Penegoes, SY20 8NN.
☎ (0654) 702054
Open: 1 March-31 October
Size: 1½ (10) acres, 10 touring pitches, all level, all with elec, 2 with hardstanding, 90 static caravans, 1 chalet. 3 hot showers, 8 WCs, 1 CWP

[icons]

Car & caravan, Motor caravan £8, plus £1 per person above 4; awn £1
Pleasant family site, developed to high standard. Wales in Bloom award, Calor Green award, Loo of the Year award, BTA Quality Grade 5 Ticks: Excellent. 2 caravans for hire (own WCs). Calor gas only. Shop and restaurant 2 miles.
At 2 miles E of Machynlleth on A489, behind Esso filling station.

MAENCLOCHOG Dyfed — Map 1 A1

ROSEBUSH CARAVAN & CAMPING PARK RAC A
Belle Vue House, Rosebush, SA66 7QT.
☎ (0437) 532206
Open: 1 March-30 October
Size: 4 (12) acres, 35 touring pitches, 5 with elec, 4 with hardstanding, 20 static caravans. 4 hot showers, 12 WCs, 2 CWPs

[icons]

Car & caravan, Motor caravan, Car & tent, M/cycle* & tent £5; elec £1
This well-kept country site, with children's play area has its own 3 acre lake for boating and coarse fishing. Restaurant 200 yards. Pitch and putt golf on site.
At 1½ miles N of Maenclochog on B4313, turn right at international sign (not at fork for Rosebush).

MANORBIER Dyfed — Map 1 A1

Foxcombe House
☎ (083 471) 404
Open: June-September
Size: 2 acres, 30 touring pitches. 2 hot showers, 4 WCs

[icons]

1 mile W of Lydstep, S of A4139.

Holimarine Caravan Park
☎ (0902) 880800
Open: May-September
Size: 3 (13) acres, 50 touring pitches. 3 hot showers, 10 WCs. Static caravans

[icons]

1 mile N of Manorbier, N of A4139.

Tudor Glen Caravan Park
Jameston, SA70 7SS. ☎ (083 482) 417
Open: March-October
Size: 6¼ acres, 28+ touring pitches. 5 hot showers, 10 WCs. Static caravans

[icons]

In Jameston (A4139), 6 miles SW of Tenby.

Whitewell Caravan Park
Near Lydstep Beach. ☎ (0834) 851569
Open: Easter-September
Size: 5 acres, 50 touring pitches. 6 hot showers, 25 WCs. Static caravans

[icons]

3½ miles SW of Tenby, off A4139. ¾ mile NE of Lydstep village.

MERTHYR TYDFIL Gwent — Map 1 B1

Bryn Bach Park
Merthyr Road, Tredegar, NP2 3AY.
☎ (0495) 711816
Open: All year
Size: 1 acre, 32 touring pitches plus 30 for tents. 6 hot showers, 12 WCs

[icons]

At Tredegar roundabout (A465), turn towards Tredegar. After 50 yards, turn right. Site ½ mile.

Grawen Farm
Cwm-Taff, Cefn Coed. ☎ (0685) 3740
Open: April-October
Size: 1½ acres, 45 touring pitches. 1 hot shower, 5 WCs

[icons]

Site S of Cwm-Taff village, 100 yards from A470.

MOLD Clwyd — Map 4 B2

WOODVALE SERVICES RAC L
Woodvale Service Station, Afonwen, Caerwys, CH7 5UB.
☎ (0352) 720330
Open: 1 April-31 October
Size: 1 acre, 15 touring pitches plus 10 for tents, all level. 3 WCs, CWP

[icons]

(1991) Car & caravan, Motor caravan £5, Car & tent,

[●] Snacks/take away [X] Restaurant [◠] Swimming pool [▥] Shelter for campers [🐕] Dogs accepted   221

M/cycle & tent £2.50; awn £1
Level site, good touring centre for North Wales, Snowdonia and the coast. Rhyl 15 miles, Brenig Dam 10 miles (boating, canoeing). Horse riding available at several stables near site. Golf and tennis at Caerwys, 3 miles away. Swimming pool 5 miles (Holywell). Fishing available on site. Calor gas only.
8 miles W of Mold on A541, to rear of Woodvale Service Station.

The Bridge Caravan & Camping Site
Dingestow. ☎ (0600) 83241
Open: April-October
Size: 3 acres, 60+ touring pitches. 4 hot showers, 12 WCs. Static caravans

At Newport, turn off M4 on to A449 to Monmouth. Continue to Raglan junction then follow camping signs.

Glen Trothy Caravan & Campsite
Mitchel Troy, NP5 4BD. ☎ (0600) 712295
Open: March-October
Size: 6½ acres, 84 touring pitches. 6 hot showers, 10 WCs

From A40, take B4293 S for ½ mile, then fork right to Mitchel Troy. Site ½ mile.

Monmow Bridge Caravan & Camping Site
Drybridge Street. ☎ (0600) 4004
Open: All year
Size: 1½ acres, 12 touring pitches. 2 hot showers, 5 WCs

In Monmouth off B4293. Access by Three Horse Shoes Inn.

ALLENSBANK HOLIDAY PARK　　　RAC L
Providence Hill, SA67 8RF.
☎ (0834) 860243
Open: Easter-October
Size: 5 acres, 11 touring pitches, all level, all with elec, 18 static caravans, 14 chalets. 4 hot showers, 8 WCs, 1 CWP

Car & caravan, Motor caravan £7; extra person 25p; elec £1.25, dogs £5 per week
A family-run site in beautiful countryside with a 200-year-old building, once a Victorian workhouse, now containing a clubhouse, 2 games rooms and the shop. Children's play area on site. 18 caravans and 14 chalets for hire (own WCs). No gas available.
Travel S from Narberth on the A478 for 1 mile, site

on left.

Derwenlas Caravan Park
Clynderwen.
☎ (0437) 563504
Open: March-November
Size: 2½ acres, 8 touring pitches. 2 hot showers, 5 WCs. 4 static caravans

4 miles N of Narberth on A478.

Dyrham Caravan Park
Robeston Wathen.
☎ (0834) 860367
Open: Easter-September
Size: 2 acres, 20 touring pitches. 2 hot showers, 4 WCs. Static caravans

In Robeston Wathen on A40, at rear of petrol station.

Quay House
Landshipping.
☎ (083 485) 262
Open: Easter-September
Size: 1½ acres, 3+ touring pitches. 1 hot shower, 1 WC

From A40, turn S on A4075. Follow signs for Landshipping.

Redford Caravan Park
Princes Gate.
☎ (0834) 860251
Open: Easter-September
Size: 12 acres, 50 touring pitches. 6 hot showers, 8 WCs. 59 static caravans

1½ miles SE of Narberth on B4314.

Hirdre Fawr Farm
Tudweiloig.
☎ (075887) 278
Open: May-October
Size: 4 acres, 10+ touring pitches. 2 hot showers, 4 WCs

1¼ miles N of Tudweiloig on B4417.

Tir Bach
Pistyll.
☎ (0758) 720074
Open: Easter-September
Size: 1 acre, 3+ touring pitches. 2 hot showers, 2 WCs

1 mile N of Nefyn on B4417.

Seasonal variation of prices

Where a single price is given it may be a low season minimum charge - rates can increase considerably at peak periods and for extra people or vehicles.
Please confirm prices with the site when booking.

Towyn Farm
Tudweiloig. ☎ (075887) 230
Open: April-October
Size: 5 acres, 3+ touring pitches. 1 hot shower,
2 WCs. 12 static caravans

[icons]

5 miles S of Nefyn on B4417, at N edge of
Tudweiloig, follow coast road for 1 mile.

Tyddyn Sander
Tudweiloig. ☎ (075887) 208
Open: April-October
Size: 2 acres, 12 touring pitches. 2 hot showers,
3 WCs

[icons]

½ mile S of Tudweiloig on B4417, take road
signposted to beach.

Wern Farm
☎ (0758) 720432
Open: March-October
Size: 3 acres, 3 touring pitches plus 100 for tents.
4 hot showers, 6 WCs. 40 static caravans

[icons]

¾ mile N of Nefyn on B4417.

NEW QUAY *Dyfed*   *Map 1 B1*

Bardsey View Holiday Park
Mydroilyn, Llanarth. ☎ (0545) 580270
Open: Easter-October
Size: 6 acres, 50 touring pitches. 4 hot showers,
6 WCs. Static caravans

[icons]

At Llanarth (A487), turn SE on to B4342. Site
2 miles.

Glynteg Caravan Site
Cross Inn, Llandysul. ☎ (0545) 560558
Open: April-October
Size: ¾ acre, 10 touring pitches. 2 hot showers,
7 WCs. Static caravans

[icons]

In Cross Inn village (A486), opposite P.O.

Llanina Touring Caravan Site
Llanarth. ☎ (0545) 580568
Open: March-October
Size: 2 acres, 45 touring pitches. 2 hot showers,
6 WCs

[icons]

In Llanarth (A487), adjacent to Llanina Arms Hotel.

Pencnwc & Pantclynhir Caravan Park
Cross Inn. ☎ (0545) 560767
Open: April-October
Size: 7 (25½) acres, 100 touring pitches. 10 hot
showers, 15 WCs. 175 static caravans

[icons]

¾ mile N of Cross Inn on A486.

NEWBOROUGH *Gwynedd*   *Map 4 A2*

Awelfryn Caravan Park
☎ (024879) 230
Open: Easter-September

Size: 2 acres, 12+ touring pitches. 2 hot showers,
6 WCS

[icons]

In Newborough, turn S at crossroads near White
Lion. Site ½ mile.

NEWCASTLE EMLYN *Dyfed*   *Map 1 B1*

AFON TEIFI CARAVAN & CAMPING PARK   RAC L
Pentre Cagal, SA38 9HT. ☎ (0559) 370532
Open: 1 April or Easter-31 October
Size: 6½ acres, 75 touring pitches, all level, 55 with
elec, 18 with hardstanding. 8 hot showers, 16 WCs,
1 CWP

[icons]

Car & caravan, Motor caravan £5-£6.50, Car & tent,
M/cycle* & tent £4; elec £1.25, awn £1.25
*Quiet site set in countryside alongside River Teifi.
Ideal touring centre, only 10 miles from sheltered
beaches of Cardigan Bay. Shop and restaurant
100 yards. Swimming pool 2 miles. Calor gas only.*
A484 Carmarthen to Cardigan. Camp found 2 miles
E before entering Newcastle Emlyn. A484 Cardigan
to Carmarthen, 2 miles E after leaving Newcastle
Emlyn.

DOLBRYN FARM CAMPSITE   RAC L
Capel Ifan Road. ☎ (0239) 710683
Open: 1 April-30 September
Size: 2 (2½) acres, 25 touring pitches, 8 with elec,
15 level pitches. 4 hot showers, 6 WCs, 1 CWP

[icons]

Charges on application.
*Family-run site in picturesque valley, with
ornamental lake, a licensed restaurant/bar, games
room and a children's play area. Close to local
beaches and in a good fishing area. Calor gas only.
Shop and restaurant 3 miles. Swimming pool
2 miles.*
From Newcastle Emlyn, travel SW as for Capel
Ifan, just over ¼ mile keep left to site on right in 1½
miles.

Moelfryn Camping Site
Ty Cefn, Pantybwlch. ☎ (0559) 370000
Open: Easter-September
Size: 1½ acres, 20 touring pitches. 4 hot showers, 5
WCs

[icons]

From Newcastle, take B4333 S for 2¾ miles. Turn
right by chapel. Site 500 yards.

NEWCHURCH *Powys*   *Map 2 A2*

Goblaen House
Rhosgoch, Painscastle. ☎ (04975) 654
Open: Easter-October
Size: 1 acre, 3+ touring pitches. 1 WC

[icons]

From Painscastle, take B4594 NE for 1½ miles to
Rhosgoch, then turn left. Site ½ mile.

Habour Farm
☎ (054422) 248
Open: March-October
Size: 2½ acre, 10 touring pitches. 2 hot showers,
3 WCs. 29 static caravans

🍴 Snacks/take away ✖ Restaurant 🌊 Swimming pool 🏠 Shelter for campers 🐕 Dogs accepted   **223**

[icons] 2 miles NW of Newchurch, off B4594.

Rhosgoch Holiday Park
Rhosgoch, Painscastle. ☎ (0497) 851253
Open: April-September
Size: 3 acres, 10 touring pitches. 2 hot showers,
3 WCs. 7 static caravans

[icons] 1½ miles NE of Painscastle.

Newgale Camping Site
Newgale Filling Station
☎ (0437) 721305
Open: All year
Size: 7 acres, 12 touring pitches. 5 WCs

[icons] On A487.

Newgale Farm
☎ (0437) 721505
Open: Easter-October
Size: 11 acres, 15 touring pitches. 5 WCs

[icons] ½ mile N of Newgale Filling Station (A487).

Rainbolts Hill
Roch. ☎ (0437) 208
Open: March-October
Size: 4 acres, 75 touring pitches. 4 hot showers,
4 WCs

[icons] On A487, 6 miles NW of Haverfordwest, ½ mile E
of Roch.

LLWYNGWAIR MANOR HOLIDAY PARK   RẬC A
SA42 0LX. ☎ (0239) 820498
Open: March-October
Size: 36 acres, 80 touring pitches, 20 with elec,
30 with hardstanding, static caravans, chalets.
8 hot showers, 12 WCs, 1 CWP

[icons] Charges on application.
*This well-kept parkland site by a river has a
children's play area and evening entertainment.
All-weather tennis court. Calor gas only.*
1 mile E of Newport on A487.

Tycanol Farm
SA42 0ST. ☎ (0239) 820264
Open: All year
Size: 5 acres, 40+ touring pitches. 1 hot shower,
10 WCs

[icons] 1 mile W of Newport, 500 yards NW of A487.

Tredegar House & Country Park
NP1 9YW. ☎ (0633) 62275
Open: All year
Size: 4 acres, 53 touring pitches. 4 hot showers,

5 WCs

[icons] 2 miles SW of Newport. Access from A48 via
Duffryn Drive.

Glandulais Farm Caravan Park
SY16 4HZ. ☎ (0686) 626532
Open: March-October
Size: 2 acres, 20 touring pitches. 6 hot showers,
12 WCs

[icons] 2 miles W of Newtown on A489.

PENYFAN CARAVAN & LEISURE PARK   RẬC A
Manmoel Road, NP2 0HY. ☎ (0495) 226636
Open: All year
Size: 4 (42) acres, 75 touring pitches, all level,
43 with elec, 40 with hardstanding. 6 hot showers,
10 WCs, CWP

[icons] Car & caravan, Motor caravan, Car & tent, all
£3 per adult, £1.60 per child; elec £2, awn 75p; WS
cc Access, Visa/B'card
*Level, grassy site with family room and new
licensed clubhouse. The site is well-planned and
was recently awarded 5 Ticks (Excellent) by the
Welsh Tourist Board. No gas available. Swimming
pool 4 miles.*
Leave M4 at junction 28 and take A467 to Crumlin,
where left at traffic lights onto B4251 towards
Oakdale. In 1¼ miles turn right and follow signs to
Penyfan Pond. Fork left to site - signposted.

Three Cliffs Bay Holiday Park
North Hills Farm. ☎ (0792) 371218
Open: Easter-October
Size: 5 acres, 20 touring pitches plus 70 for tents.
5 hot showers, 10 WCs

[icons] In Penmaen village, off A4118.

Tyddyn Du Farm
Conway Old Road. ☎ (0492) 622300
Open: Spring Bank Holiday-October
Size: 4 acres, 80 touring pitches. 2 hot showers,
8 WCs

[icons] 5 miles W from Conwy on A55, turn sharp left at
Puffin Hotel, signposted Sychnant Pass. First left at
roundabout after Little Chef restaurant. Site 1 mile.

Woodlands Camping Site
Pendyffryn Hall. ☎ (0492) 592862
Open: Easter-October
Size: 9 acres, 90 touring pitches. 4 hot showers,
8 WCs. 10 static caravans

[icons] 3 miles W from Conwy on A55, turn left signposted

WOODLANDS CAMPSITE
Pendyfryn Hall, Penmaenmawr, Gwynedd LL34 6UF
96 acres parkland, woodlands. Short walk to beach. Tourers, tents, caravanettes. Electric hook-ups. Licensed club, shop. Couples, families only. NO DOGS. SAE for brochure.
Telephone: 0492 623219

Dwygyfylchl. Site second entrance on left.

PENTRAETH Gwynedd — Map 4 A2

Pen Cefn
Llanbedrgoch.
☎ (024870) 452
Open: All year
Size: 1½ acres, 3+ touring pitches. 2 WCs. 10 static caravans

7 miles NW of Menai Bridge.

RHOS CARAVAN PARK — RAC A
LL75 8DZ.
☎ (0248) 450214
Open: 1 March-30 October
Size: 8 (15) acres, 52 touring pitches, all level, all with elec, 66 static caravans. 12 hot showers, 23 WCs, 2 CWPs

(1991) Car & caravan £5, Motor caravan £4, Car & tent, M/cycle* & tent £4.30, plus 30p per person above 2; elec £1, awn £1
A spacious, level site on a working farm with views of Snowdonia. 6 caravans for hire (own WCs). Restaurant 200 yards. Swimming pool 5 miles. From Menai Bridge town travel N on A5025 through Pentraeth. Site is ¾ mile N of Pentraeth village on left.

St David's Estate Caravan Park
Red Wharf Bay, LL75 8RJ.
☎ (0248) 852334
Open: March-October
Size: 10 acres, 120 touring pitches. 4 hot showers, 10 WCs

1½ miles N from Pentraeth (A5025), turn right signposted Red Wharf Bay.

PENYGROES Gwynedd — Map 4 A3

Talymignedd Isaf
Nantlle.
☎ (0286) 880374
Open: March-October
Size: 3 acres, 10 touring pitches. 2 WCs

At Penygroes (A487), turn E on B4418 for 4 miles.

PEN-FFORDD Dyfed — Map 1 A1

Mount Pleasant Farm
SA66 7HY. ☎ (099 16) 447
Open: All year
Size: 3 acres, touring pitches. 1 hot shower, 1 WC

Site near village P.O., 1½ miles SW of Llanycefn.

PORTHCAWL Mid Glamorgan — Map 1 B2

Brodawel
Moor Lane, Nottage. ☎ (0656) 483231
Open: Easter-October
Size: 4 acres, 40 touring pitches. 2 hot showers, 10 WCs

At N end of Nottage village on A4229, turn W into Moor Lane.

Sandy Bay Caravan Site
Sandy Bay. ☎ (0656) 782532
Open: April-October
Size: 50 acres, 250 touring pitches. 50 hot showers, 100 WCs. 400 static caravans

Enter Porthcawl on A4106, then follow signs from first roundabout.

PORTHMADOG Gwynedd — Map 4 A3

Black Rock Camping Site
Morfa Bychan. ☎ (0766) 3919
Open: March-October
Size: 9 acres, 150 touring pitches. 6 hot showers, 20 WCs

From centre of Porthmadog, follow signs for Morfa Bychan and Black Rock.

Blaen Cefn Caravan Park
Penrhyndeudraeth. ☎ (0766) 770889
Open: Easter-October
Size: 3 acres, 12 touring pitches plus 12 for tents. 2 WCs

3¾ miles E of Porthmadog on A487.

Cardigan View Park
Morfa Bychan, LL49 9YA. ☎ (0766) 512032
Open: (1991) Easter-October
Size: 1 (99) acres, 32 touring pitches. 4 hot showers, 10 WCs, 192 static caravans

At Porthmadog P.O. turn S as signed Borth-y-Gest. At ¼ mile on bear right. At Morfa Bychan turn left 100 yards after P.O. and petrol station and continue to site.

GARREG GOCH CARAVAN PARK — RAC A
Morfa Bychan, LL49 9YD. ☎ (0766) 512210
Open: March-October
Size: 1 (5) acres, 14 touring pitches, all level, all with elec, all with hardstanding, 61 static caravans. 6 hot showers, 6 WCs, CWP

Snacks/take away   Restaurant   Swimming pool   Shelter for campers   Dogs accepted   225

(1991) Car & caravan, Motor caravan, Car & tent, M/cycle & tent £3-£5.50; elec £1.20, awn £1.50
A small but well-kept family site, with good children's play area, set amid colourful flower beds and shrubs. 18 caravans for hire (own WCs). Calor gas only. Shop ¼ mile. Restaurant 1 mile.
At Porthmadog P.O. turn S as signed Borth-y-Gest. At ¼ mile on bear right. Continue to lake and ½ mile further turn left.

Glan Byl Farm Caravan & Camp Site
Criccieth. ☎ (076675) 644
Open: All year
Size: 3 acres, 20 touring pitches. 2 hot showers, 6 WCs

3 miles W of Porthmadog on A487.

Glan Morfa Mawr
Morfa Bychan. ☎ (0766) 2363
Open: Spring Bank Holiday-September
Size: 10 acres, 3+ touring pitches. 5 WCs

From Porthmadog High Street, follow road to Black Rock Sands.

GREENACRES CARAVAN PARK   RAC A
Morfa Bychan, LL49 9YB. ☎ (0766) 512781
Open: 1 March-31 October
Size: 7 (80) acres, 57 touring pitches, 57 with hardstanding, 900 static caravans. 18 hot showers, 20 WCs, 2 CWPs

Charges on application.
cc Access, Visa/B'card
Right by Black Rock Sands beach, this large site is maintained to high standards. There's a tennis court, clubhouse and children's play area.
100 caravans for hire (own WCs). Calor gas only.
At Porthmadog P.O., turn S as signed Borth-y-Gest. At ¼ mile on bear right and follow signs to Black Rock Sands.

Maes Gwyr Lleyn
Llanfrothen, Penrhyndeudraeth, LL48 6DU.
☎ (0766) 770907
Open: April-October
Size: 3 acres, 3+ touring pitches. 1 WC

N from Penrhyndeudraeth on A4085, at Garreg turn right signposted Llanfrothen. After ¾ mile, turn right by post box and follow minor road for ½ mile.

TYDDYN LLWYN CARAVAN PARK & CAMP SITE   RAC L
Black Rock Road, LL49 9UR.
☎ (0766) 512205
Open: 1 March-31 October
Size: 14 (52) acres, 230 touring pitches, 115 level pitches, 33 static caravans, 3 chalets. 12 hot showers, 25 WCs, 1 CWP

Car & caravan, Motor caravan £6.50, Car & tent £5.50 for a family, Tent £2 per person for backpackers or cyclists; awn 50p
The park is situated in a peaceful, sheltered valley surrounded by wooded slopes yet is less than a

10 minute walk from town centre and harbour. 5 caravans and 1 chalet for hire (own WCs). Swimming pool 5 miles. Dogs must be kept on leads at all times.
From Porthmadog High Street turn by Woolworths towards Morfa Bychan. After passing sign "To Borth-y-Gest only" signs for caravan park and camp site on roadside at bottom of hill. Drive for park on right immediately opposite signs.

PORT-EYNON *West Glamorgan*   Map 1 B2

Carreglwyd Camping Site
☎ (0792) 371687
Open: April-October
Size: 20 acres, 200 touring pitches. 20 hot showers, 30 WCS. 80 static caravans

Site adjacent to village and beach.

NEWPARK HOLIDAY PARK   RAC A
SA3 1NL. ☎ (0792) 390292
Open: 1 April-31 October
Size: 8 (14) acres, 112 touring pitches, 30 with elec, all with hardstanding, 100 level pitches, 47 chalets. 10 hot showers, 18 WCs, 2 CWPs

(1991) Car & caravan, Motor caravan from £6.15, Car & tent, M/cycle* & tent from £5.15; elec £1.30, awn £1.30, dogs 50p; WS
Overlooking sandy beach (4 minutes' walk), this is a family site with beautiful walks and scenery and panoramic views of the Bristol Channel and the North Devon coast. Children's play area. 25 chalets for hire. Swimming pool 4 miles.
Travelling from Swansea on the A4118, site is on left entering Port-Eynon.

PRESTATYN *Clwyd*   Map 4 B2

PRESTHAVEN SANDS HOLIDAY PARK   RAC A
Shore Road, Gronant, LL19 9TT.
☎ (0745) 66471
Open: Easter-October
Size: 200 acres, 97 touring pitches, all level, 40 with elec, 80 with hardstanding, 438 static caravans, 122 chalets. 10 hot showers, 10 cold showers, 15 WCs, 2 CWPs

Charges on application.
cc Access, Visa/B'card
Facilities at this large seaside park include a shopping precinct, children's play areas, sauna, solarium, 2 heated swimming pools and a tennis court. 438 caravans and 122 chalets for hire (own WCs).
1 mile E of junction of the A547 and A548 at Prestatyn, turn N off the A548 at crossroads (just N of Gronant), along unclassified road to site on right in ¼ mile.

St Mary's Camp
Gronant.
☎ (074 56) 3951
Open: Easter-October
Size: 7 acres, touring pitches. 5 hot showers, 9 WCs

2 miles E of Prestatyn on A548.

PRESTEIGNE Powys — Map 2 A1

Walton Court
Walton.
☎ (054421) 259
Open: All year
Size: 10 acres, 25 touring pitches. 2 hot showers,
4 WCs. 2 static caravans

| | ⚘ | 🚐 | 🅰 | | | | | | | 🐎 |

3¾ miles NW of Kington on A44.

PWLLHELI Gwynedd — Map 4 A3

ABERERCH SANDS HOLIDAY CENTRE RAC L
Abererch, LL53 6PJ.
☎ (0758) 612327
Open: 1 March-31 October
Size: 26 acres, 70 touring pitches, all level, all with
elec, 50 static caravans, 30 chalets. 10 hot showers,
10 cold showers, 20 WCs, 1 CWP

| ♿ | ⚘ | 🚐 | 🅰 | 🅿 | 🇱 | 🍴 | | | 🏊 | 🐎 |

(1991) Car & caravan £7, Motor caravan £5, Car &
tent, M/cycle* & tent £6.75, plus 50p per person
above 4; elec £1.30, awn £1.30
*Large, level site with good facilities including
heated indoor swimming pool, adjacent to beach.
Restaurant 2 miles away in Pwllheli.*
2 miles E of Pwllheli on A497.

GIMBLET ROCK CARAVAN PARK RAC L
South Beach, LL53 5AY.
☎ (0758) 812043
Open: 1 March-31 October
Size: 1 acre, 20 touring pitches, all level, 110 static
caravans. 4 hot showers, 10 WCs, 1 CWP

| | ⚘ | | | 🅿 | 🇱 | | | | | |

Charges on application.
cc Access, Visa/B'card
*A well-kept site situated at the harbour entrance,
so ideal for sailing, boating and windsurfing.
5 caravans for hire (own WCs). No gas available.
Family groups only. Restaurant ½ mile. Swimming
pool ¼ mile.*
In Pwllheli, turn S at railway station and ½ mile on,
turn left.

QUEENSFERRY Clwyd — Map 4 B2

Greenacres Farm Park
c/o Mancot Farm, Mancot, Deeside, CH5 2AZ.
☎ (0244) 531147
Open: April-October
Size: 3 acres, 50 touring pitches. 2 hot showers,
13 WCs

| ♿ | ⚘ | 🚐 | 🅰 | 🅿 | | 🍴 | | | | 🐎 |

From Hawarden (B5125), take A550 N. Site fourth
turning on right.

RHAYADER Powys — Map 1 B1

Wyeside Caravan Park
☎ (0597) 823737
Open: March-October
Size: 3 acres, 75 touring pitches. 2 hot showers,
6 WCs. Static caravans

| | ⚘ | 🚐 | 🅰 | 🅿 | | | | | 🏊 | 🐎 |

¼ mile N of Rhayader on A470.

RHOSNEIGR Gwynedd — Map 4 A2

Bodfan Farm
☎ (0407) 810563
Open: April-September
Size: 15 acres, 3+ touring pitches. 6 hot showers,
10 WCs

| | ⚘ | 🚐 | 🅰 | 🅿 | | | | | | 🐎 |

From A4080, site near Rhosneigr School.

Plas Caravan Park
Llanfaelog, LL63 5TU. ☎ (0407) 810234
Open: March-October
Size: 4 acres, 30 touring pitches. 6 hot showers,
10 WCs. 16 static caravans

| | | ⚘ | 🚐 | 🅰 | 🅿 | | 🍴 | | | 🐎 |

S from A5 on A4080, turn right at Llanfaelog P.O.
Site 1 mile.

Shoreside
Tyn-Morfa Farm. ☎ (0407) 810279
Open: Easter-October
Size: 15 acres, 110 touring pitches. 8 hot showers,
18 WCs. 4 static caravans

| | ⚘ | 🚐 | 🅰 | 🅿 | 🇱 | | | | | 🐎 |

S from A5 on A4080, turn right at Llanfaelog P.O.
Site opposite golf club.

RHOSSILI West Glamorgan — Map 1 B2

PITTON CROSS CARAVAN PARK RAC L
SA3 1PH. ☎ (0792) 390593
Open: 1 April-31 October
Size: 6 acres, 100 touring pitches, all level, 45 with
elec, 6 with hardstanding. 8 hot showers, 12 WCs,
2 CWPs

| ♿ | ⚘ | 🚐 | 🅰 | 🅿 | 🇱 | | | | 🛖 | 🐎 |

(1991) Car & caravan, Motor caravan, Car & tent,
M/cycle & tent £5-£6.50; elec £1.20, awn £1, dogs
50p; WS
cc Major cards
*Set amid some of the finest National Trust coastal
properties, ideal for walking, cycling and beach
activities. Restaurant 1 mile. Swimming pool
2 miles. 4 nights minimum stay over Bank Holiday
weekends.*
From Swansea take the A4118 SW following brown
and white tourist signs to 'Gower/South'. Turn
right at Scurlage onto the B4247 to Rhossili. Site in
2½ miles on left.

RHYL Clwyd — Map 4 B2

Cwybr Fawr Caravan Park
Rhuddlan Road. ☎ (0745) 590748
Open: April-September
Size: 6 acres, 130 touring pitches. 6 hot showers,
20 WCs.

| | | ⚘ | 🚐 | 🅰 | 🅿 | 🇱 | 🍴 | | | 🐎 |

1½ miles S of Rhyl on A525.

MARINE PARK RAC A
Cefyndy Road. ☎ (0745) 4461
Open: April-October
Size: 10 (60) acres, 25 touring pitches, 445 static
caravans, 1 chalet. 5 hot showers, 6 WCs, 2 CWPs

🍴 Snacks/take away 🇽 Restaurant 🏊 Swimming pool 🛖 Shelter for campers 🐎 Dogs accepted

[icons]

Charges on application.
cc Access, Visa/B'card
This large, well-kept site has a clubhouse and children's play area. Caravans for hire (own WCs).
From the centre of Rhyl travel S on the A525 towards Rhuddlan for ½ mile, turn right into Cefyndy Road to site.

RUTHIN *Clwyd*   Map 4 B3

Derwen
Llanerch, Pentre-celyn. ☎ (097888) 293
Open: All year
Size: 2½ acres, 18 touring pitches. 1 WC

[icons]

4½ miles S of Ruthin.

SAUNDERSFOOT *Dyfed*   Map 1 A1

MORETON FARM LEISURE PARK   RAC A
Moreton, SA69 9EA. ☎ (0834) 812016
Open: 1 March-11 January
Size: 7 (12) acres, 20 touring pitches plus 40 for tents, 15 with elec, 20 static caravans, chalets. 6 hot showers, 6 WCs, CWP

[icons]

Car & caravan, Motor caravan £7-£8, Car & tent, M/cycle & tent £5-£6; awn £1; WS
A very pleasant, slightly sloping site, 1 mile from the beach. Children's play area. New toilet/shower block. Fishing lake. Clay pigeon shooting available. Baby changing facilities. Chalets available for hire.
From St Clears on A477 turn left on to A478 for Tenby, site on left 1½ miles, opposite chapel, 400 yards under railway bridge to site. From Tenby on A478, travel under railway bridge to site. Well-signposted at entrance.

SENNYBRIDGE *Powys*   Map 1 B1

Blaen Twyni Farm
Glyntawe, Penycae, SA9 1GS.
☎ (0639) 730664
Open: March-October
Size: 10 acres, 30 touring pitches. 3 hot showers, 5 WCs

[icons]

From Sennybridge (A40), turn S on A4067. Site in 8 miles, after short dual-carriageway.

ST CLEARS *Dyfed*   Map 1 B1

Parciau Bach Holidays
Afon Lodge, SA33 4LG. ☎ (0994) 230647
Open: March-December
Size: 5 acres, 10 touring pitches plus 15 for tents. 5 hot showers, 5 WCs. 22 static caravans

[icons]

From by-pass to town centre traffic lights, continue on Llanboidy Road. After 2 miles, turn first right, then right again. Site ¼ mile.

ST DAVID'S *Dyfed*   Map 1 A1

CAERFAI BAY CARAVAN & TENT PARK   RAC A
Caerfai Bay, SA62 6QT. ☎ (0437) 720274

Open: Easter-31 October
Size: 7 (9) acres, 34 touring pitches, 25 with elec, 28 with hardstanding, 26 static caravans. 6 hot showers, 19 WCs, 2 CWPs

[icons]

Car & caravan £4.50-£6, Motor caravan, Car & tent £3.50 -£4, plus £1.50 per adult above 2, child 75p; elec £1.50, awn 80p, dogs 40p
A quiet, family-run park with panoramic views of St Brides Bay. Sandy bathing beach 200 metres and walks along the adjacent Pembrokeshire Coastal Path. Long stay reductions, also low season. Free hot water in wash basins. Shaver sockets and hairdryers. Public telephone. Shop, restaurant and swimming pool ½ mile.
Off A487 opposite Grove Hotel, St David's, signposted Caerfai Bay. Entrance to park is at end of road, 1 mile on the right overlooking the Bay.

CAERFAI FARM CAMP SITE   RAC L
SA62 6QT. ☎ (0437) 720548
Open: 23 May-30 September
Size: 5 acres, 45 touring pitches. 4 hot showers, 4 cold showers, 7 WCs, 1 CWP

[icons]

Charges on application.
Quiet, family-run site with magnificent sea views. No gas available. Restaurant ½ mile. Swimming pool ½ mile.
Take the A487 W from Haverfordwest to St David's. On entering St David's turn left into unclassified road signposted Caerfai.

East Farm Caravan & Camping Site
Tretio, SA62 6DE. ☎ (0437) 720270
Open: May-September
Size: 3 acres, 38 touring pitches. 2 hot showers, 7 WCs

[icons]

3 miles NE of St David's. Signed from A487.

Glan-y-Mor Tent Park
Caerfai Road. ☎ (0437) 721788
Open: Easter-September
Size: 2½ acres, 55 touring pitches. 4 hot showers, 6 WCs

[icons]

½ mile SE of St David's, on road to Caerfai Bay.

HENDRE EYNON CAMPING   RAC L
SA62 6DB. ☎ (0437) 720474
Open: April-September
Size: 7 acres, 70 touring pitches, all level, 32 with elec, 2 static caravans. 8 hot showers, 12 WCs, 1 CWP

[icons]

(1991) Car & caravan, Car & tent £3-£6, Motor caravan, M/cycle & tent £3-£5; elec £1; WS
Large, level, grassy site on a working farm adjacent to a nature reserve, within easy reach of the Coastal Walk inside the National Park. Riding stables. Shop and restaurant 2 miles. Swimming pool 3 miles.
From St David's travel N on the A487 for ½ mile, turn left on the B4583 for ¼ mile, turn left on the B4583 for ¼ mile, keep right for 1½ miles to site on right.

[icons] Facilities for Disabled Caravans accepted Motor caravans Tents Laundry room Shop

Park Hall Caravan Park
Maerdy Farm, Penycwm. ☎ (0437) 721282
Open: March-October
Size: 7 acres, 70 touring pitches. 4 hot showers,
8 WCs. 50 static caravans

2 miles E of Solva (A487), at signpost for RAF
Brawdy, turn N for 1 mile.

Porthclais
SA62 6RR. ☎ (0437) 720256
Open: March-November
Size: 4 acres, 70+ touring pitches. 2 hot showers,
8 WCs. 50 static caravans

¾ mile SW of St David's on Porthclais road.

Rhosson Farm
SA62 6PY. ☎ (0437) 720335/6
Open: Easter-September
Size: 10 acres, touring pitches. 2 hot showers,
6 WCs

1 mile W of St David's. Follow road to lifeboat
station.

Rhosson Ganol & Rhosson Isaf Farm
☎ (0437) 720361
Open: March-October
Size: 6 (8½) acres, 3+ touring pitches. 6 WCs. Static
caravans

1½ miles W of St David's. Follow road to lifeboat
station.

Rhos-y-cribed
SA62 6RR. ☎ (0437) 720336
Open: All year
Size: 6 acres, 20+ touring pitches. 2 hot showers,
4 WCs

Follow Porthclais road from St David's via
Porthclais Harbour. Site signed.

SWANSEA *West Glamorgan* Map 1 B1

BLACKHILLS CARAVAN & CAMPING PARK RAC A
Fairwood Common. ☎ (0792) 207065
Open: April-October
Size: 11 (21) acres, 90 touring pitches. 10 hot
showers, 41 WCs

Charges on application.
*Spacious, gently sloping site, set in woodlands in
the picturesque Gower, with children's play area
and well- stocked shop.*
Leave Swansea on the A4118 as for the airport. At
airport, turn left for ½ mile to site on left.

RIVERSIDE CARAVAN PARK RAC A
Ynysforgan Farm, Morriston, SA6 6QL.
☎ (0792) 775587
Open: All year
Size: 7 acres, 120 touring pitches, all level, 86 with
elec, 18 with hardstanding, 1 chalet. 8 hot showers,
8 cold showers, 14 WCs, 1 CWP

(1991) Car & caravan £5-£7, Motor caravan, Car &
tent, M/cycle & tent £4-£6; elec £1, awn £1; WS
*Flat, level, peaceful site, situated alongside River
Tawe (fishing available) at the crossroads of all
West Glamorgan attractions. Maximum
30 minutes' travel to all attractions. 1 chalet for
hire. Shop 200 yards. Restaurant and swimming
pool ½ mile. No motorcycles. No dangerous
breeds of dog.*
Just SE of junction 45 - M4/A4067.

TALSARNAU *Gwynedd* Map 4 A3

BARCDY CARAVAN & CAMPING PARK RAC L
Cae Bran, LL47 6YG. ☎ (0766) 770736
Open: Easter-31 October
Size: 9 (12) acres, 38 touring pitches, all level,
24 with elec, 28 static caravans, 2 chalets. 8 hot
showers, 14 WCs, 2 CWPs

(1991) Car & caravan, Motor caravan, Car & tent,
M/cycle* & tent all £2.75-£3.25 per adult, 50p-75p
per child; elec £1.50-£1.75
*Quiet family park with high standard of cleanliness.
Good facilities. Pleasant wooded surroundings
with some spectacular walks and views. A nice
combination of sea and mountains. 2 caravans and
1 chalet for hire (own WCs). Restaurant ¾ mile.
Swimming pool 4 miles. No groups. No dogs.*
1 mile N of Talsarnau on A496.

TAVERNSPITE *Dyfed* Map 1 A1

SOUTH CARVAN CARAVAN PARK RAC L
Whitland, SA34 0NL. ☎ (083483) 451/586
Open: 1 April-30 September
Size: 14 acres, 45 touring pitches, all level, 38 with
elec, 115 static caravans. 8 hot showers, 8 cold
showers, 15 WCs, 1 CWP

Car & caravan, Motor caravan £9, Car & tent,
M/cycle & tent £6; elec £1.25, awn 50p; WS
*Well-spaced site with a clubhouse and
entertainment most nights. Children's play area.
No gas available. Shop 200 yards. Restaurant
2 miles.*
At Red Roses on A477 turn NW on B4314 to
Tavernspite. Site near centre of village.

TENBY *Dyfed* Map 1 A1

CROSS PARK TENBY HOLIDAYS RAC L
Dept RAC, Broadmoor, Kilgetty, SA68 0RS.
☎ (0834) 811244
Open: Easter-End October
Size: 3½ (11) acres, 15 touring pitches, all with elec,
10 level pitches, 85 static caravans. 8 hot showers,
16 WCs, 2 CWPs

Car & caravan £6-£10.50, Motor caravan, Car & tent
£6- £9; elec £1.25, awn 50p, dogs £1
cc Access, Visa/B'card
*Award-winning, family holiday park, excellent
leisure facilities including clubhouse with nightly
entertainment for adults and children. Separate
enclosures for tourers and tents. Attractive off-peak
prices for hired static caravans including free coach*

● Snacks/take away ⊠ Restaurant ◺ Swimming pool ▣ Shelter for campers ⋔ Dogs accepted   229

tours, steam train rides, etc. No motorcycles.
From the junction of the A477 and A478 N of Tenby, travel W on the A477 for 1½ miles to Broadmoor, turn right on the B4586 for 300 yards to the park on the left.

BUTTYLAND TOURING CARAVAN & TENT PARK   RAC L
Manorbier, SA70 7SN. ☎ (0834) 871278
Open: (1991) Easter-October
Size: 10½ acres, 13 touring pitches, all level, 6 with elec. 8 hot showers, 19 WCs, 2 CWPs

(1991) Car & caravan £4.50, Motor caravan, Car & tent, M/cycle & tent £4.25; elec £1, awn £1
Spacious site with children's play area. Close to Manorbier Bay.
At 5 miles SW of Tenby on A4139, turn N, where signed Manorbier Station for ¼ mile to site on left.

Crain Cross
Devonshire Drive, Saundersfoot
☎ (0834) 812708
Open: Easter-October
Size: 2 acres, 3+ touring pitches. 5 hot showers, 12 WCs

3 miles N of Tenby, off A478.

Griffithston Farm
Westfield Road, Saundersfoot, SA69 9EQ.
☎ (0834) 813370
Open: Easter-September
Size: 3½ acres, 63 touring pitches. 4 hot showers, 7 WCs

From Begelly roundabout (A477), take A478 S through Pentlepoir and Wooden. At second crossroads, turn left for site.

Hazelbrook Caravan Park
Sageston Milton. ☎ (0646) 651351
Open: Easter-October
Size: 7 acres, 70 touring pitches. 12 hot showers, 16 WCs. 50 static caravans

Leave A477 at Sageston and take B4318 for 300 yards.

KILN PARK HOLIDAY CENTRE   RAC A
Marsh Road, SA70 7RB. ☎ (0834) 4121
Open: 1 March-31 October
Size: 20 (110) acres, 60 touring pitches, 12 with elec, 12 with hardstanding, 620 static caravans. 40 hot showers, 40 WCs, 4 CWPs

Charges on application.
cc Access, Visa/B'card
Large holiday park with a footpath to the South Beach. There's a licensed club with entertainment nightly in season. Children's play area.
500 caravans for hire (own WCs). No dogs in high season.
At ¾ mile S of Tenby on A4139, turn left as signposted.

The Leys Camping Park
Saundersfoot.
☎ (0834) 812413
Open: Easter-September
Size: 16 acres, 240 touring pitches. 14 hot showers, 36 WCs

1 mile SW of Saundersfoot on A478.

Moreton Farm
Tenby Road, Saundersfoot
☎ (0834) 812443
Open: May-September
Size: 1 acre, 30 touring pitches. 2 hot showers, 13 WCs

1¼ miles W of Saundersfoot, E of A478.

Moysland Farm
Saundersfoot, SA69 9DS.
☎ (0834) 812455
Open: Easter-September
Size: 4 acres, 3 touring pitches plus 40 for tents.

2 hot showers, 4 WCs. 1 static caravan

1 mile SW of Saundersfoot on A478. 2 miles N of Tenby, junction of Sandy Hill Lane.

New Minerton Leisure Park
Devonshire Drive, St Florence
☎ (0646) 651461
Open: Easter-September
Size: 20 acres, 200 touring pitches. 14 hot showers, 50 WCs. 120 static caravans

Turn W off A478 to Tenby into Devonshire Drive. Site 2½ miles on right.

ROWSTON HOLIDAY PARK   RAC A
New Hedges, SA70 8TL. ☎ (0834) 2178
Open: Mid March-Mid December
Size: 8 (20) acres, 120 touring pitches, 30 with elec, 4 with hardstanding, 128 static caravans, 4 chalets. 12 hot showers, 4 cold showers, 18 WCs, 2 CWPs

(1991) Car & caravan, Motor caravan £5-£8, Car & tent, M/cycle* & tent £3-£5
A sloping site with views over Carmarthen Bay, beach 10 minutes' walk. Children's play area. 12 caravans and 3 chalets for hire (own WCs). Shop 200 yards. Restaurant 300 yards. Swimming pool 1 mile. No dogs during July and August. Site 1½ miles N of Tenby on A478.

RUMBLEWAY CARAVAN PARK   RAC A
New Hedges, SA70 8TR. ☎ (0834) 3719/5155
Open: 1 April-30 September
Size: 10 (30) acres, 20 touring pitches, all level, 18 with elec, 130 static caravans. 7 hot showers, 7 cold showers, 18 WCs, 1 CWP

(1991) Car & caravan, Motor caravan £6-£10, Car & tent, M/cycle* & tent £5-£6
This site has a children's play area with swings, slide, seesaw, roundabout and sandpit, etc. We also have an amusement room, next door to our clubhouse which also caters for children. Dogs on leads - 1 dog per family. Camping Gaz only. 5 caravans for hire (own WCs). Maximum stay 3 weeks.
From the roundabout, junction of the A477 and A478, leave as for Tenby on the A478 for 3 miles to New Hedges roundabout, continue ahead for 500 yards to site on right.

Saundersvale Holiday Estates
Valley Road, Saundersfoot
☎ (0834) 812310
Open: April-October
Size: 2 acres, 30 touring pitches. 8 hot showers, 4b WCs

From Begelly roundabout, take A478 S. Fourth left turn for site.

Trevayne
Saundersfoot. ☎ (0834) 813402
Open: Easter-September
Size: 13 acres, 120 touring pitches. 8 hot showers, 18 WCs

1¼ miles S of Saundersfoot (B4316), turn E for ¾ mile.

WELL PARK   RAC A
New Hedges, SA70 8TL. ☎ (0834) 2179
Open: 1 April-30 October
Size: 4½ (6½) acres, 14 touring pitches, all level, all with elec, 6 with hardstanding, 42 static caravans, 4 chalets. 6 hot showers, 6 cold showers, 17 WCs, 1 CWP

(1991) Car & caravan, Motor caravan £9, Car & tent, M/cycle* & tent £5; elec £1, awn £1, dogs £1
A picturesque, landscaped, family-run park with beautiful views over surrounding area. First class facilities for tourers and tents, situated between Tenby and Saundersfoot, ideal for the family holiday. 14 caravans and 4 chalets for hire (own WCs). Restaurant ¼ mile. Swimming pool 1 mile. Families only.
1 mile before you reach Tenby on right hand side of New Hedges by-pass.

WOOD PARK CARAVANS   RAC A
New Hedges, SA70 8TL. ☎ (0834) 3414
Open: Easter-September
Size: 10 acres, 20 touring pitches, 12 with elec, 4 with hardstanding, 90 static caravans. 6 hot showers, 14 WCs, 1 CWP

(1991) Car & caravan, Motor caravan £4.50-£9, Car & tent, M/cycle* & tent £4-£6.50; elec £1.20, awn £1
Quiet, family-run holiday park in Tenby, 1½ miles from Saundersfoot, with shop, games room, bar, etc. 32 caravans for hire (own WCs). Restaurant 200 yards. Swimming pool 1 mile. No parties of single people. Small dogs only - no dogs end of July to August. Weekly bookings only over Spring Bank Holiday and in July and August.
From the roundabout, junction of A477 and A478, leave as for Tenby for 3½ miles, site on right.

TOWYN Clwyd   Map 4 B2

Henllys Farm
☎ (0745) 51208
Open: April-September
Size: 7 acres, 180+ touring pitches. 5 hot showers, 30 WCs

2¾ miles W of Rhyl, S of A548. Site on W side of Towyn.

TY MAWR HOLIDAY PARK   RAC A
Towyn Road, LL22 9HG. ☎ (0745) 832079
Open: Easter-October
Size: 47 acres, 238 touring pitches, all level, 76 with elec, 104 static caravans. 26 hot showers, 64 WCs, 1 CWP

Charges on application.
cc Access, Visa/B'card
A large, level site on the edge of town with plenty of activities. Licensed club with entertainment programme, discotheque, children's play area. 104 caravans for hire (own WCs). Family groups

only.
Site on the S side of the A548, 1½ miles E of its junction with the A55.

TREGARON *Dyfed*   Map 1 B1

Aeron View Caravan Site
Blaenpenal. ☎ (097 421) 267
Open: April-October
Size: 1½ acres, 12 touring pitches. 3 WCs

4 miles NW of Tregaron, turn W off A485.

Hendrewen Caravan Park
Pencarw, Llangeitho. ☎ (0974) 298410
Open: March-October
Size: 2 acres, 10 touring pitches. 1 hot shower, 3 WCs. 22 static caravans

Site on B4578/B4342 crossroads.

TYWYN *Gwynedd*   Map 4 A3

Caethle Farm
☎ (0654) 710587
Open: April-October
Size: 15 acres, 70 touring pitches. 4 hot showers, 16 WCs

1½ miles S of Tywyn, E of A493.

Llanllwyda
Llanfihangel, LL36 9TW. ☎ (065 477) 276
Open: March-November
Size: 3½ acres, 15 touring pitches. 2 hot showers, 4 WCs

N from Tywyn on A493, follow minor road through Llanegryn towards Llanfihangel for 3½ miles. Site ½ mile after Bird Rock.

Pall Mall Farm Caravan & Camping Site
LL36 9RU. ☎ (0654) 710384
Open: Easter-September
Size: 8 acres, 130 touring pitches. 4 hot showers, 16 WCs

¼ mile NE of Tywyn, off A493.

Pant-y-neuadd Caravan Park
Aberdovey Road, LL36 9HW.
☎ (0654) 711393
Open: April-October
Size: 2¾ acres, 41 touring pitches. 6 hot showers, 11 WCs

S from Tywyn on A493, site on left just beyond hospital.

Tynllwyn Caravan & Camping Park
Bryncrug. ☎ (0654) 710370
Open: March-October
Size: 8 acres, 60 touring pitches. 4 hot showers, 18 WCs. 9 static caravans

2 miles N from Tywyn (A493), turn right on to

B4405 for 100 yards. Site on right.

Waenfach Caravan Site
Llanegryn, LL36 9SB. ☎ (0654) 710375
Open: April-October
Size: 4 acres, 40 touring pitches. 4 hot showers, 16 WCs. 40 static caravans

3 miles N of Tywyn on A493.

WOODLANDS HOLIDAY PARK   RAC A
Bryncrug, LL36 9UH. ☎ (0654) 710471
Open: Easter-October
Size: 2 (25) acres, 20 touring pitches, all level, all with elec, all with hardstanding, 122 static caravans, 58 chalets. 2 hot showers, 2 cold showers, 4 WCs, 1 CWP

Car & caravan, Motor caravan £6-£7; dogs £1
Set in glorious scenery only 2 miles from the sea, facilities include licensed country club, games room and children's play area. 18 caravans and 8 chalets for hire (own WCs). Calor gas only.
At Bryncrug, 18 miles S of Dolgellau and 2 miles N of Tywyn, turn E on the B4405 for 1 mile to site on left.

Ynysmaengwyn Caravan Park
LL36 9RY. ☎ (0654) 710684
Open: April-October
Size: 7 acres, 90+ touring pitches. 4 hot showers, 10 WCs. Static caravans

1 mile NE of Tywyn on A493.

USK *Gwent*   Map 2 A2

Bridge Inn
Chainbridge, NP5 1PP. ☎ (0873) 880243
Open: March-October
Size: 2 acres, 15 touring pitches. 1 hot shower, 4 WCs

3½ miles NW of Usk on B4598.

Pantycolin Farm
Llancayo. ☎ (02913) 2592
Open: March-October
Size: 3 acres, 5 touring pitches. 1 hot shower, 1 WC

1½ miles N from Usk (B4598), at phone box fork right signposted Bettws Newydd. Site 400 yards.

VALLEY *Gwynedd*   Map 4 A2

Glan Rhyd Isaf
LL65 3HF. ☎ (0407) 740907
Open: March-October
Size: 8 acres, 30 touring pitches. 4 hot showers, 4 WCs

At Valley (A5), turn S on B4545, then left at level crossing. After ½ mile, take first right for site.

Pen-y-Bont Farm
Four Mile Bridge. ☎ (0407) 740481
Open: Whitsun-September

  ⓖ Facilities for Disabled   🚐 Caravans accepted   🚐 Motor caravans   ⓐ Tents   🏠 Laundry room   🏪 Shop

Size: 3 acres, 5+ touring pitches. 4 WCs

🚐🚙⛺   🐎

At Valley (A5), turn S on B4545 for 1 mile. Site at first farm on right at Four Mile Bridge.

WELSHPOOL Powys   Map 4 B3

Henllan Caravan Park
Llangyniew, SY21 9EJ. ☎ (0938) 810343
Open: March-October
Size: 7 acres, 10 touring pitches. 2 hot showers, 4 WCs. 55 static caravans

🚐🚙   🍴   💧   🛶   🐎

6 miles W from Welshpool on A458, take first right after river bridge. Site ½ mile.

Llwyn-Celyn Caravan Park
Adfa, Newtown. ☎ (0938) 810720
Open: Easter-October
Size: 6 acres, 16 touring pitches. 1 hot shower, 1 WC. 55 static caravans

🚐🚙⛺🍴   🐎

1¼ miles S of Llanllugan.

Maes-yr-Afon
Berriew, SY21 8QB. ☎ (068 685) 587
Open: March-October
Size: 15 acres, 20 touring pitches. 4 hot showers, 9 WCs. 68 static caravans

🚐🚐⛺🍴🚿   🐎

5 miles SW of Welshpool (A483), turn W on B4390 through Berriew. Site 2 miles.

SEVERN CARAVAN & CAMPING PARK   RAC L
Forden, SY21 8RT. ☎ (093876) 238
Open: Easter-end October
Size: 5 (15) acres, 40 touring pitches, all level, 16 with elec, 186 static caravans. 6 hot showers, 11 WCs, 2 CWPs

🚐🚙⛺   🏠🐎

(1991) Car & caravan, Motor caravan, Car & tent, M/cycle & tent £3; elec £1; WS
In beautiful countryside, this level site is on the

banks of the River Severn. Children's play area and games room. No gas available. Shop and swimming pool 2½ miles. Restaurant 600 yards. Travel S from Welshpool on A483 for 1½ miles, bear left on A490 then ¾ mile further cross river and railway, turn left for ¼ mile to site on left.

WREXHAM Clwyd   Map 4 B3

Cae Adar Farm
Bwlchgwyn. ☎ (0978) 757385
Open: April-October
Size: 3 acres, 12 touring pitches. 2 hot showers, 4 WCs

🚐🚙⛺   🐎

5 miles W of Wrexham on A525.

James Farm
Ruabon. ☎ (0978) 820148
Open: March-October
Size: 3 acres, 20 touring pitches. 2 hot showers, 4 WCs

🚐🚙   🐎🐎

5 miles S of Wrexham on A483.

PLASSEY TOURING CARAVAN & LEISURE PARK   RAC A
Eyton, LL13 0SP. ☎ (0978) 780277
Open: March-October
Size: 9 (25) acres, 120 touring pitches, all level, 50 with elec, 6 with hardstanding, 1 static caravan. 10 hot showers, 30 WCs, 3 CWPs

♿🚐🚙⛺🍴🚿💧❌🛶🏠🐎

(1991) Car & caravan, Motor caravan, Car & tent, M/cycle* & tent £5.50-£7, plus £1.50 above 4; elec £1.50, awn £1.50, dogs 50p; WS
Beautiful countryside ideally suited to people who enjoy walking with sporting amenities on site. 12 individually-run craft workshops. 1 caravan for hire (own WC). Children's adventure playground. 3 nights minimum stay over Bank Holidays. No unaccompanied teenagers.
S of Wrexham take A483 Chester-Oswestry by-pass. Take B5426 exit for Bangor-on-Dee. Follow brown and cream signs for Plassey.

Seasonal variation of prices

Where a single price is given it may be a low season minimum charge - rates can increase considerably at peak periods and for extra people or vehicles.
Please confirm prices with the site when booking.

💧 Snacks/take away   ❌ Restaurant   🛶 Swimming pool   🏠 Shelter for campers   🐎 Dogs accepted

Alderney

There is just one place to camp on the island.

SAYE BAY *Alderney*

☎ (048182) 2762
Open: For details contact the Warden (Mr W. Bohan) or the Tourist Office. ☎ (048182) 2994
Hot showers, WC and standpipe available. Charges on application.
Mainly level site close to Saye Bay. Small shop. Camping gaz only.

Guernsey

The placing of caravans and motor caravans on properties on the Island of Guernsey is very strictly controlled by permit issued by the States of Guernsey Island Development Committee, Sydney Vane House, Rue du Commerce, St Peter Port, Guernsey. No caravan camps or caravan parks exist on the Island. Trailer caravans, either of the folding or fixed types or mobile homes, are not permitted into the island at all but motor caravans may be permitted. One of the conditions required before a permit is issued is that while on the Island they are not used at any time for human habitation. For all practical purposes, therefore, camping holidays on Guernsey are tents only.

ST PETER PORT *Guernsey*

FAUXQUETS VALLEY FARM RAC A
Castel. ☎ (0481) 55306/55460
Open: Easter-15 September
Size: 3 acres, 80 touring pitches, all level. 13 hot showers, 17 WCs, 1 CWP

Motor caravan, Car & tent £3 per adult, £1.50 per child (4-14 years)
A very clean, tidy, quiet and well-organised countryside site, 1½ miles from the beach. Children's play area. Golf, tennis, horse riding, sea fishing all within 3 miles of site. Fully equipped

tents available for hire. Holidaymakers and tourists only, no seasonal workers.
Follow signs to St Andrews and Castel. Left into Queen's Road, and on to sign for Underground Hospital. Turn right, and Fauxquets is fourth lane on left.

ST SAMPSONS *Guernsey*

VAUGRAT CAMPING RAC A
Route de Vaugrat. ☎ (0481) 57468
Open: 1 May-16 September
Size: 3 acres, 150 touring pitches, all level. 8 hot showers, 12 WCs, 1 CWP

Charges on application.
Centred round a granite farmhouse which contains all the facilities, this level site is a few minutes' walk from safe sandy beaches. Campers' own boats accommodated on site. Tents and equipment for hire. Children's play area. Couples and families only, no seasonal workers.
From St Peter Port travel N on coast road for 1½ miles, turn left into Route Militaire for ¼ mile, turn left for 1½ miles to L'Islet. Continue on Rue Carre for ½ mile to Le Piquerel, continue on Route du Port Grat for ¼ mile, keep left then turn right for ¼ mile, turn left into Route de Vaugrat. Site on left.

TORTEVAL *Guernsey*

Laleur Camping Site
☎ (0481) 63271
Open: May-September
Size: 2 acres, 80 touring pitches. 3 hot shwoers, 5 WCs

1 mile from Rocquaine Bay.

VALE *Guernsey*

LA BAILLOTERIE RAC L
☎ (0481) 44508
Open: 25 May-15 September
Size: 8 acres, 120 touring pitches. 12 hot showers, 10 WCs, 1 CWP

(1991) Car & tent, M/cycle & tent £2.50 per adult, £1.25 per child, car 65p
A level campsite with a few trees and shrubs, ½ mile from beach. Shop 200 metres. Restaurant 1 mile. Swimming pool 3 miles. Fully equipped units are available for hire: £150 per week for 6 berths, £120 for 4 berths (1991 prices). 2 nights minimum stay.
At just over 1 mile N of St Peter Port, turn inland on to Vale road for 1 mile. At second traffic lights

---

234 Facilities for Disabled Caravans accepted Motor caravans Tents Laundry room Shop

QUENNEVAIS CAMPING SITE

Les Ormes Farm, St. Brelade, Jersey, CI.   Tel: (0534) 42436

Large dry flat site, swimming pool, restaurant, shop, car by tent pitches with electric hook ups, children's play area, sea view, ready erected tents for hire.

turn right into Braye Road for 200 yards and turn left.

L'ETOILE CAMP SITE   RAC L
Hougue Guilmine. ☎ (0481) 44325
Open: May-September
Size: 3 acres. 6 hot showers, 10 WCs

Charges on application.
This pleasantly situated wooded campsite is set between the river and the beach. Swimming and fishing virtually on site. Shop 200 yards. At 2½ miles N of St Peter Port.

Jersey

Import control is exercised by the Island Development Committee over trailer and motor caravans, or any vehicle adapted for human habitation (other than genuine trailer tents which are currently exempted from import control). The control policy is as follows:

Trailer & Motor caravans (e.g. Dormobiles)
There is a total embargo upon importation of these vehicles for any habitable or holiday transport use. No import licences are granted for these purposes to non-residents, nor for any vehicle in transit to enter the island (special arrangements apply with regard to Guernsey-owned vehicles in transit to St Malo, which can remain unoccupied at St Helier docks pending trans-shipment). Jersey residents only may obtain import licences for such vehicles but subject to various conditions which include preclusion of any habitable use whilst within the island.

Trailer Tents
Trailer tents of the genuine type with a trailer base and canvas walls and roof, giving the appearance of a tent when erected, are currently treated as exempt from the need to obtain an import licence. They are treated as tents and may be used only on authorised tent camp sites - advance reservations **MUST** be made. The type of trailers which have walls and roofs in a rigid material are treated as folding caravans and are not granted import licences.

Enquiries not covered by the above policy statement should be addressed to the States Planning Office, South Hill, St. Helier, Jersey.

There are no caravan sites on the island.

ST BRELADE *Jersey*

QUENNEVAIS CAMPING SITE   RAC A
Les Ormes Farm, Quennevais
☎ (0534) 42432
Open: May-September
Size: 10 acres, 250 touring pitches, all level, 40 with elec. 24 hot showers, 34 WCs

Charges on application.
cc Visa/B'card
A meadowland site with views of St Quen's Bay. Recreation and TV rooms and children's play area. Tent, car and cycle hire.
From St Helier take A1 to Beaumont and turn right on to A12, at traffic lights turn left on B36, left at roundabout, then first right and follow signs.

Rose Farm Camp
☎ (0534) 41231
Open: May-September
Size: 4 acres, 150 touring pitches. 18 hot showers, 20 WCs

From St Helier harbour, follow coast road W to St

ST BRELADES CAMPING PARK

Tel: 0534 41398
Fax: 0534 47534
Write: ST BRELADES
CAMPING PARK JERSEY

◐ Snacks/take away ☒ Restaurant ⊿ Swimming pool ▣ Shelter for campers ⋔ Dogs accepted   **235**

Aubin. Turn right up winding hill. Site 200 yards past Portelet junction.

ST BRELADE'S CAMPING PARK   🏨 A
☎ (0534) 41398
Open: May-September
Size: 12 acres, 250 touring pitches. 39 hot showers, 30 WCs

Charges on application.
This well-screened campsite just 15 minutes' walk from the beach has a swimming pool, children's adventure playground, and unlicensed clubroom with pool tables and table tennis. Tents and equipment for hire.
Follow A13 from St Helier to ¼ mile from St Brelade village. Site on right.

ST MARTIN *Jersey*

DE LA HAYES CAMPSITE BEUVELANDE   🏨 L
Beuvelande. ☎ (0534) 53575/52223
Open: 1 July-31 August
Size: 3 acres. 10 hot showers, WCs

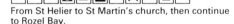

Car & tent, M/cycle & tent £4 per adult, £1.50-£2 per child (under 2 years free); dog £1
A quiet, sheltered campsite on level ground with a swimming pool, games and TV room and children's play area. Camping equipment for hire. Restaurant ¼ mile.
At 3½ miles NE of St Helier on A6 turn right into La Longue Rue, then turn right into Rue de Lorme. At end turn left to site.

Rozel Camping Park
☎ (0534) 51989
Open: April-September
Size: 3 acres, 60 touring pitches, all level. 10 hot showers, 9 WCs

From St Helier to St Martin's church, then continue to Rozel Bay.

Sark

Campsites are licensed by the Tourism Committee. There are only three such sites. Camping, other than on a site, is not permitted on Sark. No cars are allowed on the island.

Full details of the camp sites and ferry crossings from Guernsey to Sark can be obtained from: The Tourist Information Centre, Sark. ☎ (048183) 2345

Falles Barn Bar ☎ (048183) 2186
Open: Apply to site for details
Size: 30 pitches. Hot showers, WCs
Charges on application.
A simple camp site with restaurant and bar nearby. Gas available from the Gallery Stores, Sark.

La Valette ☎ (048183) 2066
Open: Apply to Mr Hilary Carre for details
Size: 40 pitches. Well-drawn water, WC
Charges on application.
A very simple campsite near the lighthouse and beach. Gas available from the Gallery Stores, Sark.

Pomme de Chien ☎ (048183) 2316
Open: Apply to Mrs J Rang for details
Size: 30 pitches. Hot showers, WCs
Charges on application.
Fully equipped tents are available for hire at this site in addition to the touring pitches. Gas available from the Gallery Stores, Sark.

Forest Sites

The Northern Ireland Forest Service operates two types of caravan sites as follows:

(1) A ring of small touring sites located in forests throughout the Province, convenient to areas of outstanding beauty. Minimum facilities are provided, i.e. drinking water, chemical waste disposal points and hardstandings for caravans. You can book for as little as 2 nights and having booked and obtained your barrier key, you can go anywhere, any time, the choice is yours. (Dates of stay to be shown on application form.) The location of these sites and details of their special features are shown in a booklet entitled *Touring in the Trees*.

(2) A more sophisticated type of site in Forest Parks provides the caravanner with toilets, showers, laundry facilities etc., and are referred to as "Extended Stay Sites". Bookings can however be accepted for short periods at the discretion of the resident Head Forester.

For further information of the above two schemes, applications should be made to The Public Relations and Education Branch, Department of Agriculture, Forest Service, Room 22, Dundonald House, Upper Newtownards Road, Belfast BT4 3SB. ☎ (0232) 650111 ext. 456.

Gas

At present 'Calor gas' is available in containers compatible with UK equipment, but it is understood that they may be phased out in favour of 'Calor gas (Cozen)' containers as sold in the Republic. These containers are not compatible with UK equipment unless an adaptor is used.

'Camping gaz international' is freely available throughout Northern Ireland.

General Information

Travellers to Northern Ireland are reminded that livestock, foodstuffs and other articles may not be imported into Northern Ireland unless they are accompanied by the necessary importation licence/certification. Items to which these restrictions apply include:

(a) meat and meat products
(b) poultry, poultry meat, poultry meat products, eggs and poultry equipment.
(c) birds (e.g. parrots, pigeons, budgerigars, canaries) and
(d) live animals with the exception of small animals such as hamsters, gerbils, guinea-pigs, cavies, ferrets, rats and mice (provided they are household pets and have not been outside the British Isles within the previous 6 months).

Restrictions do not apply to the importation of dogs and cats which have not been outside the British Isles within the previous 6 months. These restrictions are necessary to safeguard Northern Ireland's freedom from serious livestock and poultry diseases. Further information may be obtained from the Department of Agriculture for Northern Ireland, Dundonald House, Upper Newtownards Road, Belfast BT4 3SB. ☎ (0232) 650111 ext. 255/289. On sea crossings dogs are not allowed in cabins or other passenger accommodation. It is advisable to check with the shipping company concerned as to whether you are required to provide a kennel or may leave your dog in the car.

Shipping Routes to Northern Ireland

For information on routes and prices contact: B&I Line ☎ 071-499 5744
Belfast Ferries ☎ 051-922 6234
Sealink Stena Line ☎ (0233) 647047
P&O European Ferries ☎ (0304) 203388

Cairnryan - Larne (P&O European Ferries) - up to 6 departures daily
Stranraer - Larne (Sealink Stena Line) (2hr 20min) - 9 departures daily

ANNALONG *Co Down* — Map 10 C2

Newry & Mourne District Council Site
Main Street. ☎ (039 67) 68736
Open: Easter-October
Size: ¼ acre, touring pitches. Hot showers, WCs

In Annalong village, off A2.

ANTRIM *Co Antrim* — Map 10 C1

Sixmilewater Caravan Park
Lough Road. ☎ (084 941) 4131
Open: April-October
Size: 38 touring pitches. Hot showers, WCs

In Antrim (A26), take Lough Road to Lough Neagh.

ARMAGH *Co Armagh* — Map 10 C2

GOSFORD FOREST SITE RAC L
☎ (0232) 650111
Open: All year
Size: 10 touring pitches. WCs

Charges on application - permit required.
A park site with planned walks, castle and walled garden. All caravans/tents must have chemical toilets. Maximum stay 3 nights.
From Armagh take the A32 SE to Markethill. The site is adjacent to the road to the E.

BALLYCASTLE *Co Antrim* — Map 10 C1

BALLEYPATRICK FOREST SITE RAC L
☎ (0232) 650111
Open: All year
Size: 11 touring pitches. WCs

Charges on application - permit required.
Sheltered site alongside main road. Maximum stay 3 nights.
The site is on the A2, 6 miles SE of Ballycastle.

Moyle View Caravan Site
Clare Road. ☎ (02657) 62550
Open: March-October
Size: 25 acres, 30 touring pitches. 4 hot showers, 12 WCs. 252 static caravans

¼ mile NW of Ballycastle on B15.

Whitehall Caravan Park
Whitepark Road. ☎ (026 57) 62077
Open: Easter-October
Size: 2 (5) acres, 30 touring pitches. 4 hot showers, 24 WCs. Static caravans

1 mile W of Ballycastle on B15.

BALLYWALTER *Co Down* — Map 10 C2

Ballyhalbert Caravan Park
Shore Road, Ballyhalbert
☎ (02477) 58426
Open: April-October
Size: 80 acres, 40 touring pitches. 4 hot showers, 20 WCs. 400 static caravans

S of Ballywalter on A2.

Ganaway Caravan Park
Ganaway Road. ☎ (02477) 58422
Open: Easter-October
Size: 16 acres, 12 touring pitches. 2 hot showers, 18 WCs. 80 static caravans

2½ miles S of Millisle, E of A2.

Sandycove Caravan Park
Ballyferris. ☎ (02477) 58200
Open: Easter-October
Size: 10 acres, 16 touring pitches. 4 hot showers, 20 WCs. 60 static caravans

3 miles S of Millisle on A2.

BANGOR *Co Down* — Map 10 C2

Helen's Bay Caravan Park
Golf Road, Helen's Bay. ☎ (0247) 852536
Open: April-September
Size: 11 acres, 20 touring pitches. 6 hot showers, 3b WCs. Static caravans

3½ miles W of Bangor (A2), turn N to Helen's Bay. Take first right, then third left to site.

BELFAST *Co Down* — Map 10 C2

BELVOIR FOREST SITE RAC L
☎ (0232) 650111
Open: All year
Size: 7 touring pitches

Charges on application - permit required.
Basic site within easy reach of Belfast and Lagan valley. All caravans/tents must have chemical toilets. Maximum stay 3 nights.
Take the A504 towards Lisburn. The entrance is just off the road via Belvoir Park housing estate.

BELLEEK *Co Fermanagh* — Map 10 B2

LOUGH NAVAR FOREST SITE RAC L
☎ (0232) 650111
Open: All year
Size: 10 touring pitches

Charges on application - permit required.
Planned walks, picnic area, nature trail and fishing (permit necessary) available on site. All caravans/ tents must have chemical toilets. Maximum stay 3 nights.
10 miles E of Belleek on the A46.

CARNLOUGH *Co Antrim* — Map 10 C1

Bay View Caravan Site
☎ (0574) 885685
Open: April-October
Size: 4 acres, 68 touring pitches. 13 WCs

  🦽 Facilities for Disabled   🚐 Caravans accepted   🚙 Motor caravans   ⛺ Tents   🧺 Laundry room   🛒 Shop

☐ 🏕️ 🚐 🏕️ ☐ ☐ ☐ ☐ ☐ ☐ 🐕

¼ mile S of Carnlough on A2.

CASTLEWELLAN Co Down — Map 10 C2

Castlewellan Forest Park
☎ (03967) 78664
Open: March-October
Size: 6 acres, 90 touring pitches. 4 hot showers, 2b WCs

☐ 🏕️ 🚐 🏕️ ☐ ☐ ☕ ☐ ☐ ☐ 🐕

Off A25 at Castlewellan. Site signed.

CASTLEWELLAN FOREST SITE　　RAC L
☎ (0232) 650111
Open: All year
Size: 19 touring pitches

☐ 🏕️ 🚐 🏕️ ☐ ☐ ☐ ☐ ☐ ☐ 🐕

Charges on application - permit required.
Planned walks, gardens and Arboretum. Fishing is available on site (permit necessary). All caravans/ tents must have chemical toilets. Maximum stay 3 nights.
Entrance on Bannanstown Road (off A25), ½ mile E of main forest entrance.

CLAUDY Co Londonderry — Map 10 C1

LEARMOUNT FOREST SITE　　RAC L
☎ (0232) 650111
Open: All year
Size: 14 touring pitches

☐ 🏕️ 🚐 🏕️ ☐ ☐ ☐ ☐ ☐ ☐ 🐕

Charges on application - permit required.
Close to Sperrin Mountains, planned riverside walks and forest picnic areas. All caravans/tents must have chemical toilets. Maximum stay 3 nights.
From Dungiven travel SW for 8 miles on the B44.

LOUGHERMORE FOREST SITE　　RAC L
☎ (0232) 650111
Open: All year
Size: 14 touring pitches

☐ 🏕️ 🚐 🏕️ ☐ ☐ ☐ ☐ ☐ ☐ 🐕

Charges on application - permit required.
Basic site with mountain scenery and forest walks. All caravans/tents must have chemical toilets. Maximum stay 3 nights.
The site is 4 miles NE of Claudy on the B69.

CLOGHER Co Tyrone — Map 10 C2

FARDROSS FOREST SITE　　RAC L
☎ (0232) 650111
Open: All year
Size: 14 touring pitches

☐ 🏕️ 🚐 🏕️ ☐ ☐ ☐ ☐ ☐ ☐ 🐕

Charges on application - permit required.
Basic site with recreation area. All caravans/tents must have chemical toilets. Maximum stay 3 nights.
2 miles SW of Clogher on A4 (T) turn S onto unclassified road, signposted 'Fardross Forest'.

COLERAINE Co Londonderry — Map 10 C1

Castlerock Holiday Park
24 Sea Road, Castlerock, BT51 4TN.
☎ (0265) 848381
Open: Easter-October
Size: 12 acres, 50 touring pitches. 6 hot showers, 30 WCs. 190 static caravans

☐ ☐ 🚐 🏕️ 🛶 ☐ ☕ ☐ ☐ 🏠 🐕

6 miles W of Coleraine. Route signposted to Castlerock.

MARINA CARAVAN PARK　　RAC L
64 Portstewart Road. ☎ (0265) 44768
Open: 1 April-30 September
Size: 1½ (4) acres, 5 touring pitches, all level, all with hardstanding, 40 static caravans. 2 hot showers, 1 WC, 1 CWP

☐ 🏕️ 🚐 🏕️ 🛶 ☐ ☐ ☐ ☐ ☐ 🐕

(1991) Car & caravan, Motor caravan £6, Car & tent, M/cycle & tent £3-£6; awn £1
A spacious riverside town site with adjoining marina. Children's play area and TV room. No gas available. Shop 800 metres. Restaurant and swimming pool 1¼ miles.
1 mile N of Coleraine on A2.

SPRINGWELL FOREST SITE　　RAC L
☎ (0232) 650111
Open: All year
Size: 12 touring pitches. WCs

☐ 🏕️ 🚐 🏕️ ☐ ☐ ☐ ☐ ☐ ☐ 🐕

Charges on application - permit required.
Simple site in scenic area. Maximum stay 3 nights.
The site is 7 miles SW of Coleraine on the A37 (T) - entrance near forest housing site.

COOKSTOWN Co Tyrone — Map 10 C2

DRUM MANOR FOREST SITE　　RAC L
☎ (0232) 650111
Open: All year
Size: 30 touring pitches. WCs

☐ 🏕️ 🚐 🏕️ ☐ ☐ ☐ ☐ ☐ ☐ 🐕

Charges on application - permit required.
Park site with planned walks, butterfly garden, stone garden and interpretive centre. Maximum stay 3 nights.
3 miles W of Cookstown on A505 turn S on to B159, site in ½ mile.

CUSHENDALL Co Antrim — Map 10 C1

Cushendall Caravan Park
62 Coast Road. ☎ (026 672) 699
Open: March-October
Size: 1 (6) acres, 16 touring pitches. 2 hot showers, 11 WCs. Static caravans

☐ 🏕️ 🚐 🏕️ 🛶 ☐ ☐ ☐ ☐ ☐ 🐕

In Cushendall on coast road.

GLENARIFF FOREST SITE　　RAC L
☎ (0232) 650111
Open: All year
Size: 20 touring pitches. WCs

☐ 🏕️ 🚐 🏕️ ☐ ☐ ☐ ☐ ☐ ☐ 🐕

🍴 Snacks/take away ☒ Restaurant ☐ Swimming pool 🏠 Shelter for campers 🐕 Dogs accepted　　**239**

Charges on application - permit required.
Simple site in the Glens of Antrim. Maximum stay 3 nights.
The site is on the A43, 6 miles SW of Cushendall.

CUSHENDUN Co Antrim — Map 10 C1

CUSHENDUN CARAVAN PARK RAC L
14 Glendun Road, BT44 0PX.
☎ (026674) 254
Open: March-October
Size: ½ acre, 15 touring pitches, all level, 50 static static caravans. 4 hot showers, 10 WCs, 1 CWP

(1991) Car & caravan, Motor caravan, Car & tent, M/cycle* & tent £6.50
Cushendun is in a rural setting on the edge of a village, it is secluded and well-maintained, and close to beach, fishing and golf. Shop and restaurant ¼ mile. Swimming pool 12 miles. ½ mile N of Cushendun.

DUNGANNON Co Tyrone — Map 10 C2

PARKANAUR FOREST SITE RAC L
☎ (0232) 650111
Open: All year
Size: 10 touring pitches

Charges on application - permit required.
Forest Park, deer enclosure, gardens and indoor exhibition on site. All caravans/tents must have chemical toilets. Maximum stay 3 nights.
4 miles W of Dungannon on the A45.

ENNISKILLEN Co Fermanagh — Map 10 B2

The Castle Inn
Monea. ☎ (036589) 609
Open: All year
Size: 1 acre, 20 touring pitches. 2 hot showers, 2 WCs

2 miles SW of Enniskillen (A4), turn NW on to B81 for 5 miles. Turn right at Monea church. Site ½ mile.

FLORENCE COURT FOREST SITE RAC L
☎ (0232) 650111
Open: All year
Size: 10 touring pitches

Charges on application - permit required.
A park site with planned walks, picnic places and walled garden with Florence Court yew tree. Close to Marble Arch cave system. All caravans/tents must have chemical toilets. Maximum stay 3 nights.
Take the A4 SW from Enniskillen, turn S on to the A32, then after 4 miles turn W on to unclassified road signposted 'Forest Park'.

IRVINESTOWN Co Fermanagh — Map 10 B2

CASTLE ARCHDALE COUNTRY PARK RAC L
BT94 1PP. ☎ (03656) 21333
Open: Easter-30 September
Size: 10 (60) acres, 58 touring pitches, all level, all

with hardstanding, 136 static caravans. 24 hot showers, 58 WCs, 3 CWPs

(1991) Car & caravan, Motor caravan £7.44, Car & tent, M/cycle & tent £4-£7.44
Situated in a country park on the shires of Lough Erne and surrounded by woodland, this parkland site has its own children's play area and a club. There's a marina nearby. 6 caravans for hire.
From Irvinestone, travel W to Lisnarrick turn S on the B82 for 1 mile, turn right to site on shores of Lough Erne.

KILKEEL Co Down — Map 10 C2

Chestnutt Caravan Park
Cranfield, BT34 4LW. ☎ (06937) 62653
Open: Easter-October
Size: 13½ acres, 20 touring pitches. 7 hot showers, 18 WCs. 230 static caravans

SW from Kilkeel to Greencastle crossroads, then turn S for site.

Leestone Caravan Park
Leestone Road. ☎ (06937) 62567
Open: Easter-October
Size: 10 acres, 25 touring pitches. 4 hot showers, 2b WCs. Static caravans

From N towards Kilkeel (A2), turn left signposted Leestone. Site 1 mile.

Sandilands Caravan Park
Cranfield Road, BT34 4LQ.
☎ (06937) 63634
Open: Easter-November
Size: 25 acres, 50+ touring pitches. 4 hot showers, 11 WCs. Static caravans

Beach site with views of Mourne Mountains.

KILLOUGH Co Down — Map 10 C2

Minerstown Caravan Park
☎ (039685) 527
Open: Easter-November
Size: 16 acres, 70+ touring pitches. 2 hot showers, 12 WCs

Site at Minerstown on A2 3½ miles W of Killough.

LARNE Co Antrim — Map 10 C1

CURRAN CARAVAN PARK RAC L
131 Curran Road. ☎ (0574) 273797
Open: Good Friday-End September
Size: 4 acres, 29 touring pitches, all level, all with hardstanding, 4 with elec. 4 hot showers, 7 WCs

Car & caravan, Motor caravan £5, Car & tent, M/cycle & tent £3; elec £1
Modern, award-winning caravan park, within ¼ mile of sea and ferry terminals and ½ mile from town centre. Facilities within park include bowling green, kiddies' playground, putting and picnicking,

with tennis courts, swimming and squash courts nearby. *Shop and restaurant 1 km. Swimming pool ½ km. No gas available.*
¼ mile from Larne Harbour Terminal on Curran Road, travelling towards Larne town centre.

Carnfunnock Country Park
Coast Road.
☎ (0574) 270541
Open: Good Friday-End September
Size: 1 (473) acres, 29 touring pitches. 2 hot showers, 4 WCs

3½ miles N of Larne.

Browns Bay Caravan Park
Browns Bay Road, Island Magee
☎ (09603) 82497
Open: Good Friday-End September
Size: 1 acre, 29 touring pitches. 2 hot showers, 5 WCs

At Island Magee (B90), between Larne and Carrickfergus, off A2.

Benone Caravans
Benone Avenue, Magilligan
☎ (05047) 50324
Open: Easter-October
Size: 8 acres, 35+ touring pitches. 6 hot showers, 15 WCs. 10 static caravans

Site midway between Coleraine and Limavady on A2.

ROE VALLEY COUNTRY PARK   RAC L
Leap Road, BT49 9NN.
☎ (05047) 22074
Open: All year
Size: 1 (1½) acre, 10 touring pitches, all with hardstanding, 8 level pitches, 10 static caravans. 2 hot showers, 2 cold showers, 2 WCs, 1 CWP

(1991) Car & caravan, Motor caravan £7.44, Car & tent, M/cycle & tent £4
An area of birchwood close to the countryside, centre has been set aside for a small caravan and camping site together with an amenity building. Swimming pool ¾ mile. No gas available.
2 miles S of Limavady off the B192, Limavady to Dungiven road.

Lisnaskea Caravan Park
Mullynascarty.
☎ (0365) 721040
Open: Easter-October
Size: 5½ acres, 25 touring pitches. 4 hot showers, 16 WCs

3½ miles SE of Enniskillen (A4), take B514 for Lisnaskea. Site 1½ miles before village.

SHARE CENTRE   RAC L
Smith's Strand. ☎ (036 57) 22122
Open: Easter-31 October
Size: 15 touring pitches, all level, 2 static caravans, chalets. Hot showers, WCs, 1 CWP

Charges on application.
The site is part of the Share Residential Activity Centre for able-bodied and handicapped people. Sports facilities are excellent and there is an organised programme of tuition which includes sailing, windsurfing, canoeing and archery.
Travelling from Belfast on the main Enniskillen road turn at Maguiresbridge, signposted Lisnaskea. In Lisnaskea turn right towards Derrylin. Smith's Strand and Share Centre signposted on right in 4 miles.

Rathlin Caravan Park
45 Moss Road. ☎ (0247) 861386
Open: April-October
Size: 4 acres, 6 touring pitches. 1 hot shower, 12 WCs

From Newtownards towards Millisle on B172, site ½ mile before Millisle.

Seaview
1 Donaghadee Road. ☎ (0247) 248
Open: April-October
Size: 1 (17¾) acres, 25 touring pitches. 4 hot showers, 2b WCs. Static caravans

8 miles SE of Bangor on A2.

Woodlands Caravan Park
24 Drumfad Road. ☎ (0247) 861309
Open: Easter-October
Size: 8 acres, 4+ touring pitches. 11 WCs. 90 static caravans

1½ miles S of Millisle, off A2.

Moira Demesne Site
☎ (0846) 611516
Open: All year
Size: 2 acres, 15 touring pitches. 2 hot showers, 5 WCs

From M1 junction 9, follow A3 SW to Moira for ½ mile.

Tollymore Forest Park
☎ (03967) 22428
Open: March-November
Size: 8 acres, 90 touring pitches. 4 hot showers, 20 WCs

2 miles W of Newcastle, off B180.

■ Snacks/take away ✕ Restaurant ◺ Swimming pool ▣ Shelter for campers 🐾 Dogs accepted   241

PETTIGOE Co Fermanagh — Map 10 B2

CLONELLY FOREST SITE — RAC L
☎ (0232) 650111
Open: All year
Size: 12 touring pitches

Charges on application - permit required.
Basic site on main touring route to Donegal, near to Lough Erne. All caravans/tents must have chemical toilets. Maximum stay 3 nights.
2 miles W of Clonelly on the A35.

PORTBALLINTRAE Co Antrim — Map 10 C1

Portballintrae Caravan Park
60 Ballaghmore Road, BT57 8RL.
☎ (02657) 31478
Open: April-October
Size: 3 acres, 44 touring pitches. 4 hot showers, 27 WCs. 151 static caravans

From Bushmills travel W on the A2 for ¼ mile, turn N on the B145 to Portballintrae.

PORTRUSH Co Antrim — Map 10 C1

CARRICK DHU CARAVAN CAMP — RAC L
Ballyreagh Road. ☎ (0265) 823712
Open: 2 April-1 October
Size: 23 acres, 45 touring pitches, all level, 420 static caravans. 8 hot showers, 57 WCs, 4 CWPs

Charges on application.
A sheltered, spacious site, with children's play area, close to the beach. Restaurant 500 yards. Swimming pool 5 miles.
1½ miles W of Portrush, or 2¼ miles E of Portstewart on A2.

Margoth Caravan Park
126 Dunluce Road.
☎ (0265) 822531
Open: March-October
Size: 40 acres, 80 touring pitches. 4 hot showers, 4b WCs

2 miles E of Portrush on A6.

PORTSTEWART Co Londonderry — Map 10 C1

JUNIPER HILL CARAVAN CAMP — RAC L
70 Ballyreagh Road. ☎ (026583) 2023
Open: 2 April-1 October
Size: 25 acres, 75 touring pitches, all level, 10 with elec, 405 static caravans. 7 hot showers, 36 WCs, 4 CWPs

Charges on application.
Near the sea and sandy beaches, this fine site has a children's play area and offers a full summer programme of activities, including dances and various competitions. Tarmac roads. Restaurant ½ mile.
At 1¾ miles E of Portstewart, or 2 miles W of Portrush on A2.

Portstewart Holiday Park
34 Mui Road. ☎ (026583) 3308
Open: Easter-October
Size: 3 acres, 50+ touring pitches. 4 hot showers, 12 WCs. Static caravans

From S towards Portstewart, turn right at Burnside Hall for site.

ROSTREVOR Co Down

ROSTREVOR FOREST SITE — RAC L
☎ (0232) 650111
Open: All year
Size: 14 touring pitches

Charges on application - permits required.
Sheltered site with views of Rostrevor and Carlingford Lough. All caravans/tents must have chemical toilets. Maximum stay 3 nights.
The site is on the A2, 8 miles W of Kilkeel.

SHARNE'S HILL Co Antrim — Map 10 C1

BALLEYBOLEY FOREST SITE — RAC L
☎ (0232) 650111
Open: All year
Size: 10 touring pitches

Charges on application - permits required.
Basic site close to Larne ferry terminal. All caravans/tents must have chemical toilets. Maximum stay 3 nights.
Take the A8 SE from Larne for 4 miles, then take the A36 NW for 4 miles - site is on unclassified road S of A36 at Sharne's Hill.

STRANGFORD Co Down — Map 10 C2

Castleward
☎ (039686) 680
Open: All year
Size: 7 acres, 25+ touring pitches. 4 hot showers, 6 WCs

2 miles W of Strangford off A25. Site signed.

Seasonal variation of prices

Where a single price is given it may be a low season minimum charge - rates can increase considerably at peak periods and for extra people or vehicles.
Please confirm prices with the site when booking.

ⓓ Facilities for Disabled 🚐 Caravans accepted 🚙 Motor caravans ⛺ Tents 🧺 Laundry room 🛒 Shop

Animals
(1) Dogs & Cats
As a precaution against rabies, the importation or landing of dogs or cats from all countries, except Great Britain, the Channel Islands and the Isle of Man, is strictly prohibited.
(2) Other Household Pets including Birds
Queries regarding the importation of household pets from Great Britain should be addressed to: Department of Agriculture, Veterinary Division, Kildare Street, Dublin 2. ☎ 789011.
The importation of animal pets and birds from other places abroad is not permitted.

Banks
Monday to Friday 1000 to 1230 hrs and 1330 to 1500 hrs (1700 hrs on Thursday).

Camping sites
Not all of the sites in the Republic of Ireland have been inspected by the RAC but all are recognised by the Irish Tourist Board as meeting their requirements for registration. To telephone the Republic of Ireland from the UK dial 010 353 (0001 for Dublin), followed by the area code and then the site number.

Currency
Irish punt.

Gas
'Calor gas (Cozen)' available in the Republic is supplied in containers which are not compatible with UK Calor gas equipment, unless an adaptor is used, nor can UK containers be refilled without such an adaptor.
'Camping gaz international' is freely available throughout the Republic.

General Information
Under no circumstances are travellers to bring into the country, in tins or otherwise any meat or poultry, meat or poultry products, milk or milk products whether in their baggage, on their persons or in their cars and caravans. Any such commodities found will be confiscated and the owner will be liable to legal penalties.

Motoring Information
(see also **Vehicle Protection in Ireland**)

Children in front seats
Not allowed under the age of 12 years unless the child has a suitable safety restraint.

Crash helmets
Compulsory for motorcyclists and passengers.

Drinking and driving
DO NOT drink and drive.

Drivers
Minimum age for drivers is 17 years.

Emergencies
Police, Fire, Ambulance ☎ 999.

Lighting
Fog lights may only be used in fog or falling snow.

Parking
The usual restrictions apply to parking as in Great Britain. Parking meters are in use. They operate from Monday to Saturday from 0800 to 1830 hrs and the maximum parking time is 2 hours. Free use of unexpired time on meters is authorised. On-the-spot fines may be levied for parking offences.

Petrol
Leaded: super grade (98 octane).
Unleaded available: (95 octane).
A leaflet on petrol stations supplying unleaded petrol is available from RAC Touring Information, South Croydon.

Seat belts
Drivers and front seat passengers must wear seat belts, if fitted.

▣ Snacks/take away ☒ Restaurant ◩ Swimming pool ▣ Shelter for campers ⋈ Dogs accepted

Signalling
Horns must not be used between 2330 hrs and 0700 hrs on any road where a permanent speed limit is in force.

Speed limits
Built-up areas 30 mph (48 kmh); outside built-up areas 55 mph (88 kmh). On certain roads which are clearly marked the speed limit is 40 or 50 mph (64 or 80 kmh). These limits also apply to a car and trailer.

Temporary importation of vehicles
Drivers of motor caravans, caravans and trailers will be issued with a temporary importation permit in the form of a windscreen sticker and a control form by Irish Customs at the port of arrival. A temporarily imported vehicle cannot be driven by an Irish resident.

Traffic offences
If a motorist has committed an offence the Garda Siochana (Civil Guard) may issue the person with a notice instructing the offender to pay a fine within 21 days at a Garda Station. The offender has an alternative choice of letting the case go to court.

UK driving licence
Accepted.

Warning triangle
Recommended.

Passports
British citizens born in the United Kingdom do not require a passport to visit Ireland.

Prices
Prices are given in Irish punts.

Public Holidays
New Years Day, St Patrick's Day (17 March), Easter, first Monday in June and August, last Monday in October, Christmas.

Shipping Routes to the Republic of Ireland
For information on routes and prices contact:
B&I Line ☎ 071-499 5744
Sealink Stena Line ☎ (0233) 647047
P&O European Ferries ☎ (0304) 203388

Fishguard-Rosslare (Sealink Stena Line) (3½hr) - up to 2 departures daily

Holyhead-Dublin (B&I Line) (3½hr) - 2 departures daily

Holyhead-Dun Laoghaire (Sealink Stena Line) (3½hr) - up to 4 departures daily

Pembroke Dock-Rosslare (B&I Line) (4¼hr) - up to 2 departures daily

Swansea-Cork (Swansea Cork Ferries) (3½hr) - 2 departures daily (May-Sept)

Shops
Open Monday to Saturday 0900 to 1730/1800 hrs.

Vehicle Protection in Ireland
Problems just as complicated as those on the Continent may be encountered when touring the Irish Republic. The RAC is able to offer through Eurocover Ireland the same expertise and experience motorists on the Continent find so invaluable and inexpensive.

Full details are given in the RAC European Service Brochure, available at RAC offices.

ARKLOW Co Wicklow · Map 10 C3

Arklow Holidays
Ferrybank. ☎ (0402) 2156
Open: Easter-September
Size: 55 acres, 50 touring pitches. Hot showers, WCs. Static caravans

1 mile NE of Arklow.

ATHLONE Co Westmeath · Map 10 B2

LOUGH REE CARAVAN & CAMPING PARK RAC L
Ballykeeran. ☎ (0902) 78561
Open: May-September
Size: 5 acres, 10 touring pitches, all level, all with elec, 2 static caravans. 4 hot showers, 4 cold showers, 8 WCs, 1 CWP

(1991) Car & caravan, Motor caravan, Car & tent, M/cycle & tent £3 per adult, £1 per child; elec £1, awn £1; WS
On the shore of an inner lake of Lough Ree, where fishing, boating and swimming (no beginners) are all possible, this scenic site also has it own children's play area. Camping Gaz only. Shop 100 yards. Restaurant 150 yards. Swimming pool 3 miles.
3 miles NE of Athlone on T31 (N55).

BALLINDERRY VILLAGE Co Tipperary · Map 10 B3

THE TAVERN CARAVAN & CAMPING PARK RAC L
☎ (067) 22026
Open: 1 May-1 September
Size: 1 acre, 22 touring pitches, some with elec. Showers, WCs

Charges on application.
Site 1 mile from Lough Derg. Some gas available. Take the N65 SE from Portumna, just after Carrigahorig turn right onto R493. Travel through Terryglass to site in Ballinderry.

BALLYBUNION Co Kerry · Map 10 A3

PARKLANDS CARAVAN PARK RAC L
☎ (068) 27275
Open: Easter-30 September
Size: 2 (6) acres, 10 touring pitches, 6 with elec, all with hardstanding, 12 static caravans. 4 hot showers, 12 WCs, 2 CWPs

Charges on application.
Not far from the sea and beaches, this holiday site also has a tennis court and children's play area. 12 caravans for hire. Shop 150 yards. Restaurant 1 mile.
On main Listowel/Ballybunion road, 100 yards from Ballybunion/Tralee road junction.

BALLYHEIGUE Co Kerry · Map 10 A3

Ballyheigue Site
☎ (066) 33297
Open: June-October
Size: 3 acres, 40 touring pitches. 2 hot showers, 9 WCs

10 miles NW of Tralee on R551. Site by Texaco petrol station.

CASEY'S CARAVAN & CAMPING PARK · RAC L
☎ (066) 33195
Open: May-September
Size: 10 acres, 84 touring pitches, static caravans. Showers, WCs

Charges on application.
Close to beach. Some gas available. 6 caravans for hire (own WCs). Children's play area and TV room. Travel NW from Tralee on the R554, through Ardfert to Ballyheigue.

Whites Caravan Park
Sandhill Road. ☎ (066) 33284
Open: Spring Bank Holiday-September
Size: 18 acres, 40 touring pitches. 11 hot showers, 25 WCs. Static caravans

13 miles NW from Tralee on L105. Site beyond village.

BALLYHIERNAN Co Donegal · Map 10 B1

EEL BURN CARAVAN & CAMPING SITE RAC L
☎ (074) 59026
Open: 1 March-December
Size: 10 acres, 25 touring pitches, some with elec, 5 static caravans. Showers, WCs

Charges on application.
Situated on a sandy beach with children's play area. Some gas available. 3 caravans for hire.
2 miles N of Kindrum on the Fauad Head Road.

BALLYMACODA Co Cork · Map 10 B4

SONAS CARAVAN & CAMPING PARK RAC L
☎ (024) 98132
Open: 1 May-15 September
Size: 8 acres, 55 touring pitches, some with elec. Showers, WCs

Charges on application.
Site close to beach at Knockadoo Head. Children's play area and TV room. Some gas available. From Cork travel E on the N25. Turn right at Castlemartyr to Ladybridge then left to Ballymacoda. Site is 3½ miles through village to E.

BANDON Co Cork · Map 10 A4

MURRAYS CARAVAN & CAMPING PARK RAC L
Kilbrogan Farm. ☎ (023) 41232
Open: 1 April-30 September
Size: 1¼ (2) acres, 10 touring pitches, all level, 5 with elec, all with hardstanding. 2 hot showers, 2 cold showers, 6 WCs, 1 CWP

Car & caravan, Motor caravan, Car & tent, M/cycle & tent £1; all plus £1 per person; elec £1
A quiet site, an ideal centre from which to tour the South. Shop ¼ mile. Restaurant and swimming

---

■ Snacks/take away ☒ Restaurant ◺ Swimming pool ▣ Shelter for campers 🐕 Dogs accepted   **245**

pool ½ mile. Dogs must be kept on leads. "You forget your worries when you come to Murrays". Follow official signposts from town.

BANTRY Co Cork Map 10 A4

EAGLE POINT CARAVAN & CAMPING SITE ☗ L
Ballylickey.
☎ (027) 50630
Open: 1 May-30 September
Size: 20 acres, 125 touring pitches, 100 with elec, 100 level pitches, 65 with hardstanding. 16 hot showers, 2 cold showers, 25 WCS, 2 CWPs

▨▨▨▨▨▨☐☐☐☐☐☐

(1001) Car & caravan £6, Motor caravan £5, Car & tent, M/cycle & tent £5.50; all plus £1 per adult, 50p per child; extra persons £2; M/cycle £2.50; elec 50p
Spacious landscaped site. Swimming, boating, windsurfing and fishing on site. Camping Gaz only. Restaurant ¼ mile. Swimming pool 4 miles. Site 4 miles N of Bantry on the N71 (T65).

BELLAVARY Co Mayo Map 10 A2

CAMP CARROWKEEL CARAVAN & CAMPING PARK ☗ L
☎ (094) 31264
Open: 1 May-15 September
Size: 15 acres, 58 touring pitches, some with elec. Showers, WCs

☐▨▨▨▨▨▨✗☐☐▧

*Charges on application.
Fishing and swimming in river bordering site. Sport and entertainment available in nearby Castlebar. 10 miles from Pontoon and the beaches of Lough Conn.
From Dublin take the N4/N5 NE to Bellavary. Campsite is signed to the N 1 mile past village.*

BONMAHON Co Waterford Map 10 B4

BONMAHON CARAVAN & CAMPING PARK ☗ L
☎ (051) 92239
Open: June-September
Size: 8 acres, 60 touring pitches, some with elec. Showers, WCs

☐▨▨▨▨▨▨☐☐☐▧

*Charges on application.
Children's play area. Some gas available.
From Waterford travel S to Tramore. Then follow coast road W to Bonmahon.*

BOYLE Co Roscommon Map 10 B2

LOUGH KEY CARAVAN & CAMPING PARK ☗ L
☎ (044) 48761
Open: May-September
Size: 13½ acres, 72 touring pitches. Showers, WCs

☐▨▨▨▨☐☐☐☐☐☐

*Charges on application.
Forest park site with children's play area. Some gas available.
Site in Lough Key Forest Park 2 miles E of Boyle on the N side of the N4.*

CAHERDANIEL Co Kerry Map 10 A4

WAVESCREST CARAVAN & CAMPING PARK ☗ L
☎ (0667) 5188
Open: 1 April-28 September
Size: 4½ acres, 27 touring pitches, some with elec, 2 static caravans. Showers, WCs

☐▨▨▨▨▨☐☐☐☐▧

*Charges on application.
Overlooking the Kenmare River Bay, this site is a departure point for Skelligs Rock, Staigue Fort and Derrynane National Park. Some gas available.
From Kenmare take the N70 SW for 30 miles, site is on left just before Caherdaniel village.*

CAHIR Co Tipperary Map 10 B3

Apple Caravan & Camping Park
Moorstown. ☎ (052) 41459
Open: 15 May-30 September
Size: 3½ acres, 32 touring pitches. 2 hot showers, 5 WCs

☐▨▨▨▨▨☐☐☐▧☐

Site on the N24, 4 miles E of Cahir, 6 miles W of Clonmel.

CAMP Co Kerry Map 10 A3

SEASIDE CARAVAN & CAMPING PARK ☗ L
Tralee. ☎ (066) 30161
Open: Easter-End October
Size: 7 acres, 30 touring pitches. Hot showers, WCs

☐▨▨☐▨▨▨☐☐☐▧

*Charges on application.
Site on beach overlooking Tralee Bay. Some gas available.
From Tralee take the R559 SW. After 8 miles turn right onto the R560 towards Castlegregory. Turn right towards sea in 3 miles. Site signposted.*

CAPE CLEAR ISLAND Co Cork Map 10 A4

CUAS AN UISCE ☗ L
☎ (028) 39119
Open: June-end September
Size: 4 acres, 20 touring pitches. Showers, WCs

☐☐☐☐▨☐▧☐☐☐☐

*Charges on application.
Simple island site. Shop, pub and restaurant within walking distance. Some gas available.
Take the ferry from Baltimore to South Harbour, Cape Clear.*

CARRAROE Co Galway Map 10 A3

COILLEAN CARAVAN & CAMPING PARK ☗ L
☎ (091) 95189
Open: 1 April-30 September
Size: 3½ acres, 60 touring pitches. Showers, WCs

☐▨▨▨▨☐▧☐☐☐▧

*Charges on application.
Gently sloping site with views over Galway Bay. Some gas available.
Take the R336 W from Galway to Costelloe, where turn onto the R343 to Carraroe. Turn right at road signpost in village, then second left to site.*

CLONAKILTY Co Cork — Map 10 A4

DESERT HOUSE CARAVAN & CAMPING PARK — RAC L
Ring Road. ☎ (023) 33331
Open: Easter-30 September
Size: 4 acres, 36 touring pitches, 10 with elec,
14 with hardstanding, all level. 2 hot showers,
6 WCs, 1 CWP

▢ 🚐 🚙 ⛺ 🛶 ▢ ▢ ▢ ▢ ▢ 🐕

Car & caravan, Motor caravan £4.25, Car & tent,
M/cycle & tent £3.75; all plus 30p per person; elec
£1, awn £1
cc Visa/B'card
*This park is overlooking Clonakilty Bay. Families
can enjoy watching the activities of farm life.
Nearby is the historic town of Clonakilty, sandy
beaches, water sports, golf, angling and forest
walks. Shop and restaurant 500 yards. No gas
available.*
½ mile E of Clonakilty, ¼ mile off main Cork/
Clonakilty road, N71 route.

CLONMEL Co Tipperary — Map 10 B3

POWER'S THE POT CARAVAN PARK — RAC L
Harney's Cross. ☎ (052) 23085
Open: May-end September
Size: 6 acres, 19 touring pitches, some with elec.
Hot showers, WCs

▢ 🚐 🚙 ⛺ ▢ 🛗 🍴 ▢ ▢ ▢ 🐕

Charges on application.
*Site at the side of the Coneragh Mountains with
superb views. Traditional music in season.
Children's play area. Some gas available.* Take
the R678 E towards Waterford. Turn left
towards Knocknaree. Site on left.

CONG Co Mayo — Map 10 A2

Hydeoute Campsite
☎ (092) 46086
Open: June-September
Size: 10 acres, 50 touring pitches. 2 WCs

▢ 🚐 🚙 ⛺ ▢ ▢ ▢ ▢ ▢ ▢ 🐕

½ mile W of Cong on L101.

CORK Co Cork — Map 10 B4

CORK CARAVAN COMPANY LTD CARAVAN PARK — RAC L
Rathmacullig West, Farmer's Cross
☎ (021) 963749
Open: 1 April-31 October
Size: 5 acres, 80 touring pitches, some with elec.
Hot showers, WCs

▢ 🚐 🚙 ⛺ 🛶 🛗 ▢ ▢ ▢ ▢ 🐕

Charges on application.
*A rural site but within easy reach of Cork City.
Children's playground and games room. Some gas
available.*
3½ miles SW of Cork City on R600, on route to
Kinsale and Cork Airport. Follow camping signs
opposite airport entrance.

Cork City Caravan & Camping Park
Togher Road. ☎ (021) 961866
Open: All year

Size: 2 acres, 40 touring pitches. 5 hot showers,
9 WCs

▢ 🚐 🚙 ⛺ 🛶 ▢ ▢ ▢ ▢ 🏠 🐕

From Cork towards Killarney on N22, at Victoria
Cross, fork left onto Wilton Road. At roundabout by
hospital, turn left on Glasheen Road and continue
via Clashdor Road to Togher Road.

COURTOWN Co Wexford — Map 10 C3

COURTOWN CARAVAN PARK — RAC L
Ballinatray. ☎ (055) 25280
Open: 1 June-31 August
Size: 3½ acres, 35 touring pitches, all with elec,
20% level pitches, 5 with hardstanding, 150 static
caravans. 12 hot showers, 16 WCs, 1 CWP

♿ 🚐 🚙 ⛺ 🛶 🛗 ☕ 🍴 ▢ 🏠 ▢

Car & caravan, Motor caravan, Car & tent, M/cycle
& tent £8.50; elec £1
*Gently sloping family site, near holiday village and
harbour, offering many attractions including 10 pin
bowling. 40 caravans for hire (own WCs).
Swimming pool ½ mile.*
200 yards off main Gorey to Courtown L31 road.

PARKLANDS HOLIDAY PARK — RAC L
Ardamine, Gorey. ☎ (055) 25202
Open: May-September
Size: 3½ (14) acres, 80 touring pitches, 75 level
pitches, all with elec, all with hardstanding,
167 static caravans. 10 hot showers, 19 WCs,
2 CWPs

▢ 🚐 🚙 ▢ 🛶 🛗 ☕ 🍴 ▢ ▢ 🐕

(1991) Car & caravan, Motor caravan £8; elec £1
cc Major cards
*A well-maintained site with touring facilities, in a
mature woodland setting. 50 caravans for hire
(own WCs). No gas available. Swimming pool
2 km.*
2 miles S of Courtown on L31 (R742).

POULSHONE CARAVAN PARK — RAC L
Poulshone. ☎ (01) 908993
Open: Easter-30 September
Size: 4 acres, 6 touring pitches, all level, all with
elec, all with hardstanding. 3 hot showers, 10 WCs,
1 CWP

▢ 🚐 🚙 ▢ ▢ ▢ ▢ ▢ ▢ ▢ ▢

Car & caravan, Motor caravan £9; elec £1, awn £2
*A sheltered site overlooking the beach with its own
children's play area. No gas available. Shop 1 mile.
Restaurant 1½ miles.*
2 miles S of Courtown on L31 (R742) turn E at sign
for Poulshone. Site at white gates on right in
½ mile.

CROOKHAVEN Co Cork — Map 10 A4

BARLEY COVE CARAVAN & CAMPING PARK — RAC L
☎ (028) 35302
Open: 2 May-20 September
Size: 9 acres, 105 touring pitches, all level, 60 with
elec, 45 with hardstanding, 35 static caravans.
8 hot showers, 21 WCs, 1 CWP

▢ 🚐 🚙 ⛺ ▢ 🛗 ☕ 🍴 ▢ 🏠 ▢

Car & caravan £5.50, Motor caravan £4.50, Car &
tent, M/cycle & tent £5.50; all plus £1 per adult, 50p

🍴 Snacks/take away   ✖ Restaurant   🏊 Swimming pool   🏠 Shelter for campers   🐕 Dogs accepted

per child; elec £1, awn £1
Family-run holiday park at the Land's End of Ireland. Fabulous scenery, top class amenities, entertainment nightly nearby. Children's club, pitch and putt, outdoor barbecue. 35 caravans for hire (own WCs). Swimming pool 4 miles.
N71 from Cork to Bandon, R589 Bandon to Bantry, R591 to Crookhaven just before Bantry.

CROSSMOLINA *Co Mayo*　Map 10 A2

HINEY'S CARAVAN AND CAMPING PARK　RAC L
Mullinmore Street. ☎ (096) 31202
Open: March-end October
Size: 3 acres, 26 touring pitches, some with elec, 20 static caravans. Showers, WCs

Charges on application.
The site is within walking distance of trout fishing on Lough Conn. Sports centre nearby. Some gas available. 20 caravans for hire.
The site is at Crossmolina, 8 miles W of Ballina on the N59.

CURRACLOE *Co Wexford*　Map 10 C3

O'GORMAN'S CARAVAN & CAMPING PARK　RAC L
☎ (053) 37110
Open: April-September
Size: 7½ acres, 81 touring pitches, static caravans. Showers, WCs

Charges on application.
Children's play area. Some gas available. 9 caravans for hire.
From Wexford take the R741 N then turn E on to R742 to Curracloe.

DINGLE *Co Kerry*　Map 10 A3

Ballydavid Campsite
Ballydavid. ☎ (066) 55143
Open: May-September
Size: 1 acre, 26 touring pitches. 4 hot showers, 8 WCs

Take T68 to Dingle, then follow signs to Gallarus Oratory. Site 300 yards from Oratory.

DOOGORT *Co Mayo*　Map 10 A2

SEAL CAVES CARAVAN PARK　RAC L
The Strand, Achill Island. ☎ (098) 43262
Open: 1 April-30 September
Size: 2½ (3) acres, 28 touring pitches, 22 with elec, all level, all with hardstanding, 4 static caravans. 2 CWPs

Car & caravan, Motor caravan, Car & tent, M/cycle & tent £4.50, all plus 30p per person; Car, M/cycle £3; elec £1
Sheltered site, near safe, sandy, bathing beach, part level, part sloped and part terraced, all of it green except for the caravan hardstandings. The camping area is sheltered by a fuchsia hedge, the roads are tarmac surfaced. 4 caravans for hire. Restaurant 1 mile. Kosen gas and Camping Gaz.
At 5 miles W of Achill Sound on the L141 (R319) at

Bunnacurry, turn right for 3 miles, turn left to Doogort Beach.

DOOLIN *Co Clare*　Map 10 A3

NAGLE'S CARAVAN & CAMPING PARK　RAC L
☎ (065) 74127
Open: May-End September
Size: 3 acres, 40 touring pitches. Showers, WCs

Charges on application.
Site beside the quay at Doolin. Convenient base for trips to the Aran Islands. Some gas available.
From Lahinch take the L54 'Cliffs of Moher' road to Doolin.

DROGHEDA *Co Meath*　Map 10 C2

Mosney Holiday Centre
Mosney. ☎ (041) 29200
Open: May-August
Size: 3 acres, 70 touring pitches. Hot showers, WCs. Static caravans

Off T1 between Drogheda and Balbriggan. Site signed from Julianstown and Gormanston.

DUNCORMICK *Co Wexford*　Map 10 C4

St Bernard's Caravan & Camping Park
Johnstown. ☎ (051) 63109
Open: from Easter
Size: 1½ acres, 21 touring pitches. 3 hot showers, 4 WCs

From Rosslare Harbour, take N25 (T8) to Tagoat. Fork left on to L128A via Bridgetown to Duncormick.

DUNGARVAN *Co Waterford*　Map 10 B4

CASEY'S CARAVAN PARK　RAC L
Clonea. ☎ (058) 41919
Open: May-September
Size: 3 (15½) acres, 20 touring pitches, 4 with elec, 10 level pitches, 10 with hardstanding, 110 static caravans. 6 hot showers, 6 cold showers, 26 WCs, 1 CWP

(1991) Car & caravan, Motor caravan, Car & tent, M/cycle & tent £7; elec 75p; WS
A spacious site with direct access to a lovely beach. Children's play area, TV room, games room and crazy golf. Shop, restaurant and swimming pool 50 yards.
Located 3 miles from Dungarvan, 1 mile from T63 (R675), 2½ miles off N25, site near beach.

EASKEY *Co Sligo*　Map 10 B2

ATLANTIC 'N' RIVERSIDE CARAVAN & CAMPING PARK　RAC L
☎ (096) 49001
Open: Mid April-Mid September
Size: 5 acres, 50 touring pitches. Hot showers, WCs

Charges on application.

Close to beach. Fishing on site. Some gas available.
Take the N59 W from Sligo to Dromore West, where fork right on to the R297 to Easkey. Call in at village P.O. to register.

ENNIS *Co Clare* Map 10 A3

Knockatooreen
Kilkishen. ☎ (061) 72219
Open: April-September
Size: 1 acre, 15 touring pitches. 2 WCs

	🚐	🚙	⛺						

6 miles W of Limerick on T11, at Cratloe turn N for 10 miles to Kilkishen. In Kilkishen, take Broadford Road. Site 1 mile.

FETHARD-ON-SEA *Co Wexford* Map 10 C4

OCEAN ISLAND CARAVAN & CAMPING PARK RAC L
Booley Hill. ☎ (051) 97148
Open: Easter-30 September
Size: 3 (5) acres, 10 touring pitches, 6 with elec, 2 level pitches, 8 with hardstanding, 30 static caravans. 2 hot showers, 2 cold showers, 6 WCs, 1 CWP

	🚐	🚙	⛺	🚿	🔌			🏠	🐕

(1991) Car & caravan, Motor caravan, Car & tent, M/cycle & tent £5; all plus 25p per person; elec £1, awn £1; WS
A seaside site, with children's play area.
16 caravans for hire (own WCs). Restaurant 1 mile. Swimming pool 1½ miles.
16 miles S of New Ross on L159 (R734) or 20 miles W of Wexford Town, signed for Fethard-on-Sea.

GALLARUS-DINGLE *Co Kerry* Map 10 A3

CAMPAIL THEACH AN ARAGAIL RAC L
☎ (066) 55143
Open: 1 May-25 September
Size: 3 acres, 36 touring pitches. Showers, WCs

	🚐	🚙	⛺			☕			

Charges on application.
The most westerly campsite in the EC, with views over Smerwick Harbour and the mountains. Children's play area. Some gas available. Tourist information available on site.
5 miles W of Dingle follow Gallarus Oratory signs.

GALWAY *Co Galway* Map 10 A3

BARNA HOUSE CARAVAN PARK RAC L
Barna Road, Barna. ☎ (091) 92469
Open: 1 May-28 September
Size: 2 (5½) acres, 18 touring pitches, 12 with elec, 6 level pitches, 12 with hardstanding, 30 static caravans, 5 flats. 6 hot showers, 2 cold showers, 12 WCs, 1 CWP

	🚐	🚙	⛺	🔌				🏠	🐕

Car & caravan, Motor caravan, Car & tent, M/cycle & tent £5, plus 50p per person, 25p per child; M/cycle £2.50; elec £1, awn £1; WS
A secluded site, close to Silver Strand, which caters for family holidays. There's a children's play area. 14 caravans and 5 flats for hire (own WCs). Shop adjacent. Restaurant 1 mile. Swimming pool

---

1½ miles.
Situated at Barna on the L100 (R336), 3 miles W of Galway. Use the new Corrib River bridge to by-pass Galway City.

Ballyloughane Caravan Park
Renmore. ☎ (091) 55338
Open: April-September
Size: 1½ acres, 50 touring pitches. 2 hot showers, 5 WCs

	🚐	🚙	⛺	🔌	🐕				

2 miles E of Galway on T4 (N6).

GLANDORE *Co Cork* Map 10 A4

THE MEADOW CAMPING PARK RAC L
☎ (028) 33280
Open: All year
Size: 1 acre, 19 touring pitches. Showers, WCs

		🚙	⛺						

Charges on application.
Small site close to Glandore harbour. Some gas available.
Take the N71 SW from Cork to Rosscarbery where turn S on to R597 to Glandore.

GLEN OF ATHERLOW *Co Tipperary* Map 10 B3

BALLINACOURTY HOUSE CARAVAN & CAMPING PARK RAC L
☎ (062) 56230
Open: May-Mid September
Size: 4 acres, 58 touring pitches, some with elec. Hot showers, WCs

	🚐	🚙	⛺	🔌	🐕	☕		🐕	

Charges on application.
The site is part of an 18th-century estate with tennis, mini-golf, wine bar and campers' breakfast on site. Some gas available.
From Tipperary take the R664 S to Newtown, then take the R663 SE for 3 miles, estate signposted on N side of road.

GLENBEIGH *Co Kerry* Map 10 A4

GLENROSS CARAVAN & CAMPING PARK RAC L
☎ (066) 68451
Open: 8 May-6 September
Size: 2 (4) acres, 18 touring pitches, all with elec, all with hardstanding, 12 level pitches, 6 static caravans. 6 hot showers, 6 cold showers, 10 WCs, 1 CWP

	🚐	🚙	⛺	🔌				🏠	🐕

Car & caravan, Motor caravan, Car & tent, M/cycle & tent £6-£6.50, plus 50p per adult, 25p per child; M/cycle £3-£3.50; elec £1, awn £1.50
Family-run caravan/tent tourist site, close to beach and shops, adjacent to Glenbeigh Hotel. 6 caravans for hire (own WCs). Shop and restaurant ½ mile. No gas available.
On main ring of Kerry road, ½ mile from Glenbeigh village.

GLENGARRIFF *Co Cork* Map 10 A4

O'SHEA'S CAMPING SITE RAC L
Inchantaggart. ☎ (027) 63140
Open: March-October

Size: 3 acres, 30 touring pitches, 10 with elec. 4 hot showers, 1 cold shower, 5 WCs, 1 CWP

	⛺	⛟	🅰							🐕

Car & caravan, Motor caravan, Car & tent, M/cycle* & tent £1, all plus £2 per adult, 50p per child; extra adults 50p; M/cycle* £1; elec 50p
A beautiful, landscaped garden site adjacent to Bantry Bay, sheltered with friendly atmosphere. Lake, river and sea fishing close by; surfing, boat trips, forest walks, mountain climbing. Charges include hot showers. Shop and restaurant 1 mile. Swimming pool 11 miles. No gas available.
1 mile W of Glengarriff on Castletownbere Road.

Pine Cottage
☎ (027) 63110
Open: April-October
Size: 3 acres, 18 touring pitches. Hot showers, 6 WCs. Static caravans

	⛺	⛟	🅰							🐕

2 miles SW of Glengarriff on L61.

KENMARE *Co Kerry*   Map 10 A4

RING OF KERRY CARAVAN & CAMPING PARK   RAC L
☎ (064) 41366
Open: All year
Size: 10 acres, 60 touring pitches, some with elec. Hot showers, WCs

	⛺	⛟	🅰	🅰						🐕

Charges on application.
Close to Kenmare town centre. Evening entertainment including traditional music available in town. Children's play area and TV room.
The site is 4 miles W of Kenmare on the N70 `Ring of Kerry' road.

KERRYKEEL *Co Donegal*   Map 10 B1

ROCKHILL CARAVAN & CAMPING PARK   RAC L
☎ (074) 50012
Open: April-September
Size: 25 acres, 40 touring pitches, some with elec. 8 hot showers, 21 WCs

	⛺	⛟	🅰	🅰	🐾					🐕

Charges on application.
A spacious site, overlooking Mulroy Bay, with children's play area. Some gas available. Shop open July-August.
On L78 (R246) between Letterkenny and Portsalon on the E shore of Mulroy Bay.

KILCORNAN *Co Limerick*   Map 10 B3

CURRAGHCHASE CARAVAN PARK   RAC L
☎ (061) 86349
Open: Whitsun-Mid September
Size: 39 acres, touring pitches, some with elec. Showers, WCs

	⛺	⛟	🅰	🅰	🐾					🐕

Charges on application.
Country site with native trails, forest walks and historic ruins nearby. Some gas available.
From Limerick take the N69 W to Kilcornan, turn S at Coach Inn to site.

KILKEE *Co Clare*   Map 10 A3

COLLINS' CARAVAN & CAMPING PARK   RAC L
Kilrush Road.
☎ (065) 56140
Open: 1 May-31 October
Size: 4 acres, 20 touring pitches, some with elec. Showers, WCs

	⛺	⛟	🅰							🐕

Charges on application.
The site is 100 yards from the town centre and 300 yards from the beach. Some washing machines available.
Approaching Kilkee from Kilrush on the N67 take the first turning on the right after entering town.

CUNNINGHAM'S CARAVAN & CAMPING PARK   RAC L
☎ (061) 51666
Open: May-mid September
Size: 10 acres, 30 touring pitches, static caravans. Showers, WCs

	⛺	⛟	🅰	🅰						

Charges on application.
Site close to the beach with children's play area, TV and games room. Some gas available.
30 caravans for hire.
Travelling from Kilrush on the N67. Cross over roundabout in Kilkee, turn left at Victoria Hotel.

KILLALOE *Co Clare*   Map 10 B3

LOUGH DERG CARAVAN & CAMPING PARK   RAC L
☎ (061) 76329
Open: May-Mid September
Size: 4½ acres, 57 touring pitches, some with elec, 15 static caravans. Showers, WCs

	⛺	⛟	🅰	🅰	🐾	☕	✕			

Charges on application.
Rural site, mountain and forest walks nearby. Swimming, boating and fishing available on site with boats and windsurfers for hire. Children's play area. Site shop and games room open June-August. 15 caravans for hire.
3 miles from Killaloe on the Scariff road L12, signed on lakeside.

The Shannon Cottage Caravan & Camping Park
O'Brien's Bridge.
☎ (061) 377118
Open: April-September
Size: 2 acres, 14 touring pitches. 4 hot showers, 6 WCs

	⛺	⛟	🅰	🅰				🔺	📷	🐕

Follow signposts to O'Brien's Bridge. Site at E end of village, on bank of River Shannon.

KILLARNEY *Co Kerry*   Map 10 A4

Beech Grove
Fossa.
☎ (064) 31727
Open: March-September
Size: 3½ acres, 44 touring pitches. 4 hot showers, 10 WCs. 6 static caravans

	⛺		🅰	🅰	🐾					🐕

3 miles W of Killarney, off T67.

The Drive In Caravan Site
Park Road, Cork Road. ☎ (064) 31248
Open: All year
Size: 2½ acres, 40 touring pitches. 3 hot showers, 8 WCs. Static caravans

¼ mile E of Killarney on main road to Mallow and Cork.

The Flesk
Muckross Road. ☎ (064) 31704
Open: Easter-October
Size: 6 acres, 60 touring pitches. 4 hot showers, 12 WCs

¾ mile S of Killarney on N71 (T65).

FOSSA CARAVAN & CAMPING PARK RAC L
Fossa. ☎ (064) 31497/34459
Open: Easter-30 September
Size: 6 (8) acres, 100 touring pitches, all level, 45 with elec, 25 with hardstanding, 20 static caravans. 6 hot showers, 6 cold showers, 14 WCs, 1 CWP

(1991) Car & caravan, Car & tent, M/cycle & tent £7, Motor caravan £6.50, Tent only £3; all plus 50p per adult, child 25p; extra car £1.50; elec £1, awn £1.50; WS
cc Access, Amex, Diners, Visa/B'card
A lovely holiday park set in beautiful wooded area near lake and famous Gap of Dunloe. Facilities include a tennis court, children's play area, TV lounge and a games room. Cycles for hire. No gas available. 20 caravans for hire (own WCs). Swimming pool 3 miles.
3½ miles W of Killarney on the T67 (R562). Entrance at Texaco filling station.

GLENROSS CARAVAN PARK RAC L
c/o White Bridge Park. ☎ (064) 31590
Open: May-September
Size: 4½ acres, 40 touring pitches, all level, 24 with elec, 18 with hardstanding, 2 static caravans. 4 hot showers, 6 WCs

Charges on application.
Site is close to Rossbeigh Beach. Shop 5 minutes' walk. Restaurant 100 yards. No gas available.
On main `Ring of Kerry' road (N70), beside the Glenbeigh Hotel.

WHITEBRIDGE CARAVAN & CAMPING PARK RAC L
Ballycasheen. ☎ (064) 31590
Open: 17 March-30 September
Size: 3 (6) acres, 52 touring pitches, 40 with elec, 36 level pitches, 10 with hardstanding, 6 static caravans. 8 hot showers, 8 cold showers, 15 WCs, 1 CWP

Car & caravan, Car & tent £7, Motor caravan £6.50, all plus 50p-£1.50 per adult, 25p child; M/cycle & tent £3 per person; elec £1, awn £1.50
An exclusive 6 acre park situated right on the banks of the River Flesk, 1 mile from Killarney town and 300 yards off the Cork-Macroom road. Games room and TV lounge. 6 caravans for hire (own

WCs). Restaurant 10 minutes' walk. Supermarket 5 minutes' walk. Swimming pool 5 minutes' drive. No gas available.
Travelling from Limerick or Tralee turn left at roundabout and on new by-pass to avoid town centre and on to Cork road, turning off at signpost on right hand side.

White Villa Farm Caravan & Camping Site
Cork Road. ☎ (064) 31414
Open: June-September
Size: 4½ acres, 40 touring pitches. 2 hot showers, 5 WCs

3 miles E of Killarney on N22.

KILLORGLIN *Co Kerry*　　　Map 10 A4

Tunnahalla
Milltown. ☎ (066) 61154
Open: May-September
Size: 1½ acres, 50 touring pitches. 2 hot showers, 2 WCs

Midway between Killorglin and Milltown on T66.

West Caravan & Camping Park
Killarney Road. ☎ (066) 61240
Open: March-September
Size: 2½ acres, 24 touring pitches. 5 hot showers, 5 WCs. 10 static caravans

W from Killarney (T67), turn left for site. Site by River Laune.

KILMUCKRIDGE *Co Wexford*　　　Map 10 C3

MORRISCASTLE STRAND PARK RAC L
☎ (053) 30124
Open: June-3 September
Size: 16 acres, 90 touring pitches. Showers, WCs

Charges on application.
Site on beach. Children's play area. Some gas available. Families only.
Take the R742 coast road N from Wexford to Kilmuckridge village, where turn right to Morriscastle Strand, signposted.

KILRUSH *Co Clare*　　　Map 10 A3

AYLEVARROO CARAVAN PARK RAC L
☎ (065) 51102
Open: 11 May-14 September
Size: 7½ acres, 38 touring pitches, all level, 12 with elec, all with hardstanding, 8 static caravans. 6 hot showers, 15 WCs, 1 CWP

Car & caravan, Motor caravan £5-£6, plus £1 per person above 2 (under 15 years free); Car & tent, M/cycle & tent £2.20-£2.50 per person; elec 70p
An attractive site with children's play area set in wooded landscaped grounds on the River Shannon estuary. TV and games room, tennis court. 8 caravans for hire (own WCs). Camping Gaz only. Shop and restaurant 1½ miles. No dogs.
Travel 4 miles W from Tarbert-Killimer ferry

▣ Snacks/take away　☒ Restaurant　◠ Swimming pool　▣ Shelter for campers　☈ Dogs accepted　　**251**

Republic of Ireland

towards Kilrush and turn left at signpost, or travel 1½ miles from Kilrush.

KNOCKALLA Co Donegal — Map 10 B1

KNOCKALLA HOLIDAY CENTRE RAC L
☎ (074) 59108
Open: April-Mid September
Size: 14 acres, 53 touring pitches, some with elec, static caravans. Showers, WCs

☐☐🚐🚐▲🛢️🛒☐☐☐☐🐕

Charges on application.
Situated between Lough Swilly and the Knockalla Mountains with swimming, fishing and climbing available. Some gas available. 9 caravans for hire.
Take the R246 N from Kerrykeel to Ballynashannagh, then take the Knockalla coast road E. Site at base of road.

KNOCKCROGHERY Co Roscommon — Map 10 B2

GAILEY BAY CARAVAN & CAMPING PARK RAC L
☎ (0903) 7058
Open: May-End September
Size: 2½ acres, 22 touring pitches. Showers, WCs

☐☐🚐🚐▲🛢️🛒☐☐🔲🐕

Charges on application.
Lakeshore site with boats for hire, pitch and putt, children's play area and TV lounge. Some gas available.
Take the N61 SW towards Athlone. At Ballymurray turn left and follow road to lake shore.

LAHINCH Co Clare — Map 10 A3

LAHINCH CAMPING & CARAVAN PARK RAC L
☎ (065) 81424
Open: 1 May-30 September
Size: 5 acres, 62 touring pitches, all level, 22 with elec, 62 with hardstanding, 3 static caravans, 1 chalet. 10 hot showers, 16 WCs, 1 CWP

☐☐🚐🚐▲🛢️☐☐☐🔲🐕

Charges on application.
Well-organised holiday park, close to a sandy beach, with children's play area. Camping Gaz only. Shop and restaurant 200 yards.
Site situated in the village of Lahinch, well signposted.

LAURAGH VILLAGE Co Kerry — Map 10 A4

CREVEEN LODGE CARAVAN & CAMPING PARK RAC L
Healy Pass.
☎ (064) 83131
Open: Easter-September
Size: 2 acres, 17 touring pitches, static caravans. Showers, WCs

☐☐🚐🚐▲🛢️☐☐☐☐🐕

Charges on application.
Rural site with fishing, mountain climbing, country walks and pubs nearby. Children's play area and TV room.
The site is 1 mile SE of Lauragh village on the Healy Pass road R574.

LETTERGESH Co Galway — Map 10 A2

LETTERGESH BEACH CARAVAN & CAMPING PARK RAC L
☎ (095) 43406
Open: mid March-end October
Size: 8 acres, 70 touring pitches, some with elec, 6 static caravans. Showers, WCs

☐☐🚐🚐▲☐☐☐☐☐☐

Charges on application.
This site, situated close to a National Park, has good access to a wide range of sporting activities. 6 caravans for hire.
Take the N59 SW from Leenaun for 3 miles, then turn NE on unclassified road, site signed in 5 miles.

LOUISBURGH Co Mayo — Map 10 A2

OLD HEAD FOREST CARAVAN & CAMPING PARK RAC L
☎ (098) 66021/2
Open: June-Mid September
Size: 11¼ acres, 96 touring pitches, some with elec. Showers, WCs

☐☐🚐🚐▲🛢️🛒💧☐☐☐

Charges on application.
Close to Clew Bay, this site provides a base for watersports. Children's play area.
10 miles W of Westport on the R335, site signposted to the N at Old Head crossroads.

MIDLETON Co Cork — Map 10 B4

TRABOLGAN HOLIDAY CENTRE RAC L
☎ (021) 661 551
Open: March-November
Size: 3 (140) acres, 23 touring pitches, some with elec. Showers, WCs

☐☐🚐🚐☐☐🛒💧✖️⛷️🔲☐

Charges on application.
Organised holiday centre with heated swimming pool, solarium, sauna, mini-gym, also a bar, self-service restaurant, bowling centre, golf and children's playschool. Close to beach with fishing and swimming.
Take the R630 from Midleton to Whitegate, turn S on to unclassified road, site signposted.

MULLINGAR Co Westmeath — Map 10 B2

LOUGH ENNEL HOLIDAY VILLAGE RAC L
☎ (044) 48101
Open: April-End September
Size: 15 acres, 67 touring pitches, some with elec, static caravans. Showers, WCs

☐☐🚐🚐▲🛢️🛒💧☐☐🐕

Charges on application.
Site on shore of Lough Ennel. Children's play area. Windsurfing equipment and tuition available. Some gas available. Caravans for hire.
Take the N52 from Mullingar towards Kilbeggan. After 5 miles turn right at signpost `Lough Ennel-Tudenham' to site in 1 mile.

PORTLAOISE *Co Laois*　　　Map 10 B3

KIRWAN'S CARAVAN & CAMPING PARK　RAC L
☎ (0502) 21688
Open: April-End September
Size: 2 acres, 20 touring pitches, some with elec,
6 static caravans. Showers, WCs

Charges on application.
*This site is close to Portlaoise town centre and has
a children's play area, a TV lounge and dining
room. Shop open July-August. Some gas
available.*
*The site is ¾ mile out of Portlaoise on the
N7 Limerick road.*

RATHANGAN *Co Kildare*　　　Map 10 C3

CARASLI HOLIDAY CENTRE　RAC L
☎ (045) 24331
Open: March-October
Size: ¾ acre, 9 touring pitches, some with elec,
static caravans. Showers, WCs

Charges on application.
*Site is close to the Grand Canal and the River Slate.
Children's play area. Some gas available.
6 caravans for hire.*
*Take the R401 NW from Kildare. Site entrance by
Jet filling station at edge of Rathangan.*

REDCROSS *Co Wicklow*　　　Map 10 C3

JOHNSON'S CARAVAN & CAMPING PARK　RAC L
☎ (0404) 8133
Open: Easter-September
Size: 7½ acres, 24 touring pitches, some with elec,
static caravans. Showers, WCs

Charges on application.
*Tennis, TV and arcade games on site. Children's
play area. Some gas available. 11 caravans for hire.
From Dublin take the N11 S to Rathnew, then turn
W onto the R752, then left under railway bridge,
travel on 7 miles to Doyle's Pub - site signed S.*

RIVER VALLEY CARAVAN & CAMPING PARK　RAC L
☎ (0404) 8647
Open: Mid March-End September
Size: 10 acres, 75 touring pitches, some with elec,
static caravans. Showers, WCs

Charges on application.
*This site is close to the 'Motter Stone' mountain
and forest walks and within striking distance of
Dublin. Tennis, crazy golf, TV and a games room
available on site.
From Dublin take the N11 S to junction with R754,
take this SW to Redcross village where turn right,
site signposted.*

RENVYLE *Co Galway*　　　Map 10 A2

Renvyle Beach Caravan Site
☎ (095) 43462
Open: March-October
Size: 3 acres, 36 touring pitches. 2 hot showers,
8 WCs. Static caravans

12 miles NE of Clifden on T71 (N59), at Letterfrack
turn W via Tully Cross towards Renvyle. Site
signed.

ROSBEG *Co Donegal*　　　Map 10 B1

TRAMORE BEACH CAMPING SITE　RAC L
☎ (075) 45274
Open: Easter-30 September
Size: 2 acres, 24 touring pitches, 20 with
hardstanding, 60 static caravans. 4 hot showers, 13
WCs, 2 CWPs

(1991) Car & caravan, Motor caravan, Car & tent,
M/cycle & tent £6; WS
*Family site overlooking a sandy surfing beach.
Cozen gas only. Restaurant 3 miles.*
Site in Rosbeg.

ROSCREA *Co Tipperary*　　　Map 10 B3

**STREAMSTOWN CARAVAN &
CAMPING PARK**　RAC L
☎ (0505) 21519
Open: 1 May-30 September
Size: 2 (2½) acres, 30 touring pitches, 8 with elec,
15 level pitches, 15 with hardstanding, 1 static
caravan. 1 hot shower, 5 WCs, 1 CWP

(1991) Car & caravan, Motor caravan, Car & tent,
M/cycle & tent £3; all plus £1 per adult, 50p per
child; elec £1, awn 50p
*Quiet, family-run park, situated in pleasant
surroundings, not far from the Slieve Bloom
Mountains. 1 caravan for hire (own WC).
Restaurant 2½ miles. Shop 400 metres. Swimming
pool 12 miles. Camping Gaz only.*
*1½ miles W of Roscrea on the L34 (R491), near St
Joseph's Abbey.*

ROSSES POINT *Co Sligo*　　　Map 10 B2

GREENLANDS CARAVAN & CAMPING PARK　RAC L
☎ (071) 77113
Open: May-September
Size: 4 acres, 67 touring pitches, some with elec,
static caravans. 2 showers, 13 WCs

Charges on application.
*Partly sloping site with beautiful views over the sea
and hills. Children's play area and TV room. Some
gas available. 11 caravans for hire.
From Sligo take the N15 N then turn left on to the
R291 to Rosses Point.*

ROSSLARE *Co Wexford*　　　Map 10 C4

BURROW CARAVAN & CAMPING PARK　RAC L
☎ (053) 32190
Open: March-End October
Size: 13 acres, 60 touring pitches, some with elec,
static caravans. Showers, WCs

Charges on application.
*Close to Rosslare Ferry Terminal. Shop, children's
play area, tennis and pitch and putt available on*

💧 Snacks/take away　☒ Restaurant　� Swimming pool　▣ Shelter for campers　🐕 Dogs accepted　　253

site. Some gas available. 40 caravans for hire.
Take the N25 W from Rosslare Harbour to Kilrane,
then turn N on to the R736, site ¾ mile N of
Rosslare village.

ROSSLARE HOLIDAY PARK   RAC L
☎ (053) 32427/45720
Open: 1 May-1 October
Size: 6½ acres, 25 touring pitches, 20 level pitches,
all with elec, 20 with hardstanding. 6 hot showers,
8 WCs, 1 CWP

Car & caravan, Motor caravan, Car & tent, M/cycle
& tent £4.50-£5.50, plus £1 per adult above 2, child
50p; elec £1, awn free
*Close to Rosslare Ferry Terminal, this site has a
children's play area and a tennis court, and is
situated within 3 minutes' walk of the beach. Shop
and restaurant 500 yards. Camping Gaz only.*
From the ferry terminal, join the N25. At Tagoat,
turn N on to the R736. Take the third right junction
(opposite Bay Bar) for site.

ROSSNOWLAGH LOWER *Co Donegal Map 10 B1*

**MANOR HOUSE CARAVAN &
CAMPING PARK**   RAC L
☎ (072) 51477
Open: Easter-End September
Size: 5 acres, 55 touring pitches. Showers, WCs

Charges on application.
*Site on coast with views over Donegal Bay. Shop,
take-away and launderette available during high
season. Children's play area and TV room. Some
gas available.*
Take the R231 coast road N from Ballyshannon,
pass the Rossnowlagh turning and take next left,
then first right to site on shore.

ROUNDSTONE *Co Galway   Map 10 A2*

GORTEEN BAY CARAVAN & CAMPING PARK RAC L
☎ (095) 35882
Open: March-End September
Size: 14 acres, 60 touring pitches. Showers, WCs

Charges on application.
*Beach site with children's play area. Some gas
available.*
From Galway follow the N59 NE. 4 miles after
Recess turn S on to R341 to Roundstone, site is
¾ mile W of town beside beach.

ROUNDWOOD *Co Wicklow   Map 10 C3*

ROUNDWOOD CARAVAN & CAMPING PARK RAC L
☎ (01) 818163
Open: March-September
Size: 6 acres, 79 touring pitches, some with elec.
Showers, WCs

Charges on application.
*Overlooking Varty lakes and forest. Close to
Powerscourt waterfall and gardens. Supermarket
on site. Some gas available.*
Take the N11 S to Newtownmountkennedy from
Dublin, turn W on to R765, continue to

Roundwood, site in village.

SCHULL *Co Cork   Map 10 A4*

The Glebe
Colla Road. ☎ (028) 28303
Open: All year
Size: 4½ acres, 40 touring pitches. 1 hot shower,
8 WCs. 20 static caravans

11 miles W of Skibbereen (N71), turn SW on L57 to
Schull. Continue through village on Colla Road for
site.

SHANKILL *Co Dublin   Map 10 C3*

SHANKILL CARAVAN & CAMPING PARK   RAC L
Sherrington Park. ☎ (01) 2820011
Open: All year
Size: 7 acres, 50 touring pitches, all with elec,
22 level pitches, 24 static caravans, 8 chalets.
12 hot showers, 12 cold showers, 14 WCs, 2 CWPs

Car & caravan, Motor caravan, Car & tent, M/cycle
& tent £4-£5; all plus 50p per adult, 25p per child;
elec 75p, awn £1
*This well-organised site in wooded surroundings
overlooking the Dublin mountains makes a good
base for visiting Dublin (bus stop at entrance).
24 caravans and 8 chalets (own WCs) for hire.
Camping Gaz only. Restaurant 1½ miles. Dogs
must be kept on a lead.*
From Dublin follow the N11 S (10 miles) or
T44 from Dun Laoghaire (5 miles). Pass Shankill
church, over bridge through village of Shankill to
site on right. From Bray follow the N11 N (2 miles).

SHERCOCK *Co Cavan   Map 10 C2*

LAKELANDS CARAVANNING & CAMPING   RAC L
Lough Sillan. ☎ (042) 69488
Open: Easter/June-Mid September
Size: 3 acres, 42 touring pitches, most with elec.
Hot showers, WCs

Car & caravan, Motor caravan, Car & tent, M/cycle
& tent £5, plus 50p per person
*Picturesque site on shores of Lough Sillan. Ideal
family centre for water-skiing, windsurfing,
boating, fishing and swimming.*
½ mile NW of Shercock on the L46 (R192) by Lough
Sillan.

STRANDHILL *Co Sligo   Map 10 B2*

**BUENOS AYRES CARAVAN
& CAMPING PARK**   RAC L
☎ (071) 68120
Open: May-Mid September
Size: 15 acres, 88 touring pitches, some with elec,
static caravans. Showers, WCs

Charges on application.
*Site on the beach. Children's play area and TV
room. Some gas available. 12 caravans for hire.*
From the centre of Sligo take the R292 W to
Strandhill.

TAHILLA *Co Kerry* · *Map 10 A4*

The Ramblers Rest
☎ (064) 45232
Open: All year
Size: 2 acres, touring pitches. WCs

[icons]

12 miles W of Kenmare on N70 (T66). 4 miles E of Sneem.

TRALEE *Co Kerry* · *Map 10 A3*

Annagh Farm
Blennerville. ☎ (066) 21159
Open: April-October
Size: 1 acre, 20 touring pitches. 4 WCs. 6 static caravans

[icons]

1 mile W of Blennerville, off T68.

Barrow Camping Site
Ardfert. ☎ (066) 36197
Open: All year
Size: 3 acres, 20 touring pitches. 2 hot showers, 4 WCs. 10 static caravans

[icons]

From Tralee, take L105 NW for 5½ miles to Ardfert. Turn left and continue for 1¾ miles, then turn right to Barrow. Site 1¾ miles.

BAYVIEW CARAVAN & CAMPING PARK RAC L
☎ (066) 26140
Open: April-End October
Size: 3 acres, 26 touring pitches, some with elec, static caravans. Showers, WCs

[icons]

Charges on application.
Close to Tralee with children's play area and TV room. Some gas available. 12 caravans for hire.
1 mile N of Tralee on the R556 Ballybunion road.

TRAMORE *Co Waterford* · *Map 10 B4*

FITZMAURICE'S CARAVAN PARK RAC L
Riverstown. ☎ (051) 81968
Open: 1 May-30 September
Size: 1 (5½) acres, 20 touring pitches, 6 level pitches, 100 static caravans. 4 hot showers, 22 WCs, 1 CWP

[icons]

Charges on application.
Beside the beach, this site offers bathing, boating and fishing. 80 caravans for hire. Some gas available.
On approaching Tramore from Waterford take the first turn left to beach.

VENTRY *Co Kerry* · *Map 10 A3*

Cuan Pier Caravan & Camping Park
☎ (066) 59915
Open: All year
Size: 2½ (4) acres, 36 touring pitches. 4 WCs. Static caravans

[icons]

From Dingle on T68, continue W to Ventry. Follow

road round harbour to Cuan.

VIRGINIA *Co Cavan* · *Map 10 C2*

LOUGH RAMOR CARAVAN PARK RAC L
☎ (049) 47447
Open: April-end September
Size: 1½ acres, 19 touring pitches, some with elec, static caravans. Showers, WCs

[icons]

Charges on application.
Site on the shore of Lough Ramor, with children's play area and pitch and putt on site. 2 caravans for hire.
Travelling SE on the N3 towards Navan turn right at Lisduff to site in 3 miles.

WATERVILLE *Co Kerry* · *Map 10 A4*

PINE GROVE CARAVAN & CAMPING PARK RAC L
☎ (0667) 4185
Open: 1 April-30 September
Size: 3 acres, 30 touring pitches, static caravans. Showers, WCs

[icons]

Charges on application.
Situated between the River Inny, Lake Currane and Ballinskelligs Bay, this site is convenient for fishing, boat hire and swimming. Children's play area and TV room. Some gas available.
2 miles N of Waterville on the W side of the N70.

WATERVILLE CARAVAN & CAMPING PARK RAC L
☎ (0667) 4191
Open: Easter-30 September
Size: 3 (4½) acres, 56 touring pitches, 50 with elec, 50 level pitches, 12 with hardstanding, 25 static caravans. 10 hot showers, 13 WCs, 1 CWP

[icons]

(1991) Car & caravan, Motor caravan £4, Car & tent £3.50-£4, M/cycle & tent £3-£3.50; all plus £1 per adult, 50p per child; elec £1, awn £1
Four star site in magnificent Ballinskelligs Bay with a warm welcome. Children's play area. 10 caravans for hire (own WCs). Camping Gaz only. Restaurant 100 metres. Winner of award for Caravan Park of the Year 1991 - M.C.C. of Ireland.
½ mile N of Waterville, 300 yards off N70 Waterville/ Cahirciveen road ('Ring of Kerry') overlooking bay. Follow finger signposts.

WESTPORT *Co Mayo* · *Map 10 A2*

PARKLANDS CARAVAN & CAMPING PARK RAC L
☎ (098) 25141
Open: Mid May-End August
Size: 10 acres, 155 touring pitches. Showers, WCs

[icons]

Charges on application.
Part of the Westport Country House Estate, with rent-a-bike, pitch and putt and tennis on site. Some gas available.
Turn right at Westport quay, 2 miles W of Westport on the R335.

💬 Snacks/take away ☒ Restaurant ◺ Swimming pool ▥ Shelter for campers 🐾 Dogs accepted

WEXFORD *Co Wexford*   *Map 10 C3*

CARNE BEACH CARAVAN & CAMPING PARK RAC L
☎ (053) 31131
Open: Mid May-Mid September
Size: 30 acres, 70 touring pitches, some with elec.
Showers, WCs

[icons] 🐴

Charges on application.
A beach site with swimming, angling and riding available. Close to Rosslare Ferry Terminal. Children's play area and TV room. Some gas available. 6 caravans for hire.
From Rosslare Harbour take the N25 W to Kilrane, then travel due S to the coast.

FERRYBANK CARAVAN & CAMPING PARK RAC L
☎ (053) 44378
Open: 1 April-30 September
Size: 10 acres, 130 touring pitches, 29 with elec.
4 hot showers, 39 WCs, 1 CWP

[icons]

Car & caravan, Motor caravan £6, Car & tent, M/cycle & tent £3.50; extra person 50p; elec £1
A grassy site with a sauna, tennis court and children's play area. Shop open 1 June-end August. No gas available.
At E side of Wexford Bridge, ½ mile from town.

Seasonal variation of prices
Where a single price is given it may be a low season minimum charge - rates can increase considerably at peak periods and for extra people or vehicles.
Please confirm prices with the site when booking.

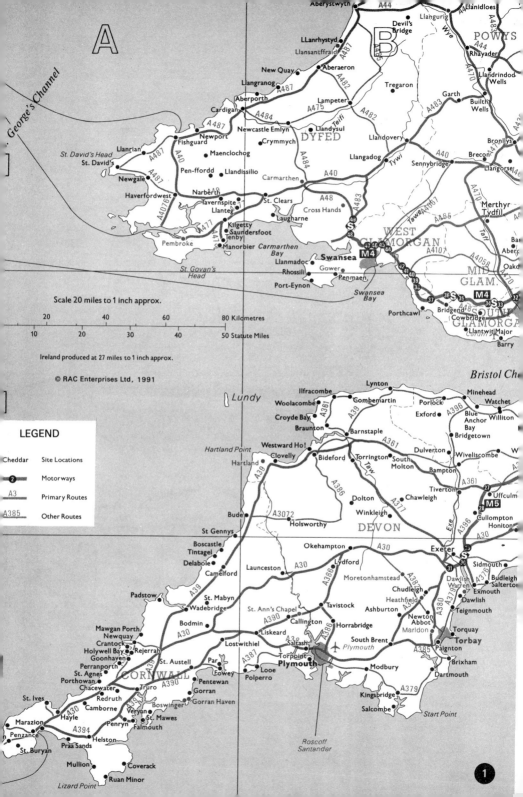

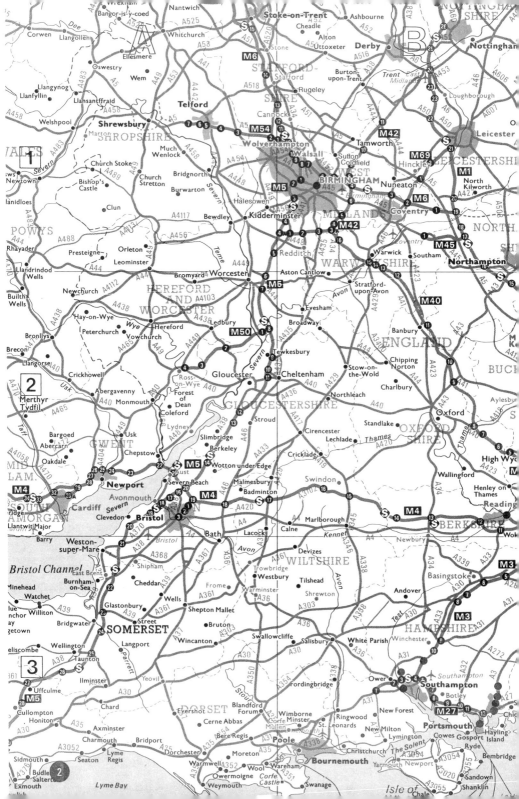

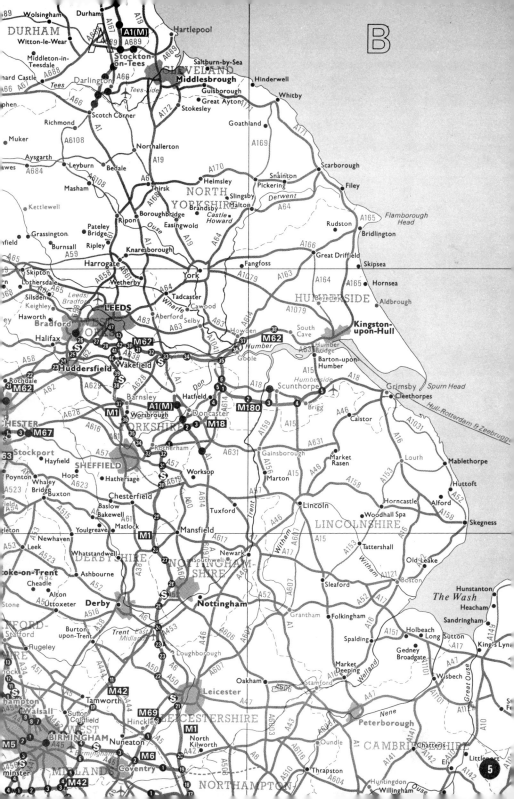

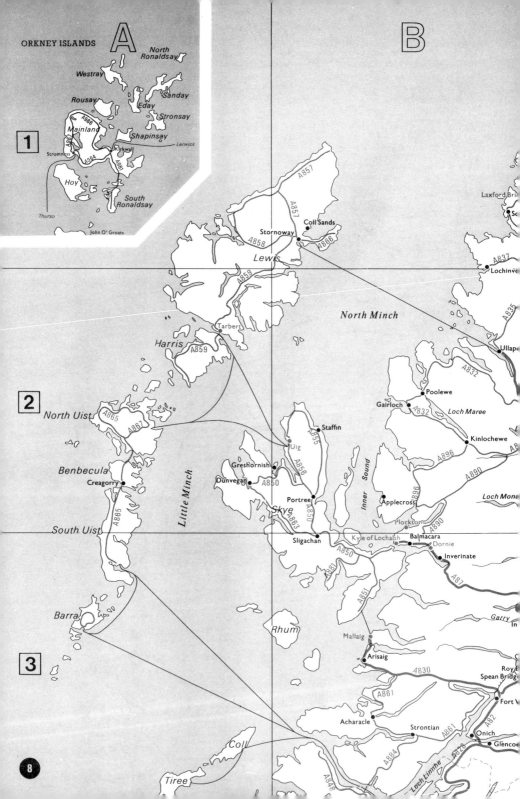

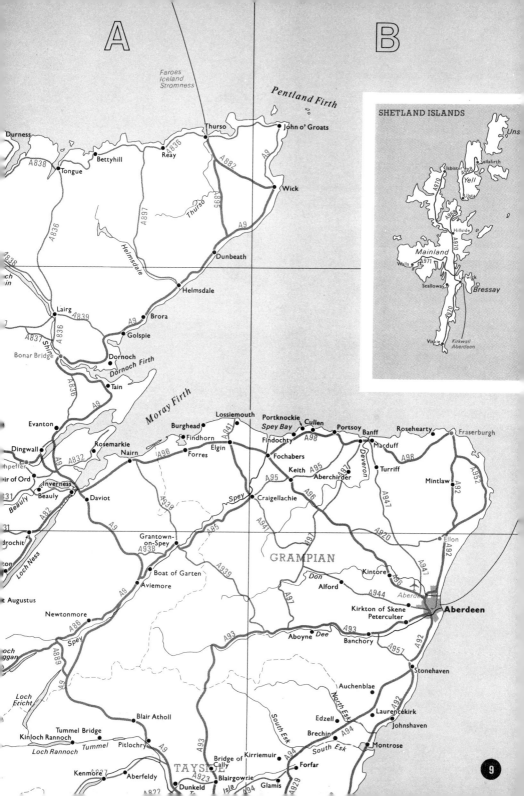

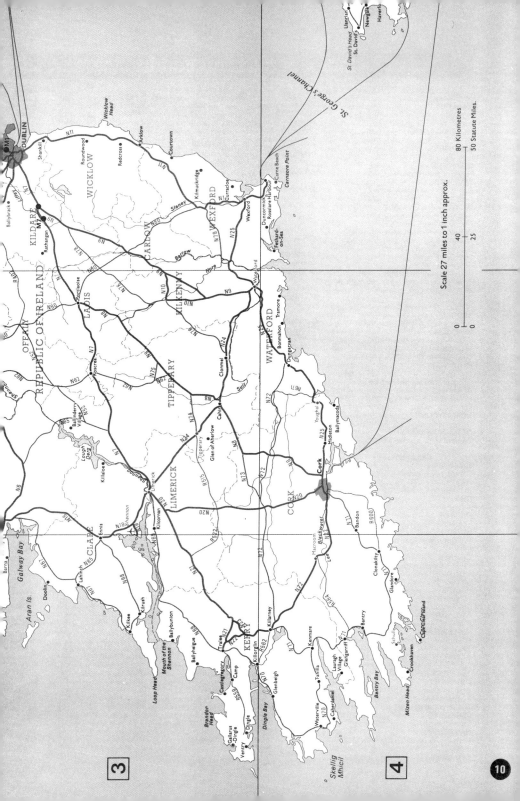

Index of sites by county

Index

270

Index

Index

Index

Index